Unbreakable Hearts!

A True, Heart-wrenching Story About Victory...Forfeited!

TRẦN HƯNG ĐẠO
(1213-1300)

In the 1200s the Mongols, under Kublai Khan, conquered most of Asia and Eastern Europe. One small kingdom, Dai Viet (Northern Vietnam), sat in the way of a complete conquest of Southeast Asia for Kublai Khan's massive forces. In 1257, 1284, and 1287, the Mongol armies invaded Vietnam, attempting to conquer the vastly outnumbered Vietnamese military, by land and sea. One great general, Tran Hung Dao, would rise up and lead the greatly outnumbered Dai Viets to defeat the Mongol hordes all three times. In the third and final invasion, the Vietnamese destroyed the entire Mongol fleet of more than four hundred ships, one of the greatest military victories in Vietnamese history.

The Vietnam Wars, from 111 BC to 1979

By the Author of CONDEMNED PROPERTY? and PAYBACK TIME!
Earl "Dusty" Trimmer
Vietnam War Veteran

First published by Dog Ear Publishing
8888 Keystone Crossing
Suite 1300
Indianapolis, IN 46240
www.dogearpublishing.net

ISBN: 978-145756-997-5

This book is printed on acid-free paper.
Printed in the United States of America

Opening Statement

"The American combat soldier-infantryman in the Pacific Theater of World War II faced an average of forty days of combat time during a four-year time period served. Amazingly, in the Vietnam War, the combat soldiers/marines were called upon to expose themselves to combat situations in just a one-year tour…for an astounding average of 240 days."

—VFW Magazine

Combat Infantry

God gives His strongest soldiers His toughest battles!
That is why He made the combat infantryman for Vietnam.

TABLE OF CONTENTS

"When you write, write in such a way as that you can be readily understood by both the young and old, by men as well as women, even by children."

—Ho Chi Minh

DEDICATION

WHEN THE CHILDREN
OF THE VIETNAM WAR HEROES ARE GONE
AND THEIR CHILDREN ARE GONE…
THE VIETNAM WAR,
ALL THAT HAPPENED THERE,
ALL THAT HAPPENED
AFTER THE WAR ENDED…
WILL BE FORGOTTEN
IN ALL LIVING PEOPLE'S MINDS,
BUT NOT IN BOOKS.
IT WILL BE BETTER
IF THE TRUTHS
OF WHAT HAPPENED TO THEM
BE LEFT
FOR GENERATIONS THAT FOLLOW
RATHER THAN BE DESPICABLE…UNTRUTHS.

—Earl "Dusty" Trimmer
Combat Vietnam War Veteran
Author

During the 1968 tet offensive in vietnam, 90 percent of all evening news in america was devoted to the vietnam war…with televised bias against the american military. The truth is the americans won that battle and they won the vietnam war, but that victory was stolen from them by their own countrymen! Nearly half a century later, most of the american species known as the vietnam war veteran have died and are closer to…extinction!

EXTINCTION IS…FOREVER !

They have been cheated out of their earned valor, betrayed when victory was won. Is the vietnam war veteran going to be robbed of the one thing they have left to leave behind them…a rightful, honorable legacy?

REMEMBER THEM…EXTINCTION IS FOREVER!

PROLOGUE

In love or war if you break their heart, you have broken their spirit, drained their soul, and depleted their passion for hope.

After I had left the Vietnam War in March of 1969, President Nixon pledged to "end the war and win peace" on June 8, 1969. The result of his actions brought twenty-five thousand soldiers home, still leaving troop strength at 484,000 that year. Many of the 509,000 troops in Vietnam at that time of the war were waiting anxiously to hear if their unit would be one of those selected and removed from the godforsaken battle-fields of Vietnam. Would they be saved or would they continue fighting an elusive enemy that never, ever quit fighting, regardless of how bad their losses were? An enemy that had become battle-hardened because of long, bloody wars before us with the French, the Mongols, and Chinese. All of them were defeated eventually. Yes, even the Mongol hordes of Kublai Khan were beaten back to their Mongolian homeland by the tenacious Vietnamese.

None of us at ground level in the Nam actually knew what or why they were always spraying stuff over there. Someone said it was for mosquitoes. Why would we think otherwise? Of course, we weren't issued protective masks as we were during some training sessions back in the States, and many of us grunts lived in the same clothing for weeks or months while in the bush. The only thing we could cover our faces with was a filthy, bacteria-drenched towel. In some ways, our enemy lived better in their underground tunnels than we did. At least they had change of clothing down in their filthy holes and a ceiling over their heads. What a depressing thought that is. No wonder so many Vietnam War veterans rarely talked about their war and most just wanted to be left alone to try to live a normal life but... the memories of the Nam would continue to haunt many of us painfully and forever. This is where I find myself today.

American soldiers had no way of knowing what they had been exposed to when low-flying C-123 aircraft flew over and sprayed deadly poisons over triple-canopy jungles, mangrove forests, and civilian-farmed rice paddy fields, the main source of food. They had no idea that what was being done around them would affect them *and* infect them long after they had physically left Vietnam behind them. Living like Neanderthals, they had survived a hundred sleepless nights, dozens of firefights, and ambushes day and night. Many had been wounded and saw death and destruction, leaving the scars of war and poisons with them for the remainder of their lives physically and psychologically.

They were told over there and back here that the skin rashes from their faces to their feet, and everywhere in between, was simply something called *jungle rot*. There is nothing simple-sounding about *jungle ROT*! I have personally had recurring outbreaks of jungle ROT from the day it appeared on my body in April 1968 to this day…forty-eight years later!

Our leaders told us that by killing the trees and thick jungles, calling it deforestation, the Viet Cong and North Vietnamese soldiers would lose their hiding places, being driven to fight in the open, where our superior firepower would destroy them, and the war would end very quickly.

They said that some herbicide spraying would shorten the war and save American lives. This game plan was hardly flawless. We presumed it was just Roundup they were spraying, as none of us had ever heard of Agent Orange at the time. They told us that our skin rashes, headaches, dizziness, and upset stomachs were just the natural results of "combat stress." If the mission was to kill trees, they succeeded. However, inside most of the spraying areas that we walked through, we also found dead birds, monkeys, reptiles, rats, and dead fish floating on the surface of streams and the rotting, nauseating smells that death and bacteria bring. We had to live with this discomfort twenty-four/seven while the heads of everything enjoyed many of the same comforts that could be had at home in America.

My book *Condemned Property?* not only stimulated and impacted Vietnam War and Vietnam Era veterans, which I prayed for; it also generated an unexpected response from our non-veteran patriotic Americans. This surprised me, but I was very happy about it. That book opened and reopened many minds that had been undoubtedly closed for decades, about what Vietnam War veterans suffered during and after that horrible war.

Less than two weeks after *Condemned Property?* went public in late November 2013, I was rocked by an earthquake-like event. They called this life-altering health disaster several titles…cerebral vascular attack, cerebral infarction, brain stroke, or just plain stroke. However, there was nothing plain or ordinary about this potentially life-threatening blow, and several permanent, crippling disabilities were left for me and others around me to deal with.

I was told the Vietnam War could accept the blame for this unfortunate ambush on my health system. Vietnam War, combat stress or PTSD, and Agent Orange-linked type 2 diabetes were all tagged with the potential causes. Secondary conditions from a severe stroke of this magnitude can leave its victim with a multitude of ugly health impairments, some temporary and some permanently devastating. I was left with some of both, including a disastrous vision impairment. As time would go on, some of the aftershocks of the stroke would change or worsen, leaving an inevitable diminishment in quality of life for me and others close to me. I feared there was something else coming down the road.

While some of the second- and third-person oral histories I used from personal interviews may not be 100 percent accurate, I guarantee that the semi-fictional bits of information entered in order to complete the message should not disappoint even the most critical reader. Invaluable information will abound in this book, factual and semi-factual. I hope that you the reader will gain a greater understanding and appreciation of the struggles required of Vietnamese to live in peace from the many unwanted invaders throughout the history of the last 2,000 years.

I have read in places and heard from sources that the Vietnamese people are known for having high IQs. In fact they have been put on the same IQ plain as the Germans, and this does not surprise me as I have found them to be exceptionally innovative. A testimonial to this belief would/could be created to how an army of 80,000 common villagers and farmers, led by two lady warriors (Trung sisters), could challenge and defeat a military force of 300,000 from China in 30–39 AD. This great achievement would be duplicated several times since, which is the only reason Vietnam flourishes today as a free-standing nation.

So, I continued on with the process of telling our story, wrote another book, *Payback Time!* and got it out while the first one was still somewhat fresh in many minds. Most Vietnam War and Vietnam era veterans (there is a difference) who I talked to or wrote me encouraged me to forge ahead with my mission. Many offered valuable suggestions, and I was open to most of them from those who were qualified to suggest them. I still am and will always hope to be.

Having to endure years of ongoing battles with the 900-pound gargoyle, the VA, writing the early books, and seeking and participating in several different post-stroke rehab programs had almost drained me of energy and finances to continue. But I knew that I must continue on or I, too, would join the massive list of Vietnam War veterans who became condemned property and died very prematurely from that wretched war long after it ended. After all, I have been bankrupt before, and in my mind, I was not at fault and I seemed to rebound each time. There were the multiple auto accidents of the 1970s, which nearly ended my life three times, but I escaped each with just concussions, cuts, bruises, and broken bones. I always bounced back, or so I thought...

CAUTION: You are about to engage in a story of anger, sorrow, respect, compassion, regret, mind-boggling passion, impressive courage, and unbelievable persistence with incomparable resilience. It is a heartbreaking true story, and yet it has heartwarming moments.

Chapter 1

SHE WAS A BAD, BAD WOMAN...

Toward the end of the first Indochina War, Ho Chi Minh would send his ragtag army of farmers and peasants, disorganized and untrained for professional combat, against the French colonial power to fight the final battle of a long, bloody, stalemated conflict. The French had a rough and combat-hardened military, including professional soldiers from the French Foreign Legion. The French were led by polished and decorated generals with a long and glorious track record of impressive victories in West Africa and Asia. The world waited nonchalantly for the certain failure of Ho Chi Minh's efforts to keep his country independent. The Viet Minh were led by a little-known general who was a college buddy of Uncle Ho himself. His name would be well known around the world after a climactic battle at a jungle outpost called Dien Bien Phu. This Viet Minh general's name was Vo Nguyen Giap. The outcome of this battle would shock the Western world as the Giap-led farmers and peasants soundly defeated the French in an embarrassingly easy manner and the European colonial adventure in the region lurched toward a permanent end.

In light of this, one has to ask why America's political "geniuses" in their ivory towers back in Washington, D.C. would make the hasty decision to resume the war in Vietnam that France could not win, and even after America itself had been held to a stalemate by North Korea and China. What could our pompous leaders have known about this new mysterious adversary that the French had apparently overlooked? What were we walking into?

The earliest years of the Vietnam War were more of a "feel each other out" game. We did not field a sizeable military force over there in 1955–1964. In 1965, the Viet Cong got our attention, especially at the battle of Ia Drang, where thousands of North Vietnamese showed up alongside their Viet Cong comrades. To this day, both sides claim a victory. In 1966, dramatic events took place and we sent more troops over there. In 1967, the "conflict"—as they referred to it back in the American Congress—then became worthy of being called the Vietnam War, as American casualties skyrocketed to 11,363. This was more KIAs than had been inflicted on the Americans in all the years of the "conflict" from 1955 to 1966...combined! Worse would follow.

The Vietnam War in 1968 needs no introduction here and little description. The Tet Offensive of 1968 would make or break the back of one side or the other or both. In 1968, American KIAs reached a staggering total 16,899 or almost 47 percent more than the bloody year before. This was shocking news for Americans, in Congress, in the streets, and to the military leaders on the battlefields. To be blunt, they were shocked

How did the American war machine get caught off guard? After all, we were the Americans, not the French. Maybe, just maybe the answers lay with the arrogant attitude of Washington's elite toward third world Hanoi. Apparently, Washington, D.C. went into this war without consulting with the French. Maybe Washington should have utilized some of its seemingly endless supply of American tax dollars and done something really smart and not too expensive, something as simple as this: **TAKE A HISTORY COURSE ABOUT VIETNAM'S WAR OUTCOMES!**

The Vietnam region's earliest known lady warriors who were significant contributors to their country's army stepped on to the battlefield (or swamps and jungles) more than two thousand years ago when the people of Vietnam's northern region fought and defeated a massive army from their northern ruler's land, China.

The lady warriors of Vietnam's northern regions have always played a major role in the defense of their homeland. Notice I said "defense of." The military forces of Vietnam have never been constructed and trained for offensive measures to invade and conquer. But in their environment, they have always known their capabilities and limitations.

As the Vietnam "conflict" was escalating in 1965–1967, the South Vietnamese were experiencing terrible and mysterious losses from very proficient Viet Cong snipers at an alarming rate. This became more than just a nuisance to the Army of the Republic of Vietnam (ARVN), and their high-ranking officers were losing their patience. Most of the sniper shots took place along the border of Cambodia in northern South Vietnam; hit and run back to safety in Cambodia. This happened to be U.S. Marine territory, and they were taking notice of the huge ARVN losses. Most sniper attacks took down officers first; if anyone else got in their way, so be it. That was a bonus for the VC ambushers.

It must have been embarrassing when the rumors came in that the leader of the most notorious sniper gang was a woman—yes indeed, a lady Viet Cong. And many of her gang members were also women. Her identity was not known, but as more ARVN officers became victims, there was a sizeable bounty put on her—something like $30,000. This seemed to motivate this lady-led Viet Cong gang, and as they grew in numbers, they expanded their target range of victims to include U.S. Marines. A fatal mistake.

Our marines named her "Apache." She was an excellent Viet Cong sniper and she did some serious damage to the American and South Vietnamese military during the Vietnam War, leaving her gruesome calling card behind...tortured soldiers and marines. Apache commanded her own freewheeling attack unit comparable to a large U.S. Army platoon. Our military would describe her as tenacious, relentless, passionate, violent, hateful, witty, and a cold-blooded killer. Yet she was also described as physically stunning with beauty—go figure.

Those who were lucky enough to survive a confrontation with Apache's raging Viet Cong have said that she made sure you knew that she did not like you and that her mission was a personal vendetta you would never forget, *if* you lived through one of her merciless ambushes along the Cambodian-South Vietnam border. Apache made it clear that she did not want Americans walking around freely in her country. She considered them the same as the French, whom she despised with extreme passion.

History books claim that Apache was as gorgeous (without makeup) as a woman could be. Sometimes her beauty would captivate an enemy, and those few seconds would be enough for Apache and her girls to pull off their ambush very successfully, notch it up, and move on to the next unsuspecting intruder. Some called her an Asiatic Medusa, that snake-haired monster of Greek mythology, paralyzing her intended victims into a temporary dazed condition and then...utterly demolishing the poor souls with a lightning quick and pinpoint attack. Some who lived to talk about it said that she knew when the Americans were coming out to find her. She knew when they left base camp and where they were at all times, waiting patiently for the perfect moment when her lady warriors could spring a catlike ambush. She seemed to welcome the inevitable confrontation. Death was of no concern to her or her mates. We Americans were in her backyard—uninvited as far as she was concerned, and she was unable to live with that.

Maybe our young, inexperienced American warriors could be forgiven for dropping their guard at the first sight of Apache because she was so stunning, staring at her in disbelief that this was the notorious killer of so many American and South Vietnamese warriors they had been told about. God help you if you were one of the few survivors of an ambush led by Apache and you were taken prisoner. You would be better off to have died as opposed to what the cruel lady warrior had in store for you. Any thoughts that a captured enemy, especially an American soldier boy, might have that he was lucky to have survived one of Apache's ambushes would be short-lived. Anyone captured by Apache's terrible, heartless bitches might live another day or even two, depending on how much enjoyment the ladies were getting out of torturing you and depending on how long you could stand it without taking your own life.

If she liked her captive, he would be forced into having sex with her again and again if she chose. But just like the female black widow spider, her male sex toy would soon be history, except Apache took longer to finish the job than Ms. Black Widow. Sadistic Apache would sometimes have her spent captive dragged to a few meters outside the fire support base he came from so that his buddies could have an early morning surprise…if they could even recognize him. Likely not and they didn't have DNA tests out there back then.

Once, as my source of research stated, after killing a marine squad that was also on ambush, the lone survivor who wasn't wounded too severely, unfortunately, was taken back to the girls' camp for playtime. First, he was stripped (of course) and hung on a bamboo rack for a couple of hours while the girls had dinner. The events that followed were standard Viet Cong torture techniques, and you can find the full details of this particular tragedy online at www.thephora.net. I am not enjoying writing this story, but as we all know, war is hell. Before the morning would come, our teenage marine would have had his eyelids cut away (no Novocain). Every time he would blink, he would cry in pain and pray to God to let him die. Unfortunately, Apache and her cronies weren't finished yet. Next, Apache's girls pried off his fingernails—all of them. Next, I am sorry to say, they began working on bending his fingers backward (while he was still conscious) and snapped them at their middle joints. Apache took care of this task herself, and she took her time, doing one finger every twenty minutes or so. I think she would have performed something comparable with his toes, but she had to get him back to where he came from before the sun came up. They weren't going to drag him back this time. He would be allowed to run back—if he could. Apache's finishing touch this night, briefly described, ended with a curved knife in her hand, with her other hand in a full grab of his genitals, and then she emasculated him, but not too quickly, I am afraid. Then he ran and ran and ran, but life would soon leave this poor marine's body by the time he ran into other marines. Imagine the disbelief on their faces.

Another story about Apache's torture of her male adversaries was if she didn't like you so much, she would have you staked in the bacteria-infested swamps—also full of poisonous critters crawling around—and leave you there to bleed to death or…die from whatever the Vietnam jungle did to you overnight or the next day and the next. If you were a lucky one, heavy rains would raise the water and drown you. This war in Vietnam was not just an average everyday war. There were no rules for either side or for a cruel Mother Nature.

As they say in the Old West movies…there is always someone faster. Fortunately, for our marines, there was someone faster, deadlier, and more determined, if that was possible. Soon, Apache would meet her match, and her long string of successful killer ambushes of marines and ARVN soldiers would come to a violent end.

Apache roamed the bush around the 1964–1965 timeframe and made it into 1966 when she finally met her match—an American marine sniper who referred to her as a **"bad, bad woman!"** Apache wasn't the only lady Viet Cong who would leave a deadly stamp on America's best soldiers and marines. However, Apache would be labeled as the trademark of one of the most vicious warriors who had ever fought on the battlefields of any war in history. To other Vietnamese she was a reminder of what the lady warriors of Vietnam were like in ancient times when bold, gallant, terribly dedicated lady warriors rose to fight alongside their male countrymen and sometimes even led them into battle and defeated a dangerous enemy that had repeatedly and mercilessly invaded their beloved homeland for centuries.

Carlos Hathcock (One Bad-Ass Marine) has often been compared to two great American heroes, Audie Murphy and Alvin York (Sergeant York). He was an expert marksman at a very young age. Audie and Alvin were Army soldiers but Carlos dreamed of becoming a Marine, and the Vietnam War would welcome him with open arms. He was to become the worst possible nightmare for the Viet Cong and the North Vietnamese Army. Carlos alone would become the communists' number one enemy, not to be underestimated because he was just one sniper.

The Vietnam War had its heroes, scores of them, and they weren't all American marines. But the man who would rise to this occasion would become known as the American Sniper of the Vietnam War. Long before another American hero, Chris Kyle, also a sniper, arrived on the scene, Carlos Hathcock was already a legend in Vietnam. But Carlos wanted the next notch on his rifle to be his taking down Apache. He dreamed of it.

I could easily dedicate the book to the American Sniper of the Vietnam War, but my mission here is to bestow credit onto an enemy that has been underestimated for two thousand years; the historians don't seem to be impressed with their stunning feats, but they should be.

Apache was a legend in her own right. Killing her victims would have been enough with her expert hunting skills—she did not need the extracurricular activities she threw in after taking her prisoners, but she was obsessed with drawing blood onto skin.

Carlos took his profession ever so seriously, and he was more often than not willing to patrol almost nonstop for many days in a row. He would take ten-minute catnaps throughout the day to provide the rest his body required. Some close to him back then started to think he was invincible. Carlos didn't mind that.

The eventual confrontation between Carlos and Apache happened when Hathcock set out on a mission that took several weeks and searched for and destroyed Apache, but he did not allow her to die slowly, as she did with so many of her victims. Her life ended in an instant from two perfect shots. In fact, his encounter with Apache was the basis for an episode in the documentary series on The History Channel titled *Deadliest Missions*.

To fully understand what Hathcock did in taking out Apache, you should read *Marine Sniper*. In his book, Hathcock says that he survived in his work because of an ability to "get in the bubble," to put himself into a state of "utter, complete, absolute concentration," first with his equipment, then his environment, in which every breeze and every leaf meant something, and finally on his quarry. After the Vietnam War, Hathcock found a passage written by Ernest Hemingway that he relished, which read:

> *Certainly, there is no hunting like the stalking of another human—who may also be pursuing you, and those who have hunted armed men long enough and like it never really care for anything else thereafter. But the memories linger.*

Hathcock commented after reading Hemingway's piece, "He got that right." There are plenty of Hathcock's adventures and successes to entertain anyone who can handle the adrenaline rush, so read *Marine Snipers*.

Apache's techniques were unique and worthy enough that they have been studied up till this day, and several more modern-day snipers have emulated her tactics and strategies. This brings me to one of the reasons I wrote *Unbreakable Hearts*: to explore where such intense fierceness and highly motivated warriors like Vietnam's Apache came from. How did they come about and what drove them?

Carlos Norman Hathcock II (May 20, 1942 – February 23, 1999) was not quite fifty-seven years old when he passed away prematurely. An Arkansas farm boy, Hathcock believed that he had killed between three hundred and four hundred enemy during his time in Vietnam, although the marines officially credit him with ninety-three kills. The North Vietnamese Army placed an abnormally high bounty of thirty thousand dollars on his life, a bounty that went unclaimed. Usually, a bounty on an opposing enemy was set at one thousand or two thousand dollars. To his knowledge, Hathcock killed every one of them who sought him out to collect the bounty. He was nicknamed "White Feather Sniper" by the Viet Cong because he wore a white feather in the band of his hat. However, after the bounty was set on his head, several of his platoon buddies began wearing a white feather in their hatband…do I need to explain why?

Carlos Hathcock was clearly a man well ahead of his time, and good for us, or Apache might still be lurking around in northern Vietnam's countryside, hunting for Americans. Fortunately, Apache's early death prevented her from breeding any future killers. Hathcock was not your everyday bloodthirsty killer as Apache was documented to be. He loved to shoot and even more so, he loved hunting, not killing. In his book *Marine Sniper*, he was quoted as saying, "I never did enjoy killing anybody. It was my job. If I don't do it, then a lot of kids dressed up like marines are gonna get killed."

Hathcock's kill of Apache was a huge morale builder for the marines and the ARVN, as she was considered public enemy number one. Among some of his other more legendary achievements was taking out a North Vietnamese general. The details on that one will wow you. Carlos stalked the NVA general for nearly a week, with his last four days and nights crawling on the ground in highly inhospitable conditions. He crawled inch by inch, becoming part of the landscape, never being detected by the many NVA patrols that walked past him. He did not take time to sleep nor did he eat during this hunting mission. During this inch-by-inch trek on his belly, he covered 1,500 yards to get close enough to get his deadly accurate shot off from seven hundred yards away. He caught the general while he was in a yawn, never knowing what hit him.

Every NVA soldier in the camp searched with a vengeance for Carlos, but he had become part of the environment. He escaped the same way he set up his stalk and ambush, by being patient and exceptionally brave. His commitment went beyond ordinary human limits. He was driven for one reason, to save American lives.

Carlos had become a major disrupting force to the communists. In some ways he reminds me of the character Robert Redford played in the movie *Jeremiah Johnson*. White Feather would find himself on the other end of an entire platoon of well-trained NVA snipers who would devote all of their attention on taking out the great American sniper.

One of North Vietnam's most treacherous generals had fourteen of his army's best shots undergo extensive training led by a man nicknamed "the Cobra." He was North Vietnam's top guerrilla warfare warrior and was also an excellent shot. Cobra's unit would be turned loose to live off the land in complete solitude till their one goal had been reached—to kill White Feather. All of Carlos's newest would-be assassins were armed with brand-new long-bolt action rifles, custom-fitted for each command with a short telescopic site. The 7.62 x 55 millimeter Mosin-Nagant rifles with their 3.5 power PU scopes were much more accurate than the older weapons used by North Vietnam.

The effect of the special NVA unit was felt immediately as marines began to die right outside their hooches or while they were standing in a chow line or showering. One gunnery sergeant was killed as he was standing outside of another sergeant's hooch…it belonged to Carlos Hathcock. Carlos and the rest of his marine buddies got the message that they were being stalked by a new breed of adversary with skills similar to the Apache's.

The stakes were raised with a 30,000-dollar bounty put on Carlos by General Tran. If that was not enough incentive, the one who would take Carlos down would also receive the equivalent of three and a half years' pay in one lump sum. But Carlos, on the prowl, along with his captain, reciprocated quickly, and two of the elite NVA assassins were eliminated.

One day, Carlos and Captain Land returned from a successful mission taking down another of the original fourteen super snipers of the NVA. But bad news greeted them as a marine captain had been done in. Carlos barely caught his breath and he and his captain went right back out to the bush. Within a few days, Cobra and White Feather faced off. White Feather would escape by a hair, but Cobra was destroyed. Both men got off a shot at each other. Cobra was half a second too late: the shot went right through Cobra's scope—into his eye. This would have a devastating effect on the remaining NVA sniper team, and each of them feared one of them would be next as White Feather was just too good.

General Tran also believed that White Feather would methodically take down each of the remaining ten snipers. So, he made a critical decision by splitting up the remaining ten, assigning each of them their own five-man ambush unit. Now there would be fifty assassins lurking in the bush with the sole purpose of eliminating the legendary White Feather.

Carlos had only a couple months left in Nam, hardly enough time to tackle and destroy the fifty snipers who were on his trail, nor would there be enough time for Carlos to be had. He would finish his tour with over three hundred kills by his estimate, and the Marines credited him with ninety-three confirmed kills. His longest confirmed kill had been at 1,200 yards until he smashed that personal record with a confirmed kill at 2,500 yards. One of his last kills was at 1,500 yards, this victim being a twelve-year-old Viet Cong boy, which would haunt Carlos forever.

Carlos became the marine everyone would go out of their way to meet. During his last two years before a forced retirement because of his failing health, he worked at training the best to become even better. He trained only the highest rated sniper instructors, Special Forces, Rangers, and Navy SEALs. While he was recommended for his country's highest military honor, the Medal of Honor, after two years of waiting for a decision, the award clerks downgraded the award to a Silver Star. He was not bitter over that (I would have been), but the men who served with him remained bitter with the downgrade.

Hathcock had a son, Carlos Hathcock III, who also enlisted in the U.S. Marine Corps. He retired from the Corps as a gunnery sergeant, following in his father's footsteps. He, too, became an expert shooter and a member of the Board of Governors of the Marine Corps Distinguished Shooters Association. Hathcock II was awarded that controversial Silver Star and a Purple Heart, not for his sniping accomplishments, but for his act in 1969 when he saved the lives of seven other marine buddies after an LXT-5 (AMTRAC) on which they were all riding struck a land mine. Hathcock himself was thrown from the amphibious vehicle and immediately knocked unconscious. However, maybe by an act of God, Hathcock woke up in time to wade through the flames and the rubble of the burning vehicle and singlehandedly rescued all his badly injured war buddies.

No matter, the legend of White Feather would live on for many decades after the Vietnam War had ended. Carlos Hathcock always called his best shot ever the one that took down the lady Viet Cong warrior called Apache. Mr. "One Shot, One Kill," Mr. Invincible as many called him, could not be taken down by the Viet Cong or North Vietnamese, but his premature death would come at the hands of a poisonous herbicide known to be a hundred times more potent than domestic weed killers... Agent Orange took the American Sniper.

When Gunnery Sergeant Carlos N. Hathcock II ended his active duty career in the Marine Corps on April 20, 1979, he was presented with an M-40A1 Marine Corps sniper rifle, complete with a ten-power Unertl I scope and a walnut and brass plaque with this inscription:

> *There have been many marines and there have been many marksmen, but there has been only one sniper—Gunnery Sergeant Carlos N. Hancock – One Shot – One Kill.*

Lady warrior, Apache, was a bad, bad woman with a nasty attitude: a cruel and unnecessarily sadistic administrator of torturous and lethal punishment onto an already wounded and defenseless enemy. Remember, we came into their homeland, where the people of Vietnam have been forced into fighting for nearly twenty centuries, just to maintain something Americans have always valued so highly, which is...F-R-E-E-D-O-M!

So, the Vietnam War's queen of the Viet Cong died, taken out by another warrior of a similar kind, a sniper legend, just like a Hollywood script would have had it. The good guy, the American wins. But did Apache's spirit die that day? Or did it live on and motivate her fellow Viet Cong brotherhood and sisterhood to never-ending ambushes of American soldiers and marines until the last one removed himself from the precious land that the Vietnamese revered so highly?

She could have been named Apache out of respect as the Apache Indians were known to be brave and ruthless in torturing their defeated enemies. They were usually stunning in appearance, not something one would expect of a vicious warrior fighting savagely to save his or her people's territory from domination by unwelcomed invaders.

America's Apache Indians looked sad, possibly because of their nostalgia for days gone by when they shared their land only with the massive buffalo herds. Our Vietnam Apache-type warriors had anything but sad expressions. After all, they had been invaded time and time again, but they rarely allowed their rude conquerors the luxury of settling in and getting too comfortable. And so it was with the lady Cong called Apache, never allowing her enemy the luxury of a peaceful night's sleep in her territory.

It is likely understood that the Viet Cong never accepted the death of this lady warrior. Her legend lives on, just as the legends of previous Vietnamese heroines, such as the Trung sisters and Lady Trieu, continue to inspire one future generation after another. One just has to know that the stories about these ladies' magnificent victories have lived on to modern times.

Here is a poem I stumbled onto that seems appropriate for this chapter's mission of…*Unbreakable Hearts*.

Under Her Spell

An Asian beauty bathed in the light of the moon broke many a man's heart and took many lives too soon, a treacherous mistress from the very start. We tried to tame her and got a bullet right to the heart.

A star-filled sky wasn't a romantic sign, it just meant more young men were bound to die. We had a relationship that was born of hell and for most of my life I've been under her spell.

Living a life in a haze, we can't get over that thrill. The only way to forget is to take another damn pill. Soon my senses dull and my rage turns to calm. I sold my soul to a bitch called Nam.

Technicolor dreams filled with night sweats, too many memories of her unwanted cares. Caught tightly in her claws held in a death grip, I vow never to return but she keeps bringing me back.

Many a Nam brother has tried to break loose. We'll have a better chance of escaping a hangman's noose, she whispers in your ear and then the tropical smell in a single heartbeat you are back in her spell.

Living haunted dreams in an Asian hell, laying there shackled and under her spell.

—Rich "Boon" Preston, Vietnam War veteran

I find such examples of human will and tenacity totally mind-boggling. If I was on the other side, the receiving end of the terrible punishment we dished out onto our adversary, I think I *might* have quit...but they rarely did.

Either way, one just has to marvel at the Viet Cong's superhuman mentality, bravery, and resilience in outlasting one super military power after another, because in the end...they would once again be the victors. I think that the Viet Minh, Ho Chi Minh, General Giap, Apache, the Viet Cong, and the North Vietnamese Army (NVA) fought their uncanny style of combat to near perfection, and this caused the American military and their allies to adapt and evolve on the spot in order to combat techniques being used against them.

KNOW THIS: I personally believe nearly 90 percent of the credit for the American soldier boys' ability to adjust and perform the way they did—in the worst imaginable conditions Mother Nature and Vietnam's geography had to offer—should go to all of the combat MOS troops from the rank of sergeant E-7 to private E-3. Of course, all of the men I fought alongside were within those ranks, so maybe I am a bit biased. I would give the E-8 on up the remaining 10 percent. This gradual evolvement was not necessarily being incorporated into the Americans' training routine in the States. It seemed to just happen on the field troops' own initiative, the ones who were sent to engage the VC nearly twenty-four/seven from 1965 to 1970. I guess it was an example of on-the-job training at its best...or worst?

Even today, our nightmares lead us to crawl around on our hands and knees, looking for VC. My wife has witnessed this often from me, once with a deadly machete in hand at 2:00 a.m. at home. Try to imagine her reaction—she was SHOCKED. Over there, it was either adapt to the unforeseen situation or, in many cases, die. Those of us who survived a year or so of the Nam experience find ourselves with memories of extremely traumatic events that will never leave us.

There was no other choice but retreat when we were hit badly by a VC ambush, and I can tell you the American grunt and marines in the Vietnam War almost always stood their ground or counter-ambushed. This was not a move the VC or Viet Minh had run into before, so it caused confusion, bewilderment, and even fear among our attackers.

Of course, this aggressive action would inevitably cause more American casualties than we would have suffered by staying put, belly down, hoping the VC would just leave, which they did sometimes. But they might advance, trying to overrun us and kill or capture us. We could never figure them out.

Something else fueled the inspiration of the Viet Cong, NVA, Viet Minh, and whatever their warrior ancestors called themselves, which was their history for more than two thousand years.

Our in-your-face jungle-fighting techniques with such an unpredictable enemy put us at our most nerve-wracked limit. We did not have the rest of our lives available to us. Sometimes a guy would become a jungle warfare expert in twenty-four hours. The Vietnam War would create a new kind of American soldier or marine; they would truly be transformed into warriors who fought like few Americans before them. This came to fruition partly due to the alarming, vicious, demonic suicidal style of warfare similar to that of Apache and her lady Cong-mates.

So, where did the true Vietnamese people come from? How did they become so resilient and almost antagonistic toward larger and more powerful invading armies? Why and how did the American government and its elite military leaders put themselves into the situation of not being prepared for the continuation of France's war with the North Vietnamese? How could such rare warrior qualities from a small and seemingly insignificant kingdom come to happen and cause such major historical changes for so many? Where did they come from?

WHITE FEATHER

Carlos Hathcock (White Feather)

Apache Soldiers

Captured / Tortured Americans

Chapter 2

WHERE DID THEY COME FROM?

Throughout the book, I bring you some of the most profound historical facts I could find from history which were written in Vietnam and America by worldly scholars and some not so worldly. But everyone deserves a shot. I have given equal coverage to those who have made history during and after the Vietnam War. As we say back on the street…"You can't make this shit up!" So, I bring it with very little fiction as most of this book has been documented.

The great rulers of China were defeated several times by that little hamlet-like nation called Vietnam. I personally cannot comprehend this, and find it almost too fantastic a story to fathom. But I am here today attempting to tell all of America that our leaders not only underestimated the heart of Vietnam's people, but also the heart of their own American soldier boys sent over there to fight a people who have always been eager to fight in a war that forced them to defend their homeland…at any cost.

How many times must they be tested? This chapter offers a question that I am not so sure anyone has answered in any historical document. Surely, the ancestors of the present-day Vietnamese fished from the same rivers, farmed in rice paddies, and built their shelters around the same time, in the same general geographical areas as other peoples who inhabited the countries surrounding Vietnam.

Where did they come from and how did they become what they became with so many hostiles around them? Vietnam is not an insignificant land and neither are the Vietnamese people. The longer I proceeded with this book and continued to search for other historical facts about these gritty, resilient, amazing people, the more I became intrigued with them. Why not? I lived with them (in the jungles), slept with them, laughed with them, cried with them, and killed them…without ever getting to know them! As I say often… **it's never too late!**

The history of the Vietnam region and its first inhabitants could be one of the longest continuous histories in the world with cultural documentation going back around twenty-five thousand years. I said, "could be." Ancient Vietnam was home to some of the world's earliest civilizations and societies who practiced agriculture. History says that as early as 2000 BC, the early Vietnamese had learned the process of making silk and by 1500 BC, they had already developed a sophisticated agricultural society.

However, prehistoric Vietnamese people can be traced back to the Paleolithic Age between 12,000 BC to 10,000 BC. The Hoa Bink culture of mostly nomads eventually settled in the Red River Valley while another group, the Bac Son people, lived in tribes in the high lands, headed by mostly female leaders.

I would suppose it is natural that when most people think of Vietnam today, they think of the Vietnam War. However, Vietnam history has an abundance of tradition, legend, heroes, villains, determination, sorrow, resilience, and adaptation that existed long before the Vietnam wars with France and America. Therefore, I thought if I was ever going to understand what made our adversary so resilient in our war with them, it was mandatory for me to understand Vietnam's rich history. The results of my research into that rich history inspired me to keep digging further and to continue with the book.

Inheriting one's traits from our ancestors, generation after generation, to me, is one very interesting, complex, and confusing process of the human race. As Americans, aside from Native Americans, we have been in this world for just a few minutes in comparison to our ancestors from other countries or continents. It remains popular to delve into the past to research who our earliest relatives were. For instance, my family tree shows a long, continuous trail of pro-military and patriotic relatives, such as a half-brother (Korea), an uncle (Korea), three uncles (WWII), a grandpa (WWI), and a great-grandpa (Spanish-American War). That is as far back as I have gone. Perhaps someday I will look into our family's history in the Civil War and our War for Independence. I have always had a notion to find out more about my mother's Norwegian ancestors. Those Vikings were real warriors.

The Vietnamese people, strange as it seems, have been the Vietnamese people for more than four thousand years, according to their traditional legends. I now understand that in order to fully and accurately understand the history and consequences of the Vietnam War, it is critical to try to grasp an understanding of Vietnam's history.

Vietnam was originally formed when King Lac Lang Quan (Dragon Lord of Lac) married Princess Au Co, who was considered an immortal from the high mountains. She bore King Lac one hundred sons, and from them, Vietnam stretched from southern China to northern Indonesia. The king and the princess eventually separated, and with fifty sons each, King Lac ruled in the southern lowlands and Princess Au Co ruled the northern mountain region. Historical information for this timeframe is difficult to find, and much of it came from exaggerated storytelling over the centuries. After King Lac died in 2879 BC, his oldest son, Hung Vuong, established the Hung dynasty, and he is regarded as the original creator and founder of the Vietnamese nation and the first Vietnamese dynasty. This is one of the legends that connects and symbolizes the importance of the unification of the two main geographical and cultural areas of Vietnam—the highlands in the north and the south's lowlands. I guess you could surmise that all Vietnamese people of pure Vietnamese ethnicity are related back to the one hundred sons, their wives, and their offspring. Anyone who has spent some time in Vietnam would become acutely aware of and impressed by how much the Vietnamese people value family. It is a tradition stretching back for thousands of years. I feel rewarded to have learned this and to understand why.

Confused? Yes, this part of the story was pretty difficult for me to write and organize; the names of kings and the kingdoms presented a problem for me since I don't communicate in the Vietnamese language. In fact, like the origins of the Vietnamese people and culture, the history of their language is also a mixture of different components. Some scholars claim that the Vietnamese language is part of what is called the Mon-Khmer branch of the Austro-Asiatic language family. The Mon-Khmer gave Vietnamese many of its basic words and the Tai languages contributed many aspects of tonality and grammar. Then, because the Chinese dominated Vietnamese culture and history for almost a millennium, much of the Vietnamese vocabulary comes from Chinese, although the pronunciations have changed. There are even a few French and English words that have found a home in the Vietnamese language. Prior to the French invasions, "Viet Nam" was changed to one word by the French, as it has remained.

Vietnam was first conquered and incorporated into the Chinese empire under the Hans dynasty in the year 111 BC. The first Vietnamese rebellion in 39 AD (to be mentioned in other chapters) was led by the legendary Trung sisters. This is when the Vietnamese as a nation began their tradition of resistance and fighting, at whatever the cost, to remain free and independent.

The Vietnamese people would continue to resist the rule of China for nine centuries until 939 AD, as China's Tang dynasty had become weak. It would be another hero rising up named Ngo Quyen as he led the Vietnamese to a lasting freedom and established the first of the great dynasties of Vietnam. This golden era would last nearly one thousand years.

THE GREAT DYNASTIES OF VIETNAM[1]

Ngo dynasty	939 – 967	
Dinh dynasty	968 – 980	
Early Le dynasty	980 – 1009	
Ly dynasty	1009 – 1225	
Tran dynasty	1225 – 1400	
Ho dynasty	1400 – 1428	
Late Le dynasty	1428 – 1776	Known as the "golden era" of Vietnam.
Trinh and Nguyen dynasty	1543 – 1776	The Nguyen lords united a divided Vietnam as the nation reached its present-day size and shape by 1757.
Nguyen dynasty	1792 – 1883	Despite revolts, the nation remained unified. The capital was moved to Hue and prospered. French missionaries became prominent even though the Nguyens were hostile against the inevitable colonization.

Some historians say that before the first written history appeared, some twenty thousand years BC, there were already people of mythological legends who inhabited the original land of what would someday be called Vietnam. Other records say 10,000 BC is more accurate. Since factual information about this is so scarce, I'll not dwell on the subject. I am just putting it out there for people to think about and maybe research for themselves.

Vietnamese people represent a fusion of races, nationalities, cultures, and languages, which have not been completely sorted out yet, as the archaeologists, linguistic experts, and other experts say. This is true for most of Southeast Asia, as the Indonesian Peninsula was a virtual highway for the migration of people. Although the Vietnamese language is a distinct language, much of it has been borrowed and merged together.

In 2879 BC, the kingdom called Van Lang (Vietnam) was founded by people referred to as Lac Viets. This area, known today as the lowland plains of Vietnam, particularly the marshy Red River Delta, was ruled under their first of many kings to come, An Durong Vurong (Loc Tuc). During this period of Vietnam, the tribes of Vietnam or Van Lang existed freely and prosperously as the Hong Bang dynasty for over 2,600 years from 2879 BC

---

1   www.asian-nation.org/Vietnam-history

to 258 BC. Eighteen separate kings ruled the area, all descendants of King Durong Vurong.

The conquering king-to-be of this expanding kingdom was Thuc Phan, who renamed the kingdom Au Lac. His capital and main citadel (a fortress) was Co Loa Citadel in modern-day Hanoi. The city was strategically placed in an area almost completely covered by rough and heavily forested mountain ranges to the north and west. Thuc Phan ruled quite successfully from 257 BC to 200 BC. Actually, at the approximate time Co Loa Citadel was built as a fortress, the Qin dynasty in China ordered the construction of the Great Wall. Note, from 217 BC to 207 BC, the Chinese Qin dynasty attempted many invasions to conquer Au Lac, but were repeatedly defeated by a highly outnumbered Vietnamese (Au Lac) military. Eventually, the Co Loa fortress was taken by the Chinese Qin, Trieu Da. From there, Au Lac became known as Nam Viet, and the Trieu dynasty ruled from 207 BC to 111 BC, when the Han dynasty, also from China, would invade and defeat the Trieu Empire. You have to put these events into perspective. They were not taking place every other year or so. It took centuries to happen.

Doc Lap is a phrase used to signify the Vietnamese spirit of independence that is traced back to approximately 500 BC. That would be a mere 2,275 years before 1776 AD when our great country earned its independence. When the massive Chinese armies were invading northern Vietnam, a group of Viet tribes called the Nam traveled southward to escape the advancing armies from the Chinese empire. The inevitable result was impossible to avoid. The Viet tribes were eventually overwhelmed and conquered in 258 BC.

Over the next thousand years, the Chinese dynasties aggressively attempted to wear down the Vietnamese race and to assimilate them into the Chinese culture as they had done so easily with many other cultures. However, the Chinese would never be able to continue their brutal domination over the Vietnamese.

One of the reasons the Chinese failed to completely and totally subdue the Vietnamese civilization was that the Viets' pre-China domination was long enough for them to develop their own distinctive ethnic traits and features. The Vietnamese racial identity was strong enough to withstand a thousand years of foreign attempts of domination. The Viets would suffer minimal cultural damage during these very forgettable years of their history.

History says that sometime between 200 BC and 200 AD, the Red River's inhabitants evolved into a distinct Vietnamese people. However, they would be ruled by their larger neighbor to the north for most of the years until 938 AD. During these years, other parts of modern-day Vietnam were separate and independent kingdoms.

It is amazing to me how Vietnam nationalism rose to and maintained the level it did from the ninth to the twentieth centuries, and that ancient Vietnamese are respected and cherished so highly by the modern-day Vietnamese people. It is amazing because of the separate identities of those people and the changes of country names and boundaries—from Au Lac to Champa to Nam Viet to Dai Viet, An Nam, Tran Nam, Dai Co Viet, Dai Nam, French Indochina, Vietnam, South and North Vietnam, and finally Vietnam again. Modern Vietnamese know that their history is rich and evocative. Sure, the American Vietnam War dominated the attention of the West, but the Viets have been scrapping with the Chinese, Khmers, Chams, Japanese, Mongolians, and French long before Americans joined the long list of powerful countries and empires that the Vietnamese outlasted and defeated. Wouldn't one think that with America's technological advances by the 1960s, our leaders and planners would have paid just a little more attention to the history of this proud nation called Vietnam before invading their beloved homeland?

Legends, fiction, or non-fiction? While I maintain that most of the material in my books happened as I have described them from the sources offered, there is one factor that is out of my control. In many cases, when you read about the prehistoric stories of a society that stretches back several hundred or thousands of years, these stories could possibly have been written as legend.

Vietnamese historians characterize the Dong Son culture as the beginning of the Vietnamese nation. This took place in 2,000 BC and included Van Lang, considered the first kingdom of Vietnam. Van Lang shows up in most history books as the correct name of the first legendary nation of what would become Vietnam. It lasted more than twelve hundred years without interruption. Van Lang enjoyed peace, tranquility, and great prosperity during this era under an extended list of some eighty-eight Hung kings. Each passed the throne on to the next ruling family member in line for the title. Only eighteen actual names of Hung kings can be found on record.

I say this here because I found conflicting accounts about the founding ruler of Vietnam, Hung Vuong or King Hung, and his dynasty, the Hong Bang (2879 – 258 BC). Regardless, today's Vietnamese honor King Hung as the ruler of Van Lang with a lavish temple dedicated to him, and they host annual celebrations of his anniversary (tenth day of the lunar calendar's third month).

Van Lang (Vietnam then) is reported to have included southern China down to what is central Vietnam today. There is an abundance of fascinating stories (legends) told by Vietnamese of these times. The Vietnamese have always been good storytellers according to several history books. Their history remains one of the important inspirations behind the many struggles to maintain their freedom from the invaders from the north.

Just for the heck of it, here is a list of Vietnam's various name changes:

Timeframe	Kingdom or Country Name
2879 – 2524 BC	Xich Quy
2524 – 258 BC	Van Lang
258 – 207 BC	Au Lac
207 – 111 BC	Nam Viet
111 BC – 40 AD	Giao Chi
40 – 43 AD	Linh Nam
43 – 299 AD	Giao Chi
299 – 544 AD	Giao Chau
544 – 602 AD	Van Xuan
602 – 757 AD	An Nam
757 – 766 AD	Tran Nam
766 – 967 AD	Tinh Hai quan
968 – 1054 AD	Dai Co Viet
1054 – 1400 AD	Dai Viet
1400 – 1407 AD	Dai Ngu
1407 – 1427 AD	Giao Chi
1427 – 1804 AD	Dai Viet
1804 – 1839 AD	Vietnam
1839 – 1887 AD	Dai Nam
1887 – 1945 AD	French Indochina
1945 – Present	Vietnam
	South & North Vietnam
	Vietnam

The Champa kingdom survived. The remains of what was a thriving region of Hindu kingdoms once called Champa barely exist in Vietnam and Cambodia. Today, the Chams are Vietnam's only surviving Hindus, an almost forgotten people of about sixty to seventy thousand. Their numbers were greatly reduced from a war with Dai Viet and persecution by the Northern Vietnamese and Cambodia's Khmer Rouge. The Khmers had set a goal of eliminating all non-Khmer people in Cambodia in the 1975–1979 timeframe until Vietnam invaded Cambodia and stopped them in 1979.

Most of present-day southern and central Vietnam, from roughly the eighteenth parallel to the South China Sea, was established by people of Malayo-Polynesian stock and Indianized culture. They were called the Chams and their kingdom was known as Champa. Chinese records use the name Champa, dating back to 877 AD. The people of Champa were a bit different from their northern neighbors, Dai Viet, which would become North Vietnam. Champa (area of South Vietnam) was eventually conquered and absorbed into Vietnam by the seventeenth century.

The people of Champa also fought the Chinese in a fierce manner, and just like the northern Dai Viets, their primary goal was to keep their land free from domination by the Chinese and Mongol invaders. From the seventh to the tenth centuries, Champa controlled trade in the Indonesian region.

To the west of Champa lived the early modern-day Cambodians, the Khmer. Relations between them were always testy. Champa fought the Khmers. Dai Viet also fought them both for centuries. Dai Viet obliterated Champa by 1471 AD and modern-day Vietnam surfaced. In 1804, Dai Viet and Champa became officially known as Vietnam…until it was renamed French Indochina.

Vietnam's history can be difficult to dissect and even more difficult to put together in an accurate chronological order, and that is not the goal of this book. I hope I have not done too badly in this section, and that degreed historians will be gentle on my efforts.

A minor example of the confusion one could run into (as I did) is when the history books talk about four distinctly separate dynasties that ruled for a long time in or around the Red River Valley where present-day Vietnam sits.

The early Le dynasty (980–1009). The Late Le dynasty (1428–1788). The Li dynasty (1010–?) and the Ly dynasty (968–1054). Try those on for size when attempting to research Vietnam history and keep it in proper order. For instance in the early writing of this book, I totally confused our typist by misplacing an I for an E or a Y. Therefore, I found myself returning to Chapter 2 several times to make corrections.

It is worth noting that the kingdom of Champa had a strong female influence, as Dai Viet did, on its rise to prominence. Cham history states that the founder of Champa was a woman named Lady Po Nagar. She actually married a powerful Chinese crown prince, the Chinese emperor's son. They had two children, and the safety of Champa was guaranteed for a few more decades. Eventually, Lady Po escaped from being forced to remain in China. She is reported to have shown up in Nha Trang, where her family was living. Near modern Nha Trang the Cham Temple Tower, built in the 700s AD, still stands in her honor. There is also the Po Nagar Festival in Nha Trang, which commemorates Po Nagar as the goddess who taught her people how to form and to weave fabric, and protected them from diseases and disasters. Her death remains a mystery, as does the complete elimination of Champa as its own identity. At one time, Champa covered Laos, half of Vietnam, Cambodia, and part of Thailand. To confuse the matter, southern Champa became Cochinchina, a French colony from 1862 to 1954 and then this area became the state of South Vietnam. Oh, by the way, in the seventeenth century, the northernmost part of Vietnam was called Tonkin and Annam with Cochinchina at the bottom.

Today, the region of what used to be called Champa thrives culturally. It can be a tourist's dream. Many of the vast temple complexes the Chams built remain strong. The site of the magnificent Son Tien Tu pagoda found on top of Mount Ba is still considered to be one of the most spiritual and sacred places in all of Southeast Asia.

Today's Cham people are not centered in Vietnam; rather they can be found throughout East Asia. They are no longer predominantly Hindu, but have transformed to Sunni Muslim, Shia Muslim, and Buddhist. Chams in Vietnam remain dedicated Hindus.

Empire of Vietnam? This was another name, but it was very short lived when, compliments of Imperial Japan, Vietnam's sovereignty was returned after France's fall in World War II. Shortly afterward, the ministers of the Empire of Vietnam met and unanimously altered the country's name to Viêt Nam. This was the first time that most patriots in the north, central, and southern regions officially recognized this name. Prior to this, the three most common names used were Dai Viet, An Nam, and Dai Nam. Vietnam…Viet Nam…Viet-Nam are all correct to use in spelling. On that note, I will move away from the historical portion about *Where They Came From* and get into the hot and heavy war history of Vietnam.

Throughout history, Vietnam has been bullied by northern neighbor China and her multitude of power-hungry dynasties. In fact, from the first century to the tenth century, the Chinese would dominate the Vietnamese as though they always owned them. The Vietnamese were distinctly different from the Chinese. Kissing cousins they are not, nor have they ever been or are ever likely to be. It would seem that the one common emotion each has for the other would be…scathing hatred.

Early rule of Vietnam began in the second century BC, as they were settling on land in the Red River Delta which had already been inhabited by the Vietnamese Dong Son. The Chinese named the area Annam ("Southern Domain"), but Vietnamese referred to their land as Van Lang and Au Loc. When the first official Chinese military invasion took place in 111 BC, the northern region of Vietnam was incorporated into the Han dynasty's powerful empire. Even though China would occupy Vietnam for much of a thousand-year period, amongst and around numerous Vietnamese uprisings, the Chinese never broke their southern neighbor's will.

Most of the time, Chinese rule was marked with brutality, slavery, and huge tributes. The Vietnamese remained stubborn and resentful in enduring the cultures that were being forced on them. I guess Vietnam's biggest treasure to China were the trade routes between Vietnam and India as well as elsewhere, such as the Middle East and access to the South China Sea.

The big plus for Vietnam was the massive construction of roads, harbors, and better irrigation methods by Chinese presence in the earliest centuries. But the Vietnamese held on dearly to their culture and their separate identity, as they were very different.

One of the mind-boggling puzzles about Vietnam's history that I had hoped to solve was the argument that spurned the American-Vietnam War: Was there ever enough sound evidence to support the argument that Vietnam was psychologically and economically two separate countries (North and South Vietnam)? This scenario in Vietnam's history has been thoroughly covered by the Vietnamese historians except that the information has not been readily available for people outside of Vietnam and I can understand why.

The Chinese invasions into northern and central Vietnam caused several periods of migration for northern Vietnamese into the lands that would become South Vietnam. Champa and what is eastern Cambodia would be easy conquests for the more aggressive northern Vietnamese. This exodus from the tenth to seventeenth century was similar to our own expansion moves in the USA until the East Coast and West Coast became our boundaries.

There was a constant growth of antagonism between the south and north. The north was far more populous and it needed more land, but of course the south's resentment was inevitably going to bring a clash between the two regions; it was just a matter of when and how. The intervention of western colonialists such as the Dutch, Portuguese, and of course the French continued from this point in time, the differences between north and south Vietnamese would widen, but there was still one country, a united Vietnam.

At this time there was strong nationalism in all of Vietnam. But the French always gave more favoritism to the southern Vietnamese. They even created a French-trained southern Vietnamese Army while the northerners wanted little to do with the French in their governing and their self-defense. Communism would plant its seeds in the north during this period of French-forced colonialism, and tensions between northern and southern Vietnamese would fester until the French-Vietnam War.

I hope that everyone who reads this book will come to understand and appreciate why such fierce and profoundly determined warrior-type mentalities like the female Viet Cong "Apache" evolved and fought in war after war from the year 39 AD to the 1970s during the Vietnam War and China's last invasion into Vietnam in 1979. I have every reason to expect that if Vietnam is ever invaded again, regardless of who the brain-dead intruder is, they would be inflicted with great pain and monstrous casualties.

On that final note, I invite you to experience the tragic, heart-wrenching disaster to glory evolution of many revolutions that would establish the character (the hard way) of the Vietnamese people. Their patriotic nationalism and "mother bear" style of protecting their cubs would become a legendary trademark of Vietnam and its people.

Chapter 3

CHINA ATTACKS AGAIN, AGAIN...AND AGAIN!

The Vietnamese-Chinese friction began from 200–111 BC with the first Chinese invasion of what was a free, independent, and thriving Vietnam. The most recent Chinese invasion of Vietnam occurred in 1979...2,090 years later. While it took the Vietnamese 150 years to become strong enough to challenge and defeat the Chinese in 39 AD, the 1979 invasion was met head-on and the Chinese were sent back to China after a twenty-nine-day bloody battle, which China did not win.

During all of the Chinese invasions, only northern Vietnam territory was involved. What is southern Vietnam today was once called Champa, a separate country in ancient times. Northern Vietnam was called Dai Viet, but the two would eventually merge into one nation.

What blows my mind is that China supported North Vietnam as if they were long-lost brothers in the war against South Vietnam and America. In fact, during the peak years of the Vietnam-American War, 1965–1969, China had sent in sixteen anti-aircraft divisions, amounting to 150,000 to 170,000 personnel, to North Vietnam. Logically, Chinese direct participation peaked during the years of 1967 and 1968. Realistically, China had been supporting the northern Vietnamese in one capacity or another from the Viet Minh war with the French and southern Vietnam's army from the 1950s until 1971–1972 when the U.S. retreated or the extraction of its military took place.

Some interested historians look at the French versus Vietnam as Vietnam War I, America versus Vietnam as Vietnam War II, and since the end of II, it has been Vietnam versus China or Vietnam War III. Border skirmishes between China and Vietnam have erupted throughout the 1970s, 1980s, and 1990s to the date of this book's beginning in 2015 and to the completion of this book in the fall of 2016. Only now, the differences are between China and Vietnam, Taiwan, the Philippines, Japan, and even the USA—the Paracel Islands and controlling South China Sea passages being the primary reason.

Bottom line—no country today weighs on Vietnam like China, and it has been that way for twenty centuries. It has never really ended and there remains little or no animosity toward the USA despite the brutal bloody war between each other and the twenty years of economic sanctions by the U.S.

I predicted fresh, smoother relations between Vietnam and the USA in my first book.[2]

China invades in 111 BC. The very ancient Chinese civilization seems to have been born with military activity since the dawn of war itself. Forming around 6000 BC, they are one of the world's oldest, longest continuing civilizations on planet Earth. It appears that the Chinese cities practiced their warfare prowess by conquering each other. At the same time, their neighbors to the south, in what was to become Vietnam, were peaceful and family-oriented and got along well with each other. They showed little war-like tendencies for centuries until the great military power from the north attacked and conquered northern Vietnam in 111 BC.

China needed to have a powerful military ready at all times because of the ongoing rivalries between the city-states. Eventually, several of these city-states would unite and attempt to take over surrounding areas like Vietnam and Korea. Other than their own farm tools like pitchforks and knives, the Vietnamese were basically rendered helpless to prevent, let alone defeat, the masses of Chinese infantry supported by an untold number of chariots. Only the hill tribesmen in Vietnam, with their early bows and arrows, could offer much resistance against the Chinese invaders, armed with axes, swords, and advanced compound bows. It was the great Han dynasty that rose to be the most powerful army ever assembled in China, and their conquest of Vietnam as well as Korea by the year 111 BC went swiftly.

With Vietnam and China as two of the world's oldest bordering civilizations, one would think that the two, with a combined existence of more than twenty thousand years, would be getting along about now. Don't count on it, and maybe the ancient ones are to blame for today's disagreements.

Long before the mighty Han dynasty rose to power, China had been a slave society; however, the Han reached a high level of prosperity, and their regime lasted 426 years.

The rise of the Trung sisters would alter Vietnam's history forever. In the earliest times of ancient Vietnam, Jesus would have been thirty-nine years old when this story unfolded in 39 AD. The birth of the Vietnam nation arrived in spectacular fashion. Please keep in mind that back then, women were seated at the rear of the bus in most countries, but not in Vietnam.

The first Chinese domination of the area of Vietnam was closing in on its two hundredth anniversary, but that domination would run into a slight bump in the path of the anticipated bicentennial celebration. During 37 AD, three brave, smart, and fearless women rose up and recruited, trained, and

---

2   www.npr.org/sections/parallels; http:/history.stackexchangel.com;
    http:/en.wikipedia.org/wiki/Chinese

organized a force of eighty thousand from the peasants and rice paddy farmers with support from the indigenous tribes from the forested hill country. The goal…to expel the Chinese rulers from their land even though they knew how badly outnumbered their quickly trained army would be.

Trung Trac, her sister Trung Nhi, and their appointed Commanding General Phung Thi Chinh, along with the Trung sisters' mother and thirty-five other lady warriors, were the captains of this new military. Most men feared the three leaders, as their fearlessness and deadly martial arts skills were legendary. Trung Trac, the oldest of the three, was the strongest warrior, and legend has it that she killed a bloodthirsty, man-eating tiger with just a "pitchfork and knife." She skinned the tiger and wore it over her shoulder as she rode into battle on her war elephant. All three lady warriors were reported to have uncanny beauty to complement their ruggedness. They were married to Vietnamese nobles. I guess we know who wore the pants in those hooches or pagodas. Even some Chinese historical records commented on how brave they were with a nasty disposition.

Trung Trac was proclaimed the supreme ruler by the people. They renamed her "Trung Vuong" or "She-King Trung." The Trungs quickly abolished the despised tribute taxes which had been imposed by the Chinese. They also attempted to restore a simpler form of government.

These early defining moments of time in Vietnamese history would be challenged by few modern-day Vietnamese nationalists. That moment of character-building and astonishing bravery of biblical proportions was, in fact, a David versus Goliath replay when the Trung sisters, with their lady general Phung Thi Chinh, raised and led a ferociously determined army and warriors from the native hill tribes to challenge their Chinese rulers. Outnumbered nearly ten to one, they fought their land's first historical War of Independence and won it in 39–40 AD.

The Trung sisters rose up while China controlled early Vietnam from approximately 111 BC until 39 AD, by assigning their own governors and overseers of the villages. Their attempt to impose complete cultural and political control over northern Vietnam was met with stiff, continuous resistance, and relations were always tense. One shocking difference to the Chinese rulers was that the Vietnamese allowed equal rights to their women, including the right to inherit and own property. In the kingdom of Vietnam, women served as soldiers, judges, and rulers of higher status.

Han Chinese rule was becoming intolerable because of feelings of extreme resentment among those being oppressed. Struggles became frequent between Vietnamese and their northern rulers. Skirmishes turned into full-fledged battles and tensions increased. Trung Trac and her sister Trung Nhi, born in a rural Vietnamese village, were the daughters of a nobleman and a military head, which allowed the sisters to grow up well versed in the martial arts. They would spend much time studying the art of warfare, weaponry, and battle strategy. They also grew up with a dislike for the ruthless way the Chinese treated their people.

One day, Trung Trac met a young prince named Thi Sac, who was also very into the martial arts, and he was not happy with the Chinese overlords. Thi Sac and Trung Trac fell in love and married, uniting two military-type families. This gave new hope to the Vietnamese people of resisting their cruel masters. When the resistance grew with Thi and Trung leading the way, the Chinese became even more savage, but the Vietnamese continued their resistance. The Chinese were so infuriated by the rebel-like actions that the execution of Thi Sac was carried out as a warning to the population. The Vietnamese did not just bow down and submit; rather they united and retaliated with a fury that caught the Chinese by complete surprise, as they did not anticipate such a violent response from conquered subjects.

Leading the cause, Trung Trac and her sister rallied and recruited more fighters, and the revolution intensified. It was in 39–40 AD when Trung's army was successful in defeating a Chinese army unit. Her rebels included a large makeup of Vietnamese women. The cause grew; Trung's army grew to one hundred thousand strong. This led to a major confrontation with a large unit of Chinese soldiers. The Trungs led from atop their war elephants, and within a few short months, their bid for independence was successful. The Chinese were soundly defeated, and the Vietnamese had recaptured sixty-five towns, which were fortified. With untrained forces and scant financial support, and without sufficient supplies or heavy weaponry, Trung and Trac, as the leading combatants, had completed a monumental feat—one that was history-changing for the tenacious Vietnamese.

During a three-year period, the Trung sisters and their allies took control of sixty-five Chinese citadels or fortresses. The victorious Trungs jointly proclaimed themselves queens of an independent state (of unknown name) extending from portions of southern China to the present site of Hue, Vietnam.

What an intolerable shock it must have been to the Chinese rulers when the Vietnamese resistance movement became more than just a nuisance to the elite and all-powerful emperor of China. I would have relished the opportunity of being present when the Chinese monarchs were informed of a very real and threatening civil disturbance—actually a revolution—that was taking place in Vietnam…and that it was being coordinated and led by two daughters of a Vietnamese nobleman from the Hanoi area.

The Trungs and their greatly outnumbered forces of native tribes and "farmers and peasants" would eventually be no match for the professional military hordes of the Han dynasty, and eventually in 43 AD, they were overcome at the battle site of Lang Bac, near what would be the present site of Hanoi. Oddly enough, the latter-day Vietnamese would place the Ho Chi Minh Mausoleum at the Lang Bac battle location, which took place nearly two thousand years earlier.

Some historians have written that the Trung sister revolutionaries were outnumbered by the Chinese army of General Ma Yuan by as much as ten-to-one. The Trung forces never had a chance in their final battle. However, there was not going to be an easy surrender, not just yet. The Trung forces retreated to what is now known as Son Tay, where they were surrounded and decisively beaten back three times, but not without inflicting massive damage onto the large Chinese army. The Trung sisters were among the last ones standing, similar to a "Custer's Last Stand" event. But their situation was hopeless. Unable to accept defeat or allow themselves to be killed by their enemy, both Trung sisters managed to avoid death at the hands of their attackers and committed suicide by drowning themselves in very dramatic fashion, in the Red River in AD 43.

While Vietnamese women have commonly been significant participants in defense of their homeland, most modern-day Vietnamese would be likely to agree on this one thing—probably the most significant women and event in their country's history are the Trung sisters and their famous victory over the Chinese army in 40 AD. Their acts of organizing the force, leading it, and fighting side by side with their outmanned army were so profoundly important that if they had not risen to such greatness and fearlessness, Vietnam would not be enjoying the benefits it now does as an independent and united country. More likely than not, Vietnam would be part of China today in 2016. It should be mentioned that the Trung sisters enjoyed years of freedom while growing up which allowed them certain liberties that were not given to Vietnamese women in the following centuries. The Trungs had the right to inherit property; they could trade with male traders and talk with male political leaders and military members.

Phung Thi Chinh was responsible for protecting the central flank, which she did in miraculous fashion. Legend says that she gave birth during the final battle and had her newborn strapped to her back as she continued to fight for the lives of her child and countrymen. It was said that when she heard of the Trungs' self-inflicted deaths, she killed her child and herself. Another legend I found was where the Trung sisters' mother fought and died in that final battle in the Red River Delta in 43 AD.

The Vietnamese women have always been in the mix during their country's resistance of foreign invaders, from the Trung sisters' victory over the Chinese to the Viet Cong in the war with America. Without their important participation, it is not likely that they would be a free Vietnam today.

Over the years, the Trung sisters' episodes became the material for legends and great poems and a source of pride for women. Today, Vietnam keeps the memory of the Trung sisters alive in a glorious fashion with monuments, books, plays, poems, posters, stamps, etc. It would not surprise me if the Viet Cong women who fought us at Dau Tieng and throughout the Vietnam War carried a memento of the Trung sisters with them, as many of them fought like the Trungs must have.

> *All the male heroes bowed their heads in submission to the Chinese;*
> *only the two sisters proudly stood up to avenge their country.*
> **—Fifteenth-Century Vietnamese Poem**

Vietnamese historians have plenty to say about the Trung sisters and their inspirational rebellion attempts against the Chinese. As Queen Trung, Trung Trac's reign lasted three years over a kingdom that she had established. It was called Au Lac.

The Chinese rule had lasted up to the Trung sisters' revolt. Regardless of which account one chooses to accept—Chinese or Vietnamese—today the Trung sisters are highly revered in Vietnam, as they led the first successful rebellion against the occupying Chinese. Vietnam honors the Trungs with an annual holiday, and there are many temples that have been constructed to honor them. Many schools and streets have also been named after them, including one of the main districts in Hanoi, the Hai Ba Trung District.

Amazingly, the Trung sisters' revolt against the Chinese was about two thousand years ago (before the discovery of America). The Trungs are highly respected national heroes. They are often depicted as two women riding two giant war elephants into battle, leading the charge while waving their swords. They remain powerful symbols of Vietnamese resistance and freedom. The Trung sisters were not your everyday housewives. Both had spent a lot of time studying the art of self-defense and warfare. They also became proficient in the martial arts, a privilege afforded them for being born into a military family.

The Trung sisters' brave acts awakened a population of people who had become accustomed to just bowing their heads to their rulers from the north (Chinese); a renewed sense of pride and nationalism had been resurrected in the Vietnam kingdom. That same pride and nationalism still exist today. This is the kind of adversary that a few hundred years later America would underestimate, and the price to be paid would last for several decades. **Never Underestimate the Heart of Your Enemy!**

It must have been extremely embarrassing for the elite Chinese military leaders to swallow the fact that the Trung sisters were able to hold off all

Chinese advances for three years. It appears that Chinese historians even went so far as to offer practically no recognition or valor to the feats of the Trung sisters. In fact, the Chinese accounts of how the Trung sisters died bear no resemblance to the Vietnamese historical accounts. Regardless, even during the decades-long struggles for Vietnam's independence in the twentieth century—against the French and the United States—the stories of the Trung sisters' brave feats have remained an inspiration to the majority of the Vietnamese population. This attitude about women has contributed to the large number of female soldiers who fought in the Vietnam wars. The sisters are honored every year in Vietnam just as George Washington is honored in America. They may be Vietnam's most revered heroes of all time.

Second invasion 43–544 AD. After the Trungs were defeated, the Han Chinese resumed their old tricks and clamped down on the people of Vietnam. Thousands of the Trungs' loyal supporters were executed. The Chinese would rule the Viets for a very long time, but there would be more champions who rose to become heroes of the Vietnam people's continuing struggles to regain their freedom time and time again.

Chinese rule over the area of present-day Vietnam resumed and continued into the tenth century even though countless rebellion attempts were carried out by the Viet people, who would never just sit back and bow to the Chinese. History was destined to repeat itself over and over from the Trungs' successful victories over the Chinese in 39 AD.

Lady Trieu, warrior woman, appeared on the scene in 248. Often referred to as the Joan of Arc of Vietnam's history, she also led a successful revolt against the Chinese after the second invasion. She was an orphan child who reportedly killed her own sister-in-law in a fit of anger. In the book *Vietnamese Tradition on Trial*, David G. Marr, an American professor, recounted the story from Vietnamese historians that Lady Trieu (Trieu Thi Trinh) was nine feet tall, had a loud voice that sounded like a temple bell, had beauty that could shake any man's soul, and could eat many rice pecks and walk five hundred leagues in a day. When she gathered up an army of rebels to attack the dominating Chinese, her brother tried to persuade her not to rebel. She reportedly told him:

"I only want to ride the wind and walk the waves, slay big whales of the Eastern Sea, clean up frontiers and save the people from drowning and never bend my back to be the concubine of whatever man."

Lady Trieu had barely turned nineteen when she led the successful insurrection against the Wu Chinese invaders. Her victory was short but sweet, and it would serve as a model of inspiration and hope for generations of Vietnamese women. In all, she is reported to have participated as the leader in more than thirty battles, most of them victorious. Vietnamese historians say that the Chinese soldiers were terrified of her and that they said this about her: "It would be easier to fight an army of tigers than Lady Trieu and her army."

Chinese sources do record that there was a serious rebellion in Vietnam at this time, but Chinese historical records carry no mention of Lady Trieu. Chinese believe in female inferiority to men and that to be defeated by female warriors is humiliating. The only mention comes through Vietnamese sources. One of those sources is *Outline History of Vietnam* by Tran Trong Kim (1920). Another description of Lady Trieu that I found read as follows:

> Lady Trieu was of the people of Nong Cong district. Her parents died when she was a child so she lived with her older brother, Trieu Quoc Dat. She was strong, brave, beautiful and smart, and after killing her sister-in-law (a hateful person), she fled to the mountains and raised a rebel force of one thousand who would follow her into battle against thirty thousand Chinese. She wore yellow tunics, had enormous breasts and fought while sitting on an elephant's head.[3]

The resistance, led by Lady Trieu, was for the Chinese, simply another resistance led by an insignificant, stubborn barbarian that was wiped out as a matter of course and was of no historical interest, so they recorded nothing of these events of 248. That might be an example of Chinese arrogance or false pride which existed back then and possibly even today. On the other hand, the Vietnamese remembered Lady Trieu's gallant uprising as the most important event of that time. Her leadership appealed to strong, popular instincts. The traditional image of her as a remarkable yet human leader going into battle astride a war elephant has been handed down from generation to generation. After her death, her spirit was worshipped by the Vietnamese. Lady Trieu also took her own life while in battle against insurmountable odds like the Trung sisters did two hundred years before her.[4]

Long after her death, Emperor Ly praised her as a brave and loyal warrior and ordered a temple to be built in her honor. It was given the title of *Bat chinh anh hung tai trinh nhat phy nhan*…or *Most Noble Heroic and Virgin Lady*. The temple exists in Phu Dien of Thanh Hoa province.

After her death, it was recorded that Trieu continued to haunt the Chinese generals. Three centuries later, she still offered spiritual support for male and female Vietnamese.

China meets Ly Nam De. Even though he was of mostly Chinese descent, Ly Nam De became increasingly frustrated with the corruption among the Chinese rulers of Vietnamese people. Upon resignation of a

---

3   Complete Annals of Great Viet
4   Keith W. Taylor, American professor

regional magistrate position in Giao Chau, an area of modern-day northern Vietnam, he organized the local tribes in the Red River Valley, convinced local nobles to support him, mobilized the imperial guard and a naval fleet, and successfully expelled the Liang-Chinese administration from 541–543. He was declared emperor by the people with the intention of demonstrating equal authority to him as the former Chinese leaders once claimed.

Ly Nam De established his capital at Long Bien (modern-day Hanoi), and surrounded himself with effective leadership in military and administrative scholars. Ly Nam De was also strongly supported by famous military commanders, such as Trieu Tuc, Tinh Thieu, and Trieu Quang Phuc (son of Trieu Tuc, later known as Trieu Viet Vurong). The latter emerged as a hero in Vietnamese history and eventually succeeded Ly Nam De as ruler in 548. Ly Nam De built many fortresses at strategic locations throughout Van Xuan (Vietnam) to fend off potential threats from China in the north and from the Champa Kingdom in the south; he also established the first national university for Mandarin scholars, implemented land reforms, and promoted literacy amongst the population. He laid the foundation for many reforms modeled after the Chinese social structure.

Again, the ruling Chinese (Liang dynasty) retaliated and reinvaded Van Xuan with more than 120,000 imperial troops, but it took three years (545–548), their third invasion, for the siege by the Liang forces to succeed. Ly Nam De continued the resistance until suffering from serious diseases due to months of living in the wilderness. His immediate successor, Trieu Quang Phuc (Trieu Viet Vuong or Trieu Viet King), continued where Ly Nam De left off, and once again, the Chinese invaders were driven from Van Xuan.

This part of Vietnam's history is a bit confusing, but I think it is being presented correctly and it is extremely important to the entire book. From 571–602, the diseased Ly Nam De's cousin, who became known as Hau Ly Nam De, would rule Vietnam (Van Xuan) as an independent nation.

The third Chinese rule of Vietnam was a period from the end of 602 to the rise of the Khuc family until 938, when the Han dynasty was defeated and expelled. In the sixth century, Vietnam gravitated more toward complete independence, and Vietnamese nationalism was growing. Vietnamese concepts of warfare also expanded during the sixth through tenth centuries. This would become one of their trademarks for future wars to be fought against invaders of Vietnam. The forested mountains, jungles, and vast swamps became their allies with such tactics as striking without warning and disappearing just as fast, stealing supplies and weapons from an invader, and then slipping back into the unfriendly environment in which the enemy was unlikely to pursue them. These were the earliest guerilla war tactics, and the Vietnamese would become the masters of the trade.

Still, the powerful Chinese had no intention of leaving the Vietnamese alone. They were expansion-crazed, and Vietnam was the most strategically positioned land from which the Chinese could launch their attacks on other lands in Southeast Asia and surrounding countries. However, the Vietnam land continued to flourish and to get stronger. At the same time, there were revolutions going on in China. The Viets took advantage of the state of anarchy in China at the famous battle at Bach Dang, where the Vietnamese destroyed a large Chinese force.

However, after another series of bloody civil wars in China, the new Sui dynasty emerged as the main power in a united China after defeating the Liang dynasty. Almost immediately, the new Sui emperor amassed a force of 200,000 to invade—you guessed it—Vietnam. Hau Ly Nam De had little fight left in him, and he was not receiving much support from his administration, which pressured him to surrender without a bloody battle and hope for a peaceful arrangement.

By 618 AD, the Chinese civil war had ended and the clear-cut winner would evolve even more powerful...the Tang dynasty. Not since the Han dynasty had there been a unified China. Since the Han fell in 248 AD and several centuries of feudal wars followed, political unrest and intermittent chaos plagued China like a never-ending game of musical chairs. Even though there was a unified China under the Sui dynasty, it was one of the shortest spans of any ruling clan, ending after thirty-six years to the Tangs. Their Kao-tsu emperor became all-powerful, and all political rivalry was quickly eliminated. Kao-tsu took on his father's temple name, Tai-Tsung, in 626 AD, which marked an era for China called...the Golden Age.

Meanwhile, to China's south, the fate of Vietnam appeared gloomy, as they could not put a lasting defeat on to this new ruling force of China. Vietnam would be a vassal state of China for another three hundred years with no end in sight to this fate. The Vietnamese would have to be patient again for a very long time. In fact, during the Golden Age, China's borders not only stretched into Vietnam and the rest of Indochina, but into Korea, Persia, Turkey, and most of Central Asia, including Tibet and Mongolia. China was officially becoming an empire of many acquisitions, all by conquest.

The Tang Empire (618–907) became the second largest and longest running empire in the world, greater than the Persian Empire and second only to the Han Empire in land mass. It is ironic that the Tangs renewed the expansion of the Great Wall that was initiated during the Sui dynasty's reign. Millions of slaves from conquered regions such as Vietnam were forced into labor to build the Great Wall. It remains one of the world's greatest wonders to this day. But was it worth the time, labor, and cost? Would it serve its purpose, which was mostly unknown at the time?

From 618 to 905, the Tangs would maintain full ownership of Vietnam along with many other nations and empires. Vietnam attempted three major revolts against the Tang dynasty between 722 and 728. The Chinese showed no mercy in the third revolt attempt in 728. The Chinese generals ordered the eighty thousand decapitated bodies to be scalped, flayed, and stacked into a Vietnamese pagoda to rot away.

Honestly, it would be easy to get deeper into the history of China's unbelievable and seemingly endless offensive war actions. Vietnam's history hardly compares, as all of their military actions were enacted for pure survival, while the Chinese killed their own by the tens of millions for thousands of years. But the phenomenon of China's long, rich, and very bloody history puts an extra exclamation on the reason I have written this story and one of its most powerful lessons: **Never Underestimate the Heart of Your Enemy**.

Ngo Quyen's power began around the year of 930. He was to become a general soon. In quick fashion, just eight years later at the battle of Bach Dang River, the Vietnamese forces led by Ngo Quyen defeated a massive invasion of the Southern Han China military, their fourth invasion, using warfare tactics that had never been used before. This monumental victory put an end to centuries of Chinese rule of Vietnam.

Ngo Quyen had called out to all of Vietnam's able-bodied warriors, including women and children, to prepare for an all-out battle against an enemy of several hundred thousand, and the Han Chinese were soundly defeated. Vietnam would experience a long period of independence for several centuries. A reminder that in the early years of Anno Domini, the population of the Han Chinese Empire was close to sixty million. At that time, Vietnam had just over one million.

The amazing victory at Bach Dang in 938 ushered in a flourishing age of rebuilding Vietnam in rapid and large-scale fashion. Some have called it the modern age of Dai Viet. Ngo Quyen, who beheaded the commanding admiral and prince of the Han Chinese dynasty, would be recognized as one of the all-time greatest saviors of Vietnam. After Bach Dang, General Ngo Quyen proclaimed himself king and established a capital for Vietnam (Giao Chi) at Co Loa. Ngo Quyen died just five years later in 944, but the following nine hundred years would bring a measure of great enjoyment and independence despite several Chinese attempts to regain control of Vietnam. However, Chinese influence wasn't all bad for the Vietnamese as cultural exchange improved the lifestyle of the Vietnamese.

Have you noticed that rarely (if at all) is there a mention of murderous rape and pillaging Vietnamese on the offensive to conquer or destroy any of their neighbors, as was a common practice in China, Mongolia, and Japan? Always, it seems, the Vietnamese were only trying to keep what was theirs or take back what was once theirs. I find this trend existing since the 39–40 AD battle of the heroic Trung sisters' forces against the Chinese invaders until the Viet Minh (Vietnamese) victory in 1954 over a huge French force of nearly thirty thousand legionnaires and mercenaries. That French defeat at Dien Bien Phu will receive due mention later in this book.

When Ngo Quyen, often referred to as King of Vietnam, restored sovereign power in the country, the Vietnamese people made advancements due to the accomplishments of successive dynasties, but not without constant turmoil by civil wars. Ngo Quyen's dynasty lasted just thirty years until 967. However, his defeat of the huge Chinese force at Bach Dang River in 938 was so disastrous to China that they would not attempt another invasion for another century. This significant victory would not be the last of many victories for Vietnam throughout the centuries. Ngo Quyen died of illness at the age of forty-seven. Nevertheless, he brought in a long-sought Viet era of independence and political autonomy. He was succeeded by a son, who was in turn succeeded by his son, and they kept Vietnam safe.

Ly Thuong Kiet (1019–1105) was another general of the Vietnamese long line of heroes. He is credited with Vietnam's first Declaration of Independence, and he was responsible for leading the Vietnamese army into China to carry out a preemptive attack against the Song-Chinese, who were planning to invade Vietnam. In 1076, the Vietnamese overwhelmed the larger Song force, defeating them in a forty-day battle.

One more time, in 1076, the Song-Chinese attempted to invade Dai Viet and one more time, the emperor of Vietnam sent General Ly Thuong Kiet to meet the invaders in a head-on collision. One more time, the result was a retreat of the invaders back to China. Following is a short poem written by Thuong Kiet.

A Democratic Vietnam
By Ly Thuong Kiet

Song nu nuoc Nam yua Namo
Ranh dinh phan tai sach troi,
Co sao lu giac sang xam pham
Chung bay se bi danh ta boi.

(Translation)
Over the mountains and rivers of the south
Lives the southern emperor
As it says now and forever in the Book of Heavens
That whoever dares to invade our land
Will be defeated without mercy.

Unbelievable as it sounds, over the next three centuries China would try repeatedly to invade their southern neighbor, with the same result each time. Maybe if the Chinese researched their own history a bit more thoroughly, it might have saved a few hundred thousand lives.

Armies and warfare played a great role in shaping the identity, character, and culture of the people inhabiting the land that became modern-day Vietnam. Looking at how many conflicts Vietnam has fought would make one think the Vietnamese were war-seeking peoples. Untrue. Warfare during the period from 39–1954 elevated Vietnam's people to the height of power as they defeated all who came to conquer them.

Chinese influence of present-day Vietnam cannot be denied, especially their cultural contributions, although I believe some Vietnamese would like to whitewash it completely. But over one thousand years of Chinese influence and, for the most part, dominating influence cannot be erased from history. Regardless, when a unified China emerged around 220–221 BC, its massive power of pure numbers would soon complete conquests of many neighboring states or kingdoms, including the Vietnam region. Vietnamese resistance to the Chinese was alarmingly fierce, considering their small numbers compared to a unified China; nonetheless, the Vietnamese revolts continued.

Three great men of the East. In multiple Far Eastern history books, the consensus appears to favor only three men as being truly great: Buddha, Confucius, and Genghis Khan.

Shakyamuni was born a prince about 500 BC in what is now Nepal. Distressed by human suffering (yes, even back then), he left his home and family and achieved enlightenment through meditation and became known as the Buddha. It is stated that at the moment of the Buddha's enlightenment, he was entitled to its immediate rewards—complete salvation (freedom from sin) and spiritual release from the bonds of existence. His teachings were optimistic (hopeful for the future). They held that every human being, regardless of his social position or past life, can through his own efforts obtain control of himself, of his ideas and passions, and of his destiny.

The Buddha first preached his doctrine at Dharma in Benares, India, a great holy city. His first mission with a handful of disciple-like followers, offering the teaching to all who would hear him and understand. According to Buddha's teachings, life is painful, the origin of pain is desire, and the end of pain can be achieved by ending desire through right living. Buddhism was spread into Tibet, where it became Lamaism, and Lamaism would reach the Mongols under Kublai Khan from 1215–1294.

Throughout Buddha's life, traveling on foot, he constantly encouraged people of all walks of life to challenge his teachings and try to confirm them through their own experiences. This Buddha statement probably characterizes Buddhism today:

I can die happily. I have not kept a single teaching hidden in a closed hand. Everything that is useful for you, I have already given. Be your own guiding light.

—The Buddha, while leaving his body at the age of eighty

Confucius—the famous Chinese philosopher, teacher, and political figure known for popular aphorisms and for his models of social interaction—was born around the same time as Buddha in 551 BC. His philosophy known as Confucianism would become the official imperial philosophy of China. His dream was to restore China to a golden age of peace. He helped to endow the Chinese with the idea that China lay at the center of the universe. His timing for China was perfect, as China was experiencing a time of ideological crisis then.

Notwithstanding the aspects of their rule that were extremely negative for China, the Mongols did initiate many policies—especially under the rule of Kublai Khan—that supported the Chinese economy at the time of Mongol conquests. Kublai even restored the rituals at court—the music and dance that were such an integral part of the Confucian ideology. Kublai also built ancestral temples for his Mongol predecessors—Chinggis (Genghis) Khan, his grandfather, and a few others—to continue the practices of ancestor worship that were so critical for the Confucian Chinese.

I remember from my childhood days into the mature years the *Confucius Says* quotes and how much fun they were. Of course, it was also fun to invent some of our own and give credit to Confucius though he could have cared not.

The will to win, the desire to succeed, the urge to reach your full potential...are the keys that will unlock the door to personal excellence. It does not matter how slowly you go as long as you do not stop.

—Confucius

Real knowledge is to know the extent of one's ignorance.

—Confucius

The actual word "Mongol" was used as a tribal name until 1206, when Temujin (Chinggis) Genghis Qahan or Khan was elevated to Great Khan. Mongol then became synonymous with the state or country Mongolia.

As China thought of itself in the thirteenth century, all Mongols thought themselves to be the center of the universe, a belief that they derived from their Shamanist communication with the spirit world type of religion. Genghis Khan was a Shamanist and he treated every Mongol equally. He did not do so with non-Mongol people. Still, the true strength of the Mongols was their unity, not their masses. The Mongol population was barely three million during the reign of the Khans and yet, they managed to defeat and conquer every nation or military force that got in their way. As a cavalry force, they were beyond compare, and soldiers were paid the highest respect among the Mongols. While Confucianism had spread to other Eastern countries, it did not impact the Mongols.

Genghis was known as a far-sighted ruler and a born diplomat who understood the wishes of his people and led them skillfully. From the state of his world conquests and his death in 1227, he killed none of his own generals with whom he built the massive empire. Even more amazing, he was never betrayed by any of them. Even though he was illiterate, he knew instinctively how to deal and negotiate with other rulers.

Genghis established his great empire and held it in place by uniting a sprawling and shifting population and created a superb fighting machine. Genghis Khan was never defeated during his reign. It would have been interesting if Genghis had lived another decade or so, and if fate brought him to a face-to-face battle with the man who would humble the relatives of Genghis in repetitive and impressive victories when the Mongols attempted to invade and destroy a small nation known as Vietnam.

Several great Vietnamese dynasties maintained the country's independent status well into the early 1200s until the Mongol armies of Genghis Khan's grandson, Kublai Khan, conquered most of the known world left for him by Genghis, and then set his sights on the Vietnamese region. Unfortunately for the Mongols, this time, the Vietnamese people did not bow their heads and turn over their villages and possessions to the Mongol hordes, despite their numbers and the reputation that preceded them. Over the last half of the thirteenth century, the Mongol armies of Kublai Khan sent wave after wave into Vietnam to reconquer it and reintegrate it into the Chinese empire. Time and time again, the Mongols' ruthless advances were met with ferocious resistance beyond their expectations. After all, they were the Mongols, so how could tribes of rice farmers and peasants with their women and children making up much of their military force defeat the mighty Mongols?

Vietnam meets the Mongols. One would have surmised back then that the reputation of the people of Vietnam was one of vicious and fearless defenders of their homeland…against any invader, against all odds, so leave them be. The aggressive Mongols' ego could not allow them to do that, so the invasions were inevitable. But the Vietnamese were once again prepared to fight to the last man, woman, and child, and the Mongols would not be prepared for that; nor did they expect that it might be necessary in order to defeat what they considered a highly inferior people.

Images on following pages will illustrate the Trung sisters and Ancient Vietnam.

The Trungs and the Ancients

Empress Nam Phuong

Chapter 4

MONGOL HORDES ATTACK VIETNAM!

I am the flails of God. If you had not committed great sins, God would not have sent a punishment like me upon you.
—Genghis Khan to the Persians

O ne of the most magnificent constructions in the history of the world, the Great Wall of China, was built to try to keep invaders out. The people who forced the need for building the Great Wall were…the Mongol hordes. The history of Mongolia is a worthy challenge for a weekend historian who would like to tackle it. Of course, it is dominated by the tales of the world's greatest and most ruthless conqueror of all time, Genghis Khan. Under the great and terrible Khan, the wandering hordes of Mongol tribes terrified all civilizations within reach, including all of China. Mongolia was also the birthplace of Attila and the terrible Huns, destroyers of the great Roman Empire.

There is little question that Genghis Khan built and ruled the world's largest contiguous empire. Rightfully so, it is referred to by historians as the Mongol Empire. Their battle strategy, implemented by their greatest leader, Genghis Khan, was pure and simple…to kill everyone in their path and anyone else who was stupid enough to get in their way. During their reign, no one could stop them…almost. Khan's conquests can be appreciated from this quote of his:

The greatest happiness is to scatter your enemy and drive him before you. To see his cities reduced to ashes. To see those who love him shrouded and in tears. And to gather to your bosom his wives and daughters.

—Genghis Khan

While most great leaders would face defeat at one time or another or be replaced, Genghis Khan was never defeated. He was never replaced until he died. I had a difficult time finding any information in history that describes stiffer obstacles to overcome in order to attain eventual greatness. Genghis was an outcast in his youth, left out in the harsh wilderness of Mongolia to die…but he didn't. He went from nothing to being a leader of other outcasts like himself, to the leader of a clan, then leader of many clans, and eventually, he united all Mongol clans under his leadership and the world would never be the same.

I mentioned Genghis was never defeated, and most who succeeded him were successful with continued conquests until the known world of the time was ruled by Mongols. If the Mongolian Empire had the strongest army in history during or after the life of Genghis, then the man who led the defeat of the Mongols three times cannot be excluded among the greatest military generals and conquerors of all time. Tran Hung Dao was that man, whom you will read about later in this chapter.

The Mongol empire lasted a bit more than two hundred years, into the mid-1300s. During the rule of the Khans of Mongolia, virtually every kingdom was ravaged, from Korea to Eastern Europe to the Persian Gulf and back. Virtually every kingdom fell except…Vietnam.

The character of the Vietnamese people can probably be described most eloquently during the years of the Mongol invasions. Historians could have been much kinder to the Vietnamese for their many victories in war. After all, theirs was a noble act in defense of their homeland against overwhelming odds. But historians like to insert glamour and sizzle into what many consider a dry subject—history. So the Mongol hordes dominated that period of history in much the same way the American media glorified the poor Viet Cong during the Vietnam War. It was around 1253 when the Mongol Empire's hordes first entered the kingdoms of modern Vietnam. Overwhelmed, the Vietnamese fled to the woods and mountains, burning their own villages along the way. Soon, the Mongols would get a taste of guerilla warfare, Vietnamese style.

During the thirteenth century from 1205–1299, the sons and grandsons of the great Genghis Khan were intensely occupied with maintaining the land conquests of Genghis, and their own grand, new conquests. One of those super conquests would be all of China itself, so at least the Vietnamese would not need to be concerned about the Chinese for a while. In fact, by 1279, Kublai Khan's Mongol hordes had finally crushed the Chinese empire, the Song dynasty, and for the first time in history, China had become a vassal state to another master. One major battle resulted in a force of 300,000 Western Xia Chinese being destroyed in 1226. However, the following year, in 1227, Genghis died mysteriously. The Mongols kept his death a secret to their subjects and the Mongol onslaught continued in his name. The Yuan dynasty was formed, which would last until 1368. Genghis Khan was credited with being the founder of the Yuan dynasty by his grandson, Kublai Khan.

The Mongols may have been the most proactive conquerors in history. For instance, during their early probes into the Vietnam frontiers during

1253–1256, they had also mastered successful conquests of Korea on the east. To the west, they were rampaging the entire Middle East, where the Islamic empire ruled. On other fronts, the Song Chinese and the Han dynasty were still providing resistance. Even worse for Kublai Khan would be the massive civil unrest, as family members were challenging him for control. Life was not a bowl of cherries for anyone who held or sought the title of the great Khan.

Keep in mind; the Mongol Empire controlled most of Eurasia, Central Asia, Manchuria, Eastern Europe, Anatolia, Northeast Asia, Tibet, and Southwest Asia. The Mongols had planned to attack and annihilate what remained of China and, as an aftermath, dispose of Dai Viet in quick fashion.

There would be three major invasion attempts of Dai Viet by the Mongols—in 1258, 1285, and finally in 1288 as described elsewhere. All three invasions had unexpected endings for the participants. Before I get to those magnificent episodes, I have to add some special hype about Genghis Khan.

A reminder—Genghis Khan is the man who almost destroyed Islam. Not many people reading this book who are not history buffs would know this. To the credit of the mighty "scourge of the east," he did not initiate the attacks on Islam. His armies (there were no marines then) were provoked needlessly by guerilla-type attacks by the Muslim Jihad. It is probable that the Muslims knew it would only be a matter of time until Genghis would try his luck at doing to Islam what he had done to the rest of the Eurasian people. Maybe they thought if they showed how brave and aggressive they were, that would influence the Mongols to invade someone else's empire and stay away from Islam. The problem with that thinking is…most of Euro-Asia had already been trampled and buried by Genghis' Mongol horde. As the history scribes say it, the Muslim Jihads tormented the Mongols with their border raids, and this infuriated the great Khan beyond his short limit of patience and mercy. Islam was going to pay, he swore to his generals.

While many historians have looked on the Mongols as looters, plunderers, rapists, and all those good things, the Mongols were like primitive Robin Hood's merry band, having a goal of looting the rich and powerful civilizations first. However, the man who would almost destroy Islam had no intentions of just looting, pillaging, and raping the Muslims. Hell no, it was not loot that drove the Mongol army to trek four thousand miles from their homeland to Baghdad when they could have walked over to Korea and then Japan, and maybe Vietnam, which were hardly a few hundred miles away. They were probably wealthier lands than what the sagging Islam Empire offered.

You gotta love this…the main reason Genghis led his army of raging killers on the brutal four-thousand-mile bivouac to Baghdad rather than east was…he felt the Muslims used "foul tactics" and extreme cruelty and needed to be taught better. Yeah, Genghis Khan, who wiped out thirty million people (mostly defenseless civilians), was harboring these feelings toward the Muslims. It was one evil empire against another of the same cruel mentality.

It is also quite believable that Genghis' hate for Islam was the motivation for his decision. Ah yes—religion comes into play again as a factor for engaging in war. Of course, one major factor was how the Muslims had exercised extreme cruelty in forcing non-Muslims to convert. Keep in mind that what took place in the savage battles between the Mongols and Muslims spanned several hundred years. If you are a walker or a hiker…take a four-thousand-mile walk tomorrow, the next day, and the next, etc. When you reach the end of the line…next year, you may not feel like jumping right in to conquering another civilization.

Special note: The Mongols were known as a peace-loving, nomadic, pastoral people who kept to themselves, very satisfied with their lifestyle. In fact, historians state that there is no record of Mongol invasions anywhere, nor was there record of ruthlessness until they were repeatedly provoked by Muslim encroachments of the Mongols' homeland. It was self-preservation that set the Mongols loose onto the Muslims and then the rest of the world.

Shortly after Genghis allegedly died from a horse-riding accident, the Islam caliph threatened the new Mongol Khan. This would be Hulagu Khan, who did not have much aspiration for continuing the conquering ways of Genghis Khan. So Hulagu Khan basically said to the Islam Khalifa… "You leave us alone and we'll leave you alone." The Islam caliph misinterpreted this as a sign as weakness, and arrogance took the Muslim caliph to a new level of overconfidence and stupidity, as he not only challenged Hulagu Khan, he insulted him greatly, and that would seal the fate of Islam's golden era.

Many history books describe the Islamic rulers as being cruel, full of trickery and dishonesty, which at the time of their reign was almost exclusively the signature of the Muslims. In fact, as it has been documented, it was for these reasons that the Mongols rose up, transforming from hardy nomads to warriors at another level. It was because of these reasons that the Mongols struck without warning, scoring victory after victory and eventually storming the Islamic Caliphate of Baghdad.

Please remember, it was the Jihadists who violated the homeland of the Mongols, so they paid back the Muslims in the same fashion with extreme cruelty, trickery without mercy, some say until there was nothing—not humans or beasts—left standing or breathing in Baghdad.

It was back then at their beginnings that it became apparent the Muslims only understood the languages of blood and death. They exhibited their gory traits throughout the Crusades. If the rest of the world today is going to stop the Islamic terror attacks and prevent Islam from becoming stronger as well as earn their respect as a more than worthy adversary, it will happen only if we are just as or more ruthless than they are. The Muslims do not accept qualities such as fair play, chivalry, compassion, and forgiveness in their bag of foul tricks. These qualities to the Muslims are examples of weakness and stupidity. When will people in the West, especially the United States, understand this?

In many respects, the Mongols were nothing like the despots and maggots of the Islamic empire. The Mongols pretty much respected all religions, even Islam. They did not embrace people who would worship a death cult. The Muslim ideology in the Crusade years was no different than it is today; their cousins are fascism and communism. We should not lose any sleep over wondering why they hate our lifestyle, or our Christian or Jewish foundation, and we need to treat them the same way we did with Osama bin Laden, Al Zarqawi, and all like them.

We need a president with a strong pro-American devotion who will not allow the deadly terrorists of modern Islam to make for hard strides. Oh where, oh where art thou, great Khan? Please arise and lead us to our own former greatness. Will our new president become America's great Khan for the next eight years and will the future of America as well as Western culture rest on his conscience?

Persian Empire burns. Even those with a mild interest in the world's history have seen movies or read about the famous Persian empires and their mighty conquests. They would become modern-day Iraq. Google.com tells us that in 1218, a Mongol caravan with food and supplies passing through what is now Uzbekistan toward the Persian Empire was stopped by Persian troops and everyone was massacred—unprovoked. After several exchanges between Genghis Khan and the shah of the Khwarezmid Empire, who had a 500,000-man army and vast reserves, the Mongols, with a force of 200,000, beat the shah to the punch, and what was supposed to be a long, bloody war was mostly over in just one battle in 1219. The Mongols then laid siege to a major city and fortress in Persia called Utrar, which was also defended by Turkish forces. The Mongols destroyed Utrar and decimated their military to the man. **The story goes on to say, Genghis Khan ordered mosques in Bukhara to be leveled and turned into stables. The cases of Korans would become manger material for livestock.**

Basically, the unplanned invasion and destruction of Khwarezmid from 1219 to 1221 just got the ball rolling for Genghis Khan and what would be the Mongols' conquest of the Islamic Empire and virtually all of Eurasia.

Isn't life humorous? It was not the intention of the Mongol Empire to invade the Khwarezmid land. They allegedly wanted to trade. In the end, several towns were destroyed after Khwarezmid was leveled to the ground. All military were shown no mercy and as Google says, "Persian scholar Juvayni stated that Genghis Khan picked out fifty thousand of his soldiers and ordered them to execute twenty-four citizens each," which would be approximately 1.2 million corpses—UNBURIED!

Iran, Persia, Iraq, Khwarezmid, Mesopotamia, Babylonia, Abbasid, Qajar, Baghdad, Syria—they were all connected from the ancient years to modern times. The Mongols conquered it all.

Islam's Golden Age crashes! With all that has been going on with Islamic terrorism since the 9/11 disaster in America, I decided to add a few words about the Islam Empire, which served in the seventh through twelfth centuries. In the Age of Islam, the Arab world had reached its pinnacle, as it became the center of culture and knowledge. Baghdad had been the capital of the Abbasid Caliphate, the third caliphate whose rulers were descendants of Abbas, an uncle of Muhammad. But Islam's glory days were numbered, as the fire from the East was coming.

At the same time, the Mongol Empire was expanding well into the cradle of civilization of Mesopotamia and the surrounding regions. Raids into Persia-Iraq had become repetitive, and Baghdad itself had been breached around 1238. It was in 1257 that the Mongols established firm domination over Mesopotamia, Iran, and Syria. In February 1258, General Hulagu Khan led a very large army, believed to be approximately 150,000 strong. History's public records state that Baghdad was "sacked" by the Mongol hordes within two and a half weeks. It had fallen by 1258.

History's Top Empires in Terms of Land Conquered[5]

Empire	% Land Area Million Km	Peak Era	% of World's Population
Mongol *	42.0	1279	25.6
British	33.7	1922	20.0
Russian	22.8	1721–1917	9.8
Spanish	19.4	1801	12.3
Umayad (Islamic)	15.0	750	28.8
Yuan (Chinese) *	14.0	1271–1368	17.1
Qing (Chinese) *	13.1	1760	36.6

5   www.listverse.com, www.businessinsider.com, www.metmuseum.org, www.travelchinaguide.com

French Colonial *	12.3	1938	5.1
Abbasid (Islamic)	11.1	1258	20.0
Macedonian/Greece	8.6	323 BC	30.3
Roman	N/A	2,214 Years	N/A
Portuguese	N/A	1415–1999	N/A
Persian (Archaemenid)	8.2	539–330 BC	N/A
Han (China's Golden Age) *	N/A	206 BC–220 AD	20.0
Ottoman Turks	N/A	1520–1566	N/A
Rashidun (Islamic)	6.0	632	N/A

*Defeated by Vietnamese in wars for freedom.

The Mongol hordes may have lost a battle or two during their climb to power and establishment of the largest empire in world history. No matter, it was never enough for Genghis Khan and his relatives to discontinue their nightmarish invasions. Shortly after setting the great Islamic Empire into flames, the bloodthirsty Mongol leaders set their sights on what was modern-day Vietnam, Cambodia, and Laos. Vietnam had long banished the Chinese from their long domination, and they were quite content with living in peace for several years.

Before the Mongols had finished with the destruction of Baghdad, the grand city had lost a third of its population. Well over one million civilians were slaughtered in barbaric fashion, and the Mongols had conquered over 25 percent of the known world's population.[6]

Military decisions and religious leaders? This one may raise the blood pressure of some Catholics, but my information can be verified with several historical sources.

Today's Islamist extremists do not like to think about the dark times when the Mongols slaughtered Muslims almost to the point of extinction. They seem to feel their mission today is an obligation to Allah, that every non-Muslim is to be converted or destroyed. Not to worry; it is not just America for which their hatred runs deep. Their massive terror attacks over the last two decades have been launched at most Western European countries and the masses of Hindus in India. Please refer to an article by a *New York Post* columnist who also contributed articles for jewishworldreview. com. One of Arnold Ahlert's articles was titled "Islam's War of Annihilation Against Hindus…India Besieged."

---

6 en.wikipedia.org/list_of_largest_empires

As much damage as the Mongols did to Islam—and they almost wiped them out—they left enough of them living that one day they would rise again and the Mongols would be expelled. It seems that the Mongols envisioned this and were smart enough to seek an alliance with the archenemy of Islam, which was Christianity. A reminder that the Crusades (Holy Wars) were raging from 1095 to the 1300s, and Islam was faring poorly against the masses of Christians who came from everywhere in Europe. The credit for this went to Genghis Khan's Muslim-slaughtering Mongols. Several sources I researched made strong references to the power-hungry Catholic popes and their part in calling for the Crusades.

It may seem like I am wandering away from the mission of the book, but I thought this point was worth mentioning. I found that on at least two instances, the Crusades could have received a shot in the arm that would have pretty much guaranteed a Christian victory, with a possible alliance between the Mongols and Christians against Islam. The first attempt to negotiate this came right after the Mongols had destroyed a large Muslim force in Khwarazmian.

Keep in mind, the Mongols were not pagans like the looting and plundering Vikings were. They had religion and showed an openness to accept other religions, even Christianity and Islam. Well, Pope Innocent IV was approached first by the Mongols to form a broad anti-Muslim pact. Pope Innocent IV never acted on the gesture. Big mistake? Maybe. But the Christians trusted neither the Muslims nor the Mongols, and who could tell which the lesser evil was at that time. One of the lost opportunities here was that Christianity would have most likely spread with the Mongols throughout their empire as well as within their own Mongol nation. But Pope Innocent's decision would only start a revival of Islam.

Pope Innocent IV was succeeded by Pope Alexander IV, and the Mongols also approached him to ally against the Muslims, who were regrouping from the massive slaughtering they had been punished with by the Mongols. The Muslims would eventually regain the power they enjoyed before the Mongol invasions. Again, a golden opportunity to contain Islam was passed by as Pope Alexander IV also refused to join with the Mongols against the Muslims.

During the Mongol stampede through the Muslim countryside, it was documented that the Shiites betrayed the Sunni and sided with the Mongols. Writers of these times referred to the Mongols' destruction of Baghdad and most of Islam in terms of a "holocaust." They also wrote as if the end of the world was near.[7]

---

7   Other sources: www.historyof/jihad.org; www.emdb.com

Conquests of Russia. It is often said that Russia has never been invaded successfully, never conquered. If Germany couldn't complete the task in WWII, certainly no other military force outside of maybe Alexander the Great or Napoléon could have—maybe it was that they had such an all-powerful military force.

As Kievan Rus' (modern-day Russia) was going through a breakup in the thirteenth century, Eastern Europe, including the East Slavic people, would eventually form three separate nations: modern-day Belarus, Russia, and Ukraine. While this fragmentation was going on, Kievan Rus' was extremely vulnerable and faced an unexpected invasion of a mysterious and irresistible foreign force coming from the Far East. No one knew their origin or what religion they practiced, if any. That was known only to God.

The Rus' leaders heard of the coming warriors and the wrath they carried. The Far East force was known for pillaging settlers and burning entire cities to the ground, which would soon include Baghdad, Kiev, and Moscow. These mysterious marauders were the Mongols. The initial invasions went surprisingly easy considering the Mongol army was usually outnumbered. The Battle of the Kalka River in 1223 was a headline battle of this invasion with convincing victory for the Mongols. Surprisingly the Mongols returned from where they came, despite the fact that they would have faced little or no opposition should they have chosen to advance and take up occupation of the Rus' territory.

Thirteen years later the Mongols returned, with a more formidable force, this time commanded by the greatest Mongol of all time…Genghis (Chinghis) Khan. All Rus' principalities submitted to Mongol domination from 1237–1240, a domination that would last up to 1480. Actually Russia did not exist prior to the Mongol invasions. Rus', as it was called, was divided into several states that feuded constantly. The Mongols' direct interference with the Russian culture united many of the principalities into Russia.

Many words of the modern Russian language were taken from Mongol Turkic languages. So the Russian state can be considered a descendent of the Golden Horde. The Golden Horde was the western section of the Mongol empire.

Slave trade between the Mongol and Ottoman Empires became prominent in the fourteenth and fifteenth centuries. The slave raids were not on the Africans, rather the predominately Caucasian Slavic peoples.

Well, as we say, for every action there is another reaction, and the Mongol domination ultimately helped to create another profound combat unit called…the Cossacks. Early known Cossacks appeared well after the Mongol invasions of Russia, around the fifteenth century. Like the Mongols, they were superb at horsemanship on the battlefield, so it is not likely these two great military forces would have clashed.

Vietnam, prepare for death! The Mongol cavalry fought best in the land of the Steppes, where there was plenty of wide-open land to carry out the broad, outflanking moves they excelled at. The Steppes also provided plenty of grass for the Mongol horses. However, the Mongols were not completely invincible.

A completely different scenario would present itself when the Mongol hordes and their dreaded cavalry matched up with the Vietnamese and their countryside of thick forests, jungles, and impassable swamps. Cavalry charges would not be as effective as they were on the plains. The Vietnamese would fight back, as their brave ancestors did countless times before. The results would be impressive, just as their ancestors' were.

Tran Hung Dao and the Tran dynasty were primarily responsible for defending against the Mongols on three major attempts to invade and conquer Dai Viet. The Tran dynasty, which began in 1225 and ended in 1400, was a long and glorious period of peace before and after the third and final Mongol invasion. The list of generals, princes, and emperors with the first name of Tran is nearly endless, and I would only confuse this chapter with an attempt to mention all of them. The founder of the Tran dynasty was Tran Thai Tong, who became the first emperor. The last emperor of this dynasty was Tran Thieu De. Others in between were Tran Hung Dao, Tran Thu Do, Tran Nhan Tong, Tran Anh Tong, Tran Minh Tong, Tran Hien Tong, and Tran Du Tong... Enough on that.

This period is one of my favorites in Vietnam's illustrious history: three historic victories over a thirty-year period which were led by the same Vietnamese commander, Prince Tran Hung Dao. To this day, the three mind-boggling victories over the mightiest conquering force of all time have military history experts shaking their heads in disbelief. The prince general of Vietnam's Tran dynasty is considered one of the most accomplished military tacticians in world history. He has shared his wealth of knowledge in several highly regarded documents.

If I were allowed the opportunity to meet only one of Vietnam's profoundly impressive and long list of great military leaders, and only one, it might come down to either Grung Trac—the oldest Trung sister who fought and slayed a six-hundred-pound wild tiger with only a pitchfork and knife in hand—or Tran Hung Dao, the legendary leader of the Vietnamese in all three of the Mongol invasions in the twelfth century. Thinking I would be hard-pressed from holding back an inevitable physical attraction to the oldest and fiercest of the fabulous Trung sisters, my selection goes to the terrible badass Tran Hung Dao.

The world's first guerrilla army was recruited and trained by Mr. Asskicker himself. Tran the Terrible then led them into multiple counterattacks against the merciless Mongols during the height of Kublai Khan's power, like Tran cared about anyone's reputation in battles. The grandson of Genghis himself was the only relative who continued with successful conquests after Genghis was gone. So Tran's ragtag vigilantes would be painfully tested.

Almost in the same instant that a Mongol emissary attempted to deliver a plain and simple offer—surrender or die—he was sent back with an arrow through his eye, sticking out of the back of his head.

Maybe the first invasion did not include the entire Mongol military, as they had other pressing issues going on from Persia to Korea and everything in between. The Mongols were half a million battle-hardened bad-asses from wars against the most powerful nations in the world, and should not have any chance of being defeated. And no one had ever heard of this Tran guy. They had every right to expect the Vietnamese to surrender. Instead the spunky Vietnamese stayed to entertain the Mongols with a new warfare strategy they had never seen.

Until this time in history the Mongols had successfully fought everywhere and under every imaginable condition (so they thought), from the steppes of Mongolia to the snowy forests of what is modern-day Russia, from the mountains of Korea to the deserts of Persia, but never in the jungles and swamps of Southeast Asia. In Vietnam, the Mongols were forced to deal with and attempt to adjust to abnormally unfriendly conditions that would eventually challenge them beyond what they were prepared for. These factors, most notably the heat, humidity, monsoons, and unfriendly wildlife, would take an unexpected toll on the Mongol military like nothing else their proud and very capable leaders had ever faced.

The Mongol style of warfare was not suited for dense, triple-canopy jungles, impenetrable mangroves, long rivers, and hostile wildlife—but nobody warned them of this. Some historians claim that in the Vietnamese victories to come, massive damage would be inflicted onto the Mongols' cavalry and infantry, with elephants hurling them into the air and trampling them. Elephants were better suited for jungle warfare than the Mongols' vaunted cavalry of small, quick horses.

And here was this very small empire on the other side of Asia, minding its own business, completely unaware of what they would be facing after centuries of invasions by the Chinese.

> The Fury That Rolls Like A Storm…
> Shattered The Old World Order, The
> Islamic Empire, The Persians,
> The Eurasians and Russia.
> Vietnam Stood In The Way
> For Future Conquests.

Next on the agenda, this story continues about how Vietnam was invaded almost immediately after the Islamic Empire was dismantled by the Mongol hordes! The Vietnamese people, unlike millions of others confronted by the Mongols, did not lay down their weapons and roll over. Other than the fact that both were of Asian nationality, the one distinct common trait the Mongols and Vietnamese shared was…unimaginable and ruthless fury when provoked. Therefore, the invasions of Vietnam and the battles of biblical proportions that followed would never be equaled up to that time or since, with one exception…the 1967 six-day war between Israel and most of the Arab-Muslim world in the Middle East. The highly outnumbered Israeli military drove forward purely in defense of their homeland and achieved an overwhelming victory against all odds. The Arab coalition that Israel was forced to square off with by themselves included military representation from Egypt, Syria, Jordan, Iraq, Kuwait, and Algeria. Israel was led by Prime Minister David Ben-Gurion and brilliant general and Chief of Staff Moshe Dayan. Israel fared well.

The first Mongol invasions (1257–1259) of Dai Viet came as the Mongols were just finishing off overwhelming conquests of central Asia and Eastern Europe. As the hordes marched south, they conquered and destroyed all kingdoms before them, and sent an emissary to Dai Viet, requesting permission to pass through their kingdom on the way to battle the kingdom of Song. Emperor Tran did not fall for this well-heard-of Mongol ploy, refused, and prepared for the invasion he had suspected was coming. The year was 1258 when the first major encounter took place between Mongol and Dai Viet armies. The initial attack by the Mongol hordes, led by Uriang-Khadai, was successful, and the King of Dai Viet fled to an island in the South China Sea. The Mongols continued their pending conquest until they had taken control of the Dai Viet capital city, Thang Long (now Hanoi). Masses of the population were massacred, as was the Mongols' custom post-victory stamp on the conquered. However, the Dai Viets' heart and will had not been conquered…not just yet.

Leading up to January 29, 1258, the Dai Viet forces regrouped under Emperor Tran Hung Dao and Prince Tran Hoang and eventually counterattacked the sleeping Mongols in the same fashion the Mongols had attacked Dai Viet initially. This time, the element of surprise was kinder to the outnumbered Dai Viet forces, and the Mongols were defeated. The Dai Viets continued their counterattacks on the retreating and panic-stricken Mongols until they were vanquished from the kingdom.

The Mongols did not wait very long to seek their revenge on what they were told beforehand was an inferior people who were not capable of standing up to the invincible Mongol horde. They reassembled, gaining reinforcements from their returning forces that had amassed bone-chilling conquests of other powerful empires of Persia, Islam, and China. They would surely teach the lowly Vietnamese people a lesson for their embarrassing treatment of the world's proudest military. The failed invasion of 1258 was simply reenacted without taking time to fully recover, and over 200,000 Mongols trekked back to the border of Vietnam in early 1259. Again, the Vietnamese defenses were caught off guard and overrun for a brief time. After all, the Mongols were known for their quick and brutal element of surprise in battle.

The pride of the great Kublai Khan would not allow such a humiliating defeat of his fearsome warriors, and history would soon repeat itself again and again, each time ending with overwhelming and valiant victories by the Dai Viets in defense of their homeland. As great as the pride was of Kublai Khan, that prize he sought so desperately would eventually bring his empire's seemingly endless conquests, pillaging, and raping to a rather inglorious end. The great Khan overlooked something about the Dai Viet people…their **iron will!**

After the Mongols' first invasion attempt of Vietnam was fought off in 1258, they would have better success in conquering other empires, including the powerful Song dynasty of China and Korea and Burma. I am trying to put the Vietnamese victories over the Mongols into the perspective it deserves.

In some way, a very small way, I could almost feel compassion for the Mongols. They had rid the world of the evil Islamic Empire, defeated and slaughtered millions of Arabs and Muslims, and I am sure they thought their excursion into little Vietnam would be a cakewalk. Besides, they needed a break from the torturous war with the Muslims and the grueling process of eliminating every living creature—man or beast—of Baghdad (two million people) and burning the ancient city to cinders.

There would be no R&R for the bloodthirsty Mongols on this conquest attempt or the next one. It must have been an ego-shattering and unbelievable shock to the Mongols in their first invasion into southeastern Asia's land of the hardy, resilient, and unexpectedly fierce people inhabiting Vietnam. Vietnam's people had enjoyed a reasonable time of peace after their last battle with the Chinese invaders, so they may have been fresh for this fight and the Mongols were not. They were also quite battle-hardened and ready for whoever else would dare to take their country from them.

The second Mongol invasion (1285) took place when an army five times larger than the 1258–1259 force lined up on the Dai Viet border and demanded passage through Dai Viet so that the Mongol hordes could invade the kingdom of Champa (modern-day central Vietnam). Again, the Dai Viets refused the Mongols and again, their emperor, Tran Hung Dao, led the defense of their kingdom, something the Vietnamese people had plenty of experience with over the past several centuries. In short, during the second invasion of Vietnam by the Mongols, Vietnamese guerillas used their country's terrain to their advantage and inflicted massive damage to the Mongol forces despite their numerical advantage.

In the beginning of the 1285 invasion, several Vietnamese posts fell quickly into Mongol control, but the Viets retaliated quickly and viciously with well-organized counterattacks. In fact, in the highlands where mountain tribes dwelled, the tribal chiefs made life totally miserable for the invaders with tormenting and effective guerrilla tactics which stymied the Mongols. In the meantime, the Mongols were now being forced to spread their forces to maintain control of the outposts they had initially overrun. The so-called conquered villages refused to act like previous Mongol victims in their many conquests.

Highly motivated by the success of the hill tribes giving the invaders far more resistance than expected, General Tran reorganized his regular army, then proceed to take back every captured outpost, killing tens of thousands of Mongols. Such a defeat would impair the Mongol military and set it back to defensive positions.

According to several historians and information found online,[8] war elephants played an important role in the second invasion's battles. Even though the Mongols had squared off with war elephants in their Persian battles, the elephants of Vietnam's jungles were different, as they delivered crushing blows. The pure number of Vietnamese elephants was staggering, and the Mongol cavalry could not maneuver around them in the thick bush. The Vietnamese war elephants were well trained—very obedient—and they were actively engaged in the battles by using their massive tusks and weight and trampling their adversary. Many of the Viet warriors sitting on top of the elephants were armed with powerful two-man crossbows, which acted as an early mobile artillery weapon. The Mongols were unprepared for this.

Add to all of the unheard-of unconventional fighting tactics facing the Mongols, the Vietnam monsoon rains began to pour down on the invaders, suffocating the second invasion attempt. Then followed the choking humidity. The Battle of Siming, as it was called, had become an all-or-nothing scenario, and Vietnam's General Tran decided to go for the kill by confronting the main Mongol force under their famous General Suboda. The Mongol hordes would again be thoroughly defeated and their great General Suboda would fall out at Siming.

---

8 factsanddetails.com/southeast-asia/Vietnam

Retreat was inevitable, but the Dai Viet leader, Tran Hung Dao, was not willing to allow the Mongols to escape so easily this time. The remaining Mongol forces were ambushed repeatedly during their retreat, completely humiliating the Khan's incredibly larger forces.

This great victory was truly a unified effort, as the Chams from Champa, the Hmong and Yao tribes, and the Dai Viet armies took turns attacking the Mongols, choosing terrain that was not "user-friendly" to the Mongols' cavalry. In fact, while part of the Dai Viet army was in temporary retreat mode to set up a vicious counterattack, the Cham were in ferocious pursuit of a large Mongol unit, and the Mongol leader, Sogatu, a naval commander, was killed during his attempted escape back to the north. The proud Mongols could not live with another embarrassing, shocking defeat, and Kublai Khan demanded the Mongol forces return in just two years. Preparation for their next major onslaught began immediately.

Third Invasion, Final War (1287–1288). Kublai Khan had resurrected the remnants of his defeated force from the Vietnam invasion of 1285, strengthened with fresh recruits from other conquered lands (mercenaries) and newly drafted Mongol youths. He was ready to unleash his 550,000-man combined army-naval force loose on the Vietnamese people for the third time. This time, he elected one of his favorite sons, Prince Toghan, to command the invasion. There were no discussions exchanged about another possible defeat.

The offer from the Mongols' commanders, Prince Toghan, and his generals would again be simple this time…surrender or watch your entire civilization be removed from the planet! If you know much about the great battle-hardened, bloodthirsty, marauding assassins led by the Khans of Mongolia back then from Genghis to Kublai, you are aware that they were not the patient, laid-back types who would sit back waiting for an answer from their intended victims. Surrender or die was their offer, and little time was offered to think it over.

Once again, the Vietnamese defense of their treasured home soil (or mud) would be led the third time by one of the finest military geniuses in history, Emperor Tran Hung Dao. The attack would come swiftly. The terms for surrender were not far behind, as the Mongols anticipated a quick and total victory this time. Why not? This invasion's force brought most of the full Mongol army and their entire navy. After all, how could a disorganized, untrained ragtag bunch of "peasants and farmers," many women included, stand up to them, the all-powerful Mongols? Initially, the Dai Viet troop's fortresses all along the border were overwhelmed by the onslaught of the Mongol cavalry and infantry. Even though each outpost was overrun, the

Dai Viets hung together and kept on regrouping, but retreat looked to be the only salvation of this day. During this time, the very existence of Dai Viet became endangered, and Emperor Tran was about ready to apprehend and execute his top general in charge of the faltered first line forces for defense. The future for Vietnam looked dim. This third invasion by the world's almighty conquerors was going as planned, as it should have, in the minds of the ruthless invaders with their blood flowing into the South China Sea. There would be no mercy this time…the Vietnamese were to be erased from the planet.

But a highly surprising and extremely inspirational event happened—the general up for court martial and execution refused to give up his command. Instead, he coordinated his defeated forces and led them safely into the Vietnam wilderness where they would reorganize and continue to fight for their country another day. The over-confident Mongols were on their way, their usual plan of destroying anything and everything in their path until there would no longer be a living thing in the Dai Viet kingdom or Vietnam was looking great, so they thought.

The third historic battle of Bach Dang was just beginning. Note that Tran Hung Dao, who was not only a prince and the emperor of the Dai Viet kingdom, was also the…Supreme Military Grand Warlord Commander of the entire Vietnamese military, a responsibility he did not take lightly. Having already done something no other country had done yet, defeating the invincible Mongols twice, Tran was undaunted by his force's early setbacks in this third and most critical life-or-death encounter.

The third battle of Bach Dang was about to get hot and heavy. As the Mongol ground forces were marching fanatically and almost laughingly toward Hanoi over, around, and through the formidable and unfriendly terrain, the large Mongol armada of five hundred large Chinese ships was also advancing deeper into Vietnam's heartland. It did not look good for the 2,000-year-old Vietnamese civilian nation of "peasants and farmers."

But Tran didn't get to where he was by being a sissy. He was known as a ruthless and brilliant military leader, especially when seemingly backed into a corner. In many ways, Tran already resembled another Vietnamese military genius, yet to be born…Vo Nguyen Giap, the mastermind of Vietnam's later victories over two great powers of the Western world: France and the United States of America.

Personally, I cannot find a way to comprehend how these people had managed to survive up to this point in history, and some of their greatest challenges to remain intact as a family-type nation were yet to face them. I am so impressed with the brave ancestors of what would one day be our adversary.

Another thing I am completely unable to grasp is why the Mongol kings or emperors drove on and on and on, seemingly for as long as there were still people out there who could be and, of course, needed to be killed. Why not just sit back with their infinite wealth of stolen loot, chill out in their jeweled clothing and gold-plated palaces, beef up their defenses, and enjoy the spoils for the rest of their lives? I guess enough was never enough for this breed who were like sharks at a frenzied feeding.

I wonder, on the other hand, why do some armies of defeated lands that turn the tables on their vicious, greedy, merciless killers not continue in pursuit of their rude invaders? Chase them all down, destroy them and their entire culture, and then live happily ever after, enjoying their newly acquired infinite riches. After all, their dreaded enemy had amassed their loot from raping, pillaging, plundering, torturing, and slaughtering everyone in their path to destruction. Better yet, make friends with what was left of the conquered civilizations around them, help them rebuild their lives, and therefore create another invincible force, one that was not aggressively looking to conquer anyone. Why not this option? Guess you had to be there.

Anyway, back to Bach Dang III, as it begins to unfold, even though Prince Toghan thinks that they have already and finally beaten their little nemesis to the south of the Great Mongol Empire. Always keep in mind that the ancient warriors you have read about so far and are about to read more about are the same basic type of "farmers and peasants" that France and the United States were unable to completely subdue. **They must have had huge "pitchforks"!**

The Mongol ground forces of several hundred thousand had already overrun all of Tran's defensive fortresses. Hanoi was standing in their way; plus, the Mongolian navy was well on its way to prevent any would-be retreaters, as if the Dai Viets had any idea of retreating—not a chance. In response to Prince Toghan's offer, here is what historians claim Tran told his army of two hundred thousand or so (including navy and militia):

> *"In the face of these dangers to the fatherland, i fail to eat during the day nor am i able to sleep at night. Tears roll down my cheeks and my heart bleeds as if it were being cut to shreds by mongol knives and swords. I tremble with extreme anger because i cannot eat our enemy's flesh...lie down in his skin...chew up his liver...and drink all of his blood till there is no more. I would gladly surrender my life a thousand times on the field of battle if i could do these things to the enemy who invades our homeland."*

Plain and simple, Tran rejected the great Mongol prince, son of Kublai Khan's generous offer of mercy, which would have presumably included the following actions or conditions: plunder all possessions, level all structures and dwellings, rape at will all of your women, then kill them so they can bear no more children, kill all of your children, and slaughter all remaining humans in ways never even imagined, some swiftly, some slowly. Some mercy!

Tran now understood completely that it was a tragic early error to match his one hundred thousand ground force army face-to-face with an enemy force five times larger, which nearly cost him any chance for victory. The Mongols' numbers were too overwhelming and their vaunted cavalry was every bit as effective as reported to him, and as he remembered from their previous invasions. Tran ordered all his ground forces to abandon their positions and disappear from the would-be battlefield chosen by Prince Toghan, and they did just that at the command of their loved and respected prince, emperor, and warlord commander.

The ancient relatives of the twentieth-century Viet Cong and North Vietnamese "peasants and farmers" retreated and disappeared with their "pitchforks" into the swamps, jungles, and wooded high country to regroup with fifty thousand of their mountain tribe countrymen, and to most definitely continue the fight…under their terms. Trust me when I say this… nobody but nobody fights in the jungle quite like the Vietnamese—except maybe a highly motivated and self-trained American soldier or marine out on an ambush patrol or a search-and-destroy mission. The twentieth-century Vietnamese would learn that the American soldier boy **DID NOT FIGHT LIKE THE FRENCH FOUGHT!**

Tran also ordered every Vietnamese city or village to be evacuated and burned to the ground, including all food and supplies that could not be carried with them into the wilderness. From their hidden camps in the woods and jungles, these "peasants and farmers" launched coordinated and vicious raids against the Mongol camps and would quickly vanish again back to their friendly jungle camps. They would do this time and time again, from several different directions. While all of the Vietnamese structures and homes had been burned to the ground, leaving a wasteland with no food or supplies for the Mongols to replenish from, there was another event unfolding which would affect the Mongol navy of five hundred giant ships. They were being set up for an unexpected surprise, a crushing…**AMBUSH!**

What happened next was plain and simple…guerilla f-ing warfare at its perfected magnificence by a highly outnumbered underdog of seemingly helpless "peasants and farmers." They were Vietnam's untrained civilian army, truly the people's army, an army with pure heart.

At the time Tran and his guerillas were reducing the Mongols' numerical advantage with relentless and unstoppable ambushes, those Dai Viets who were routed from the fortresses at the beginning of the invasion had in fact reassembled and had been working frantically, cutting down small trees, inserting sharpened bronze spear-like tips on the ends of these sturdy pole-like trees, and planting hundreds of them into the muddy ground of the Bach Dang River's bottom. Later, the armada of Dai Viet vessels (canoe-like) tricked the Mongol navy, luring them down the river, past the underwater poles in the direction of the spear-like tips. The tide of the river was up, therefore concealing the vast group of potential ship-destroying weapons which were pointing upward and forward, just beneath the surface of the muddy Bach Dang. As the Mongol armada continued their pursuit, the river's tide was retreating with the Dai Viet canoes, which of course traveled over the submerged poles quite safely, past the pointed poles, escaping completely. Along the banks of the Bach Dang, more Dai Viets were positioned, waiting patiently to launch their…**AMBUSH!**

As the five hundred heavy ships of the Mongol navy were punctured and sinking, one after another, the ground forces on the banks filled the air with their arrows, from both sides of the river, and the Dai Viet canoes turned around and counterattacked. There was nowhere for the Mongol navy to go, and methodically and mercilessly, the entire fleet was destroyed, including all living beings who were on those ships. During this historic battle of canoes against warships, the Dai Viets set many of their own dugouts on fire—they could always make more—and they directed them right into the heart of the Mongol armada. Meanwhile, those archers on both banks were also sending fire arrows, and soon, one of the largest naval invasions in medieval history had been turned into one gigantic raging inferno of charred wood and smoldering dead Mongols. The Mongols lost four hundred ships and forty thousand men in the first day of the battle. Their admiral was wounded, captured, and executed in a slow manner—kind of like the Viet Cong style of the twentieth century.

Meanwhile, Prince Toghan's army was enjoying itself back at Hanoi, having their way with an undefended and uninhabited city. When the news arrived of the armada's total annihilation and deaths of one hundred thousand men, an immediate uncoordinated and panic-driven exodus from Hanoi began and the retreat was on. At the same time, Tran's army from the woods and jungles had engaged the sizeable but confused Mongol cavalry, but unfortunately for the Mongols' cavalry, they, too, had charged into a carefully planned trap strategically designed by Tran Hung Dao. The time had arrived that Tran spent many sleepless nights thinking about. For centuries, the land known as Dai Viet had fought never-ending death feuds with the Chinese, now the Mongols, but finally Tran's enemies had made the grave mistake of taking on Tran's highly spirited warriors smack dab in the middle of the inhospitable death jungles, with swamps that were three feet deep, and water and the mud beneath would suck the Mongols' heavy cavalry down at least another foot. These were not favorable conditions for the plains-marauding Mongol cavalry. This was guerilla war—Vietnamese style.

But the fun was just getting started for Prince Tran's professional army of unwelcome conquerors. They had one more task at hand, and it would prove to be even more challenging than the failed invasion itself…they had to escape from Dai Viet alive!

Getting out of Dodge alive would be a torturous and cruel undertaking for the Mongols. The Vietnamese smelled the Mongol flesh; it was everywhere in pools of blood. What the Mongols were getting was a dose of what they had been dishing out to every living civilization they faced up with from Korea to Iran, from Europe to Siam, including China and Russia along the way. David was giving an ass-kicking to Goliath that would forever be remembered in the history books.

Bach Dang's battle would be a history-altering event, not just another major battle where one side lost and went home to recuperate, and one side won and went home with the spoils. Tran had handily defeated Mongol invasions twice before, each time allowing the defeated to retreat somewhat graciously back to their homeland. Both times, the Mongols regrouped and Kublai Khan ordered them to return to Dai Viet with more soldiers each time.

This retreat would be different. Not that the Mongols had not suffered enough already, because they had. They had been cut off from food supplies; died from cholera, malaria, and poisonous spider bites; mauled by tigers; harassed by mosquitoes the size of dragonflies, six-inch sucking leeches, man-attacking ants, and giant termites; and killed by twelve-foot-long cobras! So why did the Mongols want this land so badly?

This defeat would spearhead the inevitable demise of the Mongolian empire. Yes, you are reading correctly. A tiny kingdom of "peasants and farmers" who fought bravely, cohesively, and intelligently had once again defeated an overwhelming enemy invader. The Mongols would never return to this part of Asia. Emperor Tran, with the entire military under his control, remained loyal to protecting his homeland and had little desire to expand Dai Viet's borders.

I am grateful that Tran Hung Dai lived and fought several centuries before we Americans stepped onto his country's land. Tran was undoubtedly one of the all-time great military strategists in history. Using the terrain of his homeland and guerilla warfare to harass and defeat a much more powerful enemy, several times, Emperor Tran provided the model for Vietnamese warriors to use successfully in the twentieth century. His ability to mobilize the entire Vietnamese population for the cause of national defense to a foreign invasion undoubtedly inspired the Viet Minh against France and, of course, their brothers and sisters and offspring who would fight against the Americans ten years later.

Tran called for national unity in much the same way Ho Chi Minh would centuries later, and it worked each time. Tran Hung Dao is still an object of worship in Vietnam today, especially in the rural areas.

If there were any Mongol survivors of the 1288 invasion, they were left with dismal memories of their horrific retreat where the Dai Viets chased and attacked them continuously, smashing to pieces what remained of that once mighty force. **The Dai Viets were the ancestors of the North Vietnamese Army that the U.S. government and their arrogant generals would also underestimate in the Vietnam War.**

I got chills reading about this battle and of Vietnam's earlier heroes such as the Trung sisters. I was chilled again as I was writing the material and re-reading to enter into my book. Ngo Quyen's defeat of the Chinese in 938–939 was equally as significant as the defeat of the Mongols for the third time in 1288 by Emperor Tran, who would die just twelve years later in 1300. Ngo Quyen is known for founding the first enduring Vietnamese dynasty and laying the foundation for an independent Vietnamese kingdom, which ironically he named…Nam Viet. The Vietnamese people's defeat of the Mongols was an impressive example of a small but fearless kingdom thoroughly defeating an empire of fearsome and ruthless would-be conquerors. I can just picture this scene, the ancestors of our adversaries, the Viet Cong and NVA, challenging and beating the Mongol hordes or the Chinese hordes—either way, using the same primitive guerilla warfare tactics they would someday use against the French and Americans in centuries to come. I can visualize this, and I am amazed that my war buddies actually fought and beat such a tenacious foe.

Results of Final Mongol Invasion of Dai Viet
1287–1288

MONGOLS		DAI VET	
Mongol Strength:	550,000 500 Ships	Dai Viet Strength:	250,000 60,000 (Champa)
Casualties:	Entire Navy Entire Army Infantry & Cavalry destroyed	Casualties:	More than 50,000 including elders, women, & children
Leaders:	Mong ke Khan Kublai Khan Uriyangkhadi Prince Toghan	Leaders:	Tran Hung Dao (victorious)

The unsung heroes of the Vietnam-Mongol wars were the ethnic groups from the mountainous areas of Vietnam, Laos, Thailand, and southern China. The French were the first to call the natives Montagnards, but *Degars* is the correct name in Vietnam.

In Laos, the Hmong are closely related to the Degars of Vietnam. There are approximately fifty-five ethnic minority groups recognized by China, Vietnam, and Laos. Another major group would be the Yao people. They are officially recognized in China and Vietnam today.

Non-Vietnamese history books briefly mention the Hmongs and Yaos as peoples who fought against the Mongols, and they did much more later on. There are approximately three million Yaos existing today and about eight million Hmongs, with two hundred and fifty thousand living in the United States today. Both groups fought for the French and the Americans against the North Vietnamese communists. Their contributions to supporting the USA in the Vietnam War would be worthy of additional mentioning later in this book.

Hmong and Degar/Montagnard people have not been treated very well ever since the French Indochina War—much the same way that America's native Indians were treated. Personally, I did not have any experiences with Vietnam's tribal people, although I wish I had, as their reputation as great fighters was commonly known by most combat-tested soldiers. I would like to dedicate a few more words to these humble and brave people later in the book.

One notable Laotian Hmong hero who fought the North Vietnamese from his homeland was General Vang Pao, who I mentioned in *Condemned Property?* General Pao brought nearly two hundred thousand of his Hmong countrymen to the United States after Saigon fell to North Vietnam in 1975. But first, the general had to decide which one of his five wives would accompany him to the USA. I never heard how that worked out.

General Vang Pao earned the title of Lord Protector of the Lands from King Savang Vatthana of Laos. He was the only member of the Hmong tribes to make general in the Laotian army. His troops helped save countless American lives and helped delay the communist flow of troops and supplies down the Ho Chi Minh Trail for fourteen years. Many fallen American pilots owe their lives to him and his forces.

Vang Pao quickly recruited and trained a force of five thousand, with the American CIA backing him. The Hmongs followed him religiously, and at one time, their force reached forty thousand. They met the North Vietnamese head-on in many battles. Vang Pao was one of those leaders who led from the front in battle, even as a general.

After the Vietnam War ended and Saigon surrendered, General Vang Pao, his family, and most of his officers were airlifted safely to Thailand, as they were promised by the Americans. However, with his love and devotion to the men and women who served him, he successfully convinced the American government to bring Hmong refugee families from Laos to their new home in America. Recent counts show more than 250,000 Hmong refugees live here.

Please understand that some accounts of the Mongol invasions differ from the descriptions recorded by the Mongols versus the versions by the Vietnamese. The same goes for the China invasions and their defeats by the Vietnamese. Therefore, I attempted to informally dissect and reconnect the order of events as best I could as a weekend history buff. I found some of my information in two great sources—*Genghis Khan and the Mongol Conquests* and *The Mongols*, by Stephen Turnbull. I find the earliest years of Vietnam's history so fascinating that I wish I could have watched all of their decisive battles for freedom from a mountaintop. Trouble is I would have needed an extension in life to be there with the Trung sisters in 40 AD up to and including General Tran's three amazing victories over the Mongols in the 1280s. All were victories of biblical proportion.

After the Mongol invasions, Vietnam would enjoy two centuries of peace, tranquility, and freedom after the mind-boggling military feats in which Tran led the Vietnamese. Tran would live to be seventy-three years old, an amazing feat itself in the thirteenth century. He died in 1300. Of course, Tran Hung Dao's memory would live on forever in Vietnam as well as in the surrounding countries. After all, the Mongols had never tasted defeat before, and then this unsuspecting badass from little Vietnam defeated them three times. The Mongol Empire's glory days of massive plundering and murdering had come to a rather quick end. Even though the so-called ragtag "farmers and peasants" of the Vietnamese people had defeated several powerful Chinese dynasties in the past, as other heroes rose up, they were going to be tested again and again by a familiar invader and several new ones. As if the message they had sent around the world by defeating Kublai Khan's armies at the peak of their power wasn't enough to keep greedy would-be conquerors away until the end of time. Even then, people had very short memories.

China invades again (1427 and 1428). However, someone else stepped up to meet them. Le Loi was a wealthy landlord in Vietnam who had been recruiting and preparing reinforcements to build up the Vietnamese army for another anticipated invasion from the north. Vietnam's leadership had gone through a weak spell after the death of Tran Hung Dao in 1300. He was a hard monarch to replace, so China felt up to the task of yet another invasion of their southern neighbor in the year of 1407. However, their stay would be extremely brief this time, as the Vietnamese proved stronger than anticipated, and they were not hospitable hosts to invaders. This time, the Ming Chinese dynasty was threatening Vietnam's sovereignty. (When would these people just leave Vietnam alone?) Le Loi had power in Vietnam and he loved his land. A Vietnamese aristocratic landowner, he stepped up to his country's aid. Along with Le Loi, another Vietnamese champion stepped up. Nguyen Trai was a popular Confucian statesman, poet, and military advisor to Le Loi. Not surprisingly, Nguyen and Le used very successful guerilla war tactics to fight the unwelcomed marauders. The Lam Son uprising was a nine-year war against the Chinese Ming dynasty from 1418 to 1427. The tide-turning battle was fought at Tot Dong-Chuc Dong in 1426. The Ming larger force was humbled to an impressive loss, and Le Loi received the Ming leader's surrender. The gesture that followed this resounding Vietnamese victory should never be forgotten by the Chinese, but that is highly unlikely.

After defeating the Ming army, rather than executing or imprisoning the surviving prisoners as all Vietnamese rulers had done before him, Le Loi returned the beaten soldiers with their leaders safely back to China. He became emperor, and relations with China would run without threatening invasions for many years past Le Loi's death in 1497. Under his rule, Vietnam enjoyed great years economically and expanded its power past its southern borders into Champa.

In 1471, with Le Loi still emperor of Vietnam, the kingdom was being attacked by rogue pirates from the north (China) and from the west (Laos). The Vietnamese quickly attacked the pirates and eliminated them. However, at this same time, Vietnam was also invaded by its southern neighbor (central Vietnam area), the Champa. Their army was also destroyed and Champa was annexed to the Vietnamese kingdom. With Le Loi at the throne from 1428 to 1497, Vietnam thrived. With Le's two hundred thousand standing army, invaders were not tempted. Actually, the Le dynasty would carry on as the dominating ruling class in Vietnam for nearly three hundred years until 1788, which would be Vietnam's longest free period in their history.

Emperor Nguyen Hue (1753–1792) was referred to as the second emperor of Vietnam's Tay Son dynasty. During Nguyen's reign, Vietnam's history was confusing and restless. For instance:

> Nguyen Hue and his brothers, known as the Tay Son brothers, rose to power by defeating the ruling Le dynasty and two rival feudal houses of the Nguyen in the south and the Trinh up north. All of these accomplishments in a few years probably shortened his life as he died of a stroke at the age of forty. However, before he died, he would leave Vietnam as a unified nation, which lasted until the European invasions.

Of course, Nguyen Hue faced many challenges by potential seekers of his emperor status. In fact, there were so many episodes that I had to quit reading about them and move on, as the constant feuding had my head spinning. However, Nguyen Hue managed one major military accomplishment that clearly stood out and would embed his name into the growing Vietnam book of heroes.

In 1788, almost two hundred years after the biblical defeats of the Khan's armies, a large Chinese army had risen to become another would-be conqueror of its neighbors. The Qing dynasty had no love for the Vietnamese and still had an evil desire to dominate and enslave them again, as other Chinese dynasties had succeeded in doing in the first century.

The emperor of the Chinese Qing dynasty sent a massive army, estimated at three hundred thousand, down to Vietnam to dispose of Nguyen Hue's army and dethrone him. Nguyen Hue received advanced word of this, so he took action. He raised an army of one hundred thousand from the villages to join his regular army of one hundred thousand, and they headed north to meet the Chinese Qing army head-on. The Qing army was not aware of the advance by the Vietnamese, and the fast and furious attack that resembled the Mongol army's style destroyed half of the Qing army while they slept. *The Chronicle of Greater Vietnam* mentions that at least thirty thousand Qing died. Another fifty thousand were wounded, and 3,400 were captured, while the Vietnamese total casualties were approximately eight thousand. Yet, Nguyen showed unusual compassion and allowed the Qing survivors to return home with some honor, which contributed to a peaceful relationship with each other. Nguyen Hue was revered as the national savior of Vietnam, all this before the age of forty.

Some people have speculated that if Nguyen Hue had killed all of the invading Qing army, then marched north to finish things with the Chinese emperor, much of central and southeast Asia would be part of Vietnam today. He died undefeated in battle as one of the most popular figures in Vietnam.

Would another Vietnamese champion rise up to become a monarch and protector—savior of this special kingdom? It was almost certain that another aggressor would arrive on the scene, pay no attention to history, and attempt conquest of the Vietnamese people. History does have an uncanny way of repeating itself, and the Vietnamese have never been the aggressors.

> *Follow me if I advance.*
> *Kill me if I retreat.*
> *Avenge me if I die.*
> **—Ancient Vietnamese War Cry**

In 2018, the famous 1288 Battle of Bach Dang will be 830 years old. I know Vietnam will celebrate this monumental event as they should. They deserve to show their pride for their impressive history. I will share it with my former enemy.

Note: Genghis Khan would never allow anyone to draw or paint his image, so actual pictures of what he looked like do not exist.

Images to follow attempt to depict the Khans and Mongol warriors as well as General Tran and Viet warriors of the era.

General Tran the Great Defeated the Mongols Three Times

Ancient Viet Warriors

Genghis and the Mongols

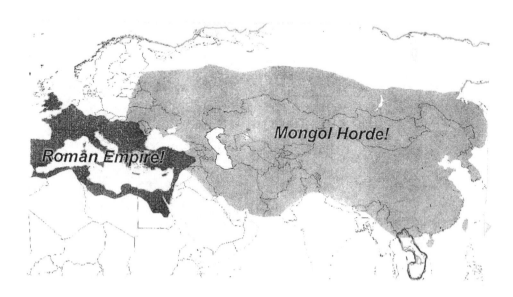

Map – Mongol Horde

Chapter 5

GIAP THE GREAT ARRIVES!

Without a people's army, the people have nothing.
—Mao Tse Tung

General Vo Nguyen Giap has been referred to by historians in many sources as the winner of both of Vietnam's wars with France and America. Several historians and writers also described some of Giap's credentials and accomplishments as superhuman.

I have clearly stated that the leaders of our country and the military fought the Vietnam War and lost it after the American military had won it due to the democratic government's ignorance and arrogance. They were flat-out inept for the task of leading a world power. However, they picked the wrong country, and picked on the wrong leader at the wrong time to make such mistakes. All they had to do was…listen to their own troops, the ground-pounding infantry who had to meet the enemy face-to-face in Vietnam and had beaten them repeatedly in the enemy's environment, their sacred homeland.

Our leaders failed to know its enemy and they failed to believe they were fighting an enemy capable of beating the American military's firepower. While we, the combat troops, learned to adapt to Vietnam's treacherous conditions, which seemingly favored an unforgiving and a very capable enemy, the *powers that be* just continued with their shallow and wrong military strategies. Sure, we had lavish firepower and the enemy did not. But using that firepower as though we were fighting WWII or even Korea all over again rather than changing action—DESPITE THE CONSTANT SUGGESTIONS FROM WITHIN THE RANKS—would contribute to their defeat.

You see, there was such a person on the other side of the DMZ in North Vietnam who could adapt his military plan to accompany his army and disorient the most recent invaders of his beloved homeland. This person had history on his side. He had heritage on his side. He also had a people's army on his side that was willing to fight for him until their last breath. And after that…his sons and daughters would carry on the fight to free their country again and again. The people's army of North Vietnam had Ho Chi Minh and a man I refer to as Giap the Great to lead them similar to many legendary god-like emperors and generals throughout their history. The American elite paid no attention to it.

Giap was born on August 25, 1911 and died on October 4, 2013 at 102 years old. His parents worked their land and lived a comfortable life by Vietnam standards. Their home had dirt floors, but was one of the few with a tiled roof. Not surprisingly, Giap's father was a dedicated nationalist and became heavily involved in uprisings against the French in the nineteenth century. However, he was arrested in 1919 for his revolutionary ideas and died while he was in prison that same year. The young Giap was home taught until being sent to a village school. His intelligence commended more challenge, and he was elevated to a district school at an advanced grade. He finished comparable high school education at age thirteen and moved on to the National Academy, a Catholic college-level institution where one of his classmates was Ho Chi Minh. Need I say more?

Giap grew up like most rural Vietnamese, helping his father, working their rice paddies. Giap's father was also a committed nationalist, having played a major part in resistance movements against the French from 1885–1888. He was arrested for subversive activities by the French colonial authorities in 1919. His activities would be considered acts of patriotism to you, me, and other good American citizens. Giap's father was imprisoned without a trial and he died in prison a few weeks after his arrest. Giap was nine years old when his father died. He would lose another family member, his older sister, who was also imprisoned by the French and died.

While Giap was attending a National Academy School in Hue, two of his classmates would become powerful figures in Vietnam. Ngo Dinh Diem went on to become president of South Vietnam from 1955–1963. His other classmate, Ho Chi Minh, took a different direction. Giap married his true love, Nguyen Thi Quang Thai, in 1939. She also became a nationalist and so did their daughter Hong Anh (Red Queen of Flowers).

Giap exiled himself to China in May of 1940, where he learned to speak and write Chinese and studied the strategy and tactics of the Chinese. Later, he learned to speak French and English. Giap's wife was arrested and sentenced to fifteen years, and she, too, would die in prison in 1943. His daughter escaped a French imprisonment attempt. Another badass was in the making, as Giap's hatred for the French grew to violent proportions.

Giap eventually remarried a beautiful Vietnamese dancer, Thuong Huyen, and they went on to have two boys and two girls.

His grand military career probably started in 1942 when he set up a camp in the mountain caves of northern Vietnam along with just thirty-four "farmers and peasants," where the Viet Minh (future Viet Cong) was born. In the summer of 1943, when Giap's first wife died in a French prison, he had amassed a formidable and well-trained military force of a thousand or so, and they were winning over the trust and confidence of the local people. Giap's "people's army" was on its way.

By April 1945, the Viet Minh had five thousand solid soldiers, and they were able to pester the Japanese posts with successful results. Giap's efforts were noticed and appreciated in the United States, enough so that they sent aid and advisors to Giap's camp in the mountains. Eventually, Giap's Viet Minh took enough territory back from Japan to form a nation, which he did just before Japan's official surrender to end WWII.

On September 2, 1945, Ho Chi Minh declared the independence of the new Democratic Republic of Vietnam, with Giap taking on high responsibilities within the government along with being in charge of the military. Unknown to them...President Harry S. Truman, Prime Minister Winston Churchill, and Premier Joseph Stalin had already taken the liberty of directing the future of the new post-WWII Vietnam. Eventually, French forces moved in, as Truman, Churchill, and Stalin looked the other way.

Giap was not just the past master of guerilla warfare; in two modern wars he would become the most successful guerilla warfare leader of all time. He taught the importance of timing, surprise, camouflage, and deception. It would be impossible to compare Giap with other legendary generals at the highest levels because of his genius-like combination of guerilla and conventional warfare. It would also be unfair to the other generals to make comparisons because Giap's accomplishments have never been seen before or since. Unprecedented success in the aspects of war, Giap was indescribably superior to his peers of this era, as many military buffs claim.

My war buddies and I know firsthand of Giap's influence on his troops, especially the things I mentioned already...timing, surprise, camouflage, deception, etc. A perfect example of how the North Vietnamese and Viet Cong were uncanny masters at concealing themselves: All too often, when we were on a search-and-destroy mission or trying to set up our own ambush, we would walk into their ambush when our point man and the next several men were allowed to walk by before the VC would open up on us. We would learn from them and return the favor, much to their surprise.

Giap had many costly failures. The 1967–1968 Tet Offensives were perfect examples. Despite every technique in Giap's brilliant military mind, the Vietnam War was almost lost and should have been lost as American troops and her allies completely turned the tables on Giap's series of surprise attacks on nearly every city in South Vietnam. Sure, we had a firepower advantage on the enemy, and we utilized it to the max from a defensive standpoint. We did not carry the fight to the enemy after fighting them off in a failed attack on our forces with a counterattack and chase after them into their hiding places in Cambodia and Laos partly because...**WE COULD NOT FIND THEM!**

The Vietnam War could have ended in 1968 by either side *if* different tactics had been used. To explain this would require an additional ten chapters, and it is mostly my opinion anyway. So, what did both sides get out of the 1967–1968 face-to-face confrontations? Over 50 percent of the war's total casualties were inflicted in those two years. Some of my war brothers will disagree on this statement, as the "gung-ho all the way" troops will tell you that our training for jungle warfare, day and night, was more than adequate. Really? How do you prepare a street kid who has been walking on sidewalks and playing baseball all of his eighteen to twenty years to suddenly become the next Francis Marion, the Swamp Fox of the Revolutionary War?

One of the bits of advice that the Yogi Bear training sergeants (Drill Sergents wore Yogi Bear type hats, therefore the nickname) told us over and over and over again was…KEEP YOUR HEAD DOWN! But as one who filled the dreaded point man position a hundred times—and lived through it—I quickly taught myself that while keeping one's head down seemed like pretty sound advice, it was difficult to do and not look down at the ground, and staring at the ground too much would shorten one's life. Our enemy was often in the trees, behind rocks or cemetery stones, or on the upper floors in abandoned buildings, and it proved to be a very healthy habit to notice their presence ahead rather than finding them two feet away as I was looking down—which we also needed to do because of booby traps. Oversimplified? Maybe. What I learned in "on the job" training was impossible to acquire in forty days of combat infantry training in spite of the almost real-life environment some of us trained in, like Fort Polk, Louisiana's "Tiger Land."

> *A man can seldom—very, very seldom—fight a winning fight against his lack of good training.*
>
> **—Mark Twain**

Don't you think General Vo Nguyen Giap was aware of how unprepared his new enemy, the Americans, were for the most part? I'm sure he learned this quickly in his early years. Then again, I think one of Giap's most serious mistakes in his war against the Americans is the same mistake the French, Japanese, Mongols, and Chinese all made by…underestimating the **heart** of the Vietnamese. Americans also had great heart.

While it became disgustingly obvious to most of America's combat troops in Vietnam that they were not fighting for the safety of their country, we were not motivated to fight with reckless abandon because some armchair colonel ordered us. Most of those who made it past the first two or three weeks out in the bush developed an instinct for survival that no stateside training could possibly instill into us. We who fought in one of the ugliest, most senseless wars in history were forced to find out in a short time what we were made of…or perish quickly!

Sure, we honed our senses, developed greater instinct and all that stuff. But something already instilled into our God-given makeup would be the difference in a lot of guys making it or not. Make no mistake, no American soldier or marine from any war before Vietnam or after it had as much drive to keep his buddy safe. The most important qualities the American soldier boy had in the Vietnam War were…his spirit and his **HEART!**

As I have mentioned earlier as well as in my previous books, every veteran's experience in the Vietnam War was different. Each of us left with different emotions. Some were more damaged than others. Some have yet to recover mentally or physically, and some have been able to adjust just fine. God bless them, but I wish more of them would reach out to their less fortunate brothers and help them along through their troubled lives.

It seems to me that nowadays people are forgetting more and more about our great country's history, especially the military history. Someone dear to me, who taught me so much about life and values, was my American History teacher, football coach, mentor, and great friend till his last day in this world. **Mr. Warder Powell** was his name. He taught and coached at Twinsburg High School in the little integrated village where I grew up, Twinsburg, Ohio. Mr. Powell was a veteran himself. He was even an all-state football player during his high school days in West Virginia. Most of his players at Twinsburg genuinely loved him. He was a really tough teacher, so I would say he wasn't as popular with the students he did not coach. Guess you had to get to know him, and luckily, I had that opportunity. Mr. Powell shared a lot of really neat pearls of wisdom with us, and we always looked forward to hearing what he would say next. One of his famous statements came when he was administering punishment by the old-fashioned paddle. He would say, "My boy, this is going to hurt me more than it is going to hurt you." Keep in mind that Coach Powell weighed about 250 pounds, and his paddling targets (me included) ranged from 130- to 190-pound students in those days. So we could never figure out how this was going to hurt him more than us.

One of the things he used to tell us was "One of the most important things I'll ever leave behind me is a legacy. Not my own legacy, but the legacy and memories of so many men from my company in the Korean War, especially so many of whom never made it back." Mr. Powell was never shy about expressing his pride for serving, although he wasn't one who would share war stories unless you were extra special to him. In case you are wondering where I am going with this, not to worry, for I am right on track with my mission.

The legacy of the Vietnam War veteran is near the top of my priority list in life these days. Naturally, at this age, other priorities need closer attention, but talking about the *heart* of my brothers over there will rank high with me until the end of my days. Many people know nothing about their own country's history, and worse yet, there is an overabundance of teachers and professors who have attempted to change our history to make my war buddies and me look like the bad guys in the Vietnam War. This is why I am dedicating a lot of my time in writing and talking about one of our country's greatest generations, the Vietnam War Era generation. There was a time, a long time, when I did not—could not openly speak about our war. Many Vietnam vets remain like that, and many died with their stories. Like I said, I am grateful to have an opportunity to write and speak about my service in Vietnam with the most amazing men and women I have ever known.

Having what it takes to engage in a surprise attack from a very capable adversary who knows his terrain better than you do, to return their fire and even reverse the battle by counterattacking them, takes a special kind of warrior. He is called a...**Combat Infantry Grunt** of the Vietnam War. Risking one's life in such situations so that a buddy does not take a bullet is something no words can describe. No one can put a value on it. Very, very few people in their lifetime will ever get even remotely close to this situation. I have been there more times than I care to say, and I am proud to say that I have served with and fought side-by-side dozens of such rare individuals.

General Giap and his Viet Minh had an indescribable hate for the French. Why not? The French Foreign Legionnaires and their mercenaries were famous for slaughtering Vietnamese civilians, so the inevitable payback time Giap had been dreaming about could not come soon enough. Fortunately, the French also made that big military error I mentioned earlier and will mention elsewhere in this book: never underestimate the will and the heart of an adversary. The end result would be a humiliating defeat of the French on March 13, 1954 at Dien Bien Phu by a bunch of farmers, peasants, hunters, and yes, women and children who contributed to Giap's historic, masterful, and overwhelming defeat of a modern Western military force. Giap's victory shocked the world, and France was completely humiliated and stripped of any heart to carry on this war or hold on to the rest of any part of their colonized empire.

Today, my perspective about the enemy my buddies and I fought against in our war with Vietnam is probably nine hundred degrees different from what it was when I was a twenty-two-year-old, 130-pound, machete-swinging point man for Bravo Company 3/22 of the 25th Infantry. I would imagine that lots of vets who served in that war have softened their feelings about those "gooks" we were being paid to kill. Doing the research for this book has me shaking my head in awe at the Vietnamese stamina, will, and heart to protect their homeland.

I'll bet Giap memorized every battle tactic his ancestors used from 39 AD until 1471 AD. He had a wealth of information about battle strategies that were tried, tested, and successful. I can envision Giap as a young officer before he organized the Viet Minh revolutionaries, sitting in a tent at a base camp hidden deep in the mountainous woods of North Vietnam. I can visualize him reading about one of his country's early heroes, Ngo Quyen. Not only did Ngo found the first enduring Vietnamese kingdom, which he named Nam Viet, but his military tactics that expelled the Chinese in 939 have been studied and reused by many Vietnamese generals throughout the course of Vietnam's history. Nam Viet would remain independent for nearly one thousand years, with occasional wannabe conquerers, until the French seized the controls in the nineteenth century.

If Giap tired of reading about Ngo's miraculous military conquests in defense of his beloved country, Giap could set the book about Ngo down, take a long walk, and when he returned to his tent, he could read on for hours and hours about Ngo's legendary exploits. But Giap also had other options to further his intense quests, to advance his aspirations, to accomplish the goals he would eventually set for earning his country's independence back again and again…simply by studying another legendary Vietnam general—Tran Hung Dao, mentioned earlier in the book. Tran Hung Dao's magnificent achievements in battle were so phenomenal that he is ranked number two among some of the world's all-time greatest military leaders.[9]

I am repeating some information here, but Tran deserves at least another mention. What the hey—if the Mongolian Empire had unquestionably the strongest army in the world during that time period, then where does one rank the general of a vastly outnumbered force who defeated the Mongols in every major confrontation? Tran Hung Dao's victory over the mighty Mongol Yuan dynasty, commanded by the great Kublai Khan, is considered by some military history experts as one of the greatest military feats in the world's history.

I find it extremely fascinating that in the Top Ten Military Generals of All Time poll, none of America's so-called super generals are ranked. Here is that Top Ten ranking:

1. Alexander the Great (Greece
2. Tran Hung Dao (Vietnam)
3. David IV of Georgia

---

9   www.thetoptens.com/top-military-generals

4. Napoleon Bonaparte (France)
5. Hannibal Barca (Carthage)
6. Julius Caesar (Rome)
7. Genghis Khan (Mongolia)
8. Vo Nguyen Giap (Vietnam)
9. Khalid Walid (Arab Muslim)
10. Sun Tzu (China)

Yes, of course there are several different ranking sources that do this. Most of them agree on who is number one—Alexander the Great. After that, they all differ greatly. But I am going with this one, which I found online (where else?). Here is a short list of others who are mentioned on **www. thetoptens.com/top-military-generals**:

Robert E. Lee (USA)
Antonio Luna (Philippines)
George Washington (USA)
Erwin Rommel (Germany)
Georgy Zhukov (Russia)
Saladin (Persia)
George S. Patton (USA)
Frederick the Great (Prussia)
Nguyen Hue (Vietnam)
Horatio Nelson (Great Britain)

Most of these are familiar names, even to the most uninterested history amateurs. Who has not heard of Alexander the Great or the Spartans of Greece, Napoleon, Hannibal, Sun Tzu, Caesar, and Genghis Khan himself? Oh, by the way, the world's top historians include two Vietnam greats in them mix…Giap and Tran Hung Dao. And we American Vietnam vets were pitted against one of those?

I wish I could have been an innocent spectator with a "safe" grandstand seat on a mountaintop while the third battle raged between the Tran Hung Dao-led Vietnamese who were fighting desperately for freedom and the future existence of the Vietnamese people, and the Mongol hordes led by their great Khan in 1288.

On the Top Ten website, at the number-three ranking in between Alexander the Great at number two and Napoleon Bonaparte at number four sits the man who halted the unfriendly advances of the Kublai Khan-ruled Mongol swarm three times. He could just as well be the number-one ranked supreme general of all time, as no one else took on the Mongols and beat them till then. Tran Hung Dao occupies the prestigious number-one position of Vietnam's Top Ten Heroes of all time. Unbelievably, this superb military leader went through his entire military life as Vietnam's ultimate protector and was never on the losing end of any battle. No wonder he was revered and studied by many of Vietnam's greatest military leaders of the future, including Ho Chi Minh and possibly the greatest general of the twentieth century, known as Giap.

Personally, my favorite generals of all time are, in no particular order, Robert E. Lee, Patton, Giap, and Sherman! From what I have read in the exhaustive research I did to assemble and coordinate much of the historical facts and stories for this book, I am led to believe that Tran Hung Dao may have personally fit the title of "The World's Bad-Ass of All Time"! And if he were living today, he would try to prove that he deserved such a title by showing us personally.

Tran Hung Dao, much like Giap, Sherman, and Lee, was fully capable of transforming ordinary citizens (even farmers and peasants) into world-class citizen-soldiers capable of doing severe damage to a seasoned, well-trained army on a battlefield. He managed to accomplish this by teaching his ragtag bands how to excel at hit-and-run, ambush-styled guerilla warfare. Anyone who cares about history or has an interest in some of the little known but monumental events should read about the fascinating life of Tran Hung Dao. You will find out quickly why Giap studied the battle strategies and victories against overwhelming odds by his famous ancestor, Tran Hung Dao.

Interesting trivia for history buffs—nothing more. Please note that none of the American generals of the Vietnam War, Korean War, or any of the American-fought wars since Vietnam are mentioned in the ranking. So what? The USA owned the air in the Vietnam War, the Navy was virtually unchallenged, and we had our helicopters. All North Vietnam had to throw at us was their iron will, their history, their homeland advantage, their heart and…**GIAP!** That was all?

Just a weekend history amateur—a rather new author with only three books under my belt—but I was one of those young Americans who was thrown to the beast, the North Vietnamese army and their Viet Cong "countrymen" who were commanded by one of the best military leaders in the world.

In the Vietnam War, we had several high-quality leaders on the American side. None of them is likely to be compared with Vietnam's Giap. In fact, one of America's most well-known leaders in the Vietnam War, General William Westmoreland, has often been referred to as "the general who lost Vietnam." That statement might guarantee me a few heated arguments in a VFW, but I am game. In fact, the topic of the Vietnam War itself remains one of the most popular discussion points in many VFWs between WWII, Korea, and Vietnam veterans.

I am certain that if I continue with this subject in this manner, I will be tempting some military experts and some not so expert to rise up from their couches to contest me. I don't mind that, but keep it level-headed, please. If you develop an uncontrollable urge to chew my ear off, don't. Consider writing your own book in lieu of challenging my statements here. I did put an awful lot of work into this.

Anyway, it does not seem fair that Westmoreland is the lone culprit blamed for losing Vietnam. He probably did his best, as much as his superiors in the U.S. government would allow him. On the other side, General Giap had virtually no restraints, and his motto was…**VICTORY AT ANY COST!**

Westmoreland asked for and received all the troops he needed until there were over 540,000 of us in-country in 1968. And we did inflict massive casualties on our enemies. His plan to seek out the enemy with search-and-destroy missions looked good on paper. Unfortunately, these missions for American combat troops also produced way too many casualties for America…more than Americans back home were willing to tolerate. Two other factors thwarted Westmoreland's search-and-destroy folly. The North Vietnamese didn't lose heart. They could also taunt the Americans at will and escape just as easily. Again, they did not lose their will. Why would Westmoreland's strategy work when the golden horde of the Mongols failed three times with these people? They had never given up against any enemy force.

The year of 1968 was not like the year of 1908 when the Vietnamese population might have been two million. In 1968, the North Vietnamese generals had that many under their command. The Americans' actual in-your-face type of combat strength on the ground was about 120,000 at peak strength. And our intelligence reports had estimated enemy strength at 270,000, meaning our ground troops would still be outnumbered by a minimum of two to one. Updated reports after the war was over put the actual North Vietnam and Viet Cong troops' peak strength at 600,000, with twice that many available in reserve to respond to Ho Chi Minh's order to report. So, the North Vietnamese army really was the people's army, and they had a substantial numerical advantage.

There can be little doubt that America lost the Vietnam War to Giap and his generals because we underestimated their military capabilities…their will to take us on no matter how many of them we killed, and our arrogant leaders paid no attention to their awesome history.

Love of their land cannot be downplayed when studying the Vietnamese people of Dai Viet or Champa. They were proud of their rice fields, the jungles, and the mountains in the horizon, just as they were aware and proud of those who came before them and defied the invaders from other countries. I saw the Vietnamese people that we were in contact with out in the raw bush as extremely poor, proud, nationalistic, stubborn, polite, and seemingly very content with their way of life. Their way of life, when we were there in the 1960s and '70s, included a small patch of land and homes most often made from mud, bamboo, and straw. I can remember a few houses in the rural villages topped with red-tiled roofs, as most village buildings were. Family was of the utmost importance to the Vietnamese, as it seems to have been for centuries and which I don't mind mentioning often in this book. Their love for each other was admirable, and most civilizations could learn from their way of life. In fact, I will be so bold to say that if more civilizations followed the Vietnamese principles of family first, there would undoubtedly be fewer wars around the world

History is abundant with great accounts of underdogs rising to the occasion to snatch a victory from certain defeat. But real-world battles in sports or wars are rarely won by the lesser, smaller, underequipped. Tanks beat horses, guns beat spears, air power beats ground manpower, ferocious beats timid, etc. The formula seems set in stone, so it seems.

Can we learn to win battles and wars from the ancients? Get this—America's own Stormin' Norman Schwarzkopf shares credit for his victorious plan in Desert Storm with a general's strategies from 216 BC. The battle was matched with the great and unbeatable Roman Empire against the ragtag Carthaginians, led by Hannibal's tactical excellence against an over-confident enemy. Rome's General Lucius Aemilius was mercilessly slain at this battle of Cannae in Italy. Confederate General Robert E. Lee was outnumbered at most of his confrontations with the Union Army, including Gettysburg, and yet Lee won more often than he lost. He simply ran out of supplies, ammo, food, and men, as the army of South Vietnam did in 1975 when Saigon had no choice but to surrender to a reinforced enemy riding Russian tanks. In the end, maybe the U.S. government was on the "other" side? Nah, after all, they put serious sanctions on Vietnam (South and North) for twenty years. That showed them.

My opinion throughout this book is perfectly clear. Our war in Vietnam was never lost on the battlefield; it was inexcusably lost largely because of America's political leadership's ignorance and…**ARROGANCE!**

Snapshot of French Dominance. Quite probably, the arrogance of the American leaders was dwarfed by the French. French involvement in Vietnam stretched over centuries, dating back to 1620 or so. What caused their expansion in Southeast Asia was their humiliating defeat in the Franco-Prussian War of 1870, and they would seek out some restitution somehow. Northern Vietnam was their target to begin a new colonial empire and return pride to France as a world power. Central Vietnam came next and Southern Vietnam fell easily. Cambodia and Laos offered no opposition, and the new

French Union in Southeast Asia was underway. As a result the nineteenth century returned pride and some honor to France.

Unfortunately for the Vietnamese people, the French ruled like true tyrants, which transformed into oppression and misery for the hardworking Vietnamese people. French laws replaced Vietnamese law. French replaced Vietnamese as the official language of Vietnam. It got worse as the French tore down centuries-old Buddhist pagodas to make room for Catholic churches, even though more than 90 percent of the population from north to south recognized Buddhism as their religion of choice. In the meantime, most Vietnamese lost their land due to the high colonial taxes. (Those were not the good old days.)

By 1930, less than 10 percent of the population in northern Vietnam (Tonkin) still owned their land. Big plantations of rubber trees replaced the Vietnamese farms, and the Vietnamese became second-class workers earning meager wages from working on what used to be their own land.

It was at this time that two Vietnams evolved under French rule. The north always gave the French the most resistance—not surprising with the likes of Giap and a man named Ho Chi Minh in the background, scheming for ideas and opportunities to disrupt the French.

In 1930, a full-scale revolt erupted, but the Vietnamese could only muster 5,500 peasants to take up arms. The French showed no mercy with airstrikes and heavy artillery; they killed most of the revolutionaries as well as any other citizens who may have been family members. The easy slaughter by the French increased their arrogance, and they made life worse for the peasants to teach them a lesson.

Like the Chinese and Mongols before them, the French did not study Vietnamese history, so they knew nothing about their previous triumphs over the massive Chinese armies. One Vietnamese poet/historian warned the French and predicted there would be a terrible bloodbath to end the French rule. None of the French leaders could see that ever happening. This stupid arrogance by the French would make them vulnerable to an unknown, but very capable military leader who would rise amongst his people and lead them to freedom. This young man would become known as…**Giap the Great.**

The Japanese Invasion. The Japanese occupation of Vietnam and most of Indonesia began in September 1940 and did not end until August 1945 at the end of World War II. Japan believed that by occupying Vietnam they could control China's southern border and eliminate the supplies of weapons and materiel during World War II. Having Vietnam in its control, Japan's militaristic hunger for more land and profit fit into their long-term plan of an all Japan-owned Asian empire. Most or all of Asia would become a group of puppets or vassal states for Japanese pleasure and would exclude the western countries. This Greater East Asia Co-Prosperity Sphere or quasi-empire would isolate itself. Japan would also benefit from cheap land, cheap slave labor, and the resources for Japanese industry. If there was ever a plan that was this imperialistic, all one had to do was look at the history of European countries like Great Britain and France.

The man born in 1880, Ho Chi Minh, and his buddy known as General Giap would not sit back like little sheep and watch the Japanese plan unfold, not in Vietnam at least. Their newly formed Viet Minh army would give the Japanese nightmares with their guerrilla warfare attacks on the so-called invincible Japanese forces.

Long before Japan's surrender in World War II, they had completely expelled the French rulers of Vietnam and executed all who attempted to resist. So, when Japan was officially defeated and surrendered in World War II, Ho Chi Minh took the brave initiative of declared independence of all Vietnam from Japan and France. In fact Ho's proclamation paraphrased the U.S. Declaration of Independence: "All men are born equal; the Creator has given us inviolable rights, life, liberty, and happiness." However, France had other ideas, and unfortunately, Vietnam would suffer from another thirty years of fighting to regain their freedom and again in 1974. Ho would not live to see that day as he passed away in 1968, during the heat of the war between North Vietnam and the American-led South Vietnamese.

The Japanese Invasion

Chapter 6

GIAP ENDS COLNIALISM!

Mid-August 1945: Japan fell; the Vietnamese independence movement was underway. Several years before the long, bloody First Indochina War began in 1946 between France and Vietnam (mostly Northern Vietnam), Ho Chi Minh had his newly organized Viet Minh national front training in China in 1941. By 1943, Ho's general, Vo Nguyen Giap, was launching guerilla operations against the Japanese who occupied Vietnam after the quick defeat of France by Germany. A little known result of the guerilla attacks, the Viet Minh army had surprising successes against the Japanese, and considerable portions of northern Vietnam were taken control of and liberated. Then after Japan's ultimate defeat in WWII under Giap, the Viet Minh seized control of Hanoi and all of the Vietnamese territory around it. With their allegiance to Ho Chi Minh, the Independent Democratic Republic of Vietnam was proclaimed.

The exiled French contributed nothing to Viet Minh's effective attacks on the Japanese, promised at first to recognize the new government and a free Vietnam, then failed to make good on their word. On November 23, 1946, the war between Vietnam and France began, as the French bombed the city of Haiphong, killing thousands of civilians. That is how and why the First Indochina War began. As for the Second Indochina War between America and North Vietnam, it never had to happen. Had France not broken their promise to Ho Chi Minh, had France not attacked the part of Haiphong (remember Pearl Harbor?), neither of these two wars, which ran from 1946–1954 and 1959–1975 should have entered the history books.

Since the first ruler of the Vietnamese people was King De Minh, I wonder if there is a connection with... Viet Minh to King Minh? The Vietnamese do relish their history, their nationalism, and their patriotism to the land they have fought to hold onto for over two thousand years. How can one not respect that? Were we any better than the French? I would like to think so; however, since we pulled out our military support from South Vietnam and left them high and dry in 1972, which set the stage for a communist invasion from the North Vietnamese and Chinese with Russian tanks, one has to wonder if any government can ever be trusted.

It is interesting to note that Ho Chi Minh was never against the Western world; he just refused to be ruled by the West or anyone else for that matter.

Ho Chi Minh was partly educated in the Western world, and today it looks like Vietnam leans much closer to capitalism than communism.

Isn't life humorous? Yes, there were two Vietnams caused mainly by French antics: North Vietnam, a free and independent state recognized by the French and China, and South Vietnam, which was French-ruled Cochinchina. However, the differences between North Vietnam and France continued. France appeared to ignore one glaring fact...the DESIRE OF THE VIETNAMESE PEOPLE, including the South Vietnamese, to achieve unity and complete independence for their sacred Vietnam.

So why did we even get involved with a war that the French were responsible for starting? We may have chosen the wrong side; I am fairly convinced of that now. But as they say, the rest is history.

In 1859, the French added Vietnam to their family of colonies, and their occupation lasted almost a hundred years to 1954. The colonization alienated the local Vietnamese population, who desperately wanted their homeland to be free again. Just as it happened under previous invaders, the sentiment to run their own country grew stronger throughout the hundred years of occupation.

When World War II broke out, Japan expelled the French from Vietnam and most of Indonesia. In 1941, a group of Vietnamese people in Northern Vietnam created the Indochina Communist Party through which the Viet Minh under Ho Chi Minh would be born. In 1945, they changed the name of the country in North and South to the Democratic Republic of Vietnam. However, after the British finally removed the Japanese from Indonesia, the French were allowed to return and retake possession of their former colony. For the Viet Minh to allow this, the French promised northern Vietnam complete independence within the newly revised French Union. The French did not live up to their promise, and they invaded Hanoi...war was on.

With France being the culprit of starting the First Indochina War by attacking Haiphong during a mutual period of peace, it would not take long for Ho's Viet Minh to show what they were made of and that they were not going to allow the French a cake walk in colonizing Vietnam all over again.

The Civilizing Mission? After reading this abbreviated description about how the colonial powers, England and France being the top culprits, brutally abused their conquered subjects, you will surely find yourself wondering why the USA supported France in their disgusting and immoral war with North Vietnam. And you will also become a believer that the Americans' war with North Vietnam was 100 percent wrong.

Like the British, the French in Africa had ruled for decades along the Atlantic coast in places like Algeria, Tunisia, Senegal, Guinea, the Ivory Coast, Gabon, and Madagascar. In the 1870s, the French pushed into Cambodia, Laos, and Vietnam. The average person in France probably had little knowledge of the conditions in their colonies from Africa to southeast Asia. But in Vietnam those who could muster up a resistance did oppose the oppressive French rulers from the very beginnings.

Throughout Indochina, the French grabbed lands and built their own plantations, producing rubber mostly. They built railways, roads, and hydraulic works to serve their enterprises, but never built any projects that served the Vietnamese population. Floods and droughts continued to reduce Vietnam's rice industry with no support from the French invaders. This created a class of Vietnamese people who slaved for the French as servants on French- owned plantations or in French-owned mines. As in their African colonies, the French overtaxed the Vietnamese and drafted them into labor. These conditions in Vietnam were creating a decline in the population as tens of thousands of Vietnamese had died.

France established monopolies in the production of opium, salt, and other products, forcing Vietnamese to buy from the French. It was the early 1900s when Vietnam resistance became a serious problem for the French. Tens of thousands of peasants picketed, protested, and became unruly. The French struck back repeatedly in southern and northern parts of Vietnam as they gunned down unarmed civilians and destroyed entire villages, shades of the Mongol and Chinese invaders before them. To be blunt, under French colonization, life in Vietnam had become a reality of horror no different than it was under earlier invaders. The Vietnamese people were once again being increasingly dehumanized because of racism at its worst. Most Americans didn't even know Vietnam existed at this time, and they didn't care—but that would change.

From the beginnings of French colonization in Vietnam, all forms of political dissent were stopped in their tracks with violent repression. Books and newspapers were outlawed and confiscated. Abusers were executed or imprisoned for life on island fortresses. I believe it was about this time that Ho Chi Minh was studying the history of America and its war for independence from England. Ruthless, grotesque violence was the mode of French rule. They took the best farms away from the rightful owners, leaving them to die from famine and disease, which was the most cruel, merciless act possible for the people of Vietnam, where they had lived and worked for over three thousand years.

France should rarely be synonymous with the word "freedom." Its history is drenched with the blood of oppressed people around the world. What I have a difficult time understanding is why Ho Chi Minh and General Giap allowed so many of the French at Dien Bien Phu to remain alive.

It must have been a sight to behold while the northern Vietnamese were secretly approaching Dien Bien Phu in 1954. They rode on bikes atop elephants and of course walked for hours and days on their way to surround the unsuspecting French inside the fortresses where a cruel defeat of the French former global power would shock the western world.

The First Indochina War (1946–1954). France's Western world-modernized military would be opposing an army of "peasants and farmers" with rifles, knives, and pitchforks…the Viet Minh organized by Ho Chi Minh. Ho's commander in chief was formerly a history teacher and journalist. He would become one of the most prominent strategists and military commanders in the history of war…Vo Nguyen Giap.

In September 1944, Ho Chi Minh decided that it was time to take their cause to the next level and named Giap his commander of the Vietnam Liberation Army. Giap's first move was to form the Tran Hung Dao Platoon, named after another great Vietnamese hero mentioned earlier in the book. This group consisted of thirty-one men and three women. Their early arsenal weapons included:

- two revolvers
- seventeen rifles
- one small machine gun
- fourteen breech-loading flintlocks
- one bow with arrows
- thirty-four knives
- eleven pitchforks

On December 25, 1944, Giap led successful attacks on French outposts at Na Ngan and Khai Phat. Two French officers were killed and all of the Vietnamese soldiers in the outposts surrendered to Giap and willingly joined his force, strengthening them substantially. Around this time, American U.S. Major Archimedes Patti parachuted into the encampment of Giap and the growing Viet Minh army. He teamed up with Giap and helped train the constant flow of new recruits to use flamethrowers, grenade launchers, and machine guns, compliments of China.

After the fall of Japan, Giap's forces had taken control of a large area of northern Vietnam, and now it was time to do some negotiating with the French. Giap accompanied Ho Chi Minh to France to pursue lengthy discussions, which provided no benefit to either side.

This extravaganza, which was supposed to be completed in one week, took a full month. All of the forty thousand Viet Minh escaped to the wilderness, and their beloved Uncle Ho and General Giap escaped with them. At the end of this very unsuccessful operation, the French reported killing ten thousand of the Vietnamese forces. Other sources say that while this may be true, the French had far greater losses compared to the Viet Minh.

The mission failed to accomplish any of its goals. Nor did the arrogant French commanders learn anything from this battle where an army of "farmers and peasants" fought face-to-face, toe to toe with a much better equipped modern-day army from the West. The French had started this war with an unexpected defeat, and they had something even more shocking ahead of them seven years later...Dien Bien Phu.

Before Dien Bien Phu. There were many battles prior to the finale of Dien Bien Phu. While the French forces enjoyed major victories in the early years of the war, once Giap's Viet Minh gained some momentum, they pursued the French forces wherever they were, like a starving tiger hunting down a badly wounded water buffalo. It would be just a matter of time until the historical confrontation would shock the world. I would like to add that while waiting for what was coming next had to be one of the worst experiences for the French in the dark, steamy jungle environment, waiting was not an inconvenience for the Viet Minh, as they were the masters of the ambush.

Cao Bang Disaster 1949. At the very outset of the French Indochina War (1946–1954), the Viet Minh were profoundly efficient at one battle technique in particular...pulling ambushes. Even though the superior French technology in military weaponry took a toll on the outnumbered and outgunned Viet Minh for the first three to four years of the war, the forces under Ho Chi Minh continued to swell as the Vietnamese rural populations continued to join Uncle Ho's army to defeat the French.

Along the northern border of China and Vietnam, French convoys were highly valuable for the French military to maintain dominance over Ho and Giap's forces. However, the level of their tenacity and determination was never more evident than in a six-month period between July 25, 1948 to February 9, 1949, when the Viet Minh harassed French convoys with twenty-eight successful ambushes.

In February 1949, five Viet Minh battalions took the French outpost of Lao Cai, and their ambush operations increased after that. On September 3, 1949, a huge convoy of more than a hundred vehicles left That Khe to reinforce Cao Bang. In typical Viet Minh fashion (and later the Viet Cong), the first twenty vehicles of the convoy were disabled, as were a dozen vehicles at the tail end. From there, the middle vehicles, trapped on the highway, were methodically destroyed. The next morning French reinforcements arrived at the battle scene, with all hundred vehicles annihilated and only four badly wounded French soldiers found alive. No doubt the Viet Minh had a purpose in leaving those four to live so that they could tell their stories. The total of French casualties of Cao Bang was never known. The French would make drastic changes in their strategy from the date of the Cao Bang massacre, but they would never regain the momentum they enjoyed during the war's first few years.

As mentioned earlier, the French had the better of things at the beginning. They even attacked and captured Hanoi between December 1946 and February 1947. This was an opportune time for a seemingly early victory as Ho Chi Minh was bedridden with a tropical fever and Giap was able to gather all of his Hanoi forces and withdraw to the highland forests. In the meantime, the "farmers and peasants" remaining in Hanoi would continue to give the French continued headaches, forcing the French to call for reinforcements. It would take over two months to assume full control of Hanoi, but that would not remain a permanent situation. Giap's guerillas in the mountains were gaining strength and preparing for counterattacks.

After Hanoi was seemingly secured, the French issued a demand for surrender, but the Viet Minh refused. The war was just getting ready to heat up. However, at the Battle of Hoa Binh between November 1951 to the end of February 1952, the French would attempt to lure the Viet Minh out of the jungles into the open where the French air force and artillery could win a badly needed victory. Actually, the French captured the strategic town and fortress of Hoa Binh rather easily, but this would be a short-lived victory, as Giap would lead a ferocious counterattack. Despite Sherman tanks at their disposal and an onslaught by a battalion of airborne rangers, French casualties were heavy. In January 1952, French General de Lattre died at the same time Giap's forces had overrun several French outposts and Hoa Binh was evacuated by the French.

Operation Atlante was a major military operation from January through March 1954, which included fifty-three divisions of French infantry and artillery, led by General Henri Navarrae. Again, the goal was to entrap what was believed to be the largest assemblage of Viet Minh in the war, some thirty thousand in between Da Nang and Nha Trang in southern Vietnam. However, there were some two to three million local "farmers and peasants" living in the marsh-swampy lagoons.

Keep in mind that during the entire First Indochina War, the Vietnamese National Army was supporting the French either by choice or force. But their performance in battle rarely matched the aggressiveness of the northern Vietnamese Viet Minh. In fact, French Chief of Defense Staff Paul Ely and Chief of the Air Staff General Fay agreed in writing that the southern Vietnam National Army was not capable of offering serious opposition against the Viet Minh…for several years.

Operation Atlante would be the final pacification attempt by the French in the First Indochina War despite the continued reinforcements for the French.

And for every village they destroyed, the counterattacks by the local population of "southern Vietnamese" and Viet Minh increased in ferocity, and French casualties mounted faster than the reinforcements could make up for.

Early French victory…almost? Based on what I read in a couple of sources, the French were given a serious dose of reality in what they might expect in their war with northern Vietnam. This happened in October and November 1947 during action referred to as Operation Lea. A large French force was led by General Valluy. In October 1947, several hundred French paratroopers landed and quickly took control of the city of Bac Kan, where it was believed Ho Chi Minh was, and capturing Ho was the mission. At the same time, approximately fifteen thousand French ground troops were moving toward Bac Kan to try to block off any Viet Minh escapes or any supplies from reaching Bac Kan. Ultimately, Operation Lea's other objective along with capturing Ho Chi Minh was to surround the Vietnamese in Bac Kan and destroy them all, civilians included.

Unfortunately for the large French force of some ten battalions, their march toward Bac Kan ended up taking too long because of the terrain of Vietnam's poor roads, mines, booby traps, and ambushes by the "farmers and peasants" of the villages on the way.

Another part of the plan failed when four battalions of French riverine forces attempted to reach Bac Kan by river but were also delayed by sandbars, mines, and ambushes. Fancy that!

Operation Vulture was the sequel of a previous attempt to reinforce the French who would be trapped at the French garrison of Dien Bien Phu. Operation Vulture was actually a proposed attempt sponsored by America that was aborted before it began. Behind the scenes lurked…Dien Bien Phu.

Eisenhower and Nixon were suggesting American ground troops, supported by B-29 bombers and fighter planes, attack the Viet Minh forces and possibly three small tactical nuclear weapons. All of this was contingent on joining participation from Great Britain, which the British declined. Eisenhower decided that the political risks were too great, as this was during the end of the Korean War, and the Soviet Union and China were helping Ho Chi Minh. Dien Bien Phu continued for seventy-seven bloody days.

The most unspoken of yet the most awesome contribution to the lopsided victory for General Giap's Viet Minh aside from Giap himself was… THE PEOPLE—you know, those "farmers and peasants." Here's how the Vietnamese people rose to Uncle Ho's call.

First of all, at the beginning of the war, the available French forces numbered 180,000 French and 375,000 South Vietnam National Army soldiers, created and trained by the French. Giap's military force was about two hundred thousand Viet Minh and one hundred thousand civilian militia volunteers at the outset; however, these numbers would swell as the war went on. Still, the French had air power, artillery, and tanks; Giap and Ho had none of these. Clearly had the southern and northern Vietnamese fought side by side, the French exodus would have been profoundly quicker.

In the end, the technological advantage would not be enough. Ho had cried out for the people, men and women, old and young, regardless of creeds or political parties or nationalities, to oppose the colonialists. But the military aid from China would balance the scales enough to keep the outgunned and outmanned Viet Minh in the game. To the people in the north and south, Uncle Ho was almost like a god. He used to live like the peasants in ragged brown cotton clothes. Uncle Ho was like a man of magical powers, and the people did believe that.

All segments of the Vietnamese society contributed to Ho's resistance, another of the many battles for freedom by the Vietnamese people. There was even a support group of "combat mothers" who took in and fed the Viet Minh soldiers. As mentioned elsewhere in this book, Ho had requested American support throughout the war only to be ignored. It would not matter. In the end, for the French, as it came for every invading army in history… the Vietnamese people were more dedicated to their cause, far more willing to make sacrifices, more familiar with the battlegrounds, more politically popular with the people (communism did not matter), and they maintained their morale regardless of their losses in defeats and victories.

Personal statement: Having witnessed the tenacity, cunningness, nationalism, and resilience in the Viet Cong and NVA that the Viet Minh possessed, I repeatedly ask myself these two questions:

1. Why didn't the southern Vietnamese fight with the same spirit and heart as the Viet Cong and northern Vietnamese?
2. Did America have any business or any reason to intervene in what appears now to be a real civil war? Why couldn't those who sent us to sacrifice ourselves for whom or what see the obvious—that the northern Vietnamese and southern Viet Cong carried deep revenge for the southerners who stood with the French?

The tenuous relationship between France and the Viet Minh of northern Vietnam was further strained when Viet Minh, assisted by Chinese forces, destroyed most remaining French posts in northern Vietnam. France began recruiting heavily after it became obvious that they were no longer facing just a guerilla war. They brought in units from the French

Foreign Legion, colonial troops from Morocco, Algiers, Tunisia, Laos, Cambodia, and southern Vietnam. At one point, in 1951, France attempted to negotiate an agreement with the Viet Minh. Once again, they made promises, but this time their suspect offers were turned down by Ho Chi Minh, and the war continued to get even bloodier. In the meantime, the Viet Minh kept winning over more of the "peasants and farmers" by providing them with rice taken from the Japanese stockpiles being hoarded by the French.

From 1952 to 1954, the war was not going well for France despite the assistance of their other colonies and America. They had gone through an almost endless loss of commanders, and each replacement was no more successful against Giap than the previous one. Finally, the French sent in the trusted colleague of France's Premier Rone Mayer to take command of French Union Forces in all of Indochina. His name was Henri Navarre.

When Nevarre arrived on the scene, he was shocked to discover that his predecessors had not set any long-range plans. Everything happened on a day-to-day response basis. He wired the premier back with these instructions: Create a military condition that would lead to an "honorable political solution."

There were a series of battles in 1953 and 1954, leading up to what would be the end of France's existence in all of Indonesia. **Next, the Waterloo of this war, Dien Bien Phu, awaited the French.** Not all of these battles were lost by the French, but most were. The main victories by the French took place a few years earlier in the war at places like Na San and Hoa Binh where the Viet Minh had suffered eight to twelve thousand casualties and French losses were considerably less at twenty-five hundred, but still a high cost.

The French leaders made numerous errors leading up to Dien Bien Phu and several more blunders after this historic battle (too numerous to name here). Some of these errors were almost comical, but I didn't laugh while reading about them. I envisioned the faces of the French soldiers who had to bear the weight on their backs. Many lives were lost as a result.

Dien Bien Phu began for the French in March 1954 and would end on May 7, 1954. However, this battle actually began for the Vietnamese at least a month before the first shot was fired by either side. The kudos for the miracle victory belong to the population of Vietnam, just as much as to the soldiers who fought it. This is the part of this battle that amazed me as I was reading about it in many sources. Dien Bien Phu did not just happen with the wave of a magic wand by Giap or Uncle Ho. For this critically important battle, tens of thousands of "peasants and farmers" contributed to building the encirclement of the French position. Through thick forests, up steep hills, over rocks, with mule-pulled carts, bicycles, and by foot, it happened. Highly fortified bunkers were built, not visible from the Dien Bien Phu encampment. Hundreds of heavy pieces of artillery were transported to specific positions all around Dien Bien Phu. I cannot begin to imagine what motivated and drove these people to throw themselves into this project, almost as slaves. To make things worse, monsoon season was gearing up, so much of the work of getting the artillery up to the top or near the top of the hills around Dien Bien Phu Valley had to pass through and over mud holes. The battle itself is worth it for military history buffs and Vietnam veterans to read about in more detail than I am providing in this book.

On May 7, 1954, the North Vietnamese Army overran the French army and their allies of **approximately twenty thousand troops.** The battle, which lasted from March 13 – May 7, 1954 marked the first time that a non-European colonial independence movement evolving from bands of guerillas to a conventionally organized army defeated a modern Western country in pitched battle. Here is a list of the damages:

Dien Bien Phu Casualties & Losses

France	Vietnam's Viet Minh
2,293 died in battle	4,020 died
8,290 died after capture	9,118 wounded
6,650 wounded in battle	
1,729 missing in action	
167 aircraft damaged	
62 aircraft destroyed	
10 tanks destroyed	
2 Americans died	

The French artillery commander, Colonel Charles Piroth, distraught at his artillery fire's inability to knock out the well-camouflaged Viet Minh artillery and anti-aircraft weapons, went into his dugout and committed suicide with a hand grenade. The specific details of this shocking demise of a large French military force is incredibly fascinating. Reading about it had me on the edge of my chair, as I almost felt like I was in one of the French bunkers with them… Fortunately, I woke up okay from that nightmare.

Approximately one month later, the French were still officially at war with Giap's Viet Minh. On June 24, Giap's Viet Minh ambushed a large French Union force of 3,500 at Mang Yang Pass with just seven hundred troops. The French losses were disastrous, as 1,900 French became casualties while Viet Minh losses were 347.

Little Known Facts about the French-Vietnam War

- In his first term, President Eisenhower decided against taking a definitive stand with one side or the other and actually favored pushing for a separate communist North and a non-communist South and providing aid to Ho Chi Minh. Of course, North Vietnam's invasion of a corrupt South Vietnam got things rolling toward a confrontation with the U.S. It could have been the mixed signals the U.S. gave Ho by sending aid that had them thinking the U.S. would not intervene if a civil war broke out in Vietnam. Ho calculated incorrectly.
- The French Foreign Legion sent roughly thirty thousand troops to assist their two hundred thousand regulars to fight in the French-Vietnam War. They were hard core and well trained, but moving from dry deserts to humid, thick jungles was not an easy adjustment. The French Foreign Legion was a poor match for the Viet Minh in the jungle, and seemed to prefer murdering civilians rather than seeking out the Viet Minh to engage them.
- Ho Chi Minh visited France several times in 1946 to try to negotiate a peaceful agreement. A second agreement was successfully completed, but the French broke the agreement when they attacked Haiphong in November 1946, killing several thousand unsuspecting civilians.
- A large force from Thailand had attempted to come to the aid of the surrounded French at Dien Bien Phu, but the Viet Minh intercepted them, ambushed, and severely mauled them. Records about survivors were never found.
- The USA was strongly considering a B-52 attack on the Viet Minh army that had surrounded the French at Dien Bien Phu.

The French military presence in the Indochina War peaked at nearly 225,000 by 1954. French military casualties were estimated at more than 47,000 soldiers. To make matters worse, a Korean Battalion (ally of France) was ambushed at Chu Dreh Pass by the 96th Regiment Viet Minh Army. Of the original 482-man force, there were just 107 men remaining, and fifty-four of them were wounded and later died, leaving fifty-three to carry the news back to Ban Me Thuot on June 30, 1954. In addition, the Viet Minh completely destroyed forty-seven French vehicles.

Three weeks later on July 20, 1954, the ceasefire was officially announced when the Geneva agreements were signed. On August 1, the armistice went into effect, sealing the end of France's hold on Indochina, and the partition of Vietnam was declared along the seventeenth parallel—similar to the end of the Korean War. However, all French troops had left South Vietnam by April 1956 at the request of their president, Ngo Dinh Diem.

Dien Bien Phu was the climactic battle in the French-Indochina War that would lead to the biggest mistake ever in America's history up to that time. After the Viet Minh's shocking victory over a Western power, France, America would make a commitment to the Vietnam predicament that was about to disrupt the world. However, ask Americans on the street today, and most likely, very few will know what you are talking about. Dien Bien Phu will live in the history books as the epic battle Americans forgot—because it actually led to the war in Vietnam for them, and who wants to remember that?

Was Dien Bien Phu the first domino down? My guess is that the Americans who invented the Domino Theory during or after the Korean War never imagined that their South Vietnam ally was going down in the same convincing manner in which the Viet Minh humbled the once mighty French colonialists in Southeast Asia. I may be wrong, but in looking back at what happened and how events took place, it seems that the USA's leaders at that time failed to be impressed by the astounding military victory led by Ho Chi Minh and General Giap.

This is so difficult for me to comprehend, as the whole world had been tuned in for two months in 1954 on what was going on at a small remote mountain outpost in little northern Vietnam. There were an estimated twelve or thirteen French army battalions being challenged to their limits by what was believed to be a highly inferior and outgunned force of fifty thousand Viet Minh warriors of northern Vietnam. They would put horror onto the faces of the French by launching crazy, almost suicidal human wave attacks every night. Years later, the Americans would be facing these eerie, horrifying attacks by Viet Cong and probably some of the same Viet Minh who fought at Dien Bien Phu.

Dien Bien Phu had been carefully and masterfully surrounded. There was no way in for French reinforcements and no way out for the outpost's defenders. The airstrip was destroyed. Airborne attempts to parachute in reinforcements proved to be a disastrous decision, as the French paratroopers were mauled by the Viet Minh's artillery, rockets, and machine-gun fire. Most of the aircraft met their demise in these futile attempts to help their comrades on the ground.

The arrogant French (just like the Americans) never gave the Viet Minh enough credit to amass and position such a force in the hills, caves, and forests around their fortress. That degree of stupid overconfidence contributed greatly to their total defeat by what was referred to as...**farmers and peasant insurgents with pitchforks and knives**.

Maybe the French had been duped into overestimating their mighty military advantages over what was surely an inferior opponent that could eventually be easily defeated. Because in the middle of 1953, Dien Bien Phu was first captured overwhelmingly by three airborne battalions, attacking by air and by ground, thoroughly routing the Viet Minh defenders of the town and outpost. Some now say that this victory was astonishingly easy. However, despite reinforcing the outpost and seemingly strengthening it satisfactorily for the French generals, the first domino came tumbling down in loud enough fashion that the explosions were heard around the world on May 7, 1954.

Today, Dien Bien Phu has become a flourishing area with tourism a strong point. Oddly enough, the area also flourished economically back in the 1950s with its famous opium traffic. Indeed, the French profited well from this lucrative business.

Located in the middle of nowhere on the border of Laos, many after-the-fact critics question why the French would set up a base in an area where the Viet Minh thrived and the local population was entirely supportive of the Viet Minh. The USA would duplicate this move when they built a base camp in the heart of Viet Cong's territory. Cu Chi was actually built on top of the Viet Cong underground headquarters. However, Cu Chi's fate would not resemble the fate of Dien Bien Phu and the French demise. This battle was heard around the world. To say the victory at Dien Bien Phu was an upset would be putting it mildly. We could very easily make a comparison to the North Vietnamese fight for independence from France to our country's own Revolutionary War against the world's greatest power at the time, Great Britain, of course.

As if one can't tell—if they have read either or all of my books, the Vietnam War is something that I've had a very difficult time getting out of my mind...for the past fifty years. Strange, but true. Even stranger, there are tens of thousands of American Nam vets who share my problem. But honestly, it is not so much of a problem for me these days. I can get a high from thinking about Nam, and naturally, I can bottom out some days. One thing is always waiting for me when the dreaming comes to an end...nothing and no one can ever take away the memories of my experience of a lifetime, serving our country during a time of serious turmoil. Most important, I can live out my life knowing in my heart that I fought side by side in that war with the greatest military force in America's history since the War for Independence. Proof in the pudding has been presented in my previous books and so far in this book—that the American soldier boy was pitted against a war-hardened, tenacious, fearless, cunning adversary in the Vietnam War and beat them at guerilla warfare. The facts do not lie.

In 1955, the South, led by Ngo Dinh Diem, experienced an uprising. Support for the uprising grew like a forest fire spreads its damage. The uprising was being supported by the North, who had grand aspirations of reuniting the North and South to one Vietnam again. The Viet Cong arose, known as the National Liberation Front (NLF). The Vietnam War with America became semi-official in 1959.

During the earliest years of 1959–1964, the war did not go well for the South. Ngo Dinh Diem was overthrown and assassinated in 1963. Around the same time President John F. Kennedy was assassinated. One of the first acts of new President Lyndon Johnson was to commit more American troops to the "conflict" as it was referred to at this time. In 1964, other countries joined in on the side of the Americans and the South. South Korea and Australia sent sizeable forces. Thailand, the Philippines, and New Zealand also joined in.

However, by 1965, the South was still losing and so the U.S. Military began to substantially step up its commitment with more troops, armor, artillery, and air power. Australia followed by beefing up their military presence in South Vietnam. Game on.

The Vietnamese defended their homeland with a never-give-in mentality for two thousand years before American troops set foot on Vietnam's soil in 1959 or whatever year our government chooses to admit to. Actually, the early 1950s would be more accurate, but Washington, D.C. has never admitted to that. But, duh—we Nam vets talk to each other, so we know what happened.

You have read a brief but accurate recap of a series of David versus Goliath confrontations, and each event ended up with David as the clear victor. The biblical David was believed to be five-foot-five or thereabouts, and he stepped forward to meet a giant of a man (in those days) who was six feet, nine inches tall, over a foot larger than David. As we know, the cunning and brave underdog won the confrontation, which motivated the Israelites to soundly defeat their enemy, the Philistines, in one battle after another, as David's victory motivated them for years afterward.

What the amazing people of Vietnam have accomplished in most every century since AD 1 has been poorly publicized for decades in the history books and the media. It would be impossible to ascertain which single victory of the Vietnamese people's numerous wars was the most awesome task to overcome. All of them were truly great accomplishments of biblical proportions in confronting and defeating a large, seasoned army of professional-like soldiers. Each victory was completed in astounding, convincing, fearlessly unmerciful fashion. I would gladly welcome a few hundred thousand of Vietnam's "farmers and peasants" to fight side by side with us against our enemies in the next war. Who knows—now that they are our ally, it might happen.

I wonder which military force that invaded Vietnam's homeland was the most serious and biggest threat to ending the Vietnamese culture completely. And which hero of Vietnam's victories was the greatest leader of all time for Vietnam? The cruel and powerful Chinese dynasties were the greatest military invaders in terms of pure numbers. Each invasion into Vietnam brought hundreds of thousands of trained Chinese warriors who had one goal in mind—to conquer the tiny land of the Vietnamese people, eradicate their culture, and turn the Vietnamese people into humbled slaves. The Chinese dynasties also dominated over the Vietnam territory for a far longer period than any of Vietnam's other enemies. Therefore, the many revolutions against the Chinese dynasties certainly had major significance in shaping the destiny of the Vietnamese culture's existence.

The Trung sisters' revolt might be my personal favorite of all the ancient wars for freedom the Vietnamese people have fought. When I read about them the first time, I found myself almost wishing that I had fought with them in their highly outnumbered makeshift army of "farmers and peasants" against their cruel rulers, the Han dynasty, back in AD 39–40. Under the Chinese domination, Vietnam would be given several name changes. The final one was An Nam and the Vietnamese despised it. An Nam meant "Pacified South." Later, the French colonialists would use it one last time as an insult to their Vietnamese colony.

Even though the sisters and their female generals would be short-lived heroes, long afterward they would be remembered and honored by women and men alike. They almost became cult figures and inspired Vietnamese women to fight well against the modern military of the French and Japanese.

I found myself envisioning two young, beautiful but truly ruthless female warrior-generals leading their army of fifty to sixty thousand into battle, straddling war elephants, waving their swords, shooting arrows into the marauding Chinese army of two hundred thousand soldiers, screaming terrifying profanities at them, and ultimately running off what was left of a once proud two-hundred-thousand-man Chinese army. I have imagined myself there when their defeat came in 43 AD and upwards of five hundred thousand very angry and embarrassed Chinese warriors were fought off twice before overwhelming the Trungs' army. But as mentioned in the beginning of the book, both sisters chose suicide over being captured and facing slavery. The sisters' accomplishments became legends passed down from one generation after another. Even the greatest Vietnamese general of all time, Giap the Great, would yell, "Remember the Trungs!" to motivate his armies in battle against the French, and yes…against the Americans as well.

The successes of Lady Trieu (Vietnam's Joan of Arc), Emperor Ly Nam De (Vietnam's first emperor), Ngo Quyen, Ly Thuong Kiet, and General Giap all led miraculous, highly unlikely, and profoundly convincing bloody victories over the invaders from China, the Mongols, the Japanese, and the French.

This author has decided to go with a prince, emperor, and supreme military warlord, but all three titles were carried by one man…Tran Hung Dao, the mastermind and conqueror of the great Mongol hordes. I have described Tran Hung Dao's insane victories, all three of them in Chapter 4, so I will not be repetitious here. I am also going with Vietnam's third time repelling the Mongols' attempt to burn Vietnam to the ground, which would be the final unsuccessful invasion by what may have been the most imposing army ever assembled in history.

The Mongol Army of 1287–1288 at Bach Dang. The Mongols had taken time out to recuperate and rebuild from the massive losses inflicted on them by the Vietnamese army in 1285. The Mongols, unlike their Chinese cousins, rarely outnumbered the tens of millions of civilians they had conquered from the year of 1206 on. Historians have estimated the Mongols' maximum strength, at their peak, at one million men. Still, their army managed to conquer most of the Middle East, including Persia, Russia, and China. Only two very small countries remained on their "yet to do" list—Japan and Vietnam. The Mongols were beaten back by both countries on the first Mongol invasion attempt in 1258–1259. Emperor Kublai Khan, grandson to Genghis Khan, decided to focus on just one of the two countries for his marauding hordes to stampede. Surely, little Vietnam could not handle a second invasion from his relentless warriors. In 1285, a two-hundred-thousand-man Mongol army with a vaunted cavalry departed south to Vietnam.

History would repeat itself. The same leader, Tran Hung Dao, would duplicate his victory over the Mongols even more impressively this time. Kublai Khan was already planning for another invasion into Japan when the remains of the three-hundred-thousand-man army he was waiting on began to return from Vietnam…piece by piece. The great Khan could not stand the news and he executed several of his generals. He then called in some of his forces from other countries they had conquered, and he could not wait twenty-seven years this time to strike. He gave his military two years to reorganize and prepare for a third invasion of Vietnam. The goal this time was not just to defeat and enslave the Vietnamese. His military had one option…to annihilate the Vietnamese civilization.

The outcome of this third and final unsuccessful invasion attempt was discussed in Chapter 2, but I have to say a few more things about the Mongol hordes of the thirteenth century and, at the same time, pay tribute to the people who beat them.

The Mongols had steamrolled over most of Europe and Asia in a hundred years' time. It has been reported that nearly one-third of the world's known population was eliminated. The Mongols took on and defeated armies and nations with tens of hundreds times the manpower of the Mongol armies. The Mongols were reported to be so unstoppable that entire towns and fortresses would often lay down their arms and surrender before the Mongols launched their attacks. History states that more often than not, those who surrendered were slaughtered. Those who fought and survived were enslaved or forced to serve in the Mongol army.

To the Mongols' credit at the time, they were being pushed past their limits by the Vietnamese. They were fighting other major wars with two attempts to conquer the Samurai Army of Japan. Both invasions ended with major defeat for the Mongols, but not at the hands of the Samurai. Nope, Mother Nature rose up to battle the Mongols by unleashing deadly typhoons (hurricanes) onto the unfortunate Mongol navy. There was also internal turmoil amongst the Mongol tribes back home, not to mention stiff resistance building with the Chinese.

Know this, the Vietnamese were outnumbered in meeting the three Mongol invasions. They won with pure heart, cunning, and resilience that future invaders would learn to respect.

The Mongols' success was due to the many creative strategies and innovative tactics that Genghis Khan and his generals utilized. They were extremely hardy and mobile and could endure tremendous hardships, as that was their way of life. It is said that those who followed the great Genghis Khan did not inherit his cunning or his determination, that the empire he built was beginning to get soft. Regardless of whether it was Genghis Khan or Kublai Khan, the world was shocked the first time, more shocked the second time, and trembling after the third victory by the Vietnamese. They did not just defeat the three-hundred-thousand-man force led by Kublai Khan's favorite son; they dismantled them. No prisoners were taken at Bach Dang in 1288. Other nations feared this new and more ferocious army from Vietnam would go on the rampage, but the Vietnamese did nothing of the sort. Their mission at hand was accomplished—again. Their beloved Vietnam was safe again…until the next dreamer arose, thinking he would try to tackle that helpless little army of "farmers and peasants."

As for Emperor Tran Hung Dao, he spent the rest of his years as supreme commander of all military forces in Vietnam, loyal only to protecting the borders of his homeland, having no desire to expand his country (Dai Viet), although he could have done that very easily. Tran's magnificent accomplishments later on would inspire another generation of Vietnam when the Viet Minh under General Giap and President Ho Chi Minh would give the French colonialists a humiliating defeat at Dien Bien Phu.

Valuable Lesson Not Learned. It needs to be mentioned that the so-called ragtag, untrained Viet Minh army often squared off against some of the best troops in the French military, so it was expected that the Viet Minh would be quickly denied of victory. That was easier said than done. The French were put into a very unkind alien environment, highly visible, often put on the defensive by abnormally determined Viet Minh guerrilla warriors. Even the weather was nothing like what the French had faced in battles before Southeast Asia. It was profoundly hostile. The monsoon seasons delivered some of the heaviest rainfalls in the world. The Viet Minh appeared to thrive in it as their ambush-style attacks never let up. To say that the misery factor was almost completely intolerable would be an understatement. It was impossible for the French military to remain prepared for and motivated to fight hard in these indescribable conditions. Endless heat, punishing rain, strange tropical maladies, malaria, and an enemy who never seemed to break, as if they were made by God with…**Unbreakable Hearts.**

Since Vietnam weather and geography factor clearly in favor of the hometown army, sometimes it was futile to call in for artillery or air support in support or rescue of French ground forces under attack. The French had the technology, the firepower, experienced, seasoned leaders, but these advantages seemed to have little relevance for the guerrilla war that was being fought in a giant swamp.

One of the main if not primary reasons the French were in Indochina to begin with, beginning in the nineteenth century, was to exploit (rob and steal) the region's rubber, tea, rice, pepper, coal, zinc, and tin resources. French plantation and mine owners made fortunes during the colonial period of "civilizing" the inhabitants of the region. When the French military and their professional mercenaries—and the southern Vietnamese they forced into combat against the northern Vietnamese—were exposed as being unable to defeat the northerners and unable to win a victory at Dien Bien Phu, the French plantation and mine owners evacuated northern Vietnam on the heels of their fleeing military.

It would have been a sight to behold when the northern Vietnamese population came together—men, women, and children secretly approaching Dien Bien Phu in 1954. But the French never saw or heard them coming.

Not a single recon patrol was even sent out. Mind-boggling arrogance or extreme stupidity?

They rode on bikes and elephants and walked for hours and days on their way to surround the totally unsuspecting French army inside the doomed fortress.

France should never be synonymous with the word "freedom," in my opinion. Its history seems to be drenched with the blood of oppressed people around the world. I have a very tough time understanding why Ho Chi Minh and General Giap allowed so many of the French soldiers at Dien Bien Phu to live.

There you are, a lesson laid out for easy learning for the next would-be conqueror of this small country of peasants and farmers.

As for General Vo Nguyen Giap, his reputation from the French-Vietnam War was that of a bold strategist, extremely skilled logician, and tireless organizer with leadership skills of biblical proportions. Giap fought for more than thirty years almost nonstop, starting with an unlikely handful of raggedy, wannabe guerilla-style fighters who became one of the world's most effective ground armies. He overcame what most military experts considered to be insurmountable odds in crushing the French military—so impressively that the whole world was shocked. But Giap wasn't done yet. His crowning achievement was yet to come when his North Vietnam army and their Viet Cong terrorist-like guerilla fighters would take on the world's greatest military power...the United States of America.

Staggering French Indo-China Casualties 1945–1954	
Army Dead/Missing	57,958
Marines Dead/Missing	1,126
Navy Dead/Missing	850
Air Force Dead/Missing	650
Total Killed / Missing	68,234
Total Wounded[10]	72,446

Included in these totals were 1,787 officers or commanders and 2,683 NCOs killed or missing.

---

10 Numbers obtained from *Teachings of the Indochina War*, edited by the French Command Far East.

Giap

Early Viet Minh 1940s

The March on Dien Bien Phu

The Attack and Victory

Defeat and Overwhelming Victory for Ho and Giap

Chapter 7

THE AMERICANS' GREATEST ADVENTURE!

There is no hunting experience that compares with the hunting of another armed man. And those who have hunted other armed men long enough and liked it, never cared for any other type of hunting thereafter.

—Ernest Hemingway

In each of my books, I get into telling our story in the Vietnam War and what happened to the war's survivors afterward. It just cannot be avoided, so please be patient with the very few mentions that seem redundant. The adventure America's soldiers and sailors were thrown into has most of us who are still living still struggling, asking ourselves this question… **What happened?** Were we really there? Did the Vietnam War adventure of our lifetime really take place? How did we survive and why did we make it when so many did not?

You have just read several historical fact-based accounts about a small primitive-like kingdom of people who stuck together and fought as one big family against all who dared to invade their beloved homeland. It was sacred to them, and they were not willing to lie down and give it up to any potential conquerors, regardless of the price. For over two thousand years, one ruthless invader after another tried to keep the Vietnamese enslaved after burning their villages and slaughtering large portions of their population, often without warning or logical reason. Most Vietnamese would consider America as one of those unwarranted, unwelcomed invaders.

This little known fact of America touching with Vietnam occurred in 1845 when the USS *Constitution* landed at Da Nang. A full company of U.S. Marines moved inland to the city of Hue and completed a successful mission, rescuing a French bishop and his followers who had been captured by the Vietnamese. This was America's first combat involvement with the Vietnamese people. About 110 years later America would be sending two full battalions of marines to Da Nang with 2.7 million troops from all services to follow. Who could have guessed this back in 1845?

It was very difficult to find recorded historical information where another country had ever come to the aid of the inhabitants of ancient Vietnam, except for the communists from China and Russia in the twentieth century, and China has been their biggest threat for centuries. Nor was I able to find even a rare instance when this kingdom would invade a neighboring country unless those people had attacked the Vietnamese first. I am convinced now that South Vietnam and North Vietnam—or Champa and Dai Viet—deserved to be and needed to be one united nation in order to become self-supporting, economically solvent, and militarily formidable enough to survive in their southeastern Asia neighborhood.

While the nation's names have changed several times, the makeup of the people has seemingly always hung on to their family heritage. This has been the main reason for their salvation. In many ways, I see another country with similar historical accounts of fighting for their culture, their individual identity, and of course, their rightful land. That other country would be Israel. Did this small, unwarlike kingdom of "peasants and farmers" in Vietnam luck out all these years? Did God reach down time and time again to help the Vietnamese and Israelis take back what was always rightfully theirs? Or did each of the all-powerful invaders of their land simply make this mistake…

Never Underestimate the Heart of Your Enemy!

That time had finally arrived for the American soldier who once played war with little plastic soldiers representing Germany, Japan, and the USA. Imagination time was over. We were finally where we had dreamed of for most of our little boy years…inserted into an adventure of a lifetime—a real war, fighting for our country against what we were told was the most deadly menace in the world… Communism.

We were in the best shape of our lives, and we believed no other military would be able to match up with us and our buddies. In fact, we expected our adversary to be in awe of our excellent physical fitness, our dead-eye shooting prowess, and the massive support of artillery, armor, and air power. Well, they should have been awed by the great and powerful military that claimed to have never lost a war. At first, things did not go the way our brilliant (or so we thought) military commanders had expected. Worse yet, we were not prepared for what welcomed us to steamy, hot, stinky Vietnam.

We grew up as either hardy country boys or tough city boys. Either way, we were here to kick ass, take names, never surrender, and get this war over with in quick mode…victoriously. It was just going to take longer than was expected.

Americans came to win. We were going to show those little fellas in the rice paddies just who we were. We were not the French or the Japanese or the Chinese or the Mongols…we were the Americans, so get ready to mix it up with or without good leadership.

They did not have to get ready. They had prepared for such a war since the early 1900s when France ruled them as their colonial masters. To the

NVA and VC Vietnamese, the American War was just an extension of the French War, and they were neither impressed nor afraid of us. I still find that hard to swallow, but now I can see why. I understand it and admire their spirit. I don't hate it, as I was brainwashed to do back in 1967–1969, and even after I came home it seemed as though no one was giving credit to our enemy. It was like people were ashamed of us, as they were led to believe we lost, to a low-quality adversary. **WRONG!**

Believe It Or Not! In recent years many different sources have become available that provide truthful facts about the Vietnam War which were previously kept away from the American people; more likely than not, this was done intentionally. I don't want to create more redundant information for my readers, so I have tried to eliminate many of the more publicized truisms over the last several years. I think many will be surprised, even astonished. Here ya go:

> When the French exited North Vietnam in 1954, the People's Republic of China and the Soviet Union reorganized and provided profound support for Ho Chi Minh's Democratic Republic of Vietnam as the official government of all of Vietnam. Of course the United States, Great Britain, and France recognized the French-backed State of Vietnam in the south out of Saigon. At the 1954 Geneva Conference, the non-communist southern Vietnamese objected strenuously to any separation of Vietnam.
>
> The surprise came when the French agreed to the Viet Minh proposal that all of Vietnam eventually be united by elections under the supervision of the United Nations, but this was quickly rejected by the Soviet Union in spite of a proposed American Plan which called for unification elections also to be supervised by the U.N. The United States had publicly reiterated its position that the Vietnamese people were entitled to determine their own future and that it would not join into any arrangement which would hinder this. In fact, President Eisenhower stated and wrote this in 1954:
>
> *I have never talked or corresponded with a knowledgeable person in Indochinese affairs who did not agree that had the elections been held as of the time of the fighting, possibly 80 percent of the Vietnamese population would have voted for Ho Chi Minh as their leader.*
>
> Communism was of little concern of the people at this time. Eventually, an election was held, with the results being supervised by Ngo Dinh Diem's brother which made it all but certain that Ho Chi Minh could not win. Diem won and immediately declared South Vietnam to be an independent state under the name Republic of Vietnam with himself as president.

U.S. President Dwight D. Eisenhower, World War II hero greeted
South Vietnam President Ngo Dinh Diem in Washington, D.C. in 1957.

Diem became the South Vietnam ruler as the French were making their exit from the country in 1954. It can be correctly declared that America's greatest adventure was under way as soon as that meeting ended.

As the Viet Cong rose up to challenge the corrupt Diem regime, the U.S. began sending military advisors to train the South Vietnamese Army. Diem had barely broken in his presidential chair when he was assassinated in a coup orchestrated by Diem's successor, General Duong Van Minh, with substantial support from the American government. FYI, it is believed that Eisenhower started the conversation about the "falling domino" principle. You have a row of dominoes set up, you knock over the first one, and they'll all fall down, with the last one falling over hard and quickly. This is still considered to be the main reason for the U.S. "invasion" of South Vietnam.

The Vietnam War followed, also known as the American War, the Second Indochina War, the Vietnam Conflict, and the Resistance War against America.

Domino Theory…to be or not to be there? This will remain an everlasting, mostly unanswered question, because "they" don't and/or won't accept the true facts leading up to the Vietnam War between America and the communists of North Vietnam, China, and Russia. This author has offered his opinions (in three books) based on diligent research and physical participation in-country during the peak years of the war in 1968–1969. But "they" who are the historians and record keepers told our story not to our liking.

The problem with that is "they" are dominated by the left and radical left. How so, or am I just spitting out sour grapes? The reporters from the left-wing media distorted the information they reported, information from or about battles "they" never witnessed themselves. But they wrote their incorrect stories anyway, sitting at their secure offices in Saigon. Then the historians educated and brainwashed others by entering distorted data into the history books. Well, that's one man's brief opinion.

I have waffled back and forth over the years since coming home from Vietnam. Should we Americans have been there? After all, we were invited by the French-made government of South Vietnam, and certainly we had to jump at the chance to come to the aid of our dear friends the French, didn't we? Hindsight now says we should have minded our own business, allowing the Vietnamese to handle their own civil war, and why not? But that domino theory thing was a scary rumor that seemed too real, especially after China's direct intervention in the Korean War.

In my previous books I mentioned that the domino theory was no myth. If one asks people from the Southeast Asia area of the Philippines, Indonesia, Malaysia, Singapore, and Thailand who remained free, they will tell you that our news media has been wrong by discounting that old domino theory. Without that American presence, communism would have wiped out one democracy after another. The Vietnam War provided a strong roadblock for the continuing spread of communism (a General Westmoreland quote).

Fortunately, not all of our scholars have resided on the left, but most of them have—especially when it pertains to the happenings leading up to, during, and after the Vietnam War. Martin Scott Catino, PhD is one of those extremely qualified researchers and authors who has told it like it actually happened. In his fine 2010 book, *The Aggressors*, Dr. Catino exposes an alarming under-reported and often ignored scenario that I've paraphrased as follows:

Ho Chi Minh's communist government in North Vietnam have admitted in their own historical documents that they never had any intention of seeking compromise for a peaceful solution at the 1954 Geneva Peace Conference. In fact, Ho Chi Minh and his communist supporters have since verified that the only reason they half-heartedly agreed to a ceasefire at Geneva in 1954 was to allow them more time to infiltrate South Vietnam, to gain strategic advantages for their coming annexation of South Vietnam, and...to enact a plan to destroy all the non-communist governments in Indochina. Essentially, due to the mere fact that the Saigon government was not under control of the communist regime of Hanoi, it had to be eliminated permanently. There was no rush for this; they would be patient.

Let's Ask the Commies. Between 1965–1971, China committed almost 330,000 troops to North Vietnam. Beijing also provided a generous supply of military equipment, weapons, missiles, rockets, artillery, trucks, and jeeps. What more proof does anyone need to become a domino theory believer?

China and the Soviet Union were convinced that they needed in order to tip the scales to favor communism over the west in the hotly contested Cold War of the 1960s. During the Vietnam-American War, neither the Soviets nor the Chinese were open or frank about the magnitude of their contributions to North Vietnam. In fact, to this day the west still doesn't have an accurate grasp on the total aid provided. I guess we've just presumed it was there.

There is no doubt about Ho Chi Minh's close ties with Moscow and Beijing. Ho pretty much was forced to gravitate toward communism, as all of his requests for U.S. support were ignored or denied.

There was some powerful history between the Chinese and Viet Minh as they fought together against the Japanese Empire in World War II. Chinese forces often took up shelter in North Vietnam when they were in retreat. In return Beijing made sure the Vietnamese under Ho Chi Minh were well armed to give the Japanese fits.

Today, we believe it was the Gulf of Tonkin incident in August 1964 and the unexpected arrival of U.S. combat troops in 1964 that forced China to escalate their support to Hanoi. Also in 1965, the Soviets stepped forward by signing a defense treaty with North Vietnam. The Soviet premier issued this public statement for the entire world to see:

> The Democratic Republic of Vietnam (DRV), the outpost of the socialist camp in southeast Asia, is playing an important role in the struggle against America's imperialism and is making its contribution to the defense of peace in Asia. The governments of the USSR and the DRV have examined this situation together…Both governments resolutely condemned the aggressive actions by the USA on 8/5/65, and especially the barbaric attacks by American aircraft on DRV territory on 2/28/65. The USSR will no longer remain indifferent to ensuring the security of a fraternal socialist country and will give the DRV necessary aid and support.

In the spring of 1967, *TIME Magazine* reported that "a river of aid" was flowing from Russia (with Alexei Kosygin as new premier) into North Vietnam. Unlike the aid from Beijing where deferred payments were expected, most Soviet assistance was supplied as free aid rather than loans. So one has to wonder, if the U.S. leadership had known what was behind North Vietnam, would they have still gone in? On that they had little or no knowledge of the massive buildup that would be waiting for us if and when we did go in? The commies were heavily committed to making North and South Vietnam an extension of their plan to own all of Asia.

My brothers and I still have vivid memories of "no-name" battles we fought in April or May 1968 somewhere between the Boi Loi Woods and the Iron Triangle area. This wasn't an all-night battle where you had to wonder if you would see another sunrise in your life, but it turned out to be a warning of what might be coming at us down the road. When the sun did rise, and we went out to check the body count of the night's attackers, I felt this blood-chilling sensation when our South Vietnamese Army troops began yelling, "Chinese, Chinese!"

Indeed there were Chinese regulars amongst the body count of that day's battle. Our reaction was typically American: **"You gotta be shitting me!"**

We never ran into Chinese army regulars again in 1968, but just their presence that night would always be in the back of our minds, like what are we really in for in this war? Trust me, a Chinese warrior doesn't fight any harder than the North Vietnamese did; in fact the NVAs might have been a more formidable adversary as they were fighting on their home dirt. So they did have more incentive to take the fight to us. I've read about the Chinese "human wave" attacks in Korea and the Japanese "Bonzai" suicide attacks in World War II and I don't think any of us would look forward to experiencing all of them and evaluating which was more formidable, NVAs, Chinese, or Japanese. I know someone who did fight against all three and in his books he was not bashful in bestowing praises on the Viet Cong and NVAs he faced off with in his third war. That was Colonel David "Hack" Hackworth, mentioned elsewhere in this book.

Hack was one of America's most decorated soldiers, having earned honors in three wars. Of the dozens of medals he received during his Andy Murphy type of military career, including multiple Purple Hearts and Silver Stars, the one award he cherished the most above all others was his Combat Infantry Badge.

If the domino theory was not a real threat, then why would the U.S. throw away billions of dollars to fight an enemy on their own sacred ground for over fourteen years? By far the worst thing they did was kiss good-bye an unfathomable body count of human lives and then almost overnight walk away, leaving the carnage behind as though it meant absolutely nothing. What kind of people do that? I think they were the same type of cesspool dwellers that the current President of the United States is trying to drain the swamps of. Think about it—it should be easy to figure out for real patriots but nearly impossible to understand why.

Looking back at what was happening in the 1954 timeframe, French colonialism was defeated, and Ho Chi Minh had come 100 percent into support of the communist plan to take their aggression to the next level. With thirty thousand Chinese communist military advisors in Vietnam, and Soviet aid flooding into Ho's army, uninvited by the governments of both countries, the United States was thrown into a situation in which they could no longer stay neutral. Communism was on the move, and all of Southeast Asia was at risk of losing their freedom.

In many ways, the phrase "never underestimate the heart of your enemy" could have led to a story about one man, Ho Chi Minh. But the heart and resilience of the Vietnamese people were in place for a few thousand years before Ho was born. Ho used his people's remarkable qualities masterfully to reach his goals.

This small, frail-looking man affectionately referred to as Uncle Ho seems to have strategically outfoxed and even manipulated the heads of the Western countries and the communist bloc. In fact, while Ho was outwitting every American president from Truman to Nixon, he was courting and winning the support of numerous countries other than China and the Soviet Union. Ho had received friendly endorsements from Cuba, Angola, Mongolia, Burma, Indonesia, Yugoslavia, and even India at that time. Cuban soldiers would be encountered by Americans in the Vietnam War. Ho had succeeded in winning support from sympathizers from all regions after his convincing victory over the French. Even in America, there was a growing faction of Ho sympathizers who praised his revolution plan.

We badly underestimated them as did the French. Just as the Chinese, Japanese, and Mongol hordes underestimated them… Who's next?

"Fighting while negotiating" was a slogan that Ho's North Vietnam lived by, learned from their ancestors in the earliest days of the Chinese invasions. There has never been a more perfect example of this than the year of 1973, the so-called ceasefire year of America's war with North Vietnam. We fell for that so badly that today it almost looks like an intentional act by the United States government. We had depleted our military in South Vietnam nearly to the point of nonexistence. In the meantime, the communists were wreaking havoc over South Vietnam, and the inevitable surrender of Saigon actually happened a year earlier than North Vietnam had expected, thanks to an American Democrat-controlled Congress!

How we underestimated these people amazes me, makes me angry, saddens me, and leaves me feeling forever betrayed. But people are still telling us to get over that war?!

How could America not love its warriors who went to defend their country under such extremely adverse conditions? They went to war to preserve the Western world's passionate will to retain their hard-earned FREEDOM! That is what we were told at first, and that is what we believed.

In my first book, I defended the domino theory, gave reasons, and I believed them. I still do to some extent. Now I am not so sure we did the right thing. It probably looked like the only right thing to do coming off the same (or almost same) scenario with North Korea and South Korea. However, knowing what I think I know now, I doubt that South Vietnam could have survived on its own for very long. Just my opinion and I am sure many former South Vietnamese would be more than eager to challenge me.

So what do we think about that domino theory of the 1950s and 1960s more than half a century later? My updated answer to that highly controversial question will be shared toward the end of the book.

My war buddies and I learned quickly that the enemy would much rather engage the South Vietnam military than confront the Americans. We were much more likely to stand our ground during an enemy "human wave" attack. We were also more unpredictable in that we often went right back after our attackers if we did not have too many wounded to take care of and protect from the initial assault on us. The North Vietnamese thought the American grunts were crazier than they were, and they wondered just what was it the Americans were fighting for anyway.

America Caught Flat-Footed? The 1968 Tet Offensive creators in North Vietnam had put together a devious and extremely aggressive plan they were sure would fool the Americans. Their plan was to lure most of their adversary's troops into the northern sections of South Vietnam through a series of diversionary attacks. The famous battle of Khe Sanh would be one of those decoys, even though it was a major onslaught. In fact it was so impressive that General Westmoreland was led to believe this was the only significant attack to be enacted by the communists. He was sure of it, in fact he believed North Vietnam wanted Khe Sanh to be the Dien Bien Phu for the Americans, and that just wasn't going to happen in his mind.

As the Khe Sanh battle raged for days, a complete surprise hit the Americans smack-dab in their noses. Viet Cong attacks on more than a hundred towns, hamlets, and outposts were carried out in a furious manner. A larger and more vicious attack on the imperial city of Hue took place. Tens of thousands of military on both sides and civilians would be killed, wounded, or captured. At least 120,000 Hue residents became homeless while over 15,000 enemy soldiers from the NVA and VC army died.

The U.S. rebounded from these shocking and completely unexpected attacks, but the way the Ameri-Cong reported the battles, Americans at home were swayed against the war. While the media reported tales of defeat of U.S. troops, which weren't remotely true, General Giap felt Tet was a communist victory. He also managed to have the Americans thinking that North Vietnam and the Viet Cong were capable of staging a repeat of the Tet

Offensive. This made Westmoreland believe that he needed another 200,000 troops on top of the 500,000 already there.

LBJ decided against Westmoreland's request. Westmoreland was ordered to return home and his replacement would be General Creighton Abrams.

On March 31, 1968, President Johnson announced his decision that he would not seek, nor accept the presidential nomination of his Democratic Party again. Needless to say, Giap and his communist cronies were ecstatic over this chain of events. They were beaten on the battlefield in the Tet Offensive, but won a decisive political victory, and total victory was near. However, there was plenty of war to be fought, and more needless blood and guts would be spilled on both sides. In fact, the communists did stage another Tet Offensive in May 1968, which would end up the bloodiest month of the war to date. The Vietnam Adventure was just heating up

I think we became the aggressor even more so in the March-August timeframe of 1968, which was also named the Tet Counter Offensive. Coincidentally, that was about the time I spent more of my days (and nights) walking way up front of the column as the point man. I can't really say if there were one or two profound events that may have changed our tactics in that we became the aggressors and took it to the enemy rather than letting them keep the initiative—as they were always on the move, so that became our agenda as well. This would increase the chances that we would face off with each other more regularly. Up until then, it seemed like they were always ambushing us, and that was getting awfully annoying. Things would change; they had to or else.

Search-and-destroy sweeps gave us a feeling that we actually were invading their turf and that we would no longer allow them the confidence of coming and going, a luxury the VC seemed to take for granted in the early 1960s of the war. With all due respect, it is quite obvious that the **shock-and-awe** tactic goes way back historically. The Mongol hordes swarmed Asia, Africa, and Eurasia with it. Germany's "blitzkrieg" was a perfect example, as were the Hiroshima and Nagasaki bombings. Then again, I would imagine Sun Tzu wrote about shock and awe in his manuscripts as he did about guerilla warfare. Just sayin'.

The mighty jungle set the stage for many shock attacks by the NVA and VC with their famous sudden and horrifying "human wave" attacks. The loud screams and the charge from almost out of nowhere made it mandatory for those on the receiving end to be at a very high level of alertness. A few seconds of falling asleep on guard duty or listening post, etc. could doom the entire unit. Unfortunately, it happened from time to time.

I know that some of the most famous shock attacks were pulled off in older wars before the mighty automatic rifle or machine gun was invented.

Think of those back-and-forth suicidal charges in World War I where each side would mow the other down in a foolish charge. Shock assault worked for the Mongols with their vaunted lightning-quick cavalry charges against a sleeping or unsuspecting army. However, with modern warfare evolving, those charges in open fields would soon become wholesale slaughters for the attackers. As I have mentioned elsewhere, in order for us to compete with and defeat the Spartan-like Viet Cong lurking in the bush, we had to learn how to return the favor by fighting in their own style, which we did often.

Imagine the charge of the Light Brigade or Pickett's charge taking place against a modern infantry battalion with automatic weapons. Germany's blitzkrieg with their tanks was one of the most successful shock attack tactics in World War II, but everyone else eventually caught on as they made faster, more maneuverable, thicker armored tanks. In Vietnam, we had the shock attack advantage with our armored personnel carriers and tanks, but sometimes even they were at a disadvantage if the VC pulled off a successful night shock attack with the variety of rocket-propelled grenades or RPGs they carried. Patton's fabled tank invasion would have been fortunate to advance in Vietnam's jungles before being cut to pieces by RPGs in every direction.

False Sense of Security. I may receive some unkind communications on this one, but it is very difficult for me to dedicate more time and information about those warriors in "the rear," the support troops, and they were warriors too. But since I spent 80 percent of my tour with combat units and since 80 percent of the Vietnam War's casualties were incurred by the combat troops, no one can ever give enough credit to the poor bastards who did not have a roof over their heads, who did not have cots, showers, daily change of clothes, daily mail, hot food or cold beer, and carried everything to their name on their backs for months and months, walking through hell every day. I must add that the majority of Americans who served in Vietnam never came face-to-face with a live Viet Cong or NVA soldier except for those captured in battles. Credit for this belongs to the entire American military team, but in large part to the combat troops who patrolled the bush outside the secure base camps, and in some cases lived out there with the enemy. My bias toward the combat troops is justified—no apologies for that—none required.

When I was over there I rarely gave much thought to who had it made, the base camp troops, or who had it rough, the combat units in the bush. Looking back on those times, I see a broader picture, at least from what I remember from March 1968 to March 1969.

Out there in the "boonies" or the "bush," the only security combat infantry had was each other. So there were rarely any racial tension-related incidents—thank God! This was not the case back in "the rear." What actually was "the rear"? Even though no place in Vietnam was ever truly safe and secure, there were different levels of "the rear" all over Vietnam. And you could be in the most protected space in all of Vietnam and still feel no guarantee that you would see tomorrow.

One of those so-called safe and secure base camps was Dau Tieng, my first official home away from home. All of our personal stuff rested in one of those safe hootches while we slept on the ground in no-man's land, somewhere near the Cambodian border. During my first six months in Vietnam, the VC attacked and attempted to overrun Dau Tieng twice. They achieved part of their mission on July 4th, mentioned elsewhere in the book. Our hootch, with all of our worldly belongings, was blown up two times. Shortly after I left Vietnam, Dau Tieng was attacked and overrun again. In 1975, the North Vietnam Army would completely destroy Dau Tieng.

So much for the so-called safe places in Vietnam. I take my hat off to those guys who were lucky enough to man the bases in "the rear" they fought too.

To the combat infantry a remote fire base with a few hundred troops was considered "the rear." From that level came temporary base camps, considerably larger and with an airfield, a PX, and hootches along with bunkers to live in. Next came the sprawling base camps, which almost never received ground attacks, but were always prime targets for mortar or rocket harassment. The largest of these types of base camps could house ten to fifty thousand troops, with artillery, several rows of barbed wire, and sandbagged walls surrounding them. You could find pretty much everything you could imagine to provide a high quality of life (even if you didn't think so), such as mess hall, service club, clinic, offices, motor pools and repair compounds, tall, protective watchtowers, drivable roads, trucks, jeeps, movie theaters, maybe a swimming pool, fresh change of clothes, socks and boots, electricity, hot showers, and hot food, and girls were often available.

Most American GIs in "the rear" lived in huts or hootches, which were quite sufficient to protect them from the monsoon rains but not the mortar and rocket attacks. If you were at one of the very large complexes like Da Nang, Tan San Nhut, Cam Ranh Bay, Qui Nhon, Chu Lai, Nha Trang, or Saigon of course, you lived and worked in larger buildings that offered air-conditioning.

To many of the fortunate troops in "the rear" at the large and very large complexes, the infantry grunt who virtually lived with the enemy in his environment, they were only fantasies or rumors and might never be seen— or hardly ever. As I have stated elsewhere, about 85 percent of the GIs lived in "the rear," while the others "camped out" under the sun and moon twenty-four/seven amongst the beast, the enemy.

As one might imagine, the larger the base or headquarters, the greater the choice of amenities, recreation, and entertainment. Just the thought of sleeping on a bed with a pillow and sheets drove us nuts "out there."

By the end of 1968, the Pentagon had built an array of clubs, post exchanges, movie theaters, and athletic facilities that rivaled some present-day resorts. By 1968's end there were forty-six main PX's similar to a large one-story department store in the States, 168 smaller PX's, twelve hall cafeterias, forty-eight snack bars, twenty-two mobile retail stores; staffed by 765 officers, 150 civilians, nine hundred third country nationals, and almost ten thousand Vietnamese. At one point in 1968 and also in 1969, nearly seventy live shows (Bob Hope type) performed. Additionally there were Filipino bands, strippers, and Australian rock groups. This period is when the infamous "black market" system reached its peak. Those who profited were Koreans, Filipinos, South Vietnamese, American GIs, and civilians who were located in "the rear" areas.

I enjoyed seeing a Filipino band perform in Cu Chi on my last evening in Vietnam before going home.

Most likely the largest, most impressive mega-base camp was where the Military Assistance Command Vietnam (MACV) headquarters had planted itself in Tan Son Nhat Airport near Saigon. The media had named MACV headquarters as "Pentagon West or East" depending on which media was reporting. This would be where General Westmoreland and later General Abrahams would be seated. Once in November 1968, an old buddy of mine also from Twinsburg, Ohio, who worked at MACV rode up in a convoy (not a safe drive) to visit me in Cu Chi. Once he arrived, Les Clemente took a quick tour of Cu Chi with me in my jeep, and he quickly said he wasn't going to stay overnight in this place. To him Cu Chi was like an outpost compared to MACV, and he wanted to get into the next convoy back to MACV the same day. Well, I appreciated his effort to come and say "hey" to me; it was not a secure drive for him.

Les Clemente died prematurely from cancers caused by Agent Orange forty-six years after returning home from Vietnam. We had lunch together several times before his death, which I treasured.

During the years after we left Vietnam, Les told me stories he had never shared with anyone else. Sometime in between my first two books, Les told me that he kept a lot of copies of some top secret operations and that he was thinking about sharing some of the information from those documents—but first he would have to organize everything so that the facts would be in order and indisputable, should anyone choose to challenge them. He knew that he didn't have more than another year to live, so he had nothing to lose, but he also wanted to make sure I was protected.

The Phoenix Program. Les talked about this operation from time to time. While people in the know outside of the CIA and MACV told some stories about this program, most were sluffed off as pure exaggerated rumors. This was a top secret program that was set up to identify Vietnamese civilians who supported the National Liberation Front (NLF) or Viet Cong. Many of these undercover Viet Cong sympathizers were considered true patriots to the admired Vietnamese leader of North Vietnam, Ho Chi Minh. Most of them were taken to rough interrogation centers and questioned about VC activities in certain areas. Sometimes they were killed upon capture and never made it to the interrogation center. Sometimes they became defectors; others were brutally tortured, imprisoned, or simply killed. How many of the suspected VC operatives were seized, tortured, imprisoned, or killed can only be estimated. The Phoenix Program was not the only organized program in action during the war, but Les thought maybe a hundred thousand Vietnamese had been captured and removed from the NLF.

I can honestly guarantee that during my twelve-month visit to Southeast Asia, neither I nor anyone I served with or fought next to had any idea of such programs. It was not until I had already been home for a dozen years (1980s) that I heard the first whisperings about these programs. The torture techniques were more creative than I care to even mention here. Most of the brutality was carried out by South Vietnamese themselves, overseen by Americans.

My take on this from what little I heard from Les Clemente was that no wonder the North Vietnamese put so many South Vietnamese into reeducation camps or prisons where many would die. Anyway, Les never got around to organizing the information he had as he died very prematurely.

Even though Les and I built tree forts, caught frogs and snakes, and played baseball together when we didn't even know there was something called Vieeee-at Nam, my fondest memory of Les was when he rode in that convoy from Tan San Nhut (Saigon) to Cu Chi to visit me that day in 1968.

Make no mistake—most grunts who did make it through a full year or more owe much gratitude to the support people in base camps who also faced the danger of a stray mortar or rocket round or a Viet Cong infiltration into their supposedly safe confines. But *if* I even considered extending my scheduled tour of thirteen months beyond that, it would have had to have been a base camp job.

Speaking about support personnel for the combat guys, I also salute the support people of our enemy. In fact, in some ways the work they did was every bit as dangerous as what their field combat compadres did. The Viet Cong had no scruples when it came to killing Americans, either by sneak attack ambushes, cold-blooded suicide human wave attacks, sniping at us from their own relatives' hamlets (trying to prod us into firing back), or maiming us for life with their grotesque booby traps. They also benefitted from an unbelievable support group.

Very often, we would talk to ourselves after a confrontation with the Viet Cong. All too often, it seemed like they knew precisely where we were, where we were going, how many of us there were, even some of our names. This is where it comes in and smacks you in the face…NEVER underestimate your underdog adversary.

Night ambush patrol was by far the most nerve-wracking exercise we were faced with out in the boonies. Our imagination started to wander at the beginning of the patrol, which was a bad thing, as we needed intense concentration on these operations…during every second of their duration. Getting a good night's sleep on these nights was generally not expected. If we were blessed with a quiet night, we felt blessed, but another day would test us all over again. The real blessing on returning from ambush patrol was when we returned with all of the guys we left with. When we were inside the good old perimeter from which we had left, we usually gave a sigh of relief and we tried to enjoy the following day's moments of safety.

As dedicated as we were and had to be, the importance of the team—squad, platoon, company, unit—was to never let your war buddy down. That same mentality operated in full force with the Viet Cong; in fact, maybe more so. They had to contend with and try to overcome our massive weaponry or firepower and our great mobility through helicopters. They managed to do this with lightning-like ambushes after dark, hit and run. The intelligence behind the scenes was uncanny and sometimes shocking to us. The Viet Cong had spies everywhere. They worked in our kitchens as hooch maids and houseboys, penetrating everything as barbers, cooks, etc. into firebases to the Embassy in Saigon. One high-ranking American officer's driver and another's hooch maid were found out to be highly active Viet Cong information gatherers.

When I see how unsuccessful or unlucky our military has been in training and motivating Iraqis to fight toe to toe with ISIS, I think back to Vietnam. Often, our South Vietnamese allies, the ARVNs, would find their ranks infiltrated from top to bottom. Then we would wonder why the ARVNs rarely fought the Viet Cong as tenaciously as we did. The answer is quite simple and scary. The one game-saver for us out there in the bush was maintaining our pride. While I was there in 1968, we covered each other's butts quite impressively, making our bond ever so important. I understand that this was not the case as the war matured in 1970 and troops became burned out. But before the burnout came…we were searching for and destroying very capable adversaries at their own game.

As I look back at those days when we fought the Viet Cong on their terms, in their style, I can envision the would-be, wannabe conqueror Mongols riding their highly athletic and well-trained horses, attempting to clear a path for their infantry's onslaught. An onslaught that would not happen. Their goal was to catch up with and destroy a much smaller force of Vietnamese and their allies from the mountain tribes.

I can see the Mongol cavalry's charge. Even their horses have blood in their eyes. Then their suicidal charge slows down as the Vietnam jungle swamp begins to swallow them.

At first, the mud was barely passable and the charge advanced a little further. Soon the mosquitoes attacked the bewildered, bogged-down, charging Mongols, tens of millions of bloodthirsty mosquitoes, some the size of dragonflies. Even though many Mongol warriors wore armor, which would also slow them down in the breath-sucking heat, the mosquitoes found their way under the armor. Still, the proud Mongols would advance. As the mud became deeper, horses could no longer run in either direction. The bloodcurdling screams of the attackers suddenly came out of nowhere; then the arrows came, darkening the skies, and they found their mark often and again, then again. The once mobile army of Mongol assassins was in a position that was all too familiar to some of them from their last invasion of Vietnam in 1285. And again, they had underestimated their adversary. Their third and final retreat was not an honorable one, and there would be no return trips for revenge.

And we, the great American military force, were about to embark on a seemingly endless odyssey—or maybe in the end it would not last long enough. Either way, in the end, we had fought one of the bloodiest wars in America's history. And we seemed to have almost had it won in an extraordinary primitive face-to-face style of warfare. But the plug would eventually be yanked on the brave American soldiers who did everything and more of what was expected of them. These courageous warriors would be sold out, actually betrayed by the same type of cowardly bureaucrats who sent them over there to begin with.

Unfortunately, these brainwashed and physically broken patriots would be treated like subhumans when they returned home, and there would be no opportunity for a rematch or forgetting even. **But…oh, what an unforgettable adventure they had!**

Destiny of a Combat Unit in Vietnam…

A typical U.S. Army company would usually start out with 160 to 200 men when they were sent to Vietnam between the war's peak years of late 1966–1970. Often, the company would leave Vietnam with half that many.

The Regulars of the 3rd and 22nd Infantry of the 25th Infantry Division featured two companies, Bravo and Charlie, that would fulfill the destiny of an infantry company in the Vietnam War. Which company took the highest casualties was a claim neither wanted to have. But from November 1966 to November 1970, Bravo and Charlie of the walking Regulars would be decimated, losing over two hundred men, with more than a thousand wounded. If every American company that served in Vietnam from 1966–1970 had suffered casualties like this, it is likely that America's final casualty totals of 58,479 KIA and 304,650 WIA might have ended up as 582,720 KIA and 3,046,500 WIA.

When the January-February 1968 Tet Offensive was launched and virtually every city of any strategic importance was attacked, the heaviest damage wasn't the I Corp where the DMZ rested or where the infamous Khe Sanh was broadcast on American televisions from coast to coast. The worst-case scenario had suddenly become reality, that the Ho Chi Minh Trail and the underground tunnels had allowed a massive buildup of North Vietnamese Regulars and Viet Cong in bordering Cambodia and III Corps, the area surrounding South Vietnamese's precious city of Saigon. American and Allied casualties in III Corps would literally shock military leaders and seemingly cause great confusion. The misnamed Vietnam "Conflict" had officially become an all-out war in South Vietnam from the DMZ to the Mekong Delta. Now Saigon had to be protected from attack from all directions for the remainder of the war. Obscure places would become well-known buzzwords of the war, such as Iron Triangle, Nui Ba Den, AP Cho, Tay Ninh, Dau Tieng, Hoc Mon, Bien Hoa, Long Binh, Tunnels of Cu Chi, Trang Bang, Duc Hoa, Phu Cong, Loc Ninh, etc.

While the importance of a support unit can never be given enough credit for bailing out the combat units under attack, it must be said that the combat units like Bravo and Charlie 3/22nd, whether Army or Marines, were constantly roaming around—sometimes carelessly or needlessly—with a goal of killing the enemy so that they could not muster up enough to launch full-scale attacks onto the support base camps.

This author served proudly with Bravo of the 3/22nd from March 1968 to February 1969. I can say honestly that it was the greatest and the worst year, a year that would haunt me for eternity. In my heart I know this…**God loves all Vietnam veterans.**

America's combat troops faced all of these "little inconveniences" while we attempted to engage an invisible enemy that considered the jungle as their best ally. Again, I wish to remind readers that about 15 percent of the 2.8 million personnel sent to the Vietnam War were classified as pure ground-pounding grunts from the infantry divisions. I have seen these figures from numerous credible sources. Using 14.79 percent as the number of real combat troops that would more than likely engage an enemy in direct battle, here are some shocking statistics readily available from many sources:

The Shocking Reality of Combat Troops Who Served in the Vietnam War...

1.	Total Vietnam Era Vets Served (USA, Europe, Thailand, Philippines, Vietnam, etc.)	11,544,000 [1]
2.	Total In-Country Vietnam War Vets Only	2,800,000 [1]
3.	Total Americans Killed In-Country	58,479 [1]
4.	Total Americans Wounded In-Country	304,650 [1]
5.	Total Combat Vets Classified Killed	34,960 [2]
6.	Total Combat Vets Classified Wounded	182,790 [2]
7.	Total Vietnam War Casualties	362,920 [1]
8.	Total Viet War Casualties From Combat Units	217,750 [2]
9.	Total Estimated Vietnam War Vets Living	875,000—1,450,000 [3]
10.	Total Estimated Vietnam War Vets Living From Combat Units	140,000—200,000 [2]

[1] These are commonly published numbers, available from a multitude of sources.

[2] These are estimates based on the presumption that 60 percent of all Vietnam War casualties came from pure combat units.

[3] These figures came from averaging out the estimates from several public online sources. There appears to be a 200,000 to 300,000 margin of error, and I find it disappointing that there does not appear to be even one source that can provide a more accurate total...not one.

Another statistic that I did not list above are the 7,500,000 to 8,500,000 Vietnam "era" vets (not Vietnam War vets) estimated to be alive. If this is accurate, approximately 25 percent of them have passed away, compared to 75 percent of in-country Vietnam War vets who have passed away during or since the war. Of course, there is room for error with some of these statistics, but quite honestly, not very much. The VA and Veterans of Foreign Wars (VFW) publish most numbers from time to time, or one can get them readily from their websites. And if one can take these figures to the bank, which seems to be a safe bet, then all of the poor souls who were forced to live like subhumans—forced to fight the Viet Cong in their style to confront and chase down the enemy until total victory was won—were sacrificial lambs then and will always be the most forgotten and unfairly treated American soldiers in the history of our country.

So, who cares? The VA should have been giving extra TLC to its Special Forces and Rangers, combat infantry, combat engineers, and Seabees from the day they were released from the service or from the day they left the Vietnam War behind them. Because they suffered from the worst physical and mental abuse possible, and on a continuous basis. That is why. They are also the ones who were DIRECTLY dumped on with deadly herbicides, which is unquestionably the primary reason (but not the only one) that so few of us remain alive today.

Senator John McCain claims that Giap said to him regarding the Americans of the Vietnam War, **"You were an honorable enemy."** I doubt if Giap was referring to the desk jockeys in Washington, D.C. who pulled the strings and gave the orders to bomb parts of North and South Vietnam into scorched earth. Hardly so. I am confident that Giap was referring to the American soldiers and marines who crawled around and mixed it up in the muck with his guerilla war experts. It was they who fought honorably and convincingly. It was the grunts, LRPs, Rangers, Seabees, Green Berets, combat engineers, and the armored divisions that, unlike the French combat troops, went out looking for Charlie (Viet Cong). It was the sergeants, specialists, corporals, and privates of the U.S. military that Giap was referring to. Giap was impressed with their spirit. How could he not be? That is what I choose to believe.

In the Christian scriptures, the physician Luke wrote, "Your young men shall see visions and your old men shall dream dreams." General Vo Nguyen Giap lived long enough to do both. His glorious legacy has been documented in several books and a multitude of other media venues. He loved his country's beauty and potential in his youth. He became part of it. He knew that his efforts brought many things to pass that had slim chances otherwise. Once he wrote, "We have defeated all invaders, gained independence and unification"…by following Uncle Ho's road.

This book was written for the Vietnamese people just as much as it was for Americans and our allies from Thailand, the Philippines, Australia, South Korea, New Zealand, and Canada. They all contributed in making this history with sacrifices that may never be understood or fully appreciated by their own country.

Vietnam War's Most Dangerous Jobs. I tend to be a little biased on this, but I would give this title to the Army and Marine combat infantry point man, having been one myself. Right alongside those guys I would put the Army medic, Marine corpsman, and of course our tunnel rats. Many books have been about them all, filled with eye-popping, heart-stopping stories of incomprehensible courage and sacrifice.

Ooooh Those Choppers…There were about 12,000 helicopters that served in the Vietnam War, 11,827 to be precise. Of that total 10,005 were

Hueys built by Bell Helicopter, and almost all were Army. Nearly 3,305 were destroyed by the enemy and 2,177 pilots were KIA. Overall, 4,906 helicopter pilots and crew were killed.

It is believed that the Huey, including the famous Huey Cobra (AH-1G), totaled 7,531,955 flight hours in-country Vietnam, the most combat flight time of any other aircraft in the history of warfare.[11]

The total number of helicopters destroyed in the Vietnam War was 5,086 or 43 percent of the 11,827 that served. In the Vietnam War there were 58,479 American casualties, of which 305,000 were wounded in action (WIA). It has been estimated by some credible experts that 50 percent of those WIAs would have become KIAs. I don't think my medic/corpsman, tunnel rats, or point man brothers will mind sharing the title of Vietnam's Most Dangerous job with the helicopter pilots and crew members, because without them the wounded would have never seen the inside of a clinic or hospital. And you know what? Those pilots got us there…**FAST!**

Every day in the Vietnam War, dozens of lives were being saved because of the amazing heroism of the pilots and crews who flew the famous Huey. The stories about them abound and I wouldn't know where to begin if I were to tell just one of them.

Military statistics say that one out of every five pilots was killed or wounded. The gunships protected the rescue and medivac choppers. Choppers were also used to spray Agent Orange and the other dioxins to deny the enemy a hiding place in the thick jungles. Of course no one was told at the time how harmful the stuff could be to the humans in the path of the spraying. And they usually flew to and back from their destinations in any and all types of weather.

I've said it before and I'll say it again and again, for as long as I can say it…**God Bless the helicopter crews in Vietnam!**

One surprise after another. I can vaguely remember how our basic training drill sergeants talked of the Viet Cong as third world farmers and peasants in black pajamas and sandals, sneaking around setting up bobby traps to engage us in combat. We were brainwashed into believing the rag-tag Viet Cong were unorganized bands of backwoods-type marauders who could never stand up to the world's toughest and best-trained lean, mean fighting machines (us) and the awesome firepower we would unleash on their helpless, sorry asses.

When two women get into a fight with each other, it is generally called a catfight and many men seem to enjoy watching them. It is sexy in a rough way. Unfortunately, our drill sergeants in basic training rarely ever men-

---

11 www.whfcn.org/stat.htm.

tioned something we should prepare ourselves for when we would meet up with Viet Cong in our initial confrontations. I will never forget our first skirmish with a small Viet Cong attack team. It was near the end of March 1968, and most American soldier boys were still walking around very tentatively, as the famous Tet Offensive of January and February 1968 was still fresh in their heads. But I was one of those f---ing new guys and somewhat eager to unleash my battle skills onto a smaller, weaker, and certainly dumber adversary. Yeah, right on one account. They were…smaller.

I still don't remember what the date was, what day it was, or even the approximate time. All I knew was that my first day out there would be in the front of our rifle team, walking "point." *Oh my God*, I thought when I was given the order. "Trimmer, get your ass on point; gotta learn sometime anyway. Might as well be now than later" were the words thrown at me. I don't remember who sent the order. I can't even remember anyone else who was walking behind me that day because I would never see any of them again anyway.

We were plodding through thick woods when we suddenly came to a small clearing, and we could see a bunker ahead. There was movement inside. I fired first, then fell flat on the ground. It sounded like nearly everyone behind me did their share of unleashing our firepower. There was no more movement inside this lone bunker. We couldn't be sure if the occupants were dead or had retreated in quick fashion. We fired a few more rounds and some M-79 rounds—still nothing—and then we advanced slowly and spread out. It was okay, and we found two dead VC inside the bunker.

Someone asked me if I nailed those two Congs, and I didn't know what to say. I couldn't remember, nor could I see if my rounds hit anybody or not. Didn't matter. We got them. Our search-and-destroy mission was already a success and we had no casualties. So, what was next, I thought. It was already a pretty full day, and maybe we deserved to go back to our base camp at Dau Tieng. This would not be an option. We were redirected and ordered to proceed to a battle going on at an ARVN compound that was overpowered by VC. This was more of a rush mission, which made me really nervous, as I did not like moving through the bush at any other speed than…slow.

When we reached the ARVN compound, the VC had complete control of it, but they had also put themselves into a sitting duck situation. Someone said we were surrounding the compound along with guys from an armored unit.

The next morning, hell was unleashed—tanks, APCs, .50 calibers, and a hundred or so small arms of M-60s, M-16s, and M-79s. The sounds were deafening. It wasn't long before all was quiet at what was left of the compound. We found several dead ARVNs and eight dead VC. That would be the end of our action for that day. I did describe this battle with more details in my first book. One thing that stood out in my mind when we went in to check out the compound is that three of the eight motionless and badly mangled corpses were very young women!

Turning over the bodies, what was left of them, was a big deal for several of us that day. We had not seen nor did we expect to see women in the ranks of the Viet Cong. The surprise wore off soon, as we would run into lady Congs again and I must say… **They fought like tigers!** We were learning things that were not taught to us during our training in the States to prepare us for what we were going to face. One of those lessons was being learned every day and night… **Never underestimate the heart of your adversary!**

Why are these people—women included, of all ages—unafraid of American might? We were never taught to be prepared for lady Viet Cong who fought like male Apache Indians. Imagine the total shock for every American when he was put into a life-or-death combat situation and then discovered he had just killed (or was ready to kill) what seemed like a dainty, sometimes pretty but vicious lady warrior. But of course, he rarely said anything to anyone about it, except to another combat Vietnam veteran. Who else could understand?

Sometimes when I receive a dose of modern-day rudeness from members of today's younger generation or some millennial-age types, I find myself almost wishing I could see them in my place during a bloody in-your-face battle—Vietnam style. Then I catch myself and withdraw my thoughts before they become wishes. That would be sinful because they would not have survived in Vietnam, not for very long, not unless the man on each side of them pulled their weight. That is an experience most of those types of Americans will likely never have the opportunity to benefit from during their lives. So those are some of the thoughts I have twirling around in my head during my spare time these days.

I don't know where I heard this—it could have been from by hundreds of combat Vietnam War veterans at different times:

We did things that the average person would have to go to the movies to believe.

—Unknown Soldier

Between 2.7 and 3.3 million American men and women served in-country Vietnam. Some were fairly stationary in one general area, and some were highly mobile, moving about the country. Tracking each of the troops' various locations has been almost impossible—hell, they can't even tell us precisely how many of us are living.

During my thirteen-year war with the VA's Comp & Pen Department, after discovering certain uncontestable facts, I have presented challenges to them as often as I feel necessary. Of course I have often approached our Congress and Senate Committees for Veteran Affairs. I continue to be persistent in keeping up to date on the next new revolutionary Agent Orange news break that would help our Vietnam War veterans.

I will be an American soldier for life. I am quite aware that in order to have a chance to get something changed within a government agency like the VA, you must persist with writing to Congress over and over. I do that relentlessly with all the passion that can be mustered. And any one of them who doesn't respond, that one will receive another contact from me, and maybe just a bit more passionate than the previous letter.

Amazingly since Donald J. Trump joined the team to help veterans, my letters to Congress get answered more frequently. What a coincidence.

Almost every one of my original platoon members and most of the replacements for our casualties have been affected by one or more of the presumed Agent Orange-related diseases. They all served in III Corps in 1968 or 1969. The strangest thing about all of this is that even the heaviest and most continuous level of Agent Orange exposure to a Vietnam War veteran may not result in noticeable problems for twenty to forty years after their in-country presence.

Over there I lost more than three dozen close brothers of mine; back home I have attended nearly as many funerals of my close brothers who died prematurely from physical or mental wounds, and in some cases both. I remember each and every one of them as though it was just yesterday. Each time I lost one over here, I continued to think of them when they were living over there, in some cases before Vietnam, and of course their shortened living days back here. Their memory never goes away, they will not go away, they cannot go away. Tears come to my eyes at all times, while I am driving, reading, taking a walk, and just about any time.

Places like the Hobo Woods, Ben Cat, Hoc Man, or even the Iron Triangle itself probably meant nothing to our Marine and Army brothers in I Corps near the DMZ and II Corps in the central highlands. After all, the Ameri-Cong media, as bad as they sucked, did manage to help places like Khe Sanh and Hue, more famous than the swamps and jungles of III Corps and War Zone C and D, where the Viet Cong operated from their main headquarters—underground of course.

Quite honestly, during the early months of my adventure in South Vietnam, I never knew from one day to the next whether we were along the Cambodian border north and west of Tay Ninh or farther down in the places I mentioned in the previous paragraph. Over time I would become extremely educated and aware of the area we were being combat assaulted into. Not that knowing would have allowed us to be prepared differently, but it was nice to be able to tell people back home in our letters where we were. The time came soon that I knew exactly where we were.

The Iron Triangle was an area of woods, swamp, triple canopy, and rivers that encompassed about 125 square miles. That was enough to lose your way, which we did sometimes. Throughout both Indochina Wars the Triangle remained a highly contested area between the French and Viet Minh and certainly the Viet Cong and Americans. The communist forces wanted to control the area, while the Americans had intense desires to eradicate it entirely and they would stop at nothing.

After the Viet Minh victory over the French, the underground tunnels already in place were expanded until thirty thousand miles of tunnels were sprawling around and under the 25th Infantry Division's main base camp. I remember the Triangle area as being the host of one of Vietnam's most formidable species of extremely unfriendly wildlife, the dreaded…**RED ANTS!** They were aggressive when bothered, the bites delivered a stinging toxin, and if you were bitten by one of them, that would be a great time to get the hell out of the area before the inevitable onslaught of the entire colony. In many ways red ants reminded me of the Viet Cong's guerrilla warfare style—attack and run, attack again, then again and again until we killed them all. We didn't have that option with the red ants; our only path to victory with them was full and hasty retreat, which sometimes turned into total panic. I can't even begin to imagine how the Mongols would have dealt with this, wearing hot, heavy armor on top of horses. Hey, how about the poor horses?

Two of the massive operations of destruction we set upon in the Iron Triangle were called Toan Thang I and II, which our 3rd 22nd Walking Regulars participated in. Nothing was held back on these multi-division assaults from five directions at once. Along with the 25th Infantry, we were joined by 1st Infantry, 11th Armored Cavalry, 173rd Airborne, 196th and 199th Infantry, and the 5th Ranger Group of South Vietnam. Working together and throwing everything we had at them…land-clearing plows, tanks, armored personnel carriers, tear gas, B-52 bombs, flame throwers, napalm, Agent Orange herbicide, and ultimately Super Agent Orange, referred to elsewhere.

In 1968 and early 1969, no other area of South Vietnam was poisoned as often and as heavily as the Iron Triangle and the surrounding areas. If you were unfortunate to be planted in the swamps and jungles of the Iron Triangle during this timeframe, and if you are still living with a comfortable quality of life…hold your breath, keep praying, and say thanks to God every day. I try to.

I hate to admit this, but it was during these operations that all principal villages were completely destroyed, rebuilt outside the Triangle, and the villagers were relocated. There was no other way to destroy the enemies' supplies and base camps. One of the saddest stories unfolded with the destruction of the village of Ben Suc as nearly ten thousand refugees were affected.

There is no shortage of stories and tales around the Triangle, and my brothers are probably describing one right this minute, somewhere. I had heard somewhere that eventually, like in the early 1970s, the entire Triangle had been removed from planet Earth. Another story told that the Viet Cong were still operating from the area all the way up to the North Vietnam invasions of 1974–75. Someday I may dig into this to find out the truth, but till then the memories of the Iron Triangle Agent Orange hotspot and the multiple health conditions I am battling will keep me plenty busy.

Many Vietnam vets will say they share these emotions but not all. Not all of them can remember or want to remember the names of those they knew over there. In some ways I look at them as being luckier, not having those terribly emotional memories. We who developed and experienced bonds of brotherhood would carry those memories for the rest of our lives. Sometimes I go off by saying, "Honey, you should have seen how Bud or Johnny or Dean or Tex or Smokey did this or that." And then I stop and move on to another subject quickly.

Don't anyone ever tell me that those guys were not just as good, just as tough, just as patriotic as any American soldier before them. They were as good as any. They were real Americans.

To Catch a Guerrilla in His Backyard. The Viet Cong were no pushovers, not on their home field, where they enjoyed a decided advantage over any adversary, whoever he might be. So, the American ground combat infantry Marine and Army grunt had to become a guerrilla too, in quick fashion if time was on your side.

My unit in the 25th Infantry Division did most of their adapting to jungle warfare in-country, in order to beat their enemy at his own game, in the jungles twenty to a hundred miles west and northwest of Saigon, often crossing into Cambodia, even though it was officially off limits during most of the war.

I think the Viet Cong and somewhat the North Vietnamese Regulars may have been caught off guard by our reversed strategy of **searching and destroying** rather than sitting and waiting. Some of our guys (not all) welcomed the change. We could have probably called it **shock and awe** as our war in Iraq was called when we began the bombing of Baghdad in March 2003, but I am sure no one had thought of it in 1968.

Our primary goal with the search-and-destroy style of battle is probably described perfectly in the title. We wanted to let the enemy know that we were not afraid to come after them in their environment and confront them under their preferred conditions. While some of us may have thought this was idiotic or insane back then, as I look back at the numbers, the enemy's casualties, it would appear that our offensive actions had worked. We most certainly succeeded in placing more pressure onto Victor Charlie (VC) than we used to, and finding the enemy became more difficult. Also reduced were the regular attacks on us as they became more sporadic. But our losses were horrendous and maybe not worth it.

Search and destroy was a shock tactic to be sure. After the January–February 1968 Tet Offensive, combat infantry units all over Vietnam were on the offensive with search-and-destroy and combat assault (helicopter-aided attacks) missions that were relentlessly punishing the enemy. Nowhere in history could I find any of Vietnam's enemies willing or capable of meeting them head-on with their own guerilla war tactics and…beating them at it!

My war buddies and I can somewhat relate to what happened to the invading armies of Vietnam from China, Mongolia, and France. But we Americans were able to use their own many centuries-old tactics against them and defeat them in most battles of various sizes. We chased them often and we counterattacked them on our terms most times, not theirs. Basically, we were facing the modern-day relatives of those Vietnamese ancestors who had become legends in Vietnam's history.

To know your enemy, you must become your enemy.
—Sun Tzu, *The Art of War*

After the bloodiest year of the war came to an end and 1969 had started off much quieter, we noticed that all of the combat units were spending less time on search-and-destroy or ambush missions, and more time was being spent in base camps and fire support bases. The war and tactics were changing, but I'm sure most of the grunts didn't mind. Everyone in my platoon finished their one-year tour in February or March of 1969. Unfortunately, our military leaders did not know until years later that we had killed off so many of the Viet Cong's hard-core cadres in 1968 and their experience would never be replaced from within the Viet Cong ranks. Oh wow, if we had only known that in January–March 1969. They could not have survived another year of constant search-and-destroy and ambush missions from us.

This is why we are so disappointed and disgusted today that historians and the media have not been kinder and more honest about how we fought and beat a fearless, smart, and resilient adversary. After all, those poor, poor godless Mongols were almost inhuman with insane emotions to kill. I can visualize them in their horrific and raging state.

Because the Viet Cong were as unrelenting as their ancestors were, when they fought off the Chinese and Mongols, we had no choice other than to take our own level of determination and tenacity to a higher level than we even knew we were capable of doing. If we did not, our end would be the result, as we were both on a dogged mission to eliminate each other and we were both in a hurry to do it.

This Was Some Enemy! Facing sinister booby traps that maimed and killed, trickery that defied any logic, relentless, unsuspecting ambushes, and grotesque treachery, we began to doubt that the enemy, especially the Viet Cong, had any soul left in their makeup. We also began to wonder in order to exist out there in their environment, how soon would it be until we had to release our souls to Satan?

During my entire tour in Nam, I never saw nor did I ever participate in battles where our guys knowingly, willingly, ruthlessly, or otherwise took the life of a child or baby. I did witness shootings in self-defense of Viet Cong who may have been only twelve or thirteen years old, girls and boys. They were also well armed with guns or grenades and rockets and they were also quite efficient at preparing booby traps. As far as sweeping through defenseless villages known to have innocent (maybe they were innocent) civilians living there and mercilessly killing them like the Mongols did, like the Japanese did, like the Nazis did, and like the Viet Cong and North Vietnamese Army did, and like the Americans with Lt. Calley did… I NEVER saw it happen.

In fact we spent a lot of time trying to relocate villagers who had lost control of their hamlets to the Viet Cong. Those villages had to be destroyed and then we might build another one for those displaced South Vietnamese, in a safer location. And by the way, it was not uncommon for the Viet Cong to ambush the Americans while they were trying to build a new village for the innocent villagers. This type of aggressive action would inevitably make the area a "free fire zone" and any living thing could be justifiably killed on sight, because they just weren't supposed to be there.

What an adventure this was for us. Not at all like playing war games back home with the other kids in the neighborhood. This was indeed not your average enemy, and in order to fight them and defeat them, we had to learn how to think like them, and to carry out the killing missions needed to eliminate as many of this enemy as possible.

Yardstick for Life. For the bush-beating, ground-pounding combat soldier and marine who slept with their loaded M-16s close by, for them, I suspect, Vietnam has been the yardstick for measuring everything in life and probably always will be because of how it was over there. Nothing on Earth will ever come close to the intensity, the adrenaline rush that we experienced over there. Nothing on Earth will ever be as hot or as humid, not anywhere. Rain will never fall as hard or for as long as it did over there. The bugs were bigger, the mosquitoes bit harder, the spiders did too, and there were more poisonous snakes than anywhere else.

We will never see water that was as dark, as dirty, as putrid as we walked in and fought in over there. The fear of walking across an open field, anticipating the crack, crack, crack of an AK-47, will never be like it was over there. We will never again be dehydrated to near unconsciousness, where the water we drank made us vomit our guts out.

Looking at the stars at night, looking for tracers and rockets, won't happen again like it did over there. The wounds, the smells, the visuals we engaged in will never repeat, not like over there. Years later, it all began to seem like an imaginary adventure.

We will never hear, nor will we ever forget, the moaning, the crying, the screaming, except in our dreams, like we did over there. That shadow of death was everywhere, all around us, so much pain, so much blood, anguish, trauma, horror, and so much deathly, heart-pounding fear that won't be there tomorrow, like it was over there. Years later, it all began to seem like an imaginary adventure, except memories and flashbacks of my visits to the Iron Triangle may last forever.

Pay Phones in Cambodia in 1968. Nightmares, daymares, hallucinations are part of being a combat Vietnam War veteran, and I have had my share of them—still do. I described a few of them in my previous books, so I'm not going to be redundant by retelling one of those bizarre events. But alas, fresh from the previous night of February 1, 2018, I experienced another one of those remarkable fantasized episodes, one that was related to but expanded on with what I guess is the creativity one suddenly finds during a dream or nightmare. While this one had scary moments, it was also humorous and far-fetched at the same time.

It was a true story that happened one night in April 1968, not too far from the Cambodian border; in fact we could have thrown a rock at it and hit it. The second squad of the 1st platoon of Bravo Co of the 3rd 22nd Walking Regulars, 25th Infantry Division were sent out on a routine night ambush mission—not that there is anything "routine" about an ambush patrol as really, really bad things can and do happen on those little walks in the woods of Vietnam. Anyway, the squad unexpectedly almost found more than we could handle as we barely avoided walking straight into a couple hundred Viet Cong soldiers, probably the remains of what used to be a full regiment that our battalion mauled pretty badly a couple days earlier. Fortunately we spotted them first and were able to take cover, where the squad of a dozen men would have to spend the entire night watching and listening to the VC force as they made camp a hundred meters or less from where we were. The nightmare for me began right about then.

Somehow I had been separated from the squad, which was really strange as I was walking point as usual. But all of a sudden, I found myself frantically and mindlessly going nowhere and changing directions often, which would guarantee I would keep going nowhere. The only thing I was sure of is that I was no longer in South Vietnam. I was definitely in Cambodia, and this was North Vietnamese Regular territory, lock, stock, and barrel as they say. I did not have a map, not that it would have mattered as Cambodia was almost a different planet. Nor did I have a compass, although I should have. But I had my trustee machete, my M-16 with two or three bandoleers of ammo, probably three hundred rounds or so and three or four grenades, so even though I was alone and obviously very lost, I would be a force to be reckoned with for a handful of enemy troops. At least I thought I was. But I was lost, had no plan, not even the slightest idea of what to do to get unlost. So I lay down to wait the night out, never sleeping of course, and as soon as the sun began to rise I would head west.

Suddenly an idea flashed by me and a voice inside me instructed me to… FIND A PAY PHONE AND CALL AN AIRLINE TO BOOK A FLIGHT HOME!

So I found myself approaching the first village I came to and began asking the villagers if there was a pay telephone close by, that I was lost and needed to contact an airline to fly me home. Several problems confronted me immediately about this idea:

- I didn't speak more than a dozen words in Vietnamese and I sure as hell couldn't speak Cambodian!
- Where was the closest city with an airport for me to book my flight from!
- I didn't have any credit cards to pay for the flight!
- I didn't have any coins to use when I found the pay phone I needed!
- What if the villagers were not friendlies? After all, they were Cambodian and we were constantly dropping bombs in their country on the Ho Chi Minh Trail!

As I continued to wander almost blindly through the thick, steamy jungle, I actually did stumble onto a remote village. I had to take a chance, so I approached the village in hopes that someone could direct me to a pay phone. As I came near the edge of the village, everyone was understandably glaring intensely at me. *Aw shit*, I thought. I made sure my M-16 was not on safe, and I resumed my advance into the heart of the village. What other choice did I have? Then two men began walking toward me; they were not armed but I was still very tense and they knew it.

Suddenly, I woke up and found myself on the floor next to my bed in a sweat and an uncomfortably bewildered state. I had just fallen out of bed, and that woke me up in the nick of time. My fall out of bed and the tumble are almost always related to me trying to escape from Cambodia. So that's it for the most current Vietnam War dream/nightmare I had, not so bad. It was sort of humorous as I look at it now. However, it put me into a drenching sweat, and like all Vietnam War nightmares, flashbacks, etc., it was all very real as I experienced it. But seriously...pay telephones...credit cards...commercial airlines and public airports in the heart of the Cambodian–NVA infested wilderness? All I can say is you had to be there and I was. What an adventure that war was for those who were thrown into it. One thing we learned very quickly was to catch a guerrilla you had to become one, which I will illustrate throughout this chapter.

Americans' Greatest Adventure...as tough as they come!

The true measure of a tribe's greatness will be remembered by the strength of their enemies in battle.
—Sitting Bull, Sioux Indian Chief

Just look at the eyes of a veteran who was a grunt in any of America's wars from Vietnam to our present war, wherever that is being fought...Iraq, Afghanistan, Syria, Libya, South Korea. If you can find one, a former grunt who saw extensive combat, pay close attention to his eyes if you can do it discreetly. They might be determined, fierce, hoping, soft, or just a blank stare. This is the face of the toughest soldier alive, whether he is an 11 Bravo infantryman in the Army, a Marine, Ranger, Green Beret, or other pure combat-trained troop. His eyes have it; that penetration into things few others can see. He sees images of horrors past, and his eyes may reflect that. His eyes will show commitment. This is why God sent his very best to Vietnam. It was a tough man's job.

God only gives his worst battles to his toughest soldiers to win! What the heck does that mean? And how would God know in advance how bad a specific battle that hasn't taken place yet would eventually be? Silly questions. Anyone requiring an answer has wasted his or her time in reading this book thus far. But I invite you to continue on. Please do. And when you have finished, please send me your thoughts. Clearly, this book has factually proven that America's Vietnam War veterans were as tough as any American soldier boys before them. We took everything that the enemy threw at us and we came right back at them, **NEVER BACKING DOWN!**

Combat troops who lived through the Vietnam War and are living yet will never forget the devastation, exhaustion, and back-breaking physical misery of a combat unit's tough and brutish ways to exist from one day to the next. Everything was one rotten and unforgettable day after another. And yet, when Vietnam vets returned to the States and stepped into a VA facility to be examined or interviewed by a young, insensitive physician's assistant…that very damaged combat vet will often be looked at and treated with disdain, not to mention disrespected. WHY?

Important Lesson Learned: In the jungles of Vietnam, when you run into a critter with fangs, you can forget about making it one of your family pets. Stories are rare about one of Vietnam's fuzzy, not so little, meanest jungle inhabitants, the giant centipede. While there are few factual accounts of human deaths from centipede bites, the pain and discomfort they can cause might make one take drastic measures to relieve the pain. Some centipede bites over the last few decades have been credited with the following:

- Ripping pain that lasts for several days
- Beet red coloration with swelling and inflammation for up to a week
- Constant, abnormal skin tingling with almost unbearable burning sensations and acute itching
- Infection of numerous muscles, requiring some type of antivenom remedy if available (I doubt this was available to the Mongols during their unwelcomed visits to Vietnam).

Similar to some poisonous rattlesnake bites, the eventual death of living cells in focused areas near the bitten area will result. Some skin is likely to turn black, lasting for a week or two. If post-bite inflammation continues for a month, treatment at a medical facility may become necessary.

During our tour in-country there was a guy in one of our sister companies of the 25th's 3rd and 22nd infantry who was bitten by an eighteen-inch-long centipede. We were told that the bite was so unbearably painful that he screamed in agony from the initial contact. He was evacuated back to a base camp for medical treatment and had to be flown to another medical facility with advanced treatment available. No one remembers his name and we never saw him again. We guessed that if he lived, it would not have been without some measure of PTSD and nightmares.

How would the Mongols have been able to cope with such dangers? They had no medics, nor was there any process for medical evacuation to a medical facility. One can only imagine the inconveniences the jungles of Vietnam must have caused the Mongols and their cavalry horses. Just imagine hundreds of bites from a multitude of poisonous, creeping, crawling, and flying critters.

Sorry if I am being overly repetitious, but some of those experiences need to be talked about again and again.

I don't have a clue as to how the Mongols endured the horrors of Vietnam's treacherous environment and the extremely dangerous wildlife with the deadly diseases they carried. I just know that nothing—NOTHING AT ALL—that I have experienced in my lifetime has ever affected me the way that single year in the Vietnam War did. Unfortunately, the memories of those nightmarish days and nights continue to haunt us; sometimes we wonder if it all really happened to us. Are these nightmares just that, images of things that are too unreal to have actually happened? Unfortunately, the physical and mental scars that the VA will eventually and continuously medicate us for will reassure us that these images that still plague us are not figments of imagination.

Booby traps had unbelievable and disgusting potential of stopping search-and-destroy missions day or night in their tracks, which opened the way for an enemy ambush on an extremely vulnerable foe…US! Obviously the Iron Triangle was a popular area to stumble onto a booby trap and spoil someone's day.

If you were not a combat infantryman of the Vietnam War, you have no idea what you missed, and you are very fortunate. Our Viet Cong adversaries were known for creating all sorts of horrifying contraptions that would give us permanent impairments if they didn't finish us off. How about this one—you are leading your twenty-man platoon one day as the point and you step into a six-foot-pit with a dozen upward protruding stakes with sharpened points, including a poison or an infectious bacteria spread on the tips. If that isn't enough, there could be a lethally poisonous bamboo viper or two lying at the bottom of the pit. Imagine yourself lying there with half a dozen poisoned bamboo stakes sticking through your body. You are numb, becoming paralyzed, in shock, but still living. Then you feel one bite, then another. Nothing else that will happen from those moments on will matter. It is a painfully torturous and slow way to die. You may be better off if one of your war buddies puts you out of your misery, as there is absolutely nothing they can do to keep you living. The snake venom works fast, but you are bleeding to death anyway.

While your platoon buddies are trying to remove your mangled, infected, lifeless body, one of the little green bamboo vipers hits one of them and then another. They need to be extracted from the pit and treated as soon as possible, but it might be too late for them, as the bamboo viper's bite has been known to kill a human within seconds. Your seventeen-man platoon is down to fourteen and not a single enemy shot has been fired. Not to worry. Mr. Charlie would never want his American foes to return to base camp without some really juicy stories of combat, so the Viet Cong suddenly gives you what you and your buddies were looking to engage in, a Viet-Cong-style **AMBUSH!**

Three men have been wounded seriously within seconds and several more are wounded, not so seriously. Maybe there are seven or eight of you left, fending off the enemy ambush, and you still haven't seen even one of your dreaded attackers. Your medic is then seriously wounded. The only way out of here now is by an extraction by helicopters. You can't call for backup artillery fire. You don't know exactly where the enemy is, and to make your precarious situation worse, the first helicopter's attempt to reach you is stopped as the VC shoots it down, and of course, kills the crew.

Your seven live and unwounded men are pinned down for as long as the enemy wants you to be. Maybe they play with you, moving to different spots to fire from, or maybe they call for reinforcements to finish off the remains of your unit. Night approaches. Mortar rounds start coming in. Earlier, it was just small arms fire, but this gives you an idea as to where to direct some badly needed artillery fire, and you do that, knowing that your own men could be hit—there is no other alternative.

During the night, the enemy, which has surrounded what is left of your platoon, subsides, but you don't dare move until daylight and then the choppers come in for another rescue attempt. However, two more of your original seventeen-man platoon are wounded during the night, leaving five well bodies left. The medevac arrives with enough choppers to evacuate your seventeen bodies, but the price paid in just one night was not worthy of telling war stories about back at base camp. Maybe thirty to forty years later, you might get together with some of those guys, but not all are overly curious as to how each has been doing. Maybe then you will relive some of the episodes that most of you all lived through together. Your original platoon of twenty on search and destroy the day of the forgettable booby trap ambush had two men left who were not killed or wounded, as nine more were killed in action later that year in Vietnam, just a few days before they were scheduled to go home. Here is a sit rep for your first ever platoon reunion:

- 17 members started out together
- 1 KIA by booby trap and snake bite
- 11 WIA from first ambush
- 3 KIA in search-and-destroy mission

This was a rather typical result for a combat infantry platoon in the Vietnam War during the bloodbath years of 1967, 1968, and 1969. Fourteen of seventeen who came home were wounded or killed. That is 100 percent casualties and enough sad memories to last each one of them a lifetime.

They will not easily forget them. Unfortunately, that war won't leave you alone as all of you who made it home, battered mentally or physically, will pass away soon from Vietnam-caused problems.

So, did this book offer some "fun" while I compiled it? Hell no and hell yes. Every time I thought of the faces as I remember them over there, before they died or back here after they died, I can honestly smile many times. I can't help but be in awe of these guys for what they did over there and have had to deal with back here.

We fought a seasoned, hardened, determined, resilient, fierce army of what some ignorant Americans referred to over and over as "farmers and peasants" with pitchforks! Well, somewhere along the way to the market, somehow the modern "farmers and peasants" of the Viet Cong stumbled onto using a few more weapons of destruction other than the old-fashioned booby trap. Please know that the Viet Cong were extremely ruthless with their ingenious variety of booby traps on land, in bushes or trees, and under-water. (Remember, we often patrolled through rice paddies and streams or canals.) Plain and simple, some of the Viet Cong took great joy in assem-bling and planting a never-seen-before booby trap that took Americans out of the war, usually permanently.

I must say that what the Viet Cong and North Vietnamese Army lacked in firepower, they made up for with their ingeniously concealed devices used to inflict serious casualties. Often, the booby trap treat would divert a search-and-destroy mission so that they could walk into another ambush. To make the booby trap war even sadder was the fact that most of the mate-riels and explosives came from discarded or stolen ammunition and dud bombs by careless Americans. I guess these weapons could be referred to as anti-personnel devices. Again, there were so many explosive types and non-explosive types that it would be impossible to describe them all.

By the time the Vietnam War had ended for us, our recon, media, con-tractors, and infantry units had identified a list of weapons used by the People's Republic of Vietnam (PRVN) or North Vietnamese Army (NVA) that included the following:

Semi-Automatic Guns	11 Types
Machine Guns	22 Types
Mortars	17 Types
Recoilless Rifles	20 Types
Rocket Launchers	9 Types
Anti-Aircraft Artillery	14 Types
SAM Missiles	Several

Rocket-propelled grenades (RPG) were extensively used by the Viet Cong and NVA to offset our armored personnel carriers (APC), and I know from firsthand experience that they were very effective and inexpensive in our war for our adversary. I have read in several sources that the RPG used against the Russian invasion of Afghanistan did not have the level of success that the Viet Cong and NVA experienced against America. This seems quite understandable because the jungles of Vietnam allowed the VC/NVA to crawl up super close to the APCs to get a better and more damaging shot off. I have ridden on APCs, but never inside one, and I am glad of it today as they could be death traps.

Surface-to-air missiles provided by Russia with qualified instructors were fired at U.S. planes in mid-1965. On July 23, 1965, a USAF plane was shot down by a Russian-built missile. Nearly seventeen thousand Soviet Russian technical operators and instructors were quickly sent to Vietnam to help the home team defend Hanoi, and at the same time, the Vietnamese ground troops were building up their numbers. Without the assistance of the Soviet professionals, by the end of 1972, the Russian SAMs had taken down over two hundred American planes.

While the U.S. air war in 1972 with North Vietnam was very intimidating, Soviet and China supplied SAM anti-air defense was winning their end, and the American ground forces had ceased to be a factor in the war. Gone were the search-and-destroy missions. Gone were the night ambush patrols. Gone were the five hundred thousand troops that had won the war in their minds by the end of 1968 or 1969. Most Nam vets back home were watching the news reports on TV every night, but they knew the American Democratic Congress had sold them out…the final result of the long, bloody, bitterly fought war would not carry on much longer. Every Vietnam War veteran still alive and still fighting that war in one way or another, please know this… **You Were As Tough As They Come!**

Is the USA irreplaceable? Fair warning, if you have been attacking our founders or if you think America is not indispensable, then you would have been offended by this book or any one of my three books. Since World War II, America's participation in all of the wars abroad have been for these abbreviated reasons, and their endings had a lot in common:

Korea	We aided South Koreans who were invaded by the North Koreans. It was a stalemate—but South Korea's freedom was preserved.
Gulf War	Quick and decisive victory against Iraq, which blatantly invaded Kuwait. Kuwait was preserved.

Vietnam   We aided the South Vietnamese, who were being invaded by
               the North Vietnamese with the support of China. Victory was
               almost certain after the complete military failure of North
               Vietnam and the Viet Cong at the close of the Tet year of
               1968. In a shocking turn of events, America withdrew all of
               its forces and ceased all military support for South Vietnam,
               resulting in 500,000 North Vietnamese steamrolling over
               South Vietnam on Russian tanks for a shocking, easy victory.

Iraq War   A self-proclaimed victory by American officials. However,
               a premature pullout by the American military paved the way
               for a reinvasion by the Islamic State terrorist military…that
               war continues.

Afghanistan   Another self-proclaimed victory by America's govern-
               ment, but Americans continued to be killed by a supposedly
               defeated enemy of Muslim fanatics. This war continued.

Who will volunteer to fight the next war? Surely, I must be kidding with
that statement. Not kidding. In spite of the obvious—that America's homeland has not been vulnerable to an in-country invasion since World War II,
as it is today—the Obama administration has been relieving troops from
their service who "volunteered" to serve their country! At the same time,
countries known to be less than friendly to the USA have been building up
their military to record levels. Still, there are those in the Obama administration who keep claiming that America still has the world's strongest military
force. The question is, strongest military force for what?

Remember the unpopular draft? If we suddenly need to build our army
back up to the strength necessary to stop or control bigger militant groups
or an overly zealous Iran, North Korea, or China, where would we get those
badly needed American soldier boys? Volunteering is no longer likely, not
after so many have been "laid off" during the last several years.

We will always be able to count on those who are eagerly willing to
fight for America's safety, but that pool has shrunk for reasons mentioned
earlier. The hard, cold truth is—America is quickly becoming a country of
un-American types, and soon we might no longer be a country that can
easily maintain a sizeable military strength advantage over our potential
adversaries, including larger militant groups.

In the Vietnam War, most of the almost three million troops who served
in-country went there on their own. They did not have to be drafted. The day
may be near when America will pay dearly to have three million warriors
like Vietnam War vets to volunteer risking their lives for the USA.

Remember the key reason the small country of Vietnam was successful at fending off one onslaught of massive invasions after another from 39 AD to 1979? The People's Army of Vietnam, their militia of hundreds of thousands of armed civilians—yes, their "farmers and peasants"—are a significant reason that Vietnam is not a divided country today. In spite of its communist government, it is one united country that is relatively FREE!

Muslim attacks of Americans in 1800! Two hundred years ago in 1815, during Thomas Jefferson's administration, the Muslim Barbary States' pirate military was completely defeated by U.S. Marines by land and by sea attacks. Today, that victory lives on in the Marines' hymn:

> *From the halls of Montezuma to the shores of Tripoli*
> *We will fight out country's battles on the land as on the sea.*

Until then, America had been paying huge tributes to the Barbary Coast pirates, up to 20 percent of America's total annual revenues. Jefferson had been against paying the tributes in the beginning, believing that only war would teach the pirates a lesson. He ended up being correct, as all previous efforts of negotiation had been a complete failure. A reminder that America had previously relied on the powerful Royal Navy of Great Britain for protection against pirates. After winning our freedom, we were suddenly vulnerable to other threats.

In fact, in a meeting of "negotiation" between John Adams, Thomas Jefferson, and an ambassador representing the Dey of Algiers, an Algerian Islamic warlord, the ambassador Sidi Haji Abdul Rahman Adja (you can't make up a name like that) told Adams and Jefferson that Islam was founded on the laws of their prophet, that it was written in their Quran that all nations who did not acknowledge their authority were sinners, that it was their right and duty to make slaves of all they could take as prisoners, and that every Muslim slain in battle was sure to go to Paradise.

Please know this—our Founding Fathers were not the alleged racists that some radicals today wrongly profess them to have been. Here are some well-documented statements by a few:

> *There is not a man living who wishes more sincerely than I do to see*
> *a plan adopted for the abolition of slavery.*
> > **—George Washington**

> *Every measure of prudence…ought to be assumed for the eventual*
> *total extirpation of slavery from the United States.*
> > **—John Adams**

I have throughout my whole life held the practice of slavery in... abhorrence.

—James Madison

We have seen the mere distinction of color made in the most enlightened period of time, a ground of the most oppressive dominion ever exercised by man over another man.

—Benjamin Franklin

Slavery is...an atrocious debasement of human nature.

—Alexander Hamilton

I needed to know everything possible about the Muslim Quran because I was going to advocate war against the Islamic Barbary countries of Morocco, Algeria, Tunisia and Tripoli.

—Thomas Jefferson

Unfortunately, there are many troubled Americans today who have formed opinions contrary to what our Founding Fathers believed and practiced. Profoundly unfortunate is the blatant ignorance by some white liberals and black radicals alike in their incoherent discussions about slavery. Here are some **FACTS**:

- One of mankind's standard fares throughout history for centuries was the trafficking of white slavery. The word slavery comes from "Slavs," referencing the Slavic peoples of Eastern Europe. Centuries later, Black slavery emerged and Black Muslims were the main culprits. Over ten centuries, Muslim pirates ravaged the African and Mediterranean coasts, raping, pillaging, murdering, and collecting millions of slaves to be sold to European countries and later, to America.
- Another rarely shared fact is that two mainly white countries, Britain and the USA, took profound measures to abolish slavery.

1807   Britain passed Abolition of Slave Trade Act.
1808   United States passed anti-slave trade legislation.
1862   U.S. President Abraham Lincoln proclaimed emancipation of slaves. Thirteenth Amendment of U.S. Constitution followed in 1865.
1926   League of Nations supported abolishing slavery.
1948   United Nations endorsed banning of slavery and slave trade.[12]

---

12 www.reuters.com/article/UK-slavery

Africa was badly drained of its most valuable resource—not diamonds, but its human population—from the fifteenth century to the nineteenth century. Most were West Africans, sold by West Africans to Western European slave traders with a minority being captured and brought to America. Actually, far more African slaves were taken to South America, Central America, and the Caribbean than to North America.

The Barbary States of North Africa's support of piracy and collecting ransoms was not so unusual at the time young America was being plagued. America was new and considered to be among the weak nations, which the pirates preyed upon. Also, at almost the precise time the War of 1812 took pace, the pirates picked on American ships more often. In one sense, a young USA had two wars on its hands within a few years after the victory in their War for Independence. Fortunately, the War of 1812 was a short one and America began beefing up its navy immediately after the war ended, with one purpose in mind…to go after the Barbary States and teach them a lesson.

Actually, the real culprits were the European countries who would reward the pirates for captured ships from any country. The First Barbary War was short, but decisively an American victory. A Tripolian warship was disabled, suffering ten casualties. The U.S. suffered none. That was that.

The Second Barbary War was little more than two ships jousting with each other. The naval fleet consisted of five battleships, three frigates, and six Dutch ships. At the same time, another attempt at negotiation was taking place, with the Algerians unaware of the large naval force on its way. The U.S. had also sent a ground force of Christian and foreign mercenaries, led by U.S. Marines. A bloody battle would begin when American land and sea forces reached the well-fortified town of Derna. This would not be an easy victory, but it would be a clear-cut lesson to be taught to the Barbary Coast pirates. Bitter hand-to-hand street fighting was required before the enemy's surrender. Shortly after the news, the pasha of Derna begrudgingly signed a peace treaty.

Casualties at the Battle of Derna were—Americans at fourteen and the Algerians at five hundred thirty-nine. Other battles took place while Derna was under siege. The result—several of the Barbary's ships were destroyed, dismantled, or captured. All captured Europeans and Americans were released. At the fall of Derna, the American flag was hoisted for the first time on foreign soil after a badly needed victory against the slave trade.

One special heroic act by the Americans was led by the U.S. Navy's Edward Preble and Stephen Decatur. The setting was a brand-new U.S. frigate, *Philadelphia*, which had been captured and beached for all Tripolians to mock. Unfortunately for Tripoli, "Remember the *Philadelphia*" became the American cry as they attacked Tripoli in full force. Tripoli would not forget this battle soon. America hailed Preble and Decatur as war heroes back home. In fact, back in Britain, the great Admiral Lord Nelson recognized the American raid as the boldest military act of the age. Pope VII declared that the United States had done more for the cause of Christianity than any of the other established and more powerful nations of Christendom had done for ages.

My dear patriots, from the War for Independence to the Iraq and Afghanistan Wars, we have fought in twenty-one major wars and in many (too many) other conflicts or operations. In each, the Barbary Wars included, our American soldiers and marines have been over eager to rise up to the occasion for the benefit of someone's freedom at a high price. That would most definitely include the battles to end slavery, which America has championed for over two hundred years, including today.

Slavery still exists…where? Modern or contemporary slavery is when someone is controlled or possessed by another person in such a way as to significantly deprive them of their individual liberty, with the intent of taking advantage of them by using them to make a profit. Today, as the Global Estimate of Forced Labor 2014 revealed, seventy-four countries contribute to slave labor in one capacity or another and well over 50 percent of the victims are women or girls.

I was unbelievably fortunate as a child to have lived in an integrated area of Cleveland's east side, called Hough. Later, after a couple of moves in between, we moved to a suburb called Twinsburg. This is the town I have referred to as my hometown all my life. I still live in a neighboring town right next to Twinsburg. Twinsburg was also quite integrated and I consider myself fortunate for this, as many of my friends today are from there, black or white.

During my time in the U.S. Army, my closest buddies were often blacks, especially in Vietnam, and I am grateful for that too, as one of them was my lifesaver in Nam. Being blessed with those experiences growing up helped me immensely for what lurked ahead in my life. I don't think I even heard the word *racist* until well after I returned home from Vietnam in 1970. Now in 2016, I hear the *R* word several times every day and I don't get it. Don't these people see what is going on all around them? Most schools are integrated. Mixed marriages are NO BIG DEAL these days, and opportunities are endless now in America with race rarely a factor.

Where is all the racism that certain special interest groups keep referencing? A third of the police force is black, and yet when a black kid is shot (regardless of circumstances) those certain special interest groups cry out the *R* word toward the cops, saying they did it (regardless of circumstances) because of the kid's skin color.

Anyway, with slavery not being an issue in America for 150 years, meaning there are no slaves from the 1850s still living here, and most of us at every level from Little League to the professional level of sports seem to be getting along just fine…where the hell is all the racism that only those special interest groups keep referring to and starting protests and rioting over and over? Those people should save those energies for what lies ahead, for what really threatens our wonderful lifestyle in grand old America. There are those who resent what we have here. They hate us for it; in fact, they have a bloodcurdling passion to see us die because of what we have.

Global Slave Index Hit 45.8 Million in 2016. This is or should seem like shocking news to many, especially black Americans who insist that the U.S. is the world's major offender of racism. Yes, about 45.8 million people around the world are still trapped in modern versions of forced labor or enslavement. It hasn't been getting any better, as some human rights groups have reported a 28 percent increase over the estimates in 2014. Walk Free Foundation is one of these groups. They also reported that North Korea had the highest per capita level of modern slavery at 4.37 percent of their population. Uzbekistan and Cambodia follow not far behind in per capita.

On the other hand, the countries that seem to receive a large part of the racism bashing have taken the most significant progress acts in antislavery. The United States amended a law to ban importation of goods made with forced or child labor. The United Kingdom introduced the Modern Slavery Act in 2015, which can penalize violators with life imprisonment.

It was my experience as well as many others I know—black, Hispanic, Native American, and white—that racism did not exist in the combat units of the Vietnam War, probably the first war this happened. We fought side by side, Martinez and Taylor and Trimmer, covering each other's backs while trying to save lives of anyone who was in harm's way regardless of skin color. I am also aware of the racial tensions that were taking place in the U.S. while we were fighting on their behalf so that their freedoms lived.

Unfortunately, there are those ignorant loudmouths berating America for its perceived or imagined total racism because they think whites today should pay for or be punished for those slave-owning ancestors from two centuries ago. While this is going on, let's take a peek at how slavery is doing in other countries. In fact, here is a current eye-opening list of the top ten nations responsible for modern slavery:

The Global Slavery Index 2016	
India	18.35 million slaves
China	3.39 million slaves
Pakistan	2.13 million slaves
Bangladesh	1.53 million slaves
Uzbekistan	1.23 million slaves
Nigeria	701,000 slaves
Ethiopia	652,000 slaves
Russia	520,000 slaves
Thailand	475,000 slaves
Congo	465,000 slaves
Myanmar	385,000 slaves

Disgusting—SHOCKING…this is 2018? Maybe those special interest groups could spend their valuable time and their donated funds on fighting the slavery problem around the world today rather than bitching about what happened in this country one and a half centuries ago.

Over one-quarter of the slave trafficking victims are children! Many of them are trafficked and sexually exploited. In some war-torn countries, child slaves can be used as child soldiers. Now that is a sad example of forced labor. Maybe our Viet Cong friends did that with South Vietnamese kids?

The old "melting pot" is still that; at least I hope it is. In Nam, we fought side by side as brothers—blacks, Hispanics, Jewish, Native Americans, and Caucasians. We had each other's backs without anyone having to order us. Many made it back because other Nam vets risked their lives or lost their lives to save lives. I have to presume that camaraderie has continued through the Middle East wars. But again, I wonder about who will be willing to fight for us in the next major war.

There has been much talk about a possible revolution, but it is unclear who would be lining up to fight whom. Many black radicals, who are as racist as anyone is, continue to instigate trouble by pitting blacks against whites and blacks against blacks. The KKK appears to be null and void these days. Thank God for that!

This great nation, which was founded on Judeo-Christian, black, white, Semitic, and Hispanic principles, is on the verge of falling from God's grace…in its infantile stage of being a mere couple of centuries old. There are many countries that have successfully owned their identity or brand for thousands of years, like Vietnam, as mentioned earlier. Americans have a long way to go, regardless of race.

One little known fact and never mentioned in our history books is…at the PEAK of slavery in 1860, only 1.4 percent of Americans owned slaves. BUT…3,000 black Americans owned a total of twenty thousand slaves in 1860. Obviously the race baiting by a very few black Americans and liberal white Americans have been fooling the rest of the Democrats for a long, long time.

I also know that racial tensions existed between blacks and whites back at the base camps. Maybe they all had too much free time on their hands; maybe more of them should have spent more time in the bush, sleeping in the jungle—on the ground—with M-16 attached. The well-known saying about the Vietnam War—we won every major battle—can be attributed to the brave and fierce fighting style of the mixed races of Americans fighting for each other, not *with* each other. For this reason alone, Vietnam War veterans deserve to be remembered as a Great Generation. Think about it, out in the bush, Native Americans, Hispanic Americans, black Americans, and white Americans slept *together*, fought for their lives *together*, experienced Agent Orange spray by their own government, ate the sprayed bananas and pineapples in the jungle *together*, were wounded *together*, cried and suffered together, and lost their lives together. No one taught them how to form and live out these special bonds; they just did it…**together.**

I don't know a single Vietnam War veteran of any color, if physically fit enough, who would not stand up for this country again. Even those with major physical or mental impairments and still able would be eager to pick up a gun and fight for America tomorrow if necessary.

What would those special interest groups causing all the problems with useless protest rallies in the streets do? Would they fight along Chinese or Russian soldiers—against their neighbors? If the latter, for what reason?

My lovely wife, Ginny, bought a T-shirt for me a few months ago, and I wasn't sure at first *if* I would wear it or where. Quickly, I canned any apprehension about when or where I would wear it. The inscription on the front of the shirt reads…

Don't Let The Grey Hair Fool You…We Can Still Kick Ass…
Proud VIETNAM VETERANS

Dear fellow patriots, America has been the global fire support base in support of freedom and opportunity for all for over two centuries. I guarantee you that most Vietnam War Era veterans know what it means to value freedom, which is why most of us, despite our persecution for decades, are still as willing and enthusiastic about picking up a firearm to defend ourselves and our family and our beloved USA.

As tough as they come for sure they were. Every one of them, whether they practically lived with their enemies in the friendliest environment imaginable, or built and supported the invaluable base camp where artillery and helicopters were safeguarded until the grunts desperately needed them. These American soldier boys were literally thrown to the wolves and vultures for the most part during the Tet years of 1967 and 1968. These were unquestionably the bloodiest years. Battle after battle was followed up with daily search-and-destroy missions by dog and squad or platoon-sized ambushes at night with the latter sometimes ending in a suicide mission.

If a combat soldier lasted the entire twelve to thirteen months he was required to serve, it is quite conceivable that he would have experienced far more combat contact in that one year than our fathers and uncles might have faced in a three- to four-year tour of duty in the Pacific theatre of WWII. Who would have ever thunk that? Few Americans believed it, especially the WWII vets, America's bestowed "greatest generation." This truth about the Vietnam War veteran would continue to be buried by the Ameri-Cong media for several decades.

So, who is going to step up to fight for us in our next war? Will the Americans of tomorrow take a pass on offering themselves up for a possible sacrifice of being wounded or killed for what past and present Americans considered an honorable cause?

Book Recommendation: *Tough As They Come*—Immediately after I heard about this veteran's book, which was not soon enough, I decided to give it a mention in my next book. All wars have generated magnificent personal non-fiction stories of heroism at the highest level. Human spirit stories can provide inspiration for all of us who have faced tough struggles with obstacles in our own lives. Some challenges are unbelievably incredible. Retired U.S. Army Staff Sergeant Travis Mills' story resembles others like *Forrest Gump*, *Saving Private Ryan* and *We Were Soldiers*.

Staff Sgt. Mills lost both his arms and both legs in an IED explosion while serving in Afghanistan. But somewhere along the line, as he explains in his book, he decided not to be known as or referred to as a "wounded warrior." He does not mean disrespect to anyone who is, and goes by the title because they are a combat-related wounded warrior. Staff Sgt. Travis Mills is one of those who never gave up. He chose to never give up. He chose to never quit. You and I can make such choices.

Tough As They Come has received dozens of five-star reviews and I will offer another one as soon as I have finished my second reading. I strongly recommend this book to anyone.

If we were faced with an in-country or out-country threat to our lifestyle, our families' lives, and our hard-earned freedom, would tomorrow's American population (loaded with illegal aliens) show their love for the land that feeds them and shelters them? Will they fight with the same passion that the Vietnamese did when their homeland was invaded over and over again? Will they have what it took for Staff Sergeant Mills to fight back? Many of us who have put our lives on the line so that others after us can enjoy their freedoms are not as confident about our great America's future with what we see on the streets these days. Just sayin'—hope we will be proven wrong if that inevitable threat presents itself.

So, is America indispensable? Is it irreparable would be a better question.

I may come off like a broken record with repetition here, but I will take that risk. As I recall, and from what my parents and grandparents used to tell me, that good old-fashioned American pride was fairly common during the presidential terms of these guys (not in order of best to worst):

Woodrow Wilson	Had many ideas that shaped the USA to become what would be at its greatest.
Theodore Roosevelt	Allegedly an honest president.
Harry S. Truman	He did what he thought was right, not politically correct.
Dwight D. Eisenhower	A military hero who helped us win WWII and end it. He got us out of a no-win situation in Korea. Was a strong civil rights activist.
John F. Kennedy	Some would say he was the most popular and most overrated president. He started the Peace Corps and the space race, stopped the Cuban missile crisis, and much more until his life was taken prematurely.

Franklin D. Roosevelt Runs neck to neck with Abe Lincoln and George Washington for the best U.S. president ever. He led us through the toughest times America has ever faced, just like our next president will need to do.

Put those terms together from Theodore Roosevelt (1901–1909) to Ronald Reagan (1981–1989); skip a few presidents during that time who were not very popular, nor were their accomplishments well heralded by historians, and those appear to be the "I love America" years. Then it would seem that the "Bye-bye Miss American Pride" began with the terms of George H. Bush during 1989–1993 and carried on by Presidents Clinton, G.W. Bush, and Obama.

I've seen a lot of true-blue American patriots during my short presence on this planet, and I hope to see a lot more before the great God almighty calls it quits for me.

What is so great about America? Why is America still so worth fighting for? I will say this—I know a lot of real combat war veterans who might have second thoughts about playing the passionate role of "I love America" nationalism they showed during the time they fought for their country...if this country continues to show attitudes such as this one:

Wearing "Unearned" Military Medal Is Protected by Constitution
—Stars and Stripes
January 12, 2016

You read correctly, and it is disgusting to most real veterans. After a long yo-yo battle over the Stolen Valor Act that lasted for several years, this eight-to-three ruling by the Ninth U.S. Circuit Court of Appeals in San Francisco stated the now repealed law against wearing "unearned" military decorations was a ban on a type of "symbolic" speech. Although the government can forbid falsehoods that can cause tangible harm like fraud or perjury, the Constitution restricts government regulation of expression based solely on its content, according to the court. "Suppressing a symbolic communication threatens the same First Amendment harm as suppressing a written communication," said Judge Sandra Ikuta in the majority opinion. "Wearing a military medal has no purpose other than to communicate a message."[13]

This was a very sad article for me to read, as tens of thousands of America's warriors were damaged for life from their wound(s) and once again, it is okay for someone who never served, never fought in a war to wear a Purple Heart, Silver Star, etc. anytime, anywhere they see fit. This means the likes of Charles Manson-type persons could be seen in public with a Purple Heart medal on their chests. Really?

Our American brothers and sisters of the 1901–1989 eras had to face and overcome some of the greatest challenges in our history, such as: World War I, the Great Depression, 1919 strikes and riots, and the Red Scare, the Wall Street Crash of 1929, Prohibition, emergence of the Ku Klux Klan, the Great Plains drought, the recession of 1937, post-World War I problems, World War II, post-WWII, Korea, Vietnam War, and its problems.

Tough as it gets...in their face. Looking back at those days of crawling around in smelly, muddy swamps, sharing the terrain with poisonous snakes, scorpions, armies of vicious ants, poisonous spiders, and a deter-

13 www.begalko@sfchronicle.com

mined enemy that could pop up out of nowhere in seconds…a smile comes to my face along with the tears.

Man, those war buddies I had the pleasure of serving with over there were magnificent bastards, and they made sure our rather invisible enemy knew what they were up against and the price we would make them pay for attacking us. This could go on for several days and nights in a row. In the end, sometimes it seemed that the "top brass" back at headquarters were interested in hearing how many casualties we took from a significant battle or operation. Usually, the first words out of their mouths were…*BODY COUNT…BODY COUNT, DAMN IT…WHAT'S THE BODY COUNT?* Of course, they were referring to enemy KIAs, as that was of the utmost importance at the upper levels. We rarely disappointed them and sometimes, not often, if the numbers were high enough, we might be given a half day off to write letters and to just catch our breath.

I remember one time when we worked out of Cu Chi with the 3/4 Cavalry, an armored unit, someone asked who we were with and when we told them we were with the 3rd 22nd Bravo Company, we could see from the expressions on some faces that they had heard of us. That reputation was earned by the guys before us in 1967 at the battle of Suoi Cut and January 1968 at the battle of Suoi Tre. Our guys killed over one thousand enemy soldiers in those two single-day battles. We didn't hurt the reputation any as February, March, April, and May were full of enough high body counts to keep everyone happy at the 25th Infantry Division headquarters, also located in Cu Chi.

I have to say that our Australian and South Korean allies were more than up to the task in what seemed like a race to report the most body counts of the day. Those guys from the "land down under" were as tough as they came in their own right. One thing for sure, none of us was out there trying to find ways to avoid the enemy. Of course, there were those times when we didn't have to look for them at all…they found us. Many of us came to believe that Westmoreland had become obsessed with the body count numbers. Unfortunately, our success rarely came about without a huge price to pay. Many of us are absolutely positive that our massive casualties in 1968 were to some degree kept quiet or delayed in reporting. But the body bags with Americans kept on coming in at shocking numbers into 1969 until the suicidal search-and-destroy missions were reduced substantially.

Unfortunately, our allies in the South Vietnamese army were not as eager to find and engage the enemy in the jungle as we were. Maybe they were smarter than we were, but we never thought that was the case. We should have paid closer attention to the results of a battle in 1963 between the ARVN and the VC.

Ap Bac was a village in the Mekong Delta, about forty miles southwest of Saigon. The Battle of Ap Bac began to develop in December 1962. Three Viet Cong companies built defensive positions along a mile-long canal connecting Ap Bac with the village of Ap Tan Thoi. The Viet Cong dug in behind trees, grass, and shrubs with clear view of the surrounding rice fields. The Army of the Republic of Vietnam (ARVN) Seventh Division attacked the position and although they outnumbered the Vietcong by ten to one, they were defeated. ARVN was characterized by incompetent officers and terrible morale. At the end of the battle on January 2, 1963, the ARVN had lost five helicopters and sixty dead, while the Viet Cong suffered only three casualties. Although American military advisers in South Vietnam tried to claim the battle a victory because the Vietcong abandoned their position, the engagement showed how difficult a guerrilla war would be and how much learning the United States would have to do about the nature of warfare in Southeast Asia.[14]

A couple of years later, Westmoreland's war of attrition was tested early in the war when Lieutenant Colonel "Hal" Moore led the 1st Cavalry Infantry Division on a combat assault drop into the Ia Drang Valley in October of 1965. They found what they were looking for on their ground search-and-destroy missions and they slugged it out with several thousand NVA regulars for several days, with the final body count from both sides ending up at:

3,561 NVA KIA   305 Americans KIA

These are the kind of results Westmorland would be looking for as our troop participation escalated. The kill ratio was a whopping twelve to one in the Americans' favor. Unbelievably, Westmoreland had sent orders to Moore during the peak of the intense battle to leave the battle early the next morning for Saigon to "brief" him and his staff on the progress of the battle while it was raging! Moore was totally dumbfounded over what was being asked of him: TO LEAVE HIS MEN, WHO WERE UNDER HEAVY ATTACK, TO BRIEF THE GENERALS?

Needless to say, Lieutenant Colonel Moore sent his regrets back to a stunned Westmoreland and his staff of generals and colonels, and stayed with his men until the battle was over and every American body, living or not, had been evacuated. How tough was that?

This war was just getting ready to heat up, and many more *tough-as-it-gets-in-your-face* types of confrontations would follow for half a decade between Americans, the Viet Cong, and NVA. As many people reading this book never heard of the majority of our battles and operations in the Vietnam War, I want to list several of them with a brief description of how they ended, along with the casualty total, killed and wounded:

---

14 www.vietnamwar.net

Some Major Confrontations 1965–1970

American/South Vietnamese

Year	Battle/Operation	Allied Casualties	Enemy Casualties	Victor
1965	Dong Xuai	816	326	NVA/VC
1965	Ba Gia	1,285	1,056	NVA/VC
1965	Ia Drang/Albany	853	2,790	USA
1966	Paul Revere	300+	1,200+	USA
1966	Hawthorn	287	1,000+	USA
1966	Prairie	1,385	3,000+	USA
1966	Masher	1,278	5,000+	USA
1966	Operation Utah	376	1,554	USA
1967	Suoi Tre	226	2,500+	USA
1967	Operation Buffalo	1,005	1,301	USA
1967	Operation Hinckley	1,038	1,234	USA
1967	Junction City	1,782	5,456	USA
1967	Cedar Falls	420	2,012	USA
1967	Dai Do (Dong Ha)	290	2,366	USA
1967	Dak To	1,802	4,664	USA
1968	Tet Offensive *	44,290	111,179	USA
1968	Lang Vei	744	400+	NVA/VC
1968	Khe Sanh	8,477	36,350	USA
1968	Hue	4,375	25,000+	USA
1968	Toan Thang	705	10,542	USA
1968	Jeb Stuart	294	3,268	USA
1968	Sheridan	229	2,898	USA
1968	Mameluke	269	5,728	USA
1968	Napoleon	353	3,495	USA
1968	Kam Duc	405	345	NVA/VC
1968–1969	Speedy Express	642	10,889	USA
1969	Dewey Canyon	1,062	5,000+	USA
1969	Hamburger Hill	444	2,400+	USA
1970	Cambodian Invasion	6,171	27,554	USA
1970	Firebase Ripcord	Americans: 1,890 ARVN: 4,205	23,850	USA

* Ranked as one of the twentieth century's deadliest battles[15]

---

15 www.army.technology.com/features, www.stripes.com

Anyone should easily be able to read between the lines from these very ugly numbers. The exodus of U.S. ground troops left South Vietnam indefensible, as the ARVN military could never go it alone. Here is a shocking but 99 percent accurate scenario of just how the war went from WINNING to DEFEATED in a very short time:

From 1956 or 1959 to 1964, the warm-up period for what was to come, there were a few skirmishes that would concern America's leaders, but nothing to be alarmed about, so they seemed to think. From 1966 to 1970, America had the war under complete control, except back home.

There were many, many more bloody battles like these, and most would produce an American-Allied victory. It never looked like we lost that war from casualty reports like this. In 1971 and 1972, the war started to get out of control and was lost in devastating fashion just three years later:

1971–1972 Battles[16]
(Without U.S. Ground Forces)

Year	Battle/Operation	ARVN Casualties	Enemy Casualties	Victor
1971	Lam Son 719	21,285	8,200	NVA/VC
1971–1972	Kontum	1,200	29,000	ARVN/US
1972	Quang Tri I	29,368	14,400	NVA/VC
1972	Quang Tri II	7,756	10,000	ARVN/US
1972	An Loc	12,500	24,000	ARVN/US
1972	Loc Ninh	36,000	2,500	NVA/VC
1972	Easter Nguyen Hue Offensive	203,307	70,000	NVA/VC

- In 1971 and 1972, most U.S. grunts had been removed from the field and were being sent home. Even with American air power still present, the ARVN forces would fare very poorly against the NVA and VC in most battles. Quite a difference when the American ground forces were there, winning virtually every battle.

At Lam Son 719, an excursion into Laos, even with U.S. air support and U.S. artillery power, the ARVNs were badly beaten. They could not even hold back the NVA's onslaughts from getting to Americans manning the artillery fire. As a result, 253 Americans died and 1,149 were wounded.

---

16 www.historynet.com, www.wikipedia.org

In addition to the human losses, the NVA destroyed 168 helicopters and damaged another 619. However, the ARVN reversed the outcome with the NVA at their next confrontation at Kontum in 1971–1972, catching the NVA completely off guard. American air support was awesomely effective at the battle of Kontum. Prospects for the ARVN living up to expectations the Americans held for them took a positive shot in the arm…for a while.

The battle at An Loc would be the last victory for the South Vietnamese. Again, there would be no U.S. ground forces in 1972, and most of the U.S. air power was being reduced. The ARVNs would be on their own from here on, but talks of a temporary truce were brewing. The 1972 Easter Offensive was a major swing in the war, favoring the NVA and VC. The communists took full advantage of the 1973 Peace Accords, as they never had any intention of living up to them. They knew the American people would not allow their military to be sent back to Vietnam, so they took this opportunity to replenish their manpower in the ranks of the Viet Cong as well as the North Vietnamese Army. They were further strengthened by war materiels and weapons supplied by the Chinese and Soviet Union—when the South Vietnamese were cut off by the American government.

Vietnam War's Last Days[17]
(1973–1975)

Year	Battle/Operation	ARVN Casualties	Enemy Casualties	Victor
1973	Paris Peace Accord in place	56,500 *	N/A	NVA/VC
1974	Phuoc Long	5,560	1,300	NVA/VC
1974	Thuong Duc	7,000	9,200	Indecisive
1975	Ban Me Thuot	65,000	2,500	NVA/VC
1975	Hue/Da Nang	100,000	15,000	NVA/VC
1975	Xuan Loc	50,000	25,000	NVA/VC
1975	Ho Chi Minh/Spring Offensive	244,000	25,000	NVA/VC
1975	Fall of Saigon	15,000	1,000	NVA/VC

The so-called "cease fire" war claimed 26,500 ARVN killed in 1973 and another 30,000 during the first half of 1974. Probably another 100,000 were wounded…some cease fire. Casualties for the communist NVA went unreported.

—Marilyn B. Young, *The Vietnam Wars 1945–1990*

17 www.historynet.com, www.wikipedia.org

After the temporary truce in 1973 and all of the U.S. firepower had departed, the South Vietnamese military was badly mauled in nearly every confrontation with the NVA/VC. The NVA/VC kill ratio over their southern foe was almost inhumane at 5½ to 1 and a total reversal of the U.S.'s battle results in the 1960s.

Ugly…ugly…ugly, especially in 1975 when the South Vietnamese military absorbed 330,000 total casualties just from five battles during a four-month period. At the same time, communist casualties were less than 69,000. It would be safe to say that South Vietnam's total casualties in 1975 alone exceeded half a million. If the U.S. Army suffered losses like that today…that U.S. Army would no longer exist! In fact, records show that 1.1 million South Vietnamese were captured or surrendered in the Spring Offensive.

Today, I am thoroughly convinced that the Vietnam War Era generation is still or has become the core of our terrific country. And if the United States were to be invaded by unwelcomed guests, twenty-two million armed Vietnam War Era veterans would rise up, band together with our active and inactive National Guard and Reserves military to confront and dispose of such a threat in grand fashion…just like our Vietnamese brothers and sisters did time and time again throughout their great country's two-thousand-plus-year history.

There is no army in the world that would have a snowball's chance in a fire to be victorious over our American militia (the people) and our regular soldiers, marines and veterans combined.

Of course, none of us of sound mind would look forward to such a deadly confrontation, but we are here just the same. It does not help America's position that our military has been reduced by alarming proportions while some of our traditional and potential enemies have not been reducing their military power. Many prayed that the November 2016 presidential election would bring us a new leader who actually loves this country as most Americans do, as most Vietnam War Era veterans do.

"*They* never quit on you then…don't you quit on them now." *They* were American soldiers. *They* were warriors and members of a team of warriors. *They* served the people of the United States, always placing the mission first, always living the soldiers' values. *They* did not accept defeat, nor were they defeated. *They* never left a fallen comrade. *They* were mentally and physically tough, trained for warrior life. *They* became experts at what *they* were trained for. *They* stood ready then, answered America's call then, and *they* stand ready today. *They* are guardians of freedom and the American way of life. *They* never quit then…please don't quit on them now! Why should all Vietnam War veterans hold their heads up high after all they have been through? Because… *they* are SURVIVORS, not victims. *They* are Vietnam War veterans.

They returned home with no one to greet them. *They* were told that their PTSD was nothing, that it would go away. *They* are still haunted by life-like nightmares and hallucinations. *They* hear familiar songs that take them back there. *They* are still fighting from Agent Orange exposure and...*they* tend to have more friends on the Vietnam War Memorial (The Wall) than there are presently in their life.

One more thought for this chapter: When those who are accepted into our homes as welcomed guests become rude and disrespectful and start acting more like intruders than guests, we ask them to leave. The same principle applies to the immigrants who are crossing our nation's borders. In fact, this principle applies especially to them, as America's overly generous hospitality should not be abused. And why is America treating those people better than we vets were treated?

After finishing this important chapter, my lovely wife and I will head to church together and afterward, we will join some patriotic friends at a local firing range to sharpen our shooting skills. **God bless the USA, OH-IO, and all patriotic Americans.**

> *When you serve in an active combat infantry unit in Vietnam for ninety days straight under constant firepower from the enemy and you make it out alive, then you can say this...you did something.*
> **—Colonel David Hackworth (Deceased)**
> **U.S. Army Veteran, Korea and Vietnam**

The Odds Against Us Were Greater Than Americans Were Led To Believe!

CHINA AND SOVIET AID TO NORTH VIETNAM[18]
1954–1971 (in $US millions)

	1954–1964	1965	1966	1967	1968	1969	1970	1971	1965–1971 Totals
Soviet Aid									
Military Aid		210	360	505	290	120	75	100	1660
Economic Aid		85	150	200	240	250	345	315	1585
Total	**365**	**295**	**510**	**705**	**530**	**370**	**420**	**415**	**3245**
Chinese Aid									
Military Aid		60	95	145	100	105	90	75	670
Economic Aid		50	75	80	100	90	60	100	555
Total	**670**	**110**	**170**	**225**	**200**	**195**	**150**	**175**	**1225**
Combined Total		405	680	930	730	565	570	590	4470

---

18 U.S. State Department 1972-1979, Edited August 26, 2015

Bob Hope was a pretty tough character in his own right. He had this to say about his experiences with close contact with Vietnam veterans in combat zones:

> *I have never faced more danger than I have in all of America's wars that I have been to than when I agreed to venture into the jungles of South Vietnam at the time the war was just heating up.*
>
> **—Bob Hope 1968**

Actually Bob Hope's initial 1964 arrival in South Vietnamese was surrounded with more secrecy than was normal for the movement of the generals or U.S. government cabinet members. Eventually the communists put a generous bounty on Mr. Hope—dead preferred. Mr. Bob Hope…you were THE man for us. God Bless You.

Being as tough as they ever were was a must in that war for soldiers. We just didn't know it until we got there and found out what kind of insane animals we were supposed to hunt down and kill or else! But being as tough as they came wasn't just about how well we fought the enemy or how quickly we were able to adjust to the indescribable elements and terrain we had to deal with twenty-four/seven. Being as tough as they came also required a lot of humanitarian actions, often when we least expected it.

Toast to the "land down under." While in Vietnam, we crossed paths with our allies, South Korea and Australia, only a few times, but both forces left a profound impression on us. It was in between Tan Son Nhut, Bien Hoa, and Cholon when we ran into and shared battle sites with the Aussies. We had heard interesting tales about the ROKS (Republic of Korea) and the Aussies. The Viet Cong respected them both. The Aussies had been assisting the USA in South Vietnam since the early 1960s as advisors. As the war escalated in 1965, Australia answered the call from the USA by sending more troops, and they were good ones for sure.

The Vietnam War showed no favorites, and the Aussies were not spared from the mind-game warfare of the Viet Cong. They were very successful in several battles during extended operations. Possibly, their signature victory came in the fall of 1966 at the battle at Long Tan, an area that touched III Corps, which was the hangout for the 25th Infantry Division, my guys. Being outnumbered ten to twelve to one did not intimidate the Aussies, as they were noted for chasing after their attackers just as we did. At Long Tan in Phuoc Tuy Province, the Aussies numbered a 110 men from D Company. This battle was described as a vintage, single-night battle of the Vietnam War. Even the Vietnam weather cooperated in making the evening more memorable as the monsoon rains pummeled the scene for most of the night. The Aussies were matched up with and pinned down by an entire Viet Cong regiment, the 275th, which offered plenty of targets for the Aussies at two thousand to twenty-five hundred strong.

At the peak time of Long Tan, nearly half of D Company had become casualties, and they were completely surrounded. Nights like this—if one was unlucky enough to experience yet blessed to survive it—will leave a dark memory that one is not likely to forget soon…if ever. D Company was rescued when UH-1B Iroquois helicopters arrived to resupply them, as they were almost out of ammo. Mind you, it was not an easy task for those choppers to get in and out that night. In many battles of the Vietnam War, helicopters took heavy damage. Resupplied, but still encircled, Aussie artillery fire began to take its toll on the enemy, at least for the time being. D Company managed to live on for the next day—well, half of them did. They were reinforced in the morning hours by cavalry and infantry from the nearby base camp of Nui Dat, and the Viet Cong force would be routed, but not without leaving behind hundreds of dead and badly wounded Viet Cong comrades. The Battle of Long Tan was a victory the Aussies would be proud of, but their losses were depressing for the entire unit. D Company would settle down at a base camp to lick their wounds and wait for the "f'ing new guys" to replace the KIAs from Long Tan. Eventually, they would return to the field at full strength and try to finish where they left off. It would not be fun; of course it wouldn't, as the war was just picking up steam, and D Company would be sent to one of the most heavily infested Viet Cong areas, **the Iron Triangle.**

The American and Aussie soldier boys were up to the task, whatever the challenge was. It would have been really nice if the American media had the decency to tell the truth of what we were doing, to our family and friends back in America.

Winning hearts and minds was an official ongoing program created in the 1966–1967 years by the military's leadership. But the American soldier boy didn't need to be led to the water to drink it; we knew how to find it and drink it ourselves. The same went for the ground troops who were meant to find the path of pacifying the hearts and souls of the Vietnamese people. Sure, we had some really bad eggs out there in the bush, and being out there where the "beast" was just made those guys worse. Some would get out of control, but those jerks were by far the minority of America's tough combat veterans of the Vietnam War.

The soldiers I saw in Nam were more likely than not eager to reach out and do a good deal of humanitarianism for the rural village people, as much as they were quick to respond to an enemy ambush. Unfortunately, sometimes that ambush might come from one of those villages we just helped the previous day. That was a tough tug of war—which way do we go this day and the next? Of course, our number one priority was to preserve number one…each other. Otherwise, we may not ever see America again, and many times we had doubts if that day would come.

Try to imagine how difficult it was to do the good deeds for the locals to try to earn their trust when their village was attacked by the Viet Cong because they were friendly to us. And maybe the next day we were forced to shoot into that village as there was enemy fire coming at us and we lost a couple of our brothers.

The following day, we went back to the same village with our engineers to build a new village for the people. Then a week later, we would pull out a search-and-destroy mission…you guessed it—around the same village. That merry-go-round and cat-and-mouse game would never end, and it was going on all over Vietnam. Until 1968–1969, I think our guys were always outnumbered by the NVA and VC out in the bush. I doubt that General Westmoreland cared about how many times we helped the local villagers. His main concern was…BODY COUNT!

Westmoreland would be relieved of his command, and with his departure, so went the search-and-destroy mission insanity. And ten years after the first American military advisors arrived in 1962, at the end of 1972, they were all gone.

Heroes of My Lai? Most who will read this book won't remember any other names who were involved in the My Lai Massacre, other than Calley. I had just arrived in-country in March 1968 when this disgraceful and unforgivable happening occurred. Sorry for mentioning My Lai again. And I'll bet no one reading can name even one Vietnamese victim of that day.

In 1998, thirty years after the highly controversial massacre, three men were awarded the Soldier's Medal, our nation's highest award for bravery not involving direct contact with the enemy. Lawrence Colburn, Glenn Andreotta, and Hugh Thompson, Jr. (all deceased) became known as the "Heroes of My Lai" as it was their actions in defending innocent villagers from continued slaughter by Lt. Calley, the main culprit of the gruesome event that would darken opinions and memories of the entire Vietnam War.

In December 2016, Lawrence M. Colburn, a helicopter gunner in the Vietnam War, died as Agent Orange caught up to him decades after he left Vietnam. Coburn was a young sixty-seven years old and the last survivor of the "Heroes of My Lai." He was diagnosed with Agent Orange-related cancer in September 2016 and lost his last battle with the Vietnam War on December 13, 2016.

On January 6, 2006, at the age of sixty-two, former U.S. Army Captain Hugh C. Thompson Jr. was also taken down by the poisons of the Vietnam War as his battle with cancer ended his heroic life. Thompson was the captain of his Hiller OH-23 Raven Observation helicopter crew along with Colburn (gunner) and Andreotta (crew chief).

Glenn U. Andreotta, the helicopter crew chief for Warrant Thompson at the My Lai incident, never left Vietnam alive. During his second tour in Vietnam as Andreotta was serving as a door-gunner on a combat assault mission, he was killed by enemy fire on April 8, 1968.

Warrant Officer (at the time) Thompson was quoted to say this about Andreotta:

> - *Glenn Andreotta—if there was a hero, I don't like that word, but if there was a hero at My Lai, it was Glenn Andreotta, because he saw movement in that ditch, and he fixed in on this one little kid and went down into that ditch. I would not want to go in that ditch. It's not pretty. It was very bad. I can imagine what was going through his mind down there, because there was more than one still alive—people grabbing hold of his pants wanting to help. "I can't help you. You're too bad off." He found this one kid and brought the kid back up and handed it to Larry and we laid it across Larry and my lap and took him out of there. I remember thinking Glenn Andreotta put himself where nobody in their right mind would want to be. And he was driven by something. I haven't got the aircraft on the ground real stable. He bolted out of the aircraft into this ditch. Now he was a hero. Glenn Andreotta gave his life for his country about three weeks later. That's the kind of guy he was, and he was a hero to his last day.*

Until Thompson's crew intervened, people were being executed and thrown into the ditch Thompson refers to. He intervened, even threatened to shoot any of Calley's platoon if they attempted to kill any more of the fleeing children. The full story of My Lai can be easily researched from multiple sources as books and movies about it resulted.

Thompson, who reported the massacre in progress, also testified at court hearings after the "cover-up" of the tragedy became known to the public. In 1998, Thompson and Colburn returned to the scene of the crime of 1968 to the village of Son My, where they sought out and met with some of the people they had saved. Even though Thompson would testify against twenty-six soldiers for My Lai and some were charged with criminal offenses, all were acquitted or pardoned.

I've chosen to make no further mention of Calley, but one can find his entire story on multiple sources if they wish..

Unfortunately, Thompson was condemned and ostracized by some in the military and United States government, and even by some of the public citizens. I guess the feeling was…after all, they were only "gooks." How very, very sad.

Hugh Clowers Thompson, Jr., as a direct result of what he experienced in Vietnam and after Vietnam, suffered from severe PTSD, alcoholism, divorce, and a severe nightmare disorder until the day he died. I would have been proud to serve with him and his buddies; they were perfect examples of being **as tough as they come—and I love them.**

Major General Flint, Author, Platoon Member Martino

How Tough Were They? This is a fairly simplistic analysis but I think it is a fair and honest one as the numbers don't lie. From 1962–1965 before Americans had much of a presence in Vietnam, the south Vietnamese were getting beaten badly and often by the Viet Cong/NVA forces. From 1966–1970, the South Vietnamese were aided by superior American firepower and tens of thousands of combat-trained soldiers and marines who were not bashful in taking it to the enemy in head-on confrontations. At the end of this period, especially 1967–1969, the once mighty Viet Cong who terrorized South Vietnam at their pleasure were no longer a formidable fighting force. In fact they had been nearly exterminated, and the Vietnam War seemed to be coming to an end. It should have come to an end, but the incompetent politicians in Washington, D.C. came through with enough stupid moves that would allow the communists plenty of time to recover while our forces were being downsized way too prematurely. Quickly North Vietnam would have the Viet Cong back as a serious fighting force, along with hundreds of thousands of new recruits for North Vietnam's army. In 1973–1975, there was no longer an American-allied military force and there would be a very weak and toothless South Vietnam military left to fight on their own as they were pretty much doing from 1959–1963.

- 1965 was the year of several major confrontations, causing both sides to suffer more casualties that year than in 1959–1964 combined. The conflict was pretty much a stalemate between the allies and communists.
- In 1966–1969, over two million Americans fought in the war. This was 80 percent of the total 2.8 million who fought in-country from 1959–1972. In more than thirty major battles where Americans met the enemy head-on, enemy losses would end up at a 1-5 advantage to the Americans.
- In 1971–1972, American ground forces were pretty much nonexistent, but American artillery and air support remained. The casualties on each side were almost even again, with a slight advantage to the South Vietnamese, but that would be short lived.
- In 1973–1975, all American-allied forces were removed. Those last few years would prove just how effective American soldiers and marines were during the bloodiest years of 1966–1969. In 1973–1975, the North Vietnamese/Viet Cong snarled the South Vietnamese, inflicting casualties at an alarming 5-1—almost a complete reversal of the American ground forces' 4-1 advantage over the enemy.

The Tet Offensive from January to March 1968 was one of the largest and deadliest all-out ground ambushes in military history. Virtually every city and hamlet in South Vietnam was viciously attacked by unannounced Viet Cong-style ambushes with the support of North Vietnamese Army Regulars (NVA). This would be the ultimate test for the American troops and the allies as they had not faced anything comparable to this in the Vietnam War up till that time.

How fiercely did the United States military respond to this monstrous ambush? Ameri-Cong media portrayed this bloody event for both sides as a victory for the communists. A bigger lie that was topped when that same Ameri-Cong media would label their fellow Americans as being conscienceless, ruthless…**Baby Killers.**

Yes, the Americans counterattacked with a vengeance that the enemy attackers had never imagined. In fact, so fierce was the American/allies' response that several Vietnam veteran officers who had fought in Korea and even World War II stated they had never seen Americans fight more bravely and as intensely in face-to-face combat as the combat Vietnam soldiers and marines did in that war.

Jungle Warfare and Green Faces—Beware! Rumor has it that the U.S. Navy SEAL Teams were created at the insistence of Mr. PT-109 himself, John F. Kennedy, in 1962. Great timing as the greatest guerrilla war in history was barely into its infancy stage in South Vietnam.

The Navy SEAL Teams were established and designed as the maritime counterpart to the Army Special Forces Green Berets and the Airborne Rangers, also of the Army. Almost immediately they were thrown into action with a critically important mission to work with the Phoenix Program to capture high-ranking Viet Cong leaders in southern Vietnam. The SEALs were so tough and so effective that the Viet Cong quickly learned to recognize them with their green faces…if and when they were fortunate to actually see them. Usually that was after being ambushed and/or captured by those green-faced men.

The Navy SEALs tried to help turn the war around in the early 1960s, but Americans didn't have the upper hand. Their most important contribution was probably their ability to effectively disrupt the enemy's lines of communication. You couldn't put a price tag on that. Operating primarily in the Delta region where there were thousands of rivers and canals, they would often get in the way of night-traveling Viet Cong on waterways.[19] At Normandy's D-Day invasion they were referred to as the Scouts and Raiders Team. In the South Pacific on the island of Tarawa, they were known as the Navy Combat Swimmers and Raiders as well as Naval Combat Demolition Teams. In the Korean War or the "forgotten war," the Underwater Demolition Teams (UDTs) fought heroically, and as usual, few ever knew about their accomplishments. They targeted bridges, warships, tunnels, and sea mine disposals. The UDT also built a strong relationship with the Republic of Korea (ROK) in training their own Navy SEALs, who are still active today.

The UDT's skills for conducting beach and river reconnaissance, inserting guerrillas behind enemy lines, had tested their traditional activities, expanding their capabilities that suited them perfectly in the Vietnam War. The South Vietnamese who were trained by the new Navy SEAL teams were called "soldiers that fight under the sea" or in Vietnamese "Lien Doc Nguoi Nhia" (LDNN).

It was obvious that the U.S. government had a bias toward the Army Green Berets. So the Navy, feeling this favoritism from the administration, established their own guerrilla and counter-guerrilla units, which would become the official Navy SEALs. These units quickly adapted to the jungle warfare style that was necessary in Vietnam. These newly organized units would become efficient from sea, inland waterways, air, and by land.

---

19 https://navyseals.com/nsw/navy-seal history

By the 1963–64 timeframe, the LDNN was starting to be recognized for success with their missions, so their area of operations was expanded into central South Vietnam and even to the DMZ area operating out of Da Nang. The SEALs and Brown Water Navy Boat Crews made it their job to impede enemy troop movement by the waterways. Combat with the Viet Cong became very close and personal, like it already was for the Army's infantry grunts and of course the marines. Killing at close range and responding, counter-ambushing, etc. without hesitation became an absolute requirement in order to stay living.

In 1967–68, a SEAL unit was formed to operate the mixed US/ARVN units which became known as the South Vietnamese Provincial Reconnaissance Units (PRU). The PRUs were intensely active with the Phoenix Program.

I had the opportunity of participating in a few combat recon exercises or Mobile Support Teams. They were the guys who operated the patrol boat, riverine (PBR) units, and swift boats. Later in the war from 1968–1971, they were highly successful in training South Vietnamese soldiers into a special unit called South Vietnamese Commandos. Everything I've read on this points to a very successful venture with this program. Even before the SEALs arrived in South Vietnam, the Army's Special Forces were having good results with their training of ARVNs into Vietnamese Special Forces Rangers.

The green-faced Navy SEALs of the Vietnam War were said to have been established in 1962. SEAL Teams One and Two were to bring Navy Unconventional Warfare capability as soon as possible to the Vietnam War. The obvious and most important mission for them was to conduct effective counter guerilla warfare against the best guerilla fighters in the world at that time, the resilient Viet Cong.

Twinsburg, Ohio's, SEAL Connection to three well-known Navy SEAL brothers, accompanied by their mother Susan McDonald Andexler and step-father Charles Andexler: I grew up with Suzy and Chuck in Twinsburg, and we're proud of her sons' famous exploits with SEAL Team 6 and other teams.

I never ran into the SEALs when I was in the Vietnam War, and oh God, would I have cherished the experience. Honestly, my war buddies and I were not even aware of their presence in-country when we were there. In my post-Vietnam years it's been a pleasure to meet several of those Bad Frogs. In fact my ears have been burned from one of my best friends since our early teen years when we were Little League baseballers together and against each other. Billy McDonald grew up or lived in the same towns I did, Aurora and Twinsburg, Ohio. He was one of those famous "we fight too" Navy Sea-bees in Vietnam when I was pounding my boots on the ground as an Army grunt. Anyway, amongst the baker's dozen of McDonald kids in their fam-ily—I knew them all—was Suzy McDonald, whom every red-blooded boy had a crush on at one time in their life. If they were really lucky, she may have noticed you. I was not one of them. Seriously, Suzy McDonald was probably the cutest, friendliest, and loveliest little blonde to ever walk the halls of the Aurora and Twinsburg school systems. Today she is known as Suzy Andexler, and she married her high school crush and my good friend Charles "Chuck" Andexler, the second time around for both of them.

Suzy did her best to contribute to the security of our great country; in fact she made three generous contributions that America is still benefitting greatly from. Her three stupendous contributions have names, boy names. Suzy's three sons are Adam, Jake, and Luke Newbold, all three lifetime and highly accomplished U.S. Navy SEALs.

I don't have enough space to elaborate on their adventurous careers, but anyone interested can look them up by conducting a little online research. Official SEAL Teams never existed. In the 2014 book *Navy SEALS: Their Untold Story,* the U.S. Department of Defense almost never publicly acknowledges the existence of the Naval Special Warfare Department Group.

As I understand, the general Navy SEAL organization includes nine unclassified teams. SEAL Team Six has been well-known for carrying out some of the more risky missions that combat military units are involved with. One of those missions was the seeking, capturing, and killing of Osama Bin Laden. Since September 11, 2001, Team Six and the other Navy SEALs have been more active than ever, participating in missions from Afghanistan to Iraq. Many of their operations are so high-impact that it would be difficult for the larger, conventional forces to engage.

Adam, Chuck, Suzy, Luke, Jake

Nearing the end of the Vietnam War, a small group of SEAL teams were sent on a mission in June 1972 which began off the coast of North Vietnam. The leader of this mission, called Operation Thunderhead, was Philip L. "Moki" Martin. This highly classified mission was meant to locate and rescue American prisoners of war who were in the process of attempting to escape a North Vietnamese prison in Hanoi. If this reminds any readers of the series of *Missing in Action* movies starring Chuck Norris, I got the same notion when I read about Operation Thunderhead. This mission was so highly classified, like many SEAL missions are, that it was not declassified and made available to the public until 2008, some thirty-six years later.

Initially Operation Thunderhead called for several four-man SEAL teams to begin their mission in darkness in mini-submarines to a small island nearly two miles off the main coast where they had hoped to meet up with the POW escapees. Disaster would strike and prevent this mission from the success everyone had planned for. The twenty-foot Swimmer Delivery Vehicle (SDV) was tested with unforeseen difficulty because of unexpected surface and tidal currents which forced a premature termination of the SDV's battery. Dry and Martin and the other team members together swam the SDV further out to sea to keep it from the North Vietnamese. Waiting in the water for another seven hours, when a Navy rescue helicopter finally arrived, they sank the SDV and were taken to the cruiser *Long Beach*. Quickly Martin and his team contacted and warned the other SEAL teams about the rough currents.

A day and a half later on June 5, 1972, the helicopter carrying Dry, Martin, and the rest of the team spotted a signal at sea from another team. Operation Thunderhead had been aborted but Martin's team hadn't received the news yet. Poor weather conditions presented poor visibility, and altitude reading was too difficult.

Dye and Martin made jumps anyway, with Dye being killed on impact of the water. Martin survived the bone-crushing impact, but his leg was badly damaged and he was left barely conscious. Martin had already rescued two injured SEAL team members and recovered the dead body of team member Dye. This mission was finally awarded the Navy and Marine Corps Commendation Medals with the prestigious "V" for valor.

On March 18, 2008, a medal ceremony took place in Coronado, California. Moki Martin was physically decorated with his award. He accepted while in a wheelchair as a quadriplegic. After his discharge from active duty in May 1983, Martin remained an active member of the Naval Special Warfare community, giving lectures to Basic Underwater Demolition/SEAL students. His primary lecture topic was "Lessons learned in Vietnam."

Approximately fifty SEALs died in-country during the war, and a similar number were wounded. That doesn't seem like a significant amount of casualties since 58,479 Americans died overall during the war. But the SEALs' contribution was felt. I guarantee that it was…I saw it.

The last SEAL platoon departed from Vietnam in 1971.

Marines Fix Bayonets at Dai Do! The Battle of Dai Do would barely allow the Americans in I Corps enough time to catch their breath from the huge battles at Khe Sanh and Hue. The siege at Khe Sanh lasted seventy-seven days. America's upper-level military leaders, Westmoreland included, would repeat an ongoing mistake by underestimating their adversary's resilience and tenacity. Communist casualties during Tet I 1968 totaled over 100,000 killed, wounded, or taken prisoner. These staggering numbers gave the Americans a dangerous false sense of security, arrogance, and overconfidence, which was nothing new to western militaries.

Quang Tri Province in northeast I Corps was always under threat of attack because the area was directly in the path the North Vietnamese Army needed to take in order to advance further south, down the east coast. But once again few military minds believed the NVA would be able to launch another attack of the magnitude during the Tet Offensive. I Corps was commanded by Major General Rathvon McClure Topkins, with Colonel Milton Hull the 3rd Marine regiment commander and Lt. Col. William Weise the 2nd battalion commander. A biography of Weise, now a retired brigadier general, is scheduled to publish in November 2018, titled *One Magnificent Bastard*.

The Battle of Dai Do could just as easily be titled in the Latin or Zulu languages. I hope the information I have scraped up about it, with the limited space I have here, will do proper justice to it and the great American heroes who fought and died in that place in Vietnam. Honestly, many thousands of lives were affected by these small nameless battles, and the legacy of their iconic warriors can never receive enough mentions in American history.

By the end of May 1968, I had already survived two months of heavy combat exposure and was starting to wonder how much longer my luck would hold out. But that was in God's hands as I just went about doing my job as a combat infantry point man. I had just missed the January-February Tet Offensive, but things were stirring up for another one, Tet II they were calling it. And it came as more than 120 provincial and district capitals, military firebases, and major cities from Danang to Saigon were targeted. While Tet I was mostly a Viet Cong planned uprising, Tet II was going to have an all North Vietnam Army participation.

On April 29, 1968, it was the 3rd Marine Division's turn again, and their headquarters at Dong Ha had the entire 320th Division of NVA licking their chops. No one could have guessed that May 1968 would end up the bloodiest month of the entire war. Again our military leaders had underestimated our very worthy adversary.

First In—Last Out? Dai Do wasn't Iwo Jima nor does it matter who were the first troops in or the last ones out of Vietnam. Most marines probably believe their own motto…"first in—last out," and few of us non-marines care to dispute that from earlier wars. So then, since I opened the story of this book featuring the legendary marine sniper Carlos Hathcock, it would be quite fitting to finish this chapter about uncommon heroism with a marine story, and there are plenty to select from. The old Army-Marine rivalry should be a healthy one, not a competition for who was the greatest of all time in something. After all, we wouldn't ever pit Daniel Boone against Davy Crockett or George Washington against Dwight Eisenhower. Of course not. But pitting a liberal against a conservative is different.

Army, Air Force, Coast Guard, Marines, Navy—members of these branches all have very important jobs and are trained specifically to perform those jobs in order to complete an important mission successfully. And in Vietnam, I believe it was actually the Army's Special Forces/Green Berets who went in first during the 1955–1959 time frame. But Army or Marine, we all pretty much went everywhere the other went, and we were usually a formidable team. None of our battles in Vietnam went down in history as being world-changing or famous for turning the tide of a war, such as Yorktown, Gettysburg, Normandy, Iwo Jima, Chosin Reservoir, etc. So most people reading this book will not be familiar with most battles I have mentioned. Nor will you be likely to have heard of the Battle of Dai Do. I hadn't until a marine buddy of mine mentioned it at a 2016 American Legion meeting in Chagrin Falls, Ohio. I have been testing other non-marine veterans, but so far I have not found even one who could tell me they had heard of the Battle of Dai Do. I say to that…**Do your research on your war troop!**

The hardly remembered Battle of Dai Do[20] was documented as one of the fiercest, bloodiest, and most complex in-your-face brawls of the entire Vietnam War. The initial activity which was to set off the battles to follow happened in the morning of April 29, 1968, when two full battalions of an ARVN infantry division were ambushed by an unknown-sized NVA force. The ARVNs were in a critical fight in a retreat-or-die predicament. A task force of one rifle company and a full armored company with tanks was summoned to back up the seriously troubled ARVN division. The task force was ambushed almost immediately by another large NVA mob. The task force was mauled, taking forty casualties in quick fashion, and four tanks were destroyed, forcing the task force to lick their wounds and retreat.

---

20 amtrac.org

One survivor in the task force described things in this paraphrased fashion:

It was nothing like I had experienced in Nam so far. The noise was deafening. I saw smoke and red dust clouds rising higher than the trees. I had fired all kinds of weapons in my short time in Nam but I had to ask guys what it was that I was seeing. It was NVA-fired artillery and mortar shells, and crew-served enemy rockets. I didn't know the NVA had such weapons. I thought all of the other guys looked much older than they said they were; they were filthy, grungy, torn fatigues, had boots on that looked like a thousand miles had been put on them and me…well, I looked like a polished penny. Then suddenly I was rattled and jumped up as I heard the order to saddle up. We were going back out. I thought we would get a little break after limping back in from the earlier battle…not a chance.

—U.S. Marine Corporal (paraphrased), Battle of Dae Do 1968

Dai Do Survivor
Ted Rood, Marine
Chagrin Falls, Ohio

By this time the village of Dai Do itself was filled with dead and critically wounded everywhere—dead NVA, dead civilians, dead animals, and dead marines. The NVA had fortified bunkers and tunnels in place, and it was one ambush followed by another. There were 130-millimeter artillery shells pummeling the village that sounded like freight trains coming down to disintegrate any living thing that was still walking or crawling. Despite all of this heavy fire and heavy presence of NVA soldiers, the marine companies continued to advance. The setting was now…hundreds taking the fight to thousands. These marines kept advancing and taking ground by counterattacking the NVA ambushes.

By this time into May 2nd the marine companies were operating at 50-55 percent effective strength, and there were still thousands of NVA rampaging around Dai Do and other hamlets nearby. As I read well into the stories of this battle, I could understand and appreciate the abnormal, near superhuman tenacity of a few hundred marines turning loose onto an entire division of battle-hardened North Vietnamese Army regulars.

Fortunately, the F-4 Phantoms were working overtime with their Napalm, the navy gunfire, and artillery crews weren't taking any breaks either, and so the small marine companies continued their aggressive counterattacks, taking more turf from the NVA.

Good grief, I can visualize and feel the pain, anguish, and adrenaline of these men as I continue reading about Dai Do. Damn, what supernatural force motivated these men to advance, take a wound, get up, advance some more, and hang tough on the turf he has gained? **Where Did America Get Men Like This?**

If there are still those out there who continue to doubt the credibility, heart, and bravery of America's Vietnam War veterans, they should study up. They can easily find recently updated facts provided willingly by the government of modern-day Vietnam:

Hanoi now admits to losing 1.4 million soldiers compared to the 58,400 Americans who died in-country during Vietnam's war with America.

Back on the battlefield around Dai Do, the companies of the 2nd and 4th Marines were pulling off nothing short of more than one miracle as they out-maneuvered and out shot the confused NVA attackers. It was now almost as if the roles had been reversed as the marines were no longer playing defense. Creating bold and brilliant diversions, they broke out of situations where they were pinned down or even surrounded on three sides, and repelled one enemy advance after another. These marines kept fighting with an attitude. The results of this battle would reward the marines for the extra time they spent on the shooting ranges back in boot camp.

Late in the day on May 2nd, frustrated at being outmaneuvered and out shot, the enemy suddenly launched a massive human wave onslaught in a cleared area. It would be a fatal mistake they would regret. Aircraft arrived and pinpoint artillery was called in, taking full advantage of the NVA's irrational decision. Hundreds of enemy bodies drenched the open clearing with blood and body parts. When the third day of the Battle of Dai Do had finally ended, NVA casualties would number in the thousands.

At the end of the day on May 2, the 2/4's numbers had been reduced: Company E had forty-five men, Company F had fifty-two, Company G thirty-five, and Company H had sixty-four live bodies remaining. These marines have been memorialized by the 2/4 Association and are affectionately known as the "Magnificent Bastards." The total losses from April 30 to May 3 for this unknown but epic battle were shocking;

3rd Marine Division…	233 KIA	821 WIA
The Navy…	15 KIA	22 WIA
ARVN losses were	<u>42 KIA</u>	<u>124 WIA</u>
	290 KIA	967 WIA
North Vietnamese	2,366 KIA	N/A WIA/POWs

The exact body count of the NVA force is still unknown as the NVA were known to drag their dead away from the battlefields whenever possible. Regardless, Dai Do was a major victory in that it was another devastating setback in North Vietnam's plan to invade South Vietnam. Of the remaining men of the 2/4 Marines, most of them had been wounded at some time in the battle. In fact, it became a tongue-and-cheek, humorous comment that the Purple Heart had almost become the unit badge for the 2/4th.

Obviously many troops were bestowed with well-deserved awards for valor at Dai Do. Two heroic warriors were awarded the Medal of Honor, Captains James E. Livingston and Jay R. Vargas.

Retired 2/4 Battalion Commander Brigadier General Bill "Wild Bill" Weise would last for thirty-one years as an active duty marine; his last whereabouts had him in good health in Florida in December 2017.

A fighting spirit against all odds has been almost standard mentality with the Marine Corps. An example of this, whether true or a tale, takes us to the Belleau woods in WWI. After a major German breakthrough in 1918, the marines had just arrived to help when a French officer frantically approached them, explaining a general retreat was ordered. The marine commanding officer was reported to yell back…"Retreat, hell! We just got here." Then the marines proved their worth and forced a German retreat. Oh, those marines were sure something.

After the Battle of Dai Do was long over, where one-half day of hand-to-hand fighting took place, there was an enduring reminder discovered at the scene of where the marines had advanced their position. Among the dead bodies of NVA and marines lay one marine sprawled across the battlefield with his head on the edge of an NVA bunker, the bayonet of his ammo-empty rifle planted directly in the dead NVA machine gunner's chest.

I dare anyone to try to tell these Vietnam vet marines who fought against and profoundly overcame overwhelming odds that they didn't fight in a real war, that they were not as tough as the marines before them. Worse yet, I dare anyone to step up and refer to them today as baby killers!

Where did we get such men? Simple answer might be their bloodline could be traced back to those heroic marines of World War II, the men they emulated…their dads. Are marines tough enough?

Marines—Love 'Em or Not? The U.S. Marines are said to have originated at an old tavern in the Philadelphia area called Tun Tavern. This was
the local watering hole where a committee of new U.S. government offi-
cials-to-be founded the Marine Corps. The resolution was officially approved
on November 10, 1775, which formed the Continental Marines. Therefore, I
believe every November 10th is a big day for them; it's their birthday.

Samuel Nicholas became the marines' first commander, and they were
ready for action in 1775. Tun Tavern was open for business in 1686 at the
intersection of King (now Water) Street and Tun Alley. Tun Tavern's fame
doesn't rest solely on the backs of the new marines. There were a number
of lesser known organizations that were born at this location, such as the St.
George (Sons of Liberty) Society, the St. Andrews, and most notably the
Free Masonry Masonic Lodge of America. That tavern had really good beer.

Tun Tavern burned down in 1783 near the end of our American Revolution. Tun Alley no longer exists either, having been replaced by Interstate 95.
There is a marker commemorating this historical structure at Front Street.

There is another pub now located in Atlantic City, New Jersey, called Tun
Tavern Restaurant and Brewery. The U.S. Marine Corps National Museum
in Quantico, Virginia, contains a Tun Tavern-themed restaurant. Some legends will always keep living on, especially if it happens to be marine related.

So, how can you not like the marines, created in a bar in the city of broth-
erly love. And…THEY WIN BATTLES! I rest my case; let's keep them.

The 25th Infantry's Walking Regulars 1967–68. We weren't in the
most famous battles, like Hamburger Hill, Khe Sanh, Hue, Dak To, or Dai
Do. Those were all fought in the northernmost provinces of I Corps, where
arguably the most intense fighting of the Vietnam War took place from 1965
to 1967. We take our hats off to those brothers who really mixed it up at
places close to the Ashau Valley near the Laos border and even the DMZ.

A few hundred miles south where the war "seemed to be" a little quieter, a real storm had been brewing in an area where the Ho Chi Minh Trail
ended, dumping tens of thousands of well-trained, eager-to-kill North Vietnamese Army Regulars. Eventually places like Tay Ninh, Loc Ninh, Katum,
Cu Chi, Nui Ba Den, Trang Bang, Duc Hoa, and Dau Tieng would command
more attention from the American military leaders and their allies. All of
these places sat in between Cambodia and Saigon: Bien Hoa, Cholon, and
Tan Son Nhat, where the allied forces' main command and the South Vietnamese government resided. From 1967–1969, the combat units from the
1st Infantry and 25th Infantry Divisions would be called on to bear the brunt
of the repeated NVA attempts to reach the Saigon area, especially in 1968.

Soon MACV heads began to relocate reinforcements from I Corps
by sending thousands of troops from the 1st Cavalry Air Mobile Infantry

Division. This area of III Corps was known to harbor the underground headquarters of the Viet Cong. There were no marines or 101st Airborne combat troops here, Walter Cronkite would never be seen here, and rarely were there any Associated Press reporters. But significant warfare raged here, and on-the-scene casualties in III Corps would shock the military leaders and the bureaucrats back home in Washington, D.C. Although the Ameri-Cong media would show up to report on activity around the Saigon area, they would rarely be present when a small base camp in the Iron Triangle or Bolor Woods was hit with a deadly "human wave" attack out in the boonies where safe and secure outposts, firebases, and LZs just did not exist outside of Cu Chi, the 25th Division's main headquarters.

In 1967, 1968, and 1969, the NVA Regulars and their VC allies would be confronted twenty-four/seven by brave, ferocious warriors from units like the Wolfhounds, Manchus, ¾ Cav, and the Walking Regulars from the 3rd Battalion 22nd Infantry, plus many other key support combat companies including artillery armor and assault helicopters.

I was initially assigned to the 2nd Battalion 12th Infantry for a few weeks before being transferred to Bravo Company of the 3rd 22nd, both 25th Infantry Division Brigades. Of course I did not know this at the time, but one of our war buddies from Bravo 3rd 22nd would later become a famous actor, producer, and writer named Oliver Stone. His movie *Platoon*, part fiction, part nonfiction, was his story of what an infantry battalion might have experienced during its one-year tour of duty. I never met Oliver Stone over there, but it is very possible that we participated in several missions together in April and May 1968.

As the Vietnam War was shocking the world in 1967 and 1968, the Walking Regulars were building a reputation within the 25th Infantry and all of III Corps, and I wish to describe some of the activities the 3rd 22nd was heavily engaged in.

Suoi Tre, March 1967. This would become known as the largest single-day battle of the war to this point. At the war's end, Suoi Tre kept that distinction. For ten hours, four hundred men of the 3rd Battalion were under a nonstop human wave attack at night, by 2,500 hard-core guerrillas from the 272nd NVA Regiment with Viet Cong support. A Company, B Company, and C Company were heavily engaged as the enemy force attacked all sides of the fire base perimeter. On occasion Firebase Gold was overrun and certain elements of the battalion became surrounded, requiring reinforcements. At one point Bravo Company's first platoon was completely overrun. A Cessna O-LE Bird Dog directed one airstrike but was shot down immediately after, killing pilot and observer. Howitzers were blasting, and the 2-77 Artillery was responding viciously to reinforce the surrounded first platoon. A company managed to send a twenty-man rescue force to help B Company's first platoon. But another human wave attack had put all of Bravo Company in serious danger, and the twenty men from A Company were caught in the attack. An AC-47 Dragon Ship showed up with Gatling guns firing at the enemy who were in open spaces. F-100s and F-4 Phantoms began to arrive as Artillery batteries were running out of ammunition, as was Bravo's first platoon. VC and NVA had penetrated close enough to force bayonets to be fixed for use in face-to-face combat.

In the nick of time a force of infantry men from the 2-12th Infantry arrived and joined up with Bravo 3rd 22nd and together they reestablished the original perimeter. To make matters worse for the NVA and VC, elements of a sister battalion of the 3rd 22nd, the 2nd 22nd Mechanized Infantry and Army, arrived and swept forward almost unchallenged. Soon the attackers would be in full retreat. Mopping up began, and medivac helicopters did their job.

Total Enemy Casualties Estimated	841 KIA	1,300 WIA
Total American Casualties	31 KIA	187 WIA
	872 KIA	1,487 WIA (2,359)

The rest of 1967 would be like one big Suoi Tre for the 3rd 22nd of the 25th Infantry. Wherever they went, it seemed there was an ample supply of Viet Cong or North Vietnamese Army Regulars available to keep things interesting. In 1968…things got worse!

Soui Cut, January 1968. Firebase Burt sat near the Soui Cut River near the Cambodian border not far from the scene of the crime at Suoi Tre nine months earlier. Only three days after the fire support base had been built, four battalions of Main Force Viet Cong conducted an all-out attack, attempting to overrun the newly built base.

Again the attacked defenders were members of the 25th Infantry's 3rd Brde same one at Suoi Tre. The VC at Soui Cut were also part of the same VC battalion (272nd) at Suoi Tre—reinforced of course! This huge one-night battle unfolded and ended in similar fashion to Suoi Tre. The 3rd 22nd was outnumbered by 12-1 odds, but the Americans would be victorious. Oliver Stone fought in this battle.

Total Enemy Casualties (estimated)	382 KIA	600 WIA
American Casualties	23 KIA	153 WIA
	405 KIA	753 WIA (1,158)

Ap Cho, February 1968. This significant battle had a different script for the 3rd 22nd who were actually called on to seek out and destroy what was believed to be a large communist force positioned a few kilometers from Cu Chi. They were already well dug in with fortified bunkers. They were also aside a main supply route for convoys, so this was completely unacceptable. The fact that they were hidden in thick woods made it even more difficult for the American infantry men to take out this unknown-sized enemy force. The 3rd 22nd Walking Regulars with Charlie Company in the lead had only one choice, to attack the fortified positions daily for as long as it took, at whatever cost for the Americans. The battle would not end in one day; it lasted almost two weeks. Inch by inch, hacking away from hootch to hootch. Little by little the Americans gained more ground, taking bunkers one by one in marine-style combat. But there were no reporters here for this battle, not while the 1968 Tet Offensive was rampaging all over South Vietnam, occupying TV sets back in America.

The full thirteen-day battle was fiercely fought by both sides. It became obvious that the enemy on this day had no backup plan of retreating to their tunnels. These were NVA Regulars who had no intentions of surrendering or fleeing. They were prepared to fight to the end, just like the Japanese often did in WWII. These were North Vietnamese, they had their own pride and heritage to protect and live up to, and besides, it was their country that America invaded.

The 3rd BN 22nd went out each morning, bayonets fixed, freshly supplied with hand grenades and M-798 law launchers. Later, during the thirteen-day battle, they were joined by the 4-23rd Mechanized and ¾ Cavalry Mechanized units. The last day there were over thirty airstrikes unleashed, and the final assault was on until the battle ended.

Total Enemy Casualties	288 KIA	N/A WIA
		300 Estimated WIA
Total American Casualties	50 KIA	134 WIA
	338 KIA	434 WIA (772)

Good Friday, April 11, 1968. The 3rd BN 22nd Walking Regulars took to the air for this one, climbing aboard choppers into a remote jungle halfway between the outpost of Dau Tieng and the Cambodian border. Pulling a search-and-destroy mission after they landed, the Walking Regulars had few daylight hours remaining, but they hastily dug foxholes and filled as many sandbags as they could. They made themselves as comfortable as possible, pulled a few shifts of guard duty, and at 4:00 on Good Friday morning…**All Hell Broke Loose!**

The enemy launched over 125 mortar rockets, 61- and 82-millimeter mortar rounds. The rounds were usually accurately directed, almost all of them falling inside the small camp's perimeter. As usual a massive ground assault followed, with Bravo Company in the direct path of the main thrust of the attack. Despite the arrival of artillery rounds called in by Battalion Commander LTC Roy K. Flint, the Viet Cong kept coming, intensifying the human wave attack.

Bravo Company was pushed back, but comrades from Charlie and Delta Companies rallied to their backsides, and the north perimeter line was taken back. Once again the 3rd BN 22nd's sister battalion, the 2nd 22nd (Triple Device), came rambling to the battle, fighting off one ambush after another through five miles of triple-canopy jungle at night to aid their brothers. The rout was on as the enemy was pursued in their retreat, and more of them would die.

Total Enemy Casualties Estimated	206 KIA	WIA-N/A
		300 Estimated
Total American Casualties	15 KIA	47 WIA
	221 KIA	347 WIA (568)

Overall from these four battles for the 3rd BN 22nd, casualties for both adversaries totaled up to:

$$1{,}836 \text{ KIA} + 3{,}021 \text{ WIA} = \qquad 4{,}857 \text{ Total}[21]$$

ABSOLUTION is the title of a book authored by one of our own Walking Regulars, Charles J. Boyle of Charlie Company 3rd Battalion, 22nd Infantry. I am going to respectfully share one of his final messages from his fine book.

Between 1960 and 1978, hundreds of thousands of young men, many of them barely teenagers, were thrust into the barbarity of an Asian Civil War. They were inadequately trained for jungle warfare, and initially armed with a defective weapon (M-16), so they acquired their "killer skills" by instinct and imagination. Transformed by necessity, these genteel sons quickly became fearless gladiators that their government's politicians sent them to be. Then, undermining their gallant service, a powerful and highly biased news media created negative myths that quickly spread across America. "The only war we ever lost," Americans began saying. They (the media) wanted Americans to believe that the Vietnam War's soldiers lost the war, when in fact, we lost only our youth, our innocence and way too many

---

21 https://C322 association.org

of our brothers. The Vietnam War veterans were some of the finest soldiers that ever served America…believe that, America. Vietnam veterans served. They fought. They died. Vietnam veterans received neither their country's glory nor their country's compassion.

So went a typical twelve-month tour for the combat infantry men of the 3rd BN Walking Regulars, handpicking just four battles of the dozens this 25th Infantry Battalion engaged in. They took several casualties, earned dozens of high military awards, and inflicted massive destruction onto an enemy that was relentless, resilient, and respected.

Participating in just one of these battles would most definitely leave permanent memories, especially the images of the men you watched helplessly die in front of you…from both sides.

How tough were these men? As tough as they needed to be or were forced to be! Think about it the next time you meet up with a Vietnam War veteran who fought with one of America's proud and honorable combat units in the war that most of America has been trying to forget. We who were there have not forgotten. It is simply not possible to do that.

There is no gloat here. I am simply comparing apples to apples to illustrate how well the Americans fought in direct combat on foreign soil in an extremely unfriendly environment. Needless to say the North Vietnamese/Viet Cong forces fought with far more conviction, determination, and ruthless vengeance than their southern countrymen.

Nearing the end of America's presence in Vietnam, 1970–1972, the war was changing almost weekly because of the massive support of the war machines and supplies from China and Russia. The North Viets were taking down B-52 bombers and fighter jets with anti-aircraft missiles. American mechanized units, even tanks were being hit hard by rocket-propelled grenades (RPGs), and our helicopters were being knocked out of combat by the hundreds, sometimes in just one month.

My point in this section is that the disparity in casualty numbers during the early years compared to the peak years and then to the end, when Americans were at home while the war raged, seems to provide profoundly powerful evidence that America's combat troops were well challenged by an underrated enemy. But the Americans most definitely stepped up to the plate. Their motivation certainly was not spurred on by the non-support they were getting from the home front. The fury for which they fought as well as any American ever fought in a war was sure and simple…they fought for the brotherhood that had been built in those long days and nights in the swamps and jungles of a country with vicious, unforgettable, unfriendly elements.

Our enemy's brave and witty leader was also gentlemanly enough to compliment his American adversary. One of those compliments was mentioned earlier; here is another:

> Do not fear the enemy, for they can only take your life. Fear the media far more for they will destroy your honor. At the battle of Tet, Americans defeated us. Then we became elated with new hope to see your media helping us and causing more disruption in your own country than we could inflict on the battlefield.
>
> **—Vo Nguyen Giap**

Maybe General Giap had intended these words for the American leaders to learn a valuable lesson from. If he did, it had been ignored in the same arrogant manner it was during the French war with Vietnam.

How Tough Could They Be? I am surprised that this figure isn't much higher, but it's impressive as it is. A study from Health Research Funding on Veterans and PTSD[22] stated that Vietnam War veterans are three times more likely to be suffering from PTSD than veterans of the Gulf War, the Afghanistan War, or the Iraq War.

Still, over 90 percent of Vietnam veterans state they are glad they served, and 75 percent of them would serve again if called. The total number of veterans from the Vietnam War who have been diagnosed with some degree of PTSD is almost 500,000, and nearly 200,000 were still receiving disability compensation for PTSD. Nearly 98 percent of Vietnam veterans were discharged under honorable conditions, which is equal to or surpasses honorable discharge statistics from other wars Americans fought in.

Vietnam's POWs endured more brutality, horror, and a mortality rate of 50 percent, which is higher than other wars, even higher than the merciless Civil War POWs suffered from at Andersonville.

Hal Kushner spent six years as a POW from 1967–1973. Some of his statements that have been published elsewhere are astonishing to say the least:

> Once home I saw television and movies with grossly frank profanity and even sex. When I left for Vietnam Luci and Desi Arnaz slept in twin beds. Ozzie and Harriet were replaced by Taxi Driver. What had happened to our country I thought? When my aircraft crashed on November 30, 1967, I collided onto one planet and then I returned to another one. It had changed forever. Our country had lost its innocence.

---

22 healthresearchfunding.org

This war, which had such a great impact on all of us who served there, is a dim memory today. Over 58,400 Americans died over there, over 300,000 were wounded, and over one million have died since coming home, and yet our high school history books will offer but a couple of pages about this war. The Vietnam War is as remote to Americans as the War of 1812. This is so depressing because today's young people have no idea just how tough the Vietnam War veteran was…had to be.

1968 Damn That Year! It was the year that an American soldier in Vietnam became a dreaded casualty of the war. Those brave souls in the early years, sent by John F. Kennedy, are always willing to tell us how bad the war was in the beginning as there were very few real base camps built yet, just little outposts in remote areas. It must have been like it was in Daniel Boone's days when Boonesboro was completely surrounded by hostile Native Americans.

America's serious buildup had not started yet and there weren't enough American soldiers to risk them by daring search-and-destroy missions by day or ambush patrols at night. This brings me instantly to "Hell Year," the unforgettable Tet year of 1968—my year there. Almost immediately when the New Year rolled in, all hell broke loose. The Viet Cong unleashed totally unexpected attacks all over South Vietnam, hitting every major city including Saigon, their biggest target. Americans, however, were not caught off guard, and their retaliation was immediate and merciless. But casualties would not escape either adversary as men died in every town and hamlet from Saigon to the Mekong Delta to the DMA.

On January 31, 1968, Vietnam exploded as "345" Americans were KIA, the worst day of the war till then. Unfortunately, that wasn't the end of the Tet Offensive of 1968. In fact the communists escalated their attacks across the country, and the rivers would run red from blood during the spring months of March and April. There would be no letup, and it seemed like the VC and NVA had an endless supply of men (and women and boys) to put onto the suicidal battlefields.

The month of May would get worse. How was that possible from this small country of North Vietnam? We often wondered what it was that motivated them. The Tet Offensive II in May 1968 would send "2,415" American warriors back to America in…body bags! This would be the largest loss of life for any one month of the war. Guess what? It was only May and there were another seven months of 1968 to deal with.

The year of 1968, the "Twilight Zone" year, would drag on and on with countless combat assaults thrown at the evasive VC and growing ranks of NVA, and when December 1968 ended, "16,899" body bags had been sent home to America.

While the war would begin winding down in 1969–70, too many Americans would die in the swamps and jungles of Vietnam up till 1972. It seemed that 1968 had set the outcome of the war, no matter how much longer it might last. Without hesitation I will always remember 1968 as that year we lived in hell. I'll hate that year to my grave, and in some ways that year will be the cause of my meeting with God.

February 3, 1969

TROPIC LIGHTNING NEWS

Ready To Strike.... Anywhere, Anytime

| Vol 4 No. 5 | TROPIC LIGHTNING NEWS - | February 3, 1969 |

Third Brigade Records Another Bountiful Year

DAU TIENG - The 3d Brigade has drawn the curtain on a year in which the Tropic Lightning infantrymen killed more than 4,200 enemy.

In 12 months of fighting which ranged from the streets of Saigon to the jungles of War Zone C, the brigade captured more than 426,000 lbs of rice and countless weapons and ammunition.

The year was highlighted by counterpunches at Soui Cut, where more than 350 enemy died in a single night; near Saigon in the enemy's abortive Tet offensive; around Trang Bang and Tay Ninh City during the enemy thrusts in May and August, and in the area near Dau Tieng base camp during the closing months of the year.

As the year began, the brigade's forces were positioned in Fire Support Base Burt, on the Soui Cut, a small stream 60 miles northwest of Saigon.

In the second largest single day action of the war, forces of the 2d Battalion (Mech), 22d Infantry and 3d Battalion, 22nd Infantry dealt death on enemy human waves hurling themselves out of the jungle on the night following New Year's Day.

Aided by guns of the 2d Battalion, 77th Artillery, helicopter gunships and tactical air strikes the infantrymen killed 382 enemy.

During the days following Tet, the brigade's forces were split between the areas around Dau Tieng and Saigon. While the 2d Battalion (Mechanized), 22d Infantry Triple Deuce ranged Dau Tieng to Trang Bang in road sweeps and combat operations, the brigade's other two battalions fought in areas between Cu Chi and Saigon.

In fierce fighting less than 10 miles from Saigon and in Cholon, infantrymen of the 2d Battalion, 12th Infantry and 3d Battalion, 22d Infantry, dealt with enemy in house to house fighting and in battles across rice paddies.

In April, Regulars of the 3d of the 22d, backed by the Triple Deuce, killed 137 enemy in a night battle near the edge of war Zone C.

As the enemy tried yet another offensive in May, Tropic Lightning organized Task Force Daems, bringing

https://www.25thida.org/TLN6n4-05.htm

numerous units of the Division under operational control of the 3d Brigade.

In 13 days the Task force accounted for more than 600 enemy in sweeps ranging from Hoc Mon and the Saigon area toward Tay Ninh City. In all, the force accounted for more than 800 enemy killed.

At the conclusion of the summer operations the brigade held the enviable record of not allowing a single enemy rocket or mortar round to be fired from its area of responsibility. Earlier the area had been notorious as part of the enemy rocket belt.

With its return to Dau Tieng near the edge of War Zone C, 45 miles northwest of Saigon, the brigade has concentrated on thrusts into the Boi Loi Woods and Trapezoid areas.

Tropic Lightning News

Americans' Greatest Adventure...Unheralded Lady Hellcats

I suppose this chapter could have led off with the story at the beginning of Chapter 1 about Apache, the despised and feared but somewhat respected Viet Cong leader of a death squad who tormented the American Marines and the South Vietnamese military from 1964 through 1966. However, I also thought that a real eye-opener introduction would give the readers a wake-up call at the very beginning. Apache was for real, and other female warriors of Vietnam both preceded her and followed in her footsteps. They were an amazing breed and I am proud to have fought on "their" battlefield, even if it was as their adversary.

> **America's Congress Offers Praise—Women in Combat.** December 2015's decision to open all military jobs to women—including combat roles—earned both praise and promises of closer scrutiny from members of Congress. At a Pentagon press conference, Defense Secretary Ash Carter announced that the military will open all combat jobs to women early next year with "no exceptions." Congress has thirty days to review the move, and leaders from the House and Senate Armed Services Committees promised to give "proper and rigorous oversight" to the decision's potential long-term effects on the force.

> In a joint statement, Rep. William "Mac" Thornberry, R-Texas and Sen. John McCain, R-Ariz., said the move will have a "consequential impact on our service members and our military's war-fighting capabilities." Without offering any specific support or opposition to the move, the two said that they want defense officials to quickly turn over all research and rationale for the move—including a 1,000-page Marine Integrated Task Force report critical of allowing women in combat roles—to ensure that lawmakers fully understand the process that led to Carter's decision.

> Rep. Joe Heck, R-Nev., Chairman of the House Armed Services Committee's personnel panel, offered praise for the women with whom he served during his time in the Army, but added that "our first priority must be ensuring the safety and security of our troops" and that "this must be the foundation of any changes to the structure of military units."[23]

That offers an almost perfect modern-day example of just how advanced General Giap was with his warfare strategies. As you have already read in this book, Vietnam's women have been defending their homeland in close combat since 39 AD, when the Trung sisters made life miserable for the invading Chinese.

---

23 *Military Times,* December 3, 2015, Leo Shane III, Staff Writer

Hooch maid...friendly or Viet Cong? A hooch maid in South Vietnam was a woman employed to clean the shelters for American servicemen who resided in base camps or cities. I barely remember the hooch maids during my first nine months in-country. We didn't have any hooch maids out in the bush.

Cam Rhan Bay in March of 1968 was my introduction to them. Since I was a freshly arrived new guy to Nam, the only things I paid much attention to were the spiders and snakes on the ground and rats and lizards. In the background was the artillery, day and night, and that took a little getting used to. However, the time would arrive soon when we would hardly notice the background noises of a battle in Vietnam and we would become part of that noise. I think the women and kids were the first Vietnamese people who greeted us when we got off the plane on that first day. There was no cheering or brass bands to greet us, and most of the facial expressions were not warm and fuzzy smiles.

During the intro to Nam days at Cam Rhan Bay, we filled sandbags... ALL day. I guess it was better than what was to come when we would be reassigned to a combat unit out "there" in the real Vietnam. So we really did not mind sand bagging. We would soon learn and the time flew as we listened to stories from other vets who had been there a few days more. Their stories originated from the other GIs before them.

Every soldier and marine who spent at least thirty days in-country ran into and maybe even fell in love with a Vietnamese lady named Mai, pronounced "My" or "May." I had met many, but there was one who would stand out, and I still remember her pretty, smiling face and cute sense of humor.

I never knew how much the hooch maids were paid. Sometimes, they were just given goods from the Post Exchange, which would often be turned into money for the black market. Generally, the hooch maids were provided for officers and some higher-ranking non-commissioned officers (NCOs). I remember them as being more efficient at cooking than washing uniforms as they would sometimes wash without using soap.

Most of the hooch maids I came into contact with were actually good Catholics. Although they might have flirted with us in their unique sense of humor, most of them did not date or have sex with American soldiers. Mai was one of those, and I did not mind when she flirted with me. Despite their small stature, the Vietnamese women were unusually strong and hardy.

I met Mai for the first time in November 1968, after being transferred to the 25th Infantry Division's headquarters in Cu Chi. I had been in Tay Ninh Hospital, healing from bad leg and foot infections, when I heard there was a permanent base camp job available in Cu Chi, working for Headquarters Company, performing a multitude of duties. I got the job. One of my assignments was to pick up and drop off hooch maids who worked for the adjutant general and inspector general. I didn't think much of the assignment, not after spending my previous eight and a half months out there with "the beasts" living like a Neanderthal. Besides, they were cute, but Mai was really cute and I already had a soft spot in my heart for Vietnamese girls named "Mai" because of a small Vietnamese girl, also named Mai, whom we had previously rescued from her Viet Cong captors. We entered the scene after her village was blown up by Viet Cong; they had killed the poor kid's entire family. This was not going to be another Mai Lai massacre—we were going there to save the people from the dreaded Viet Cong, but we arrived a little too late to save everyone. Fortunately, we were able to find some of Mai's relatives in a neighboring town in Hoc Mon Province, and she had a new home.

Mai was a common name in Nam. I think it was the name of a pretty flower that grows in Vietnam or China. The rule was strict about not having any relationships with the hooch maids, especially those who were working at Division Headquarters, where a lot of secret information was floating around. I also noticed immediately that the hooch maids always had their ears tuned in to our conversations. Gosh, they were smart. They loved to tease us from time to time to the point of flirting with us. The thought of crossing that line never stayed in my mind for very long; going home healthy and breathing was more important.

Mai seemed to get the best of us in the teasing and did not seem afraid of us at all. Besides, they could see how much we liked the Vietnamese kids, and they seemed to have fun with us right back. At least their laughter would indicate that they got the better of the jostling back and forth. One of Mai's favorite ways to tease would be to say me... "Trimmer, you like me, but you no can have Vietnamese girl because VC will get you." Of course, her words were issued in a joking manner; I hope they were. Anyway, I was leaving for R&R to Australia with my buddy Messmer. As soon as we returned to Nam, both of us would be real "short-timers," having less than two weeks left in-country.

Messmer and I left for Sydney together on or about February 20, 1969. We were scheduled to return on February 27, which would be way too soon. Sydney went oh so fast—it seems like we got off the plane and back onto it the very same day. Our R&R was everything a couple of wounded, battle-weary combat soldiers could have dreamed of. I remember very little about that week with the Aussies—wish I did.

Our return to Cu Chi seemed a bit eerie to us, even more so than usual. It seemed so quiet. Well, Messmer and I were exhausted from our R&R activities and the flight back, so we hit our cots right away. I had to be up, bright-eyed and bushy-tailed, to pick up the girls in the morning, and I always needed to be sharp for Mai's quick wit. Man, those girls were smart. I could see how Mai would have been a good sister to me back in America, and she would have blended in really fast. She also spoke good English.

On the way to the hooch girl pickup station on the morning of February 28, 1969, I noticed several heavily damaged Chinooks (large choppers) and knew something had happened here while on our R&R in the "land down under." I waited at the front gate for about twenty minutes, but no hooch girls. I asked the Military Police. They just nodded an *I don't know* head move. The girls had never been a no-show before. In fact, they had never even been late before. Oh well, I guess they were sick and I would catch them tomorrow. I drove back to Division Headquarters and before I could tell the colonels about the girls, one of them told me what happened while I was sunbathing on Bondi Beach in Sydney. Cu Chi was hit with a serious ground attack the evening of February 26. There were many casualties for both sides—at least thirty U.S. KIA, twenty-eight U.S. WIA, and at least thirty enemy KIA and eight POWs. We lost thirteen Chinook helicopters, and an ammunition dump was blown up. Then I was told that our Mai may have been one of the Viet Cong casualties, but this was not confirmed just yet. This shocked me, but I was so worried for her too.

The next morning, I showed up at the gate and two of the three girls were there, but Mai was not one of them. Neither of the two who showed up was related to Mai, and they did not know where she was. Still no word from my colonel on whether Mai was one of the VC casualties, which was updated to thirty-one KIA, but the blood trails leading out of Cu Chi indicated more KIAs were possible.

During this time of uncertainty, I was most uncomfortable, worrying about Mai—she was just a gook hooch maid. Right? I kept tormenting myself, wondering whether she was a VC or not. And if she was, I wanted to see her. I wanted to know why. *SHAKE OUT OF IT!* I shouted to myself. We lost many good Americans on February 26, and if Mai had participated or supported the VC in any way, she was just as much a killer as those who shot the RPGs and AKs and threw the satchels of explosives. And who drew the maps and sketches of the base camp that were found on some VC KIAs? Mai was very capable.

I had about eight days left in-country—was Mai MIA or KIA? I just wanted to know the answer. A couple more days passed, but still no Mai at the pickup gate in the morning. I was really getting psyched for my BIG going home day to get here when I would jump aboard the Freedom Bird and say my final words to what had become my homeland for a full year…
GOOD-BYE, VIETNAM!

Actually, I caught myself quietly practicing those three words. There was no way I could shout them out until I was on the airplane ramp. I was afraid of jinxing myself and everyone else. I heard of stories where the enemy managed to get some last-minute shots in as planes were taking off. It was said that they got a real kick out of it. I could believe it.

It was now March, and I was down to just two days in-country; today would be the last time I would pick up the girls at the front gate. I was reading *Stars & Stripes* during the wait for them when I heard them jumping into the jeep. I also heard one of them say, "Hey, Trimmer, you miss me?" That voice…I knew it was Mai. My head was pounding like a giant drum. At least it sounded like that to me.

I replied, "Naw, I didn't even realize you had been gone—so where were you?"

"I visit my sister in Saigon. No one tell you that? I am sorry."

Moving on, I took the girls to their jobs for the last time, told the colonel that Mai was back, and then I went to clue in my replacement. He was supposed to have been in Cu Chi a couple of days ago, but his old unit ran into a mess with some NVA. I certainly understood. So he was to ride with me that evening when we took the girls back to the gate—the last time for me.

"Hey there, short-timer," Mai said to me as the three girls stepped into the jeep that evening. I introduced their new driver, and the ten-minute ride to the front gate seemed like seconds. Mai was the last one to step out of the jeep. She stopped, looked at me, took her hat off, and said, "Trimmer, I have something for you," and then she kissed me gently on my left cheek and said, "I will miss you, Trimmer. Me glad VC not get you." That was a heavy good-bye and great closure to some doubts and worries I had about my good friend, Mai the hooch maid.

That was how my last evening in Vietnam ended, about 980 degrees different from so many other evenings for the past year. I was already packed, ready to go, except I had no idea how I could get to sleep that night. The next morning was quite fitting—our chopper from Cu Chi to Saigon actually received gunfire, probably from some of the locals who turned into Viet Cong in the evenings, but we made it. **GOOD-BYE, VIETNAM!**

Coming home, no one said thank you. This was a phenomenon commonly reported by the troops returning to Canada and the United States. After the horror of Vietnam, another hell awaited them that they were not prepared for at home. They heard "Baby Killer" and some were spat upon, fact. Most of us were greeted gladly by our families, but one thing was missing… **WELCOME HOME!**

May 1969 at Fort Hood was my next and hopefully my last stop as an active duty American soldier boy. I looked forward to my final day in the

U.S. Army with mixed emotions. In fact, as the bullshit of stateside duty, playing war games, and saluting the asshole lieutenants got under my skin, the thought of "re-upping" and requesting to go back to Nam crossed my mind from time to time. Fortunately, that thought did not linger for very long.

I was settling in at Fort Hood, Texas, just fine, trying not to think of what was going on in Vietnam. Then one day, I received a letter from one of my buddies in Cu Chi who was with the Wolfhounds. They were a tough grunt unit. Here is the shocking note he sent me:

Hey Trimmer, you missing the Nam yet? Just kidding, of course. Then again, you seemed like you were starting to really like it here. Nah, just kidding again. But listen up, buddy, I have some news for you and I'm not so sure you will like it. One night, one of the Wolfhound platoons went out on an outer perimeter stay for the night, just a couple hundred clicks outside of a firebase in the Boi Loi Woods. You surely haven't forgotten that place already? Well, the Wolfhounds got more than they bargained for or they got exactly what they were looking for with their ambush set-up. First, their Claymores were set off and it was on, one helluva firefight. Our guys had three casualties but here is what they found after a morning search of the area. They found dead VC soldiers and get this, pal—their leader was a fresh, sweet Viet Cong—girl. Trimmer, it was that hooch girl you used to pick up and drive around. Think you kind of had a crush on her. Mai was her name? Sorry if this is disturbing news for you, but thought you should know.

Stay out of trouble, bro.
Gene

Holy shit! I should have seen that coming but for some reason I did not. Now suddenly, thoughts were bouncing back and forth inside that hard head of mine. Reality had smacked me right between the eyes, that I had been escorting a ruthless female Viet Cong around Cu Chi for three months. Not my fault, right? The U.S. Army gave me that job and I had no choice but to do it day after day, week after week.

What kind of bullshit was that? Who gets put into a life situation like that one? I mean geez, I made it through the better part of a full year where every day required every ounce of energy we could muster to complete one search-and-destroy mission after another, and there was no resting at night. So what if I had taken it (been killed) back in a base camp, supposedly a highly safe one as Cu Chi was considered to be? What if my throat was no longer breathing when they found me? What if one of those little Cong darlings had booby trapped my jeep? I would have never been prepared for something like this. Maybe it was safer out here in the Cong's element where we were always on guard, never taking the next minute for granted.

Oh, that would have been a great story for everyone back home…Dusty Trimmer went down, taken out by a couple of hooch maids!

What if I had been put into a situation where I had to take one or two of them out? Sure, I could do it; I had killed before, but not like this. I couldn't believe what I was doing to myself with those far-fetched thoughts that were hitting me after reading Gene's letter.

Chalk it up as just another experience during the most *Twilight Zone-*like war in American history. Forget about what might have happened, what didn't happen, and just remember what did happen.

Obviously, here I am in 2019, fifty years later, and forgetting about that time with the hooch maids hasn't happened yet. I can never think of Mai as a cold-blooded terrorist, nor was she a communist; she didn't know what communism meant. She may have been brainwashed into leaning toward her North Vietnamese countrymen than the corrupt South Vietnamese and I'll never hold that against her.

Well, I was adjusting pretty well to Fort Hood. Heck, the weather was comparable to Nam in some respects. But that note from Gene shook me up a bit, as I just couldn't put two and two together. Mai always showed up on time. Her work was excellent. She had a great sense of humor with me. She was always smiling and it was kind of moving. How could this sweet young lady be such a doll during the day with us and then revert to the role of a Viet Cong killer of my war buddies? I will probably never forget that one; still makes me sad.

Moving on, I found a couple of letters written by others which I felt would fit into this chapter quite well. I think they will touch many readers.

My Brave Enemy…Forgive Me Please. Tay Ninh Province, 1967—I walk the paths my ancestors wore clean, and the pride swells in my chest with the courage and allegiance they had shown in defending our country. The Chinese, Mongols, Japanese, and French had met their match and were expelled from Vietnam in our past. Now it is my patriotic duty to swear allegiance to my country and defend it against the Americans. Not because of political reasons but of pure patriotism and the knowledge that blood had to be sacrificed by my ancestors before me. I would shame them not to offer my own blood or life for my country.

I had been forced into womanhood at age thirteen, proudly trained and tutored by our top military minds of Vietnam, China, and the Soviets. Without hesitation, I accepted command of a Viet Cong group operating in South Vietnam when I was almost fifteen years old. We patrolled and defended a large area the Americans called the "Iron Triangle." We had been credited for the taking of many American lives. We accepted citations and medals as only doing a duty to country. The taking of an American life was our highest priority and I was obliged to do that. We just watched them during the daytime as their superior firepower was instantly damaging to our attacks. The Americans were unlike the French before them, my elders told me. The Americans were hard to kill.

Strange feelings went through my mind as I watched the enemy's actions during the day. They showed emotions from happiness to dreadful sorrow, not unlike the emotions of my group. I could almost share my enemy's loneliness they felt, being away from their families and in a way, I regretted the suffering I would try to inflict upon them tonight. Having watched and studied the Americans personally, I hesitantly doubted the teachings of my teachers from the north, that they would rape our women and kill our children. I followed the training I was taught.

This night I would lead our group for a recon of a local American firebase, which I considered safe and easy duty. We walked with confidence as we had done on many previous nights. Good luck was not on our side this night. As we moved through a familiar rice paddy, avoiding the berms we had set booby traps in, for some reason, as we approached our ambush site, we forgot the intervals we were supposed to keep and for a few seconds we were bunched up and easy prey.

Never did we imagine walking square into an ambush by the Americans that was patterned as one of our own. The first blast came from one of their claymores, which we were very familiar with, as we had many that we took from them. Emotions ranged from terror to panic to hatred and revenge and of course, survival. The second claymore blew towards us, then the third claymore. At the same time, their M-60s and M-16s had already mowed down half of my very young group. They would never get a chance to kill Americans after this night. The rest of us were stunned, blinded, and dazed. When we saw more of us blown away all around us, our fate was sealed. There would be no escape and none of us would survive.

As I felt the first of the claymores, concussion from the impact, the burning pain from hot metal into my body, I could not help but to admire the precision of the Americans' deadly ambush and in some ways, I thought we trained them well and thousands of deadly steel balls ripped into the fragile bodies of my entire group. The sky suddenly let up on this dark moonless, "perfect for an ambush" night with their flares and heavy automatic fire followed to eliminate us completely. We would have done the same to them.

I was weak, but with one last gasp of air, I heard him faintly through my painful eardrums, as he whispered to a buddy...dead at about fifteen. Can you believe it?

Not so bad...as death eased the pain, as I faded away, I faintly watched an American walk guardedly up to me and surprisingly, even in the flickering light flares, the anticipated look of hate in his eyes was not there, but a look of sorrow. It is as if I looked into my own eyes as if standing over my trophies of my enemy dead, and in my heart regretted having taken a life. How strange that he, an American, might feel...as I feel.

Tiredly, I looked into my enemy's eyes...and in reflection, I see my enemy. I was on the surviving side of this ambush in 1967 and I still pray that my enemy may forgive me as I have forgiven them. May we all someday...rest in peace.

Written by Pat (Beanie) Camunes
Tay Ninh Province
South Vietnam, 1966–1967
D/4/31 Lt. Inf. Bde.

Hooch Maid or Viet Cong? Smiles can be deceiving.

Viet Cong Camaraderie. *I was about to return from Hanoi to my combat unit, what used to be the green jungle, a part of Vietnam most Vietnamese were proud of, but it would now be scorched earth from battles and Agent Orange spray. I had just finished my last training with the Regular Army and I was eager and happy to get back. I was starting to understand something that has been inside me for a long time. I've discovered that I regarded the combat base in the jungle as my home now. The soldiers were now my new family. It was almost like I was about to return to my old village and my family. All were gone now except for my brave husband, Tranh. He had been in almost continuous combat for twenty grueling years with the French and the Americans and could barely get around on one leg.*

Why did we put ourselves through this for so long? Our ancestors never rested until their freedom was won from long and hard fought wars with the people from the north (China). And even today we have yearned all of our lives for independence and freedom and we had pledged to bear arms and fight until the final objective was reached. So the battlefield had become our lives. We were fighting for our lives and our sacred homeland. We hated the French. Defeating them so badly was our justice. We had a beautiful and noble goal of liberating the homeland and the people. But why were the Americans in our country now and why did they fight as hard as we did? This was not their home.

I understand the sacred comradeship created by our goal. During the hard days of hunger and thirst, we shared each piece of jungle root, each bit of hard to find firewood, each rotting apple, and each swallow of spring water we had brought from the mountains. Each human life was precious to us, no matter what the Americans may have thought. We were all of the same family. We were all soldiers for Uncle Ho.

I still remember my first killing of an American. I still have nightmares, anxieties. Not sure I ever got used to it, but the resistance had to live. We were indoctrinated with the necessity of killing. I wasn't sure who was good or who was bad, but we were killing for our country. The whole year of 1968 after Tet, we were on the move, avoiding the Americans as they had increased their vengeance to kill more of us. Moving our artillery units wasn't as easy as moving the army. Even our rocket tubes were heavy.

Our health was shattered in mid-June 1968 after six straight months of attacking and avoiding the Americans and their Vietnamese slaves (South Vietnamese soldiers). Our morale was not good, especially when the B-52 bombs were dropped. Our resting places outside of the tunnels were not bomb shelters. They were just a couple bamboo posts with bamboo poles tied to them. We had no place to hide from the B-52s. The tunnels were too far away.

As we moved on, we passed five comrades, dead from the shrapnel of B-52s. This was the sacrifice, our way of life, and we would never give up to the invaders.

—Kim Van Tra
Lady Viet Cong (1968)

The main reason for this chapter was, of course, to give credit to Vietnam's valiant women warriors, and credit to Giap the Great for recognizing their immense value—because I figure most of America would not be aware of this very important part of Vietnam's long history of ongoing wars to keep their freedom.

During the American-Vietnam War, there were numerous opportunities to contribute to the war. Working on the Ho Chi Minh Trail was a career, and many Vietnamese women lived their last days doing this work for the cause. Contrary to what I used to think, and so did a lot of other Americans, the female soldiers, age twelve or thirteen on up, were not working to defend communism; rather they were doing whatever they could to defend their homeland, as their ancestors did. Of course, they performed all of the combat duties when they were needed. They built booby traps, conducted ambushes, and shot down American planes.

The initiation to become a bona fide lady Viet Cong or "long-haired warrior" was quite unlike the basic training that our American military enlistees might receive. No one knew how many of them joined up with a pack of them or were aggressively recruited, then abducted and initiated with rough love—well, sort of.

Vietnam has a long history of female warriors since the symbolic importance of the Trungs. During the French occupation, Vietnamese women were brutalized and sexually exploited by the French, which created a savage hate for the French. Then, when the Americans arrived, they displayed a macho attitude and did not show much regard for women and girls as threats in a war. This attitude was a great mistake.

Most likely, our young, feisty, and very resilient future female VC were born and raised in poor peasant families, learning to work just as hard as their brothers would. Their other choices in life might be this array of glamour careers in no particular order: future wife and mother or unwed mother working by day as a bar girl and prostitute, and then by night as a Viet Cong who might end up killing Americans or Australians she served during the bar hours.

During the Vietnam War, there were many restaurants and bars blown up without warning. Almost every terrorist act was well planned, well timed, and well executed at a time when the targeted establishment was overflowing with enemies of the VC...unsuspecting soldiers and marines who were looked at as invaders, not saviors. Of course, the terrorists could not possibly have known when the timing for their ambush with explosives or rockets and mortars would find the largest gathering for their intended victims. How about unintentional aid from a drunken soldier, marine, sailor, or airman who was deceived and smitten by one of the cute and overly friendly bar girls. Done deal—all too often that happened to our guys.

Then again, if the young peasant girl chose the bar scene for her occupation, which offered much higher pay than rice paddy work, she would be forced to go through unimaginable experiences. Rape would be her thank you for doing her job. Raped VC girls weren't just treated as such by their own VC comrades; you could also count on the South Vietnamese Army as willing rapists if fortunate to capture a lady VC alive. Yes, a few Americans, Australians, and South Koreans would do their duty if they had the chance. After all, "everything is fair in love and…war!"

Many of the girls who lived long enough (few actually would) could mature into deadly VC terrorists and maybe even leaders among the men, as the storied VC Apache once did. However, Apache died by the sword she lived by, being killed by another sniper. She was only in her early twenties when her life ended.

Obviously, there would be no beauty parlor visits, no getting her nails done or massages in the local health spa. Her evening of comfort and relaxation would come from sleeping in a tunnel along with the other inhabitants such as rats, scorpions, giant centipedes, poisonous snakes, and the local flock of malaria-carrying mosquitoes, and nowhere to go to avoid all of this. During the day, they might not leave the tunnels, not for very long, as daytime was when we were looking for them. They might rest during the day and then turn themselves loose on us. What a life of charm for a lady. These were truly the forgotten warriors of the unforgettable Vietnam War. Just another memory that we who fought there will never forget.

Apache II. The photo on this page was taken in 1972 of the female Viet Cong soldier Lam Thi Dep. As mentioned throughout this book, it was not uncommon for Vietnamese women to fight for the Viet Cong cause. Note that in this picture, when she was about eighteen years old, she was armed with an American M-16A1, the updated model of the weapon, obtained either through the black market or from a killed American soldier. But Viet Cong were also known to receive M-16s from South Vietnamese soldiers sympathetic to their cause against the American presence in their country. That sure sucked.

Unlike Apache discussed in Chapter 1, who terrorized the I Corps area where the marines operated, Apache II roamed in the Mekong Delta's IV Corps area, which was as far south as the Vietnam War was ever active in the Provence of Soc Trang, where ambushes were frequent.

Lam Thi Dep was noted for her warrior skills with Viet Cong ambushes, but she was also invaluable at getting jobs inside American base camps obtaining secret information about American and ARVN troop positions and their strength. Her prowess was no secret to her adversaries, so I nicknamed her Apache II.

A Vietnamese woman's journey from war to peace

A Vietnamese woman's journey from war to peace. Here are the words of a Vietnamese-American woman who came to America as a victim of the Vietnam War. I think her words ring loud and clear as to who the Vietnamese people were and will probably remain throughout time:

*For my first twelve years of life, I was a peasant girl in Ky La, now called Xa Hoa Qui, a very small village near Danang in what is now central Vietnam. It was northern South Vietnam during the war. My father taught me to love God, my family, our traditions, and the people we could not see—**our sacred ancestors**. He taught me that to sacrifice one's self for freedom—like our ancient kings who fought bravely against invaders, or the manner of our women warriors, including Miss Trung Nhi Trung Trac, who drowned herself rather than give into foreign conquerors—was a very high honor. From my love of my ancestors and my native soil, he said...**I must never retreat**.*

—**Le Ly Hayslip**

Le Ly was a Viet Cong soldier from the ages of thirteen to fifteen against American and South Vietnamese soldiers. Everything she knew about the war up until that age she learned from the Northern Vietnamese leaders in their hidden camps in the swamps. Most of her southern Vietnamese colleagues assumed everything they heard to be the truth because the Viet Cong in the south always said the same thing, and those were the beliefs she grew up with. One of the first things Ly was taught by the northern Vietnamese was that Vietnam was a sovereign nation which had been held captive by the Western imperialists for over a century. That all nations had a right to determine their own destiny also seemed beyond dispute since the farmers subsided by their own hands and felt they owed nothing to anyone but God and their great ancestors for the right to live as they saw fit.

Even the Chinese, who had made their own disastrous attempts to rule Vietnam in past centuries, had repeatedly learned very painful lessons about the people's determination to remain free and independent. The Chinese created an old saying that profoundly summarized their unsuccessful attempts to conquer and dominate Vietnam... **Vietnam is nobody's lapdog!**

Lady Viet Cong like Ly, at just twelve or thirteen years old, may have been trained initially only in setting booby traps. They could string the trip wires and attach them to grenades or other explosive devices, and then set them on the most often used patrol routes by the American infantry. They could also plant what we called the "Bouncing Betty" land mines that detonated several feet above ground when pressured. Maybe their favorite and most gruesome booby traps were the "punji pits." When our guys fell into one of these, they did not die instantly but were maimed for life. Their screams inflicted a psychological wound that would hang with us for life. That was as much a part of the Viet Cong's goal along with the traps' physical damage. Yes, I think the punji pits were the VC's bread-and-butter tactic, as they also allowed them to spring a lethal ambush on the victim's unit as they came to his rescue. I was never introduced to that particular nightmare, so I cannot explain what happens next, as a happy ending is not likely. Because Americans are so devoted to their buddies in battle, sometimes saving themselves just isn't going to be an option even though it is the safe act.

If you have further interest in learning more about the agonizing life of a female Viet Cong during the Vietnam War with America, I think you would be rewarded immensely by reading Ly's 1989 book called...*When Heaven and Earth Changed Places.*

Nguyen Thi Dinh with Nguyen Thi Bien, Bien with Fidel Castro,
Dinh with Mao Zedong

Madam Nguyen Thi Dinh was a twentieth-century warrior leader. Several of the history papers I read refer to one Vietnamese woman as the most important revolutionary in the Vietnam War, and she was also one of those "peasant farmer" warriors you have been reading about in this book. As a young teenager, she fought with Giap's Viet Minh against France and was captured and imprisoned for three years. After that war ended, she started right where she left off in 1960 and was one of the founding leaders of the National Liberation Front (NLF), the Viet Cong. Soon, she was appointed deputy commander of the Viet Cong forces. In her memoirs, she describes attacks on American and South Vietnamese troops while they were sleeping and so was their guard.

After the Vietnam War with America and South Vietnam and the Reunification of the two Vietnams, Madame Dinh served on the Central Committee of the Vietnamese Communist Party and became the first female general of the Vietnam People's Army. She and Madam Nguyen Thi Binh were two of the most prominent female Vietnamese Communist leaders in Vietnam's history.

Madam Dinh writes about the "long-haired army" which she helped organize and of which she was so proud. They worked very hard on keeping the Viet Cong's actual strength a secret from the Americans, which might explain why our intelligence reported how the Viet Cong were nearly put out of existence during the 1968 Tet Offensive. I guess we'll never know, which is the way Madam Dinh wanted it. She represented the Viet Cong at the Paris Peace Accords in 1973. She passed away in 1992. When asked what drove her, she was once quoted to say, "I want a peaceful life and control of our own country."

She was a founding member of the NLF in her province and became an official within the NLF. In 1965, she became chair of the South Vietnam Women's Liberation Association. At the same time she was appointed deputy commander of the Viet Cong Army, the highest-ranking combat position held by a member during the war. In 1967, she was awarded the Lenin Peace Prize. Her memoir is *No Other Road To Take* (1976). In 1995, she was posthumously awarded the title of Hero of the People's Armed Forces.

Nguyen Thi Binh was right behind or next to Madam Dinh, another Vietnamese warrior and yes, she was also a member of the Viet Minh and later the Viet Cong. She was also imprisoned by the French in 1951 and 1953. In the American-Vietnam War, she became a high-ranking member of the Viet Cong's Central Committee. Madam Binh was one who signed the Paris Peace Accords and was elected to two terms as the vice president of Vietnam from 1992 until 2002.

Under the leadership of such warriors as Madam Dinh and Madam Binh, women were motivated to join the armed forces. They even had groups called the Volunteer Youth Corps, and one million young women served in the North Vietnam local militia units. The women's contributions and sacrifices throughout Vietnamese history are incomprehensible to me, and I witnessed it firsthand during my tour in South Vietnam.

Continuing my research, I found no shortage of lady warrior heroes among the Vietnamese people. This chapter presents a small sample of the many.

Ho Thi Ky, born to a poor peasant family, began participating in the revolution in her early teens, working as a courier. In 1968, she entered the Youth Union and earned herself into a ranger team near Ca Mau town, experiencing many battles with excellent battle performance. Admitted into the Communist Party of Vietnam in 1969, Ho would die in battle one year later in 1970 at the age of twenty-one. The commune that Ho was born in was renamed after her, as were several schools and other institutions. She was posthumously titled a Hero of the People's Armed Forces.

Vo Thi Sau was a schoolgirl when she first began combat training as a guerilla fighter against the French. When she was just fourteen, she threw a grenade into a group of French soldiers, killing or wounding thirteen of them. She managed to escape, but when she threw another grenade at a local Vietnamese official who was responsible for executing many Viet Minh sympathizers, it did not explode. She was apprehended and imprisoned until 1952, when she turned nineteen years old and was executed. Escaping twice, she was imprisoned in three different facilities before the execution. Sau is revered as a heroic nationalist martyr and a symbol of revolutionary spirit to Vietnamese people today. Some believe she has returned as an ancestral spirit.

Nguyen Thi Doan is a modern-day example of Vietnam's respect for their women. She has been an educator, legislator and politician, having served as the Vice President of Socialist Vietnam from 2007 until 2016.

Nguyen Thi Duc Hoan was a highly successful actress, director, and film-maker with most of her work completed between 1978 and 1991. Before all of that, she had left home as a young girl with hopes of joining the anti-French resistance and became a successful guerilla fighter. She survived that war and then the Americans came. She had a daughter who trained for the militia. Duc Hoan was a true-to-form lady warrior, of whom her ancestors would have been proud.

Imagine this scenario for a minute—if the North Vietnamese were able to recruit a million lady volunteers into their militia during the American-Vietnam War that was fought in South Vietnam, I don't think Americans could imagine how many patriotic Vietnamese "peasants and farmers" would rise up and leave their rice paddies ASAP if we had physically invaded their country as some so-called military experts in the United States were suggesting. I would fight for my country with my life again, but had we physically invaded North Vietnam, I would not have wanted to be part of that, and I am glad today that we did not do that. As of late 2016, Vietnam had the world's largest civilian-ready militia of five million.

Here is a short list of bibliographical or historical sources that might be helpful if interested in the focus of this chapter:

Even the Women Must Fight (1998)
Vietnamese Women at War: Fighting for Ho Chi Minh (1999)
No Other Road to Take (1976)
The Long-Haired Warriors (1989)
After Sorrow (1995)

Full Metal Jacket was a critically acclaimed and Academy Award-nominated film directed and produced by Stanley Kubrick. The plot's setting is the year of 1968 in the Vietnam War in the ancient city of Hue, Vietnam. The movie starts out with a disaster to a platoon of marines during their combat training at Parris Island, South Carolina.

Assigned to the action at Hue as the 1968 Tet Offensive is underway, the platoon's command leader is killed by an enemy sniper in Hue. Mistakenly, the marines declare the area secure after a few successful enemy encounters. Soon after, while the platoon is on patrol, one of the squad leaders is killed by a Viet Cong booby trap. The platoon becomes lost and while they are trying to find their way, two more men are badly wounded, including the medic. Against orders, another platoon member attempts to save his brothers and he, too, is wounded by a sniper. Two more marines are killed when they are attempting to determine where the sniper fire is coming from and how many enemy soldiers are at the location.

One of the marines discovers which building the enemy fire is coming from, but he, too, is shot and killed as he attempts to point out the enemy location to his remaining platoon buddies. With a newly appointed leader, the team launches an attack on the enemy location. One of the marines gets inside the building as the others provide fire support for him. He makes it up to the floor where the enemy's shots are coming from, which has devastated an entire squad of marines. He discovers there is just one enemy sniper that has done all of this damage to his brothers. He does not hesitate as the sniper is firing at his buddies who are pinned down. His attempt to kill the enemy is unsuccessful when his M-16 jams, which alerts the sniper, who turns around and constantly fires AK-47 rounds at the terrified marine hiding behind a post or beam made of thick lumber. The face on the Viet Cong startles the marine as he fumbles around trying to unjam his weapon. What the marine sees will live with him for the rest of his life: The Viet Cong sniper is a teenage girl, and the expression on her face gives the marine chills as she continues to keep him pinned from her AK-47 fire.

Another squad member makes it to the scene and manages to mortally wound the teenage Viet Cong, but she is still living by the time the rest of the squad arrives. They, too, cannot believe what they see lying on the ground…a very pretty VC teenager with the hateful expression on her face of a killer, and that is exactly what she has succeeded in doing. She begs the marines to shoot her to put her out of her agony, and finally after arguing among themselves, one of them reluctantly performs the deed.

R. Lee Ermey plays the gunny drill sergeant in the combat infantry training. He received an Oscar for that performance. I found him to be absolutely perfect for the role, very similar to the one drill sergeant I had in basic training at Fort Knox, Kentucky.

While most reviewers gave favorable responses to the movie and the actors, particularly Ermey (Gunny), several reviewers were harshly critical of the final scene around the young killer's demise, a female teenage Viet Cong. They referred to it as an unreal and muddled message. Guess what, folks, that was the Vietnam War—so different, so pointless, tragic, and heartbreaking. Several scenes of *Full Metal Jacket* hang around inside my memory…the men who were killed by the invisible enemy, Gunny Ermey (I would watch this movie again just to see his entertaining and extremely real performance), and last…the expression on the teenage Viet Cong. I have seen that look before in real life.

When I think of the lady Viet Cong over there and their unheralded participation as field combat warriors, thrown out there to do in-your-face combat with professional, trained French Foreign Legion and American soldiers and marines, all I can say is…**Oh my God, they were awesome!**

One major advantage for the North Vietnamese military commanders (actually, it was more like a secret weapon and a monstrous disadvantage for America and her allies) was our arrogant, high-ranking leaders' lack of respect for the Viet Cong women warriors. Such a shame. If our brass had done some research—just a little—they would not have believed what they were reading. Unfortunately, our generals hardly took the lady Viet Cong as more than a silhouette standing out there, waiting to be shot. Oh, and our elite leaders' opinion was…if they shot back, what would they hit?

As a result of our arrogance and ignorance, there were thousands of Americans who would never see their soldier boys alive or in the same physical or mental shape as the way they saw them before flying off to Vietnam.

The Viet Cong women pulled deadly ambushes on us, reminiscent of their ancient relatives in the many wars against the Chinese and the Mongols. If we captured one of them, believe me, we would not turn our backs on her with a simple rope tie of her hands. She was ready to die in one last attempt to take down at least one of her captors.

It would be extremely difficult to train people to develop an attitude like that, and even more difficult to change it again. The ongoing trouble in Iraq is the perfect example. Our guys try to train the Iraqi troops. The Iraqis go through the motions, but when a real firefight erupts, they might be more worried about their uniform being gashed and ripped than they are about their wounded and dead Iraqi comrades.

This scenario brings me back home to where there has been a flurry of attention given to the subject of our American women becoming warriors in combat overseas, fighting next to the men.

I guess I am a chauvinist, as I do not think most American women have the "attitude" to jump out of a helicopter (with incoming rounds hitting it), then crawl around with poisonous critters of all sorts in leech-infested swamps. And your reward, if you make it with the guys and reach the objective, is to engage in a vicious firefight to the death. I rest my case on that subject, but life moves on.

Today, Vietnam honors their female warriors of the past with an impressive Vietnam Women's Museum in Hanoi, which honors the women from the south and the north. My fading memories about these unique and rare warriors reminds me of how feisty and quick-witted they were. And don't turn your back on them after you have pissed them off.

How mind-boggling that the Americans and the French got another vital aspect of the Vietnam War wrong by underestimating the lady Viet Cong! Again, because we did not understand Vietnamese history and we did not put forth much effort to study it before launching our military onslaught into harm's way.

After the Geneva Accords, a collection of documents relating to Indochina from the Geneva Conference of April 26–July 21, 1954, Vietnamese women were virtually thrown into the role of carrying out the Viet Cong resistance of the south while most men went north to join the Viet Minh against the French. Women in the south assumed any role necessary, such as spy, porter, tunnel digger, booby trap engineer, and of course, soldier and even sniper. By the time the Americans had arrived in the south, Cong women had become the soldiers and backbone of the resistance. After centuries of continuous war, the Northern Vietnamese had developed hardened attitudes toward whatever they did in work or battle.

We showed them too little respect. Sometimes I relate Custer's bold, arrogant, and careless trespassing into the heart of Sioux territory with our own massive invasion of South Vietnam. Why were we brainwashed into thinking that the Viet Cong were not to be taken seriously as much of a threat against the mighty, all-powerful American military? How the hell could American soldiers and marines be led into horrible ambushes that decimated entire platoons and even companies…in just a few minutes' time? How could our superior officers in Washington and Saigon not have anticipated what we were about to walk into over there again and again and again?

Miss Apache wasn't the first lady warrior in Vietnam's long, war-torn history, but she served as a perfect warning example of what America and her allies would have to deal with and what must be done in order to defeat the new and underrated enemy who was, after all, fighting in their own back-yard. Before America arrived in Vietnam, most of the male Viet Minh (VC to be) who fought against the French were sent to North Vietnam. This left or created a surprisingly formidable, hard-core force of Viet Cong women in South Vietnam. They fought as spies or informants and assisted in killing or capturing Americans. Mai, the hooch maid and VC, was the perfect example of how brave and cunning they could be.

They should have been recognized and maybe even respected as dedi-cated, vicious, and efficient killers of America's soldier boys. I ask myself over and over, why did our smug leaders ignore these lethal soldiers? Why were they brought into the military base camps to work in headquarters of senior officers where they would gather enough information that would bring down scores of our brothers out in the bush and inside so-called "safe" base camps?

I guess Westmoreland and his minions believed these "primitive" people would be so overwhelmed and defeated by the devastating damage Vietnam would be handed that they could not possibly remain much of a fighting force. What a horrible error.

In this strange unpopular war (on both sides), we would unleash a hell onto the Vietnam countryside like no other country had ever suffered from in the world's history, including Germany or Japan. Vietnam was poisoned… gassed…burned and blasted away until half of its pristine forests were gone and nearly a similar proportion of its agricultural land was rendered unsuit-able to farm and produce food.

Agent Orange did much more damage than erase our enemy's ability to hide from our relentless search-and-destroy missions. Agent Orange starved an enemy and half the population of South Vietnam. And yet, the will of our adversaries could not be broken. Why couldn't our generals come to realize this? Or why did they seem to refuse to?

Almost fifty years later since Tet of 1968 shocked Washington, most of America, and the world, I still feel the effect of that single year of my life. When people ask us if we would do it again if asked to, and most Vietnam veterans have allegedly replied with an absolute yes, I just say…really?

There are probably some great images hidden somewhere in the muse-ums of Vietnam, showing a group of teenage girls and women scampering and ever so cautiously crawling around in the jungles of their country. They would not be playing war games like American boys did in their pre-teen years. They would be going through serious, intense, grueling training exercises to fight for the Viet Cong army against the South Vietnamese, Americans, and allied military forces. Men against girls? Go ahead and laugh, then remember Apache in Chapter 1 and multiply her several thousand times…and watch your buddy's back.

The Viet Cong women were in many ways the backbone of the Viet Cong's resistance forces. These gals spied, took prisoners, built booby traps, and of course, they did not hesitate to take down an American soldier or marine with a well-placed shot from their carbines or AK-47s.

To say that the lady Cong were hardened combatants would be an understatement. Unfortunately, they were also very well-trained (by life experiences) actresses at a scary young age of twelve or thirteen. If you had the opportunity to sleep with one of the little cuties while on an R&R in Vung Tau or other resorts on the coast of the South or East China Sea, you would have found ladies who were extremely willing to accommodate you. However, it was an unwise decision to think she actually liked you when she said, "I love you, GI!" If you bought that and stayed the night…that could have been your last one. These girls were sure hard core and would have no problem slicing up a GI while he was sound asleep.

Oh my, there were so many different ways to die while you were in-country, South Vietnam. So it is quite true when someone tags all of South Vietnam as a total war zone. There were no 100 percent safe zones… this enemy was indeed everywhere and it was twenty-four/seven.

Many Vietnamese historians have given credit for victory in both wars against the French and against America and her allies to the women warriors of Vietnam. One such person would be a well-known author, Lady Borton. She was an American Quaker who documented numerous stories about heroism among the women of the Vietnam Wars. One of Lady Borton's masterpieces, which I have read, is *After Sorrow: An American Among the Vietnamese*.

By the time the French-Vietnam War had ended, North and South Vietnam (it was France who split Vietnam) were blessed with—or cursed with—an abundance of war-hardened, professionally experienced lady warriors. Had our bureaucratic leaders in Washington paid attention to this rather than ignoring it, maybe, just maybe, they would have told France they were on their own instead of wasting hundreds of millions in ammo and supplies for France. Maybe then, Vietnam would have had its own election without intervention and rigging from the U.S.

Honestly, any one of four so-called friends, from France to Australia, could have done us a huge favor by advising the U.S. to stay out of Indochina completely. It's not speculation or armchair quarterbacking for anyone to easily come to this decision:

- Had the U.S. stayed out of Indochina's politics and allowed Vietnam to have their own elections, it would not be an exaggeration to say that…between twelve to sixteen million people who died in that war might still be living today.

Isn't that a sickening thought? Not one easy to digest in an entire lifetime if you are lucky enough to be one of the few surviving combatants or victims of Vietnam. Well, our know-it-all leaders did not mind their own business, and basically they extended the war in Korea over to the Southeastern Asian Peninsula simply because they were the Americans, the freshly self-anointed superpower of the world. Maybe they were searching for a war where an easy victory was granted after the embarrassing draw in Korea.

Who pretty much built the Ho Chi Minh Trail? Who pretty much did the digging of the tunnels of Cu Chi? Vietnamese women did, as they stood beside the men. These are the people who awaited the next wannabe conqueror…the Americans. An easy victory for them did not carry a guarantee.

In a strange sort of way, because I know now what I did not know back then in 1968, I have begrudgingly come to understand and even admire the lifestyle and missions of Mai and her hooch maid comrades. Their commitment, bravery, and unwavering willingness to sacrifice their lives for a cause is now understood, regrettably.

The Trung sisters, Lady Trieu, Phung Thi Chinh, Apache, Mai, and many more: For what it is worth at this point, this old combat Vietnam War veteran salutes your heart and courage by writing this book.

America's Lady Tigers. While the Ameri-Cong media and the radical antiwar protestors were putting despicable, degrading labels on its own combat warriors, something else was going on during a heated, violent war; American women were risking their lives, and few back home would ever know it.

Engraved on the Wall (Vietnam Veterans Memorial) on Panel 23W, Line 112 is the name of U.S. Army Lt. Sharon A. Lane, an Army nurse who died from enemy 122-millimeter rockets fired into the 312th Evacuation Hospital at Chu Lai, South Vietnam, on April 29, 1969. There is a life-sized statue of her in uniform located on the grounds of Aultman Army Medical Center in her hometown of Canton, Ohio. Sharon Lane was a decorated combat soldier of the Vietnam War, who was awarded the Bronze Star Valor medal and the Purple Heart, posthumously.

Every one of America's combat nurses who served in Vietnam had volunteered to be there. When they came home, the same unfriendly reception was waiting for them, just as though they, too, were some of those…Baby Killers.

At least one nurse was known to have been spat on by an antiwar protestor while standing in line at an airport in San Antonio, Texas. This is mentioned with more details in the excellent book by B.G. Burkett and Glenna Whitely, *Stolen Valor*.

Sharon Lane met her fate as she was trying to move patients from a vulnerable area to safer quarters. A rocket struck her neck, which killed her almost instantly. Shrapnel from the Viet Cong attack injured twenty-five already wounded patients and killed one Vietnamese patient...a baby!

The names, rank, and age of America's Lady Tigers who lost their lives in-country during the Vietnam War deserve mentioning in this chapter as they saved tens of thousands of American and Vietnamese lives, even babies:

- 1st Lt. Sharon A. Lane, twenty-five, killed 1969
- Capt. Eleanor G. Alexander, twenty-seven, killed 1967
- Lt. Col. Annie Ruth Graham, fifty-one, killed 1969
- Capt. Mary Therese Klinker, twenty-seven, killed 1975
- 1st Lt. Hedwig D. Orlowski, twenty-three, killed 1967
- 2nd Lt. Pamela D. Donovan, twenty-six, killed 1968

I guess the only positive out of this is that the Ameri-Cong media played no favorites in their false reporting of the Vietnam War. Woman or man, if you were an American soldier in the Vietnam War, you were undeservedly and almost automatically tagged as...Baby Killers!

The Vietnam War could very well be referred to as the Americans' Greatest Adventure...a war that started on lies and ended on lies. Here is an infamous quote by one of America's leaders at this time.

Vietnam I would classify as a fourth-rate power.
—Henry Kissinger, Secretary of State

Vietnam 1959–1975: It was the best of times; it was the worst of times. It was the age of judgment; it was the age of the unthinkable. It was the epoch of disbelief; it was the epoch of doubt. It was the season of night; it was the season of day. It was the spring of hope. It was the winter of our disillusionment. We had everything before us. And we were left with almost nothing. We were all going directly to heaven. We were all going through hell first. In short, it was so far removed from the present that many of its survivors couldn't help but remember it for good and for evil as an era that compared with no other before, or so far, after. It was the Vietnam War era. Promises were made, promises were broken, and the greatest promise ever made that affected the Vietnam War was undoubtedly this one, by four presidents:

We are not about to send our American boys some 10,000 miles away from their homes and families to do the job of and to risk dying for the Asian boys who ought to be doing what is necessary to protect themselves.

Paraphrased from…

> Lyndon B. Johnson
> John F. Kennedy
> Franklin D. Roosevelt
> Woodrow Wilson

JFK's withdrawal plan from Vietnam in October 1963 had already been decided on, whether the South Vietnamese appeared to be winning or losing its war with the communist insurgency. A detailed plan had been drawn up to accomplish this, and it had already been implemented at the time of JFK's assassination. It is believed that in the fall of 1963, Robert McNamara and Maxwell Taylor returned from a trip to Vietnam with a specific date of when we were going to accelerate the troop withdrawal. Instead, six months later when Johnson was president, the same two went to Vietnam again, but this time they came back with a message to LBJ that more troops were needed!

From 1960 to 1964, the U.S. State Department seemed unaware or unconcerned as to whether or not North Vietnam was infiltrating the south with their troops. They apparently did not sense a state of urgency, as was the case when North Korea overran South Korea, and China joined in when the U.S. was threatening to invade China from North Korea. In fact, just three years before all hell would break loose with the 1968 Tet Offensive, a 1965 report was completed on the estimated levels of infiltration of North Vietnamese troops into South Vietnam in support of the Viet Cong guerrillas. This report was criticized from every direction as being propagandistic by overestimating the enemy's level of infiltration. The war hawks were delighted with this report, and they demanded an escalation of American troops.

Well after the damage was done in 1967 and 1968, when the VC and North Vietnamese rampaged the countryside by springing ambushes and all-out human wave attacks Chinese-style, it was learned that the State Department report had significantly *underestimated* the levels of North Vietnamese infiltration into the south. A critical mistake and a price would be paid beyond expectations. That 1965 report had estimated that approximately 27,000 communist troops had been ushered to the south during all of 1959 through 1964. **WRONG!**

A 1994 history book by the Vietnam People's Army, translated by Merle L. Pribbenow, stated that 40,000 to 44,000 troops from the north had been sent southward between 1959 and 1963. But communist troop strength had been so badly *underrated*, not overrated, that by the end of 1965, the Viet Cong had built their force up to nearly 300,000 fighters—backed up by a North Vietnamese army of 250,000 and growing.

Strangely, back home, no one was complaining about the massive invasion into the south by the communists. I guess the peace lovers and protesters were too high at the time. As long as the north continued to deny their secret invasion, that was enough for the liberal left in America. Bad mistake. When the Viet Cong attacks increased and American casualties were suddenly catching Americans off guard, President Johnson ordered retaliation by hitting targets in North Vietnam with our air force. At this time, it was said that the Soviet communists advised the growing population of American communists to increase their pressure so that U.S. public opinion against the war would cause internal strife at home. And now…you know the rest of the story, as the horrors of the Vietnam War would spiral out of control, affecting millions of families in Vietnam and America for the rest of their lives. Otherwise, I would not be writing this book.

Who is Merle Pribbenow? There have been hundreds, maybe thousands of books written about the Vietnam War since Saigon's surrender in 1975. Most discuss how the United States military performed during the war. Why not, as the Ameri-Cong media did not do it right when it counted most, and America's soldier boys were being sent home in body bags or wheelchairs by the tens of thousands.

There was another story to that unfortunate war—the North Vietnam side, which is explained in books by Vietnamese authors—in the Vietnamese language, of course. For the United States government, the Vietnam War was an extended struggle from the Korean War against the horrible advances of communism in the Asian region. For the North Vietnamese, this was a "great patriotic" battle against a military Goliath, similar to what their great ancestors faced from the Chinese, the Mongols, and the French.

Merle Pribbenow II, who I stumbled onto by accident, graduated from the University of Washington in 1968 while the war in Asia was peaking. Earning his BA degree in Political Science, he went on to spend twenty-seven years as an officer in the CIA and a successful author of military papers, including projects for the Cold War International History Project. He is well-known for the translation of *Victory in Vietnam: The Official History of the People's Army of Vietnam*. It was first published in Hanoi in 1988, revised again in 1994 (also in Vietnamese), and then translated and published by the University Press of Kansas in 2002 by Pribbenow. Some of the book's critiques were complimentary—*an important book, well worth reading…a unique addition to the history of the Vietnam War…if for no other reason, scholars and students will be able to reference it to understand or discover the viewpoints of the North Vietnamese during the war… the importance of this book is that it provides the viewpoint of our enemy during the longest and probably most controversial war in America's his-*

tory...while heavily Marxist based with socialist viewpoints, the book still offers unique and surprising insights...the book is a definitive statement of the Vietnamese communist point of view, and many of the so-called facts presented in American history books are wrong...it is a boring gap in the endless literature on the Vietnam War...it contains a load of details never before presented in English.

The way I see it now, our brilliant bureaucrats misjudged communist troop strength that was well entrenched and literally lying there in the weeds— waiting for us. When American troop strength peaked in 1968 and 1969, giving the enemy more live targets, the holocaust of the Vietnam War was on as both sides mercilessly slaughtered each other.

I have tried to make it clear in each of my books that the Vietnam War has had a profound impact upon my life and all those whom I served so proudly with in Vietnam. But the impact that war has had on our lives after it ended continues to challenge many. For instance, as the "after the fact" or "I told you so" historians have written, America made too many mistakes with our policies toward Vietnam during the aftermath of World War II and up to the beginning of the American-Vietnam War. At least two presidents, Franklin Roosevelt and Dwight Eisenhower, had expressed their beliefs that Vietnam should be allowed the right to self-determine their own destiny rather than sitting back and watching France reassert itself in Vietnam as their colonial master. This major blunder was exactly that, so we turned a self-groomed ally of World War II into our enemy, and France hightailed it out of the scene in Indochina entirely, then sat back and watched, safely and soundly, as America stepped in to fight France's battle.

This book has been a difficult book to write and put together. The entire subject is controversial as it draws a line between friends and family just as the Civil War did.

It is pretty much understood and agreed upon by most who are knowledge-able that the South Vietnamese government did not win the hearts and souls of the "farmers and peasants" in the south. Although they also feared and despised communism, the South Vietnamese government administration was more con-cerned about making themselves rich than helping the poor. Most of them were Catholics, trying to run a civilization of mostly Buddhist faith.

People nowadays constantly express their frustration and disgust with the American media. Many kid themselves into believing it was never this bad, that it is finally out of hand...gone too far. Well, it depends on when you were born, where you were born, or why or how you were born. (Don't try to figure that out.)

I was born at the right time to remember this incident as reported:

Our Destroyers Attacked Second Time. American Planes Retaliate with Hit on North Vietnam

Washington Post
August 5, 1964

President Johnson has ordered retaliatory action against gunboats and supporting facilities in North Vietnam after renewed attacks against American destroyers in Gulf of Tonkin.

New York Times
August 5, 1964

I could probably get a really active donnybrook in an American Legion or VFW pub if I walked in, brought up this subject, and after the talks got a bit warm, I spoke this out loud:

"THERE WAS NO SECOND ATTACK—NO RENEWED ATTACKS AGAINST US!"

More air strikes were ordered in "retaliation" for a North Vietnamese torpedo attack that supposedly never happened. In the classic book *The Uncensored War* by Daniel Hallin, it suggests that there was "a great deal of information available which contradicted the so-called official account of the Tonkin events," quoted by Lyndon Johnson, President of the United States at that time.

So maybe the real escalation of the impending Vietnam War was caused by rumors? About four years later, another lie was unfolding…the Tet Offensive of 1968.

On January 30, 1968, more than a quarter million North Vietnamese soldiers and 100,000 Viet Cong irregulars launched a massive attack on South Vietnam. But the public didn't hear about who had won this most decisive battle of the Vietnam War, the so-called Tet Offensive, until much too late.

Media misreporting of Tet passed into our collective memory. That picture gave antiwar activism an unwarranted credibility that persists today in Congress, and in the media reaction to the war in Iraq. The Tet experience provides a narrative model for those who wish to see all U.S. military successes—such as the Petraeus surge—minimized and glossed over.

In truth, the war in Vietnam was lost on the propaganda front, in great measure due to the press's pervasive misreporting of the clear U.S. victory at Tet as a defeat. Forty years is long past time to set the historical record straight.

The Tet Offensive came at the end of a long string of communist setbacks. By 1967 their insurgent army in the South, the Viet Cong, had proved increasingly ineffective, both as a military and political force. Once American combat troops began arriving in the summer of 1965, the communists were mauled in one battle after another, despite massive Hanoi support for the southern insurgency with soldiers and arms. By 1967, the VC had lost control over areas like the Mekong Delta—ironically, the very place where reporters David Halberstam and Neil Sheehan had first diagnosed a Vietnam "quagmire" that never existed.

The Tet Offensive was Hanoi's desperate throw of the dice to seize South Vietnam's northern provinces using conventional armies, while simultaneously triggering a popular uprising in support of the Viet Cong. Both failed. Americans and South Vietnamese soon put down the attacks, which began under cover of a cease-fire to celebrate the Tet lunar New Year. By March 2, when U.S. Marines crushed the last North Vietnamese pockets of resistance in the northern city of Hue, the VC had lost 80,000-100,000 killed or wounded without capturing a single province.

Tet was a particularly crushing defeat for the VC. It had not only failed to trigger any uprising but also cost them "our best people," as former Viet Cong doctor Duong Quyunh Hoa later admitted to reporter Stanley Karnow. Yet the very fact of the U.S. military victory—"The North Vietnamese," noted National Security official William Bundy at the time, "fought to the last Viet Cong"—was spun otherwise by most of the U.S. press.

As the Washington Post's *Saigon Bureau, Chief Peter Braestrup documented in his 1977 book* The Big Story *the desperate fury of the communist attacks including on Saigon, where most reporters lived and worked, caught the press by surprise. (Not the military: It had been expecting an attack and had been on full alert since Jan. 24.) It also put many reporters in physical danger for the first time. Braestrup, a former marine, calculated that only 40 of 354 print and TV journalists covering the war at the time had seen any real fighting. Their own panic deeply colored their reportage, suggesting that the communist assault had flung Vietnam into chaos.*

Their editors at home, like CBS's Walter Cronkite, seized on the distorted reporting to discredit the military's version of events. The Viet Cong insurgency was in its death throes, just as U.S. military officials assured the American people at the time. Yet the press version painted a different picture.

To quote Braestrup, "The media tended to leave the shock and confusion of early February, as then perceived, *fixed as the final impression of Tet" and of Vietnam generally. "Drama was perpetuated at the expense of information," and "the negative trend" of media reporting "added to the distortion of the real situation on the ground in Vietnam."*

The North Vietnamese were delighted. On the heels of their devastating defeat, Hanoi increasingly shifted its propaganda efforts toward the media and the antiwar movement. Causing American (not South Vietnamese) casualties, even at heavy cost, became a battlefield objective in order to reinforce the American media's narrative of a failing policy in Vietnam.

Yet thanks to the success of Tet, the numbers of Americans dying in Vietnam steadily declined—from almost 17,000 in 1968 to 9,414 in 1969 and 4,221 in 1970—by which time the Viet Cong had ceased to exist as a viable fighting force. One Vietnamese province after another witnessed new peace and stability. By the end of 1969 over 70% of South Vietnam's population was under government control, compared to 42% at the beginning of 1968. In 1970 and 1971, American ambassador Ellsworth Bunker estimated that 90% of Vietnamese lived in zones under government control.

However, all this went unnoticed because misreporting about Tet had left the image of Vietnam as a botched counterinsurgency—an image nearly half a decade out of date. The failure of the North's next massive invasion over Easter 1972, which cost the North Vietnamese army another 100,000 men and half their tanks and artillery, finally forced it to sign the peace accords in Paris and formally to recognize the Republic of South Vietnam. By August 1972 there were no U.S. combat forces left in Vietnam, precisely because, contrary to the overwhelming mass of press reports, American policy there had been a success.

To Congress and the public, however, the war had been nothing but a debacle. And by withdrawing American troops, President Nixon gave up any U.S. political or military leverage on Vietnam's future. With U.S. military might out of the equation, the North quickly cheated on the Paris accords. When its re-equipped army launched a massive attack in 1975, Congress refused to redeem Nixon's pledges of military support for the South. Instead, President Gerald Ford bowed to what the media had convinced the American public was inevitable: the fall of Vietnam.[24]

Vietnam's Long-Kept Secrets...

1950	
August	U.S. sent ships (unknown numbers) of arms and supplies to aid the French and Indochina.
1951	
August	U.S. stepped up their aid to France to $500 million.

---

24 *Wall Street Journal,* February 6, 2008

1953	
August	France recruited mercenaries and French Legionnaires to help fight the Viet Minh. Atrocities by the French aroused the Vietnamese people and they rushed to join the Viet Minh in masses. Days became numbered for France's colonial empire.
1954	
May	It happened—what nobody around the world anticipated—a third world military soundly defeated a western power at the battle of Dien Bien Phu!
1955	
February	President Eisenhower sent U.S. troops as "advisors" to South Vietnam. North Vietnam protested.
1961	
May	President Kennedy escalated the Vietnam situation by sending 5,000 U.S. Army Special Forces to train in Thailand and set up a base.
1964	
October	Hanoi reached out and submitted a peace proposal to USA—denied.
1965	
February	Rolling Thunder launched bombing.
May	Hanoi restated another peace proposal to the U.S. It was also rejected.
November	IA Drang—The battle was won by the Americans and yet, it convinced Ho Chi Minh he could win eventually. He would simply outlast the Americans, which he did.
1965–1970	The American military had a favorable kill ratio against the communist forces of almost 6 to 1.
1967	American forces had earned a series of hard-fought victories until October 17, 1967, when a Viet Cong ambush was successfully sprung on a first infantry battalion. Although this would not rank as one of the war's longest battles, it was one of the more lopsided defeats and bloodiest for Americans. At the stream of Ong Thanh, the VC ambush inflicted casualties on the Americans at a ratio of 142 to 22, a kill ratio advantage for the VC of 6.5 to 1. **U.S. Army's news services and some mainstream media reported the battle as an American win?**

1st Infantry's Alpha Company of the 2nd-28th (Black Lions) was wiped out in twenty minutes while Delta Company took 50 percent casualties. 2nd Battalion Commander Lt. Colonel Terry Allen was killed.

1969	President Nixon declared that the Vietnam War was over. He did this at a news conference from 25th Infantry Division headquarters on December 8, 1969, saying that the war was coming to an end soon. He said a new program called "Vietnamization" was working, as the ARVNs had become more capable. The war lasted until April 30, 1975.
May	Peace plan offered by North Vietnam and Viet Cong—denied.
September	Ho Chi Minh died before the end of the war.
October	Vietnam Moratorium, estimated one million Americans protested in antiwar rallies.
1970	
September	Peace plan talks resumed again—remained at stalemate. War continued. North Vietnam invaded South Vietnam. U.S. responded with heavy air bombardment. Americans filled the streets with protests.
1971–1972	The American ground troops were barely used, primarily as advisors as they were in 1962–1964. American air power helped the South Vietnamese fight to a stalemate in those years. Neither side had the advantage over the other.
1973	
May	U.S. Senate cut off any future funds for air-bombing support of South Vietnam.
1974–1975	After the 1973 Peace Accords Treaty was broken repeatedly and there was no longer any American firepower to keep the North Vietnamese under control, North Vietnam and the Viet Cong dominated the ARVNs with a phenomenal 9-to-1 kill ratio edge. In fact, in the final year it would be worse.
1975	
March	North Vietnam launched largest offensive of the war. Without American air power to stop them, South Vietnam's military was devastated and surrendered within two months.
1977–1978	Khmer Rouge invaded Vietnam relentlessly, killing Vietnamese villagers. Despite warnings by Vietnam, the Khmer Rouge slaughtering continued.

1979–1989	Vietnam invaded and controlled Cambodia until a new government was set up. The Khmer Rouge were destroyed. The horrors of the "Killing Fields" was fully recognized.
1979	China invaded Vietnam again—perfect timing when most of Vietnam's army was fighting in Cambodia. Vietnamese militia successfully fought off the Chinese army while their military continued with their battles in Cambodia until 1989.
1991	Vietnam and America exchanged friendly gestures for the first time since the end of the war. U.S. normalized relations with Vietnam. Trade embargo was lifted by the U.S.

This was preventable—except for the lies of Tet, reported by the Ameri-Cong media. Vietnam War veterans who fought over there, who managed to survive the battles, were in disbelief when Saigon surrendered. They repeatedly asked of each other, **"WHAT THE F- - - HAPPENED? WE WERE WINNING THAT WAR WHEN I LEFT THERE!"**

Abandoned in Vietnam…American children? They aren't kids anymore. When the last Americans evacuated Saigon on April 29, 1975, left behind was a country scarred forever by an unforgettable war of unbelievable damage to both adversaries who fought in it. What could be worse than that? Well, another horrible example of deceit and flagrant heartlessness would be the thousands of half-Vietnamese and half-American offspring who were born during the war. They are called Amerasians, and most never met their fathers and more than likely never will. These innocents became victims just like the rest of their countrymen. Some are half black, half white, born from bar girls, hooch maids, laundry workers, general laborers who filled sandbags all day to protect Americans or…lady Viet Cong.

As I mentioned at the start, they aren't kids anymore, and most have done okay for themselves since being left behind…but not all of them. I believe that most Americans are very aware that there is a sizeable Vietnamese population in the U.S., many coming here after the fall of Saigon. What few Americans would know about these Amerasian kids from American fathers was the hardship they had to endure because their faces resembled the enemy of their friends and relatives…the Americans. Many of these Amerasians would suffer from Agent Orange spray or their own PTSD, and any medical treatment was highly unlikely, especially since the Americans had left, closing down their clinics behind them.

Human byproducts of war was not a new thing with the Vietnam War. Nonetheless, their stories are extremely sad, many times tragic. Imagine being discriminated against by your own kind—same nationality sort of, born in the same country, same village, and thrown into a sad life of prejudice and shattered hopes for the future. Even those Amerasians who did make it to America faced similar problems of prejudice. That goes on everywhere in the world.

Poverty, homelessness, starvation, hostility, and extreme neglect describes the plight of many Amerasians who were left behind in their own homeland. While many did fare well, many also disappeared without ever having a chance to make their mark on the world.

I personally know very little about Vietnamese Amerasians, and I am not even sure I saw any of them when I was in Vietnam. They weren't likely to be out where we were. To be perfectly blunt, few American soldiers would even know if they had fathered an Amerasian. Most encounters with the Vietnamese women were not motivated by love. They were more of the "one-night stand" hook-ups. However, I did look into the possibility of adopting a young Vietnamese girl who lost her parents from a battle between us and Viet Cong. I don't know to this day who was the killer of her parents, as the Viet Cong were using the villagers as shields as they were shooting at us. If I had been the one who killed her parents, I would not have felt guilty, as we had no choice under the circumstances.

I don't know why I have come into a love affair with Vietnam, its culture, and its people after all these years, especially when I have spent so much time and tried so many things to help me forget everything there was about Vietnam. Especially since I never saw its former beauty, only its darkest hours. Especially since I was brainwashed into thinking so terribly about people I had never met. That is how I have come to feel over the last decade or so, regardless of what happened to me and my war buddies over there. Make no mistake. Not only did our government act irresponsibly toward the Amerasians, so did many of the soldiers who fathered them. This resulted in condemnation of those children to lives of prejudice, discrimination, poverty, and instability.

Reminder—these children we abandoned were South Vietnamese. We fought a long war on behalf of these people, so you see, the decision by our government to leave South Vietnam high and dry—unlike South Korea, whom we still protect—caused much more damage than most Americans could possibly be aware. Okay, the harm was done. So how have the Amerasians in general managed their lives?

For the most part, Amerasians who came to America adapted well, learned English quickly, and have become model American citizens. They have never protested in the streets or caused riots for what our government did to them or did not do for them. Just like their half-Vietnamese ancestors who fought off multiple invasions from Chinese dynasties, Mongol hordes, France, and America, they bounced back because of the resilience bred into them.

Our Amerasian brothers have blended into American society with little assistance from us, and many have served in our Armed Forces very honorably, I might add—as I would have expected. If they fought with half the tenacity their relatives and ancestors did, any American should feel proud and safe serving next to an American-Vietnamese offspring. I know I would.

As of the most recent Global Census, Vietnam is now a country with almost one hundred million people. Here is a thought—wouldn't it be nice to have this country and its very formidable military on our side now as an ally?

I think that when my Vietnam War buddies read this book, they are going to say something like "You must have been Vietnamese in a previous life." If I was, I hope that I was fighting with the Trung sisters in the fourth century when Vietnam fought its way out of being dominated by the huge Chinese dynasties. That would have been an honor indeed…yeah, dream on, Dusty.

Like many other war buddies, I never talked about Nam—NEVER— for at least twenty years after coming home. No one cared. So I went on with my life, thinking I could block the Nam out of my life…wrong-o! Recently, I have even entertained thoughts of returning to Vietnam for different reasons than most Nam vets have gone back there for, like some kind of "closure" or something. There is no closure for anyone who was deeply involved with that war and the people over there. Still, I have thought about it, not seriously though. Actually, I don't think I could handle the anxiety and anticipation on that *very* long plane ride. I wouldn't sleep a single wink, so I would already be in a near hypertensive state at landing time in Tan Son Nhat Airport or wherever.

Next, I would have to de-board the plane, looking at Vietnam again— fifty years later—and I don't think I could make it any further without collapsing. Seriously, my heart and soul is so much into that place where I spent just one year of my seventy- plus years on planet Earth. So, going back remains *not* on my bucket list.

We need to look at Vietnamese Amerasians as a living legacy of our longest and most unpopular war in America's short history. To our country's credit, in 1987 (fourteen years after our war there ended), Congress did pass what was known as the Amerasian Homecoming Act. Under the conditions of the act, Amerasians and their immediate family members were offered the opportunity to immigrate to the U.S. at U.S. government expense, where they would receive priority refugee benefits such as job training, language classes, housing, health care, and other special attention to help them adjust. Nearly 100,000 Amerasians and family members accepted the offer as an opportunity to escape Vietnam and live in that dream country they had always heard of…*the* United States of America. Many other Amerasians did not take advantage of the Amerasian Resettlement Program, as they were unreachable where they lived, in the forests and mountains.

Unsaid until now, many Amerasian babies were quickly abandoned by their mothers. Are you surprised? When a poor kid was able to talk, of course, he knew absolutely nothing about his mother—most definitely not his father—or even what an Amerasian was.

I mentioned earlier that Agent Orange affected Amerasians, and they were met with a shortage of health-care professionals, an unwillingness to treat them, or a lack of knowledge or technology. Roger that. Being disabled in Vietnam in the post-Vietnam War years of 1970 through the 1980s and after was difficult beyond words of description. In the traditional Vietnamese family, mostly rural, a disabled family member was shameful to the family and to the unfortunate being who was inflicted. Amerasians who were cursed with a noticeable disability were shameful to their family, and they were often kept from exposure to the public…more so because they were Amerasian, but being disabled made them look more unnatural or freakish to others who were ignorant around them.

Unfortunately, my research found that only a few of our Nam brothers were able to take responsibility for their Amerasian children. The reasons had to be insurmountable, and why would an American soldier or marine care to openly discuss this with anyone when he returned to America?

One Amerasian named Quyen told her story to another American U.S. Army vet about her mother's unfortunate episode with falling in love with an American soldier:

My mother worked in a canteen at an American base where my father was a helicopter pilot. He flew with the red crosses that would pick up and bring back the many wounded Americans after they were in a bad battle with the VC. He was married, but my mother did not know that. She was about three months pregnant with me when he was transferred to another American base. She never heard from him again. I asked how my mother's parents had reacted to her relationship with an American. They were very mad and sad, she said. You are supposed to be married before you get pregnant, especially if the man is a foreigner. All of our friends looked down on our family.

Then my mother was forced to leave home and she was told to give me away, but she refused. So, we had to leave their home.

This did not make me feel hatred for my American father. My mother was here for me and I loved her so much. She went through so much for me. I had to respect her for that. We were so innocent at the time. My mother always said he was a great guy and she believed he would come back for us some day to bring us to America, but he never came. My mother waited for him for twelve years before she died.

—Quyen, Amerasian

Hail to Castro? Few of us who served in Vietnam were aware that Obama's good buddy Fidel Castro and his murderous military were participants in the Vietnam War…on the side of the North Vietnamese communists, of course. I have paraphrased some of the House of Representatives Committee on International Relations' report on the "Cuban Program" in Vietnam to note facts for this section. Our Vietnam War veterans deserve to have this information.

Cuba was not just a bystander during the war. They were heavily involved with lethal actions that would contribute to the death of many American soldier boys. In fact, Cuba's participation in the war was so heavy that they had set up a consulate with a medical treatment center deep in the jungles between Cambodia and Laos.

Cubans in Vietnam were responsible for maintaining a large portion of the Ho Chi Minh Trail's critically important supply line that ran from North Vietnam through Laos into Cambodia and eventually South Vietnam's northern sector in I Corps. They were accompanied by a large contingent of well-trained and battle-hardened combat engineers and combat infantry soldiers. Unfortunately, the Cuban responsibilities stretched into other areas such as piloting Russian M16s against our American pilots in air combat actions.

The Cuban Project, where American POWs were held at a POW camp called the Cu Loc POW camp, was also known as "the Zoo." The well-concealed buildings were French-built during their war with North Vietnam. It is known that American POWs were tortured mercilessly and killed by Cubans at the Zoo. But hey! Didn't Hanoi Jane Fonda swear that American POWs were not treated badly? Of course, she only visited "the Hanoi Hilton" POW camp. Hanoi Jane needed to get out more during that war; she may have become too comfy at the Hilton in Hanoi.

In reading about the condition of some of those POWs in the Cuban Project, *ungodly* is the best way to describe their appearance and what was done to them. Judicial Watch President Tom Fitton stated this when Obama was making his visit to Cuba to chum with the Castros: "The Obama administration admires Castro's Cuba so much that even the fate of American POWs from the Vietnam War are of little concern to him." What kind of American supports this demagogue? Certainly, not anyone who is proud to call himself or herself "American."

According to former POW Air Force Colonel Donald "Digger" Odell, "Two American POWs left behind in a Cuban-managed camp were so brutally tortured that they were left behind when the 1973 Operation Homecoming took place. They were indescribably tortured into a senseless state by the Cubans to be released. The North Vietnamese did not want the world to see what had been done to them."[25]

If you are getting the notion that not all of our living POWs from the Vietnam War have been returned to us, your suspicion is right on, unfortunately. Some people believe there may be a dozen or up to nineteen. Obama was pressed to bring this important topic up with the Castros during his spring 2016 visit. I could not find any reports that he did do that on his trip. How bad does that stink…you Obama lovers?

A piece published in *Accuracy* by John Lowery described at least seventeen U.S. airmen captured during the Vietnam War were reportedly brought to Cuba for "medical research experiments" in torture techniques. Please imagine what an opinion-enhancing move it could have been if Obama had returned from Cuba…with our American heroes who have been POWs for forty years longer than our guys were held in North Vietnam. It appears Obama has no interest in that.

However, on Obama's visit in March 2016, during a speech at the Gran Teatro in Havana, he said… "I have come home to bury the last remnant of the Cold War with America." But patriotic Americans wanted to know if that "remnant" included American service members still living or buried on the island. As I mentioned earlier, most Americans were unaware that Cuba was so heavily involved in the Vietnam War, and I am happy to have mentioned it in this book.

At least John McCain issued challenges to Fidel Castro back in 2008. Actually, he issued strong accusations about his torturous treatment of our men. McCain was in his presidential run at the time and of course, he, too, was a POW at the Hanoi Hilton. When do the cover-ups and lies about the Vietnam War ever stop?

During one of Obama's meetings in Cuba, thirteen Cuban dissidents at the U.S. Embassy in Havana gave him names of political prisoners whose existence in Cuba's prisons were denied a day earlier by President Raul

---

25 Free Republic, February 14, 2004

Castro. There was no record of Obama pursuing this subject during his stay in Cuba.[26]

Then, according to the Voice of America, in one of those meetings, Elizardo Sanchez, president of the opposition group called Cuban Commission for Human Rights and National Reconciliation, gave Obama another list of eighty-nine political prisoners in Cuba's prisons.

My question of this weird news—as I did not know this until early 2017—is…why weren't the American POWs held by the Cubans released and returned home with the other POWs in Operation Homecoming in 1973? This blows my mind that I am just now learning this and that no one has ever brought it up. The news about the Cuban Program is not new. It has been a well-kept secret, but a few scattered articles did publish in 1977, 1981, 1992, 1996, 1999, and 2008, and now in March/April 2016.

Obama stated that the U.S. continues to have deep differences with the Cuban government in the area of human rights and democracy.

One of the eye openers about the Cuban Program tragedy is that many of these guys should still be living as they would be fairly young men in the age group of sixty-five to seventy-three, with a number of years left to enjoy at home in America…if they are still living. But the President of the United States didn't seem to have much compassion.

Anyone who viewed the September 2017 ten-part narrated series called *The Vietnam War* by Ken Burns and Lynn Novick should now be convinced that our American combat soldiers and marines were as tough as any military that America has ever put onto a battlefield. They were unbelievably courageous, tenacious, hardy, and dedicated to one purpose…to preserve each other. The close brotherhood of the Vietnam war veterans today is living proof. But…were they also "baby killers"?

NO! Yes, the tragedy at My Lai happened. Yes, there may have been similar incidents as there have always been in every war since the Israelites slaughtered many of their enemies, innocent civilians. I personally know not even one other Vietnam vet who experienced the act of the Calley-led soldiers. In Chapter 20 (Vietnam's Greatest Lie), I will address this very sensitive subject with surprising details and end this book with heart-stopping images.

Many Vietnam vets, especially those who experienced the ugly combat of that war's in-your-face style, are often maligned by other Americans as carrying too much anger. The people who should be the most understanding toward us work at Veterans Affairs and hospitals. They are not that. Another lie received a shot in the arm in September 2017 when the left wing rag

26 www.voonews.com/content/cuba-dissident

The Washington Post published an article by journalist Colby Itkowitz in defense of poor "Hanoi Jane" or Jane Fonda. I responded to Ms. Itkowitz with a fact-laden three-page rebuttal. Let's just say that I put our beloved Ms. Fonda into the same class as these sweet and revered ladies: Tokyo Rose, Hanoi Hannah, and Saigon Sally. To me and many Vietnam vets, that is Hanoi Jane's legacy in history that she deserves till her last day on Earth. In fact she denounced any warm feelings toward our country during a public interview in mid-October 2017 which only solidified her legacy with patriotic America.

"When Lyndon Johnson pulled out, the war was metaphorically over. The grunts sensed it right away. We were never going to win, but we had to withdraw with a semblance of dignity. That semblance of dignity took four more years of deceit and unnecessary deaths. And in the moral vacuum, there was never any clear reason to us why we should be dying. Dissention, even mutiny grew in the ranks between the enlisted men— the grunts and officers, so fraggings escalated. Black/white relations grew worse. The ultimate corruption was President Johnson sending only poor or uneducated to the war—in fact practicing class warfare wherein the upper classes could avoid the war by going to college or paying a psychiatrist. I am sure that if those upper classes had been sent to Vietnam and began to return in body bags, those upper class parents, politicians, and businessmen would have demanded an ending to the war a hell of a lot sooner. In fact, politicians' sons, if not the politicians themselves, should be sent to every war first."

Oliver Stone, Writer and Director
U.S. Army 25th Infantry 1967–68

What were our children told? Because, we were anything but losers. And we sure weren't baby killers! Ask any Vietnam vet who had a part in actual battles against the communist-backed NVA and VC from 1965 to 1972 what happened over there, and they will most likely say to you…Hey, We Were Winning When I Left!

I've watched the last days of the Vietnam War on TV several times, and each time I was more angry at our politicians (majority Democrats) and I have not been able to curb that anger to this day, regardless of countless hours with VA psychologists. Combat PTSD and severe anger seem destined to plague me and many others who fought "victoriously" in hundreds of firefights and full-blown battles during those bloody years of 1967, 1968, and 1969. Nearly 75 percent of all Americans casualties (killed/wounded) occurred in just those three years (1959–1973) of American participation in the war. In 1974 and 1975 the casualties taken by the South Vietnamese military were almost embarrassing, without American combat troops on hand to back them up.

Justifiably so, my memories of this great adventure of a lifetime will always be of victorious battles against an enemy that was far more cunning, brave, persistent, and resilient than our son of a bitches in Washington ever warned us about, ever prepared us for, and to this day they still seem to discredit that extremely formidable adversary an unworthy opponent. **BULL!**

It was not a secret that the NVA and VC would begin to roam the countryside of South Vietnam after they were sure our departure was final. But no one expected the South Vietnamese military would be dominated so quickly and convincingly. Although Americans were not victorious in every battle, we undoubtedly won most of them, and even in defeat we usually held our ground.

In 1968–69 I remember South Vietnam troops cheering us; the villagers were less enthusiastic toward us, although the kids were friendly. During Vietnam's last days, the South Vietnamese were not cheering the departing Americans. They were jeering them and in some cases shooting at them! Hard to blame them as thousands of Vietnamese who had been promised safe passage to the U.S. were left behind to whatever fate awaited them with a revenge-motivated North Vietnamese Army, thanks to a Democratic majority Congress in 1975. So be it. Nuff said on this.

After all, one of the main reasons to step up and become a soldier or marine is to experience adventure and travel to other countries.

Poisonous snakes were not the only creepy, deadly critters that the Vietnam War veteran had to be wary of as they were conducting search-and-destroy missions day and night in the jungles and swamps of Vietnam. There were also killer hornets, giant centipedes, ferocious and extremely aggressive red ants, scorpions, and an overabundance of spiders and snakes with venomous bites to large body-crushing boa constrictors. Vietnam's jungles were no tropical paradise. In 2017, over 30,000 Vietnamese farmers were reportedly bitten by snakes.[27] The Vietnamese mosquito doesn't take a backseat to those in other tropical areas as they cause their fair share of malaria, yellow fever, and dengue. The giant huntsman spider may look like just a little old tarantula, except that it is twice as big, faster, and meaner. The giant huntsman spider is the world's largest spider by leg span, which often reaches one foot or more. Laos, Vietnam, and Australia are home to huntsman spiders, which by the way hunt down their prey rather than spinning a web and lying back, waiting for the meal to trap itself. A soldier would hate

---

27 hubpages.com

to wake up one morning in Nam with one of these things in their boot or walking on their chest to start a day off. But hey, wait a minute. I did wake up with some of these creepy crawlers in my boots and on my body from time to time. Once is enough.

Fortunately, the giant huntsman spider wasn't discovered in Vietnam until a few years ago, long after the Vietnam War had ended in 1978. Quite possibly the destructive war devices reduced their numbers back then. But there were plenty of cobras, bamboo vipers, and tigers to ruin one's sleep in Nam.

Soldiers were given (forced) opportunities to be stalked and hunted by a large variety of the Vietnam's environment while they were trying to perform the specialty they were trained for, to hunt, capture, or kill communist-backed soldiers. None of us were prepared for the shock of what was in store for us in Vietnam's unique environment and rough geography.

Every day and most nights, it was the same anticipation…what's next? Where will it come from and when? What will it be? This constant scenario of stress and tension was enough to elevate and maintain our blood pressure at high levels. Then the actual confrontation with the danger it brought skyrocketed our blood pressure, as our adrenaline must have been raised to almost life-threatening levels. But you know what?

I don't remember, nor do any of my war buddies recall, ever having a blood pressure check by a medic after a battle!

The life-threatening hazards of Vietnam's wildlife and unfriendly environment could sometimes be just as tasking as our efforts to stay alive as the battle confrontations we were sent to Vietnam to deal with. We also got free on-the-job classes on what it may have been like for our ancestors, the Cro Magnon and Neanderthal humans, and what they must have had to overcome during the Stone Age.

Pick Your Poison…So have at it. To follow are a couple dozen pages of images of what we may have run into each and every day and night during the Vietnam War. And, trust me, there was no training offered to us, nor was it even available to prepare us for these unforgettable and extremely unpleasant experiences. I hope the following images remind Vietnam vets of what they definitely don't miss about Vietnam. For the non-Vietnam vets, these images should get you thinking that you were extremely lucky to have avoided the Vietnam War.

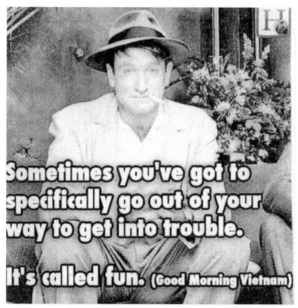

America's Greatest Adventure Begins

Marines Arrive I Corps, Claymores Out

Adventure Begins with Breakfast at the Ritz Then Air Assault

Air Assault and Endless Search-and-Destroy Missions

Searching for Him, a Barefoot Guerrilla Viet Cong

Short Break But...Stay Alert

And so, we became blood brothers, having each other's back 24/7!

Ambush!

Counterattack Unleashed!

Keep Your Head Down

On-the-Spot First Aid

Casualties Add Up

Brothers Saving Brothers...

The enemy also took care of their own with unusual dedication.

At the End of the Day,
Was It Worth It?

Our Great Adventure Continues. Even though Ho Chi Minh died in 1968, leaders Le Duan, Phan Van Dong, and Giap kept regrouping after every brutal battle and always showed up again the next day willing to take more punishment from us.

The War and the Great Adventure Continues for Five More Years

Our Awesome Firepower

Mobile Riverine Patrol

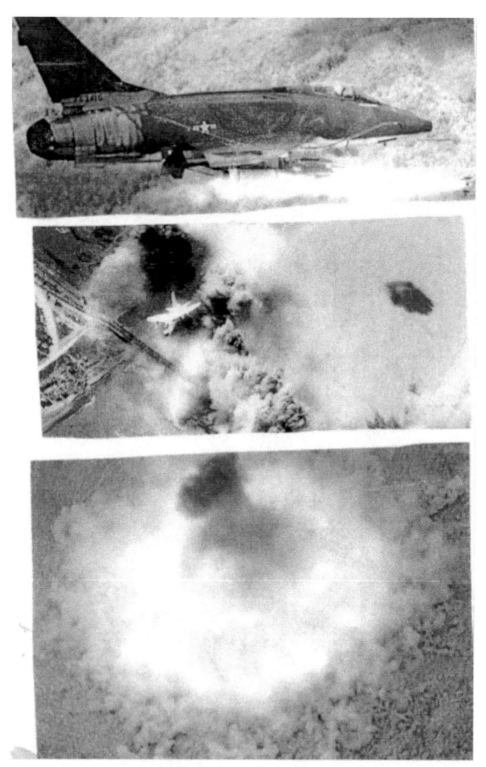

Hell Unleased from Above

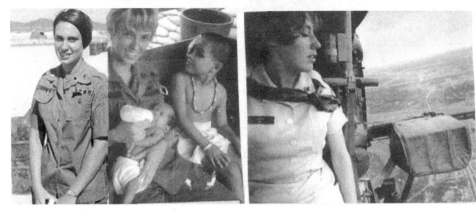

More Firepower Support, Unsung Heroes

Tet II Offensive in Saigon, May 1968

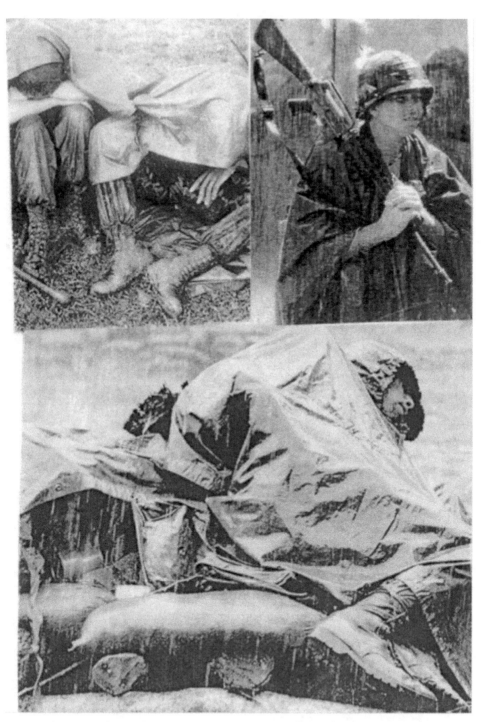

Monsoon Season, Wet 24/7

Fate of a Convoy...Ambushed

Bad Ending

The Tunnels

The Dreaded Booby Traps

Pick Your Poison...

Bamboo Viper, Cobra, and Croc

Big Lizards

The Bananas, Spider

Pineapple and Coconut Spiders

Giant Black Widow and Scorpions

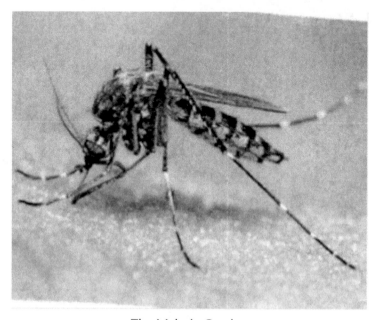

The Malaria Carrier

map

Venomous Ants?

Godzilla Centipede

Even Rhinos, Elephants, and Water Buffalo

And This Guy Too

Misery Road—Ho Chi Minh's Trail. In my first two books, I barely mentioned one of the Greatest Wonders of the World, so I've given it some coverage here. The trail was a profound part of our Greatest Adventure. Personally I never set my boots onto its dirt and mud, but we came close a few times when we entered into the Cambodian sanctuary for NVA and Viet Cong. We also viewed it from the top of the Black Virgin Mountain just a few miles away in Tay Ninh Province. We probably flew over the trail a few times while on a combat assault mission by helicopter. And unfortunately three of the trail's busiest exits into South Vietnam emptied tens of thousands of NVA back and forth between the areas known as the Fish Hook and the Parrot's Beak. It would be an understatement to say that without the trail the North Viets and their VC buddies could have never waged extensive warfare as they did during the Tet Offensives of 1967 and 1968.

In fact, without the trail there would not have been a war of much significance past 1965 when the troops' escalations took place from 1965–1968. But it was built by almost the entire North Vietnam population in one way or another. Now I will defer to the images on the next few pages to finish the story of the trail.

American's Great Adventure Ends

The curtain closed on our great adventure two months after the signing of the so-called Peace Agreement with North Vietnam and the Viet Cong. While the U.S. pulled out all combat troops, this simply rose the curtain on the DMZ for NVA's to inviltrate South Vietnam at a greater rate, with nothing to stop them. Despite winning 99.9% of the major battles, despite handling the communists a crushing defeat at the 1968 TET Offensive, Americans were forced into retreat mode from a war they were clearly winning. So the Vietnam War continued … reverting back to the Civil War it was before we invaded the country. Some will always say that we fought on the wrong side, the side the French set up to fight against the northern brothers of the south.

On April 30, 1975 the extended Vietnam War came to a breutal end as Russian tanks, manned by North Vietnamese rambled into and over Saigon, almost unchallenged by an army that had no more ammunition to fight with or gas to fuel their tanks and aircraft with … thanks to an unsympathetic Democratic controlled American government as well as the dirty deeds by the Ameri-Cong Media, now unaffectionately and properly labeled as the …
Fake News.

> Troops who served in the so-called safe areas, the base camps etc. He pisses on the notion that they were traumatized and even had a right to claim they suffered from PTSD.

Of course there is no doubt that the support troops in large basecamps faced anything even close to the constant dangers that the field treoops did on a daily basis. And I have even mentioned this in each of my books. But for sure, the cooks, clerks, vehicle drivers etc. sleeping in tents or flimsy hootches that enemy mortar rounds decimate like toothpicks put together by string earned their name placement on The Wall just as every other poor soul did. Bottom line, Hastings and Burns have presented valid reasons why I need to write this book for my brave brothers and sisters of the world's most senseless and misunderstood war.

Ho Chi Minh Trail

• Path along borders of Vietnam, Laos, and Cambodia to supply arms to Vietcong

The Hartford Courant

ESTABLISHED 1764, VOL. I · J. CXXXVI · No. 23 · HARTFORD, CONN., WEDNESDAY MORNING, JANUARY 24, 1973 · 44 PAGES

Nixon Announces Peace Accord

LBJ Eulogized

Says Goal Of Honor Achieved

Conflict Ends On Saturday

Part of Ho Chi Minh Trail—2018

Our Part of the Greatest Adventure Ended in 1973,
but the War Continued On

Going Home to What Awaits Us

The Final Invasion in 1975

April 30, 1975: The Fall of Saigon

Ho Chi Minh's Dream Comes True Seven Years After His Death!

The Ho Chi Minh faithful came out. And those who were afraid—ran.

Many had to leave.

Chapter 8

CAMBODIA/CHINA INVASIONS

The China-Vietnam scenario is ancient. It has been tumultuous, with China being the pure aggressor every time from 111 BC to 1978–79. Put aside all those bloody invasions by the Chinese and the successful counterattacks fiercely launched by the Vietnamese people to regain their freedom. Their relationship continues to be one difficult puzzle to figure out. At least I found it that way.

China sent tens of thousands of troops to North Vietnam during the course of their war with America. They weren't sent into direct combat against us, not officially, but more so for advising, training, and building and repairing the damage by our bombing attacks. This helped to free up the North Vietnamese Army to fight the Americans and their allies. I've read various reports where China gave North Vietnam several million firearms, 70,000 artillery pieces, 17,000,000 artillery shells, over a billion rounds of firearm ammunition, nearly 600 tanks, 170 aircraft, over 150,000 other vehicles, 30,000 radio transmitters, 40,000 rocket-propelled grenades, and tons of food. Clearly North Vietnam could not have waged the war they did against South Vietnam and its allies without such generous support from their age-old adversary.

At the same time, the USSR was contributing in the billions of dollars to help North Vietnam fight their war. And believe it or not, China resented the Soviet contribution and continued to pressure North Vietnam to break ties with Moscow. In 1969, there was a skirmish between China and USSR along the Soviet-Chinese border. After this the Soviets actually stepped up their military aid to North Vietnam, and the People's Republic of China's relations with North Vietnam soured.

After North Vietnam took over South Vietnam in 1975, China began supporting the ruthless Khmer Rouge in the Cambodia civil war, and there was no love affair between Cambodia and Vietnam anyway. Even though the Vietnam civil war was barely over, their military was far superior to the Chinese-backed Khmer Rouge. Even so, the Khmer Rouge intentionally antagonized Vietnam with vicious raids along their borders. The Khmer Rouge thought China had their back and they did, sort of. When Vietnam had enough of the insulting raids along their border with Cambodia, they conducted a full invasion into Cambodia. China was outraged and prepared to take action.

Cambodia-Vietnam War (1978–1989). The American-Vietnam War ended in 1972. The North Vietnamese reconquered South Vietnam in 1975, and the reunification of Vietnam was complete. Next for Vietnam? The invasion of its neighbor, Cambodia. Why? Weren't they both "commie" buddies under the arm of big brother, China? Wasn't the domino theory meant for these Communist nations to become fraternal brothers and steamroll over the rest of Southeast Asia? Wasn't that one of the reasons why Presidents Kennedy and Johnson sent 2.8 million American soldier boys over to Vietnam? Wasn't it?

Until 1975, the final year of Vietnam's civil war, Cambodia and Vietnam had always tolerated each other, with an occasional border scuffle taking place. But with Vietnam's economy drained, its military depleted and disoriented after thirty-plus years of war with Japan, France, America, and their civil war within, it was assumed by the ruling party of Cambodia that Vietnam was in no position to take on another conflict. Cambodia (Kampuchea) was also the brat child, protected by China, which explains why Vietnam held back from major retaliation to the increased Cambodian border attacks from 1975 to 1978. In one border encroachment by Cambodia, over three thousand Vietnamese civilians were massacred. Still, Vietnam tried over and over again to negotiate a peaceful resolve, but the Cambodians were not in a negotiating mood. After all, the two countries had been squabbling for centuries, with Cambodia losing territory and Vietnam gaining more territory each time.

I suppose the ruling communists of Cambodia, the merciless Khmer Rouge, and their leader, Pol Pot, the dreaded culprit who created the "killing fields," were afraid of a stronger, reunified Vietnam looking for expansion. On April 30, 1977, the Cambodian army shocked much of the world by launching a major surprise attack on Vietnam. While Vietnam retaliated, they did not do so with intent to conquer. In fact, they attempted more negotiations to try to settle down their neighbor's border attacks. Even China attempted to mediate peace talks between the two, but little progress was made.

By then, the whole world was finding out that the Khmer Rouge was a ruthless, vicious regime that had committed genocide not seen since the twelfth century when Genghis Khan was in the process of annihilating one-third of the known world's population at that time. It is mind-boggling that it was the Vietnamese who stopped the continued advances of the Mongol hordes by defeating them in battle not once, but three times. And it was the Vietnamese who defeated and vanquished the evil Khmer Rouge.

While the Khmer Rouge were slaughtering their own and any other people of any nationality in an alleged ethnic cleansing, Vietnam continued to see its borders crossed and many of the Vietnamese villages destroyed mer-cilessly, without provocation. As this went on, the world stood by and looked the other way, including America, again, probably because of the Demo-cratic Congress that betrayed the Vietnamese people and their own warriors who fought there, and China kept supporting its little brother in the Vietnam border attacks. It was not until Cambodia launched its largest attack ever against Vietnam (about sixty thousand troops) that Vietnam would tolerate this no more, even though the threat of an angry China loomed in the back-ground. Vietnam counterattacked in full force and declared a full-scale war with Cambodia in 1977. The Khmer Rouge ran to the border of Cambodia and Thailand without any protests from a weakened Thailand government. The Khmer Rouge continued to peck at the Vietnam army, which continued to occupy Cambodia until 1991, and China continued to supply the renegade Khmer Rouge. Honestly, as I view this, Americans might have had far more justification to step in on behalf of Vietnam this time than we had in the civil war between North and South Vietnam. Remember, the French were the bastard colonialists (invaders) of Vietnam, and we made the wrong decision to step in for them.

Vietnam should have been seen as a savior by the citizens of Cambodia as well as their own people on the borders and to the world. But the longer they remained in Cambodia, they were looked at more as a conqueror than a savior; even the United States teamed up with China with the protests at United Nation meetings. Painful economic sanctions were increased against Vietnam. Therefore, the war with Cambodia is not a war that is remembered and celebrated as all of Vietnam's wars still are today. Eventually, Viet-nam would turn Cambodia over to its people and with guidance from other nations, a new government and a new country would be created. It would be called Democratic Kampuchea. But Kampuchea could easily have become a barren, human-less vacuum in Southeast Asia had Vietnam not acted.

On December 25, 1978, the Vietnamese army invaded Cambodia again. This time, it was an all-out invasion, quickly and masterfully resembling a skilled, highly organized, lean, mean military machine. The advance was prolific and unstoppable. After all, going back to their ancestors, up until then the Vietnamese had become like professional soldiers. They were prob-ably handed a sword at birth in the ancient days and taught quickly how to use it. Led by seasoned and highly talented generals who may have fought the Americans and French, the Vietnamese army methodically sent six coor-dinated columns of regiment size across the Vietnam-Cambodia border. They were complemented by a full naval division, attacking from the sea. Airstrikes, using captured or abandoned American aircraft, would seal the doom of the Khmer Rouge even though they fought back with suicidal-like fanaticism. This war would not carry on like the American or French wars did. This brief conflict between two communist nations was watched by the entire world, as the Vietnamese army made short work of the genocidal Khmer Rouge.

Within just two weeks, the Cambodian army (Kampuchean Revolutionary Army) was completely overrun. Pol Pot and his entire military were exiled or destroyed, and Vietnam began their unpopular ten-year period of occupation of the country they had just defeated with relative ease. It was not until September 1989 that Vietnam withdrew its military from Cambodia. The aftermath of this war was estimated at twenty thousand KIAs for Vietnam and fifty thousand KIAs for Cambodia. As for the "killing fields" of Pol Pot, the ghastly reality of what went on in the prison camps of Cambodia under the Khmer Rouge, where millions of Cambodian and Vietnamese civilians were murdered in gruesome fashion, came to an end.

Some Cambodians believed that after exiling the Americans, Vietnam was scheming to form an Indochina Federation, with Vietnam as its leading member. Therefore, the acts of aggression by the Khmer Rouge were launched on Vietnam in 1977 and 1978 more out of fear of what Vietnam *might* be up to. There has never been any evidence found of this suspicion.

After Vietnam's humanitarian sacrifice to rid the entire region of the Khmer Rouge, even the United Nations continued to recognize the Khmer Rouge-Democratic Kampuchea as a legitimate government, which was incomprehensibly wrong. The right and moral act to proceed with as soon as possible would have been to join in and support the Vietnamese until the threat by the Khmer Rouge was completely eliminated.

Looking at things from the Cambodian Khmer Rouge viewpoint, Vietnam had colonized Cambodia in 1830 in much the same way France did with Vietnam. The Vietnamese stranglehold on Cambodia was maintained during the French colonization. Cambodia was forced to cede much of its southeastern area, which included Saigon (Ho Chi Minh City), the Mekong Delta, and Tay Ninh Province. These actions would seemingly justify the mass extermination of civilians in unfathomable proportions by Pol Pot's army.

Vietnam was warned several times to vacate Cambodia, but the Viets remained until a reliable and patriotic faction was voted in as Cambodia's leaders. It wasn't until 1990 when Australia joined in and helped organize the Third Jakarta Informal Meeting. Representatives from both political parties agreed to a mutual power-sharing arrangement. However, the Khmer Rouge continued to make things very difficult by disrupting elections with military attacks on official UN peacekeeping forces, and the killing of ethnic Vietnamese resumed. The Vietnamese military remaining in Cambodia would act as police until 1991.

For the record, while some anti-Vietnam critics often compare America's invasion of Iraq to Vietnam's takeover of Cambodia, that comparison is still a bit bewildering to me. The U.S. invasion of Iraq was not based on any provocation or direct military action on the United States. On the other hand, Vietnam's border had been encroached often, and Vietnamese civilians were massacred by the Khmer Rouge. Clearly, the U.S. supported the bad guys in Cambodia when the right thing to do was condemn the Khmer Rouge killings and put economic sanctions onto Cambodia.

If you have not seen the movie or read the book *The Killing Fields*, I respectfully recommend that you do one or the other. The story starts out in the 1973 timeframe when the regular Cambodian national army is in a civil war with the Khmer Rouge. This occurs largely because of the Vietnam War spilling over into Cambodia.

Why did the Khmers kill so much of their own civilization? Their mission was very similar to Hitler's Nazis, to purify the Cambodian race. The total damage may never be known, as remains of those murdered are discovered to this day. The conservative estimate is at least 1.5 million Cambodians and tens of thousands of Vietnamese and Laotians. One village in Vietnam that was attacked and destroyed by the Khmer Rouge lost three thousand dead in an overnight massacre. There were several more murderous raids like this.

The Vietnamese government has never confirmed official casualty totals from the Cambodian War. However, some online sources provide estimates without any specific sources mentioned. They all differ, slightly to greatly, so I took the average from several online sources and came to these estimated casualty totals:

Vietnamese Army	30,000 KIA	50,000 Wounded
Vietnamese Civilians	20,000 KIA	35,000 Wounded
Khmer Rouge Army	70,000 KIA	90,000 Wounded
Cambodian Civilians	2,500,000 KIA	750,000 Wounded

As I mentioned, the total casualties varied from source to source across the board. Make no mistake; the Vietnamese invasion and occupation of Cambodia had a mission which would not come to an end until the Vietnamese were satisfied with the outcome. This was not a little skirmish anymore.

Funny thing about this—while the Viet Cong and NVA of North Vietnam were considered to be bad people by U.S. officials, compared to the Khmer Rouge, our Viet Cong adversaries were like altar boys in terms of pure ruthless, torturous, murdering assassins.

And so our former enemy who we labeled so negatively, as though America was the white knight in shining armor, had intervened, taking heavy casualties and stopping the blatant slaughter of their neighbor's civilians and freeing Cambodia. This was an unexpected move by the Vietnamese. So was the awesome manner of their successful attack on a formidable army of fanatics. Another surprise came when the southern and northern Vietnamese pulled together. After all, they were once again facing another dangerous threat against their peaceful nation. The united Vietnamese fought well together as they pounced onto the Khmer Rouge like a wounded mother tiger protecting her cubs. But this mother tiger had no mercy left in her heart for these victims. They had to be eliminated.

Bottom line—the Vietnamese taught the rogue Cambodia regime a lesson they should not easily forget. As for the sixty thousand Khmer Rouge and another eighty thousand comrades who plundered countless Vietnamese villages, burning them all to the ground, the Vietnamese army made short work of defeating them and destroying most of them. This war epitomized the statement—*an eye for an eye and a tooth for a tooth.* Right or wrong, retaliation in self-defense of yourself or others close to you cannot be a crime, not in the eyes of the law or in the eyes of the almighty power…God.

Shame on the USA. The U.S. government is almost unequaled at keeping the truth of what it does globally from the American population. Examples abound throughout our short two and a half centuries of existence. One such example that I can relate to is the stand our government chose or did not choose to take during the Pol Pot "killing fields" tragedy. The entire world knew what was going on in Cambodia during and after North Vietnam defeated South Vietnam after the U.S. exit from that war. We chose to invade a country because of a bona fide civil war, and yet we ignored a situation in that same region that was delivering cruel, ruthless genocide of its own population by the millions.

While the U.S. did nothing to help the victims of the killing fields, neither did the rest of the world, not even the UN. So Vietnam stepped up to the task in spite of the real threat of an invasion from China, Cambodia's ally at the time. Vietnam had no choice but to attack Cambodia; it was sure self-defense. The rest of the world should have supported them, and yet China invaded Vietnam on behalf of their murdering ally Pol Pot.

Personally I actually love what the Vietnamese (Southern and Northern) did. They were certainly suffering badly from the French and American Wars, fighting us tooth and nail for over a decade, and still rolled into Cambodia and dismantled the Khmer Rouge in two weeks. Unfortunately, the exiled Pol Pot's Khmer Rouge was allowed to seek sanctuary in Thailand, which was a terrible act.

Another sad and well-kept secret by the U.S. government was when they seemingly sided with China against Vietnam and voiced heavy protests against Vietnam for invading a sovereign nation. Seriously?

This kept many Americans in the dark, and they simply believed that Vietnam deserved America's sanctions on that country. Those sanctions damaged Vietnam's economy and kept it from regrouping and moving forward.

All that happened around this time after the U.S. was completely out of Vietnam can be credited to the same Democratic-controlled Congress, the same group that left South Vietnam high and dry in 1973.

I, for one, am impressed that the Vietnamese people seem to harbor few if any ill feelings toward the USA. No country has done more damage to Vietnam than the USA has from the 1950s into the 2000s.

Sadly I find that many (not most) Vietnam War veterans still carry bitter feelings against Vietnam's northern population. I think this anger deserves to be directed entirely at our government and/or the Ameri-Cong media. ALL OF IT!

Although I once used the word "gooks" when referencing the Vietnamese, I have stopped that completely. In fact my eyes and ears are tuned in when I hear a black person tag them as "gooks." That's pretty racist, isn't it—no matter if it's a white or a black person uttering the word about Asians. On the other hand I am unable to recall ever hearing a Vietnamese person refer to a black person as "nigger." God, I detest these slang words.

Today, just like American, Australian, and South Korean/Vietnam war veterans suffer from various degrees of post-traumatic stress disorder, so do our adversaries of that war. Life is a bitch and war is hell!

You should see by now that I have positioned the Vietnamese in this book not as an aggressive conqueror of anyone's land. They eventually left Cambodia several years later; however, their struggles were not limited to Cambodia. China loomed in the background, as it always has considered Vietnam a stepchild that belonged in their family.

The Vietnamese were well aware of the threat of China intervening if Vietnam and Cambodia ever tangled in a serious manner. That happened; China acted and Vietnam would be invaded yet again. The 1960s and 1970s were not good years for America to be active with any country in Southeast Asia. It seems as though we picked the wrong side every time.

The last time Vietnam was forced to defend its homeland against a Chinese invader was in 1406–1407, when the Ming dynasty crossed into Vietnam. That invasion was repelled, and Vietnam retained its freedom.

Five hundred and seventy-three years later came another Chinese invasion of Vietnam in 1979, which didn't catch Vietnam by surprise. However, the Vietnamese Regular Army was in Cambodia, preoccupied with teaching a lesson. Remember, China favored Cambodia, which was the reason for their invasion into Vietnam—to teach them a lesson. This conflict would last almost a full month, but why did it last that long when the Vietnamese military was fighting a war with the Khmer Rouge?

While sources vary greatly as to just how large the Chinese invasion was, it was substantially large and quite capable of doing harm on a civilization of unprepared, untrained "farmers and peasants" whose regular army was not available. As expected, the Chinese crossed into northern Vietnam pretty much unopposed and enjoyed some immediate success in capturing a few cities. Their mission to punish the Vietnamese was going well at first, but would fall short of original goals.

China's force was estimated at a low of 300,000 to a high of 600,000 with five hundred tanks. Vietnam was not completely defenseless, as an estimated 150,000 very brave and capable militia ("farmers and peasants") gave the much larger Chinese forces all they could handle. They met the Chinese head-on at several locations where significant battles took place unexpectedly, and the Chinese were dealt extreme casualties. In the meantime, two other scenarios were unfolding. As they had done successfully during previous invasions, thousands of militia and mountain tribesmen waged a lethal guerilla war using the Vietnamese jungles and swamps to their advantage, and these guerilla warfare tactics again inflicted massive casualties on the Chinese forces just like the last Chinese invasion in 1406 and 1407 and the Mongols three times before. The Chinese claimed victory anyway and pulled their battered forces back, saying that Hanoi was taught a lesson and there was no need to advance further. Of course, China's retreat might have been influenced when they were alerted that 200,000 Vietnamese regulars with three hundred Russian tanks were on their way back from Cambodia to support their "peasant and farmer" militia.

The best way to describe the Vietnamese militia's stand against half a million Chinese regulars could be to say that China underestimated the heart of their stepchild adversary again would be a laughable understatement. This invasion should never have happened. Granted, China and Cambodia were allies. Vietnam cozied up to the Soviet Union rather than China, and Cambodia was the unquestionable instigator and cause of everything between Cambodia versus Vietnam and Vietnam versus China. In the background of all this was a little known episode on China's northern border. The Soviet Union was amassing an increased military force on the Sino-Soviet border, which could have been another factor for the early Chinese withdrawal from their invasion of Vietnam. Imagine this scenario, which could have happened:

- They rose up to defend their country from yet another invasion from China and <u>with</u> very few Vietnamese regular troops. To defend them, 150,000 "farmers and peasants" emerged as a formidable roadblock to the waves of Chinese. Their Vietnam nationalism smoldered with high-pitched anger. What was supposed to be a cakewalk for the big, bad Chinese military over a defenseless, unprepared, and highly outnumbered adversary suddenly turned into a frienzied, violent, and bloody battle for which the Chinese were not prepared.
- Vietnam's army attacks China from the south.
- Soviet army attacks China from the north.
- An all-out war results among the three major commie armies of the world.

China's retreat from Vietnam was not completed without inflicting horrible collateral damage as villages were reduced to rubble. Roads and railroads were severely damaged. The relations between China and Vietnam have not improved. This can be better exemplified by a statement made by a Vietnamese businessman who conducts business with China:

I fear that someday the Chinese may return. I remember at the end of the 1979 war how they killed our livestock, destroyed villages, killed defenseless villagers, and burned all available food stocks. Our hatred has been sown, yet I have to do business with them. But I have to work with caution. Politics between them and my country do not interest me, and if the Chinese ever came knocking on our door again like they did in 1979, I would pick up weapons without hesitation and fight them. Of course, I would because...I am Vietnamese.

—Nguyen Huu Hung
Vietnamese Army Veteran

During the Cambodian-Vietnam War, Pham Van Dong was prime minister of the Democratic Republic of Vietnam (North Vietnam) from 1955–1976 and of the Socialist Republic of Vietnam Reunified Vietnam from 1976–1987.

One major series of events before the Cambodia-Vietnam War of 1978–1989 were the ambush-type attacks by the Khmer Rouge on villages in what was South Vietnam. Only now, the Khmer Rouge were spitting on the newly reunited Vietnam. At this time the military force of Vietnam was still comprised of NVAs who fought against South Vietnam. It didn't matter. Pham Van Dong's military might was unleashed onto the murderous Pol Pot's Khmer Rouge terrorists. Clearly it can be said that Northern Vietnamese came to the rescue of Southern Vietnamese. I have rarely heard people make this reference to what happened here and how it came about, not even Vietnamese people whose background is Southern Vietnam, where most Khmer Rouge massacres took place.

Uncle Ho Meets Giap and Pham Van Dong. Giap met Ho Chi Minh in 1940 when he was only twenty-nine. Pham Van Dong, a man Giap had met five years earlier, had accompanied him on this historic meeting of three men who would someday rule Vietnam as a free unified country. Historians have passed down that an everlasting bond was formed from this meeting and that Giap and Pham Van Dong both knew instantly that Ho, who had been studying with Mao Tse-Tung's people, should be the leader of their independence movement.

Sometime during the bonding years of these three, Le Duan was already in the picture. He had studied with Pham Van Dong and was considered the most radical believer in the Communist Party. You could say that Ho and Giap were best buddies as Le Duan was with Pham Van Dong. There may have been some rivalry, but one thing kept that from getting in the way of their mutual goals. They loved and respected Ho Chi Minh. And why not? Uncle Ho was reported to be quiet, humble, and very impressive to all who would meet him. But later in the years when Ho's health would begin to fail him, Le Duan would rise to power and even Giap would fear his ruthlessness. Eventually Le Duan became powerful enough to have Giap and Pham Van Dong set aside.

BTW, the Vietnamese do not date their national independence to 1954 by defeating the French, nor do they credit it to 1972–73, when American military forces departed. Nor do they date it to 1975 when the civil war ended between North and South Vietnam. The Vietnamese date their official national independence as 939 AD, when they ushered the Chinese military out from their country's borders.

France and the United States in some ways acted as though they were God and their intervention into Vietnam's long history would be the best thing the Vietnamese people had ever experienced. The Viets were not impressed.

Forget France, Uncle Ho, Giap, the Viet Minh, and the Vietnamese villagers and farmers military handed it to them in 1954. From there Vietnam should have lived on happily ever after as one free and unified nation. But the Vietnam-American War would rudely step in and delay the inevitable which exists in Vietnam today.

So the painful question keeps coming up from those who are interested or who accidentally stumble on to the subject: what would have happened in Vietnam if the U.S. had never intervened, or pulled out by 1965?

It seems obvious to me that Ho Chi Minh never wanted to team up with China. His disdain for the Chinese has been passed down to modern-day Vietnamese and is well documented by Vietnamese historians.

The Southern Vietnamese favored by the French would have laid down their arms almost immediately if the U.S. had withdrawn all its forces in 1965, which unfortunately was the year the military presence was increased substantially. The Diem regime would have fled to Europe then, most likely France. Very little resistance would have faced Ho Chi's invasion of 1965, and the game would be over almost ten years earlier. The lives of at least 150,000 American soldiers would have been spared along with the two to three million Vietnamese (south and north) who died. And the problem that still exists, that participants from the Vietnam War are *still* dying prematurely from old wounds and ongoing illnesses, would not be happening.

Ho Chi Minh and Giap would be smiling today.

LBJ and Westmoreland would not be.

In 1999, 2007, and again in 2014 and 2015, tensions between China and Vietnam flared up, and this relationship appeared to be like a time bomb just waiting to explode.

The research I conducted from several sources provided estimates of casualties for both sides in this latest confrontation between a huge army and a much smaller one. So, I take the low and the high estimates and average them out for this story. Not very scientific, but then I trust the Chinese figures less than I do those from the Vietnamese.

Invasion or Rescue? It is so wrong and extremely senseless for anyone to condemn Vietnam for its invasive action into Cambodia a few years after its war with America and their allies. Even the present prime minister of Cambodia totally rejected those vile rumors. In January 2015, Hun Sen praised Vietnam's actions in the 1970s as an action of "reviving" his country.

Looking back at the Vietnam invasion of Cambodia today, I see a country of feisty, humane warriors who went after the Nazis of Southeast Asia, and they really had no other choice or the attacks on thousands of Vietnamese (in South Vietnam) would have continued. If the Khmer Rouge became and remained the sole power of Cambodia (Kampuchea) then that old domino theory feared by America's presidents could very well have come about as China so favored the Cambodians over Vietnam regardless of who was the Cambodian ruling party.

So Vietnam's risky act to attack Pol Pot's renegade communist military brought the Chinese military upon them. What a fine reward for saving an entire country from complete destruction.

An untold fact about these terribly death-ridden times was not revealed by the media nor the history book writers until thirty years after the last Vietnamese troops left Cambodia.

Just how bad was life for Cambodians during the China-supported Pol Pot killing fields era? It might have been nothing to what Pol Pot's ultimate plan was, his dream of an urban utopia. Entire cities were being forced to thrive in urban areas where citizens would toil on the land owned or confiscated by Pol Pot. The working conditions were extremely brutal, and many would be overworked until they simply died or were killed due their inability to work anymore for Pol Pot.

All money would be taken from the peasants, with the ultimate plan to abolish money availability entirely for all peasants and slaves. Why would they need money? Pol Pot would provide them with edible scraps from the fields the peasants used to own but now slaved on for the almighty king/emperor.

The last thing the peasants once had to fall back on that provided the hope they needed to carry on was also abolished entirely. Religion of any belief was outlawed; if the people needed to worship, they could worship Pol Pot's grandeur.

Hun Sen, prime minister of Cambodia in 2018, knows the tragic history of his country during the Pol Pot era. Hun Sen became one of the Khmer Rouge military officers, and he would learn from them how to deal with future political adversaries in the Cambodian government. He learned well as he showed no mercy for anyone who would challenge his rule.

Actually Hun Sen abandoned his lofty position as a Khmer Rouge battalion general and led many of his fellow Khmer Rouge military officers into Vietnam in 1977. Here he would help raise a rebel army that Vietnam sponsored, and they would fight alongside the Vietnamese army when their invasion of Cambodia took place. After the Khmer Rouge were soundly defeated, Vietnam rewarded Hun Sen's loyalty as he became deputy prime minister and foreign minister of the Vietnamese-installed People's Republic of Cambodia. In 1985, he was elected by the people as chairman of the Council of Ministers and prime minister of Cambodia.

Controversy surrounded Hun Sen's ruling years as the elections were disputed. So, he simply executed those who dared to utter false and uncomplimentary rumors about him. He seemed unconcerned about criticism from leaders of other countries. In fact, in 2003, Hun Sen declared himself as the ruler of Cambodia until he would reach the age of seventy-four. Regardless of his self-declaration, demonstrations by tens of thousands of protestors took place to defy him and the biased elections that he always won.

In 2014, U.S. Congressman Ed Royce called for Hun Sen to relinquish his hold on the leadership of Cambodia's government. Hun Sen seemed to respond to Congressman Royce's unwanted intervention without fear or respect, as he had a part in all of the following actions: He warned all would-be adversaries that should he die mysteriously, the Cambodian military would spin out of control and no one could control them but him. He ordered the National Assembly to abolish the Minority and Majority leaders to reduce his opposition's strength. In early 2017, Hun Sen barred his opposition from even questioning some of his decisions or viewpoints, despite outside pressures accusing him of undermining democracy in Cambodia. Hun Sen seemed to ignore the criticism and threats as bluffs.

Pol Pot died in exile in 1998, leaving a legacy worth forgetting, but the painful memories he created will endure time. A few years after the book *Hun Sen: Strongman of Cambodia* was published, Hun Sen himself came out and defended Vietnam and their invasion of Cambodia with the following statements, which I have paraphrased:

- Vietnam's presence in Cambodia was to meet an urgent need of the Cambodian people for the purpose of survival. Has any other country ever helped Cambodia as much as Vietnam has? Only Vietnamese people and their army have helped us when we faced our worst difficulties.

- They murdered so many people; why should we not accept a rescue gesture from Vietnam? They responded and I strongly reject any such allegations that they may have overstayed their welcome in our country. Vietnam promised they would leave whenever we became stronger as a country. What people do not understand, or they choose not to recognize, is Vietnam could have very easily annexed Cambodia and then the Americans' fear of that so-called domino theory would have become a reality. They did not overstay in our country; actually they left mostly in 1989, and they have not returned since.

Hun Sen has categorically rejected any notion that Vietnam was an unwanted invader of his kingdom in the 1970s, saying Vietnamese soldiers sacrificed their lives for a stable Southeast Asia and pure survival of Cambodia.

I myself cannot explain all the meanings of the word "Vietnam." In brief Vietnam means the revival of Cambodia.
                              —Hun Sen, Prime Minister Cambodia 2012

It should be told that some political opponents of Hun Sen have in the past tried to accuse him of being a puppet for Vietnam. Today Hun Sen and his political party hold total dominance over the mainstream media. Hun Sen's Cambodian People's Party has placed bans on public gatherings.

Hun Sen's father, Hun Neang, was a resident monk in Kampong Chan province before defrocking himself to join the French resistance led by Ho Chi Minh and northern Vietnam.

China's last invasion was a disaster…for China. Both sides still say they were the winners. Vietnam clearly won an unexpected victory without their regular army, which was fighting another war in Cambodia. China still claims that the Vietnamese were taught a lesson and that was all they had intended to accomplish. The real loser was the Cambodian people. While they were being slaughtered by the heartless Khmer Rouge, Vietnam came to their rescue when China should have done so. Instead, they invaded Vietnam and temporarily thwarted the Vietnamese army from their mission of saving the people of Cambodia from continued suffering.

Cambodia's rogue regime, the Khmer Rouge, under their Mussolini-Hitler-type dictator, started the war with Vietnam. There is no questioning this.

Remember, it was the Chinese army that drove our military forces out of North Korea and forced America to settle for a stalemate rather than a victory. Some twenty-five years later, that same Chinese army could not finish the job they started with their Mongol-like human wave onslaught into Vietnam. Had they gone further by entering Hanoi, many military experts and historians believe the Vietnamese would have retaliated with the same vicious fury as their heroic ancestors did time and time again. China's forces were lucky to escape back to their homeland with just about 30,000 casualties inflicted by the Vietnamese militia of "farmers and peasants."

When the Vietnamese military was doing the whole world a huge favor by dismantling the "killing fields," Khmer Rouge, Hanoi, and Ho Chi Minh City were smoldering with good old-fashioned nationalist anger. The people exploded into a frenzy in the streets, knowing the Chinese had launched an attack on them when their country was in its most vulnerable state since the French invasion after World War II ended.

The Vietnamese people did not have time to grab anything or go anywhere to be safe. They did not have time to conduct several months of combat training as most combat forces do in other countries. This was history repeating itself from past centuries, and the primary culprit was pretty much the same, their neighbor to the north, China.

Villagers along the border woke up to artillery barrages from the Chinese Army, accompanied by their huge ground force of several hundred thousand trained combat soldiers. At that time, there was little affection in Vietnam for the Chinese, even though China supported Vietnam militarily against the Americans and the French. Their history together is full of dark times, as the Chinese launched several large-scale invasions across the Sino-Vietnamese border with the intention that France had to conquer and dominate the Vietnamese people.

After the Vietnam War with America ended, instead of a domino theory effect moving forward, which could have easily happened, the socialist nations began bickering and competing with each other. The historic animosity toward their old foe rematerialized. So, Vietnam took steps to cover its back and strengthen its alliance with China's great rival, the Soviet Union.

As was reported in a *time.com* story in May 2014, "more Chinese soldiers were getting killed than Vietnamese militia because they were fighting like it was the older times [Korea maybe?]. Chinese had been slaughtered by battle-hardened Viet-Cong type militia as they fought from jungle positions and tunnels as they did so successfully in both Indo-China wars."

The bold boast from a high-ranking Chinese official, "We will be able to take Hanoi in a week," became an embarrassment that could have never been anticipated, not with the Vietnamese having dedicated themselves to the war in Cambodia beforehand.

For such a war, the death toll was staggering. The Chinese casualties of 30,000 were far more than the Vietnamese casualties of 20,000. Even though China claimed victory and that the Vietnamese were taught a lesson, the Vietnamese military remained in Cambodia until their mission had been completed. If China gained anything out of this battle with their southern neighbor, it was that China's inability to prevail against Vietnam's smaller militia force demonstrated the need to modernize its military—a process that has continued to the present.

Some news outlets referred to this short war as the 27 Days of Hell, when China and Vietnam went to war.

As mentioned earlier, when the Chinese military was leaving (retreating) from Vietnam in 1979, they pretty much destroyed any chance of having a friendly relationship with Vietnam, as they destroyed villages and slaughtered defenseless livestock on their disgraceful exodus. The hatred was cemented then, where it stands today. I think our government is watching this scenario and the opportunities that may present themselves for maintaining global stability.

Other sources echo what I have stated here, such as:

The 1979 war between China and Vietnam was arguably a potential disaster for China. Vietnam outperformed China militarily. China underestimated the Vietnamese and their heart...again.
**Paraphrased from *Blinders, Blunders, and Wars*
by David C. Gompert, Hans Binnendijk, and Bonny Lin**

In 2017, both countries maintained substantial forces at their borders, which is a drain on each country's economy. Occasional mini-battles are not uncommon, which festers the hatred for each other.

Imagine these scenarios for a moment—the United States invades Canada. Who would stop the American military? Who would come to Canada's aid…England or France? What if the USA did the same with Mexico? Who could stop the American military might? Canada has vast natural resources like uranium and oil. In fact, Canada is second to Saudi Arabia as the most oil-rich country.

How about uranium-rich countries? Our dear ally down under, Australia, has nearly 33 percent of the world's uranium. Canada is up there too, with 10 percent of the uranium in the world. Overall, the world's most resource-rich countries are Russia and the United States. How much of Canada's military is at their border with the USA? And vice versa? In fact, it has been said by many Canadians that they almost consider themselves part of our country. Then, there are some Canadians who resent that idea. The odds are about one hundred trillion to one that Canada and the United States would ever square off militarily with each other. What about China and Vietnam's odds for mixing it up again in the near future? Odds are pretty high if history between the two countries means anything.

Vietnam and China continue to spit at each other. It is mostly China, as they have been so overly ambitious in claiming more than their share of the South China Sea. If China would engage Vietnam again on Vietnam's homeland, they would have to face the Vietnamese people's same vestiges of nationalism and standing up to foreign aggressors—something with which Vietnam has a long and very successful track record.

What if China invades Vietnam again? Vietnam never invades other countries unless attacked first—they just rise up when it is necessary for the people to defend their homeland. So, what *if*? Would the USA become involved or stay out of it, and which side should we support? If the Soviets were still on Vietnam's side, it might become a golden opportunity for the USA to side opposite the Chinese. Just a thought.

Quite simply China's cruel and ruthless 1979 invasion of a civilian army was met by a militia of all ages to defend their homeland. Today Vietnam has one of, if not the largest militias in the world at five million volunteers presenting any invader with an over-imposing challenge they would most likely regret. It seems, in this author's opinion, that the Vietnamese government, communist led or not, has the best intentions in mind for the protection of their country and its hundred million people. God bless the Vietnamese.

Pol Pot's Khmer Rouge Attack
Vietnam Villages

Pol Pot and the Killing Fields
of Cambodia

Le Duan, Pham Van Dong, General Giap —Vietnam Leaders 1975–1979

Vietnam Strikes Back—
Invades Cambodia

Vietnam Picks up Another War!

Vietnam's Militia Counterattacks the Chinese Army

Chapter 9

THE BAD WAR—FIFTY YEARS LATER?

We were winning in '68 and '69...what happened?
—Vietnam Vet, Unknown

Vietnam was a bad war to the American public. In their eyes, it was immoral, with unnecessary death and destruction. That is, those who were never forced into the horrible experiences of severe battle felt that way. The result of this with the Vietnam War could be stated in this manner:

- **The good war, World War II**, was reported by newspaper and radio broadcasts with all references of the enemy as the "bad guys." We (our fathers and uncles) could do no wrong with the pro-war media at that time. Americans were then allowed to form their images of the war on their own. There were few actual vivid images of battle or carnage. That wasn't portrayed positively and heroically for the Americans.
- **The bad war, Vietnam,** was dominating television in the media as entire families around the world could sit down in front of their TVs and watch it as the media chose to portray it. Brutal images of suffering Americans and Vietnamese were thrown into living rooms every night. Negative opinions were inevitable as the media reporting was largely anti-American and inaccurate. They tended to portray the South Vietnamese as victims, caught in between the heroic revolutionary Viet Cong and the American colonialists.
- A bad war allegedly produces bad veterans, bad citizens, and bad people, and the public that believes and accepts this ridiculous opinion will seek distance from those bad boys of the so-called bad war.

The image of a good war, free from immorality and immediate destruction, exists in the minds of those who never experienced the horrors of battle. The news of atrocities reported from the good war was accepted as necessary damage. The actual events that took place in combat during the good war are simply accepted but rarely discussed in detail. That keeps the good war glorious. The good war image of World War II lives on forever, just as the newspapers and magazines reported it and as the WWII post-war movies promoted. Long live the greatest generation from the good war. And the media guaranteed that, right or wrong.

The media-biased images of Vietnam became the pre-written history of the war before the American soldier boy even came home. He was also receiving an earful about what people thought about a war that the Ameri-Cong media had falsely reported since it began until it ended. As strange as this seems, when Vietnam War veterans began talking more openly about their war thirty years or so afterward, that was about the same time many WWII veterans started to talk about their battle experiences and the PTSD they had been dealing with. You see, they fought in the good war and they weren't supposed to have nightmares, flashbacks, depression, suicidal thoughts, etc. Twenty to fifty years later, the post-traumatic stress affected them in droves. Those problems were reserved for the survivors of the bad war; they were the crazy ones, not strong like the WWII heroes. There was no adjustment back into society for WWII veterans just as there wasn't for Vietnam's veterans. So, the WWII veterans, still living and troubled, began reporting their problems openly much later (like sixty to seventy-five years) than the returnees did from the bad war. However, it has been proven that because WWII was the good war, that alone helped the veterans reintegrate more easily into society until PTSD struck them in the 2000s.

Reminder—the bad war, as well as the good war, is determined by people who never participated in live battle. Here is a thought to ponder:

- We, the Vietnam War era generation, grew up and matured in an America that was created by the World War II generation, our parents and relatives. The World War II generation's growing-up years were drastically different from the years of the Vietnam generation. The good war returned heroes. The bad war did not. So, the Vietnam generation really did grow up in a different world, one of darkness and total silence.

Another uncanny difference from America's good war versus its bad war was the unexpected, undesired state of warfare that American soldiers were forced to revert to: primitive guerilla warfare!

With our presumed invincibility through superior technology, America was not prepared to fight battles from hamlet to hamlet with innocent villagers living in them, or to crawl around in jungles, looking for someone to kill. Plus, sometimes the villagers would be the enemy. Confusion ran rampant because of this odd style of battle.

To Survive, We Had to Act Immediately and Decisively. The Vietnam War has earned itself many titles or distinctions; some of them are not so complimentary and we know that. But one thing that made the war so unique by the standards of warfare of the 2000–2010s can be said simply: The Vietnam War was the last of its kind where both adversaries fought an IN-YOUR-FACE STYLE OF COMBAT.

Mano-a-mano, with only a ditch or bushes as cover, in swamps and jungles, from trees, the combatants sought each other out in the most stressful, grueling, horrifying, demanding way possible. This would more often than not leave men permanently damaged goods physically or mentally or in some cases BOTH. Or, they ended up just dead sooner and that was that. Call it primitive or even Stone Age warfare, but know that being an active round combat soldier or marine in this war and coming out of it in one piece brought true heroes home who did not deserve the cruel and painful abuse that so many Americans would so heartlessly welcome them with.

In addition to the confusion we veterans felt in Vietnam between all of the contradictions, few Americans were able to adapt well enough to make it through an entire year of guerilla warfare. Earlier in the book I described some of the confrontations between the Vietnamese "farmers and peasants" against massive armies from the Chinese dynasties and the Mongols as well. You may think that the tactics used by the Vietnamese in the thirteenth century did not differ greatly with the wars fought by the Viet Minh against the French or that of the Viet Cong against the Americans. You would be almost correct.

Because of Vietnam's style of guerilla warfare, whether in 938, 1288, 1954, or 1968, victory was achieved regardless of their adversary's numbers or their advantage with weapons.

We had to fight battles with them far from home…if we did not produce quick and decisive victories and if our casualties became excessive, our home population would begin to recall us. Time was not on our side. The war dragged on, and the enemy just waited and waited…using their country's climate, jungle, diseases, and forest mountains to wear us down and discourage us.

That is how it happened, and we still don't understand how it happened that way, not to us…not to the Americans!

Today, as I see it, a combat infantry Vietnam veteran who has been in contact with thousands of Vietnam war veterans and their families, I believe many of us have forgiven our country's people while still harboring revengeful feelings toward our political leaders. There are also those Vietnam veterans with angry, unforgiving attitudes for what happened to them, but mostly what happened to their war buddies who died over there or back at home. More of them may die with these unhealthy feelings—and that is so sad.

My tour in the bad war over there began in March 1968, right at the end of one Tet Offensive, but just in time for another one and another and another. To my war buddies, it seemed like 1968 was one continuous Tet Offensive with no end in sight, except the unthinkable. The Vietnam War of the twentieth century began unofficially in the 1950s and ended officially for Americans in 1973. For our adversaries, the Viet Cong, North Vietnamese, and the Chinese, the seeds of war had been planted several centuries earlier. American leaders did not know that or they paid no attention to the fact. They would regret that major oversight.

As a result of our long imprisonment, some of today's survivors of the Vietnam War from both sides suffer from another form of psychosis, an obsession with making their story right, telling it over and again until it is accepted or at least heard by the masses who have blocked Vietnam out of their minds for so long.

Americans have been trying to get a handle on the Vietnam War for over fifty years, and despite thousands of books written about the subject, most of America is right back where they started from in trying to understand the Vietnam War. *Unbreakable Hearts* will not answer all or even most of the questions or misunderstandings about this tumultuous time in America's history. However, this book will attempt to help you appreciate those who participated in the war…on both sides.

Understanding the most unpopular war in America's history, fought abroad, would take volumes of information, more than anyone could ever browse through in a lifetime. The Vietnam War occurred in Vietnam, Laos, Cambodia, and America officially from 1959–1975. However, many refer to it as the war that just will not end. The war was fought between the communist allies (including the Viet Cong in South Vietnam), who historians say won the war. The government of South Vietnam was the opposing force along with its allies, including the United States, who eventually lost, as many historians have reported without providing believable reasons for their ignorant reporting.

Should we have won this war? Could we have ever won this war? I used to be one of those who often argued with anyone who cared to engage me that the Vietnam War (second one) could have been won if political constraints had not existed from day one till the last day. No more do I believe that, not after committing myself to thoroughly studying the history of the people of the Vietnam region, from the later BC years into early AD and up to the 1979 conflict with their centuries-old nemesis to the north, China.

Fighting Spartans Like a Spartan! As I look back to the 1968–1969 timeframe, knowing what I know now, here is one simple suggestion I would have made to General Abrams, who was Westmoreland's replacement…PROMOTE Colonel David Hackworth to the highest command position possible so that every U.S. Army infantry division's commander could report to Hack.

That is a bold, controversial suggestion and certainly an example of "hindsight has twenty-twenty vision." Being a mere E-5 buck sergeant, two-year draftee, what could I know? I do understand this…when LTC Colonel David H. Hackworth landed in Vietnam in January 1969, he had just completed an impressive writing, a tactical handbook for the Pentagon to review and hopefully take seriously. So now, Hack was being given the opportunity to put his own writings into action. He would be the commander of an infantry battalion that was at this time considered the worst fighting battalion in the Mekong Delta area, if not the entire army. They had earned their reputation because of their monstrous casualty rate. They were the 4/39th, and the Mekong Viet Cong had been feasting on them.

As I will mention elsewhere, the search-and-destroy strategy was beginning to wind down in 1969, but for a short while that plan would be put on hold in the Mekong. The 4/39th's new commander would work a miracle by quickly transforming a sorry, ragtag bunch into one of the Vietnam War's finest fighting outfits. Soon, they would be known as the ferocious, hardcore Recondos of the 9th Infantry Division.

The 4/39th was picking up steam, as they no longer believed the Viet Cong were superhumans and nine feet tall. However, General Creighton Abrams relieved Hack of his command in May 1969. Here is how it came down—Hack was relayed a message that Abrams had ordered him to be relieved of his command of the 4/39th immediately. He could have any other job in Vietnam as long as it was not in direct combat. Yes, he was devastated as he loved the 4/39th, but he was told that he was considered too valuable and he was still taking too many chances.

While Hack was shocked into disbelief, part of the reason for Abrams' decision was that another commander in the 9th who also led from the front, as Hack always did behind the point man, was killed in an ambush. With these unfortunate events taking place, it was inevitable that the high risk and high casualty rate program of *search and destroy* was on the way out.

Hack had very high respect for his enemy. He had been quoted more than once that in his opinion the Viet Cong (women or men) were the best infantry soldiers the American infantry had ever faced. A reminder that Hack was a veteran of three major wars, including WWII.

The Viet Cong, in Hack's eyes, were no different from the Spartan warriors of ancient times. The Viet Cong bred their future fighters, the little brothers and sisters of their herds. Their big brother and sister Viet Cong were involved in the Spartan-like on-the-job guerrilla war-training program. The young Viet Cong-to-be grew up spying on their enemy (us), carrying food and supplies, growing food, setting up deadly booby traps, caring for wounded, and burying dead Viet Cong, maybe even from their own family. Then as twelve- to fourteen-year-olds big enough to shoulder, arm, and fire a weapon with proficiency, they became official soldiers of the Viet Cong army.

Spartans fought as teammates with prestige and honor. Although they strived to become individual champions in battle, they knew that individual talent was never as great as those who worked to support each other. Spartans were elite warriors, at the cutting edge of a battle. Their teammates expected them to fight harder, move faster, hit harder and more often at their opponents. I, too, could see this in some of the Viet Cong we faced in Vietnam. They did not seek individual glory. They fought unselfishly and with a vengeance to defeat the opponent on the battlefield…at any cost.

We have all heard the phrase *attitude is everything*. Well, the Vietnamese "farmers and peasants" that the great dynasties of the Chinese and the Mongols fell to over and over, despite huge numerical advantages, had that attitude thing. They expected to win regardless of how big the enemy was or how many there were of them.

Dear readers, the Viet Minh of the First Indochina War and Viet Cong and NVAs of the American-Vietnam War challenged themselves harder. They hit harder; they came at us over and over again, seemingly without fear as if this day of battle would be their last. And that, my dear fellow Americans, is exactly how your American soldier boys fought them right back…like Spartans!

Molan labe! Going back to the often-shown movie *300* and the historic stand by the Greek Spartans at Thermopylae Pass, you may recall the Spartans' reply to the Persian king, Xerxes, when he called for an immediate surrender… ***Molan labe,* meaning "Come and take it!"** Another old saying about the legendary warriors of Sparta was this… "Spartans never die. They just go right to hell and prepare for their next war."

I learned that the most reliable men were those who lived long enough to become an experienced grunt. They knew what was happening but very few of the officers gave them that credit. They were just dumb enlisted men. What could they know? I did not feel this way to the men under me. In fact, it became my experience that if we could get more of the f-ing new infantry replacements through the first few weeks of combat, their chances and our chances of making it as a unit were improved big time. The trouble is, when things didn't go right and we took heavy losses, it meant we would be getting replacements in faster than we could break them in. When I look back, it is truly amazing that in 1969, the grunts hadn't blown away more of the high-ranking officers. Then again, those sorry bastards never stayed out in the shit with their men. And when they got the medals they were after, most of which were not earned, they couldn't get transferred quick enough.

**—Paraphrased from *Steal My Soldier's Heart,*
by Colonel David H. Hackworth**

American leaders and trainers would tell (brainwash) us that these kids were abducted and forced into the ranks of our enemy. While that may have been partially true, more often than not they volunteered willingly into the program and they were proud to be the best Viet Cong they could be. There you have it—other views about the enemy Americans fought and, more often than not, defeated in battles using their own tactics.

What I found from extensive research through an assortment of documents about the Vietnamese people is that although they have lost many battles and have often been ruled by other countries, the Vietnamese people have never lost any of their wars, no matter how long they lasted. Having fought alongside them, having slept with them, eaten with them, cried with them, shared with them, protected them, and killed them, I feel as qualified as any American to tell their story.

The Vietnamese people and the American soldiers were thrown at each other. The Vietnamese had no idea what was coming, and the Americans had no idea what they were getting into, but…their leaders should have known. The result was indescribably disastrous—over five million civilian and military casualties during the war, millions more who died prematurely after the war, and millions who will continue to suffer from that war until their final days in this world.

What makes this horrible time in history even worse is the well-kept secret from the American people that America may have had an opportunity to prevent Ho Chi Minh from taking sides with the communists. He reached out for our partnership long before the first Indochina War had roots in the ground.

On February 28, 1946, Ho Chi Minh wired the following telegram to the President of the United States, appealing for America's assistance in negotiating with France:[28]

Hanoi, February 28, 1946

Dear President,

On Behalf of the Vietnam Government and Vietnamese People, I Beg To Inform You That In Course Of Conversations Between Vietnam Government And French Representatives The Latter Require The Secession Of Cochinchina And The Return Of French Troops In Hanoi Stop. Meanwhile French Population And Troops Are Making Active Preparations For A Coup De Main In Hanoi And For Military Aggression Stop I Therefore Most Earnestly Appeal To You Personally And To The American People To Intervene Urgently In Support Of Our Independence And Help Making

---

28 Telegram from Ho Chi Minh to President Harry S. Truman (National Archives Identifier 3052631)

the Negotiations More In Keeping With The Principles Of The Atlantic And San Francisco Charters.

Respectfully,
Ho Chi Minh, President, Vietnam Democratic Republic

This is one of several telegrams from Ho Chi Minh to U.S. President Harry S. Truman, requesting support for their independence from France; none were ever responded to. Two wars would follow.

Understanding and/or teaching the Vietnam War presents a multitude of almost unanswerable challenges for teachers and all others with an interest. Since my own combat infantry platoon brothers began dying off prematurely after coming home from Vietnam, I became intrigued and then incensed with trying to understand more about the war my brothers and sisters fought in, risked our lives in, and died for. *Unbreakable Hearts* is in some ways dedicated to a brave, sometimes ferocious, but always resilient enemy that just would not quit. Yet we defeated this very capable enemy, and quite honestly, America was lucky to have men and women who answered the call to take on this formidable opponent on their terms, and in their backyard. A reminder—we were sons and daughters of *America's Greatest Generation*, weren't we? And yet, our homecoming was unspeakably cruel, especially given the unbelievable price we paid in Vietnam.

As the killing of Americans in Afghanistan, Iraq, and elsewhere in that region continued to drag on at the writing of this book, with no definitive sign of a full-blown victory in sight (even though America's President Obama had claimed a false victory), comparisons to the Vietnam War have continued to be aired out. They all seem to have this one-word description in common...*quagmire*.

Among the many problems with drawing lessons from the Vietnam quagmire and applying them to Afghanistan, Iraq, etc. is that the history of the Vietnam War is more often than not misunderstood. Each war's history is constantly evolving as new information emerges, particularly from our adversaries. Think about it—how often do we pay much attention to understanding the enemy's motivations? We tend to have an incomplete or inaccurate picture of that enemy and that war.

Who could have seen it coming? America's intervention with Vietnam's politics has obviously produced some unfortunate and unforeseeable results, resulting in decades of butting into other people's affairs. America's influence on South Vietnam's future might have been more instrumental in its demise than we may ever comprehend. However, it appears South Vietnam's destiny was written by its own people. If leadership is important to the success or survival of a struggling country to achieve stability, then please take a look back with me to the history of Vietnam's (both) political leadership. I found this to be an eye-opener if my research is accurate:

History of Vietnam's Presidents from 1945 to Present

North Vietnam (1945–1975)		*Cochinchina (French Name)*	
Ho Chi Minh	1945–1969	Van Thinh	1946
Ton Duc Thang	1969–1975	Vin Hoach	1946–1947
		Van Xuan	1947–1948
		Provisional (Army)	1948–1949
The Socialist Republic of Vietnam (1976–2016)		*South Vietnam (1945–1975)*	
Ton Duc Thang	1976–1980	Bau Dai	1949–1955
Hua Tho	1980–1981	Diem	1955–1963
Chinh	1981–1987	Minh	1963–1964
Chi Cong	1987–1992	Khanh (Army)	1964
Durc Anh	1992–1997	Minh	1964
Lurong	1997–2006	Khanh (Army)	1964
Triet	2007–2016	Provisional (Army)	1964
		Minh	1964
		Suu	1965
		Thieu	1965–1975
		Huong	1975–
		Minh	1975–

The eye-opener here is that communist-controlled North Vietnam showed a great deal more stability with the leaders of its country than democratic South Vietnam did. Then, after the reunification of the two back to one Vietnam, that stability continued impressively. In fact, only eight presidents have held office in modern Vietnam in forty years, while South Vietnam went through twice as many during a shorter timeframe of just thirty years, from 1945–1975. At this writing, the president of the Socialist Republic of Vietnam is still Truong Tan Sang, serving since 2011.

North Vietnam Presidents	1945–1975	2
South Vietnam Presidents	1946–1975	16
The Socialist Republic of Vietnam	1976–2016	8

It is difficult to believe that North Vietnam made it from 1945 to 1975 (and beyond) with just two presidents, while South Vietnam went through six-teen…mind-boggling! Taking the journey through history was fascinating and a bit nerve-wracking. How in the hell did we support the government that would treat the office of its top executive and commander of its military like a game of musical chairs?

Just as mind-boggling is the possibility that in many Southern Vietnam-ese officials' minds, President Diem, assassinated in 1963 with the alleged blessing of the USA, was most likely the best and most qualified person for the presidential position he was so rudely removed from. In the two years following Diem's termination, the critical function of president of South Vietnam would resemble a carnival merry-go-round, as an embar-rassing turnover took place eight times during the critical start-up years of the Vietnam War. No wonder we got a slow start in training South Vietnam's military!

Even more disgusting is looking at the record of longevity of the South Vietnam presidents after Diem was murdered by his own with America's head turned the other way. During 1964 and 1965, the revolving door with Diem exiting until someone finally lasted for more than one year, eight dif-ferent presidents would come and go in just two years!

Nguyen Van Thieu entered the scene on June 14, 1965 and lasted until Saigon fell in April 1975. There would be two more presidents chosen to fill that position in 1975 before it was terminated in what must have been one of the fastest changes in presidents of any country ever, shortly after Thieu escaped the country before the North Vietnamese entered Saigon on Russian tanks. Then, Ton Duc Thang, president of North Vietnam since 1969, would assume the presidential position for the new Socialist Republic of Vietnam until 1980.

Some of the basic topics to research for anyone interested in understand-ing the Vietnam War could include the following, covered to some extent in all of my books:

- Lyndon B. Johnson
- The Cold War
- The Domino Theory
- The Military Draft
- Guerrilla Warfare—Viet Cong
- Rolling Thunder—Bombing Missions
- Chemical Warfare—Agent Orange
- The Tet Offensive
- The My Lai Massacre

- Ho Chi Minh
- American Anti-War Movement—Kent State Shooting
- Gulf of Tonkin Incident
- Pentagon Papers
- Paris Peace Accords
- Post-Traumatic Stress Syndrome (PTSD)
- Search-and-destroy Mission

If we were to learn from the past (ha—fat chance!)…then maybe we would be able to pass on a better, more secure world to future generations. Easier said than done, as the underlying reasons or excuses behind every war are extremely complex. The Vietnam "thing" continues to evolve, in that we are constantly uncovering masses of misconceptions about the Vietnam War, and no doubt, these eye-opening bits of information will continue to be rediscovered and create more controversy. The same goes for Korea, Afghanistan, Iraq, etc.

Misconceptions or questions about the Vietnam War continue to be many. Here are a few questions for you to ponder and maybe do some research on for yourself:

- Was Ho Chi Minh the uncontested leader of North Vietnam?
- Was there ever a chance of negotiated peace in place of a total victory for North Vietnam?
- Who was the real architect of the 1968 Tet Offensive?
- Could we have escalated the intense rivalry between China and the Soviet Union for influence over Hanoi and altered the war's outcome?

One question that I constantly ask of my war buddies and myself is… *why did the American government leave us over there for so long?* Whether it was right or not to send us there will always meet with serious debate, and there are no wrong answers that I have heard in my lifetime. However, I will never understand what the strategy was for our ground combat forces to remain in an increasingly hopeless situation. It was criminal to throw young Americans into a combat arena without full support. It was insanely and viciously criminal to leave us there for what seemed like an eternity to many of the combatants and our families who waited for us.

I realize that not every living Vietnam veteran will entirely agree with some of the things I have said in my books, and that is okay. That is everyone's privilege and I respect that. But facts are just that…facts, and I stand with strong convictions that most Vietnam veterans will agree and even appreciate the cause for which I wrote *Unbreakable Hearts.*

Most Vietnam veterans will never accept the label by the American media that Vietnam was the first war the United States lost. I pray that all living Nam vets are in agreement with me here. How can you lose a war unless you are defeated? That did not happen. The truth about Vietnam is… it was the first war America withdrew from before it was over. Then again, was it ever winnable?

How could Americans understand Vietnam when they were fed a steady diet of World War II documentaries depicting great clashes with great victories? Our sacred marines became legendary from the post-World War II movies. And yet, I'll bet if this question was asked of one thousand Americans at random, 99 percent would answer incorrectly—and there are just two choices. Maybe this war was never winnable after China and the Soviet Union "unofficially" entered the war and became heavily committed to preventing an American victory—Korea déjà vu?

In which war did America's marines suffer their highest total casualties?

Answer: Vietnam War (101,700)
World War II (86,940)

There was no Iwo Jima or Okinawa or Battle of the Bulge in Vietnam. In Vietnam, American soldiers had to face endless days and nights of exhausting patrols, defending isolated outposts under constant harassment with an occasional large-scale battle in between, such as Khe Sahn, Ia Drang Hue, Suoi Tre, or Dak To—battles almost never heard of by non-Vietnam War veterans in America. In some ways, Vietnam was more intense than any war ever fought by Americans. Something else about the Vietnam War that was misreported even to this day is…the tenacity and resilience of our enemy. Many of our battles resembled this one, although many of them were much larger and deadlier.

In the early hours of July 4, 1968, the 25th Infantry's base camp, Dau Tieng, more like an outpost, came under a full attack from the Viet Cong and North Vietnamese Regulars. Before this battle would come to a glorious end for us, this would be the largest assault of the entire Vietnam War on Dau Tieng until the day it was destroyed in 1975. I was there that day of July Fourth. The onslaught began with a shower of mortars and rockets; officially over four hundred rounds landed inside Dau Tieng before the ground attack followed. The noise was deafening. I hear it loud and clear to this day. Dau Tieng would be overrun by a regiment-sized unit of mostly Viet Cong. Although we did prevail that night (it would take another book to describe it), the one thing that sticks out in my mind from that battle was the look on their (Viet Cong) faces. There was no fear in their eyes even though death was inevitable for many of them before daylight would come. They still kept coming…the damage would be incredible on both sides…and then it was over.

I have always wondered what really drove our adversaries to the frenzy I saw that night and more nights to follow. Some said they were doped up. Some said they were just crazy commies and didn't have much of a life anyway. Whichever, it made a lasting impression on me, that icy, heartless, cold stare with a grin-like smile. They looked like they were already dead and we had to kill them again, similar to the movies about zombies today. But I knew there was more to it than just their heartless look because they fought with as much heart as anyone I ever saw. WHY? This is one of the reasons I have been inspired to do the research into Vietnam's history and write my third book about the Vietnam War. *Unbreakable Hearts* attempts to show why an outgunned enemy would fight until the last man was standing and why this combat infantryman admires and respects the Vietnamese people.

Our Washington leaders had absolutely no chance of discovering or understanding some of the reasons why our adversary fought with unbreakable hearts and intense passion. These reasons would not have motivated Alexander the Great, Genghis Kahn, Saladine, or the likes of Hitler. Some of these reasons the Vietnamese fought with such passion include:

- Their parents' teachings about myths and legends of their ancestors
- Their fear of embarrassing the ancients
- Uncle Ho Chi Minh, who commanded them to fight
- Their love for their land and passion to survive

How were America's leaders going to get it about a small third world country? But the communist leaders made a similar mistake in thinking the Americans would be just like the French and lack the will, determination, passion, and dedication to fight on. The unsuccessful Tet Offensives of January 1967, Jan/Feb 1968, May/June 1968, and Aug/Sept 1968 showed the North Vietnamese that they had more to fear and overcome than the American firepower. They had undervalued the American soldiers, who also fought with unbreakable hearts. So the war was destined to continue on for several more years until finally South Vietnam gave up in 1975.

North Vietnam, under Ho Chi Minh, General Giap, and later General Secretary Le Duan, knew what they wanted and they were going to fight for it to the last man, just as their great ancestors did every time the need arose.

When Ho Chi Minh's health was failing in the latter 1960s, Le Duan assumed more of the responsibilities and was just as committed, just as nationalistic toward reuniting Vietnam again as Ho was. When Ho died on September 2, 1969, Le Duan became the most powerful figure in North Vietnam. He continued with the aggressive strategy just like Ho Chi Minh.

My war buddies and I might have still been over there fighting had our left wing politicians not turned tail and run away.

After the end of the Vietnam War, Le Duan began to trust the Soviet Union and rely less on China. It was Le Duan who ordered the 1978 invasion of Kampuchea (Cambodia) after Kampuchea attacked several defenseless Vietnamese villages, most infamously the Ba Chuc Massacre. China would then invade Vietnam, leaving the Vietnamese in a war on two fronts, still in recovery from the American War.

Although 1959 is still often marked as the beginning of the Vietnam War, the first American soldier killed in Vietnam was Air Force T-Sgt. Richard B. Fitzgibbon Jr., who was killed on June 8, 1956. His name appears on The Wall in Washington, D.C. The last casualty in the war occurred on May 15, 1975.

There is no easy war. War is simply hell, period. But the Vietnam War was so different from any war America had ever fought in until then. In-your-face, savage combat separated Vietnam from the other wars. Attacks and ambushes would strike from anywhere, nowhere, at any time of day or night with absolutely…NO WARNING!

Both sides fought constantly in a tenacious, almost maniacal fashion. Nam's warriors who fought in the bush that the Viet Cong called their home had to be willing to put their lives in harm's way and battle a fanatical enemy like no American force did in *any* other war, for so long. Our leaders in Washington had little understanding of this, and they proved this so many times by showing their lack of workable military strategies that would at least have a chance of helping the American ground grunts who often had to confront their enemy in face-to-face battle. America's young soldiers and marines were asked all too often to follow young, inexperienced, and poorly prepared officers from ROTC and rarely West Point. I apologize for repeating myself here, but this topic deserves to be stated again and again. The American officers in Vietnam, in general, seemed to be more concerned about "getting their tickets punched" by recommending each other for career-enhancing medals of valor.

Fortunately, my war buddies and I were blessed with some non-commissioned officers (NCO or sergeants) who were more concerned about their men than they were about getting a career-enhancing medal. I can remember five or six such NCOs in Bravo 3rd 22nd during my 1968 experience in Nam. We broke some rules set by the top brass, and the result was that we killed more of the enemy and fewer of us became casualties. I know that most of us would do it our way again, regardless of the potential penalties. This style of fighting that some combat units would employ probably confused our enemy, and that was to our advantage. For the most part, all this meant was that we might pick a different (better) ambush site than our original orders had directed us to. Or it could simply mean that we might spring an ambush onto our enemy without receiving a green light to fire yet. This worked out well for us more times than not.

We would find out from those we captured during a battle that the enemy really respected the American ground combat troops. They told us that there were specific units of grunts that the Viet Cong tried to avoid. Ours became one of those units on the VC's radar. The 9th, 4th, 1st, 101st, and other units of the 25th infantry were mentioned by our enemies most often. Of course, there were other units that performed bravely. Bottom line was…the American grunt, ground-level combat troop was never afraid to mix it up head to head with our formidable enemy.

Please, just try to imagine if you are a non-combat veteran of Vietnam and you say something like this to someone who did fight and survive combat:

"We should never have fought that war."

"You fought against peasants and farmers, not soldiers."

"Your war wasn't as intense as WWII, and you lost."

Things like this should never be mentioned to a combat Vietnam War veteran, not without ducking. I, for one, will no longer engage in a discussion if it becomes argumentative about the first topic. I know now that we should never have fought that war. My stance on this has changed 180 degrees, and it will stay that way, but this is one of those hindsight scenarios: If we knew then what we know now, we could have done things differently.

Sadly, and mysteriously, those who write the history books have almost completely ignored the fact that the People's Republic of China and the Soviet Union supported North Vietnam as powerful allies. It looks to us now that if we had gone into Vietnam in full force in the earlier years before China and the Soviets became so heavily involved, we probably could have ended the war before it picked up steam. However, after China and the Soviets stepped up their support, had we made an actual invasion of North Vietnam, we would have been in direct combat with three countries—North Vietnam, China, and the Soviet Union. All-out war would have been the result. This is unquestionably a fact.

We tried to destroy North Vietnam's industrial capacity and their flow of supplies and weapons into South Vietnam with Operation Rolling Thunder as well as Linebacker II. Neither was successful, and might never have succeeded because North Vietnam's industrial base was in China and the Soviet Union. The two great communist powers funneled supplies and weapons to North Vietnam over land, by rail, and by convoy through China and also through Laos and Cambodia, a satellite of China.

On the other hand, by far the most effective battle actions which administered the most damage onto the communist forces along with air power were America's search-and-destroy missions conducted on the ground with awesome fire support nearby, which were designed to find, confront, and kill real enemy soldiers. It is now a known fact that the Viet Cong army had been almost annihilated by the American soldier boys by the end of 1968. Unfortunately, America itself and Americans at home were not prepared for, nor could they accept the massive American casualty count of 1968. More Americans were KIA or WIA in just 1968 than in all wars America has fought in after Vietnam…combined! To say that America's combat marines and army ground troops were put through a shocking experience like no other American military before them or after is not an exaggeration by any means. The facts vouch for that loud and clear.

Vietnam vets fought just as courageously as any American soldier did in any previous war. In fact, it has been said and proven by many that *no* **American force in *any* other war or conflict fought with more determination or sheer courage than the combat Vietnam War veteran.** Furthermore, it was Secretary of State John Kerry (alongside Jane Fonda) who was directly responsible for creating the false image of Vietnam veterans as a "barbarian horde" which raped and murdered innocent Vietnamese civilians daily as a matter of policy. Give us a break, Kerry!

Yes, Kerry is a Vietnam veteran, but he has never been embraced by most Vietnam veterans as one of their own. Reasons for that are too numerous and would require too much verbiage; and it would waste the space where more valuable information could be used. I will just end this topic by sharing the words of another true combat Vietnam War veteran and bona fide hero:

When John Kerry decided to transform truth into fiction and honor into dishonor, we had to take action. We had no choice. It was our duty to protect and defend not just our honor, but the honor of every past, present, and future member of our armed forces.

Fellow prisoners-of-war and I came forward to speak the truth about our imprisonment and to explain the detrimental consequences of electing John Kerry, a man who defaced both our country and our warriors, to be our president.

— **Colonel George "Bud" Day**
Medal of Honor recipient
Prisoner of War, Vietnam

I mentioned Bud Day several times in *Condemned Property?* and a man like him, a true hero, can never be mentioned enough. Bud Day spent five and a half years as a POW in Vietnam and was Senator John McCain's cellmate. He became one of America's most highly decorated military servicemen, right up there with General Douglas MacArthur and Colonel David Hackworth (mentioned elsewhere). He did not stop fighting after he was released from the Hanoi Hilton in North Vietnam. He kept right on sticking his two cents in for the benefit of veterans' rights. During his stay as a POW, he was tortured so badly that his arms were torn from their sockets. His hands and arms never functioned properly again. Colonel Day passed away on July 27, 2013 at the age of eighty-eight.

I would like to add that Colonel "Bud" Day and Colonel "Hack" never received the rank of general. If you research their stories, you will understand why. Neither of them was bashful about standing up to his senior officers, especially when the subject matter would be likely to affect veterans. In other words, neither of them was "ass kissing" material.

In my lifetime, if I am able to help veterans 1/100th as much as Bud Day or Hack did, not much else in this life could please me more. When I say "help" veterans, that help includes restoring one's honor and stolen valor to assisting troubled or wounded veterans receive the care or attention they also deserve because they earned it. And that just continues to remind us that nearly fifty years later, Vietnam remains unfinished business. It is still greatly misunderstood by most of America.

Who understands them? One of the reasons I have never returned to Vietnam is simply because I have never wanted to. Why I have never wanted to when others have returned is a bit more complex to answer.

Even more heartbreaking and downright disgusting to me is what has been going on back here since we came home. I had no clue how many of our Nam brothers have been so badly troubled, psychologically as well as physically, since coming home from Vietnam. After I woke up from the 1970s, my post-Vietnam years, I was able to see things much more clearly. You see, pretty much all of the 1970s were a complete blur for me, which I described in *Condemned Property?* Maybe the 1980s weren't much better for me, not until I met my lovely wife-to-be in 1984 and married her on my fortieth birthday. I still carried a lot of baggage, which was tough on her and possibly her children, who came into my life with her. Anyway, Ginny was by my side then and Ginny is still by my side thirty-two years later. I love her back and in my own strange way, I love all four of her children, who along with their children have had a tremendously positive effect on my survival. They still have a difficult time understanding me. Many families have experienced mild to impossible adjustment problems with their Vietnam veterans.

During the last thirty years, especially the last fifteen years, I have been able to reach out and make personal contact with more Vietnam veterans and try to talk with them about their problems, many of which I have experienced. I tell them that they are not alone, that we are brothers and we should not only reach out to others, but also be ready to accept a reach-out attempt by another brother or anyone who shows a *genuine* concern for us. I have benefitted from this exchange in a huge way.

Going back to Vietnam physically has never become a high priority for me, not as long as there are troubled Nam vets back here and my team of Nam buddies or I can help them in some way. One never knows…I might return to that country someday, but right now I am quite busy dealing with my *mental* returns to Vietnam. A day never passes without thoughts of Vietnam, and sometimes they are problematic.

If I returned to Vietnam tomorrow, what would I see? I don't see that visiting some of the places where my war brothers fought, were wounded, or died would be a problem for me. I don't feel that there would be any closure resulting from such a trip. As I said, I think talking to and hanging around more Vietnam vets back here who could use some camaraderie is more important.

If I returned to Vietnam tomorrow or next year, I would be more afraid of what I would see in the eyes of the population of the Vietnamese themselves than anything else. We did a lot of damage over there, not so much us soldiers and marines, as we were sent there for two reasons—number one, to fight to preserve our own lives and number two, kill our adversary before they killed us. Those were our choices. There was no in between. But our government did a lot of damage. Maybe most of it was necessary, then again, maybe not.

If I returned, would I notice some of the civilians my age and a few years younger? Would I notice their deformed bodies from Agent Orange-caused birth defects? I think so. Would I notice the damaged bodies from the massive firepower we unleashed on them? Yes, a lot of innocents were hit. I think so. Would I be able to detect the psychological effects that many of the Vietnamese elders are still carrying around? I think not, unless I sat down and talked with some of them. But I can do that with some of the American-Vietnamese refugees who call the USA their home now. This makes me wonder how many of the Vietnamese-Americans long to return to their homeland, a homeland that the Vietnamese people have been forced to fight for since before Christ's years. I wonder about these things often. You bet this weighs on my conscience. My country's politicians have made me feel ashamed of what we did in a war for which we were supposed to come home as proud warriors. I have so much empathy and pity for the mama sans, papa sans and baby sans who never knew what hit them when our mighty bombs erased so many of them from their homeland. The reward for many who survived the bombing felt our wrath from Agent Orange poisoning or from being burned to death by napalm.

It may be too difficult to believe that our little conflict across the ocean in the little backward country defended by "farmers and peasants" with pitchforks would inflict more damage onto our vaunted U.S. Marine Corps than any previous war ever fought. Hard to believe because our country's Ameri-Cong media misreported this war from its beginning to the sorrowful end. Then, many of our country's left-wing-slanted, liberal historians continued to brainwash Americans with false and negative recounts of what truly happened in Vietnam. Pardon me, please, if I expound on this sore subject too often, but hey, it is tender and it still hurts.

Our Dads Should Have Been Proud of Us... We were so proud of them; we were raised that way. Anyone who served in WWII could walk on water, and whenever one of them spoke...everyone listened. That's the way it was as we were growing up; we were the most patriotic generation in America's history...who would want to make John Wayne mad? We never wavered; we never doubted; we never spoke ill of our fathers, uncles, or our WWII leaders. And when the national anthem was played, everyone (even our pets) stood at attention and prayed silently for a father, uncle, or older brother fighting "over there."

I've read and heard many sources say that there were many Americans who did not like Franklin Delano Roosevelt, but the nation was more unified during those years than most anyone could remember, so I've been told. Hell, FDR might still be president today if he had lived long enough and if the congressional rules could have been altered for him to be re-elected. Wonder how FDR would have fared as President of the USA during the Vietnam Era, or even today?

With virtually every home and business flying an American flag during and well after WWII, how could any real patriotic American make any decision other than go and serve if or when our country called on us during the escalating conflict in Vietnam?

I broke my mother's heart by dropping out of college to enter the U.S. Army in 1967. I also broke my own heart as I had to quit the sandlot baseball team I was playing for—my childhood dream was to be a professional baseball player. Vietnam prematurely ended that fantasy.

At that time how could anyone blame us for going? Worse yet, how could so many turn their backs on us when we (who lived) returned home? Oh, let it go, Dusty…let it go and get over it.

The Vietnam Era has been celebrating its fiftieth birthday one year at a time since 2012 and will continue the anniversary until 2022. The fiftieth birthday of the 1968 Tet Offensive is in 2018. So is the My Lai tragedy. The 1970 Cambodian Invasion's fiftieth birthday takes place in 2020. April 30, 1972 was the official end of America's participation in the Vietnam War, so 2022 will be its fiftieth birthday.

A well-kept secret about many Vietnam vets' welcome home is that not many of their fathers or uncles who served in WWII ever reached out to us with an "atta boy," "nice job," or "I'm proud of you." Could the blame for that be put onto the negative images the Vietnam War was poisoned with by the news media, especially TV? There is little doubt that the term "fake news" would have been perfect back then in the 1960s and '70s.

When Johnny Comes Marching Home, remember that? The WWI and II vets got that greeting, not sure about the Korea vets, but there is no doubt the Viet vets were left alone to welcome each other home…many still do that.

I can't remember ever having a conversation with any family members about Vietnam, not even once. And so I copped out by becoming a full-time alcohol abuser for the entire decade of the 1970s. Basically ten years went down the drain. This was the period when I became a professional job seeker, going through seventeen employments until 1980. Of course I never accepted responsibility for the bad, bad things that happened to me in the 1970s. I simply blamed them all on Vietnam, which seemed like the right thing to do. I still regret those wasted years when my judgment wasn't just clouded, it was totally nonexistent.

Oh BTW, I should mention that it was my biological father who provided me no comfort or encouragement for my war service. My stepfather was far more understanding and to some degree appreciative for any patriotism, and I'll always remember both of their attitudes toward the Vietnam War.

"Hey…look what's getting off the plane fresh from Vietnam. The f**king Baby Killers!" I'd also remember derogatory comments like that from the war protestors at the airports. You see, unlike others who were ordered to change out of their uniforms, I decided to keep mine on during the entire trip, a very long one, home.

We were told how the Australian moms and dads gave their sons welcome home parades. Also, that the soldiers of the North Vietnam Army were cheered in the streets by Vietnamese in the south as well as the north. Well, I guess they thought they won the war, so why not welcome home the winners and ignore the losers. And those scenes of the Russian tanks carrying NVA soldiers crashing into Saigon in 1975 are still being shown on TV around the world. **WHY?**

Both my father and stepfather are gone. I guess in a way I feel cheated in that my father never asked me about any of my medals for valor, how I got them—what happened on those days. And of course they did not live long enough to read my first book, *Condemned Property?*, and I am still saddened by that.

Almost as tragic is the fact that I was never allowed the opportunity to talk about those fantastic men I served with to either of them. I would have liked my father and stepfather to get to know my Nam brothers. They should have gotten familiar with them. I wouldn't be here if it wasn't for them. Almost makes me feel cheated.

We have been deprived of so much of life's joys because of a war that should have never happened. It has been nearly impossible to not dwell on the past, as Vietnam had an indescribably negative and lasting effect on our outlooks for our remaining years. I suppose this bores some people as I repeat these things over and over, but it cannot be avoided.

Vietnam's horrors, and it was predominantly horror, are going to be with many of us for as long as our brains are still in a function mode. I just wish most of my war buddies could come to terms with that rather than letting it get the best (or worst) of them. I also wish others would leave us alone about it and let us get through the depression times; we really cannot help it. The reminders are endless. If only our fathers had been proud of us, but the endless media lies reach them too.

We were delivered onto the enemy's homeland, some twelve thousand miles away from our home—American marines and soldiers—and we fought with a tenacity and dedication that may never be fully understood or appreciated by the generations to follow. This can be summed up in someone else's brief statements as follows:

> *To this day, it stuns me that their own countrymen have so completely missed the real story of their service, lost in the latter confusion of the war itself.*

—James Webb, Senator
Former Secretary of the Navy
Vietnam Veteran

Over the years since I have been home, I have done an enormous amount of soul searching. Not so much about what my Nam brothers and I did; we did what we had to do. On the other hand, my feelings about our leaders in Washington at that time while we were constantly in harm's way and how they have not done their best to take care of us to this day really trouble me.

Vietnam could have been a fun place for many of America's military personnel. Yes, I mean that. Life back at the large, very secure base camps such as Cu Chi or the cities with military stationed there had to be an absolute dream for some. They had pretty much everything available to them that the States could offer them, if you could get used to the noises of the battles going on ten to twenty miles away. Not to dwell on that anymore, Vietnam was a total combat zone for everyone who stepped onto its soil.

So much has been said about how the Vietnam War was like no war before it or any war since. I do believe that, but then, I did not fight in any other war, so I can only go by what the military historians put on paper for us to read. I know this about the Vietnam War and how it differed from every war prior to it:

- The severity of combat injuries to the wounded in action (WIA) were, as a rule, more vicious than in America's previous wars. The artillery used on both sides during the Vietnam War was specifically designed to inflict massive multiple injuries on the intended targets. Many times, we were on the targeted end from our own weapons, which the enemy captured and had no qualms using on us. It doesn't sound fair, huh? That is war.
- Along with our guns, there was napalm, white phosphorus anti-personnel bombs—always meant to hit the enemy, but that wasn't always the case. Napalm and phosphorus would burn skin clear down to the bone. You think getting burned from your oven or stove at home is painful—try getting hit with napalm. I would not like to run into the Vietnamese who were on the receiving end of American napalm attacks. I don't want to imagine what they look like now.
- Add this to it all—Vietnam was a very small country, and the use of helicopters to airlift and medevac the wounded to a hospital meant that there were far more injuries to treat than in previous years because many of them would simply die before treatment.
- I remember talking to a new nurse in Cu Chi about her job. Even though she was trained well in the States, she and many other nurses found it extremely traumatic to see the level of carnage. They would have to get used to treating wounds they had never seen before or were prepared for. Then there were the diseases that the wounded were very susceptible to—typhoid, malaria, tuberculosis, bubonic plague, dengue fever and a few others, compliments of the bacteria in the air and water of Vietnam.
- I have read in many reference materials, history books, and books written by other Vietnam veterans who served in the war after I came home about how drug addiction became a serious problem. Maybe this is mostly rumor, as I have come across so few who have actually talked about it. Well, the nurses had to treat these casualties as well, and they probably received little or no training. The most common addiction was reported to be heroin. Other drugs caused addiction problems as well—marijuana, cocaine, amphetamines, and opium.

Again, I wonder often how the elder population in Vietnam is doing. Stressed, depressed, angry, confused, forgotten? Pretty much how we American vets feel at times. Trying to understand Vietnam almost fifty years later is something about one million Vietnam vets are faced with, and I believe with all my heart that most of them can do that with better results today than twenty years ago.

I think that I understand the Vietnamese people much better now and that they are very special people. I no longer see them as "gooks," but I also understand why our U.S. Army instructors tried to embed it into our heads that they were not real people; they were just "gooks" and our job would be to take them out. I am so much more sympathetic toward our former adversary and what they were put through to defend their homeland so often, long before we showed up. I even think about what today's Vietnamese might be going through in their country and elsewhere in the world, especially in the USA.

Pitchforks and knives did not sink the American ship the USS *Card*, an escort aircraft carrier that went down in 1964. Two Viet Cong commandos with ninety pounds of high explosives and other parts to assemble two very powerful bombs completed the unlikely mission. The charges killed five crewmen, wounded seven others, and this proud ship, which survived several U-boat attacks in WWII, sank to the bottom in unusually quick fashion.

Supposedly this was the last U.S. aircraft carrier in history to date sunk by enemy attacks. Several fixed-wing aircraft and helicopters went down with the ship. Reminder, the culprits were not skilled U.S. Navy SEALs; they were simply Viet Cong terrorists.

Aircraft carriers have always been a symbol of a nation possessing great power status. As one can imagine, the North Vietnamese celebrated this event as a great victory at the highest level. And the U.S. government refused to acknowledge the ship's sinking, telling the American public only that it had been damaged in battle. North Vietnam would not allow this great propaganda.

Admiration is clearly the one word that comes to my mind when I now think of the Vietnamese people in general, whether they are from the northern or southern regions. Respect is the next word that describes my feelings toward them, and it makes me want to do something for them other than just saying it in this book. The Vietnamese people are possibly the most resilient people I have ever come in personal contact with…right alongside our Jewish friends in Israel.

The admiration and love I have for everyone who fought over there at the ground level can never be put into words. However, whether this is rumor or fact (I tend to believe it), when our fearless leader, General West-moreland, was asked by a news correspondent what he thought of how the French fought their war with Vietnam and had he studied the lessons of the French, Westmoreland's response allegedly was… "Why should I study the lessons of the French? They haven't won a war since Napoleon."

America's leaders had decided or were ill advised that Ho Chi Minh was beyond approach, that he was a die-hard, cruel communist. They felt communism had to be stopped in Southeast Asia, and why not use Vietnam as the battleground. But Ho Chi Minh wanted to meet with American politicians, and none of his attempts were ever acknowledged. Here we go again with that arrogance factor from a white capitalist world power; this time it almost caused an entire civilization to perish, as well as poisoned a generation of American soldiers and many of their family members.

Well, putting aside whether or not we were justified in being there and doing what we did in the first place, there was a much easier solution and a safe, more logical path to take which would have prevented the greatest disaster in American history from taking place…the Vietnam War!

You see, what America's brilliant leaders did not know—or maybe they did but didn't care—was that Ho Chi Minh was a dedicated nationalist to his country and its people *first* and a communist *second*. As I've mentioned elsewhere in *Unbreakable Hearts*, Uncle Ho made several attempts to communicate with American presidents long before all hell broke out, and he was willing to accept help where he could get it for his goals to be achieved peacefully. Had the U.S. been willing to show any interest in supporting a united, independent Vietnam, it was quite possible that Ho could have been negotiated with, and he might have backed off on taking his unified country toward communism. However, when his forward gestures to take a different direction toward a free democratic government were rudely ignored, Ho knew what North Vietnam needed to do. They were willing to do it and they were prepared to fight a war to the last man.

South Vietnam was divided and confused at this time. The majority of South Vietnam's people wanted to be ruled under Ho Chi Minh. The U.S. intervened in South Vietnam's elections (sound familiar?), and this worsened the divide between North and South Vietnam, bringing on a genuine civil war. North Vietnam was not confused, nor divided; their leaders were committed to the same goal…a united Vietnam regardless of who or what stood in their way.

Taking a page out of someone else's playbook so to speak, here are some mind-boggling facts I'll bet most Americans are not aware of:

Staggering Numbers. Since the Vietnam War's end, veterans and veterans activists have claimed that somewhere from 250,000 to two million of the approximate total 3.3 million men and women who served in the Vietnam War theater (Vietnam and Thailand) of operations were suffering from PTSD. There are astonishing figures, especially since fewer than 15 percent of those were ever exposed to direct combat, outside of the secure base camps and installations they were assigned to. This figure remained consistent throughout the duration of the war. Non-combat or support personnel in "the rear" were badly needed, and they might also suffer from some PTSD because of the mortar and rocket attacks that happened during the night. And occasionally a ground assault would scare the dickens out of these support personnel, but the attacks were almost always fought off... almost always. During the Tet Offensives of 1967 and 1968, many base camps were in danger of a ground assault, and some of the smaller outposts were physically overrun. That would cause PTSD for anyone for a lifetime, if they survived.

In 1988, a four-year study by the Research Triangle Institute in North Carolina, the National Vietnam Veteran Readjustment Study, found that 15.2 percent of male Vietnam theater veterans, about 480,000, suffered from PTSD.

The study also showed that an additional 11 percent of the Vietnam War's veterans were suffering from "partial" PTSD at the time of the study, bringing the total to 830,000 or 26 percent of all Vietnam veterans who served in-country. This included non-combat along with actual direct combat troops. This study tied PTSD to high levels of combat exposure, and most Vietnam War veterans rarely saw any combat.

Paraphrased from *Stolen Valor*
B.G. Burkett, Glenna Whitely, 1998

Stolen Valor told the sad but true story of how the Vietnam War generation was robbed of its heroes and its history. This 692-page gem should be on the shelf of everyone's library who was ever touched by this war in any way. I do not agree with everything in this book, as many Vietnam veterans will take issue with portions of my books, but very few have so far. B.G. Burkett is a Vietnam War veteran who served around John Kerry. Neither Kerry or Burkett experienced what my war buddies did as combat infantrymen, as we did not do much of what they did on the Mobile Riverine patrols of Vietnam's inland waterways. However, despite its length, **Stolen Valor** captivated me when I read it almost twenty years ago, and I still refer back to it from time to time. If you've never read it—do get it as it will be well worth your time.

Some of the facts and stories seem almost impossible to believe, even for another combat veteran like myself. But some of the mentions in my books are so truthful and real that they become almost unreal. Believe it, neither **Stolen Valor** or any of my books (**Condemned Property?**, **Payback**

Time! or *Unbreakable Hearts!*) are fictional. If I leave a reader shaking his or her head in disbelief, so be it. I did my job well.

This seemed to be the American attitude of those that all of us at ground level from sergeant E-8 on down had to follow. This was the attitude of disgusting and unforgiveable arrogance. Unfortunately, this bird-brained ignorance prevented Americans from really understanding a quality about the people of Vietnam. Our leaders failed to recognize that the Vietnamese victory over the French was not about technology but of human determination. Their unique technology was their inner strength to overcome the most demanding physical and psychological hardships imaginable. Their tolerance for pain and suffering is what prevented a quick and decisive victory for American technology. Our leaders' misguided arrogance and the incomparable strong will of the Vietnamese forced America into the longest war in our country's history. As another American general once said:

> *Wars may be fought with weapons, but they have to be won by the people.*
>
> **—General George Patton**

Nobody cared. Despite these huge obstacles to overcome, the sons and nephews of America's greatest generation won their battles anyway. Think about these roadblocks for the Vietnam War warrior:

- LBJ stopped bombing the Ho Chi Minh Trail at the peak of the war.
- The South Vietnamese government was corrupt and more dangerous than the communists of North Vietnam. Why were we helping either of them?
- The Vietnam War was a civil war and we had no business being there.
- American bureaucrats and generals badly underestimated a tenacious adversary.
- The American government left us out to dry after sending us over there.
- The American media stabbed us in the back as we risked our lives or died for them.
- The American people swept us under the rug after we came home.
- The Vietnam War never had a plan for victory.
- The American Service Clubs, American Legion, VFW, etc. blackballed us.
- The American antiwar movement was not about bringing us home. It was against what we were sent there for…before anyone knew why we were being sent there.
- The American public (our families and friends) were never told the truth about what we were up against or how we survived.

Nobody else cared, so how did the Vietnam War veterans beat such odds and survive? The answer is…MOST HAVE NOT!

Vietnam will always dwarf everything in my life up to this point. Nothing has ever required the intensity that forced us to stay on the edge at all times. We could be taking a relaxing walk in the forest with our dog and then the unexpected crack of a branch could put us right back to a particular day or night in Nam. But over there, we had each other, nothing else. Our camaraderie, shared with the pain, anger, and sadness, will most likely never be equaled again. However…***One Day We'll Be Together Again…***

Dear America,

One day we will be together again.
I don't know when. I don't know how.
But there is one thing that I know for sure.
My loyalty to you will never end.

Bring back the magic that we used to share—tell me that you honor me and you still care.
Let me stand proudly by you again until the end of our time.

I'll always admire you and I hope that you realize that all I feel for you is genuine and written in stone.
You'll always be in my thoughts wherever I am, deep in your heart I hope you understand.

My heart longs to be in your thoughts.
My soul cries out for your recognition.

If only you could somehow see all of the emotions that still remain.
What did I do to turn you away?
Please tell me that I can finally come home.

Open your heart and let me in.
Please honor my salute again.
Open your eyes and see who I am.
I bled and died for you when others damned you.

Dear America, tell me those words I've longed to hear
That someday we will be together again…soon.

          —Vietnam Veteran to America

No one can know what will be discovered someday about the future health problems our brothers and sisters who served in the Middle East wars will be faced with. I am concerned for them. But right now, there is older business that deserves to be taken care of: helping neglected Vietnam War veterans while they are still living.

One of the saddest tragedies about the Vietnam War is that it continues to kill so many who have been struggling to survive Vietnam's aftermath… after they came home

Sometimes when I am talking to God, I still ask him, Dear God, why did you allow those bureaucrats in Washington, D.C. to send us to hell…while we were still living?

Regardless…we can't go back and change the beginning, but we can start all over where we are right now, and change the ending with the support of a loving family and great friends.

Chapter 10

THEY NEVER GAVE UP ON AMERICA

*The bravest thing we ever did was continue our lives when we wanted
to die.*

—Unknown

I think the greatest victory in my life was every time we walked out to
the jungle looking for the beast, always giving it everything we had out
there—and making it back the same day—all of us! That was a magnificent victory for us. We couldn't go out and win a bowling or golf match, a
baseball game, or a girl's heart. All we had over there was this unbelievably
strong desire to make sure that as many of us as possible made it the whole
year so that we could come back to see our beloved America the beautiful
again. None of us ever thought that what we did over there for our country
wouldn't be good enough for many Americans when we came back, and oh
my, were we in for the shock of our lives!

Try to imagine this series of totally unexpected events in your life:

Your best friend is making it with your girlfriend while you have been in
a major battle in the Iron Triangle of Vietnam, which is the headquarters of
the Viet Cong. There is reason to believe that you might not survive the day,
as you have watched dozens of your buddies go down and the battle is still
raging. Finally, a combat assault of a dozen Huey Cobras land successfully
with a full company of infantry to bail your badly mangled company out of
there. Your company is mauled, there are almost too many to rescue, and
more of your guys are hit trying to pull guys out. The company of reinforcements is now taking casualties while trying to remove the wounded from the
battle scene. One Huey is loaded with wounded and it takes off, but while
your brothers are loading the first Huey with wounded bodies...the second
helicopter is shot down, blown to bits.

Another combat assault of a dozen Hueys lands in an area behind the
enemy's location. Now the enemy is surrounded with no escape, so it seems.
Suddenly, you black out as you are hit in the neck. Hours later, you wake up
in a hospital near Saigon, and your first words are...*How are my brothers?
How many made it?*

The news you receive is somewhat of a relief in that your guys prevailed
in the battle and every wounded or dead American body was recovered.
Two of your best buddies did not make it, which makes you wish that

you could have been there to save them. Next…it is mail call time and one letter is handed to you. You are a wreck. Your wound is throbbing with almost unbearable pain, and you are so upset over the loss of your brothers, but maybe the letter from home can bring you a bit of cheer. God knows you need it right now. The letter provides you with absolutely no uplift whatsoever. It is a "Dear John" letter from your girlfriend, saying she has fallen in love with your best friend. You and he were best buddies since you were both ten years old. He remained in college and avoided the draft. You didn't.

There were thousands of stories very similar to this one during the Vietnam War and most wars. As a soldier, you are loyal to your country, loyal to the war brothers who fight next to you for a full year or for whatever amount of time you all last together, and you get that heart-breaking letter from your girl. You will spend the next three months in rehab, surgery, more rehab and then…you should be ready to be sent home. But are you ready to go? Do you even want to? You have been watching the news reports on TV and in the newspapers; the news is full of protests, anti-Vietnam War marches, and you feel like writing a message to your country, maybe like this one:

Dear America,

I am a husband, father, and grandfather.

I may have been a coworker with you at one time during the last thirty years.

I may have coached your kid's baseball or soccer team.

Once, I fought for America in one of the most horrible wars the world has ever seen.

I still have problems with that war due to a poison called Agent Orange and a very bad illness called PTSD.

Chances are your entire family is much safer with me around you than when I am not, but we are treated like outcasts.

I am a…proud Vietnam veteran and we will never give up on America.

—Vietnam Veteran

They never gave up on America…Vietnam veterans! One of the goals of this book is to make a connection with a small southeastern Asian country's people, their resilience over two thousand years of fighting off hordes of vicious invaders, and to show how the Vietnamese people have hung on to something that Americans were known for from the beginning of their country, but I don't know anymore.

Nationalism is what Americans carried so proudly on their faces and in their hearts after the War for Independence, during and after WWI, WWII. And yes…even when our heroes came home from an unpopular war in Korea, and then Vietnam without a warm welcome. Even so…VIETNAM VETERANS HAVE NEVER GIVEN UP ON AMERICA. That's a fact, Jack.

It was America's much-maligned Vietnam veterans who inspired people to gather at airports from Boston to San Diego, from Seattle to Fort Myers and everywhere in between, where our heroes from the Gulf War were returning home. Same scenario for our gallant guys returning from Iraq, Afghanistan, and the war against the Islamic State terrorists. Today's veterans know this to be true.

Vietnam veterans buried their anger as best they could because they loved their country more, the country they went through hell for. The love for America has been unconditional for most of us, and we have more reasons than any group of Americans, any race, any nationality, any generation, to remain mad as hell for the rest of our lives. Of course, many of the soldiers and marines coming home from the 1990s and 2000s wars are our own sons, daughters, and grandchildren. Regardless, we would be supporting them anyway. No question about that.

America has been so very fortunate. Only twice before have troops from another country invaded our land—the British with the War of 1812 and the Confederacy in the Civil War. Of course, Pearl Harbor was undoubtedly a serious encroachment on our home turf. All situations were taken care of.

Danger…Danger…Danger! Our beloved America is being invaded right now by unfriendly soldiers loyal to the Islamic States. They are not looking for a new beginning in life for their families or new jobs, and with it to enjoy the American dream. No sir, no ma'am, their only goal in mind is to attack us from within and bestow as much destruction onto our culture as they possibly can. This invasion has been going on at an alarming rate since the beginning of the Barack Hussein Obama administration.

This silent invasion is no longer a secret and it has caused Americans of all kinds to arm themselves in preparation of what seems inevitable violence in the streets of our neighborhoods.

Hey, we are still the "good guys" in this world. Don't ever disbelieve that despite the crap you will hear and read from the left wing dominated media. Hell, they have been preaching the virtues of socialism over a free democratic America since the 1950s. Please keep this old saying in mind, whether it applies to you or someone you know:

Definition of STUPID: Knowing the truth, seeing the truth, but still believing the lies.

—Author Unknown

Modern Vietnam War Hater. I wanted to put something here that matches up with the above quote, and I found it. A gentleman (?) named Laurence M. Vance wrote an article published on April 29, 2013, which was titled "Should We Honor Vietnam Veterans?" Not knowing what to expect in an article with a title like that, I was a bit skeptical; however, I still attempted to keep an open mind as I began digesting Vance's opinions on this subject. It didn't take long for my open mind and positive expectations to turn sour. I don't want anyone to take Vance's comments out of context, as they say, so I will simply hand-pick a few of them in the very same words he used. Here are some:

> *I for one will never forget what Vietnam veterans did—they traveled half way around the world to fight an unjust, immoral, and unnecessary war against people they didn't know who were no threat to them, their families, or the United States.*

I have little problem so far with his opening, but he ruins it as he carries on. I swear this man hides behind the name of God and speaks out more like the anti-Christ rather than one of God's children. This man needs to beg for forgiveness from God before he dies. We, who he so disgustingly disrespects, do not need nor would we seek out an insincere apology from a creature such as this. We would just prefer that he keep his distance from us in face-to-face life. He is a flaming jackass.

> *The Vietnam War was a monstrous evil in every respect. And as Nick Turse* [presumably a Vietnam vet] *documents over and over again in his new book* Kill Anything that Moves: The Real American War in Vietnam, *the whole war was one murderous My Lai incident, with lots of rape, torture, and mutilation thrown in.*

> *So, why should we honor or respect Vietnam veterans? Because, as Turse documents, they killed, poisoned, raped, beat, tortured, burned, mutilated, abused, drowned, and sexually exploited the Vietnamese? Of course (it is said), only a few bad apples did those things.*

> *How about because of their courage, sacrifice, bravery, guts, and valor? How about because they did it for "duty, honor, country"? Nice try, but as Fred Reed recently wrote: "There is no honor in going to someone else's country and butchering people you don't know because some political general, which is to say some general, told you to; a hit man for the Mafia is exactly as honorable."*

As he continues on elsewhere:

> *Because of the nature of the Vietnam War, Vietnam veterans as a group should not be honored any more than Iraq and Afghanistan war veterans as a group should be honored. That means they shouldn't be honored at all.*

Author Vance and author Turse must have listened to John Kerry's tapes from The Winter Soldier on April 27, 1971. As he continues on:

> *There are, however, some individual Vietnam veterans that should be honored—but not because they fought in the Vietnam War. We can honor those who acknowledge that their participation in the war was a terrible mistake. We can honor those who regret the lives they took and the property they destroyed. We can honor those who now realize that the war was a great evil. We can honor those that refused to kill once they arrived in Vietnam. We can honor those who have publicly denounced the war. We can honor those who have returned to Vietnam and apologized to the Vietnamese. We can honor these individual Vietnam veterans—but not because of anything they did while fighting in Vietnam.*

I shared this article with members at the American Legion Post I belong to as well as three VFW Posts which with I am active. One hundred percent of those who read Vance's piece voted thumbs down. The most common verbal response was…**F_ _ _ ING BULLSHIT!**

My dear readers, Vance has put out similar crap about American veterans, but when I look at his credentials in his biography, which are impressive, I cannot figure out why he would be writing such despicable junk about us, other than he is obviously antiwar, and he could not measure up to serve in our military, and that he is envious. But that is just a guess.

> *No man is worth his salt who is not ready at all times to risk his body…to risk his well-being…to risk his life…in a great cause.*
> **—Theodore Roosevelt**

If your blood boils at such anti-military, anti-soldier, anti-patriotic "opinions," you can find a lot more of Vance's work online. Here is quoted material from a more current article of his, titled "Thank Them for What?"

We fought side by side, back to back, in tight quarters like few other American soldiers have had to in previous wars, disillusionment on a daily basis in the muggy inferno of the Nam. As we say to people who ask us about it…you had to be there, but good for you that you weren't.

We will grieve forever for our war buddies who were sacrificed during that war and who were allowed to die after its end. How dare anyone question our loyalty to each other and to our country, and NO APOLOGIES if we tend to dwell on that time of our lives that happened so long ago…when we were soldiers once, and very young.

Unfortunately, there are still some very troubled Americans who remain bitter and even hateful toward us, and give us no credit for our sacrifices. I am not far off base making this statement, especially when that war damaged so many Americans' entire families. While Jane Fonda and John Kerry have pretty much shut up with their moans and groans about Vietnam and have even half-ass "attempted" to apologize to us for their sinful actions during the war, there remain others like them who continue to spit at us for what they were led to believe we did over there. Laurence M. Vance is one of the worst of these types, but he also has other demented America-haters to keep him comfortable.

Before I provide you with a long list of Vance's one-liners about his dislike for those who have stepped up to do what he is too cowardly to do, I have to share an abbreviated but fairly impressive resume with you, so you can see that he is not psychologically insane, as he seemingly knows what he is doing:

About Laurence M. Vance

Laurence M. Vance is an author, a publisher, a lecturer, a freelance writer, the editor of the **Classic Reprints** series, and the director of the **Francis Wayland Institute**. He holds degrees in history, theology, accounting, and economics. The author of twenty-four books, he has contributed over 600 articles and book reviews to both secular and religious periodicals. Vance's writings have appeared in a diverse group of publications including the Ancient Baptist Journal, Bible Editions & Versions, Campaign for Liberty, LewRockwell.com, the Independent Review, the Free Market, Liberty, Chronicles, the Journal of Libertarian Studies, the Journal of the Grace Evangelical Society, the Review of Biblical Literature, Freedom Daily, and the New American. His writing interests include economics, taxation, politics, government spending and corruption, theology, English Bible history, Greek grammar, and the folly of war. He is a regular columnist, blogger, and book reviewer for **LewRockwell.com**, and also writes a column for the **Future of Freedom Foundation**. Vance is a member of the **Society of Biblical Literature,** the **Grace Evangelical Society,** and the **International Society of Bible Collectors,** and is a policy adviser of the **Future of Freedom Foundation** and an associated scholar of the **Ludwig von Mises Institute.**[29]

Not bad credentials, huh? So, how much further can his hatred for us nosedive? Take some solace, my brothers; it appears that he shares his unpatriotic opinions with all of America's veterans. Please take a few seconds to read a more current display of his demonic feelings toward my brave comrades.

---

29 www.vancepublications.com

Thank Them for What?

By Laurence M. Vance

November 27, 2015

"Thank You Veterans" said the sign out in front of my local Harley-Davidson dealer on Veterans Day. The owners of the veterinarian practice across the street from the Harley dealer are obviously more patriotic: They kept their "Thank You Veterans" sign up all the way to Thanksgiving.

Beginning on Veterans Day and running through Thanksgiving Day there have been stories on the news and during football games about the poor U.S. soldiers we should thank in Afghanistan and the Middle East who won't be home to celebrate Thanksgiving with their families.

Some churches had on Thanksgiving Day, or had the night before, special services in which the congregations were reminded from the pulpit to not forget to thank both veterans and the troops.

Thank them for what?

It is generally never said. Sometimes we are told that we should thank veterans and the troops for "their service." Other times we are told that we should thank veterans and the troops for "defending our freedoms." On other occasions we are told that we should thank veterans and the troops for fighting "over there" so we didn't/don't have to fight "over here." And still other times we are told that we should thank veterans and the troops for "keeping us safe."

But above all we are just bombarded with "Thank You Veterans" or "Thank You Soldiers."

Again I ask: Thank them for what?

It doesn't seem to matter where the troops go, why they go, how long they stay, what they do when they get there, how much it costs to keep them there, how many innocent foreigners die because they went there, what physical and mental condition they will be in when they return, whether they will create more terrorists by going, whether whatever they accomplish is worth one drop of American blood, or whether they should go in the first place.

So again I ask: Thank them for what?

Should we thank them for creating more terrorists every time they maim and kill in some other country?

Should we thank them for killing thousands of civilians and keeping some of their body parts?

Should we thank them for drone strikes that regularly miss their targets?

Should we thank them for helping to carry out a reckless, belligerent, and meddling U.S. foreign policy?

Should we thank them for safeguarding the American way of life when they have nothing to do with it?

Should we thank them for following orders when the orders are immoral?

Should we thank them for fighting unjust wars?

Should we thank them for serving Uncle Sam and not the country?

Should we thank them for sacrificing their families on the altar of the god of war?

Should we thank them for their high suicide rate?

Should we thank them for going where they had no business going?

Should we thank them for fighting senseless wars?

Should we thank them for serving as the world's policeman, bully, and troublemaker?

Should we thank them for defending our freedoms when our freedoms are steadily eroding?

Should we thank them for expecting military discounts on all major holidays?

Should we thank them for helping to waste a trillion dollars of the federal budget every year?

Should we thank them for fighting unnecessary wars?

Should we thank them for maintaining our First Amendment rights when they are slipping away?

Should we thank them for avenging 9/11 by maiming or killing hundreds of thousands of people who had nothing to do with it?

Should we thank them for making hundreds of thousands of widows and orphans?

Should we thank them for preserving, protecting, and defending the Constitution when they do just the opposite?

Should we thank them for fighting immoral wars?

Should we thank them for being a proud member of the U.S. military?

Should we thank them for going to a country they couldn't locate until they were sent there?

Should we thank them for being invaders?

Should we thank them for being role models for our children when they are anything but?

Should we thank them for expecting special preference in employment, and not just for government jobs?

Should we thank them for keeping us safe when their actions make us less safe?

Should we thank them for engaging in offense instead of defense?

Should we thank them for being heroes because they kill and maim?

Should we thank them for fighting undeclared wars?

Should we thank them for destroying Iraq and Afghanistan?

Thank veterans and the troops? Thank them for what? What in the world should we be thanking them for? Americans have a lot of things to be thankful for at Thanksgiving. U.S. soldiers "serving" in some foreign country is not one of them.[30]

Unbelievably, Vance continued on and on with these idiotic and despicable rantings. I had to wonder who dropped him on his head again and again and again. Hard to believe that a man who hides behind the name of God could bear such satanic feelings toward so many of America's bravest men and women. It makes me wonder if he married, had children, etc. I searched long and hard to decide on one or two words to describe my anger with Vance's public degrading of such fine people. But he doesn't deserve any more space in this book than something like this:

The lowest form of life is an organism called a *prokaryote*, which includes disease-causing bacteria and slimy blue-green algae. Prokaryotes are very simple, single-celled organisms. So it seems to me that Vance could easily come from their family tree. Then again, the lowest form of life I was aware of until now was your good old-fashioned blood-sucking, swamp-dwelling LEECH!

Moving on quickly and as far away as I can from what you just read—this is 2016, not 1968, so it is painful to witness such anti-military hate at Vance's level. Sure, it happened in the 1960s, 1970s, and 1980s, and even into the 1990s. This kept many Vietnam veterans from shedding the shame they carried for so long. For too many decades, ever since the high point of

---

30 The Best of Laurence M. Vance https://www.lewrockwell.com/author/Laurence-m-vance/

antiwar fever during the 1960s and 1970s, too many American Vietnam era veterans have been ashamed or afraid to display their military or especially their war services with pride. How sad.

Nationalism Vietnam Vet Style...I remember the feelings I had after the shock of my conscription (draft) notification wore off. New emotions were taking over my thoughts. I was actually getting excited about the opportunity coming to me, to serve my country at a time she seemed to need me. I hoped that I would be up for it when the real thing (battle) faced me. I wasn't burning any draft cards. I respected, admired, actually loved the American flag. I wanted to punch out those ingrates who spat on Old Glory, let alone desecrate it in far more insulting fashion...like putting on flag-burning demonstrations. I was certain that most of the young men riding the bus with me to Fort Knox, Kentucky, in the fall of 1967 felt like I did. Then again none of us had any inclination of what was waiting for us in that very strange place called Vietnam.

BRING IT ON! was the feeling most of us had, and a lot of the guys even cheered when we arrived at our first location, where we would spend the next eight and a half weeks, sharing barracks with dozens of complete strangers. But what the hey, how bad could it be? We were all Americans, there for mostly the same purpose, those of us who would end up in Vietnam, that is.

I tipped the scale at 180 pounds the first day of check-in. I thought I was in pretty good shape too, with a thirty-two-inch waist. Two months from then I would weigh close to my high school weight at Twinsburg High, right at 160 pounds with a thirty-inch waist. I hooked up with and bunked with another Cleveland boy, John Victoryn, who went to Cathedral Latin High. His attitude about it all was a mirror image of mine; in fact Johnny was even a little more gung-ho about the army and said right at the start that he was going "all the way Airborne." Johnny would do just that and would end up with the legendary 101st Airborne. My destination would take me to a similar type of combat unit known as the 25th Infantry Division. We were both grunts, tuned at Fort Polk, Louisiana, or as it was affectionately called..."little Nam."

Fort Knox was basic training. But a day never passed without our drill sergeant mentioning the Viet Cong and the Vietnam War. Some of them had been there and survived it. But none of them ever shared their experiences over there; they just trained us and went their own way at the end of the last training day. Gosh, I wanted to talk to them so badly. So did Johnny, but it never happened. Actually, except for a few faces, I cannot remember anyone else's name at basic training except my pal Johnny Victoryn. I have never seen anyone from that training company since.

I've often wondered how some of them fared in the rest of their lives. Most of us got along well then; you always have your standard brand of assholes, some of whom challenged the drill sergeants and even went absent without leave (AWOL)! All that got them was a prison cell. I definitely never saw any of those characters again, and that was fine with me.

After basic training, it was on to "Tiger Land" in the north part of Fort Polk, noted as the best place to be if your next stop was V-I-E-T-N-A-M. Polk Advanced Infantry Training soon clued me in that I was not in the best shape of my life, but I would be if I made it out of Polk, Oklahoma. That was not a guarantee as Polk's training in the Louisiana swamps and jungle-like terrain was too much for some to handle. Polk's training was so tough, it even killed some before they got to Nam.

As a very brash and immature twenty-two-year-old, I was so curious back then. How were they going to prepare us for jungle warfare? As it would turn out, no one could quite prepare us for our next destination's 24/7 activities in the real swamps and jungles of Southeast Asia.

I thought that some of us were ready for our next assignment after four weeks or so at Fort Polk. We were in even better physical shape than when we left Fort Knox. I did not believe how fit many of us were. In our final physical training context, I ran my one mile even in four minutes and fifty-eight seconds…in full army fatigues and heavy combat boots. Man, did I feel ready for those Viet Cong we kept hearing about day after day, night after night. I found myself wanting to meet and shoot my first VC and get that out of the way. As for all those guys I trained with at Polk, I would only see one of them ever again. His name was Roland Broussard, a home-grown Louisiana boy. He was actually one of the other platoon leaders at our infantry company at Polk, although I rarely saw him back then. This would change as Broussard and I would end up with the same combat infantry outfit in Vietnam, Bravo Company 3rd 22nd of the 25th Infantry Division. I am thankful to say that both of us made it over there. He still lives in his home state of Louisiana and I still live in mine, Ohio. I would never see Johnny Victoryn again after we went home on leave together from Polk. Vietnam took his life in quick fashion during a Viet Cong ambush.

My new family and I would meet soon enough, at a small fire base not too far away from our main outpost called Dau Tieng. Other than being scared and uncertain of what we were in for, most of the guys were pretty cordial to each other and we would get to know each other a little bit more every day.

We had some guys mixed in with the rest who wanted to be the next Audie Murphy. We also had some guys who were scared stiff 24/7; fortunately, I wasn't either of those types. Both of those types seemed to be amongst our earliest casualties, as we would come to realize later. One thing that remained a constant with most of us was the special feelings of admiration, respect, and love we would share with those of us who were still in one piece or mostly one piece at the end of our tour.

We all came home separately. It would have been better if we had each other again to face what was waiting for us at the airports in the USA. But we had to face that unexpected experience alone. It is an experience I have never forgotten, and I doubt that I ever will...unfortunately.

Unbelievably we were "advised" to change into civilian clothes due to the likeliness of negative reactions if we still had our military uniforms on. I was one of those who refused to come home without my uniform on, with the medals I had *earned*. I was a proud soldier and proud to be an American—still am—always will be.

Without going into any details—I've done that in previous books—let's just say that MY PATRIOTISM WAS CHALLENGED. My patience was tested. The memory of that time when I returned to America would be nothing like what I had hoped for, what I had dreamed about. For me and too many of my Nam warrior brothers who had survived the worst and longest possible living nightmare of our lives, we were not greeted with either Welcome Home or Thank You for Your Service!

Aside from this depressing neglect when we came home, most Vietnam vets remain loyal, patriotic, and proud to be an American. We did not avoid going to a war when we were called and we still stand up for our sacred National Anthem—God Bless America!

Another example—during the Vietnam War, it became almost impossible to distinguish between propaganda of the so-called peace movement in America and the war propaganda machine coming directly out of North Vietnam. In fact, the anti-American progressive peace movement activists (socialists) were not bashful about spreading North Vietnam's bogus, hateful propaganda about America's evil role in the war. Simply, the left wing liberal Americans teamed up with the communist North Vietnamese to condemn the truths about the war and...promote the lies as though they were the truth.

It is unfortunate but true that many "peace advocates" in America gave aid and comfort to the enemy of our soldiers and marines in the Vietnam War. Whether they were aware of their crime or not, anti-American communist-leaning citizens played a profound part in influencing or supporting acts of treason.

American soldiers and marines were vilified as brutal, immoral, merciless, and unjust doers of the worst possible atrocities imaginable against an innocent, defenseless victim, the Viet Cong. Therefore, the American media earned the name "Ameri-Cong," compliments of patriot Dr. Roger Canfield in his book *Comrades in Arms*.

We have come to know that many American history books used in schools and colleges were printed with much of North Vietnam's political propaganda, inserted and almost unedited into the history books. The damage done to future nationalistic opinions of our country has made its mark. A disgusting example of this damage could be—our streets were filled with protestors of the action taken against Iraq's Saddam Hussein's invasion into an unsuspecting Kuwait. What possible notice could those protestors have had other than they were just plain old America haters from the left.

Somehow, we have to stop the cruel history makers in their tracks from infecting history books with the maliciously harmful lies that were told about the Vietnam War and the heroes who fought there. NOTHING I have stated in this chapter will matter if there is not a major change in the November 2016 Presidential election. If Americans vote for another president from the far left, then this book will be rendered useless and I will pull it from the bookstores and never write another on this critically important subject of…America's future. I will revert to writing a book about man's best friend instead…dogs. They rarely let us down.

However, my fellow patriotic Americans, if the November 2016 Presidential election comes out with someone who loves America like you and I do, this book might have helped that. I advise you to hang onto it, read it again, and share it.

During all of 2016, I prayed for an American victory with the November 2016 Presidential election, hoping we would put someone into the office who could provide us with the hope we have been looking for to see a resurrection in the attitude of Americans. We'll find out soon enough what our new president is made of.

Now I would like to share a short story from another Nam brother.

Remember us? As my year of living nightmares was drawing to a close, hell was about to get even hotter as the Mini-Tet of May 1968 exploded onto the scene. We couldn't see how it could get any worse here, but it did. Same shit, just more of it—find 'em, kill 'em, count 'em, bury 'em, then do it again, hoping we don't become the ones getting buried. Now I really, really began to get scared that I would not get out of this place in one piece. The choppers were bringing in body bags every other hour now, day and night. What the hell was going on out there in the bush? Everyone was getting ambushed before we could pull the ambush on them. We needed more men out in the field and the base camps were full of 'em, not doing much of anything. I almost went to the first sergeant to ask him to send me back out there to help kill those bastards, but better sense prevailed…I only had nine days left in-country and what the heck, I did my time out there, battling the beast in life-or-death situations day in and day out. Man, I couldn't wait to GET OUT OF THIS PLACE!

Yeah, right, and oh, by the way, there were these constant guilt thoughts about leaving my buddies behind. After all, they had been my family for the last year. Well, I'm sure I'll see some of them again back home after this war has ended. At least I hoped I would see them.

My last few days in Nam couldn't have gone better. They left me alone and that was fine with me, as I was prepping my brain on what I thought it would be like when I got home. I would need to catch up on things as fast as I could, and I was looking forward to that—who wouldn't? I wanted to tell everyone what great soldiers were here risking and giving their lives for Americans back home, and how proud I was to have fought side by side with these guys. I wished we could have all gone home together, but it just doesn't work that way.

*Those last few days in-country I spent a lot of time trying to get back to my buddies still out there in the bush, to say good-bye properly. I did that by trying to hitch rides on dust-offs or slicks or courier choppers. I'm glad I did that. I will remember those guys for a lot of reasons, one of them being...**they were some of the toughest men I have ever seen in my entire life.***

I never got the chance to thank my mom and dad for hanging in there with me when I needed them and for not bugging me when I needed time to myself. I miss them terribly.

Again, I thank Dusty for my chance to say some things. Most important of all, I gotta thank my wife number five, Rosa. Man, did she come into my life at just the right time and she stuck to me like glue while I was trying to screw my head on right. I can't ever thank her enough for hanging in there, trying to understand the damaged mind of a grunt from Nam and always being there ready to help me get through a painful moment. Maybe it's time for me to do the same for her...love ya so much, Rosa. I could not have made it without you, honey...I love you.

*After seeing Bob Hope and Martha Rae once at Lai Khe, I became an immediate member of their fan clubs for as long as they both lived. God, they were the perfect epitome of...**Great Americans.***

Forty-eight years later, and I am still not comfortable talking to anyone about Vietnam who wasn't a veteran. No one else ever wanted to hear about it anyway, so I'll probably die never having the chance to tell those who need to know what happened over there. I'm grateful for Dusty's books. They tell things as they were and they are a tribute to what many of us believe was the greatest army in America's history that most Americans never got to know the truth about.

As my years progressed, for the first two decades after Nam, I look back at four failed marriages, a short prison term for assault, and countless attempts to make something out of my life for my fifth wife of twenty-eight years and myself. Had she not found me and rescued me and cared about my Nam experience, there just is no way to tell what would have happened to me. A lot of my brothers from over there are gone, leaving not so happy lives behind them.

How can you tell people that weren't there how it really was when the newspapers back here were reporting things differently than how they actually happened? I got so tired of arguing with people over that, eventually I blocked everyone out of my life who wasn't a Nam vet, and I'm happy with that decision. Unfortunately, my brothers who died since the war ended will have died as betrayed heroes. Vietnam veterans were betrayed by this country—lock, stock, and barrel. Add PTSD, Agent Orange, and an incompetent and heartless Veterans Administration working against us, not for us.

The Veterans Administration has been screwing Vietnam veterans every way we turn since our war ended, and they are still selling us out. I was brought up to believe in my country, right or wrong. Now I look back at my blind loyalty and wish I could get even somehow because of the sorry treatment we've gotten from them right down the line. We gave all we had; VA shut us out while America turned its back on us. To me, this was the greatest or worst injustice in our country's history, and the story goes on and on for us.

I'm sixty-nine years old, look like eighty-nine, and I feel older. I have diabetes from Agent Orange exposure, very heavy exposure, had a heart attack, lost a home and a business, and I still fight with demons from Vietnam at night.

At long last, I'd like to thank a few people. First of all, I'd like to thank my kids for eventually coming around to me after they read Dusty's first book, Condemned Property? *a couple years ago. I guess, as Dusty always says...* **IT'S NEVER TOO LATE!**

P.S. Dear America, despite the anger that many Vietnam War veterans still are not able to let go of, I personally don't know even one "real" Vietnam War veteran who wouldn't pick up a weapon tomorrow if American needed them again...to put their lives on the line to protect our freedom.

—Robert W., South Carolina
Nam Vet
U.S. Army, Ben Cat 1967–1968

Condemned Property? was the most difficult book for me to begin and complete. It took me back to Vietnam like nothing else has done since coming home. My war buddies and I either experienced or were influenced by much of everything that was put into that book. The book took me nearly two and a half years to complete, but honestly, I had begun putting it together from the first day I stepped on to the "Freedom Bird" on my trip home in March of 1969. At the end, *Condemned Property?* took a great toll on me as I suffered from two cerebral vascular attacks within a few days after the launch.

Payback Time! gave me much satisfaction, but like most sequels to anything, it may have been a bit anticlimactic coming out on the heels of my first book, which had a profound impact on its readers, whether they were real Vietnam War veterans, family members, or non-veterans. Eyes were opened at all levels, especially with VA employees as well as many of our country's Congress members. Both books served their purpose, achieved the goals and expectations I had for them, and they are both still selling on Amazon.

Many of us have carried these feelings of guilt and yes, almost shame. When will it stop? How can we stop these feelings? I see thousands of Vietnam vets adorning baseball-type hats with slogans referring to their past as being a proud Vietnam veteran. Wearing a baseball cap is fine, and you are entitled to at least that display of pride about who you are. I know that this is also a message to others that you are indeed a very proud American. I understand that, I really do.

I wish that more Vietnam veterans would or could brag more about their pride in having served in the Vietnam War. I think our fallen comrades would like us to do that. I think their families would embrace that. I am told that the post-World War II years commonly had America's veterans proudly wearing their military ribbons, buttons, and medals publicly. This practice is believed to have ended at the end of the Vietnam War, and I pray that we will start doing it again.

About ten years ago, I came out of hiding, so to speak. I went on a nationwide search to find a dress-green U.S. Army uniform that I could squeeze into. Eventually, after visiting every Army-Navy store between Baltimore, Atlanta, Houston, Kansas City, and Cleveland, I finally found a coat (in Cleveland) and trousers (in Houston) that I could ease into. Since then, I have worn that uniform in parades, funerals for other Vietnam vets, and public events where I was invited to speak. I plan to continue for as long as the garb fits. Right now, I've had the trousers let out as far as they can go.

The fear of showing your pride that you served needs to come to a screeching halt! Veterans—Vietnam veterans as well—should stand at the top of our country's social ladder. The 1960s and 1970s military haters, draft dodgers, antiwar radicals, and racist cowards have lived on too long. This can be speeded up by more American veterans displaying their service and beginning to show their pride as our forefathers and mothers who served did.

Your military ribbons should be worn on the left side of your suit, jacket, or coat lapel, shirt collar or left shoulder and left shirtsleeve. But…NOT on T-shirts, costumes, or politically driven garments and maybe not at your place of employment if your employer is anti-military. But by all means, put them back on after leaving work. I am paraphrasing from an article that was printed twenty-some years ago and reprinted several times since, "America's Vietnam Veterans Should Stop Being Ashamed or Afraid for Having Served."

My dear war brothers, I have felt your pain and, sadly, even the undeserved shame of having served as a combat soldier in America's most controversial war abroad. I wish that someday, we could all step up and end these painful and undeserved feelings. The 1960s and 1970s are long gone, but I, too, carry those memories as many of you do. I remember things like the following that we were a part of as brothers. Could it be that people like Vance may have been jealous for the love we had for each other? Regardless, no one who does not try to understand us will ever receive understanding of what they do, from us. Here are some things we did, things that still haunt us, that few others will be able to appreciate:

- Giving up our C-rations to homeless Vietnamese children whose parents were murdered by Viet Cong.
- Walking through a burning village, looking to **rescue** villagers wounded and maimed by VC or North Vietnamese Regulars.
- Carrying some of those Vietnamese children to another village, hoping they would be safe there and knowing that the platoon might get ambushed after doing that.
- Participation in the rebuilding of a village demolished by VC/ NVA or our own errant bombing missions.
- Forced to fight in a war that may have been unjust or facing a court martial and dishonorable discharge either way, leaving as a permanently damaged person.
- Witnessing countless American brothers shot down, massacred by unsuspecting ambushes from VC/NVA, sometimes right after coming to the aid of Vietnamese villagers also under attack.
- Watching a medic being picked off by a VC sniper as he was administering medical aid to save the life of a wounded enemy.

- Helplessly watching an entire column of brothers (ten to fifteen men) being shot from an enemy ambush and then seeing more buddies being mercilessly shot down as they made unsuccessful rescue attempts.
- Watching helplessly as enemy snipers shot down helicopters on a medevac mission to get the wounded to a hospital.
- Our thoughts after the war…were we helpless pawns of the U.S. government?
- Wondering for the rest of our lives if they died for a lie.
- Wondering for the rest of our lives if we may have been duped or brainwashed into doing something we have regretted ever since.
- Living with daily memories of the premature deaths of our war buddies from Agent Orange, PTSD, or suicides, wondering who is next.
- Wondering if we can ever trust our country's government again.
- Wondering if we were sent to Vietnam as the invader or the savior.

Damned right, these things have been on our minds, and it has created problematic phobias and insecure feelings about wearing our medals and ribbons. This suffrage has been pitifully cruel for those who felt that way, and it may never go away for some. If you are one of those who just cannot bring yourself to wear a special medal or two for 365 days a year, why not just pick one full month to wear them. May with Memorial Day, July with Independence Day, and November with Veterans Day would be quite appropriate for that.

OUR PROUD HISTORY WAS ABANDONED BY THE FEARFUL. IT DEMANDS RESTORATION BY THE FEARLESS.

My dear brothers and sisters, our demons are just a whisper. We *are* bad-ass Vietnam War veterans and we should never give in, we should never give up. We should not let our loved ones down and we should no longer keep our story to ourselves. Please tell your story for love of our fallen war buddies to anyone you care about.

"More Than 200,000 Vietnam Vets Still Have PTSD"[31]

---

31 www.TIME.com/Vietnam-veterans7/22/15

Anti-Patriots of 1968, 2008, 2018

Author with some
vet buddies after the
Vietnam War

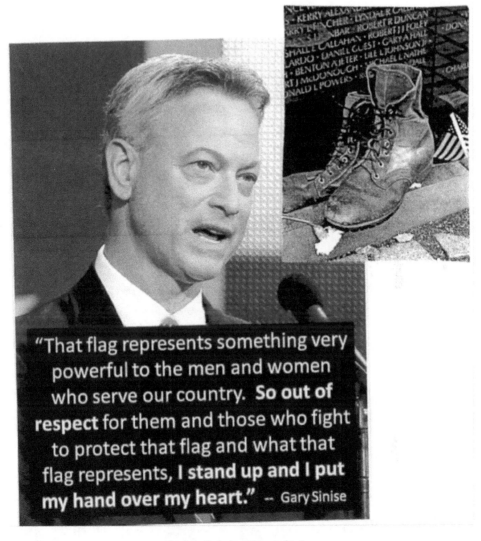

"That flag represents something very powerful to the men and women who serve our country. **So out of respect** for them and those who fight to protect that flag and what that flag represents, **I stand up and I put my hand over my heart."** -- Gary Sinise

Super Patriot Gary Sinise,
also a Vietnam veteran

More vet buddies

Rolling Thunder—Vietnam Veterans in Washington, D.C.

These men have never given up on America.

Chapter 11

VA IGNORES THE EVIDENCE

It was mid-April 2016 as I began to write this chapter, which became an Agent Orange story from the "twilight zone." Then I kept updating to it into early 2018. These stories will seem more like something like "Tales from the Dark Ages." Maybe I should have used that for a title.

I know of way too many VA horror stories than I am able to divulge in just one book. I did share several of them in my two previous books. They both had sad but factual endings. There was Jack "Bud" Gainey, age 59; Robert "Smokey" Ryan, age 62; Gary "Tets" Tetting, age 62; Curtis "Tex" Daniels, age 63; and scores more who were part of my life up to and at the time they died prematurely from complications directly attributed to Vietnam War-related killers.

As I stated earlier, there are just too many tragic VA horror stories to describe here, and unfortunately, the list is not going to stop growing anytime soon. I could write about the premature deaths of some Vietnam War veterans' wives who had their lives shortened by secondary exposure of PTSD from their husbands. Martha Gainey and Kathleen Bellemy are two whom I knew very well, and the Vietnam War could have been written on their death certificates as probable cause of death. Marty and Kathy each lived out their lives, married only the man each woman loved, and dedicated her life to sticking with him, covering his back. They provided emotional support to their troubled Vietnam War veteran husbands, both great friends as well as Nam brothers of mine.

Several of my other Nam brothers were not as fortunate in hanging on to their wives as long as Jack and Bud did. In more instances than not, the fault rested on the shoulders of my Nam brothers. But to tell the absolute truth, most of the fault could be credited to that little patch of land in Southeast Asia where millions of people died because of one very badly reported war, causing critically wrong misunderstandings and PTSD for spouses as well.

I was privileged to be around for Bud when Marty died first, and I was there for Bud when he left us not too long afterward. I am here for Jack and always will be, and he is still suffering from heartbreak and trauma from Kathy's death. Jack is also one of those Vietnam War veterans who has been suffering from PTSD, but will not admit it and chooses to deal with it more or less on his own, so he likes to believe. At least he had Kathy's ear while she was still with him. That marriage began in 1964 or 1965 and lasted into 2015 (forty years) with Vietnam always a present topic in their lives.

Jack Bellemy and I knew of each other before the Vietnam War, which swallowed both of us up like an evil people-eating cookie monster, and refused to spit us out until we both came home a year or so after the Tet Offensive with its mark stamped on our heads permanently. Jack and I talk Nam stuff together all the time; it is the best possible therapy we can get. Unfortunately, this keeps refueling our anger. Then again, maybe that is not so unfortunate. So far, we have managed it for the welfare of others around us...so far.

In 2005, I was first introduced to the Department of Veterans Affairs or Veterans Administration, and I became one of their patients with a PTSD problem. There seemed to be nowhere else to go for help, not that I could have afforded financially. A VA shrink and a private sector psychiatrist diagnosed me officially with severe PTSD in 2006. As a result, the VA begrudgingly awarded me something I was not looking for, a service-connected disability rating for my PTSD, and believe you me, I had it at a full-blown stage when the VA "awarded" me with the lowest rating they could.

And that is when I officially entered the Delay, Deny and Delay Till You DIE program of the Department of Veterans Administration's **Waiting for them to Die!**

A Vietnam War veteran checks into a local VA for the first time since coming home because he had no reason to until this point. He's diagnosed from his initial physical as having high blood pressure and hypertension (so who doesn't at our age) and so he files a claim for PTSD disability with the VA.

Until Donald J. Trump arrived it would be one to two years before that claim might even have a Comp & Pen exam scheduled. And then, when that long-awaited C&P exam actually happens, it may be six months before the results are made available to you. The decision comes back and your claim is...**Denied!**

Okay, next step is you file a Notice of Disagreement, and it may be another one to two years until you are given another C&P exam. If you don't have new evidence, don't be too disappointed with another decision...**Denied!**

Next step is filing your appeal. It may be another two or three years before your hearing is heard. Warning: I am in the process of waiting for appeal hearings for two claims, and I've been engaging the VA in this war for thirteen years.

Keep your HOPE up, baby. There wasn't much else to fall back on until Donald J. Trump popped up. And I really believe we can thank the Lord Almighty for delivering President Trump to us. Until he arrived we had just two options, hang with the delay or die.

There are so many horrible, unforgettable memories, and most of them find little or no understanding at the VA. Forget about getting any sympathy. One of those unforgettable memories happened over forty years ago on April 30, 1975, when the Ameri-Cong media reported something many of us will never forget:

SAIGON SURRENDERED! . . . BAD MEMORIES!

I remember the general news release that probably read like this:

> *South Vietnam unconditionally surrendered to the Viet Cong today, ending thirty years of bloody warfare. Communist forces began moving into the city within two hours after President Duong Van Minh spoke to the nation. A jeep flying the Viet Cong flag drove along the street a block from the abandoned U.S. embassy at noon. The cheering Viet Cong in the jeep, in civilian clothes, carried an assortment of weapons including communist AK-47 rifles.*[32]

Third Indochina War 1974–75. U.S. forces departed in 1973, and that would cost the ARVN dearly as they incurred nearly a hundred thousand casualties (23,000 KIA) that year, their highest number of casualties since 1968. Clearly the withdrawal of U.S. forces left a huge void the South Vietnamese were unable to overcome on the battlefields. Ironically during the Vietnamization program from 1969–1972, the South Vietnamese were taught how to fight by and like the Americans, with superior air power. The loss of American air power along with the withdrawal of all ground combat troops spelled doom and gloom for South Vietnam. In fact the last significant victory for the South Vietnamese took place in III Corps' Parrots Beak area inside Cambodian borders. With sufficient air support during that battle in April–May 1973, communists casualties exceeded three thousand, with 1,200 KIA.

After the May 10, 1973 victory, the well quickly ran dry for the South Vietnamese in 1974. With air power gone, supplies and ammo reduced from America despite a million-man army, South Vietnam defeats became common. Eventually the South Vietnamese would run out of fuel, and air missions or sorties came to a screeching halt before the end of 1974. The Third Indochina War as South Vietnam President Their labeled it, would be the shortest of the Indochina Wars.

As 1974 was drawing to a close, behind the scenes, North Vietnam's military presence in the south was growing rapidly, while the South Vietnam military was suffering troop losses for a variety of reasons. Along with the devastating

---

32 Agence France-Presse

shortages of materiel, fuel, and ammo, troop enlistments were dropping, combat losses were skyrocketing with few replacements coming in, and desertions were on the rise, weakening all military units. Soldiers' wages had to be cut, forcing many to seek other part-time jobs to feed their families. Hospitals were also facing shortages of medicine, antibiotics, bandages, etc., leaving many of the wounded vulnerable. How were the South Vietnamese soldiers going to "defend till death" under such morale-crushing circumstances?

By the end of 1974, desertions had increased to an astonishing number, averaging nearly twenty thousand every month. When 1975 came around, the South Vietnam military had been reduced to about 65 percent of normal strength, and the desertions continued, with many joining the ranks of the Viet Cong. By this time the situation had truly become a civil war, and the result would be a unified Vietnam once again, as it was before the French colonization.

A dozen Russian-made tanks had rolled into Saigon, flying the flags of North Vietnam and the Provisional Revolutionary Government (Viet Cong). Saigon radio was taken off the air, leaving the airwaves to the liberation radio of the Viet Cong, as reported by Agence France-Presse.

North Vietnam's General Nguyen Huu Hanh, deputy chief of staff, went on the air to order all South Vietnamese troops to turn themselves in immediately to avoid further and unnecessary bloodshed. Most seemed willing to comply. Saigon then fell silent as the Viet Cong stopped their bombardment of the Saigon airport.

American choppers evacuated all of the nine hundred or so Americans and as many South Vietnamese officials and professional people as possible, some fifty thousand. As the Americans were being evacuated almost in panic mode, from the roof of the fortress-like American embassy, the thousands and thousands of South Vietnamese booed and jeered the Americans, showing their displeasure in how America had stopped supporting them.

Four American marines died during the final hours of the U.S. presence in Vietnam, which received hush-hush coverage. Meaning that Americans died in Vietnam from 1959 to 1975 or sixteen years.

Embittered South Vietnamese soldiers, feeling betrayed by the American withdrawal, fired their weapons at buses carrying American and South Vietnamese evacuees to the embassy for escape. Shots were also fired at helicopters carrying evacuees, with two marines killed when their helicopter was shot down.[33]

What were our discussions in response to that most unforgettable catastrophe? Plain and simple, many dreamed about another opportunity to blow up something, preferably with government politicians inside. Others

---

33 Peter Arnett, Pulitzer Prize Winner

talked about going to Washington "loaded for bear" and making a last stand on top of a government building and taking out people walking in and out of the White House. Bad thoughts causing terrible talk that ended a long time ago…or did it?

Trust this Vietnam vet, to this day thoughts of the final days in 1975 as Saigon fell and hundreds of thousands of South Viets of every age could be seen on television, scrambling frantically to get out of the way of the expected wrath of the North Vietnamese Army. Those images anger many of us to this day, which may be one of the many causes of PTSD for my brothers and me. I guess we'll just chalk it up as another bad memory that we'll die with.

VA Ignores the Evidence…My first book, *Condemned Property?*, was finally done after three and a half agonizing but satisfying years. It was to publish December 2012, which it did not do until a full year later. Unfortunately, I did not benefit from the exciting launch, as I was struck down with two strokes, one week apart, in November and December 2013. Hospitalized, operated on, and undergoing several months of rehabilitative therapy, I missed those first critical months of book promotion, which should have delivered a quick death to the book. But for some reason, I believe, with God's help, *Condemned Property?* caught on and early sales, while I was fairly inactive, were quite encouraging. At least that is what several close friends told me, and I chose to believe them because I wanted to and because I needed to. Believe this, I would much use the information provided to me by another Vietnam veteran in distress or any veteran for that matter. However, by sharing my own experience in my own book, you will have the comfort in knowing the content is undeniably factual from every word throughout.

Condemned Property? was written for the finest, bravest, and toughest men I had ever known in my life, my Vietnam War buddies. Some of them died over there. One was too many. Some died back here. These were slow and torturous deaths unlike how Nam killed them in-country real fast. Three of them died while I was still writing *Condemned Property?* and yes, all three were victims of something the war did to them when they were living in Nam. Their deaths weren't any easier than those quick and unexpected losses in battle. In fact, it was almost unbearable, watching during their last few years, knowing their time would be up soon, and knowing what killed them would never be vindicated. Other Nam buddies of mine died while I was frantically trying to speed up the book's finish. I did not want to do that, but it was always in the back of my mind that I was going to see more of them die before getting the book out.

Condemned Property? was all about them—those who had already passed away prematurely after leaving Nam and even more important, for those still hanging in there, still intensely battling the diseases and illnesses they came home with.

Fortunately, the book did reach the public in time to influence, motivate, and help preserve some of those guys. Whether I managed to enjoy a great sales experience with the book was not nearly as important as the copies that did sell and impacted someone's life. That mission was accomplished beyond my wildest dreams.

About seven months after *Condemned Property?* was out there in the public and a couple thousand people had read it, the so-called VA scandal became a public shocker to many Americans. I would like to believe that the content and the message of that book delivered a helping hand in exposing a badly needed story about VA and Vietnam veterans' long, painful relationship together. I believe some people at VA view that book as a thorn in their sides, an instigator if you will, as the American people became louder than they had been in decades about their shock and disappointment with VA's unimaginable treatment of most veterans, not just Vietnam War veterans.

Some comments dished out to me about the book by VA staff members riled me enough that if I were twenty years younger, I would have shared a well-placed left uppercut, and that would have cancelled out future visits to the VA for me. But I contained myself.

On the other side of the fence, I received far more compliments from VA employees than I did negative or condemning statements. What counted most was how Vietnam War veterans accepted the book, and many of them took the time to share their feelings of appreciation and gratitude for having the guts to follow through with such a project.

Up to this point in my life, things were on the upside of an up-and-down relationship with the Veterans Administration. At least I can say that the medical care was not disappointing as it often was in the earlier years from 2005 to 2009 when I became a regular VA patient. The last few years from 2010 to present have been quite pleasant for me, with the medical staff, that is. On the other side, the benefits, compensation, pension, and administrative side has created nightmares that have continued in very depressing fashion. There are many signs of that improving soon, from my standpoint and from what my vet buddies tell me.

Seven months after my stroke in December 2013, I filed claims with the VA for the following service-related health problems:

- Transient Ischemic Attack, changed to Cerebral Vascular Attack (CVA).
- Unable to sustain full employment, I was finished as of December 2013.

- Post-stroke after-effects, including: stress, complete loss of functional vision in right eye, loss of equilibrium/balance—causing falls, depth perception, memory damage, word association deterioration, muscle strength depreciation, headaches more common, and basically my life had taken a full 180-degree turn since.
- All physical activity had been downgraded to walking short distances only.

My claim for the above conditions was filed in July 2014 with all medical notes, exam results, and therapy information stored in the VA's records and completely available to the VA's Compensation and Pension examiners to research. These records would include numerous vision examinations with the VA organization as well as consultations outside the VA with private medical facilities—authorized by VA doctors.

Regardless, the "bean counters" at Compensation and Pension decided they needed more evidence to substantiate my claim for an indisputable loss of vision in my right eye, directly resulting from either or both CVAs. Mind you, now I had been to some of the most credible vision centers and ophthalmologists in northeast Ohio, including the VA's own vision specialists at the VA's Low Vision Department. Still the Comp and Pen staff insisted on another eye exam as well as other opinions about the other post-stroke effects or damages which had been officially documented by several highly credible VA professional medical staff members.

The specially requested exams took place at Parma, Ohio, Veterans Administration location. I received a consult of questions pertaining to my headaches, another full eye exam, my eighth one in 2015, and had x-rays on a knee for another ailment.

In regard to the CVA's residual vision damage and headaches, etc., only, here are the decisions that the Comp and Pen examiners or raters came up with:

- Rated my right eye (the useless one) at normal vision!
- Decided the headaches were not caused by strokes!
- No decision on the physical and mental residuals from the strokes.
- Decided that the CVA with residuals including an impaired right eye's vision would not affect my ability to perform normal full-time employment.
- Assigned me a disability rating of…10 percent.

All of this was incomprehensibly inadequate, and caused more stress on me and my family. These denials have been ongoing for thirteen years up to early 2018.

The CVA was recognized as a secondary illness related to my primary service-connected disabilities of Diabetes Mellitus II (Agent Orange caused) and my PTSD, also service-connected.

In the VA optometrist's exam results, she specifically noted that my right eye was "severely damaged." Unbelievably she rated the eye at 20/40, despite the fact that a colleague of hers at VA had already rated the right eye at 20/3000 vision!

Seemingly the Comp and Pen raters ignored some of the exam results of the VA optometrist they set up for me to meet with, and they completely ignored the vision testing results from VA Medical Hospital, VA Low Vision Center, Beachwood Ophthalmologists, Akron Vision Center, and another direct VA employee, an optometrist. The VA Comp and Pen staff ignored all of this and instead rated a useless eye at 20/40 and noted that none of my other problems from the two strokes warranted more than a 10 percent service-connected disability rating. The basis for the conclusions they came to…OPINIONS!

Never one to sit back when wronged, I sent five certified letters to the VA's Regional Office in Cleveland. After four and a half months, the VA sent out a letter to me, I presume in response to those five certified letters. Okay, this VA horror story continues to get better—if I can call it that. The VA letter I received pertaining to these topics included some of the following comments notifying me of my options. Please read carefully:

> Mr. Trimmer,
>
> We will not take further action on your request (Request for Reconsideration) unless you do one of the following [one of three options that were offered]:
>
> - Identify a clear and unmistakable error in a prior VA decision. Clear and unmistakable errors are undebatable so that reasonable minds could only conclude that the previous decision was flawed at the time it was made.

Clear and unmistakable errors are undebatable so that "reasonable" minds could only conclude that the previous decision was flawed at the time it was made?

Oh, I responded ASAP to their shallow advice, with additional credible evidence. VA ignored it again of course.

So what remote chance do we veterans have with such unreasonableness as shown here? And the VA is not even afraid or ashamed to put comments such as this in writing? As of April 10, 2017, we had not received any communication with an apology, not even admission of "clear and unmistakable errors" or that "the previous decision was flawed." We sent an official form with additional evidence with letters written by three doctors. They were not even private practice doctors. They were…VA DOCTORS! I had also sent another certified letter dated March 29, 2016 to the three highest-ranking staff members at the department of Veterans Affairs, Cleveland Regional Office.

There you have it, a real example of how veterans (especially Vietnam veterans) have been treated over the years by the VA and obviously are still being treated. So many of my brothers have received far worse treatment that has cost them their lives, and I continue to fight in their memory.

Will God allow VA into heaven? The night of July 13, 2017 was very disturbing—another nightmare that did not seem to make much sense—and the event caused me great unrest. There were no Viet Cong, North Vietnamese, or weapons. There was not even a jungle in this nightmare. But…I had passed away in my sleep (in my nightmare) and found myself traveling endlessly in no particular direction, similar to some of my sales trips throughout my former business career. I was not aware of what was happening or that I had died during my sleep. I just sort of kept traveling through space, going nowhere that I could tell. It wasn't painful, but I had no idea what was guiding me on this trip or why. Most of my life had been full of seemingly endless and even senseless happenings with ongoing challenges to confront and overcome without direction or support from others. So here I was again on one of those trips, but of course, this trip was unlike any I had ever experienced before…in my "living" world.

At last, I had settled down on something. It looked like a large cloud, but it had enough substance to sit on. I wish I could say it felt like a cloud, but who knows what clouds feel like? Suddenly, sunrays burst through the clouds ahead of me, which created a scene of beauty I had never seen in the living world. There were sounds also unlike any I can ever recall from the living past. Then it hit me that I was no longer in the old world where I had spent a few minutes of time; the notion came to me that I was approaching the heavens of God himself. But I wasn't quite there yet. Those "Pearly Gates" I had all heard about and read about suddenly appeared, and they began to open, but I could not see what was inside or if there even was an "inside." The sounds were harp-like and soft, and something was moving, coming from whatever it was the gates were protecting. These were not normal gates. In fact, they were so high that there was no seeable end to how high they were, but I was not afraid, just very much in awe of what was happening around me.

Then…I saw an image approaching me and I heard a voice. It was in an indescribable tone like I had never heard before, kind of like a bunch of deep baritone voices merged into one and with a firm, calm tone. The voice said,

"WELCOME, DUSTY. YOU HAVE MADE IT! We will get you processed in, and then you can go around and visit everyone you have loved. Be well, my son. You are out of harm's way now."

The image, which had no form to it then, seemed to fade away into the background while an array of angelic voices escorted him to his next meeting. I was guessing. Before leaving, he said this to me…

I would need to be "processed in"? Whatever would that entail and would it require that I have to stand in another line? No matter, I thought; this wait would certainly be worth it. I waited just a few more minutes, not sure if I could advance forward, so I waited a few more minutes, then a few more. Finally, after standing there for well over half an hour and without a clue what to expect next, I could see movement ahead of me and the clouds were opening up. Finally, there they were—my "greeting into heaven" party, so I thought. I could not quite make out the features of their faces. They sure did not look like angels that one would expect to greet and welcome one into heaven.

I was asked to sit down and heard something about getting me processed, but there was a long waiting line for the final approvals for entrance. Long waiting line for approval? What the heck, and who are you people? I demanded.

"Mr. Trimmer, we are from the Department of Veterans Administration. We handle the processing into heaven. Now, what is your Social Security number so we can get started. Others will be waiting behind you." Then I thought, *VA… You are here from the VA and you guys are here to process me into heaven?* I mulled this thought over. There are just three possibilities that could result from this processing-in thing. Still, I would have a problem with the leniency given to the VA because so many of the VA acts were criminal against veterans, homeless, and disabled as well…how could they go unpunished? And why did I have to stand in line yet again waiting for the VA to process something? Uh oh, was this really heaven?

For those reading this book who have been fortunate enough to live a life of good health, safety, fun and recreation, financial stability, more food than you could eat, more clothes than you could wear, please take a moment to envision this unfortunate but very real-life scenario for those who have sacrificed or relinquished all of what even the simplest of life necessities could have provided for them. This dream had become very frustrating.

Suddenly, I woke up, well before the VA Administration was able to complete the required paperwork for me to cross over in heaven. Then I thought …**Even in Heaven There Is a Wall, a Gate, and Extreme Vetting**.

Imagine if you can, soldiers and marines who were forced to live like cavemen for an entire year except that our Neanderthal or Cro-Magnon ancestors probably had better living conditions. I personally know of hundreds of combat infantry grunts who would have given up their entire paycheck to have a cave to shelter in during those horrendous missions in the swamps and jungles of Vietnam.

Oh, dear God, if we could only have had a dry place to build a campfire to dry out our "drenched with stench" socks and pants…without being ambushed by our VC friends (who lived in even worse conditions). Oh dear God, I so wish that you would have intervened and put a halt to the Vietnam War, as no human being should have been punished like Vietnam's combatants from both sides were with such unbearable living conditions. No one except maybe the Nazis or Mongols who annihilated entire civilizations while they were on the rampage, probably one hundred million lives between the two of them.

How could I possibly write an entire book without dedicating some material to our not-so-friendly villain—America's Department of Veterans Affairs or Administration, especially the Compensation and pension examiners and raters?

My first two books told true stories about other veteran brothers of mine who were literally tortured by the VA till their death. I have been the recipient of their torturous, inhumane, cruel actions. But many of the brave men I served with, fought with, and shared the same rice paddy dike as a bed with have experienced worse horror from their dealings with the VA. Unfortunately, that list of just those I have known is too long to put into one single book…way too long.

Dear God, I am going to pray that you find a way to read this chapter in my book, *Unbreakable Hearts.* If there were some way to deliver it to you personally, I would spare no expense to do so. But praying for it will have to do for now. Heck, I don't even know what time zone you are living in these days. Silly me, of course you would have a presence in every time zone, twenty-four/seven. I will send this prayer often.

Soon after *Condemned Property?* launched on November 25, 2013, the book began delivering unexpected responses from all walks of life—Vietnam veterans, veterans of other wars, and non-veterans as well. The letters, cards, emails, and telephone calls nearly overwhelmed me. I still go back and read those letters and cards. The stack is over a foot high, but I love them.

What I got out of this was that I had made a difference in lives on both sides of the tracks by spilling my guts into such a book and publishing it. In some cases, it had a profound impact on people's lives—Nam vets and non-veterans. I needed to continue the mission.

Realizing this unexpected phenomenon, I decided to continue promoting the book as I was consumed with getting *Condemned Property?* out to as many people as humanly and economically possible. Unfortunately, I was dealt a major setback as I was hit with those cerebral vascular attacks (CVA) just a couple of weeks after the book launched, which would disqualify me from working my regular job anymore, and also prevent me from traveling. This snuffed any chance of promoting the book across the country with personal visits to book signings, trade shows, etc. This was a shocking setback and, of course, totally unexpected, but that's how life is. Up until the CVA, I was living up to a similar schedule of activities as I had led for much of the previous thirty-year period. I had been enthusiastically engaged in canoeing, kayaking, trekking in the Florida Everglades, with some fishing as well, and an occasional rattlesnake hunt in Pennsylvania, Colorado, or Texas, and even Florida's 2013 Python Challenge. I biked ten to fifteen miles daily and walked three to five miles every other day along with dog walks in the woods for sightseeing. A couple of hours in the yard on a weekend and a round of golf every other week or so. The batting cages with grandkids had been a routine since they were nine or ten years old. Now, three are in college and no longer needing tutoring, nor can I offer it. By the way, I was still working, covering twenty-seven states and Ontario, Canada, to which I dedicated sixty hours a week.

I had slowed down from 2010 to 2013, and in 2014 all of those activities had come to a halt. I was beginning to feel the effects of my diabetes and I was tiring a lot easier and sooner than I used to. But I can honestly say that I was heavily engaged in all of those activities and some others up until the age of sixty-seven. I was a happy puppy with such an agenda, and I was still excelling at the true love of my life, sales on the road.

The signs were there, but like many pig-headed men, I felt invincible and felt I could keep up the grueling but fulfilling lifestyle for many more years in spite of the fact that the big one, seventy, was approaching more quickly than I was prepared to accept. How does one prepare for a stroke, let alone back-to-back strokes? They rarely announce themselves ahead of time.

Fast forward to 2017, almost four years later. Nearly everything in my life that required any physical endeavor, including walking, would be different the day I was released from the VA Medical Center in Cleveland, Ohio, on December 13, 2013. Deterioration has accelerated in 2017–18.

Here I was, one of the tough American warriors who had fought and lived through a war and helped defeat an enemy whose ancestors had defeated large empires to save their freedom, including THE largest and most blood-chilling empire in history…the Mongol Empire. And I was becoming almost housebound.

Needless to say, my ability to carry out the demanding functions of an outside sales representative who used to drive nearly as many miles as I flew (about 75,000 each) was no longer an option. I had to fold my company, an independent representative firm I named after myself, of course, The Roland Group Inc., which I had operated very successfully from 1987 to 2015. I kept it open until February 2015, just to wrap up unfinished business, which I was able to do by telephone and the computer, but I had stopped nearly all travel after the strokes hit.

My battle with the VA to receive benefits that I deserve, that I earned the hard way, continued as 2017 closed and 2018 rolled in.

Heaven or Hell? Sometimes I wonder if I'll ever get to heaven, and I don't have time or the right to spend much time thinking about the VA's chances. This is what I can bank on if I go to hell: I'LL BE A FEW HUNDRED FLOORS ABOVE THE LIKES OF ROBERT MCNAMARA... LBJ...JOHN KERRY...JANE FONDA, AND HUNDREDS OF EXAMINERS FROM THE VA'S COMP & PEN DIVISION! But of course, it will be solely up to God Almighty to sort everyone out.

During the ten-month period leading up to mid-August 2017, several profound events took place that would affect the VA, and these happenings could almost be looked on as acts of God.

- Trump defeats Hillary
- Robert McDonald, Secretary of VA is fired by Trump.
- David Shulkin, Under Secretary of VA, is promoted to Secretary by Trump
- The Veterans Complaint Hotline, promised by Trump, went live June 1, 2017. It actually works.
- Trump begins removal of corrupt VA managers.

This is where we stood by mid-September 2017. I don't mind saying—in fact, I am compelled to say that President Trump has already accomplished more for veterans than the last six presidents combined. But of course, these prolific good deeds by Trump were all but ignored by the mainstream/left wing media. This is fact, not opinion. Even Ronald Reagan, who loved the military and they loved him, was not able to do as much for the veterans as Donald Trump has already.

IF Hillary had become president, the socialist world of the Democrats would have been extended and more likely than not strengthened to a level that only a full-fledged revolution or a direct act of God could have saved this country from its continued demise. As for us veterans, our brothers and sisters would simply continue to be treated as third class citizens by the bureaucrats at the VA under Hillary's regime. By no means has the socialist world of the Democratic Party disintegrated. But we now have a man in the White House who really loves our country, respects our police, firemen, and military. Guess what...the liberals hate it.

While Donald Trump may not be the best person for the most important job in the world, in the eyes of millions of "real" patriotic Americans, he has been a welcome change from the swamp dwellers who've been in charge for way too long.

President Trump has given America's veterans solid reasons for hope. He has temporarily derailed the socialistic march of the Democrats, giving "real" Americans precious time to reload and be better prepared for the evils that will continue to threaten Americans who are committed to putting America first. For you staunch Republicans in office, you better not choke on your gloating. You, too, have been put on notice by the American people that we're fed up with the swamp-sucking leeches from both parties. Republicans did not win the 2016 Presidential Election...**AMERICA WON THAT ELECTION!**

Up until the Trump era, I have watched in horror as the VA Comp & Pen bean counters have ignored most of the real and most credible evidence that a veteran could present. Worse than that, I have been a witness to their malicious negligence being turned into almost criminal acts as they have managed to create their own evidence and overrule the veterans' indisputable facts. Not to bore readers with my VA problems, but here is a case in point about evidence presented and ignored:

Exhibit A—Brain stroke strikes on December 10, 2013; partial permanent loss of vision suffered immediately was operated on. Noticeable diminished strength and coordination throughout entire body—never recovered. Walking is affected. All physical activities ceased aside from casual walking. Driving reduced to daylight only and short distances. Cognitive damage minimal but obvious. No longer working, closed down personal business. <u>Disability for employability claim filed.</u>

> <u>Support Evidence</u>: Multiple exam results from four different optometrists declaring my vision loss as severe and permanent. Vision 20/300 in right eye. The VA Low Vision Clinic rates right eye as useless.
>
> <u>VA Evidence</u>: On November 15, 2015 two years after stroke, VA appoints their only optometrist to examine me. A statement arises somehow that I have 20/40 normal right eye vision. I have to file a Notice of Disagreement.
>
> <u>Support Evidence</u>: I am instructed not to work in any capacity by VA provider. Statements recorded by two other VA doctors that my disabilities would prevent me from full-time employment. Two MDs had PhDs.
>
> <u>VA Evidence</u>: It is determined by a VA-appointed physician "ass-istant" that in his opinion I should be able to perform sedentary employment.

Claim for Unemployability DENIED. Notice of Disagreement filed, claim was again DENIED.

Support Evidence: Diminishment of feeling in feet makes walking diffi-cult. Several falls occur, some quite painful and dangerous for additional injury. One fall causes huge gash above left eye, requiring several sutures by a VA doctor. Two more falls cause painful bruises to both hips, pain lasting for months. Another fall causes injury to my lower back, requir-ing multiple therapy sessions to relieve pain. It is not uncommon for me to bump into something, knock something over, or fall down over and over on a weekly if not daily basis.

Exhibit A presented overwhelming evidence of the after-effects this vet-eran suffered from 2013 strokes, presumed to be connected with diabetes II and Agent Orange exposure. In spite of the obvious, including several highly credible letters from the regular VA doctors who I have been seeing for ten years, the VA's Comp & Pen Department stalled my claims repeat-edly with delays and even denials, ignoring irrefutable evidence.

In 2015, the year after the 2014 VA Scandal was uncovered nationally by multiple sources, veterans were fighting back on their own with the help of determined advocates like Pete Hegseth, Jeff Miller, Gary Sinise, and Chuck Norris. In June 2015, my book *Payback Time!* was also launched with one mission: to motivate and support troubled veterans to overcome the unfortu-nate resistance from a stubborn and non-sympathetic Veterans Affairs and to get the benefits and health care they deserve. Veterans' Town Hall meetings were organized from coast to coast to exchange battle strategies and to com-pare horror stories with VA experiences. One Vietnam veteran took it a little further as he spent his own money by advocating his message on multiple billboards in Florida with this simple message:

VA is LYING. Veterans are dying!

The VA Health Care Scandal Is Still Happening.

If the VA is just prone to failure—our country's "real" heroes will continue to pay the price. To say that veterans deserve better is a monumental under-statement, and Webster doesn't offer enough words to describe it.

"VA officials dump $40 million in sketchy bonuses on...EACH OTHER YEARLY!" That headline appeared in several medical sources less than one year ago, in June 2017. I'll explain this one in more detail:

VA officials routinely gave each other huge recruitment, relocation, and retention bonuses to move from one city to another or just to keep the job they have, wasting a cool $40,000,000 annually, according to a govern-

ment watchdog. In just 2014 alone the VA's Office of Inspector General
audit concluded that all nineteen relocation incentives awarded to senior
executives were very improper. And the VA often seemed uninterested in
recovering the funds when the recipients failed to fulfill the obligations
that accompanied the payments.[34]

During the scandal year of 2014, dozens of reports were unveiled about
unethical practices at the VA from the East Coast to the West Coast.
Waiting times and delinquent appointments were discovered in shocking
amounts, and veterans did die because of this. And yet, it was uncovered
that in 2014 alone, the Department of Veterans Affairs handed out nearly
$145 million in bonuses to their executives and employees for sub-par
performances.

One of this veteran's biggest complains is that some of those recipients
of bad bonuses were those employees who worked with the claims for benefits (including disabilities) to recessors from Philadelphia to Wisconsin to
Arizona from $300 to $5,000 each. I have good reason to suspect that VA
Comp & Pen staff at Ohio locations may have benefitted from illegal and
unethical bonuses for influencing or finalizing wrong claim decisions which
would have saved tens of thousands of dollars that the VA would not have to
pay to the deserving veterans.

Please know that this author has received wonderful medical care from
most of the VA's providers—they are not the problem in my case. And I like
to believe that the majority of VA employees are committed to serving us
well. But corruption and incompetence have existed within the VA's bureaucracy for decades.

One of the champions for veterans during the scandal years around 2014
was Florida Republican Representative Jeff Muller, chairman of the House
VA committee. I described some of the problems I have had with the VA
Comp & Pen process. One of the worst examples I can swear to went like
this:

- I was in the Parma VA in 2016 for a couple of VA C&P exams.
Nearing the end of the day, my final C&P exam turned out to be a mere
ten-minute question-and-answer exam. I can remember answering only
two or three questions to the C&P examiner, who was not a doctor; he
was a physician's assistant. While I was very tired and frustrated from the
previous day's exams, I was not paying close attention to this last exam
for the day. As I mentioned, it was surprisingly short...almost too short, I
thought afterward.

---

34 http://dailycaller.com/author/luke-1/6/17

When the C&P Rate Report from that day's exams came to me, I was appalled at the inaccuracies of the contents. There were wrong answers to the questions I was asked. Just as irritating to me were the examiner's answers to questions, about half a dozen, which to the best I can recollect... HE NEVER EVEN ASKED ME.

As is my style, I wrote to that C&P examiner at the Parma VA presenting my concerns and doubts about the information from his exam that day. Of course he never responded and I have had to live with the unfair rating decisions his "opinions" caused.

There is absolutely no doubt that veterans have been denied and cheated out of millions in benefits by the VA's Comp & Pen Department. One report dated October 1, 2016, on the *Military Times* website claimed that the IG reported nearly 200,000 disabled veterans as of March 2015 were affected by errors or delays in their rightful compensation. Some delays were only weeks or months old; however, others went unpaid from one to six years.

While much of the ineptness and corruption was human caused, some of it occurred because of outdated technology, which for the most part seems to have been corrected as of this writing in 2018.

Office Inspector General. To file a complaint about your VA problem, call or contact the main overseer of the VA—the Office of the Inspector General (VAOIG)—through the following avenues:

- Call VAOIG Hotline at 800-488-8244 8:30 AM to 4:00 PM EST Monday to Friday
- Write VAOIG Hotline at VA Inspector General Hotline (53E) P.O. Box 50410, Washington, D.C. 20091-0410.
- Fax the VAOIG Hotline: 202-565-7936

It is important that your complaint includes information about the subject matter; do not exaggerate your complaints, and keep records of any contact you may have with the VAOIG Hotline.

Your complaint should include one of the following areas:

- VA employee misconduct
- Patient abuse
- Serious safety violations
- Theft by VA employees
- Misuse of government property
- False claims by employees
- Systemic problems with VA
- Gross waste of funds or time

To obtain more information on how to file a complaint with the Department of Veteran Affairs, please refer to https://legalbeagle.com

The physical mailing address of the VAOIG is:

VA Inspector General Hotline (53E)
810 Vermont Ave., NW
Washington, D.C. 20420

Veterans for the Truth. In each of my books I have dedicated sad but undeniable situations where veterans have been wronged by the VA's Comp & Pen Department. I do this to support and encourage other veteran warriors who speak up about their unfortunate experiences with the VA. There aren't too many things that frustrate me than veterans not stepping up to tell their story, either about their service or especially about their problems with the VA.

The late US Army hero from the Vietnam and Korean Wars Col. David "Hack" Hackworth was not only a legendary army guerrilla fighter in Vietnam; he continued fighting for veterans as a hyperactive advocate. He formed a company called **Soldiers for Truth.** Through this foundation he carried the torch in helping our stories be heard by Congress, which is the only way to get action on our behalf actually done. I did not dedicate the statements in this chapter for my cause, as I am very concerned for my veteran warrior buddies. As Col. "Hack" once stated…"all the reporting in the world won't cause a lick of change unless you, the veteran victim, get your facts together and scream to Congress and the White House with your facts." I have been trying to carry the torch for people like Col. "Hack" and I can honestly say it has paid off for us.

Before the close of this chapter, I would like to share the full MWSA review of my last book, *Payback Time!*

Vietnam Vet Trimmer Cluster Bombs the VA

Author "Dusty" Trimmer delivers this credible PAYBACK TIME message across the VA's minefield of issues that get stepped on by veterans deserving proper healthcare access and benefits. Aging Trimmer still brings the fight! Taking careful aim and switched to automatic fire, Dusty sprays and stitches the VA with valid complaints from every direction, with a major focus on the dying Vietnam-era veterans' horrific dilemmas.

Armed heavily with research, a useful index, and an extensive glossary, Trimmer shoots-scoots-communicates through multiple VA obstacles that returned warriors face. He lays down suppression fire to cover current-era war fighters, provides insight into the political landscape that has/

will create the VA obstacles, and triggers through multiple other VA fights, including insightful views on current VA Secretary Bob McDonald. From a very personal perspective, Dusty Trimmer empties his heart out to help our veterans in a VA system that lacks much. Way to take up the battle![35]

Just a few of the more influential people I have written to or talked to about our problems with the VA, and who have responded, are Pat Sajak, Gary Sinise, Jeff Miller, Bob Peterson, Secretary Shinseki, Secretary McDonald, Secretary Shulkin, two undersecretaries, President Donald J. Trump, and a dozen Congressmen/Senators. The Squeaky Wheel Does Get Greased— Believe It.

At Last . . . My Hopes are Fulfilled. On February 17, 2019 I received a surprising and unexpected envelope from the VA's Board of Appeals Office in Washington D.C. Fear as well as excited anticipation were my reactions before opening it. Lo and behold my 13 year war with the V.A.'s Comp & Pen dept. was seemingly ending. Actually this BVA report addressed seven health care claims that ranged from 3 to 13 years old. **Denials** of three minor conditions but **Approvals** of four major health problems were added to my long list of service connected disabilities. By golly, the long, long wait had finally paid off **I WON!!!**

An unexpected bonus to my patience in surviving the VA's waiting game of **Delay Til You Die** was that the BVA judge included important details from all of the previous Comp & Pen exams for PTSD for the last 13 years. This allowed me to realize where, why, and how the Denials were "opined" by C & P examiners and that they had clearly been wrong for 13 years. How depressing this could have made me, but since I knew the C & P examiners decisions were incomplete, incompetent or both now I became excited that I could prove it if I chose to.

HOPE is the big word here dear brothers and sisters. It pays off for you to stick with your claims if you live long enough. And if you feel that you have tried everything and still not getting the results from VA C & P or your advocates why don't you do what I did, write a letter to Prez. Trump. He seems to have a soft spot in his heart for Vietnam Vets and he is not bashful in taking on his bureaucratic subordinates.

Go for it my brothers, you have nothing to lose and never, never lose your **HOPE!**

---

35 Military Writers Society of America, Book Review, July 26, 2016

Chapter 12

AGENT ORANGE'S TRAIL OF TEARS

So we were exposed to the most toxic chemicals known to science from 1962 to 1970—WOW! In talking with hundreds of my brothers, it seems many of them have limited knowledge of the extent and duration of their exposure. And the VA is unable or unwilling to assist us. The VA has always just presumed that if your boots touched the ground of Vietnam, regardless of how long, you are exposed too, and that's that.

But there were more herbicides tested and used during the early 1960s: bromacil, diquat, diuron, dalapon, monuron, and Tandex. The case of the Vietnam veteran's exposure to dioxins through Agent Orange and the whole family of poisonous chemicals can present extremely complex epidemiological problems. If you are a Vietnam War veteran who served in III Corps in 1968 and early 1969, to what degree is the ultimate harm of that exposure going to be?

I wonder how many Vietnam War veterans are aware today that they were also sprayed in 1968 with a...**Super Agent Orange. Seriously?**

Agent Orange's Trail of Tears! Rightfully so Vietnam is still referred to as the war that just won't end as it stalks its victims for decades after contact with them. The common end result is too often a premature funeral for the Vietnam veteran. To put it mildly, this seemingly endless postwar phenomenon for Vietnam veterans has created deeply trenched feelings of mistrust and lingering anger toward the obvious culprit, the Department of Veterans' Affairs bureaucrats. The unspeakable avoidance of honesty by the U.S. government in studying and fully recognizing the damages done by Agent Orange and the full family of rainbow herbicides as incomprehensibly cruel. The conscious cover-ups, rigged test results, and bogus studies have put way too much grief onto Vietnam veterans and their loved ones. Yeah, it is still going on.

To be sure many lawsuits were filed by various veterans' groups after finding out the results of certain studies were in fact rigged in favor of the government—against the victims. Even during the Reagan administration, cover-ups were substantiated. A particular example was a cover-up of charges against the White House that was substantiated in 1990 by the House Government Operations Committee.

Rainbow Herbicides Launched January 13, 1962. When several Air Force C-123s began Operation Hades (later called Operation Ranch Hand), the defoliation began. In the fall of 1962, the spraying was intensified and the mission was fully endorsed to continue. From 1963 through 1966, the pilots were able to visualize the effects of their work, and some of them were more dismayed than pleased.

Danger to Humans Known. The hundreds of thousands of exposed Vietnamese, Americans, and their allies had no idea what was happening as they were living, breathing mist of the rainbow herbicides. The makers were well aware of the danger these poisons presented but suppressed the knowledge. In fact in March 1965, officials from Dow, Monsanto, Hooker, Diamond Alkali (to become Diamond Shamrock), and Hercules met to discuss the possible toxicological problems of the samples of 2,4,5,-T and 2,3,7,8 TCDD, a highly toxic compound. This meeting and its results were kept secret for several years. The U.S. government and the chemical companies united to maintain there was no adverse health danger to humans.

But the air force knew as early as 1967, when it was uncovered that military officials were aware of the potential long-term health risks of being exposed to frequent sprayings.

Military Covers Up. In March 23, 1968, high-ranking General Brownfield sent a memo to all senior U.S. advisors in the IV Corps zone, ordering that all "helicopter spray operations will not be conducted when ground temperatures are greater than 85° Fahrenheit and wind speed is in excess of 10 mph." This precaution was for the benefit of the rubber plantations (cash cows), protecting them from the drifting mists of the spray. There was apparently little or no concern for the safety of the troops in the area.

Defoliants Dumped Carelessly. Because of the unexpected "mist drift issue," herbicide damages hit non-targeted areas from navigational errors as mentioned above. In late 1965, "Project Pink Rose" was a secret mission to destroy forest and jungle growth by large fires. Unfortunately this meant that areas already hit with Agent Orange would be increased in toxicity by burning. In 1967, several areas were bombed and sprayed when ground troops were operating. This technique was terminated by mid-1967.

In October 1967 and January 1968, it was recorded that emergency dumps of herbicide into the Saigon River as well as the Dong Nai River, just fifteen kilometers from heavily populated Saigon, were made. But rivers rarely sit still; they move things downstream. So, people and water supplies were officially dumped on, and guess what? The Agent Orange spraying was just gaining momentum as 1968 and 1969 would receive nearly 50 percent of the twenty million gallons dumped from 1962 to 1971.

The cover-ups would continue until the use of Agent Orange finally ended on June 30, 1971. But the denials and cover-ups would continue for another couple of decades, and people were dying. Veterans were clamoring for help from the VA, but their response was breathtakingly slow, or not at all. Sound familiar?

Finally in 1979, a National Veterans Task Force on Agent Orange was formed and legislation eventually passed by Congress at the insistence of Representative Tom Daschle (D–SD), a Vietnam veteran who had been exposed to Agent Orange. This would be just the beginning of another war for Vietnam War veterans, and it lasts to this day with some veterans.

These are sample news headlines of what Vietnam veterans would be faced with, repeatedly and from several directions: State Department Exonerates Chemical Companies; EPA Banned Use of Agent Orange at Home in the U.S.; Chemical Companies Employees Develop Skin Problems, Class Action Suits Filed; American Medical Association Downplays Dioxin Danger, Then Rose Test Results to Still Mixed Hidden Evidence of Mortality; Decisions Made—Changed Without Authorization; White House Cover-Up; Reagan Has No Interest in Agent Orange Studies; Fraudulent Study Rigged; House Veterans Affairs Bottles up Legislation; Deliberate Course of Misconduct by Chemical Companies; Flawed Research Continues; Ill Health Effects Suppressed; Politics and Money More Important than Human Lives; Manipulated Decisions; Government Waiting Game Continues.

How sad. The next time someone visits the Vietnam Memorial, they should envision the Wall with ten times the 58,489 names that are engraved there. Imagine the wall with at least 584,890 names on the wall to include all of the victims of the Vietnam War after it had ended, just imagine. WOW, HOW SAD!

Agent Orange Hits Home! This story proves that Agent Orange had no bias as it struck down navy guys as well as the boots-on-the-ground soldiers and marines. This brief recap of the Elmo Russell "Bud" Zumwalt Jr. story is a tearjerker, as most Agent Orange stories end up being:

- Elmo Zumwalt Jr. served in the U.S. Navy from 1942 to 1974 during World War II, Korean, and the Vietnam War. He earned the rank of admiral, chief of naval operations, and was a highly decorated warrior during his renowned thirty-two-year career. During the Vietnam War the admiral had been "ordered" to have a substantial amount of Agent Orange sprayed over a heavily vegetated area in the Mekong Delta so the Viet Cong would be forced to seek cover elsewhere.

- The admiral's oldest of four children, son Elmo Zumwalt III, served as a lieutenant on one of the patrol boats under the admiral's command. Unfortunately, Zumwalt III's area of service was in the heart of the area that his father was ordered to dump Agent Orange onto. In 1983, Zumwalt III was diagnosed with lymphoma and just two years later in 1985 he was diagnosed with Hodgkin's disease, Only three years later Zumwalt III passed away in 1988, at age forty-two, from the combination of both diseases—there was no recorded history in the family trees of his parents for either. The admiral was convinced that his son's life was shortened substantially by his heavy exposure to the herbicides he was ordered to spread generously in Vietnam. Both of these diseases would eventually be recognized as Agent Orange related...**but not until 1991.**

In the meantime Zumwalt III's son Elno Zumwalt IV had been born with severe learning impairments. Admiral Zumwalt continued on with a profound lobbying campaign with Congress to recognize the lethal damages caused by Agent Orange. The admiral and husband, together with writer John Pekkanen, wrote *My Father, My Son*, published by MacMillan in September 1986. In 1988, the book was made into a TV movie with the same name, starring Karl Malden and Keith Carradine.

Elmo Zumwalt III died three months after the TV movie was shown. The United States Navy's DD (X) guided missile destroyer program was named after the Zumwalts, and its lead ship bears the name USS *Zumwalt*.

Unfortunately for Vietnam veterans, there are many ways to leave this earth prematurely, and one doesn't have to get too creative or search too far to find the method of choice. I'm talking about the taboo subject of...**SUICIDE!**

The easiest way for us to be buried prematurely was to be mortally shot or blown up during the war. Or we might be allowed a choice of one of the many other avenues that may take our lives over there, such as malaria, snake bite, centipede or spider bite or tiger attack—or we could become a POW and be tortured to death or just die an accidental death, and the odds were generously likely to find us.

While my war buddies and I have experienced far more pain, grief, and pure stress than the average non-veteran, I have a difficult time understanding or believing the horror stories of those Vietnam veterans who had to battle for their lives in the early years coming home from the Nam. Literally NO ONE, no organization, offered them any assistance or understanding. They had to suck it up as they died off. And some people have had the nerve to refer to the Vietnam veteran as "whiners"?

Most of our fathers and uncles who fought in World War II have passed away by now, but at least many of them were allowed the opportunity to live out their lives well into their eighties or nineties and beyond and generally died a fairly natural death. On the other hand, five decades after the 1968 Tet Offensive, Agent Orange still ravages Vietnam veterans who have lived to their late sixties and seventies. HEY…I'm one of those. I made it up to my seventies and I'm still ticking. So bring it on, I say from here on out. And from here on out may be exactly what is waiting for us as Agent Orange has been proven to be an "accelerator" for the worsening of PTSD and the multitude of diseases related to Agent Orange exposure.

Prostate cancer strikes one of every six American males, making it the second leading cause for cancer death. Academic researchers have recommended that physicians should screen Vietnam veterans and perform biopsies more often than their average patient as the Vietnam veteran is a "high risk." Agent Orange cases finally have doctors and scientists accepting it as fact that exposure can predispose the veteran's body to lethal diseases later in life.

How do we prepare ourselves for what's coming since the seed was planted into our bodies back when we were nineteen to twenty-five years old when we were still innocent, die-hard patriots and healthy as newborn babes?

What's next? It seems like every year lately, there is a new disease popping up in Vietnam veterans that the VA is forced to consider adding to the growing list. What a bummer for us seventy-year-olds. Agent Orange will continue to accelerate our cancers, ruining our quality of life to say the least. And just when the traditional treatments begin to work, our nemesis finds a way to make us sicker. Hardly seems fair. Of course it's not fair. So when will the government start to care?

Many Vietnam veterans also were exposed to other carcinogens that were used on military base engines and equipment. Basically we were thrown into a "toxic soup" over there, and we've been fighting to keep from drowning in it ever since. Hell, the guys and gals in the so-called "secure" base camps might have been in more contact with the stuff. The stationary planes and choppers were dripping Agent Orange, and people would walk on it, carry it to other places, the AO drums would like—it all over their hands and other parts of the body, etc.

Life After Cancer. It has become almost impossible to strike up a conversation within family, amongst circles of friends and even acquaintances who we may meet on the street without this dreaded word being discussed… cancer. Vietnam War veterans are known to become diagnosed with cancer earlier and more often than the average American. Unfortunately, I fit into these discussions most appropriately as of December 28, 2017, when I was operated on at a VA hospital for kidney carcinoma.

I did not expect this sudden and critically important necessity in order for me to continue on living into 2018. But the surgery was successful, all for the goals the VA doctors had in mind. And even though I am still not out of the woods, God has given me enough reason to keep my hopes up. Finishing this book was a higher priority after I left the VA Wade Park Hospital on December 31, 2017. I won't dwell on this situation, even though I am grateful to be able to. I'm going to end this chapter simply by including a VA doctor's letter. He wrote this to provide me with clinical support and evidence to convince the VA Comp & Pen Department that my recent illness was serious enough that close and constant observations were required and additional surgeries would be necessary.

VA | U.S. Department of Veterans Affairs
Northeast Ohio VA Healthcare System

NORTHEAST OHIO VA HEALTHCARE SYSTEM
RAVENNA OUTPATIENT CLINIC
6751 N CHESTNUT STREET
RAVENNA, OH 44266
P: 330-296-3641
F: 330-296-5297

January 22, 2018

To Whom It May Concern,

I am Joseph Orzechowski MD and I am Mr. Roland Trimmer's current primary care physician at The Ravenna VA Outpatient Clinic. Paul Fantauzzo DO was my predecessor within the clinic.

This letter is intended to provide my clinical support for Mr. Roland Trimmer's consequences of his strokes (brain attacks) that occurred December 2013. There have been a number of complications related to his strokes including vision loss in his right eye, resulting in reduced driving capability, difficulty with sensory integration, depth perception loss, and falls. Mr. Trimmer also has disequilibrium and vertiginous dizziness, requiring a cane for assistance and causing him to list into walls as he ambulates. Other physical effects include muscle weakness, arthralgias, headaches, and word finding difficulties.

In addition to his strokes, that has now been diagnosed with chronic kidney disease and renal cell carcinoma. He is status post open right radical nephrectomy that was done December 2017. He is now being followed by urology and nephrology.

The psychological manifestations of his chronic medical conditions are being managed by Ravenna's mental health team and include PTSD, anxiety, sleep derangements, fearfulness, depression, stress, loss of short-term function, and confusion.

It is my opinion that Mr. Trimmer's strokes and chronic kidney disease were more likely than not caused by his diabetes mellitus type 2 which has been linked to dioxin exposure in Vietnam. Diabetes has been demonstrated to be linked to causing strokes and kidney disease. It is also more likely than not that his renal cell carcinoma was caused by his exposure to dioxins in Vietnam also. The dioxins have been linked to multiple other cancers which suggests that his dioxin exposure may have led to this renal cell carcinoma. Mr. Trimmer has been unemployable at an active and sedentary job due to his diabetes which led to his 2 strokes in 2013 which has caused his disabilities.

Sincerely

Joseph Orzechowski MD

Joseph Orzechowski MD

Letter from Doctor

While the cancer was removed successfully, it can always return at any time as cancer does. Continuous maintenance will be critically important with bi-monthly lab tests, CT and PT scans, ultrasounds, etc. Unfortunately, chemotherapy and radiation are not options to clearing the type of cancer that invaded my right kidney.

Standing in line is the left kidney, also infected from chronic kidney disease and also requiring vigilant medical observation. Not trying to sound like a doomsdayer, because I am anything but that, but there is always the threat of another stroke hitting me, and my diabetes II is capable of stimulating complications to another level.

Who has time to worry about PTSD with all of this negative activity abounding all around me? Ha and trust me, my PTSD condition has only gone in one direction…it worsens weekly.

Now, with our lives continuously in danger from deadly illnesses whose seeds were planted in our bodies half a century ago, and we are constantly taken to task by the VA Comp & Pen Department, can anyone blame us for showing outward anger toward those we believe have betrayed us?

We Vietnam vets did our jobs and we did it much better than historians have given us credit for. We have every right to be proud of our time served in Vietnam, against an extremely underrated, highly resilient adversary. But sometimes many of us wonder if it was worth it. Was it a waste of time and the lives of good patriotic Americans who had the backbone to fight for America while most Americans backed off?

How can VA's Comp & Pen staff ignore a doctor's letter like this one? Well, they did and I find it criminal.

Fortunately, I wrote much of this book before my episode with right kidney cancer and left kidney failure Stage 3-B. So please understand that I was forced to jump back and forth to complete the book from this point on.

Beware of Dr. Orange! It's bad enough that the VA waited for more than twenty years to recognize what was already known by the U.S. Air Force, that Vietnam veterans' exposure to dioxin through Agent Orange presented one of the most complex problems ever imagined. It wasn't until November 9, 2000 when the VA announced that Vietnam veterans with Type II diabetes were eligible to file a claim for disability benefits.

Lawsuits and a dozen research projects carried on in the 1980s and 1990s. There were efforts to get comprehensive Agent Orange legislation through Congress to right the many wrongs of the cover-up. These efforts were stonewalled by an unlikely foe: Representative Sonny Montgomery of Mississippi and chairman of the House Veterans Affairs Committee. He had claimed to be the true friend and champion of veterans, and yet he had almost singlehandedly bottled up Agent Orange legislation. He did this while air force scientists and other military had already been aware as early as 1967 of the potential long-term health risks of frequent spraying. Disregarding this, over the nine-year period Agent Orange was sprayed throughout much of South Vietnam **at a rate of six to twenty-five times the rate suggested by manufacturers.**

In spite of the powerful opposition against the victims of Agent Orange, receiving any disability compensation finally became official by Acts of Congress. By 2017 the VA recognized fourteen or fifteen diseases as being linked to Agent Orange exposure. That number may have increased by the time of this writing and increased again by 2018's and…

Not Out of the Woods Yet? Several years ago an article was published that read like this: NEW ACTING VA BENEFITS UNDERSECRETARY SAYS AGENT ORANGE HARMLESS! When will the VA quit trying to take earned benefits away from veterans? This time, because of numerous personnel changes, a new acting undersecretary for Veterans Benefits was appointed. Despite being a veteran himself, Mr. Thomas Murphy showed determination (threats) of "holding the line on veterans' Agent Orange claims." However, his mission was to target only these two groups: Blue Water Navy Veterans and the C-123 Veterans Association. This squabble has carried on for nearly six years with no clear-cut winner as of today.

Jim Sampsel, an analyst within the Department of Veterans Affairs compensation service, as recently as March 2017 opened up a hornet's nest when he told a VA advisory committee that he believed much of the renewed attention on Agent Orange is a result of media hype and hysteria. "When it comes to Agent Orange, the facts don't always matter." Sampsel is a Vietnam veteran who had an opinion that Agent Orange contained very, very small amounts of dioxin and that U.S. planes did not spray it when American troops were in the area. Of course he is in error here. I know it personally.

Many lessons can be learned from the history of the Agent Orange panic. One is that when a government offers presumptive compensation for diseases (as by the Agent Orange Act of 1991) many will show up to collect. Some will not even have any related diseases.
—2006 article "The Agent Orange Fiasco"
Co-author Alvin Young

Dr. Orange became Mr. Young's tag shortly after that, and it became evident that he was on a mission. Known as the government's go-to expert on Agent Orange, he has maintained this belief that few veterans were exposed to Agent Orange, which contained the toxic chemical dioxin. And even if they were, it was in doses too small to harm them. Some vets, he wrote in a

2011 email, were simply "freeloaders," making up ailments to "cash in" on the VA's compensation system.

As anyone could imagine, Mr. Young's opinionated influence caused a flock of angry opposition, including veterans, credible scientists, and powerful government officials and Congressmen. Note that Mr. Young served as an "expert" for Monsanto and Dow when Vietnam veterans sued them in 2004.

Mr. Young was also met with stiff resistance from Linda S. Birnbaum, director of the National Institute of Health, and Jeanne M. Stellman, professor at Columbia University. All Vietnam veterans during the "hot spot" years of 1968–69, when Super Agent Orange was presumed to have been dumped mostly on III Corps, need to be kept in the know about the history as well as the foreseeable future of Agent Orange illnesses. Fortunately, we have some very powerful government leaders in Washington who seem to have our backs. I wrote about one of them in Chapter 20, President Trump.

Statement from Secretary on Agent Orange. On November 1, 2017, U.S. Secretary of Veterans Affairs Dr. David J. Shulkin (appointed by President Trump) announced that he is considering new presumptive conditions that may qualify for disability compensation related to Agent Orange exposure. What has influenced this is a recent report by the National Academy of Medicine regarding veterans' exposure to Agent Orange.

More Options in Claims Disagreements. On November 2, 2017, the Department of Veteran Affairs announced that it will launch the Rapid Appeals Modernization Program, which will provide expanded opportunities for veterans to enter the new, more efficient claims review process outlined in the Veterans Appeals Improvement and Modernization Act of 2017, signed into law by President Donald J. Trump on August 23, 2017.

At this time President Trump and Secretary Shulkin were making me feel more trusting that the VA we veterans have to rely on so heavily is becoming the VA it needs to be. That we need it to be. That trust has not been there, nor was it deserved, for decades.

Vietnam veterans were not able to begin filing for Agent Orange disability claims until 1977, if they even knew that they could, which most did not. My book *Condemned Property?* attempted to shock Americans by telling them the truth of what's been happening to us since coming home. Unfortunately, a lot of really great Americans have suffered premature deaths because their country's government carelessly exposed nearly 3.3 million American soldiers and millions more Vietnamese soldiers and civilians with…**THE MOST TOXIC CHEMICALS KNOWN TO SCIENCE!**

My Fellow Vietnam War Buddies, if you served over there during 1968 into early 1969 and you were anywhere at any time in III Corps, not only were you exposed to the most and heaviest concentration of Agent Orange use, but you were also in the paths of Super Agent Orange Dioxins.[36]

Here are the hot spots where the heaviest amounts of Agent Orange exposure were recorded by the Congressional Record, the U.S. Air Force Ranch Hand Study, 1984–2000, the U.S. Air Force CHIECO Reports, 1965–1971, the Centers for Disease Control, Health Status of Vietnam Veterans 1989, Institute of Medicine-National Academy of Sciences, Veterans and Agent Orange Update 2000, the Development of Impact Mitigation Strategies Related to the Use of Agent Orange Herbicide in the Aluoi Valley, Vietnam, and others.

Agent Orange/Super Agent Orange Hot Spots 1968–1969

III Corps and I Corps	Orange I & II	White	Blue	Total Gallons
1 Phouc Vinh (III Corps)	484,383	146,676	12,810	643,769
2 Katum (III Corps)	299,420	239,395	20,000	558,815
Firebase Jewell/ LZ Snuffy (III)	219,500	145,010	7,300	372,680
4 Nha Be (III Corps)	119,725	121,925	6,000	247,650
5 Ben Cat (III Corps)	87,250	83,640	20,105	190,995
Others				
6 Fire Base Rakkassan (I Corps)	150,145	23,900	2,510	176,555
7 Bien Hoa (III Corps)	35,345	124,525	3,950	163,820

This list recorded the number of gallons applied by fixed-wing aircraft only. It does not include any other aerial or ground spraying, nor does it include dinoxol, diquat, trinoxol, bromacil, Tandex, monuron, duiron, or dalapon. It does *not* include these deadly agents either: Agent Super Orange, Agent Pink, Agent Green, and Agent Purple, which some people say was the worst of them all. The amount represents gallons within eight kilometers of the area. Each area was approximately 9.6 miles in diameter.

As you can see six of the top seven areas dumped on were in southern Vietnam's III Corps, and most of it was active in 1968–1969 in an area between Cambodia and Saigon where the Ho Chi Minh Trail emptied into South Vietnam. **VA IGNORES THE EVIDENCE** is the label that I chose to get this chapter rolling. So I'll close it with same. And tens of thousands if not hundreds of thousands of veterans from all wars have suffered through or died during the VA's **Delay, Deny, Delay Till We Die process**.

---

36 United States—Vietnam Scientific Conference on Human Health and Environmental Effects of Agent Orange / Dioxins, Hanoi, Vietnam Mar. 3-6, 2002.

It is November 18, 2017, and just as I was beginning to feel good about the pencil pushers and bean counters at VA's Comp and Pen departments…
AMBUSHED!

You grunts and Special Forces guys out there know all too well what the word *ambush* does to our minds even to this day. It arouses us. We can hyperventilate. Anger of the worst kind can settle in. But fortunately, since VA already has us "pill popping" for mega stress and maybe depression issues, we are almost able to fend off the killer anger and the thoughts it brings. I'm always wondering when I will notice the benefit of taking all these prescriptions from the VA. I guess they are working or I would be in jail or in the grave.

The ambush by the VA Comp & Pen Department arrived in the mail on November 18, 2017. This warm and fuzzy report from C&P included a not too shocking DENIAL. Been there before and the reasons shouldn't have been too alarming as I've experienced similar responses well over a dozen times since my very first day at the VA's Cleveland Ohio Regional Office in December 2005. That was the day I took my first Agent Orange physical.

I feel this setback in my twelve-plus-year marathon saga with VA's C&P is not by any means to be blamed on the Trump/Shulkin plan to establish and enforce the accountability needed here, which their administration is so dedicated to pursue.

Not only did the ambush from VA deliver a rude and wrong denial to a credible claim, it also included a real shocker. They did an extremely rare reversal on a claim that they had previously approved just one year ago. I have my work cut out for me. I will not allow them to beat me down as they have done to so many of our veteran brothers. Trust me, comrades, I will engage the VA's Comp & Pen hacks with every ounce of energy I have left in my body. I owe it to the many, many brothers who died so very prematurely due to long waiting times for health care or the disgusting Comp & Pen system of **Delay, Deny, Delay Till We Die!**

I won't waste more space in this book on the new and very disappointing VA rating decision. But I was hoping to end this chapter on a positive note, in sharing some upbeat news about positive experiences other veterans have shared with me regarding their VA treatment. While these good news stories do exist, it is obvious that the VA's problems remain uncured. But we have to hang in there and keep the faith.

If this book's story does nothing else, I just hope that it shows America, Vietnam veterans as well as non-veterans, that the Vietnam War's combat veteran is a unique individual. They fought and repeatedly defeated a well-armed, highly determined, and vicious enemy without the support or understanding of the American people and without a policy or strategy to win the war from their civilian and military leaders. At least WWI, WWII, and Korean War veterans faced an enemy with identifiable uniforms on and were easily identifiable as someone who was trying to kill you.

It has been said before, but I need to say it again…the way our country ignored the Vietnam veteran's sacrifices will always remain nothing less than shameful. WWII and Korean War vets should have known better. If a man fought in just one battle of a war, he has immediately become a unique individual who deserves honor and respect.

In actual battle America's Vietnam veterans were almost instantly thrown into likely combat situations, and they were most likely going to stay there for weeks or months before getting a break. Some might remain out there in the bush for an entire year if they stayed healthy enough. If their units were hit hard, they would most likely stay out there accompanied by a constant flow of "new guys." Those who somehow made it through their tour unharmed physically would have the privilege of going home with their mental wounds and hopefully receive badly needed understanding, appreciation, and therapy. Most of them received neither when they got home—so that's how their war ended for them—or did it?

Super Agent Orange and the Iron Triangle. We know about the many ways and means that the boots-on-the-ground troops were exposed to the deadly herbicides in Vietnam. We're also aware of a variety of poisonous herbicides that were used, with Agent Orange being the most widely used chemical. In the early years of the war, only fifteen thousand gallons were sprayed in all of Vietnam, most of which was concentrated in I Corps near the Demilitarized Zone (DMZ). As the military demand increased, the manufacturing processes were greatly accelerated in quantity and in density of dioxin contamination. (More Agent Orange coverage in Chapter 13.)

Over the next nine years, an estimated twelve million gallons of Agent Orange and related herbicides would saturate the jungles of Vietnam from the DMZ to the Mekong Delta. And yet, there were many questions that went unanswered until many years after the war ended. How quickly did the chemicals diffuse in the atmosphere? How long would the herbicides linger on the ground? Could it be burned off? How would it affect water? They already knew it would kill the Vietnamese crops—depleting their food supply. But who cared. After all, they were just **gooks.**

Similar herbicides had already been used in the United States, much more diluted with water and oil than in Vietnam. The issue of "mist drift" caught the U.S. military off guard as it inflicted lethal damage in areas that weren't being targeted. Still, the military continued its spraying, increasing dosage and strength year to year. In 1964, 175,000 gallons were dumped, then 621,000 gallons in 1965. In 1966, the total spraying across Vietnam totaled 2.28 million gallons. The military insisted there would be no adverse impact on civilians or military personnel on the ground, and the spraying continued to escalate. In 1967, 1968, and early 1969, the heavily populated provinces surrounding north and northwest of Saigon became the primary targets. This was III Corps, where the Viet Cong headquarters were located underground. The area was also called the Iron Triangle, which would be nonexistent by the end of 1969.

The United States scientific community warned against increasing the strength. By early 1969, the strength of the Agent Orange dosage being used was up to twenty-five times stronger than the original recommended dose. It wasn't until the 1980s that scientists discovered there was strong evidence that military officials were aware of the potential long-term health risks of frequent, heavy spraying back in 1967. An air force scientist, Dr. James Clary, wrote that the air force knew Agent Orange was far more hazardous than anyone had admitted to at the time. Dr. Clary wrote in a 1988 letter to Congress...

"We were aware of the potential damage due to dioxin contamination and that the military formulation was even greater in dioxin concentration. However, because the stronger material was to be used primarily on the enemy, no one was overly concerned. It was never considered that our own personnel would become contaminated. And if we had...WE EXPECTED OUR OWN GOVERNMENT TO GIVE ASSISTANCE TO VETERANS SO CONTAMINATED."

So many fine and thorough books have covered this subject, so I am touching on it ever so lightly. Well, the spraying would continue to 1971 and would be stopped permanently with the war winding down then and the military quite satisfied that their mission had been accomplished. It would be another twenty years before the massive human health damages were to be known. The damage continues as I write this book in 2016–2018.

If there are any Vietnam veterans reading this book who served in III Corps, in 1968 and 1969, if you aren't aware, you and I and our brothers/sisters in III Corps were treated to inhaling something much stronger, even more lethal than regular old Agent Orange itself. If you did not know this, we ate pineapples, bananas, rice, and fish treated with it. We drank water that was contaminated by it. Ladies and gentlemen, our government gave us the special treatment with **SUPER AGENT ORANGE!**

While I was not able to locate information about how much stronger this brand of lethal chemical, Agent Orange II, was, it is fairly easy to conclude that it was considerably stronger and more lethal for its intended targets. Not long after my brothers and departed from III Corps in early 1969, there was an article that appeared in the 25th Infantry's monthly newsletter *Tropic Lightning* as well as the U.S. Army's newspaper *Stars and Stripes,* which announced the final elimination of the Viet Cong hot bed or sanctuary, a woods and jungle area called **The Iron Triangle.**

Honestly, if they had been able to destroy the vegetation earlier, like before Tet 1968, literally thousands of American lives would have been saved from death by combat. However, since they had been heavily exposed and often to Agent Orange I and then Agent Orange II, their expected life span would have been shortened anyway. But they were cheated from the opportunity to live out the rest of their days back home. Of course no veteran "gets" Agent Orange; it's not a disease in itself. It causes diseases and they can be lethal. There was a host of herbicides used during the Vietnam War:

- Bromacil used between 1962–1964
- Tandex used between 1962–1964
- Monuron used between 1962–1964
- Diuron used between 1962–1964
- Dalapon used between 1962–1964
- Dinoxel used between 1962–1964
- Trinoxol used between 1962–1964
- Agent Purple used between 1962–1964
- Agent Green used between 1962–1964
- Agent Pink used between 1962–1964
- Agent White used between (unavailable)
- Agent Blue used between (unavailable)
- Agent Orange used between 1965–1970
- Agent Orange II used between 1968–1969 (also referred to as Super Agent Orange, most often used in III Corps areas around Saigon, mentioned in Chapter 13)

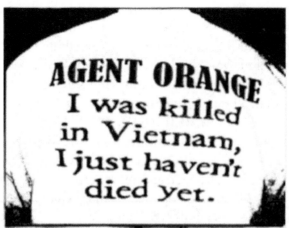

Vietnam Generation Fading as Death Rate Rises for Vets

AGENT ORANGE: Painful legacy

Agent Orange, a combination of herbicides and defoliants, was used by the U.S. particularly during the Vietnam War. The substance caused extensive medical including cancers and birth defects, among people exposed to it.

In 1991, the Agent Orange Act made veterans exposed to the chemical eligible for compensation and medical care. The U.S. Department of Veterans Affairs recognizes a 'presumptive' link between Agent Orange and a range of illnesses:

Dark areas on the map show Agent Orange concentrations.

Vietnam Jungle—1967 Before Agent Orange

After Spraying 1969

Chapter 13

THEIR GREATEST DAY...I'LL NEVER FORGET!

Maybe the reasons for sending 2.7 million of America's soldier boys to Vietnam don't hold water. Maybe the two million South Vietnamese and two million North Vietnamese who were sacrificed was for nothing. Maybe the corrupt governments of the United States and South Vietnam should stand trials for war crimes. Maybe? What cannot and must not be forgotten is how the brave and gutsy soldiers and marines fought like wounded tigers out there with little reason or any motivational factors whatsoever, except for just this one...**TO COVER EACH OTHER'S BACK.**

Most of our platoon became casualties during the post-Tet Offensive months of 1968—March, April, and the dreaded month of May, the bloodiest month of the entire war. Even after that, we all had to get through nine more months. I remember that some of the guys were starting to talk crazy shit about what they were going to do when they got home and that kind of stuff. As the point man I wasn't even thinking about home. I was more concerned with what was behind the next bush or what all that noise was in a palm tree ahead.

We had spent the entire time out in the bush—eighty-eight days straight, and no one had heard of any plans to relieve us. We were badly needed out there, and our sister companies had lost more of their men than we had. I guess that after three months in the jungle with the beast and still living, we were considered irreplaceable because of our experience. I wondered—how could they consider a bunch of scared soldier boys like us as the experienced guys? What did that tell us? It flat-out told us that no one expected a grunt to make it into his fourth month, let alone six months to a full year.

We had already been through full-blown "human wave" attacks from the NVA and VC, and what seemed like never-ending sniper pot shots, which picked a few of us off one by one. The night attacks on the fire support bases we were helping to defend in those first three months took major attacks in the Iron Triangle and the Boi Loi Woods, which were infested with Viet Cong. At neither battle did it ever appear that we were in danger of losing. We had the superior advantage in every way possible. We outnumbered them, and yet they were attacking head-on into our superior firepower, not to mention we had sufficient protection from our bunkers and the barriers we had set outside the base. We were able to call in outside firepower from our base camps at Cu Chi or Dau Tieng and even helicopters with firepower. That was almost shameful as the VC ran in every direction to escape the torrential spray of bullets into their suicidal charges. In the morning, after the battle was finally over, we found enough bodies to report that the heads back at headquarters would be dearly satisfied with us…for this day.

The night attack on our fire support base in the Iron Triangle was similar to the Boi Loi action. It just didn't last as long, and of course, our enemy body count wasn't the cheery news the prima donnas back in Cu Chi were expecting. Hey, so what? We survived another risk of not being here the next day, and that counted for something or at least to us it did.

For a while casualties were light for Bravo Company, and I suppose that meant to the top brass that we weren't living dangerously enough to suit their appetites. It didn't seem to matter to anyone at the top that those evening battles did cost us some lives and that we had no chance at all to grab some sleep—not even a catnap. Most of us agreed that it would not be a good idea to take a nap while we were being shot at and charged at by a few hundred doped-up, screaming Viet Cong that we did not expect any mercy from if they had succeeded in overrunning our fire support bases.

One day word came down that Bravo Company was going out for a search-and-destroy mission very early the next morning. We would be walking into the same area that our brothers from another company explored a couple days ago. They had walked into a bad, but very effective enemy ambush. It happened in some of the thickest bush, in one of the swampiest woods any of us had seen in Nam up to that point. Not making it back to the Iron Triangle fire support base for a couple of days, when they got back, many of them were missing. They were still out there, either dead, wounded, or pinned down with every direction closed off, and unable to escape.

Bravo was being sent out to locate and rescue any Americans still managing to hold on out there. What we would find that day would not be anything to write home about and I'm sure none of us did that. But we didn't ask. We set out on a typically hot and muggy day, and I swear to this day that our feet never touched dry land until the day ended and some of us made it back to the base.

There wasn't anything special about this day. It pretty much looked, felt, and smelled like most others—the stench was nauseating—but we were used to it by now. It would be often that we dropped our guard as we stumbled, fumbled, got back up, then stumbled again. I swear the mud kept getting deeper, blacker, and smellier. How could that be, I wondered back then as I wonder about it to this day. We humped for a couple of hours, which seemed like dozens of hours Nam time. So far, there were no visible signs of any survivors or KIA from that company. Naturally, we continued with what seemed like a suicidal search-and-rescue mission, fearing at all times that it would become us, Bravo Company, that might need to be rescued. We were more focused on finding some of the poor souls from that group who never made it back to the base the day before.

I was walking point this day, and it would mostly be up to me to lead us through the most ungodly-looking terrain we had ever seen ahead of us. There was no other passable way to get to the approximate location of where our brothers were ambushed. We wondered how we would be able to carry our guys if we found any of them; what we were about to walk into was certainly not very user friendly for our medevac choppers. No matter, our mission remained the same. After all, if it were us still out there, still breathing, lying painfully in our own blood along with the critters of the Vietnam jungle, we would have tried to keep our hopes up that there were guys out there trying to find us.

Dealing with and accepting reality in a war is something your average American soldier boy handles well, when other American lives are at risk, even though we really didn't know very many of them. Then it hit me— because of so many f-ing new guys over the last three months, I could not remember half the names of our second platoon who were also humping with us about twenty meters away, which seemed more like two hundred in the mud and sloppy terrain. I thought about our morale. Did we have enough left to make it through one more day, knowing that there would be so many more ahead of us, waiting to torture us physically and psychologically? What was it that kept us motivated to carry on when it could have been much easier to roll over and let a mortar round or stream of AK-47 fire end our miseries? Thoughts like that were all too common amongst the combat guys who were forced to adapt to our hostile environment.

Even today, when I think back at some of those days and nights that we made it through, I just shake my head. It awes me to think of how we managed to maintain our resolve when in fact, our bodies were in full-scale revolt mode. I think enough of us realized how important it was to cling to whatever morale that we could. As sad as this sounds, we needed to have morale in order to handle the psychological mentality we needed to prepare for killing in battle day after day.

Back in the world (home), society taught us not to do that, and then we were forced to be the opposite. Why didn't the government invest as much into us after we came home as they did in training us to get ready for the darkest moments of our lives? Why?

Suddenly, something happened, and all of this took place in about eight seconds, I swear. First, I saw unusual movement ahead, which froze me for a couple of seconds before I dropped to the ground, facedown. I heard the sickening sounds of enemy fire, a ton of it. I heard guys yelling out. Some screamed, and I heard enemy chatter back and forth, which seemed so close to me that I kept my face buried in the mud. **ALL HELL HAD BROKEN LOOSE!**

Those few seconds were over in a flash, even though it seemed like an hour. How frightening could that be to a bunch of teenage kids? The ambush was on, and it was an instant success for the Viet Cong. I was able to spot the movement ahead, and by hitting the ground immediately, all the guys behind me also hit the ground in time to allow a lot of bullets to fly harmlessly over their heads. Unfortunately, and possibly because I failed to yell out as I hit the ground, a lot of guys not directly behind me who couldn't have seen me dive to the ground were not able to get out of the way when the first volley of enemy rounds found their targets. One body after another went down in just five or six of those short but critically important few seconds. If I could have two or three of those seconds back in my life, maybe that entire day's outcome would have made a huge difference in the lives of many. Only if!

What happened next that day deserves to be described in at least a dozen separate books. What had become an average, forgettable day in June 1968 instantly became a totally unforgettable day for those who made it out alive and are still breathing today. What happened—what those men did over the next few hours (I have no recollection of time here)—made an impression on me that no description can do justice to.

Helmets were literally flying through the air like wounded Frisbees, as two of our guys were grazed in the head by enemy fire (I was one of them) and their helmets landed about twenty feet away in the mud. It didn't matter. We were all focused on one thing and only one thing at that moment in time…we had to get our wounded guys out of there.

The unfriendly terrain would make it difficult to pull any wounded or dead out of there. It didn't seem even remotely possible for any medevacs to get in and out of this area safely. Well, my war brothers proved me totally wrong. As some of us advanced our positions to gain more favorable shots at our attackers who were not backing off, several other members of Bravo Company's platoons also advanced without much regard for their lives with only one goal in mind—to rescue and save as many wounded Americans as possible. This day would not end with any Bravo Regulars left behind. That is the last memory I have of that day.

Most people have heard the expression "I was so scared that I shit my pants." Well, many of your American soldier boys who were in this extremely precarious position on this day were suffering from many other inconveniences while they were attempting to fight off a vicious enemy ambush and save the lives of the war buddies around them. Imagine them stressed out in battle, suffering from dysentery, bloody diarrhea or dehydration, and no safe drinking water available. If they made it through the day, there would be no fresh, dry, clean fatigue pants to replace the pants they had just uncontrollably shit in. I can't put enough emphasis on the deplorable living conditions that our government sent us to live in, fight in, become wounded and die in. Oh wait, I believe Obama made a brilliant statement about the dangerous and poor living conditions of America's fighting men and women. "They joined up for this, knowing full well what they were in for, and after all, they did get paid for their service." Yes, his statement went something like that. To Obama's credit for his statement, I checked back to my first book, in which I documented that the U.S. Army issued a new pay rate increase in May 1968 for active duty private E-1 soldiers of a whopping $6.60 per month. This brought my gross monthly pay to the sub-poverty level of **$102.30 PER MONTH!**

Never mind the "minor inconveniences" of sleeping with rats, centipedes, poisonous snakes and spiders, lying in your own shit, breathing napalm and Agent Orange, being undernourished for most of the year, flat-out living as an ape in Africa lives, and being sent home with illness, diseases, and injuries that you would have to live with the rest of your life. Never mind the ugly fact that the government that put you through all of this then refuses to take care of your Vietnam War-caused health problems and in many cases, even challenges that you have such bad health or that it may not have been service connected (in their opinion) from your battle experiences. Never mind all of this; we were Americans with a job to do, and if we made it through all of that, certainly America would welcome us home with hugs and kisses. Then all would soon be well again…so we thought.

Back on the battlefield in June 1968 where Bravo Company of the 3rd 22nd Walking Regulars were ambushed and badly mauled just one day after a sister unit was badly mauled from a VC ambush, the Bravo Regulars were trying to prevent a bad, bad day from getting much worse. Their only goal at this moment was to rescue a dozen of their fellow American soldier boys. One heroic act after another was performed by these guys in relentless fashion with almost no regard for their own lives. Some were wounded trying to rescue wounded buddies. Some of the already wounded were wounded again as they refused to leave the battlefield while they still had buddies lying there in excruciating pain. Helmets were shot or blown off heads from enemy rounds or shrapnel. Some of them were not even fazed and continued on with what needed to be done at that moment.

Martino guardedly helped others to pull Paris to safety. Jenner did the same with another, while Ryan, who was hit twice already, stubbornly remained to help carry or painfully drag men to reasonable safety. Taylor fended off any advance from our attackers with his deadly M-60 fire as Turner did with his well-placed, devastating M-79 rounds. Daniels and Best advanced from the rear along with several others to assist in carrying the many wounded to medevac choppers that made amazing landings and extractions during the battle. One chopper did not make it. Neither did those soldiers who were inside. They were all KIA. But an even dozen—twelve men who had been wounded during the battle—were rescued to live another day.

The attack never really stopped, which was unusual for a VC ambush team. Then again, we never figured out how many of them there were because we never clearly saw them, not until later that day when we returned to search the area after B-52 bombs were dropped. Even then, we did not find an actual body count, just a lot of thick blood trails and body parts. So we knew that we inflicted a lot of damage on our attackers.

All of the initially wounded men during the initial few second burst from the ambush were wounded critically and required immediate medical attention. Four more men who were attempting the rescue process were also wounded. Fourteen men were medevac'd that day. Twelve more replacements, the f-ing new guys would be filtering in over the next few days. Some of them would not last more than a couple of days and then they would need to be replaced. Obviously, an infantry unit in Vietnam rarely operated at full strength.

This day stands out in my mind and this day is what I think of when someone makes mention of the Vietnam War. As anyone can surmise, negative references of any degree made about Vietnam or the unbelievably courageous soldiers and marines who fought like wounded tigers over there is very likely to draw a dangerously negative response from me.

Long after the ambush at Catholic Village in Hoc Mon Province on June 15, 1968, I overheard Lieutenant Graves and the platoon sergeants discussing who should be recommended for a Silver Star, Bronze Star, or Commendation Medal. I was one of the Silver Stars written up for that day. I think there were three Bronze Stars–Valor submitted, and justifiably so. There were many Purple Hearts earned for that, way too many, and we would never see some of those guys again.

A couple of months later, I heard a couple guys got their awards for their heroic actions that day, so I asked the brigade clerks about the Silver Star I was put in for. "We lost it," I was told by one of the clerks. Then it dawned on me that I had won about three hundred dollars from that clerk in card games called Tonk and Hearts. Oh boy, he was trying to get even with me, I thought. So, I made mention of this situation to Staff Sergeant Daniels, who had replaced Staff Sergeant Maines as our platoon sergeant. He told me that he would take care of it and re-submitted it, as he clearly remembered what happened on June 15, 1968. I let it go and moved on from there. Well, the award finally came down, but it was reduced to a Bronze Star Valor and I figured that punk clerk had something to do with that. I didn't pursue the Silver Star recommendation, too busy trying to stay alive during my last few months in-country. BUT...I never forgave what that "base camp warrior" did to me, and I even developed a bad taste in my mouth toward the troops in the rear. After all, they had no idea what we went through out there, and the clerk had no right in keeping that Silver Star from me. Others who were in that hideous battle never let me forget what came down that day; they always made me feel really good. That was enough for me. (Still wish the Silver Star was on my chest...)

I see those men's faces of that day, some nameless, most with nicknames. No one can ever tell me that there were better and braver warriors than these. I don't care which war is being referred to—any Middle East war, Korea, WWII, WWI, Spanish-American, the War Between the States, or the War for Independence. The Vietnam War veterans I served with on that day in June 1968 all deserved a Medal of Honor!

Americans back home would have been proud of their soldier boys who battled for their lives at this small insignificant hellhole in the middle of nowhere in June 1968, had they been told the truth. America's gritty soldier boys fought valiantly, brilliantly, stubbornly, and then again not so brilliantly, as they repeatedly exposed their vulnerable bodies to be shot at, trying to save one another. It was days like this when combat veterans of the Vietnam War formed a brotherhood that would last for their entire lives.

All who were thrown into being present that day and heavily involved with the saving of many men's lives probably experienced the most unusual and extreme emotions of their lives. I remember that I did. From ecstasy to crying like a baby in one instant after another with the last emotional feeling probably being anger of the highest level in that we now wanted to kill someone. I found myself afterward praying that the feeling would never take control of my senses like that, putting my mind into an indescribable state of frenzy, helplessness, and desire to do great harm to another human being. Unfortunately, that horrible day would be repeated again and again.

A couple of weeks later, our 25th Division base camp, Dau Tieng, was attacked early on July 4 with an initial barrage of approximately four hundred to five hundred rocket and mortar rounds followed by repeated Viet Cong-style human wave attacks. Eventually, the good guys prevailed, but we would take many casualties before the last VC was disposed of. Just a couple of weeks later at a place called Trang Bang, we were working with the 25th Division's 3/4 Cav Armored Unit and we were hit pretty hard there too by a large enemy force. Several more battles would take place, including massive human wave attacks around Tay Ninh and Nui Ba Den. Heroics were plentiful at all of these confrontations as well as scores of smaller "skirmishes."

That year, 1968, will be embedded solidly in my memory bank, no matter how much mental therapy or medication the VA takes care of me with. I will never get out of my mind what the guys of Bravo Company 3rd 22nd Regulars of the 25th Infantry did on a scorching day of tropical heat, 100 percent humidity, in an unfriendly environment, to say the least, and a dogged enemy that just would not quit…not until we were gone.

After our tour in Vietnam was over in 1969, I am happy to say that most of the men who were wounded and rescued on that sweltering day of one-hundred-degree heat and humidity, on bacteria-infested terrain, came home alive to their families, yours truly included. Except, many of them have died prematurely since.

Unfortunately, they did not receive the welcome home they had hoped for and dreamed about. They never will because it's too late. Many Americans, especially WWII veterans, including our fathers and uncles, went so far as to degrade our war and what we did over there by referring to Vietnam as a mere "conflict," saying we fought against a bunch of "farmers and peasants" who fought with "pitchforks."

The references became worse as the term "baby killers" became a popular way to describe us. Those who did that know who they are—or were. I hope you have been forgiven for those sins, that is, if you asked the Almighty Power above, our dear Lord, if he would forgive you.

My mind wandered off again, thinking—am I finished with this book or will another memory pop into my head? Then it happened when another Nam vet told me about his VFW post sponsoring an event to commemorate the fiftieth birthday of the war. Wow, just when would that be, I thought. Well, here comes that one more story.

I no longer wonder what the effect has been on all of us—from those days of unimaginable horror. They will be with us for the rest of our lives. And yet, here I am in November 2017, trying to complete this book, and people, especially at the VA, keep saying things like **"That war was so long ago. Why can't you guys get over it?"**

Well, the fact that I am deeply engrossed in and committed to yet a fourth book about that "unforgettable" experience over there should suffice to anyone who ever thinks about asking such a forbidden question again of a combat Vietnam War veteran. **"THAT WAR WAS SO LONG AGO. WHY CAN'T YOU GET OVER IT?"**

I have known hundreds of men who returned to society from the Vietnam War with these feelings inside of them that might make them a danger to others as well as to themselves. From the 1970s all the way to the 2010s, these feelings have overtaken me sometimes, causing an argument over something, and it might not even have been Vietnam related; most times it was. I guess my PTSD was showing itself for what it is…mega stress.

There is little doubt in my mind that a higher power stepped in and saved me from causing terrible harm to others, including myself. Yes, I believe that God saved me in those near catastrophic confrontations. I hate to say this, but it is a fact for many veterans who experienced moderate to severe combat that killing was done as easily as flipping Tiddlywinks in a little boy's game. Their emotional state made them dangerous to others around them.

I don't think this is an overstatement, so I'll go ahead and say it—most war veterans who were exposed to in-your-face combat where death and unbelievable, almost intolerable visuals occurred will be cursed with PTSD. Fortunately, several caring mental health professionals at the VA reached out to me several years ago and have helped me become a better person and a safer person to others around me and to my own self. Unfortunately, an enormous number of Vietnam War veterans and other veterans have not benefited from such wonderful life-saving TOC from the VA as I have found. Too many of their lives ended prematurely and tragically.

Vietnam War's Fiftieth Birthday. For forty-four to fifty-four years, some of us have been looking back at our Vietnam experiences like a bad, bad love affair—on again, off again, on again. Some of us have already recognized the fiftieth anniversary of our Vietnam experience from 2009 back to 1959. Some will not celebrate their fiftieth until the year 2022 or maybe even 2025. Whichever, America's longest war's actual starting point could be labeled 1959, as America's military was put in harm's way that year. The official ending point could be labeled 1975, as that was when Saigon surrendered and there were Americans in-country at that time. So 1959–1975 and fifty years beyond each year, Vietnam veterans will be recognizing their anniversary with the war they fought in Vietnam. Actually, it gets more complicated, as America was very involved with supporting the French during their war with Vietnam from 1945 until 1954. Officially, we have had "boots on the soil" of Vietnam from at least 1950–1975 or twenty-five years.

Sometimes we look back with a passionate love to that war and its people we fought with and against. Neither was responsible for the beginnings of what are called by some as the Indochina Wars between France and Vietnam and the USA and Vietnam.

Many of us have never returned to that war with a passionate love, and many of us have. All of us have distanced ourselves from its memories and how the war was allowed to fail miserably, especially after it appeared to be won after the bloody Tet year of 1968. To this day, many of us cannot understand it—how we became involved and, certainly, how our government chose to allow it to end. Anyone interested in reading the truth from a valid source needs only to look up the Pentagon Papers, which were kept top secret for decades. Most combat Vietnam War participants would prefer not to read them, I am sure. There remains enough anger that has been harbored inside us for decades without finding a healthy outlet. Some Nam vets seemed to find a release or some sort of settlement with themselves by returning to Vietnam for a vacation-like visit. I cannot see the benefit in that, as I have mentioned elsewhere in this book. But things change.

The one painful question that remains unanswered is—WHY DID THE AMERICAN GOVERNMENT LIE TO US ABOUT VIETNAM? I would think that a great movie could be made about the history of Vietnam, beginning with the Sino-Vietnamese kingdom that existed in the northern Red River delta of Vietnam from 207 BC until present. The movie would, of course, show the centuries of great struggles between the Chinese forcing their culture onto the Vietnamese, and then the wars with the Mongols, French, and Americans, as well as the China war in 1979.

I attempted to do my best with earlier chapters of this book, but the history of Vietnam is long and complicated, especially for a non-Vietnamese-speaking American who is not a degreed historian. And much of Vietnamese history has been protected by their government.

Although the early ethnic Vietnamese originally lived only in Northern Vietnam, today the country is indeed a melting pot with a multitude of nationalities and an endless number of dialects. But Vietnam became what it is today in the late 1400s when the ethnic Vietnamese completely conquered and absorbed the kingdom called Champa. For more than four hundred years, Vietnam was ruled and protected from the northern cities of Hanoi and Hue. It was the French who brought the unification to an end by the first half of the nineteenth century.

Although the French helped to improve some things, such as communications and health, the French refused to allow the Vietnamese to educate their young and demonstrated blatant racism toward them. Outraged, the Vietnamese began a formidable nationalistic movement. This movement would be crushed. The only alternative was to reform the group underground and remain based in China. Its name became the Indochina Communist Party. Ho Chi Minh would rise as their leader. Ho Chi Minh's nationalist desire was so much stronger than this desire to court communism for support that in 1943 he temporarily disbanded the Indochinese Communist Party. Eventually, "Uncle Ho" had gained massive support and admiration from communists and non-communists.

Ho had expected support of his newly decorated free and unified country, called the Democratic Republic of Vietnam. He was a big fan of the United States and, reportedly, at one time showcased a portrait of George Washington on his wall and kept a copy of the Declaration of Independence on his desk. Ho did not see what was coming from his next opponent after disposing of the French. The Americans would be a formidable adversary, one he could not afford to underestimate.

Americans had been looked up to by most Vietnamese, but the French had no concern about that. In fact, they resented it. I also discovered that at one point, Ho Chi Minh's new military, the Viet Minh, actually had to fight against a combined force of British, Indian, Japanese, and French. Together, they looted the Vietnamese countryside while the USA sat back and did nothing. Remember, as I mentioned earlier, Ho Chi Minh had sent several letters, at least eight, to President Truman and the U.S. State Department, asking for the U.S. to step in to help Vietnam maintain its freedom from the French.

By the beginning of 1948, the French had started to believe that a military victory over Ho Chi Minh's Viet Minh was going to be more difficult than planned. Therefore, the French set up another Vietnamese ruling faction in the south to rival Ho Chi Minh in the north. France would control them, but they did everything possible to create a perception to the world that these Vietnamese in the south wanted their own free state, as they did five hundred to one thousand years ago. This ploy worked as they attracted international support away from Ho's Viet Minh.

It appears that the U.S. government may have panicked when China sent troops into Korea at the same time the Viet Minh, with Chinese support, had taken the initiative against the French. The thought of a Chinese-controlled Korea and all of Vietnam caused enough fear in Washington that they now felt compelled to support the French as the Viet Minh army appeared to be an extension of China and communism. Looking at all of these events in history, I can easily see how our leaders in Washington were led into the wrong direction. The domino theory seemed real, considering the circumstances.

Now, please read this carefully. The plot thickens. The Truman administration allegedly managed to keep Washington convinced that the French role against Ho Chi Minh was helping to hold off a communistic takeover of Vietnam, which could not be afforded. In fact, it became a policy of Washington to urge the French to continue on, and even though Ho Chi Minh had extended peace offers, the U.S. pressured France to reject them and carry on with the war.

From 1950 to 1954, Washington was sending military "advisors," combat troops by the hundreds, as well as dozens of American bombers and other military equipment. In the meantime, the great propaganda resources of the west had most of the international community brainwashed that the Viet Minh were the invaders, pawns of Chinese communism, and that the French, along with their southern Vietnamese subordinates were the ones being threatened to lose their independence.

Another great lie, and this one bothers me very much—the west's propaganda machine had the world believing that a French victory was unstoppable, that Ho Chi Minh would be defeated any day. Sound familiar? Allegedly, this idiotic perception was still being promoted up to the day before the great and complete defeat of the U.S.-supported French military at Dien Bien Phu in 1954.

The propaganda from the west did not stop with the Viet Minh's victory and destruction of colonialism itself. But the damage had been done in turning world opinion against Ho Chi Minh's evil army of Viet Minh when, in fact, they were the only faction that should ever be referred to as true revolutionaries. Many of the Viet Minh became Viet Cong, and the new North Vietnamese Regulars Army was well under construction.

I doubt that you could muster up half a dozen Vietnamese today who would agree with this great American-created lie about the great leader of Vietnam…that Ho Chi Minh's primary interest during both Indochina wars was the promotion and spread of communism. Anyone who would believe that, Vietnamese or American, is lying or…they never did any research on Ho Chi Minh's entire life's work.

The people at the top of our government in Washington who participated in creating and promoting this great lie knew that what they were doing was terribly wrong.

I suppose my fiftieth anniversary in remembering the Vietnam War would have to be fifty years from when I came home, which I think was in March of 1969. When March 2019 comes, if I am still living, I will celebrate that month in some private manner. Because sadly, there may not be any of those guys left that I served side by side with to celebrate with.

Tough and Misunderstood. Coming to closure of this book is going to be difficult, and I have a ways to go. I hope my sometimes disorganized writing style has somehow managed to pull all of this information together so that regardless of who you are, you will have a newfound or increased level of respect for the Vietnamese people as well as the only combat force that has ever managed to defeat them…the American military.

I have bestowed great adornment onto our brotherhood and how that precious family environment kept us going day after day and night after night. But ya know what? I can look back to those unforgettable moments and now I can give credit to an unlikely inanimate object, a dirty, worn, and sometimes torn paper envelope which would deliver a special message from home. It was our mail.

Mail call in Vietnam was much more special to us than it was at a home base like Fort Knox, Fort Hood, Fort Polk, or Fort Bragg, where the letters from home usually arrived more often and in a cleaner, undamaged state. Out in the bush where combat-trained soldiers and marines spent much of their time, sometimes there would be no mail call for many days in a row. It could be too dangerous for the helicopters to deliver the mail, or food, or fresh clothes. Still, I can remember how the soldier's facial expression changed instantly as he ripped his envelope apart and physically attacked his poor little defenseless letter from Mom or his honey or any family member. He couldn't read it fast enough, as though there was a time limit. Letters with loving words, while they didn't cure our homesickness and cold-stone loneliness, did keep our inner spirits alive, giving us an added reason to survive the night and maybe even motivating us enough to wake up the next morning with a smile. But my eyes may have been swollen from tearing in the night.

It was also upsetting to many of us seeing those who rarely received a letter or a box of homemade cookies, so we used to pass them around, hoping to make them feel better. Imagine the effect on a soldier who received a perfumed letter from a sweetheart!

Americans, how could you have treated these homesick, war-weary young heroes as badly as you did? And how could you continue to be so distant, so unsympathetic, so unkind for so long after they came home? I wonder often how many Vietnam vets who died prematurely, died without a thank you or a welcome home? Unfortunately, I have a pretty good idea...too many.

While the fiftieth anniversary may be recognized on different dates by many Nam veterans, the majority of us do share one thing that remains a symbol of our time over there. And although some of us were fortunate to come home physically, we often make return visits mentally, especially when we hear some of the music that came out in the 1960s. We had one song, the "Vietnam Veterans' National Anthem," while we were over there. Whenever we hear it today, our minds will wander off back in time, and Vietnam will appear. **"WE GOTTA GET OUT OF THIS PLACE, IF IT'S THE LAST THING WE EVER DO!"**

Many of us remain locked in the past and have been trying to get out of that place for five decades. Imagine having their nightmares for fifty years. One has never lived until one has almost lost a life in battle, and for those close to the fight, life has a weird but special flavor that the protected will never know.

On May 23, 2006, just before Memorial Day, *USA Today* printed the following profound headline:

USA VIETNAM: ONCE ENEMIES IN WAR, NOW PARTNERS IN TRADE...

While this revitalized relationship was already under construction before the Obama reign, it was under his watch that it became official that two former enemies in a long, bloody war had become partners in business and military. It was in 1954 that North Vietnam put the finishing touches on their unlikely victory over France and their South Vietnamese colony. Around the same time, the Korean War came to a climax, but a new war was already underway between the North Vietnamese and the USA, and again the South Vietnamese supported the invaders from the west.

Once again the Vietnamese would be challenged by another world superpower, to fight for their lives and to preserve their country from being eliminated. Once again the peasant-farmers of Vietnam would change over to warrior mode, for as long as it was required.

Many of my Vietnam War brothers were skeptical or even angry when the announcement came that the USA and Vietnam (a united North and South) were forging ahead with a strong trade relationship. I must admit that this writer had doubts about this happening, but I came to favor the deal as being a great thing for both countries, and I still feel that way. So do many Vietnam War veterans from both countries. However, there was one country that objected to this new and unlikely partnership...mainland China.

Unfortunately, around the same time Vietnam and the USA were buddying up, the Obama regime either fell asleep or just did not care, and a very, very old and dear ally, the Philippines, was distancing itself from being a USA buddy. Their relationship with China became the talk of the area in the Far East. Chalk one up for Obama and scratch one off for Obama and the USA. Maybe the new American president's staff can repair this once treasured relationship. I had an uncle, a U.S. Air Force captain, who fought alongside the Filipinos in World War II, and he always spoke highly of them. BTW, the Philippines supported the USA during the Vietnam War for twenty-three years, 1950–1973.

While China was a major supporter of North Vietnam against the U.S., China has also been one of the Vietnamese' oldest adversaries. But that was the past, and the Vietnamese appear to be focused on the future, with the U.S., Japan, South Korea, Thailand, India, and Australia as allies.

Aside from being the birthplace of two of the top military generals in the world's history, Vietnam can brag about its modern-day military capabilities as well as its economic future, making them a great ally to have on our side. Over the history of planet Earth, only two names are consistently ranked ahead of Vietnam's two monster generals—Tran Hung Dao and Vo Nguyen Giap. They are Alexander the Great and Napoleon Bonaparte. Even Genghis Khan and Julius Caesar rank behind Tran and Giap.[37]

Not far behind was another monster Vietnamese general, Nguyen Hue or King Quang Trung, who was credited with never losing a battle during his entire life. One of his most famous military victories came in the late 1780s when he led fifty thousand soldiers on a Sherman-like march of more than five hundred miles on foot in three days to confront thirty armies from China and defeat over two hundred thousand Chinese invaders. His victories were legendary to the Vietnamese even today...230 years later.

That extraordinary decade is celebrating its fiftieth anniversary one year at a time. The 1967 Tet Offensive turned fifty in January-February 2017; January-February 2018 will mark the fiftieth anniversary of the Tet Offensive of 1968. This is hard to swallow—fifty years ago we were fighting one of the most awesome yet primitive militaries in history. Whatever history chooses to call it, the Vietnam War was America's signature catastrophe over the last two and a half centuries. Therefore, it is just that America could be so heavily influenced by that little country of extremely hardy and resilient people.

Vietnam's economic growth through 2024 was projected to be at 4.8 percent per year higher than Canada, Mexico, or the USA. The population of Vietnam is pushing one hundred million people, not far behind the Russian population of 140 million.

Military strength of Vietnam in terms of quantity fares well with the rest of the world. I for one am very happy about this and that they are on our side. Here is how Vietnam compares militarily with the top six militaries in the world of one million or more:

Country	Active Personnel	Reserve Military	Paramilitary	Total
N. Korea	1,190,000	600,000	5,889,000	7,679,000
Vietnam	482,000	5,000,000	400,000	5,882,000
India	1,325,000	1,155,000	2,288,407	4,768,407
China	2,333,000	510,000	660,000	3,503,000
Russia	845,000	2,000,000	519,000	3,364,000
USA	1,492,200	843,750	14,000	2,349,500

---

37 www.thetoptens.com/top-military-generals

Not a surprise here that North Korea has the largest military force on the planet. This would indicate their intentions to invade South Korea again someday. Vietnam's military overall is larger than any other country in the world. Their 5,000,000 militia number is probably because of their history of invasions from the North. Vietnam is still poised to defend their country, not invade another. Still I find it refreshing to have them as one of our allies in the east, along with India, Thailand, Japan, and South Korea. FYI, outside of Vietnam there are more Vietnamese people living in the USA than any other country, and most of them are very positive contributors to our country.

People's Army of Vietnam (PAVN). Also known as the Vietnam People's Army (VPA), the PAVN is the military force of the Socialist Republic of Vietnam and is a part of the Vietnam People's Armed Forces. During the French Indochina War (1945–1954), the PAVN was Ho Chi Minh's Viet Minh. During the American Vietnam War (1959–1975), the army was referred to as the North Vietnamese Army (NVA). According to Hanoi's official history, the southern communists, or Viet Cong, were a branch of the VPA.

The first record of historical data showing the Vietnamese military as an organized force was in the ancient Hong Bang era from 2879–258 BC. Vietnamese history thereafter has not been peaceful. In fact the word *turbulent* is a common description used by educators and historians. The Vietnamese armed forces were generally credited with being one of the most professional, battle-hardened, and well-trained armies in all of Asia.

As most military buffs know, Ho Chi Minh and self-appointed General Vo Nguyen Giap initially put together what became the backbone of what the Vietnamese military machine would become from fighting the Japanese in World War II and other world powers in future wars. What many people are not aware of is it was an American OSS agent who trained, armed, and led the Viet Minh those days in fighting the Japanese. Archimedes Patti has been referred to as the founding father of the PAVN. The 2018 version of the PAVN is a formidable force, capable of making their ancestors proud if needed.

They Still Like Us. Usually when Vietnamese are talking about America, they are talking about freedom. Many are still fascinated by America: its freedom, its energy, its robust work ethic, and its robust economy. They do have some doubts about our overpowering role around the world. To many Vietnamese America is still the best country in the world, even though they also see Americans acting like they are the head of the family, doing things without asking or listening to anybody. They see America imposing its ideas on the rest of the world. While they seem to admire us, many have become cautious over how and how much to embrace our way of life. They are wary of copying too much of the American way of life, like relations between men and women and between children and parents. Everything seems so loose that personal relationships in America do not run as days and as sentimental as with Vietnamese people. These days they may be right.

Vietnamese see America as a country with a lot of violence amongst its population, but our massive immigrant cultures seem to blend better than other countries. Our society is well organized in the eyes of many Vietnamese.

They tend to agree that they did not defeat us on the battlefield, as our firepower was too great. But defeating the U.S.-backed South Vietnamese government set up by the French is good enough for them to celebrate as victors. Since the end result served their purpose, honestly, most of the younger Vietnamese don't really care about what happened in the French and American wars. They just want to enjoy their freedom and have fun. However, one would find many young Vietnamese who have lost grandparents in those wars, and their absence is felt.

We talk about our POWs and MIAs of the Vietnam War, whose numbers pale compared to the estimated three hundred thousand Vietnamese soldiers still missing from the war. While the older people still reminisce about the wars, the young people usually mind their own business as they cannot relate.

As Vietnam has become one of the fastest growing economies in Asia and around the world, communism still rules, but more capitalism is allowed than some people think. Many Vietnamese actually relish the great personal freedom they have in modern-day Vietnam. In fact a fairly recent Pew Survey found over 90 percent of the Vietnamese people support free market capitalism.

By 2014, approximately 1.5 million Vietnamese immigrants resided in the USA. The USA is the top destination country for Vietnamese migrants, with Australia a distant second, followed by Canada. Compared to other foreign-born citizens of America, Vietnamese tend to have higher incomes and lower poverty rates.

Over half of all Vietnamese American immigrants reside in California (38%) and Texas (15%). As one would expect, the largest influx of Vietnamese immigrants followed the year of 1975, when the Vietnam War ended. The ties to the mother country remain strong as Vietnamese from around the world send over $12.5 billion back to Vietnam, which is equal to 6 percent of Vietnam's annual GDP according to data from the World Bank. The United States Vietnamese-born citizens send approximately $8 billion to

Vietnam annually. This equals a greater amount of money being sent to Vietnam from all countries in the world combined.[38]

I personally found a desperate need for more information about the Vietnam War with America. But it is not easy to access from the Vietnamese viewpoint.

It seems most Americans who lived in the 1960s would prefer to white out every troubling memory of the Vietnam War and just recognize it with a "welcome home" or "thank you for your service" comment. And that's all right…sort of. But the truths of Vietnam were barely or rarely confronted. People turned their heads and focused on what was next…just like that. But how do you throw away millions of memories of KIAs and many, many more millions who were wounded mentally and/or physically? You can't, and I won't do it here, not on this section. But see how a Vietnam veteran's mind wanders off? This paragraph almost became a whole new subject. Can't help that, sorry. I just don't want to leave this world without doing something to keep the Vietnam War era from going down for the count, being left as a dark family secret that no one will ever talk about again. God, that thought scares me.

Gotta Love Them "Gooks"… First I need to clarify that calling an Asian, particularly a Vietnamese, a "gook" is no different than referring to a black person as "nigger." Neither of those two words are part of my vocabulary. However, during the Vietnam War and for at least a decade afterward, my most common reference to the Vietnamese adversary I fought against was a "gook." But no more. And honestly, having grown up in mixed neighborhoods, I have never adopted the "N" word into my vocabulary, even if others around me commonly used it. I just never accepted it, still don't, never will.

With Vietnam being such a common topic in the news during the 1960s and 1970s, why have the Vietnamese not been major news topics around the world or in the United States over the last couple of decades? How/why has Vietnam gone from being the most dangerous place in the world during the 1960s–70s to being one of the "safest places on Earth"?

I mean, once a gook, always a gook, right? This is what was pounded into our brains as we were going through our military training and then were sent as sacrificial lambs to become avid killers of the gooks. Shame on the politicians in Washington, D.C. (the swamp) responsible for this… May they get their punishment in hell.

Vietnam today, as it was in past centuries, is a homogeneous country, the Kinh Viet being the dominant ethnic group with 90 percent of the population. So there is little ethnic tension and there are few terrorist acts. Religion

---

38 www.thenation.com as well as paraphrased from U.S. Census Bureau statistics 062014.

is practiced freely. The society is not plagued by criminals as the people are not violent. They are very content and comfortable with their heritage and having their own country. In fact Vietnam is often called the safest and most stable country in Southeast Asia. Despite being governed by communism, the people hardly know it, and the one political party state makes Vietnam rarely fazed by negative news.

The worst threat today's Vietnamese are faced with might be the unexploded bombs and artillery rounds that threaten the countryside. Or the continuing effects of Agent Orange and what it does to Vietnamese children. China continues to be a nemesis to Vietnam as it has been for over two thousand years. But the Vietnamese never back down, they never have, and I would be shocked if they ever do.

The Vietnam War / Civil War lasted almost twenty years, ending in 1975. The Cambodian and Sino-Vietnamese followed, lasted another ten years and hindering the development of the Vietnamese economy. Then the American trade embargo further held them back.

Over the last fifteen years, Vietnam has moved forward as an economically developed and friendly country. This is a young country; over 50 percent of their hundred million people are younger than thirty-five as of 2016. Vietnam will continue to shine as an ally, which is far better than not. I would think that combined with its large organized society, it is likely that Vietnam will be more newsworthy internationally in a positive way.

Please take in some comments I discovered online from some recent travelers who visited Vietnam:

"There was a noticeable stoic politeness that my wife and I found very appealing."

"One of the first things we noticed was that Vietnamese people are very reserved."

"As a foreign visitor, I found Vietnam to be a wonderful country. I can look forward to a return visit soon."

"Money is inflated; it was difficult to keep track of all the zeroes in the exchanges. I thought Saigon (Ho-Chi Minh City) was quiet. People were surprisingly friendly, always trying to feed us—then await our reaction."

"As a Vietnam veteran I felt compelled to visit the Cu Chi tunnels. I could see other tourists not liking their experiences, so I doubt many return visits happened with them. Even to me it was terrifying just as I thought it would be. They were like miles of endless giant rat holes and hard to believe that entire families and entire armies lived there for much of their lives. Dirt kept falling in on my hair and eyes and I found it difficult to breathe let alone see. I imagined the unfriendlies down there, like poisonous spiders and snakes. I don't mind admitting that I did not last even ten minutes on that tour."

"The rest of Vietnam was very pleasing and I would return, leaving Cu Chi out."

—American Vietnam vet, tourist

Since the war's end, the Vietnam government has done a miraculous job of replanting the areas that were devastated by hundreds of thousands of explosions, napalm, and of course Agent Orange herbicides. Vietnam over time has enjoyed a rebirth of sorts in that it is once again referred to as a land of exotic beauty. I am glad and anyone reading this should be too.

Here is one friendly bit of advice if you plan to visit Vietnam some day: Don't ever ask a Vietnamese if they came from ancient China.

From what I can gather, most of the people of Vietnam came from northern and central Vietnam. I have done extensive research on this, have spoken to several Vietnamese about it, and there is little doubt about this. If the Vietnamese originated from China, there would have to be evidence of a noticeable genetic change, but none has ever been found. If anyone doesn't want to simply take this author's statement as enough proof, please conduct your own research and share the results with me.

I love the pride most people have toward their country, and yes, it is a form of nationalism without even a hint of racism. Too bad that the liberal Americans call conservatives who show off their nationalism as being racist. They could learn many lessons from the Vietnamese.

"It is an established fact that all Vietnamese in Vietnam share a common gene, culture, and traditions and a common history. Cultural differences came mostly from the western presence in the south, the French and Americans."

—Luong Manh Tuan
Ethnic Vietnamese

During the Mongol invasions in the thirteenth century, Dai Viet and Champa joined forces to fight off the Mongols; otherwise, all of Southeast Asia might have become part of Mongolia or China. However, Champa and Dai Viet would go to war with each other often after the Mongol threat was over. Eventually Dai Viet (North Vietnam) would conquer Champa (South Vietnam), and so Vietnam stands strong and united today, and the Vietnamese are by no means "gooks."

Le Cong Huan was a patriot from birth. He was born in the heart of Southern Vietnam, the Mekong Delta region, before his country was forced into a divided nation of South and North Vietnam. As a teenager he made an easy choice and joined Ho Chi Minh's army of Viet Minh guerrilla fighters. He thought it was right to fight against those responsible for the split of the country he loved, and that meant going against the despised French imperialists.

He had been trained in North Vietnam to become a combat infantry officer and lead his comrades of the Viet Cong army in the south. Although first wounded at the 1963 battle of Ap Bac against a combined American/South Vietnamese force, he returned to the battlefield to resume his leadership role once he was healed. Le Cong was already looked at as a hero, as the Ap Bac battle was an unexpected victory for the Viet Cong. Even though he would be wounded again and then again, he returned to battle each time, where he fought on until the end of the war came in 1975.

Over fifty years from the day he was wounded at the battle of Ap Bac, he is still reminded of the war by his physical wounds, fragments embedded in parts of his body. Those wounds, as painful as they were, do not plague him like his mental wounds do. He rarely complains to anyone and he has tried so hard to put his past behind him. In fact he has met several American veterans of the same war as they were visiting his country. He harbors no ill will toward them; he felt quite happy to meet them. He has never met a French veteran who he fought against when he was with Uncle Ho's Viet Minh. Maybe they could not face us, he thinks, but he could meet with them if the opportunity came.

Today, he is still in 2018 a Vietnamese citizen, a patriotic nationalist to his country. The communist rule has not been as bad as some people have reported, and their ways keep getting better—most Vietnamese know this. He thinks it was the right thing to do for the communists to punish the South Vietnamese who fought side by side with the French and Americans. He is still confused why the Americans invaded his country after the French left.

Le Cong Huan is very enthusiastic about the present relationship his country has developed and nurtured with the United States. He remembers how Ho Chi Minh had admired the U.S. and that he came to the American presidents first, his pleas landing on deaf ears—forcing him to seek support from the communist countries to battle the French. That was so long ago and now Uncle Ho's dream seems to have come true half a century later. He looks forward to an even greater relationship and a brighter future with the Americans, where Vietnamese children are visiting America and get to know the Americans.

Vietnam in 2013 was talked about around the world—how it had been transformed from one of the poorest countries in the world into a lower-middle-class-income country. Suddenly Vietnam was being looked at as one of the most dynamic emerging countries in the entire East Asia region.

Economic and political reforms under Doi Moi, which began in 1986, had boosted rapid growth and development. Since 1990, Vietnam's GDP per capita growth has been among the fastest in the entire world, with a dramatic reduction in poverty and improved social outcomes, and more than forty million people escaped from poverty over the course of just two decades. Remember that Vietnam was doing this despite the long and hard sanctions put on their country by the U.S.

In 2015, Vietnam had a young labor force, one that was well trained and highly educated. It was one of the highest information technology growth countries from 1995 to 2008. It has progressed in its industrialization and modernization to catch up and keep up with neighboring countries. In 2016, China was slowing down.

In 2017, Vietnam's GDP rate in the third quarter hit a record high of 7.46 percent. Almost out of nowhere, its tourism sector shot up, and Vietnam hardly even tried to make it grow. But continued development challenges and limitations remain for Vietnam in order to keep pace with their phenomenal growth.

A couple of decades ago, Vietnam could easily have been referred to as a third world country, as our U.S. presidents called it during the Vietnam War. In the 1990s, only 84 percent of the population used electricity as their main source of lighting, and now (2017–18) that figure has shot up to 99 percent. Only 36 percent had access to sanitation facilities, while that has grown to 67 percent in 2017–18. Clean water was shared by a mere 31 percent of the population in the 1990s with that figure doubling to 67 percent. The government has continued to show reform commitment with its 2011–2020 Socio-Economic Development Strategy (SEDS).

Anyone visiting Vietnam today would be impressed by its natural beauty. Most of the Agent Orange-damaged forests and jungles have grown back, and Vietnamese people in general are warm and hospitable—unless someone visits with invade-and-conquer plans. The Vietnamese have a long history of expelling invaders no matter who they are.

By the end of 2017, almost five million people with Vietnamese ancestry lived in the United States. Reverse migration back to Vietnam is very small compared to the incoming flow every year. So I guess they haven't found the good old USA such a terrible and racist country? I am not surprised; I just wish more Americans recognized this. God bless America!

Why is it that the people of Vietnam today do not hold the ill feelings toward American Vietnam veterans as so many American citizens did for decades after the war ended and even today, like Laurence M. Vance mentioned in Chapter 15? Why?

Samsung makes Vietnam's farmers and peasants "richer than bankers" in 2016—WOW! The South Korean electronics giant moved into the rice paddies of Bac Ninh province of Northern Vietnam and started rolling out smartphones around 2008. This and other invented gadgets forced the sleepy province into Vietnam's second-biggest exporting center after Ho Chi Minh City. And this is just one example of what has been happening in Vietnam for the last couple of decades.

Farmers have become business people. Samsung spurred the economic growth of the entire nation. This move was called the first stage in Vietnam's plan to inherit a slice of the manufacturing mantle of their northern neighbor China. And before China woke up, Vietnam had struck again and again. Is that good "payback" for all those invasions or what?

Vietnam plans to continue to strengthen their businesses and long-term haven of investment have created a healthier working environment. People who have moved from the rice paddies to production lines receive much higher earnings, social security benefits, pensions, sick leave, etc. Is this how communism works? Ha, ha, ha. So I say, is the joke on Ho Chi Minh or the United States or China? Think about it long and hard, seriously.

Hard to believe, but despite the horribly infamous history of Vietnam's war with America, Vietnam today (2018) seems to be one of the most pro-American countries in Southeast Asia or the world for that matter. Who would have predicted this twenty to forty years ago—that diplomatic relations would be heading in this direction with a country that named itself the **Socialist Republic of Vietnam?**

Well, both our countries are republics, and Ho Chi Minh himself had always been an admirer of the USA's path to becoming a free republic. So what else does Vietnam have in common with its former adversary, the United States of America?

In the earlier part of 2018, Vietnam surprised many global leaders by holding a ceremony that featured some key developments in Vietnam's recent plan to be a part of what the United States does—involvement in international peacekeeping. Uncle Ho must be smiling if he is still watching the country he reunified.

Even though Vietnam's participation in the United Nations' peacekeeping operations just began five years ago, they have made great strides forward in the development of its relations with the international community. I wish more of the Vietnam haters would enlighten themselves on what Vietnam has become since ridding its country of foreign intruders from the late 1940s (France) into the early 1960s (USA).

An interesting move that took place in March 2018 saw Vietnam and Laos take larger steps to work together with joint military positions, mainly to manage the borders between their countries. Maybe Mexico and the United States should try the same thing? Why is it that two longtime democratic countries have not been able to do what two one-party communist states have been doing very successfully...*working together*?

Our politicians should take ego-reducing pills and do now what they should have done before engaging in a war without end, with a country that had already fought and won dozens of wars before the USA was even born.

The present generation of Vietnamese Nationalists have quickly come of age since the aftermath of the war. They may have done this because they have carried on the tradition of Tran Hung Dao. Following his example wouldn't be such a bad trail to navigate. All Tran Hung Dao did was... **exterminate the Mongol hordes three times!**

One more profound example of the persistence and resilience of the Vietnamese when fighting for their homeland happened in the war with France in 1941–1954.

In January 1951, General Giap launched a new offensive against the French and South Vietnamese pro-French army. With an expanded army of forty thousand Viet Minh supported by millions of villagers on call, Giap attacked French garrisons near Hanoi with human wave attacks which were advised by China. Fortunately, Uncle Ho intervened and directed his Viet Minh to revert back to guerrilla war before the entire Viet Minh army was removed from the face of planet Earth by a devastating attack from the sky of deadly American-supplied napalm bombs. Over six thousand Viet Minh were killed, their bodies burned to a crisp. As horrible as it was to die this way, guess what? Giap reorganized his battered and confused Viet Minh army and counterattacked the French, catching them completely off guard repeatedly. This may have been the beginning of the end for France as their vaunted combat forces were demoralized. The war ended just one year later.

This time the Viet Minh were joined by Laos Pathet Lao guerrillas and Vietnamese mountain tribes to confront the French and French-backed South Vietnamese army. It wasn't long before Uncle Ho's tenacious forces led by Giap wore down the French and overran them at several battles with Dien Bien Phu the climax.

As I have said, I am glad to have Vietnam as an ally, not an enemy, and I would fight with them against anyone unfriendly to them, except my own country of course. I think if Ho Chi Minh could see his country today, he would be all smiles as his dream has come true.

Brief Look at Vietnam Military 2018

Vietnam's Future Global Military Value. On the 2018 Power index score listed on Global Firepower.com, Vietnam ranks twentieth when it comes to waging a prolonged campaign against another country. A reminder that outside of the Cambodian War of the late 1970s, all of Vietnam's wars over their three-thousand-year history of wars had been purely defensive types. In each situation the Vietnamese were fighting off an enemy invader of their homeland. Going beyond fighting strictly a self-defense war, here are some of the key factors to consider Vietnam's chances of succeeding in a different style of war:

Total Population	96,160,163
Manpower Available	50,650,000
Fit For Service	41,505,000
Reaching Military Age	1,650,000
Total Military Persons	5,488,500
Active Military	4,448,500
Reserve Military	5,040,000

Vietnam's modernized air force includes fixed wing and rotary wing (helicopter) aircraft from their air force, army, and navy. While Vietnam's military's main strengths are more suitable to ground wars, their aircraft strength is on the rise; they currently have over three hundred total aircraft, including nearly a hundred attack aircraft. Their helicopter strength includes 164 craft.

On the ground Vietnam currently has 3,150 armored fighting vehicles, including 1,545 combat tanks. They also have over 2,700 artillery pieces and 1,200 rocket projectors. It appears that Vietnam's navy strength is not overpowering. They have no aircraft carriers or destroyers.

Vietnam was the first Southeast Asian nation to arm its submarines with deadly land attack cruise missiles. North Vietnam did not even have submarines in the Vietnam-America War.[39]

Vietnam's best days as a global military power may be ahead of them. But for now, they do just fine as any country's ally, hopefully the USA's.

---

39 TheDiplomat.com4/30/15

Chapter 14

OLD SOLDIERS' STORIES,
AMERICA'S HISTORY...PLEASE LOVE THEM

Who cares about Vietnam today? Some snide Americans might ask this question if they happen to stumble on this book, or any of the other Vietnam War books; there are thousands of them. Obviously a Vietnam War veteran would still maintain an interest in what people are saying or writing about the Vietnam War era. Relatives and friends of Vietnam War vets would also be a given.

Those who took a staunch antiwar stand back in the 1960s and 1970s may not carry much of a desire to be reeducated about those troubling times. I can understand this but I also strongly believe these are the people who should have an interest in Vietnam Era books. Unfortunately, my experiences have shown me that the Vietnam Era's antiwar population does not have much interest in someone opening up those years, so why should I bother trying to keep telling the Vietnam War veteran's story if half of America does not want to know what really happened so long ago?

Anyone who doesn't recognize that the Vietnam Era is still referenced often in the news has probably been in denial that the earth is round, or they have been in a coma for the last couple of decades. Believe me, they are out there.

Many younger people continue to express an interest in knowing more about the Vietnam War and the Americans who were touched by it. Doesn't it seem like the media has gagged each president with their own Vietnam? Iraq was Bush's. Afghanistan is often related to the Obama administration. President Trump's Vietnam, as of today, January 24, 2018, hasn't been designated yet. The options for this one remain frightening to even think about.

Believe it or not, there are many people from the Vietnam War era who are still open to and are searching for the truth in support of the decisions they chose to live with back then, whether they fought in the war, ran away from it, supported it, or protested against it. Many Americans have just recently discovered that the information fed to them by the Ameri-Cong media is not real or complete. If people have little or no interest in learning the unquestionable truth about incorrect beliefs which they have chosen to accept and live with, no matter what the other evidence tells them...maybe God can help them.

The struggles of Vietnam War veterans and all veterans are not just stories. They are the heart and soul of our great country's history. Without these stories to tell and share, all Americans could easily be speaking English... as a secondary language!

Since we are not required to speak another language as primero uno like German, Japanese, Russian, or Chinese (Vietnamese was never a threat), the proper thank-you belongs to those Americans who have been making stories for the rest of us to hear or read about over and over for as long as we are breathing and speaking English today.

It is discomforting or even funny how certain situations are different when we were actually living them out versus once we are out of the episode and how they are looked at or described in hindsight. Our feelings and perceptions about those situations will change over time and they will continue to change unless we cling to the past with a death grip. For those who find it difficult or impossible to let go, that could end up being the death of them.

The events, actions, and results of the stories we tell from our experiences in the Vietnam War will or should remain the same. Notice that we may tell the same stories a little differently each time, but the ending remains as it was. What happens to misreported stories like when a medic person recounts a battle he or she witnessed portions of and then documents what he or she saw from their perspective. An example being...I have talked to some soldiers who claim they were actually there as participants at the famous 1965 battle at Ia Drang in Vietnam. Each story has varied quite a bit and that is all I say on that. Know that a very credible warrior who fought at and survived Ia Drang contacted me as he was reading my first book, *Condemned Property?*

As we know, approximately 2.7 to 2.9 million Americans served at varying times in-country during the official years of the Vietnam War from 1963 to 1972. Of that estimated total, less than 20 percent were assigned to a bona fide front line combat unit—about 580,000 troops in total. Even less were actually trained and sent to the field to engage in face-to-face combat situations, leaving that total at 12 percent and less than three hundred thousand. Keep in mind, 80 percent of the war's casualties, 362,924, were from these units. That total resulted in 290,339 casualties from the field and 72,584 from the so-called "secure" base camps and cities. So, depending on who is listening when a Vietnam vet is talking about how it was over "there," you could get a couple million variations of stories and not all are credible.

There could be some Nam vets who disagree with some things in my books. Fortunately, I have run into very, very few of those so far—about three, I think, and even that low number bothered me as I tended to think they were the phony "wannabe" Nam vets. Too bad. Please know that this writer has received hundreds of letters from "real" Nam vets expressing their satisfaction and appreciation for doing my first two books. Only one negative review was entered on amazon.com or barnesandnoble.com. That opinion carries very little merit with me, but hey…freedom of expression goes both ways.

Endorsements have come from virtually every veteran's organization, which made me feel really good. It would be difficult to pick out just one review that stood out above all others, and I do not have just one favorite. But here are the thoughts and opinions toward my first book sent to me by a Nam brother, a survivor of the 1965 battle of Ia Drang, that I treasure very much, paraphrased below:

Dusty, I recently came across your book, Condemned Property? *while researching for a forthcoming event. For me,* Condemned Property? *has been a great read and déjà vu. I know firsthand and absolutely identify with the exasperating experience of dealing with the Veterans Administration and coincidentally, identical to some of your experiences with having been finally diagnosed (it took years) with service-connected diabetes II. I look forward to talking with you, but I am writing you today on a more upbeat tone to obtain permission to include some of the text from your book in connection with a forthcoming 50th Anniversary Honorarium Tribute to one of our unit's battles in 1965.*

Dusty, I am one of the survivors of the Ia Drang Valley battle of 1965 and I have been nominated by my fellow veterans to serve as the representative of these survivors for the 50th Anniversary Celebration Honorarium of 2015. This is a project of the U.S. Army Entertainment Detachment (Soldier Show) based at Fort Sam Houston, San Antonio, Texas. The 2015 Soldier Show will travel from May to November 2015 to 35 army bases in the USA and abroad. I intend to use excerpts from the book We Were Soldiers *by Lt. General Hal Moore and co-author Joe Galloway. I know them both personally. We have also asked Mel Gibson to appear in a special salute. As you may know, he appeared in the 2002 movie of the same name,* We Were Soldiers.

Please accept this as my request for permission to use excerpts from your book, Condemned Property? *I cannot promise credit recognition for the use of your writing yet, but I can promise that I will request permission for inclusion of your book title if possible in the video credits portion of the Soldier Show. Please feel free to call me anytime; would love speaking with you.*

Best Regards,
Patrick Stephenson
7th Cav—1st Cavalry Infantry
U.S. Army, Vietnam, 1967–1968

FYI, the Battle of Ia Drang was one of our war's bloodiest battles for both sides, and it should have been a real eye opener for the bureaucrats in Washington, D.C., as well as the top brass officers with stars on their shoulders, but it was ignored and filed as a great victory. Anyway, Patrick Stephenson, who fought in this historic battle, became the narrator at the shows. Patrick's grandfather served in World War I, his father served in World War II, Patrick in Vietnam, his son served in the first Gulf War, and a grandson served in Operation Iraqi Freedom. **I wonder how writer Larry Vance (mentioned in Chapter 15) would behave if somehow he had to face the entire Stephenson five-some.**

Who are these guys? The Vietnam War produced a bushel or two of rough and tough, in-your-face type of warriors. Most proud Americans would be eager to bring them home for dinner and some of Mom's apple pie, if they only knew who they were. I've served with a few of them, but I can hardly say that it was a pleasurable experience. Blood, pain, and death never are. But who are these guys?

Most of us are familiar with the likes of Col. Bud Day, Col. David Hackworth, Gen. Colin Powell, Gen. Norman Schwarzkopf, and Col. Oliver North, but Vietnam's ugly and extremely unpopular war produced a slew of genuine heroes who remain unknown to much of America today.

Major Leo Keith Thorsness took on the unenviable assignment of seeking and destroying the dangerously accurate surface-to-air missile (SAM) sites where our B-52 bombers were killed from. Needless to say he had to be a very capable flyboy to avoid being shot down himself, and that danger presented itself on every mission. So, one might think it was just a matter of time before his number would inevitably be called out on one of the F-106F fighter bombers he piloted.

On December 2, 1966, Thorsness earned a Distinguished Flying Cross for one of his dangerous missions. That was the first of six of these super valorous awards. One year later in early 1967, he received his first of two Silver Stars.

On April 19, 1967, shortly after he destroyed two SAM sites, he noticed another F-105 fighter had taken hits from anti-aircraft guns and was going down. The two occupants, Maj. Tom Madison and Maj. Tom Sterling, were descending with opened parachutes when a Russian MIG-17 started to bear down on them. They were sitting ducks. Thorsness responded to the situation instantly, engaging and destroying the MIG and then proceeding in a dangerous "catch me if you can" with several other MIGs, leading them away from the parachuters. The actions that followed Maj. Thorsness solidified his nomination for the Medal of Honor.

Unfortunately, less than two weeks after the April 19th mission, he was shot down in a rear attack by a MIG-21. He and Capt. Harold E. Johnson managed to parachute safely into the hands of North Vietnamese ground troops and became POWs for six years. They were tortured to the point of permanent bodily harm, as was the case for many American POWs from the Vietnam War.

On March 4, 1973, Thorsness was freed during Operation Homecoming, and President Nixon presented the MOH award to him. After retiring from the air force, he entered into a political career, winning an election for a Washington state senator position in 1988. In 2010–11, he served as president of the Congressional Medal of Honor Society and lived the rest of his life in quiet dignity; however, he died prematurely on May 2, 2017. So that's who this guy was.

Beyond normal sea warfare. Some of the first Americans sent to Vietnam were Seabees, as early as 1954. I used to chuckle whenever one of my Vietnam vet Seabee brothers would say, "We fight too." In Nam I did not have any experience with Seabees; we had our counterparts with the U.S. Army's combat engineers, and I know firsthand what they were called for in Vietnam. Infantry grunts and combat engineers often shared dangerous combat situations.

One of my best friends to this day, Jack Bellemy, was a combat engineer who worked and fought with our unit, the 3rd 22nd Walking Regulars of the 25th Infantry. Two other very good friends of mine to this day were Seabees in the Vietnam Wars, Bill McDonald and J.R. Wager. Trust me, these Nam vets were tough. The Construction Battalions were created during World War II and were assigned to the marines. They were building camps and runways for the U.S. Army's Special Forces (Green Berets) in the late 1950s into the early 1960s.

On February 1, 1965, Petty Officer 2nd Class Marvin Glen Shields appeared on the scene during the Vietnam War just as America was beefing up its forces to confront the communist Viet Cong and North Vietnamese Army. From March to June, Shields and his fellow Seabees built the Special Forces camp at Ben Soi. The base included a total of nine Seabees, eleven Green Berets, and about three hundred local tribal fighters.

On June 5, 1965, the Seabees began construction on a runway for the camp at Dong Xoai. Still under construction, the camp received a full attack by two regiments of Viet Cong, about two thousand soldiers with artillery and mortar support. Over four hundred rounds hit the camp in the first three hours, killing two Green Berets, several Vietnamese tribesmen, and one Seabee. Shields was wounded in the initial attack.

As the VC fanatical assault intensified with repeated human wave attacks at around 2:30 a.m., the first line of defense was overrun and the defenses had to fall back, including Shields.

Shields was wounded in the face for his second wound, but he kept firing at the enemy. He stopped once to rescue a wounded man and drag him to safety. Of major concern was a VC machine gun nest that had inflicted heavy casualties in the early stages of the attack. Shields, already wounded twice, volunteered along with Special Forces 2nd Lt. Charles Quincy Williams, who had also been wounded. Together with a 3.5-inch rocket launcher, they destroyed the machine gun and its crew. While returning to their main defenses, both men were wounded again. Shields' wound was more serious and he had to be dragged by Williams. Most of the Vietnamese natives had been killed or captured, and fourteen of the fifteen Americans still alive were wounded.

Helicopters were called on to rescue the remaining Americans who were at their last line of defense. Two choppers were shot down, killing both crews, but three choppers were able to complete their mission and rescue the fourteen wounded Americans. Shields did not survive the battle. On June 23, 1966, President Johnson presented the Medal of Honor to Williams on behalf of Shields. Williams then presented the posthumous medal to the widow of Marvin Shields, the only Navy Seabee awarded the nation's highest valor award. So now you've heard of this guy.

Long Live the Medic! In the marines, they're called corpsmen. Medic or corpsman, to the combat grunt, they were like human gods to us in battle, and I have never met a medic I did not absolutely love.

On November 8, 1965, again when the Vietnam Conflict was maturing to actually be called the Vietnam War, the 1st Battalion, 503rd infantry Regiment of the 173rd Airborne Brigade was attacked Viet Cong style—surprise ambush. Nearly fifty Americans would die in this battle with almost a hundred wounded. This is how a perfectly conducted ambush can work with quick and massive casualties.

This battle earned its own song by the country stars Big & Rich, called "8th of November," with the introduction read by Kris Kristofferson.

The KIA total would have been worse, but one medic of the 173rd would have none of it as he performed above and beyond what he was trained for…
SAVING LIVES!

Specialist Lawrence Joel, a black man who did not see the color of a man's skin, fought furiously, inflicting heavy casualties on a fanatical enemy. But he did much more than fight and kill the adversary warriors who had ambushed his beloved brothers. What Lawrence Joel did that day takes a backseat to none of America's long list of Audie Murphy-type heroes. Someone must not have told him that there were three battalions of Viet Cong out there trying to kill him, especially him, as he was running around during the battle, patching up the wounded until he ran out of supplies.

Joel resisted the order from superiors to stay low to the ground, and risked his life over and over, even after he was shot twice in his right leg. Then he continued hobbling around the battlefield with a makeshift crutch, searching for medical supplies from dead comrades, and he continued improvising efforts to keep the many wounded living a while longer until they could be rescued by medevac helicopters after the daylong battle ended. Joel would be placed onto one of those choppers with his brothers and eventually had to be sent to a major hospital in Saigon and then Tokyo.

The strategic base of Bien Hoa could have been the ultimate target for the Viet Cong that day, but Lawrence Joel's 173 Airborne unit stood between the enemy and Bien Hoa. Lawrence Joel was the first living black American since the Spanish-American War to receive the United States Medal of Honor along with a Silver Star and a Purple Heart to go with it.[40]

Navy's Audie Murphy. Even though I spent my tour in Nam as a pure grunt, a unique opportunity was presented to us in July 1968. We were pulling bridge security while the engineers were doing extensive repair on the Phu Cuong Bridge in III Corps. For several days we were directed to ride with the navy's riverine patrol boats (PBR). At first some of us thought we were being given a break from our search-and-destroy patrols, which were grueling and dangerous. However, on the second day of my ride on a PBR, we took enemy fire from both riverbanks, and guess what? There was nowhere to hide!

While we were firing back and calling in airstrikes, at the same time the skipper, captain, or whatever they called the guy steering the boat put it into high gear, and we got out of the line of fire without any KIAs, although three men were wounded. There were four navy guys and two infantry riflemen aboard. After that some of us weren't as eager to jump on board as a rifleman on the next PBR ride. In the jungle, when you were ambushed you could usually find cover behind something. Well, this brings me to sharing a very brief version of the story about one of the most decorated enlisted sailors in the navy's history: James Elliott "Willy" Williams, a Vietnam War veteran.

Will Williams was one of those guys many people have read about, as he enlisted in the U.S. Navy with a phony birth certificate in 1947 long after WWII had ended. But the "skirmish" on the Korean peninsula would present him the opportunity to serve his country during wartime. He served at that time on the destroyer USS *Douglas H. Fox* and some duty on other vessels from 1953 to 1966.

Then in May 1966, just when another "conflict" in Southeast Asia was hinting at becoming a war, the South Carolina-born boatswain's mate first

---

40 Paraphrased from *Purple Heart Magazine*

class served with a Patrol Boat River 106 or PBR. As I stated earlier, this duty on the inland waterways was not a joy ride. This duty would not allow Willy and his mates much time for reading or sightseeing. From July 1 to the end of August, Willy was thrown into precarious situations which would earn him several medals of valor quickly and furiously as they say. Bronze Star–Valor number one, the Bronze Star–Valor number two, and then a Silver Star along with a Purple Heart, which few if any except maybe John Kerry really would want to get. But this Navy hero was just getting started. The following awards of valor, honor, and distinction would find a cozy spot on Willy's chest: the Medal of Honor, the Navy Cross, the Navy and Marine Corps Medal of Honor, the Legion of Merit-Valor, Two Navy Commendation Medals-Valor, and he ended his epic career with three Purple Hearts.

Mr. Williams was personally active in the saving of many American lives. He was no Tinker Bell when forced into face-to-face combat situations. On several encounters with the Viet Cong in 1966 and 1967, just when the conflict really became a genuine war, Willy was directly involved with or assisted in the demise of more than a thousand enemy soldiers and the destruction or capture of dozens of enemy watercraft.

Willy Williams is often referred to as the Audy Murphy of the river.

James Elliott "Willy" Williams passed away on October 13, 1999, and just four years later in 2003, the U.S. Navy launched the Arleigh Burke-class destroyer USS *James E. Williams*.

I would be wrong if I tried to paint the image of Vietnam veterans as not having a mean streak in them. Mean streaks were inevitable for most combat-trained troops, especially those sent to engage the Viet Cong in face-to-face, intensely cruel, violent combat. During a life-threatening ambush and a firefight that followed, it was not a time to turn the other cheek and expect to survive the moment. Know that this is a fact: even though there were times when a village of seemingly innocent civilians fell victim to our own firepower, more often than not, the American ground combat warriors found themselves in save-and-rescue mode, trying to preserve the lives of women and children from merciless slaughter by their own Viet Cong countrymen. If anyone found themselves caught in the middle of undesirable situations, it was the American combat-trained soldier boy in the Vietnam War.

How could Americans back home not love their own victimized warriors in this war? Because the real truth was withheld from them until well after the war had ended. The untold truths about the Vietnam War were never more damaging to the American ground troops than during the six-year period in the 1960s, heading up to what was never expected with the bloodiest year of the war in 1968. While it may have been true that the VC strength in South Vietnam was a mere five thousand in 1959, intelligence gatherers had fallen asleep during 1960 and 1964, as their reports showed that less than forty thousand VC existed by 1964. The truth is that at least a hundred thousand were now in place. That number would skyrocket upward in 1967 and 1968.

Since the heavy American military build-up had not gotten underway until 1967, the primary targets for the Viet Cong were the innocent villagers in the countryside. Those who would not join up with or agree in some way to support the VC were punished. In fact, by the end of 1965, a Radio Hanoi broadcast announced publicly that the VC had been successful in destroying more than 7,500 South Vietnamese hamlets. This is what many of us came to believe was our purpose over there…to save lives. But in order to do that, we had no choice but to take lives along the way to protect the villages from destruction. Had the Ameri-Cong media reported these stories of the Vietnam War instead of painting a story of poor little patriotic Viet Cong being sense-lessly killed by Americans…America would have loved us—not hated us.

Fifty years later, even more for some, many Vietnam War vets are unable to forget that love we never received on our homecomings. I ask those of you who were not returning Vietnam War veterans at eighteen to twenty-five years old—put yourselves into that situation and try to think how you might have dealt with it.

If two countries with powerful militaries went to war and they both badly underestimated each other, the inevitable outcome would spell disaster. The after-effects would last for decades for both adversaries. They could even be called catastrophic for both sides.

This is precisely what happened, and the after-shocks of this unusual war remain in motion, seeming like they will never go away. Only now, many of the so-called survivors have become victims, and those wounded old soldiers are still hoping for just a little love before their time is up.

Having overcome and soundly defeated one of the most formidable military forces in history in terms of relentless determination and cunning-ness, tenacity and resilience, the American soldier boy was in many ways a hero above all the rest America has ever sent to battle. And yet, they were not respected, not appreciated, not accepted, and rarely honored when they returned from living hell. Here is an old soldier's tale about his war:

Three Aces! This Vietnam War veteran's military decorations include multiple awards, except the Medal of Honor. Just like Colonel David Jack-worth, Brigadier General Robin Olds (deceased) was rated as a Triple Ace pilot, having shot down seventeen enemy aircraft during two wars, Vietnam and WWII. He completed 152 combat flying missions in Southeast Asia in his F-4 Phantom II. On two separate missions using air-to-air missiles, he shot down two Russian Mig-17s and two Mig-21s, earning him the nick-name "MiG Killer." He also had 107 combat missions in WWII.

Some of this highly decorated Vietnam veteran's awards are:

- Air Force Cross
- Distinguished Flying Cross (6)
- Silver Star (4)
- Distinguished Service Medal (2)
- Legion of Merit
- Distinguished Flying Cross—United Kingdom
- Distinguished Flying Cross—Croix de Guerre—France
- Air Medal (40)
- And many more.

General Olds graduated from the U.S. Military Academy, West Point. He was an All-American tackle on the Army football team in 1942.

Olds flew his first plane at the age of eight in an open cockpit biplane. He came to be known as the best wing commander of the Vietnam War, and obviously it would be impossible to dig deeply into some of his heroic accomplishments; his decorations do that loud and clear. He was dedicated to "Duty, Honor, Country." However, he once was compelled to admit he had indulged in alcohol in New York City and was demoted from the rank of cadet captain to cadet private. He mentions this in his memoirs and that he was "only the second cadet in the history of West Point to earn that dubious honor."

His inability to achieve higher rank—not that brigadier general is anything to sneeze at—was generally blamed on his maverick views and his fondness for alcoholic beverages. Many staff members also resented him for a rapid rise in rank and his impressive collection of combat decorations. He faced a career-long battle with superiors he viewed as not being warrior-minded.

One of his closest friends both professionally and personally was Daniel "Chappie" James Jr., who would become the first African-American four-star Air Force general. James and Olds worked closely together, including on combat assignments. Olds and James became a popular combination, earning them the affectionate nickname of "Blackman and Robin."

One might catch some of Olds' acts of combat heroism by tuning to the History Channel *Dogfights* series. Nearing retirement time, when Operation Linebacker began in May 1972 over the skies of North Vietnam and when the Americans struggled with a poor one-to-one kill-loss ratio, he offered to take a voluntary reduction in rank to colonel so he could return to active combat and straighten out the problem. However, his offer was denied and so he retired on June 1, 1973. Olds is regarded among aviation historians and his peers as the best wing commander of the Vietnam War. He lived for another thirty-four years after retirement, passing away on June 14, 2007. RIP Robin.

The Vietnam War veteran in general deserves to be referred to as a great American. He had to deal with enemies from all fronts. He was different. Still, to this day, those who were old enough and are still kicking tend to act like cowards, ignoring or buying their shame that was unloaded on us. Vietnam War vets have a courage that those people who were hostile toward us will never know.

We kept telling ourselves that God still loved us. But letters from home were telling us what was being said about us, and it was not very inspirational. Often, we lost our faith over there as our hearts suffered untold agony due to the reality of darkness, coldness, and emptiness so terrible that nothing positive touched our souls.

I believe Vietnam War veterans as a group will always be one of our greatest generations. I maintain my faith in them; so should everyone else.

I would be just a wee bit off if I denied that combat veterans from the Vietnam War could be a little problematic or overly feisty; just ask a VA clerk. I am afraid it is our nature, caused by a war over there and the war back here. Our war back here has been even more lethal than the one over there. Americans have become aware of the sad, sorry fact that **veterans have died at the hands of Veterans Affairs!**

The mission of my 2013 book *Condemned Property?* had a couple of goals, and of course, many sub-goals. One major goal was to make sure more Americans became aware of what was being done to us by some VA centers. The other major goal of the book's passionate message was to describe to Americans in a shocking and angry manner just how shamefully and horridly the Vietnam veterans on both sides were mistreated. Their living conditions could be likened to the Dark Ages. Both sides sent their soldier boys into a war often described as the Twilight Zone, primarily to be sacrificial lambs. All of their earned valor was then stripped away from them when the war ended in complete shame, as the Ameri-Cong media painted it. Therefore, at this time, I find it an absolute *must* that I refer readers to the great book *Stolen Valor* by B.G. Burkett. Simply put, this book, written in 1998, is about how our generation was robbed of our heroes and our history from the Vietnam War. I have read it twice.

Casting our burdens onto God. My lovely mother was a Baptist missionary who left this earth much too prematurely, just like so many of America's Vietnam veterans have. She devoted the last twenty years of her life to trying to save the souls of others, including mine.

Although I last saw my mother physically alive on --/--/--, an evening at Brentwood Hospital in Warrensville Heights, Ohio, the image of her loving face has made appearances in my life many times. Often, it was during times of trouble for me when she appeared. Therefore, I have come to believe that Betty Mae Jensen Robinson has been a guardian angel to me for the last thirty years of my life.

Earlier in this book, I presented this question—**does the VA deserve to go to heaven?** Obviously, the final decision on that is not my call, but honestly and emphatically, I pray that the Lord God Almighty shows no favorites (which he will not) when judgment day comes for each and every VA employee who has had a part in the premature killing of any of our veterans. Who am I to speak of this? After all, I have devoted such a small mention about our great and wonderful God in this book. Going back to my saintly mother, Betty Mae, I remember her mentioning this biblical passage (among many) to me specifically:

Cast your burden on the Lord and He shall sustain you.
—Psalm 55:22

Mom also reminded me to keep this in mind and try to live by it: *God grant me the serenity to accept things I cannot change, the courage to change the things I can, and the wisdom to know the difference.* This is a powerful prayer, one we should all pray and attempt to live by.

I accept that some things in life cannot ever be changed…but many can. Some things God has given to us as fixed realities that we should accept. Some things he would have us not accept, but work to change (with his help). If we fail to do both of these—to accept some things and work to change others—we will end up burdened with worry, undeserved guilt, and of course, frustration and stress. That being said, I have come to accept that I did not seek help from God during the long and tedious compilation of information that went into *Condemned Property?* I wrote that book with a vengeance, trying for two years to get it done and out to the public, mostly on my own. The result came within weeks after the release of *Condemned Property?*…two almost back-to-back transient ischemic attacks and then the big one, a cerebral vascular accident known as a brain stroke. I am not putting blame on God here, not by any means, and I did come close to death when the second CVA struck. Maybe it was God's way of slowing me down.

Since I woke up from the Vietnam War's deadly influence on my life through the entire decade of the 1970s—I had been racing through life from 1980 to 2013 (thirty-three years) at lightning speed, stopping or slowing down for nothing or no one, trying to make up for all of those lost or wasted years after the Vietnam War. I had the feeling that having escaped from dozens of near-death events in Vietnam and then dozens more death-defying experiences (accidental and intentional) during the 1970s, I came to believe for a variety of reasons that the 1980s were my last chance to make something of my life. But I never took a breather. It felt that my time could run out any day, so I felt compelled to cram thirty hours into every day. In my mind, knowing how I had lived my time in Nam (1968–1969) to August 29, 2013, that on my sixty-ninth birthday, I had already lived 109 years and that I would expire at any moment and someday soon, I just would not wake up the next day. That sure kept my guardian angel (my mom) busy. How selfish and inconsiderate I was, as I look back on those days now.

As described in Chapter 15, my entire life came to a screeching standstill as I checked myself into the emergency room of the Department of Veterans Affairs medical institution in Cleveland, Ohio, where I would spend the next four days recovering from a devastating CVA. How weird or how lucky was it that I was on my way to VA anyway for other reasons, and the brain stroke hit me just a couple of miles away from the VA hospital—wow! Nice work. Way to go, Mom. You were there again in the time of trouble and you would guide me through this terrible brush with death as well. Thanks, Mom. Thank you, dear Lord.

Lying in a hospital bed for four days, I had no idea how the stroke had altered my life…and the lives of everyone around me. When I got out of bed, I tried to dress myself, but could not quite do it (my wife helped). I sensed that something major had taken place with my body, my brain, and all that went with them. On the way out of the hospital, after getting out of the wheelchair, I bumped into a wall more than once, stumbled a few times, and was so relieved to sit down in my car again…on the passenger's side. The next six to twelve months would bring some of the biggest tests of my life. It was a no-brainer that I could no longer perform full time at my job as a traveling advertising salesman and consultant for publishing companies. I was forced to stop traveling immediately and reduce my workload to working on a computer (which I was not very good at). I made one desperate attempt to travel, but it ended up being an exercise in futility and I was forced to return home, having gone just halfway to my final destination in Terre Haute, Indiana. I had made that trip dozens of times, driven there and back four hundred miles each way, and never gave it a thought. I was done with my career in traveling sales, a career I loved so much and thrived on. People were always amazed at the battle stories I would tell after a challenging sales trip. They would just shake their heads and often say…and you love this shit?

I came to believe that my life as a combat infantry point man in the Vietnam War had prepped me for the many, many battles I would encounter in the sales profession. Indeed it did. I was in my element of guerrilla warfare and I believed nobody could be better at this than I could…**NOBODY!** I could write an encyclopedia-sized book about those sales battles, which did not always end in victory, but I have to focus on *Unbreakable Hearts*.

Facing the fact that I was now a disabled veteran and that Agent Orange and PTSD had teamed up to unhinge me has not come very easily. VA has DENIED my claims for full service-connected disability twice, and at this writing, just minutes before Veterans Day 2017, my fight with VA's dreaded Compensation and Pension division continues. Little do they know that I will never, ever give up and allow them to sit back, relax, and enjoy a feeling of defeating me. Damn it…I am a surviving combat Vietnam War veteran and we **NEVER GIVE UP!**

I have come to realize that I am at war with the same institution that betrayed my war buddies and me when we were sent to Vietnam to be sacrificed for the inflated egos of the United States government. Here they are again; after betraying me over there, they are now trying to finish me off for good by denying and delaying my quest for full service-connected disability benefits which are unquestionably owed to me.

So yeah, here they are again. This time it is not the Department of Defense trying to end my life; it is another unit of the U.S. government, the Veterans Administration. Why are they still trying to kill us? We answered the call, we fought the fight few others were willing to fight, and now we just want to be left alone and live out our lives as comfortably as we can…that is all we want.

The VA medical staff takes pretty good care of me. I rarely have anything to complain about to them. Most doctors and nurses stand in our corner and sympathize with our plight with the VA Compensation and Pension ogres who insist that I should be able to find employment at a sedentary job. Heck, I would agree with them—*if* I could find the training course and complete it at my age. Who is going to hire a seventy-plus-year-old who has very limited motor and physical skills and needs to be trained all over again?

I am presently in communication with one Veterans Service officer, a couple of Disabled American Veterans service officers, all VA doctors who treat me, several congressmen, and two legal institutions about my situation with a very stubborn VA Compensation & Pension division. I am trying my absolute best *not* to take this to the courts and I want this to resolve itself with as little pain for the VA and myself as possible. I just do not believe that the VA C&P division has the same empathy for most Vietnam War veterans or me personally.

If some miracle happens and VA C&P comes around and does what should be done by granting my claim, I may delete this section. Then again, since my battles with VA C&P for service-connected disabilities have been going on for nearly *four thousand days*, maybe I owe it to them and my war buddies to leave this story where it is. Naturally, I will write a happy ending at the end of the book if VA C&P gives me the justice that I deserve.

Cast your burden on the Lord and He shall sustain you. In other words, I believe God prefers that we learn to trust in him, especially in times of trouble. I have to remind myself of this every time I receive a letter from the VA C&P.

One day in mid-summer of 2017 as I was walking slowly in a parking lot, wearing a Vietnam War veteran T-shirt, a young man stopped to ask me if I was really a Vietnam War veteran. Of course I nodded that I was. Unexpectedly and almost immediately he shook his head and uttered these words to me..."Wow, dude, you guys are so old!"

I glared at him and shook my head in disbelief of how disrespectful he came off. And it wasn't like I asked for his opinion about Vietnam veterans or the war we fought in. Then I simply walked away saying nothing and so did he. What I wanted to do was spank him; obviously his parents never did. But better thinking took over—never mind he was about six inches taller, had much larger muscles, and was about one-third my age. Good decision, Dusty.

What I really would have liked to do was give him an autographed edition of *Condemned Property?* and leave him with words something like "Many Vietnam veterans still see that war as a recent happening in our lives." After all, to us it was just yesterday when we stepped off the plane in March 1968 at Cam Ranh Bay Airport. That war will always live on in our thoughts, like events that just happened last week, or yesterday.

We do not want to be remembered as those who fought in a mistaken war, a war historians continue to say was lost by America. Maybe, just maybe, someday Americans will remember their Vietnam War veterans in this manner:

We who participated in that war are warriors who wrote out a personal blank check payable to the United States of America for an amount of up to and including our life!

—Unknown

After Vietnam, Secret Battles Raged! After Vietnam, battles raged on. On Palm Sunday 1968, that lovely year a marine was wounded three times at a bloody battle in the Sarrh. On the day before, this marine and his brothers were scheduled to head out for a search-and-destroy mission, and a Catholic priest was sent to administer the last rites to Gary Rodd and his fellow marines as they were being sent to an area that had repeatedly been the site of several heavy casualty battles.

Gary Rodd barely survived the Palm Sunday mission; his unit was ambushed by an unknown enemy force, and he was shot in three separate places. As of the date of this story,[41] he was still carrying a small plastic container with those same bullet fragments that were removed from his body. To add insult to injury, this marine also received extra shrapnel fragments from an

_____

41 poststar.com/news

enemy grenade which he barely escaped a direct hit from as it exploded a mere ten feet away from him. Needless to say this marine was shot up pretty bad; in fact he needed to be hospitalized for recovery procedures for six months and then returned to Stateside, assigned to a unit in the New York City area.

Gary Rodd arrived home after his hospital time carrying other scars, the invisible ones. These emotional scars would not heal as easily as his bullet and shrapnel wounds. Adding insult to injury were the protestors who abused him at the airport on his first day back to home sweet home.

One day Gary Rodd was asked to be a marching participant in a large parade in New York City to honor the Apollo astronauts who landed on the moon. He was honored and could hardly wait for the experience, as he had not marched in any parades since coming home. What Gary has a difficult time in forgetting about the day of the parade, which was supposed to be a patriotic and glorious time, went like this:

"As soon as the Vietnam veterans appeared in full dress uniforms with medals visible, we could hear the boos from the crowd almost instantly. Soon to join in with the boos, which were depressing enough, were those who screamed at us those unbelievable words…**Baby Killers!"**

Gary goes on to say how he put his uniform and medals into a chest and stashed them in a closet where they would be forgotten.

Stories like Gary Rodd's were a dime a thousand from Vietnam War and even Vietnam Era only veterans who dared to wear their uniforms when they returned home from hell in Southeast Asia. The only people who have forgotten what happened on our return are those who treated us with inhuman cruelty.

It's not that we could do what we did and few others couldn't. It's that WE DID IT and others did NOT. We will never forget those hot, steamy, wet, miserably uncomfortable days and nights, being tired twenty-four/seven, hungry most days and sleepless most nights, and highly underpaid. What we all do miss is…THE BROTHERHOOD!

Ending a story that refuses to end itself is an impossible task. I suspect that the Vietnam story will come to an abrupt and uneventful ending on the day the last official Vietnam War veteran dies. How much time do we have left to tell our stories, to right the lies? Unfortunately, not very long. As of the summer-fall time frame of 2016, a consensus of estimates states that less than 33 percent of the estimated three million Americans who served in-country during the Vietnam War (1959–1973) are living. Well over half of them have been hanging on with health issues caused directly from their service over there. Sadly I must admit that most of those who served there survived to come home and who died back here or are still fighting to survive on a day-to-day basis will have never told their stories to other Americans. How sad.

There, I have just shared several old soldiers' stories, one of my own, one that is still running. Is our story over? I pray it is not. Will I ever write another book about it? I am undecided, but I hope my brothers will want me to. My heart breaks every day, sometimes more for what Vietnam War veterans have been through. Sometimes I feel like this...that which we loved and fought to defend has betrayed and destroyed too many of us. The two most important days in our life are the day we are born and the day we find out why. None of us knows when our story might end or how, but nowhere will anyone ever read where we stopped serving America or gave up!

Obviously someone in high places has been paying attention to what is happening and not happening to America's veterans, especially Vietnam War Era veterans. In fact, the *New York Post's* Michael Walsh thinks that the media has the wrong definition of "chaos." Throughout President Trump's first term, the media threw the word "chaos" around as if it's the perfect description for what took place in the White House. The only problem with this idea is that chaos implies that things are a mess and nothing can be accomplished. In reality, the exact opposite is the case. President Trump has actually been able to accomplish more of his agenda, in less time, than any president in recent memory. Walsh goes even further and states that President Trump has actually accomplished more, in less time, and with greater opposition than any other president since Franklin Delano Roosevelt! Time will tell on this, but one thing is certain: he deserves to be left alone so that he can keep us safe from our enemies. But I'll talk more about this in the next chapter.

Saigon then (1968)

Ho Chi Minh City 2018

The Faces of Vietnam 1968–2018

Chapter 15

UNLIKELY CHAMPION FOR VETERANS

Nearing the end of President Obama's second term, active military, veterans, and defense policy experts had been accusing him of dangerously gutting the U.S. military through massive and continuous funding cuts and warned that it was sending our armed forces into a "death spiral" if it was not stopped and reversed. Of course the Obama administration downplayed these accusations even though the facts supported them then, as they do now.

Some critics warned that these cuts would painfully endanger the country's security, and harsh consequences would be inevitable.

President Trump walked into this serious situation where the USA could no longer repair or replace military weapons and equipment that had been wearing out over the last couple decades, making our military increasingly unable and unprepared to face the possible challenges of a major conventional conflict should the U.S. find itself faced with one. Almost immediately President Trump made this situation—the defense of the U.S. and taking care of our military's veterans who had been badly maligned by the U.S. government itself, the Department of Veterans Affairs—his highest priority. He promised he would do this, and despite what his political adversaries say…these promises were being kept continuously during his first one and a half years.

I would love to dedicate an entire chapter to someone in the long, long line of champions for veterans who have come forth to stand up for us, but I'll list here an abbreviated but impressive list of names:

Gary Sinise	Hal Moore
Pete Hegseth	Joseph Galloway
Bob Hope	Oliver North
Robin Williams	Rocky Bleier
David Hackworth	Denzel Washington
Chuck Norris	Chuck Hagel
Chris Noel	George "Bud" Day
Every combat medic or corpsman	And many others

I could quadruple this list, but space is limited. Another list I could prepare, also a short one, would name some well-known people, mostly celebrities, who could have helped veterans but did not, in my opinion. Most of America's past and present veterans do not revere these people:

Jane Fonda	Lyndon B. Johnson
John Kerry	Nancy Pelosi
Robert McNamara	Richard Nixon
John McCain	Hillary Clinton

When *Condemned Property?* was published between Thanksgiving and December 1, 2013, it joined the heated attack on the Department of Veterans Affairs for their unspeakable crimes against America's veterans. The casualties were mind-boggling as various media was reporting on throughout 2014–2016. People were shocked as one despicable story after another reached the American public. Sadly it was discovered that the group of veterans being ignored and victimized the most were those good old boys of the Vietnam War. Not a surprise, but still a shameful sin.

As of January 2019, Vietnam War veterans make up to 36 percent of the present pending compensation inventory backlog within the VA![42]

I know oh so many of those Vietnam War veterans who were waiting and waiting and waiting for treatment or a claim's decision for disability benefits they deserved and earned. I was one of them and I was delighted to see that my book was helping to expose the culprits at VA.

Since Vietnam War veterans had always received second-class treatment from the VA, this statement was not much of a surprise to us. In fact, many of us believe the 36 percent figure is too low, as most Vietnam vets were not being treated well or in a timely fashion by their respective VA. While most Vietnam vets have been euphoric over the VA being exposed finally, the ugly fact remains that tens of thousands of Vietnam War Era veterans have died much too prematurely while waiting and waiting and waiting to be taken care of. Because of this, with the generous assistance from our friend Agent Orange, Vietnam War veterans have become an endangered species…on the verge of ultimate extinction, I'm afraid.

The Veterans Health Administration Scandal of 2014 should have been uncovered decades ago. What an evil, inexcusable, criminally immoral, continuous cover-up that has amazingly been allowed to exist without aggressive action taken until 2017.

---

42 Backlog claims pending longer than 125 days. Department of Veteran Affairs, 4/15/14

The negligence in treatment did not stop there. Recordkeeping was not only done improperly, but in many cases records were falsified to show that targets were being met on schedule. Again these were criminal acts with tragic results…dead veterans. So why did it continue for so long? It was not a democrat or republican thing, as the criminal acts at VA happened during the presiding of both political parties.

In the last Obama year, the daily suicide rate of American veterans reached the disgusting all-time high of twenty-two per day.[43] Much of the problem or the cause if you will was the documented fact that more than one-third of calls to a VA suicide hotline for troubled veterans were NEVER ANSWERED because of the overwhelming internal problems at the Department of Veterans Affairs.

From my personal observations, when President Obama chose Robert McDonald to replace Eric Shinseki as VA Secretary in May 2014, I had many reasons to keep my hopes up that my most troubled veteran brothers and sisters were finally going to be more highly thought of, and long overdue attention was just around the corner! I had already benefited from the fine and sincere care of a VA suicide prevention staff professional, Dr. Robert Marcus, a psychologist who worked out of Ravenna and Youngstown VA offices. But Dr. Marcus was not a creation of McDonald or Obama; he was his own man who simply cared for us. Dr. Marcus and I have remained friends for about ten years, and I hope it will last much longer.

Our New Best Friend? The lives of my brothers and me have been controlled by politics throughout our military service, so the topic comes up in our circles often. Well, here I am plodding unintentionally at a slow pace with this book. It's mid-October 2017, and the man in the oval office is Donald J. Trump. The Democratic Party has not recovered from the shock yet. I voted for Trump. Yes, I did. I set aside most of the hate comments made by the "never Trumpers" and I judged the man by what he was saying about the things that mattered most to me and most Americans I know…NOW!

I did not care for one of the Bushes or Obama, nor did I see much future for another Clinton receiving the baton from Obama. Hope for my great country to regain some of the luster it once had did not look good for the conservative and die-hard patriots of America. Was there really a reason to believe President Trump could be the man to make America great again?

The real question is will America remain patient and allow the controversial Trump to do the job he was legitimately elected to do? At this writing there were impeachment rumors floating around amongst Democrats and some of Trump's own party. This is sad, very sad and I will continue to pray

---

43 www.militarytimes.com

for America, its leader—whoever it is—and of course the American people. Yes, I would have prayed for Hillary if she had been elected. Begrudgingly of course.

Being a veteran, my primary wish for an American president is to put the hammer down on the VA's lack of accountability, which has existed for the past thirty years or so. Guess what? President Trump has come through for us and has become a true champion of veterans, even us forgotten outcasts, the Vietnam veterans. He has also helped our homeless vets.

Unfortunately, the good old Ameri-Cong—or fake media as they are referred to now—has kept nearly every good accomplishment by Trump pretty much a secret from the public.

Dr. Ben Carson has been a favorite of mine and he is nobody's Uncle Tom. He made the following statement in one of his newsletters, *Ben Carson News*: "I have never seen in my life a more outrageous media bias against an American president! This president is under siege."

Trump condemns neo-Nazis and white supremacists as well as the Antifa, and the media says he does not go far enough. Elitist experts in the Democratic Party say the president is crazy or suffering from dementia. Seriously?

What Happened? Hillary Kept Asking. One evening in November 2016, when most of America went to rest their heads on their pillows, Barack Obama was still president, with Hillary Clinton waiting to take over the world's most powerful office. When the sun arose the next morning, the shock of what happened then was the most profound result since Pearl Harbor was attacked. Hillary Clinton was defeated by the most unlikely candidate in American history. The shock has not worn off yet with most Hillary lovers; the unthinkable happened, as Donald J. Trump became our new president.

Since that historical event, our new president was served notice by the opposition party that he was officially under siege. Imagine, the President of the USA, a country under siege by multiple unfriendly countries, enemies, and alleged allies having to watch his back from a country he is trying to protect from the America haters.

But hold the fort! It seems we have been breeding our own homegrown America haters, and they have been around for decades since WWII—the far left and the far right, although neither group will admit to their unpatriotic attitudes. Well, this is no secret to anyone who can see and hear if they use those senses. This has touched my heart and the hearts of many veterans…especially those forgotten from the Vietnam War.

I have attempted to bring the crimes of VA against Vietnam veterans public for a couple of decades, as many other crusaders have. Why not… The **VA has been lying while veterans have been dying—FACT!**

Tragic horror stories have mounted since the Korean War veterans came home. But no one in the White House in the last twenty years has done much about it. They must not have cared or the political walls were just too massive to knock down. As I said it has been like this for over half a century, so we veterans, those still living, had almost given up the only thing we had left...**HOPE!**

Amazingly, during the few months leading up to the November 2016 election, Hillary somehow was able to bring several high-ranking military officers before a national audience, showing their support of her presidential run. Although these were legitimate highly decorated military officers, much of the American public was not aware that these were a mix of Obama's "chosen few." He had fired or forced out hundreds of military officers in his deliberate dismantling of America's military, keeping those most loyal to him. Verification of my implication above can be sourced from credible figures, such as:

> "Obama has been weakening the military in unprecedented ways. Budgets have been terribly slashed. Officers have watched other high-level officers (generals included) being relieved of duty at an unprecedented rate—and most that remain have been virtually silent. Because everyone must follow orders or else, the military is no longer a conservative leaning institution. It's on the cutting edge of being a socialistic experiment."
>
> **—Elaine Donnelly, President**
> **Center for Military Readiness 2013**

Former Florida Congressman Allen West called for congressional oversight hearings into what he described as an "alarming trend of dismissals and firings of high-ranking military officers by the Obama administration, firings that appear to be political."

Former Army Major General Paul E. Vallely called for nationwide rallies and protests to demand the resignations of President Obama and other administration officials for the systematic political purge of hundreds of senior military officers. He was also quoted as saying..."Our federal government continues down the path of destroying America."[44]

As it came closer to the election, most veterans remained or moved over to help elect Trump. One year later and as other Trump voters seem to have abandoned him, the veterans remain among his most loyal supporters. Wasn't he one of those who avoided the draft during the Vietnam War? They did not seem to care, or had they forgiven him?

---

44 www.wnd.com

I am one of those Vietnam veterans who still stands by President Trump. Maybe my veteran-warrior buddies and I have more distrust for the Hillarys and those swamp politicians. Maybe we are not offended nor appalled by his blunt attacks, including the one he directed at Senator McCain when he was a candidate for president. I have news for you McCain supporters, most of whom seem to be liberals and other left wing fans: McCain is no longer looked up to by many Vietnam War veterans—quite the contrary. Granted he served his country, risked his life for her, may have endured torture while a POW. But the things he has done or not done for veterans or for America's welfare have given many of us a justifiably bitter taste in our mouths.

The Trump Inheritance. To many of us veterans the Trump legacy began during the second week of January 2017 when he made the decision to keep Dr. David Shulkin on board, replacing Robert McDonald as secretary of the beleaguered Department of Veterans Affairs. With President Trump leading the way by removing long-established obstacles, the two of them in quick fashion have addressed and found partial solutions to some of the problems that have poisoned the VA, such as:

- Long wait lists to receive health care
- Veterans can seek health care outside the VA
- Underperforming VA staff and those committing fraud and negligence and wasting resources can be punished with termination

This may not sound like much, and the Ameri-Cong media has downplayed anything positively good for America's future if Trump may have had a hand in it. Some of the things these two would be able to take credit for, I'll list later. But first to fully appreciate what the new president had quickly accomplished, one should dig deep into the long list of problems he walked into.

- The VA Scandal of 2014 revealed that at least forty veterans had died while waiting for long overdue health care at the Phoenix, AZ VA Hospital. A criminal investigation was initiated by the inspector general.
- To follow was a criminal investigation by the Justice Department legislated by Congress. On May 16, 2014, the top Phoenix VA official, Dr. Robert Petzel, was forced into early retirement, which was not enough for most veterans. Just two weeks later the secretary of the VA, Eric Shinseki, also resigned, and the scandal was just getting started.
- In June 2014, several more VA medical centers from coast to coast were identified with similar problems, and the investigations wid-

ened by the DOT and the IG. On June 27, 2014, President Obama ordered a White House investigation for criminal actions by the VA. By August 2014, it was discovered that significant and chronic system failures existed in a corrosive culture.

- Unfortunately, further research revealed that the IG reports of patient wait time delays had been unreliable, even manipulated, back in 2005 and every year since. In June 2014, after Shinseki was relieved, Acting VA Secretary Sloan Gibson made attempts to fire some VA executives, but Congress took its good old time in giving him such authority.
- On June 30, 2014, former Procter and Gamble CEO and U.S. Army veteran Robert A. McDonald, as the new and permanent VA Secretary under McDonald, and Obama the next year showed virtually no progress on the VA Scandal of 2014. It only extended itself through 2015 and well into 2016.
- On November 20, 2013, my book *Condemned Property?* launched, and almost immediately it reopened closed wounds. I got copies into the hands of hundreds of influential people at my cost, and I received acknowledgments from many of them, mostly congressmen and senators from both political parties. This motivated me, so I borrowed and borrowed so that I could advertise the book nationally. Again I received encouragement from congressmen, senators, and celebrities like Chuck Norris, Gary Sinise, Charlie Daniels, Pat Sajak, and Oliver Stone.
- Well into 2015, I launched my second book, *Payback Time!*, borrowing more money to promote it as well as continue marketing *Condemned Property?*

On February 15, 2013, I read where President Obama and the VA bureaucracy had been sabotaging the VA reform law that was passed in August 2014. One of the headlines I saw online read…***Obama Betrayal: Effort to Snatch $10 Billion from Veterans***.

A die-hard veterans' advocate and veteran, Pete Hegseth, then CEO of Concerned Veterans for America, stated that "vets were getting the runaround when they tried to use the Choice Card. The VA was making a concerted attempt to undermine anything that looks like choice." Pete has since become a regular contributor on Fox News.

Too bad, so many lives have been at stake—the lives of those who took an oath to risk their lives for the country they loved. On December 10, 2013, I suffered from a severe cerebral vascular attack (stroke) which followed lesser transient ischemic attacks in October and November. My ability to continue the battles with VA were diminished substantially from that time, but I did not give up. My heart was still in it, and although it had been cracked and weakened a bit, it was still an **Unbroken Heart!**

So the foundation had been solidly entrenched for the next President of the United States to tackle, or to ignore. I saw little reason to expect the VA problems would be ignored. Practically no one had any idea of what was going to happen, as everyone seemed convinced that Hillary was a shoo-in and few people had much confidence in Mr. "You're Fired" Donald A. Trump.

Most veterans pretty well knew that Hillary would be a continuation of what was in place. But what did we know, huh? We knew this…

Nearly a hundred patients died waiting at Los Angeles VA!

Number of veterans who die waiting for benefits skyrockets!

VA's relationship with veterans is strained with untruths!

How the VA devalues veterans!

Veterans denied $110 million in benefits by VA!

Suicide rate for veterans far exceeds civilians' rate!

Those are a few pickings I chose to illustrate what the incoming president was going to run smack-dab into. Add to it all, the suicide rate among veterans has increased more than double that of the civilian population. Approximately one in every five suicides nationally is a veteran. And Vietnam veterans top the list percentage wise, as they have for decades.

So, do you never-Trumpers really believe Hillary would have continued the fight for us? If you did, you are dumber than whale dung. Trump may fall short in many ways as being what people have come to expect as a president, but I wish we had him as our president instead of LBJ or Nixon during the Vietnam War Era.

And there you have it, how the dishonesty at the VA among everyday employees and their leaders is routinely tolerated, leaving the veterans high and dry without their meds or homeless. Oh, by the way, the taxpayers also get shafted, left to deal with and pay for the consequences.

That statement was proof to me that this gentleman cares for us in that he wasn't bashful about mentioning what VA's major negative was. They are too adversarial to veterans. In a nutshell, the VA's employees constantly devalue your sacrifices and mine.

Worse yet, various government watchdogs (we can never have enough of those) have found that the investigations by the inspector general were inefficient and biased. If true, the only persons left to trust in getting the VA thoroughly cleaned up are the President of the United States and his secretary of VA.

Veterans from coast to coast (even California) of all eras have been cheering Trump's actions for us. His promises to fire corrupt officials at the

Department of Veterans Affairs has been most impressive. Just as those who served in Afghanistan and Iraq are proud of their service, so are the rest of us who served in Korea, Vietnam, and of course World War II. We became so frustrated and angry with how previous administrations kept on ignoring us and by how insensitive our fellow Americans seemed to feel about our problems with the VA.

President Trump has quickly brought new hope to the veterans. We have liked the way he calls it out, showing little or no fear in defending what he thinks is the right thing. Has Trump made a lot of mistakes? Probably too many and he may hurt our country more than help it, just like so many previous presidents have. I just hope he receives the chance he earned to prove himself as a worthy president for all of America, not just the veterans. He deserves the chance, but too many Americans have not been willing to step back and allow him to perform his duties for our great country.

While Democrats kept their 2017 focus on so-called Russian collision with Trump, he was quietly building on his potential voter base by reversing the massive military cuts by the Obama administration. Of course the mainstream media gave this little coverage. Regardless, he was cranking up our military strength and increasing his popularity with America's active warriors. Great move, Mr. Trump.

Trump's own appointed secretary of VA, Dr. David Shulkin, the third change in that critical position in three years, has already done more positive things for the vets than the last three of his predecessors managed to get done.

Under Dr. Shulkin, with Trump's approval, the new Veterans Coordinated Access and Rewarding Experiences (Vets CARE) Act allows medical appointments to all veterans who seek specialty care not provided by the VA or who might face a longer wait time than would be clinically unacceptable. The Vets CARE Act also expanded telehealth options (mentioned elsewhere for veteran patients, and has eliminated restrictions on where doctors and patients must be located to perform online sessions.

While some of them may loathe Trump, by far the majority of active military and veterans have favorable feelings for him. They have his back because he's proven to have their backs. Keep in mind there are twenty-two million veterans in the USA, all of voting age.

Like many other veterans who have held onto their warrior-soldier mentality, I have written, emailed, faxed, and placed calls to every president since Jimmy Carter. Also every VA secretary and undersecretary since the late 1990s and dozens of congressmen and senators going back to the mid-1990s. While many of the government officials were quite responsive to my communications, not even one president ever wrote back to me, until finally in January 2017, one of my letters to the various men in the Oval Office was finally answered by Mr. Donald J. Trump. I am sharing Mr. Trump's memo with all of America; it appears at the end of this chapter.

What has Mr. Trump done or attempted to get done for veterans since he has been in office his first year? Since the mainstream media has kept things like this a secret, I am sharing this abbreviated but very impressive list with anyone who cares about veterans:

MR. TRUMP DID WHAT?

March 9, 2017 Mental Health Care Expanded for Veterans…**Promise Kept again**

VA Secretary David Shulken, appointed by Mr. Trump, said that the additional coverage was urgently needed for former neglected service members who were experiencing mental health disorders. He told Mr. Trump that a large number of stressed-out veterans needed care now, and waiting for legislation to run its course would cause loss of lives. The president acted quickly on the VA secretary's request. This critical move brought immediate assistance to veterans in danger of suicide.

April 19, 2017 Bill Giving Veterans Access to Private Health Care Signed…**Promise Kept**

This was a well-kept secret but a proud moment for America just the same. How could it not be as veterans have poured out their blood and sweat for so long, and it was way past due for them to be recognized in this way. **The Veterans Choice Program Improvement Act** speaks for itself. This bill extends and improves the veterans choice program so more veterans can finally see the doctor of their choice.

June 20, 2017 President Signs VA Accountability Act into Law, Guaranteeing Veterans Better Care…**Promise Kept.**

This law made it easier for the VA to fire employees for wrongdoing and added protection for whistle-blowers in the VA. Responding to an Obama-era scandal where veterans died while being put on delay for medical treatment and claims decisions for deserved benefits, President Trump said this law would make sure that a VA scandal like this would never happen again.

July 21, 2017 Veterans Hotline Launched…**Promise Kept.**

August 17, 2017 WWII Veterans Receive Help with Denied Claims for Exposure to Mustard Gas…**Promise Kept.**

Unbelievably, the VA's denials to WWII veterans exposed to mustard gas remained unsettled. President Trump signed a bill in rapid fashion to help survivors of that war. This required the VA to reconsider all of those claims.

August 23, 2017 Veterans Appeals Improvement Act Signed…**Promise Kept**

Bill signed to speed up disability appeals. This measure signed by President Trump was meant to accelerate the long and backed-up appeals process for disability claims with five-year "average" wait times for decisions. This was a big one for us. At this date there were nearly five hundred thousand appeals cases pending, including mine. I still have hope for a fair and just decision.

September 1, 2017 President and secretary announce telehealth improvements for Access Care…**Promise Kept.**

Veteran telehealth initiatives are approved that will expand access to health care across the country with telehealth technology and mobile applications. This act benefitted any veteran with a complaint or a suggestion on VA reforms. FYI…it worked!

September 20, 2017 New Accountability Law Voted…**Promise Kept.**

U.S. Dept. of Veteran Affairs Secretary Shulkin undertook action provided by the VA Accountability Act, which President Trump signed in June 2017. Washington, D.C. Medical Director Brian Hawkins removed.

November 1, 2017 President Proclaims November Veterans and Military Families Month…**Promise Kept.**

November 2, 2017 Program Passed for Providing Veterans More Options in Claims Disagreements…**Promise Kept**.

PFC Vietnam Veterans Medal of Honor. Usually when the news of a Medal of Honor recipient is announced, more often than not we see the rank of this hero to be from the officers' lieutenant to colonel cadre. And it is not uncommon to find men from the Enlisted Men's ranks of sergeants and specialists serving under or alongside this MOH awardee who think that someone else was just as deserving, if not more so, than the officer was. I am not saying that this is how I have felt in Vietnam. I was not there when that act of heroism took place. On the other hand, I have seen soldiers doing things during a battle that in my opinion were deserving of the MOH, but it didn't happen. These were almost always specialists to sergeants or E-4 to E-9.

But in June 2017, a hero of the Vietnam War received his valor award for courageous actions on the battlefield of a remote place called Hui Yon Hill, in 1969. James McCoughan was a twenty-three-year-old private first class when he risked his life along with eighty-nine of his buddies who were ambushed by a much larger enemy force. PFC McCloughan was the company medic for his U.S. Army unit in this battle which lasted for forty-eight hours.

President Trump was given the honor of awarding McCloughan, the president's first person to be awarded our nation's highest valor award. Despite being wounded himself during the battle, McCloughan stayed with his brothers until the battle was won and every American was safe. He was credited with being personally responsible for saving the lives of ten of his warrior buddies. He called the battle "the worst two days of my life." I can relate to that.

This example of uncommon valor exemplifies most of the Vietnam War's combat warriors I vividly remember over there. He makes us all proud to call ourselves Vietnam War veterans.

Most of America's veterans willingly served their country, prepared to accept harm or even death. What we were not prepared for was being forced to wait and wait or, worse yet, to be denied proper and timely care from the VA.

Under the Trump administration every day has been like a new day of hope for veterans, and God knows we deserve it after all these years. President Trump's Accountability Act of 2017 gives power to the secretary of the VA to remove (fire) bad VA employees and replace them, fulfilling an overdue obligation by America to veterans.

As recent as late November 2017 when I wrote this portion of Chapter 18, I was still running into dozens of Americans who had no knowledge of these positive acts by our president.

The rest of the international community has been confused and in some ways shocked by some of Trump's actions during his first year as President of the USA. Back home the left block has opposed him on nearly every issue he presented, even when his suggestions make good sense for America. The mainstream media hasn't been warm and fuzzy to Trump either, and that's a no-brainer as well. Then there have been the GOP liberals who have managed to stick a monkey wrench into several important legislations by a mere vote or two. Still, the president has been quietly taking care of our country's veterans, almost catching them off guard. Well, we shouldn't have been surprised because he promised we would be taken care of, and that promise is seemingly being kept.

The American Dream...on Its Way Back? On October 31, 2017, a survey said that 82 percent of Americans now had renewed faith that the American Dream was achievable, or that they were achieving it today. Just as impressive, the same survey stated that 51 percent of Hispanics shared these warm and fuzzy feelings about this country.

The American Dream was first exposed to the public in 1931 when author/historian James Truslow Adams published *The Epic of America*. Coincidentally, this was when the Great Depression was causing so much suffering in the United States. Eventually it became a widespread term to identify the American way of life in general. But it has its original roots in the Declaration of Independence, which proclaimed that "all men are created equal" with the right to "life, liberty, and the pursuit of happiness."

Martin Luther King Jr. in a 1963 letter rooted the Civil Rights movement in the African-American quest for that American Dream.

Americans must work together in order for the American Dream to be realized by many. For some people only wealth is their connection to the dream. For others it is much more than having money. They have found their dream from simple living, finding happiness and a fulfilling life along with deep faith. Putting it as simply as I can, the American Dream is about liberty and belonging to a country of unlimited opportunities.

Country of unlimited opportunities? If President Trump can make that happen again in the USA, then he would truly succeed in making America great again.

Unfortunately, Trump walked into a country that had become as divided as it was during the Vietnam War era. He was also smacked immediately by Trump haters, possibly because of past mistakes in his life. No one can possibly predict where this situation will be going as it seems for every step forward he takes for America, there are always oppressors actively fighting him, and this sets his good efforts back a step or more.

This writer knows that Trump is in the corner of America's veterans, and for me that means so much as it should to every other American.

Trump keeps promises, media cares not! On November 14, 2017, Congress agreed with President Trump that our military must be strengthened as Congress passed the National Defense Authorization Act. This bill increased defense spending by $74 billion and granted the largest pay increase for the military in eight years. This included $15 billion for missile defense, which was badly needed. It also provided for $110 million for another critically neglected area for the military, the modernization of our country's B-52 bomber program.

America's Department of Affairs was a very dark spot during the Obama presidency. Corruption was running rampant, and those who did the ground fighting in wars were being cheated, lied to, and flat-out betrayed. Believe it, under the Trump regime, congressional Republicans have been reversing the trend of poor or no care for our veterans. In fact the trend in late 2017 had become one of expansion of care and benefits for those in need of it the most… **Finally!**

Our new champ's signing of acts and laws favoring troubled veterans is long overdue—not Trump's fault. His expansion of more and better care is also long past due. Something else needed to be done to right all the wrongs, and he has attended to it. Under the president's administration in just its first year, sources have stated the VA has been forced to fire over five hundred employees, suspend another two or three hundred, and demote dozens more. In fact, to prove a new transparency policy was in force, the VA became one of the first agencies to post information about employee disciplinary actions online and at the same time protect its whistle-blowers.

In his short but powerful note to me on January 26, 2017, Trump used one statement which impressed me beyond my expectations of his commitment to us vets: "I am honored to embark on this new chapter to make the country you have selflessly served great again."

We are blessed to have a country. It is yours and mine. Nobody outside of its borders from anywhere has the right to be part of it without following legal procedures. This means we must defend our borders, stop illegal immigration (no exceptions), and keep potential terrorists from known America-hating countries out of here. **PERIOD!**

The media is so against President Trump that they would rather see him fail than succeed and better our country. He is following through on his promises to veterans.
—Dakota Meyer, U.S. Marines, Medal of Honor Recipient

"Mad dog" Takes Us Back to the Future. At first he seemed like a sure fit. Trump man, James Mattis, retired Marine Corps general, named Secretary of Defense. His resume had no weak links and needed no checking up on despite a few pot shots at him from a few weak-minded Democrats. Unfortunately, Mattis inherited the results of a neglected military by a slew of presidents and many other American bureaucrats in Congress who had lost touch with the direction the U.S. military was going. Although many of the country's top leaders in government positions seemed unaware or unbelieving of our military's backward steps, both Trump and Mattis were greatly motivated to put the U.S. military back on the map so to speak. And while it is wonderful what Trump has accomplished so quickly for our veterans, of course correcting the decade-long neglect of our active military capabilities was also at the top of the president's to-do list. Rightfully and critically so.

Mattis quickly showed that he was the man people thought he was, an outstanding combat officer with first-rate intellect to deal with what must be dealt with in proper order. Make no mistake that Mattis and Trump did inherit the world's finest military force, but our lead over our primary adversaries had been downgraded under the previous administrations, most glaringly under Obama.

Mattis's position had been filled for one general mission, to rebuild and modernize America's pride and joy—its military. The army was first in line for this rebirth, so to speak. The budget reductions hurt the army more so than the other armed forces over the previous eight years, eroding its ability to fight and win decisively over another comparable force.

Mattis's rebuilding and modernization program, with Trump's blessings, has included equipment upgrades to counter and defeat new weapons, including armed drones, long-range missiles, antiarmor munitions, and even newly improved soldier training changes. In a sense, the army is going "back to the future," and the time to do it was yesterday. Mattis accomplished this before retiring at 2018's end.

ENOUGH IS ENOUGH. We can't afford any more mis-steps in the defense of our country and our freedom. The stakes are way too high. My fellow veterans had been too quiet for too long. The time had come for immediate change when Trump entered the presidential race. Fortunately, and it was extremely pleasing to me, veterans stepped up, got involved, and made it happen by electing a very new kind of president...Donald Trump.

At this book's publishing it was too premature to gauge results from all of these actions influenced by Trump. However, in a January 3, 2018 article by Leo Shane III, *Military Times*, it was stated that VA employee firings jumped in the second half of 2017 after the new accountability legislation was signed into law. Till then outdated laws kept the government from holding those who failed our veterans accountable. Today many of those useless, outdated laws have finally changed.

From February to the end of July 2017, before the new laws took hold, 566 VA workers were terminated (an average of ninety-four per month). From August to December, the figure rose to almost eight hundred firings, or over 172 a month.

In 2015, under VA Secretary Bob McDonald, an Obama appointee, about 1,500 employees were terminated, an average of 125 individuals a month. Looking in from the outside, this veteran sees the legislation this president has passed has been the most significant in decades and has been helping instill real accountability, the type veterans and taxpayers have deserved for so long. As I stated, at this date, it is much too early to come to a credible conclusion on how effective the Trump laws have been. It depends on who is getting fired and why. But this president isn't sitting back waiting for the axes to chop by themselves. Chop away, Mr. President.

It seemed most Americans radically thought one way or the other about the November 2016 election. Voting for an out-of-control egomaniac like Donald trump would be like playing Russian roulette with the future of this country. Voting for someone with a track record like Hillary Clinton would be like putting a .357 magnum with round chambered and pulling the trigger. Then there was the other choice of not voting at all and simply giving up. At least with the Trump option you still had several chances. And that is how the situation stood after President Trump's first year...we still have a lot of opportunities left to avoid that bullet. Now, if only more of America's sour grapes left would allow our president the chance he deserves.

Many more Americans would be pleasantly surprised, if they would just let him do his thing for veterans. Oh how I wonder how it will have turned out if Americans support him and allow him to serve a full term...and then pass their judgment.

There are people who actually think Trump is not fixing the economy? This question was plalstered throughout the media during the early months of 2018. From newspapers to magazines, television/radio and online. Donald Trump's promise to ilmprove the economy by bringing more jobs to America was being challenged, even ridiculed. However on March 10, 2018, this headline was appearing in media outlets[45]: **The Number of Employed Americans Set an All-Time Record Under Trump In March/ April 2018!**

The stock market was soaring. The jobs report of March 10, 2018 said there were 155,215,000 Americans employed during February and January 2018, both record-setting months. There were also recorded highs for two subgroups—black Americans at 19,087,000 and women sixteen and older at 72,530,000. In terms of new jobs, economists came to agree that an increase of 200,000 non-farmworkers could be expected. Surprise, that number was totally obliterated as 313,000 new jobs were recorded. This news remained a well-kept secret by the main news media.

Throughout 2016 and in his first year of 2017, if there was one single theme behind Trump's message, it would seem to be a call for a renewed nationalism and patriotism. He really sounded like he was the man who could make America great again. If he lasts through an entire term, no doubt the world will have become a much more interesting arena, with the USA as the featured gladiator. **Maybe, just maybe, "Trumpism" will become our new nationalism. Then again, maybe not.**

Credit to Obama. Vietnam came closer to the U.S. partly from President Obama's doings. This surprised me but also elated me. Unfortunately, that "attaboy" got taken away when the Philippines announced they were breaking away from the U.S. and a fifty-plus-year friendship was ending. Their new big brother would be China—not good.

---

45 www.bix.gov/news.releasel/lpdf/empsit.pdf

Credit to Trump. The Prez immediately set out to strengthen the newly formed bond between Vietnam and the U.S. and he did it very convincingly.

Credit to Trump. As of April 20, 2018, the Philippines were reported to be leaning back to the U.S. and pushing away from China. This is very excellent news for the U.S. and all our allies.

In my humble opinion these moves have shifted the balance of power in Eastern/Southeastern Asia over to the U.S. and the following staunch allies: Australia / New Zealand, Japan, South Korea, Vietnam, Thailand, and India.

Getting things like this done are what will help make America great again. Believe it.

Trump Kept on Trulmpin… As I was attempting to close this book, for the umpteenth time, Trump had the entire world in a buzz from the North Koreans, Russians, Canada, Mexico, and more. Fighting off the highly biased opposition from the left back in America, he just kept motoring on and on with one accomplilshment and kept promise after another. I almost wished I could keep this book open, keeping an eye on his actions. In my eyes he truly looks for ways every day to help the little guys;; if only every- one could realize this and give him credit for it.

Think about this—hasn't he exposed hypocrisy at a record level within the swamp or deep state? Yes, indeed he has. Especially when the unqualified accusers are as dirty or dirtier than the person they are accusing. Hypocrisy stands loud and clear. Trump seems to attract thousands of these types, and maybe it's justified.

He can expose the ultra-loud critics who try to stomp on everything he says or does, exposing their own selves as liars, cheaters, or even criminals. Example: when the Democrats, who constantly talk of possible collusions, completely ignore what they or their fellow democrats have done. Some of these same people defend Bill Clinton while they accuse Trump of being a sexual predator.

Coincidentally it seems that those who accuse Trump of something vile quickly and disgustingly expose their own vileness. Trump can cause things to boil up, and the scum rises to the top to be skimmed off. He continues to unveil one hypocrite after another. Way to go, Prez! Here is a copy of a emo he sent back to me. Where he lands next after his first term is unknown, but I will always treasure his personal and thoughtful note to me on January 26, 2017.

January 26, 2017

Dear Mr. Trimmer (Dusty),

I appreciate your kind words: and thank you for your service to our country.
Your support means so much to me.

Melania and I are inspired by the sacrifices made by our remarkable service
men and women. I want you to know that I will always be your voice, and I
will always be your champion. I am honored to embark on this new chapter
to make the country you have selflessly served great again.

Working together, we will create a better and brighter future
for you and your family.

With best wishes,

Donald J. Trump

Why not Vietnam? The Vietnamese people emerged early as a coherent community, and the people have now spent much of their twenty-five centuries in fighting off one powerful invader after another. The Vietnamese people have been blessed with a long list of nationalistic and courageous leaders. The U.S. would do well to have Vietnam as a loyal ally. Somewhere, sometime, if and when Vietnam needs him most, you can be sure that a leader with the makeup of the Trung sisters, Tran, Hung Dao, Le Loi, Ho Chi Minh, or Giap will arise to lead the Vietnamese against whoever that unwanted marauder might be.

Presuming that the man who seems most capable and ambitious enough to make America greater, Donald Trump will complete an entire presidential term—at least—I think that Prez will need the staunch support of America's veterans. In particular, I see the Vietnam Era veterans stepping up to cover the Prez's back. And guess which of our allies may also need to play a more important role with teaming up with the USA? I'll step up and say it…Vietnam.

$55 Billion More to Vets June 30, 2018. Just as I thought this chapter was ready to close, the Prez finds time to sign another bill as he continues his staunch efforts to overhaul the Department of Veterans Affairs and provide more and better health care options for us veterans. Does this man ever sleep?

The money will change how the VA pays for private care, expand the VA caregiver program for "pre-9/11" vets, and speed up the process of reviewing the overall infrastructure of the VA itself. This bill actually received overwhelming bipartisan support from the House and Senate. This legislation also followed through with one of Trump's major campaign promises to insure more options for health care in the private sector.

Prez Trump was quoted as follows in *American Military News*: "It seemed like if the vets were waiting in line for several days or weeks and can't see a VA doctor, why aren't they going outside the VA to see a doctor and take care of themselves and we pay for the treatment? It works out much better, and it's immediate care and that's what we're doing. So we're allowing our veterans to get access to the best and quickest care available, at VA or at a private provider."

Whether Prez Trump makes it through an entire term or if he's even eligible for a re-election run, I could not possibly know. However, I felt it necessary and by all means entirely justified to give credit to his TLC toward the American military and its veterans. Very few (if any) American presidents have done more for America's warriors.

Note: Just as I finished this book, I received another letter on 7/31/18 from Mr. "Drain the Swamp" President Trump. How great is that?

Negotiating with China leader

I am one Vietnam veteran who stands by what Prez. Trump has accomplished for all veterans. In his extremely short time, his direct attention to the VA's incompetence and negligence has caused overnight improvements in many areas. I know this ,my experiences are living proof. And, I am in constant contact with many Vietnam vets around the country who share far more compliments about VA healthcare service than I would hear 3-20 years ago. I have had two life saving surgeries at VA attending to my terminally ill conditions. Just as impressive; I have written to every President, every VA Secretary back to the Reagan years with NONE of them responding back. I have heard this way too often from other Nam vet buddies. So it should be no mystery to anyone as to why many vets, particularly Vietnam vets hold a high regard for Prez. Trump.Why not.....he has given us new.... HOPE FOR OUR FUTURE AND OUT FAMILIES.

Chapter 16

UNCOMMON HEROISM

How far can a soldier/warrior be pushed? How much should be expected from the men and women who take the oath to serve their country? After all, everyone has a limit to how much mental or physical pain they can endure until the inevitable breaks their spirit and they crack!

Unbreakable Hearts! has delivered a brief recap of the true impressive history of a small kingdom of tribes from the land now unified under the name Vietnam. For centuries of facing overwhelming odds from massive invasions of their land, they showed remarkable courage, tenacity, and resilience and fought them off every time. Today Vietnam can hardly be referred to as a tiny kingdom, not with a population of a hundred million and with a military of active and militia types almost seven million strong.

American soldiers, drafted from farms and cities, were sent ten thousand miles from home to fight a seasoned, hard-core advisory who they knew little about and certainly were not trained properly to fight. They were led to believe these rebel Viet Cong fought with primitive weapons, mere pitchforks, shovels, and a few booby traps. They went over there as boys used to hunting small game with slingshots and bee bee guns but came back as matured men who were forced to kill humans without ever knowing WHY. Their hearts were as unbreakable as the native Vietnamese who were fighting to preserve their families and country. The Americans soon learned why they had come to fight like wounded tigers—because they had a new family to fight for. This new family became known as the **Brotherhood!**

This chapter should touch everyone who has an ounce of patriotism in their makeup. I could have easily merged this story into one of the earlier chapters, such as "As Tough As They Come," "They Never Gave Up on America," or" Old Soldiers' Stories Are America's History." However, as I dug deeper into the subject, it became quite obvious to me that a separate chapter was needed. I just hoped that I would do it justice.

I have taken a bold step by indicating that our controversial president could become a champion for America's long-neglected veterans. God knows we need someone to step up and stop the inexcusable mistreatment by the Department of Veterans Affairs. Neither of the last several presidents did much for us. Time will tell.

While the Vietnam War was raging in South Vietnam for over ten years, thousands of American Soldiers were fighting their own little war behind the big show. They were rotting and dying in Stone Age prison camps in North Vietnam, Laos, Cambodia, and even China. They were America's prisoners of war and missing in action. They were our ultimate heroes who had **Unbreakable Hearts!**

Imagine a scenario much like those mentioned earlier in the book. Your home, if you care to call it that, is a mini-base camp, actually an outpost—located in the thick brush of Laos or Cambodia. One night all hell breaks loose. The outpost is surrounded and easily overrun by hundreds of fanatical Viet Cong assassins. Everyone is yelling, screaming, and crying out as men are going down all around you and then it's over for you. You are wounded and knocked unconscious. You aren't dead yet, but you could very well be dying soon, and the worst night of your life up to then will be painfully ended. But you do not die that night and you have not seen your worst night yet.

You wake up two days later and it hits you immediately that you are not in South Vietnam, nor are you in a hospital. You are squeezed in a three-by-four-foot cage on muddy ground. There are five of your buddies, all wounded, also lying in tightly fitted cages. No one has received any care for their wounds. Your anxiety level continues to rise as you see dozens of armed NVA guards, and none of them look pleasant to be around. You are now a prisoner of war in North Vietnam, and your future is cloudy.

Your captors leave you caged for a couple more days, feed you rice once a day, ration out small doses of water. You lie in your own urine and feces. Finally you see other American POWs being ushered from a stockade to somewhere. All are in irons, and none look healthy; in fact they look like they are starving, and the marks on their bodies show beatings have been common. Wherever they are being ushered to, in your mind, it would have to be better than a cage on the ground rain or shine.

A couple more days go by. Your buddies are moaning from their painful and infected wounds. You start to wonder if it might have been a blessing if you had died in that night battle, which now seems like a long time ago, but it was just a few days. Why didn't they just finish you off that night like they did to the others? What would they possibly gain from keeping you living in such agony? No one is telling you shit and when you try to utter something to the other caged Americans, you are told to shut up and they kick your cage around.

The heat might kill you, and you almost welcome the rain when it begins pounding on you, but this is no ordinary rain shower. Monsoon season has begun and it may pour down for days and nights. You will be left to lie in the puddles and mud for as long as your captors are entertained by watching you suffer, whine, and scream at them with a rage you didn't know you possessed. Life is not being kind to you, leaving you wondering what you will have to face next.

Morning comes one day after five or six days in the bamboo cage, and a miracle happens as your captors come to you, stand you up FINALLY, and you can barely rise up, but you must. They waste little time and lead you off to a bamboo hut and lay you down on a poor resemblance of a bed. Ecstasy comes over you as you can actually stretch out your legs, and they begin cleaning your wounds, but you wonder if it's too late as the infections have set in, you can feel it.

This scenario could have easily been what many of the American POWs experienced during their first few days in a North Vietnamese prison. For some of them things might have gotten better, but not for the following few brave Americans:

- John Thomas Anderson: U.S. Army Sgt. Captured February 5, 1968 near Hue. Made three escape attempts. First one he passed out from wounds, recaptured. Second time captured quickly. Third escape, captured and beaten by locals but survived until being released in 1973.
- Edwin Otterburg: USAF Pilot shot down August 12, 1967. Escaped May 10, 1969, recaptured. Died May 18, 1969 as a result of beatings/torture.
- Harold Bennett: U.S. Army Sgt., captured March 24, 1969 when his base camp was attacked and overrun. Escaped day of capture, recaptured same day. Next day attempted second escape, was executed same day.
- Donald Cook: USMC Capt., captured December 31, 1964. Escaped March 1965, recaptured immediately. Died in captivity in December 1967. Awarded Medal of Honor posthumously.
- George "Bud" Day: USAF Major, shot down August 26, 1967, captured. Escaped often, evaded North Vietnamese for two weeks with arm broken in three places and banged-up leg. He made it across the DMZ back to S. Vietnam but was shot and recaptured. Awarded Medal of Honor, survived until release in 1973.
- Dieter Dengler: USN Lt. JG, shot down February 1, 1966, captured. Escaped February 12, 1966, recaptured same day. Escaped again on June 29, 1966, living in the jungle, evading captors for three weeks. **Rescued** on July 20, 1966.
- Dennis Hammond: USMC Cpl. Captured February 8, 1968. Escaped April 1968, shot in the leg and recaptured. Locked up in stockade, beaten every day until he died in captivity March 1970.

- James Michael Raj: U.S. Army PVC, captured March 18, 1968. Credited with two escape attempts, awarded Silver Star, died in captivity November 6, 1969.
- Lance Sijan: USAF 1st Lt., shot down November 9, 1967, evaded enemy for forty-six days with serious injuries in Laos. Captured on December 26, 1967, escaped next day, recaptured immediately. Died in captivity January 22, 1968, awarded Medal of Honor posthumously.
- Len Tadios: U.S. Army Sgt, captured December 11, 1964 when overrun in Mekong Delta. Escaped June 1965, recaptured in three days. Escaped October 1965, recaptured next day. Died in captivity March 1966.
- Dennis Thompson: U.S. Army Sgt, captured February 7, 1968 when camp near Lang Vei was overrun. Two attempted escapes, captured and beaten severely. Escaped third time February 18, 1968 in Laos, evaded for full week, carrying another escaped POW, both captured February 25. Fourth escape attempted March 1968, captured immediately and beaten to near death but survived. Released in 1973.
- Floyd (James) Thompson: U.S. Army Capt. Captured March 26, 1964 near DMZ, moved to Laos. Made three escape attempts in April 1964. Fourth escape attempt in May or June 1964. Recaptured on June 21, 1964. Fifth escape attempt made and captured on July 21, 1964. Escape attempt number six on October 1, 1971, recaptured next day. **Remained locked up for two years, being the longest held American POW of the Vietnam War. Released in 1973.**
- Humberto Versace: U.S. Army Capt. Captured October 29, 1963. First escape attempt late November 1969, immediate capture. The Viet Cong executed him on September 25, 1965 after at least three more escape attempts. In 2002, he was posthumously awarded the Medal of Honor. Other POWs say he attempted to escape at least five times.
- Donald Cook: USMC Capt. Captured December 31, 1964. Two escape attempts failed, died in captivity in December 1967. Awarded Medal of Honor posthumously.
- John Graf: USN Lt. Comdr. Shot down and captured November 15, 1969. Escape attempt made, failed, and he was killed in the attempt. Listed as MIA.
- Ben Purcell: U.S. Army Col, shot down (helicopter) February 8, 1968. Escaped December 7, 1969, recaptured. Second escape attempted March 18, 1972, recaptured. Was released in 1973.
- Betty Ann Olsen: Nurse at Ban Methout hospital, captured February 1, 1968. She was constantly moved back and forth across the borders of Cambodia. She became seriously ill with dysentery, malaria, and beriberi, and passed away in prison in September 1968 as a POW.

I could share more of these stories with most ending very sadly, but not all of them. There were thirty-four American POWs who were rescued by U.S. Forces after escaping. One of those was Issac Camacho, U.S. Army SFC, captured west of Saigon on November 24, 1963, when his camp near Hiep Hoa was overrun. Three other Americans survived that battle and were captured: Claude McClure, Kenneth Roraback, and George Smith. On July 12, 1964, Camacho escaped successfully, aided by his buddies who covered for him. Camacho was the first U.S. military POW to be **Rescued!**

The American military attempted at least fifty raids to rescue American POWs, the most well-known being a raid on a camp near Son Tay in North Vietnam. Only five Americans were actually rescued from POW prison camps during the entire war. Two were American civilians who were accidentally rescued when their communist guards stumbled into an American ambush. There were at least five hundred South Vietnamese soldiers rescued during these raids. However, some sources say that the involvement of American politicians and even senior military officers actually hindered the rescue efforts more than they helped. That is not shocking news, but very disheartening. One American POW died shortly after being rescued.

- Larry D. Aiken, U.S. Army. E-4, captured on May 13, 1969. He was reportedly seen alive in a Viet Cong hospital. A rescue attempt was carried out July 10, 1969, when he was found lying on the ground outside the evacuated hospital, unconscious from head wounds. Although he was returned to an American hospital, he remained in a coma until he died on July 25.

During the Korean War, of the 7,190 Americans captured (mostly during the first nine months of the war), approximately three thousand died in captivity, a mortality of 43 percent, largely due to forced starvation. This compared with a WWII mortality rate of 4 percent U.S. POWs in Germany, reflecting the Geneva Convention. However, POWs in Japan had a mortality rate of 34 percent. Special Note: German POWs held by Soviets died at 45 percent and Soviet POWs held by Germans had a mortality rate of 60 percent. U.S. POWs officially held in North Vietnam (1965–1973) had a reported mortality rate of about 15 percent. However, there were at least a hundred MIAs presumed to be POWs who died unreported in captivity, bringing the unofficial rate to more than 20 percent.

Prior to the Korean War, our captured soldiers had no information, no training on how to handle themselves except to reveal only "name, rank, and serial number." The most important information asked of our POWs to gather were names and identification of other POWs, as many as possible. This could make it less likely the captors would feel comfortable in killing the POWs. Vietnam War POWs, particularly, kept in solitary, were ingenious in finding ways to acquire and transmit this information back and forth to each other by Morse code. The North Vietnamese military would become infuriated with this and constantly searched for ways to isolate them and silence them with unhuman torture.

Even though the Chinese and North Koreans spent a great deal of time and effort to indoctrinate and reeducate (brainwash) the POWs, the North Vietnamese did not see the value and stuck with pure torture in an effort to break a POW into collaborating with them. This could mean signing anti-American documents, making anti-American radio broadcasts, telling highly classified information, and/or holding administrative posts that only a few POWs could benefit from. The name of POW John McCain enters many discussions around this sad subject. While fellow Vietnam veteran McCain is not a favorite of mine, I'll not go into details. Let's just say, I put him right alongside Jane Fonda and John Kerry as many Vietnam veterans do, but not all.

The Department of Defense publishes a list of every American listed as POW or MIA in Southeast Asia. I don't know if the 1995 version has been updated. This is not classified information and it is readily available by contacting the Defense Minister of War and Missing Persons Office. Other sources with more specific information about our POWs and MIAs from the Vietnam War are mentioned at the end of this book.

Over a dozen prison camps were used to house U.S. prisoners in North Vietnam, and the most famous was Hoa Lo Prison, or "the Hanoi Hilton." All living at the time were released after negotiations concluded in early 1973 when the first of 591 POWs began to come home on February 12, 1973. This was referred to as Operation Homecoming. At that time there remained 1,350 Americans as POWs or MIAs, and the U.S. had hopes of the return of roughly 1,200 Americans reported as KIA, but their bodies had not been recovered.

The cruel torture techniques used by the North Vietnamese were common knowledge, with their only intention gaining a propaganda victory around the world. Three-by-four-foot cages and pits in the ground were used to hold some prisoners. Heavy and permanently tight rope bindings, irons, various types of beatings that left broken bones, and inhumane, prolonged periods of solitary confinement of three to four years were often exercised.

Near the end of 1969, the torture process suddenly softened up to a great extent for many reasons. Ho Chi Minh passed away, and the infamously unsuccessful rescue attempt called Operation Ivory Coast took place. No prisoners were rescued on this raid, but the effort itself was extremely motivational for many POWs, and it put the North Vietnamese on edge, cautious of future raids to come.

As recently as 2008, some Vietnamese officials were still claiming that no POWs were ever tortured. The POWs' versions disagree drastically.

The return of POWs from previous wars in U.S. history was not celebrated as it was for the Vietnam War's POWs during Operation Homecoming, and it initiated a surge in patriotism not seen before during the Vietnam War. This warm and fuzzy feeling waned quite rapidly as the Ameri-Cong media continued to blast the war, and then the Watergate scandal put all feelings of "welcome home, Johnny" on temporary hold, which seemed to linger on for at least thirty years or more.

Regardless of how America feels about that long-forgotten war, I hope and pray that we will never forget the Vietnam War's veterans, including of course our POW brothers, who in my eyes are the perfect example of what has made the USA a great country. To me, those POWs mean resilience. They showed heart and spirit that only they can understand, but it can be and should be appreciated by every American who loves this country.

For those interested, please circle these dates on your future calendars—February 12 through April 30—as Operation Homecoming for our POWs.

While the majority of American POWs in the Vietnam War were air force officers, shot down in North Vietnam, many of the POWs who were most likely to attempt an escape were U.S. Army men. I won't speculate on that other than this makes me extremely proud of my army brothers, and I suppose this story would have been a perfect fit in Chapter 8: They Were As Tough As They Come, but Unlikely Heroes is fine too.

I keep asking myself over and over, how did one of those courageous lost in the Vietnam jungle survive for forty-six days? How does one evade and outmaneuver the Viet Cong who live in the bush? There had to be dozens of search parties sent from the NVA. Imagine nearly everywhere you step, there is the likelihood of making contact with one of the thousands of poisonous critters that swarm the bushes, grounds, and waterways of Vietnam. Hell, one night alone in the Vietnam bush could seem like a full year, but forty-six days and forty-six nights?

What would have possibly motivated those men of iron will to carry on? Their long odyssey of nightmares began (and could have ended) the night before they were captured after their base camp had been overrun, or shot out of the sky in their plane or helicopter. Maybe if they knew what treachery awaited them, they might have chosen to die in that base camp with the rest. Or they might not have ejected and parachuted to avoid the unforeseen nightmares ahead.

How many "do or die" crises can a human overcome and do it all over again and again?

Why are there fewer than thirty of 175 SEAL candidates remaining after several weeks of intro-training? Most likely, most of the other 145 went in with strong qualifications and a burning desire to make the cut, but they did not. So what drives those thirty to excel, to find that uncommon resolve when they are pressed to the wall?

My company Bravo of the 3rd 22nd Walking Regulars lived out in the jungles and bush of Vietnam for periods of ten, thirty, and eighty-six straight days at a time. You read correctly, eighty-six days once with no conveniences like showers, toilets, clean water, decent warm meals, no roof over your heads when it rained, and many other minor inconveniences. But honestly, this doesn't compare to those guys who had the guts to attempt one escape after another and live in the bush all alone, no supplies, no decent food, no clean water, no clean clothes, no shoes, for days and weeks in an unfriendly jungle.

I don't want to know how those who perished before finding other Americans or before they might have been captured. The ways one could have died out there all alone are endless, I can appreciate this, but I don't know if I would have had the metal to undertake such an ordeal by myself. There had to come a time, more than once, when the easy way out was self-inflicted death. It would have been so easy. So why didn't more soldiers take themselves out of this nightmare of all nightmares? The one single reason why they might have stuck it out and gone past normal human limits over and over may be so they could return to the beloved USA, their true HOME!

James Nicholas "Nick" Rowe. In 1962, the U.S. Army formed the U.S. Army Special Forces Vietnam (Provisional) to advise and assist the South Vietnamese government in the organization, training, equipping, and employment of the Civilian Irregular Defense Group (CIDG) forces. James Nicholas "Nick" Rowe was one of the Special Forces (Green Beret) advisors. He was a West Point graduate who would make a career out of the U.S. Army. When his country became involved in Vietnam, he answered the call and served there. He was remembered by his family as a brave man who knew what he was getting into. His cousin John Ford once said of him, "He walked like an army officer, he talked like an army officer, and he died like an army officer."

The initial United States Special Forces Provisional/CIDG network included fortified, strategically positioned outposts, each one with a small airstrip. Eventually this program developed into combat operations and border and surveillance. These were isolated camps in the middle of heavily active enemy operations that were always vulnerable to attack, and the Viet Cong would gladly oblige.

On October 29, 1963, First Lieutenant Rowe, Sergeant Daniel Pitzer, and Captain "Rocky" Versace were accompanying a CIDG company on an operation. The team were chasing a small enemy unit of Viet Cong, but instead they found an ambush waiting for them. Much of the CIDG company of South Vietnamese soldiers became casualties, and the three Americans were wounded and captured. Nick Rowe would be a POW for sixty-two months but not without causing grief for his captors. He battled the usual inconveniences of the Vietnam jungle: beriberi, multiple fungal diseases, dysentery, physical torture, and psychological torment. Every day he woke up, he thought this would be the day he was going to be executed. Imagine having that thought on your mind each day for five years.

Rowe constantly schemed for the day he would be able to escape. In fact he made four quality attempts until he finally succeeded the fifth time. Ironically, his Viet Cong captors never knew who he was or that he had highly classified information that could benefit them. After his capture he convinced the Viet Cong that he was a mere "draftee" engineer who worked on civil affairs projects. Actually he was a West Point graduate and had access to loads of information about outpost defenses, names of key people, unit strength, locations, etc. Neither torture nor trickery made Rowe reveal his true value to his captors.

Unfortunately, his marathon display of iron will and resilience for five years suddenly crashed as he was betrayed by other Americans. A group of college student war protestors like the SDS at the Kent State riots and today's Amtifa groups researched Rowe's background and fed information to his captors. They were known as the National Liberation Front. "Mr. Trouble," as the Viet Cong named him, was closer to execution, he feared.

Nick Rowe was scheduled to be executed in late December 1968. The VC were fed up with him and no longer wanted to waste time feeding and torturing him. He was not going to break. Rowe refused to go along with the communist ideology, and his continued escape attempts would be put to a halt. When he was being led to the execution location in the forest outside the outpost, his guards were suddenly startled by an American B-52 bombing raid, scattering his guards into different directions. He was left with just one guard, who Rowe was able to take out by striking him with a log, and he made a successful getaway into what was known as the "Forest of Darkness." Again he would be tested to evade his pursuers.

Rowe spotted a group of American helicopters and ran to a small clearing to wave at them. Ironically, since he was dressed in Viet Cong-type black pajamas, the helicopters almost fired at him, but fortunately he was recognized in time and rescued.

Rowe's experience as a POW was an ordeal that few humans could survive. His faith was never shaken in the American system. He was a superb example of the American fighting man during the Vietnam War. He was as tough as they come. None were ever better. He was as good as any.

Rowe remained in the army, and what he had learned in escape-and-evade techniques, he shared when he came back from Vietnam as a major. The army promoted him twice during his POW years. In 1987, as Lieutenant Colonel Rowe was assigned to the Philippines, where communist insurgency was a growing problem—remember the domino theory?—he assisted in training in the fight against the communism threat.

Near the end of 1988, the U.S. State Department's Intelligence and Research Bureau had assimilated credible data on the profound intensity of the Communist Party's penetration into the Philippine government. Prior to that Rowe had often warned his colleagues of the threat, but these warnings appeared to have fallen onto deaf ears. What a shame as Roe himself would become a victim of his own government's ignorance and negligence.

Rowe had been working closely with the CIA. He was also made the chief of the army division of the Joint U.S. Military Advisory Group (JUSMAG) providing counterinsurgence training for the Philippine military. Therefore, the State Department had known for months about the Philippine Communist Party's efforts to identify CIA-backed agents who had infiltrated the party's ranks.

Responding loyally to the request from leaders of the Communist Party in North Vietnam, members of an antiwar group in the United States searched for information about the POWs. They found revealing information, including Nick Rowe's biography. When his Viet Cong captors were handed this information from "the peace and loving friends" of the Viet Cong—the National Liberation Front—his fate was doomed.

On April 21, 1989, Colonel "Nick" Rowe was assassinated, gunned down when a machine gun sniper killed him instantly. The Vietnamese communists never forgot Rowe for the embarrassment he caused them during the Vietnam War. Of course he was never forgiven either. In fact he was a desired target for this terrorist murder. It was learned that they specifically wanted to kill an American Vietnam veteran, and they took out one of our best. In a sad way the Vietnam War took Rowe's life twenty years later.

Rowe had been targeted from the day he arrived in the Philippines because of his confrontations with the North Vietnamese and Viet Cong. Rumors floated around after Rowe's death that the American State Department ignored the threat Rowe faced on April 21, 1989, but for whatever reasons never warned him. His chief regret was said to be his inability to spend more time with his son, who was conceived on a conjugal visit. He was an Uncommon Hero who should be remembered as a legend in American military history.

James Nicholas "Nick" Rowe is buried in Section 48,
Arlington National Cemetery.

Where Did America Get Men Like This? The Vietnam War required a
unique breed of boots-on-the-ground warrior. Take your pick…Army Infantry Grunts. Army Rangers, Army Green Berets, Marines, Navy SEALS, and
the medics, corpsmen, engineers, and Seabees who complete the combat
teams on the ground. Or the air force crews who provided backup support
when the ground troops ran into inescapable situations. But with or without the awesome firepower from the air, armored machines, and artillery,
the communist guerrilla fighters had clearly met their match in their own
in-your-face combat style and in their environment.

Of course our fathers and uncles from the "greatest generation" deserve
some credit for passing on their genes to their sons and nephews. But hered-
ity alone never won wars. Our fathers and uncles fought and won their war;
no one can take that from them, nor would any of us Vietnam veterans
ever want to. It was what they did in WWII that inspired us to answer our
country's call to Southeast Asia. I don't believe America had ever fought
in such a sustained, hard-core guerrilla war against an adversary that had
built up their resilience for over two thousand years. I also do not believe
that eighteen- to twenty-five-year-old Americans deserved to be thrown to
the wolves, so to speak, into the ultimate twilight zone of all wars. This war
had no front lines, no rules, and no ethical boundaries for our enemy. The
only way to defeat them was to fight them back harder, using their unconventional tactics. We were forced to adapt because the stakes were much,
much higher for the VC and NVA than they were for the Americans and
their allies. The northern Vietnamese people had been backed against the

wall before. They had lost their country and their freedom before to foreign invaders. They weren't going to let it happen again. They were not going to let their brave ancestors down.

From my experience and from what I witnessed the hard way, it did not take very long for American ground combat warriors to learn what had to be done and how to do it quickly. To this day I have an extremely difficult time when I look back and realize just how well and how quickly we adjusted to an unknown style of war.

One day we landed in Hawaii for a day of paradise. Nothing seemed real there. Two days later I was walking in an infantry rifle team on a search-and-destroy mission with the U.S. Army's "grunts." There weren't any smiling faces there, no tropical music in the background. That was replaced by explosion background noise. I had a loaded M-16 with live ammo and the gun was not on "safe." Gone were the sights and smells of fragrant flowers. There wasn't anyone with you that you knew; you were kind of on your own. All of the sounds in the forest were magnified. A rat sounded like a water buffalo on the move or another human putting you on edge, ready to pull the trigger.

Most made it through the first day, but those who did not will pop into your mind for as long as you live. But you made it the first day, so what's next? Barely finished with your meager and unappealing C-rations, you hear the command to "lock and load and saddle up." You have to down the C-rats and jump up to join the first platoon to join a night ambush patrol. "What the hell," I uttered on my first night, and I was quickly addressed by a squad leader who said, "We don't sit around waiting for the VC. Those days are over. We're going out to find them. This is Vietnam troop."

You want this first ambush to be successful, which would mean some enemy died that night and not you or your buddies. We did lose a couple of men that night from mortar attacks. This meant, unfortunately, that the VC knew our position and we did not know theirs. Obviously, I made it through that night as most did, but there were casualties, and for the second straight night I got zero sleep.

The rule for survival through more days and nights in the future was this simple…learn to be a guerrilla warrior as quickly and as efficiently as you could. Your training started yesterday, so treasure what you learned. After a couple of weeks had gone by, which did not go fast, those strangers with you on that first day—you now know each other's entire life history, and they are your brothers. A few months later about half of your platoon has been replaced by new guys. You have now been out in the bush for a 25th Infantry Division record of eighty-eight consecutive days. You have aged a couple of years, lost about fifty pounds, your skin is rotting away in multiple areas, diarrhea is a given on a daily basis, some guys get malaria, and now you are one of the seasoned combat grunts, and it's your duty to help the new guys who keep coming in. They have to learn quickly as you did. It's life or death.

Then one day several months later, you wake up on the Freedom Bird, on your way home…FINALLY! Oh wow, you want to step on American soil so bad that you go sleepless a couple more nights. You ignore (try to) the protestors at the airports. Going home is all you can focus on for now.

You make it! You're home, BUT? People have been questioning you about your mission over there. Your character is being challenged, Did you guys really do the things the media told us about? Even some veterans from Korea and World War II provide unsolicited comments about how incredible your war was, in comparison to their war. What the hell is going on here? You taught yourself to be a guerrilla war fighter for a full year. You and your guys won pretty much every battle against a tenacious and unbelievably resilient enemy in the most inhumane conditions imaginable. Why are you being treated so coldly and rudely as though you were the communist enemy you had just defeated in dozens of bloody battles?

This you never expected; it is so wrong. Anger becomes an uncontrollable emotion and yet no one can understand why or try to. The other dominant emotion you feel is probably the most painful. You have begun suffering from…a **Broken Heart!**

Decades go by, many of you retain the anger as well as the broken heart, although the severity subsides—BUT…it is evident that your inner feelings of being betrayed and dishonored can easily be brought to the surface if/when some unworthy troll offers up an unsolicited and unwelcomed opinion about your war and your brothers.

Undoubtedly you are suffering from post-traumatic stress disorder, and you take on mental health therapy at the Veterans Affairs. You find out that tens of thousands of other veterans suffer from PTSD, from all wars and at varying levels. Many more Vietnam vets have died prematurely back home than those 58,479 who died in Vietnam. This doesn't help you feel any better.

No one knows of any other culprit to blame for this phenomenal punishment the Vietnam veterans were given, except this one logical suspect. The Ameri-Cong media or fake news, and a Democratic Congress and Senate jointly own this distinction.

The New York Times

U.S. Forces Out of Vietnam; Hanoi Frees the Last P.O.W.

War Role Is Ended After Decade of Controversy

Thousands Watch 67 Prisoners Depart

Chapter 17

VIETNAM'S GREATEST LIES...DESTROYED!

M aybe the reasons for sending 2.8 million or so of America's soldier boys to Vietnam do not hold water. Maybe the two million South Vietnamese and two million North Vietnamese who were sacrificed was for nothing. Maybe the corrupt governments of the United States and South Vietnam should stand trial for war crimes. Maybe? What must not be forgotten is how the brave soldiers and marines fought like wounded tigers over there with little reason or any motivational factors whatsoever except for this one...**TO COVER EACH OTHER'S ASSES!**

No one wanted the U.S. to be in Southeast Asia fighting a war. Plus, everyone was able to watch the "living room war" on their home TVs. But the TV cameras covered mostly the base camp battles or the large city attacks at places like Hue, Khe Sanh, and Saigon, where the reporters could cover the action more easily and safely. During most of the war, the "bush"—jungles and swamps—remained remote, where only the Viet Cong and alien wildlife resided. Agent Orange would change that, and eventually, the grunts and marines became fixtures in the bush. They were unwelcome inhabitants who would disrupt the Viet Cong's unique guerilla war style, which they'd had two thousand years to perfect.

Most of the battles fought in the bush rarely lasted more than one day or night. Too many times, there were few or no survivors from the American or South Vietnamese side, especially from 1967 to 1968. So America rarely witnessed the behind-the-scenes action where most of the blood was shed. Had the media ventured off into the night with the evening ambush patrols, rubbed elbows with the real heroes of that war, America would not have betrayed their own who fought for their lives so often. The army's grunts and marines became more than a match for the VC and NVA, who had the decisive advantage of fighting in their own backyards. Again, those Americans never got to see those guys in action from their warm and cozy living rooms.

Our single-day or -night battles which I am familiar with took place at non-household named places such as Suoi Tre, Soui Cut, Dau Tieng, Nui Bau Den, Trang Bang, Hoc Mon, Duc Hoa, Phu Cong, Prek Klok, and Go Dau Hau. Only a handful of readers will be familiar with those places and what happened there. I don't remember any reporters or movie cameras around.

So, the big lies about that war flowed back to America as well as the world. The living room home movies showed burning villages and wandering Vietnamese, but the viewers were never told who caused the villages to burn down or who made the people homeless. Nor did the home viewers get to see the American engineers going in to rebuild the destruction from the Viet Cong. In the end, the Viet Cong only did what they had to do, and probably what the French and Americans forced them to do in order to survive.

Somebody ought to make a movie about these people, as I know of no other group or nationality of people who have been so often faced with invasions by global powers that had one or two goals in mind...to enslave an entire culture or to completely eliminate them from the face of the earth. Only once did a global power actually defeat these people in a ground war on their homeland. In 1967 through 1969, the American military soundly and repeatedly defeated these people in combat. Only one thing went wrong...NO ONE TOLD THEM THAT THEY HAD BEEN BEATEN, SO THEY FOUGHT ON!

What was the fantasy or passion for the world's greatest superpowers' repeated invasion attempts to force their will and their way of life onto a small peace-loving population of farmers and peasants like the Vietnamese? Even more bewildering to me is the result of all of these invasions. Some invasions were successful by the Chinese and the French but not for long, as the Vietnamese people refused to remain a conquered nation. Looking back to around 113 BC is when China's first major invasion of the Vietnamese people's homeland was successfully accomplished. This domination would last until 39–40 AD, when two unlikely heroines would get the ball rolling for Vietnamese nationalism to be born and for it to last until the day this book was completed.

Every day, so it seems, another great myth about that hard-to-forget war in Southeast Asia is uncovered and disproven beyond any shadow of a doubt. Because of reasons already mentioned in this book, after the North Vietnam defeat of France and colonialism itself, our American presidents were seemingly misled into resuming a war the French could not win (even with hundreds of millions in support by the U.S.). So we stepped in, making one of the most catastrophic decisions in the history of warfare on planet Earth. The U.S. and several other countries chose to support the horribly corrupt country of South Vietnam, formerly a part of the country of Vietnam, before the French invasion. Another blind and stupid blunder was made very obvious—that the South Vietnamese military leaders were just as inept as their government leaders were corrupt. And we were going to train and motivate these losers to do things they were just not capable of doing. Right out of the gate, as our military was increasing its unfortunate commitment of American troops to Southeast Asia, the Viet Cong welcomed our guys by showing us that they were ready for us and that they did not fear us.

Viet Cong victories in the early years of 1963 and 1964 shocked our elite military leaders. Ap Bac, Hiep Hoa, Cha La, An Lao, and Binh Gia (and the first battle of Pleiku) were decisive victories for the VC and they came quickly and furiously. The war (still referred to as a *conflict*) did not favor the U.S. and its allies until some of the battles fought in 1965, such as Song Be and Ia Drang. However, Viet Cong determination was never thwarted as they continued to notch victories to their credit. But this war was just beginning to heat up.

Yes, the U.S. won the majority of the more publicized battles. Maybe that is the reason they were publicized. But 1967 and 1968 were brutal years for the Viet Cong and their NVA brothers, as our search-and-destroy missions crippled them with ferocity that I am sure no Vietnamese military force had ever suffered in their two-thousand-year history of fighting major wars.

I think the Vietnam War can be divided into four phases, and I have described them by using the casualty totals of the one hundred largest battles of the entire war and listing the won, lost, and draws for the period. Keep in mind that the element of surprise favored the enemy more in the smaller battles when they pulled the ambush. They did not lose many of those, but our counterattacks were brutal. None of those hundreds of skirmishes are included. Chapter 14 lists the titles of about fifty large battles (an amateur history buff's Vietnam War analysis of major battles results):[46]

Phase I   **1959–1964**

Fought primarily between South Vietnamese or ARVN forces against primarily Viet Cong communist sympathizers. U.S. troops were filtering in, but would not reach peak strength until 1969.

- ARVN/USA Victories	10
- VC/NVA Victories	8
- Indecisive/Draw	2

Phase II   **1965–1969**

The bloodiest years—U.S. troop strength would be at its maximum in 1968 to 1969. U.S. troops took control of the war in most large battles. Ho Chi Minh knew his army could never win the war if this pattern continued.

- ARVN/USA Victories	35
- VC/NVA Victories	1
- Indecisive/Draw	2

Phase III 1970–1973

The phasing-out years as U.S. ground troops were pretty much out of the war from 1972–1973. South Vietnam was left to fight their adversary alone on the ground with some temporary American air and artillery support.

- ARVN/USA Victories   12
- VC/NVA Victories   12
- Indecisive/Draw   2

Phase IV 1974–1975

All of the major victories by the communists were waged against South Vietnamese forces only, as VC forces were never able to reach their peak strength of 1968. In 1974–1975, it was more of a North Vietnam war against South Vietnam. China and the Soviet Union had increased their military support of the NVA and VC by the billions while the USA's liberal democratic Congress had withdrawn all U.S. support for South Vietnam. Communist victories were now the rule until the very end.

- ARVN Victories   1
- VC/NVA Victories   13
- Indecisive/Draw   2

Perfectly clear here, in the earliest years, the Viet Cong—former Viet Minh under Ho Chi Minh and General Giap—continued with their momentum from their victories in their war with the French, and they appeared to hold their own against the South Viets and early American forces. Had the war continued as it was with minor American ground forces in-country, it was believed that South Vietnam would not be able to survive as an independent nation and that communism rule was inevitable. As the U.S. ground troops poured into Vietnam, the war looked to be very winnable for the U.S. Although the U.S. soldiers and marines were often outnumbered in the major ground wars of 1967, 1968, and 1969, the Americans were winning often and convincingly as the grunts and marines had no problem with taking the battle directly to a formidable enemy in his environment. As the search-and-destroy missions were all but ceased in 1969 and 1970, and the plan of *Vietnamization* was stepped up, victories for the VC/NVA resumed their commonality. In 1975, the final year, the South Vietnamese, alone against the North Vietnamese, were horribly overmatched.

This book has focused on destroying one of those great lies that was created and built upon by our country's Ameri-Cong media. Along the way, several other lies were inadvertently exposed and completely disproven. I apologize for any duplication here, but I must review these important historical events in chronological order to stress the importance of this book's main mission:

The Brave and Resilient Vietnamese People's Almost Three Thousand Years of Being Underestimated by World Powers!

- 40 AD—The Trung sisters led a small army of farmers and peasants to a shocking victory in a war for independence over their powerful rulers from China.
- 248 AD—The Han dynasty of China, Vietnam's latest conqueror, was caught off guard as Warrior Lady Trieu led a highly outnumbered ragtag force to victory.
- 543 AD—As another invader ruled them for several decades, a knight in shining armor, Ly Nam De, led this successful rebellion over the Liang dynasty.
- 930 AD—The reign of General Ngo Quyan began as once again, China's Han dynasty took control over Vietnam. His war would successfully banish another military of several hundred thousand from the world power Han dynasty.
- 1076 AD—One hundred fifty years after Ngo Quyen defeated the Han Chinese, the Song Chinese dynasty rose to be a world power and Vietnam was invaded again. One more time, another Vietnamese general stepped up, leading a preemptive attack and overwhelming the Song forces with a stunning victory over a massive force.
- 1259—A new scourge of Asia erupted onto the scene, the Mongol hordes of Genghis Khan. The Mongols defeated the Persian Empire, the Song-Chinese dynasty, burned Baghdad to shambles, and slaughtered millions in Asia and Eurasia. Vietnam was in the path of the hordes from Mongolia. That imminent invasion was coming soon. This would mark the first defeat of a Mongol military in battle.
- 1285—A second Mongol invasion of Vietnam was led by their famous naval commander, Sogatu, but another expected victory was thwarted decisively. The Vietnamese did not pursue their defeated invader, a mistake they would not make again.
- 1288—The third and final Mongol attempt to conquer and annihilate the entire population of Vietnam. Kublai Khan even sent his favorite

son, his top general, and 550,000 men to take on the Vietnamese "George Washington," General Tran Hung Dao. The third battle was the most historic of the battles and wars in which Vietnam had ever been engaged. Victory was almost in the hands of the Mongols twice, but each time the Vietnamese regrouped and then counterattacked repeatedly until most of the Mongol generals were slain or had surrendered.

With the entire Mongol navy destroyed, most of their ground forces dead or wounded, the Vietnamese followed the remnants of Kublai Khan's once proud forces well into their homeland, continuing the counterattacks for hundreds of miles. This awesome bludgeoning of the most fearsome military force in history would allow three hundred years of peace for Vietnam.

Their Mind-boggling Victories Continue

- Fifteenth century—The Vietnamese held off another unsuccessful invasion by the Chinese military in an attempt to re-conquer Vietnam, as it was then. The invasion failed.
- Seventeenth century—Most of what is now Cambodia, Laos, and Siam/Thailand was taken control of by the Vietnamese.
- As far back as the seventeenth century, there was a divided Vietnam. In the late 1700s, the south conquered the north, and by 1802, there was a united Vietnam. In the interim, a united Vietnam fought off another invasion attempt by China.
- Vietnam's long history was one of violence and, more often than not, successful resistance against overwhelming odds (Chinese—Mongols).
- The French again divided Indochina, including what was then Vietnam, into three parts: Northern, Central, and Southern.
- 1920s—The Vietnamese continued unsuccessful efforts to drive the French out. It was in the late 1920s that a Vietnamese named Ho Chi Minh had formed the Vietnam Revolutionaries...all thirty-five of them.
- 1930s—Ho's forces had multiplied into the tens of thousands and conducted wave after wave of strikes against the French. French legionnaires and other mercenaries were brought in, and the assault, rape, robbery, and slaughter of close to a hundred thousand Vietnamese commenced. Tens of thousands of innocent civilians were also deported, imprisoned, or executed. The conduct of the legionnaires and mercenaries was indescribably merciless.

- 1943—Viet Minh guerilla operations were launched against the occupying Japanese, successfully led by Ho Chi Minh and General Vo Nguyen Giap. Their Viet Minh army expelled the Japanese and liberated a considerable portion of what is northern Vietnam today. At first, the French recognized the new government as a free state, and then reneged on that. The U.S. chose to support France.

- 1945—The U.S. sent aid and supplies to the French. Few Americans appeared to appreciate Vietnam's history. In fact, in 1945, President FDR was quoted as saying, "The Indochinese are people of small stature…and not very war-like." This misperception was undoubtedly handed over by the French, who had conquered most of Indochina.

- 1954—Just a decade later, some thirty thousand legionnaires were outwitted, outfought, outgunned, forced to surrender, and slaughtered by the sons of those same so-called farmers with pitchforks at a place on the Vietnam-Laos border called Dien Bien Phu in 1954… shortly after the Korean War ended in a stalemate.

- 1959 to 1972—**The Americans entered** a long, bloody war of attrition with North Vietnam, led by Ho Chi Minh and General Nguyen Giap, who were fighting the world's greatest superpower, the United States of America and her allies from South Vietnam, Australia, Thailand, Philippines, and South Korea to a "draw" until the Paris Peace Treaty of 1973.

- 1974 to 1975—North Vietnam defeated South Vietnam in a civil war and the two countries were united again as one Vietnam.

- 1977 to 1979—Vietnam invaded Cambodia, defeated the rogue military of the Khmer Rouge, and freed Cambodia from brutally ruthless acts of genocide.

- 1979—China invaded northern Vietnam while most of Vietnam's military was still in Cambodia fighting the Khmer Rouge renegades, trying to free the Cambodian people. Vietnam was left with one-tenth of their active armed forces and an all-volunteer force of military comprised of farmers and peasants to fight five hundred thousand Chinese Regular Army troops. Both sides claimed victory, but clearly, the Chinese incurred heavier casualties and suffered the great shame of not being able to subdue an untrained, outnumbered militia of civilians (including women) who worked in rice paddies in their day jobs. Again, the tenacity and strong will of the Vietnamese people defeated a superior force of invaders in the same spirit as their historic ancestors did over and over to protect their land.

Whether today's Americans care or not about how great the people of Vietnam have been for over ten centuries, as a combat infantry U.S. Army veteran who "mixed it up" with them, who was brainwashed to despise them and to disrespect them, I have almost come full circle with my feelings toward those phenomenal people and the awesome history of their beloved kingdom.

Most of us know that we should never underestimate the heart of a dog—man's best friend. Well, one world power after another has made that mistake for a variety of reasons with the Vietnamese people. The American bureaucrats who inhumanely led us off the cliff like an army of lemmings, who led us to believe our purpose in life was a noble one, are guilty for the cruel and unforgivable destruction of millions of people during and after that war. They deserve to spend eternity in purgatory, but of course, that is not my call.

So, is Vietnam communist? For those American politicians who believed that in the 1960s and for any who still carry such a notion…you are mostly wrong.

I already mentioned Ho Chi Minh's efforts in reaching out to America for support with their resistance from the Colonial French to regain their independence. And since we ignored Ho's attempts in favor of supporting the French with their inhumane domination over most of Indochina, communism was brought to Vietnam because it was the only way Vietnam could lay claim to their country's total freedom. Most of the South Vietnamese people who swore their loyalty to Ho Chi Minh and North Vietnam were called Viet patriots rather than communists. To the people of Vietnam, kicking out the invaders from France and the U.S. was worth accepting communism to do it.

The Communist Party of Vietnam didn't just suddenly show up one day and take over North Vietnam. Ho Chi Minh had formed one of the original umbrella groups of mass movements in Vietnam aligned with communism, forming the North Vietnamese government. Uncle Ho's group, founded in May 1941, was called the League for the Independence of Vietnam, which was later merged into the Vietnamese Fatherland Front, founded in 1955.

The Vietnamese Fatherland Front was solidified in 1977 by mergers with Viet Cong groups, the National Liberation Front of South Vietnam, the Alliance of National Democratic and Peace Forces of South Vietnam, and of course the Communist Party itself. As for the Viet Cong, contrary to some sour grapes reports by American writers, the VC were embraced and respectfully merged or united into society. The Viet Cong flag remains a respected symbol today and is used as a symbol of national pride.

The Vietnamese government today sees the Vietnamese Fatherland Front as the political base of the people's power. It has a significant role in

Vietnam's society, promoting nationalism and unity of mind in political and spiritual matters. The Front is a major influence in programs that reduce the long-standing poverty in Vietnam.

Nationalism and patriotism were the motivating factors for the Viet Cong and the NVA, and the furthest thing from their minds during battle was finding a paradise of communism. They also cared about being able to work their rice paddies in peace again and providing a couple of good square meals for the family. They weren't asking for too much. With that dream achieved, at a horrific cost, Vietnam has never really been a communist state. And it isn't now, say most Vietnamese citizens.

Communism had to be brought into Vietnam in order to claim back independence for a united Vietnam. Repeating myself here because it is so important, the Vietnamese people who went to war under the name of communism, the Viet Cong, at the very heart, were patriots and nationalists. Also, after the war ended and Vietnam became one country again, the leaders who were devoted communists rewrote the country's constitution that Ho Chi Minh had pretty much constructed, to make sure that they are never challenged again from within.

Hate to say this but I think it is true at this point that China and Vietnam are the fastest growing economies in the world. It is quite possible that Vietnam under Ho Chi Minh would have become like Vietnam is today, had the two separated Vietnams been allowed to fight it out between themselves. And Ho Chi Minh's North Vietnam would have easily dominated the corrupt South Vietnamese government.

Vietnam's economy is flourishing today, and it is not following the communist models. Neither is their society even near communism; they don't really care and they don't need any outsiders to try to save them. Save them from what?

Despite what many Americans choose to think about so-called communist countries, it has become quite evident that most Vietnamese citizens have become supportive of their government; after all, the postwar years of the late 1970s have been gone for four decades. In the many communications I have enjoyed with Vietnamese people during the last ten years or so, I've learned that they show little concern if any about the bad propaganda about communist-controlled countries, as they just don't feel like one of them.

It is the opinion of this Vietnamese War veteran that there has been a resurgence of the centuries-old nationalistic pride. If their country was ever invaded again by anyone, China included, the Vietnamese people would fight and defend their homeland with the same resolve that their highly respected ancestors did for hundreds of years.

Chosen people? Throughout the world's history, various groups of people have considered themselves to be *chosen people* in reference to God. Israelite ancestry has received claims from the Christians, white Jews, and black Hebrew sects. Some Christians (Catholics included) put claims on being chosen people based strictly on their religion and their belief that their particular church has replaced Israel as the true people of God.

If you have already determined that I know little about this subject, I confess it. But I am entering the zone anyway with a few of my own God-given rights to offer an opinion. There are mounds of literature available in nearly every language, and I have hardly even scratched the surface of those written in or translated to English.

Some of the many groups that have claimed to be God's chosen people would undoubtedly surprise you.

The Mormons believe that many of their faith are from one of the tribes of Israel. Some Christians claim descendants of the ancient Israelites are of Anglo-Saxon, Germanic, Nordic, and kindred peoples of the world. Some sources of Jewish biblical tradition and Ethiopian legends say that Israel's King Solomon and Ethiopia's Queen of Sheba conceived a child, making the Ethiopian people the true children of Israel and the chosen people. And yet, Sun Myung Moon taught that Koreans were chosen to serve a divine mission under God, and the Koreans would be the last of the birthplace of "Heavenly Tradition," bringing in God's kingdom. Elijah Muhammad, the founder of the Nation of Islam, taught and called for the establishment of a separate nation of black Americans and the adoption of a religion based on the worship of Allah on the belief that blacks were God's chosen people.

People of God is a term used in the Old Testament or Hebrew Bible that applies to the Israelites. In the New Testament, which refers to Christians, we see the terms *people of God* and *His people*, meaning God's people. The popes have often continued to use the expression *the people of God*. Pope Paul VI used it with regard to his profession of faith. Pope John Paul II used it in his teaching that the Church is the new people of God. The catechism of the Catholic Church devotes a section to describing the Church with characteristics of the people of God that distinguishes it from all other religious, ethnic, political, or cultural groups found in history. Membership of the people of God, it says, comes not by physical birth but by faith in Christ and baptism. Being married to a dedicated Catholic, I know that Ginny Trimmer does not accept some of the beliefs mentioned in this section, nor do I. I am a Christian and baptized a Christian.

Why not me, Lord? All of God's people...does that in fact refer to all civilizations, all religions, and all races of all time? Maybe, but there can be little doubt that the Nazi Germans could never be considered the chosen people. What about the Mongols of the twelfth and thirteenth centuries? How could God allow Genghis Khan's empire to thrive at the cost of forty to fifty million innocent people's deaths? Then again, it is recorded that when Genghis Khan's armies conquered a land, he demanded freedom of religion be put in place immediately. So, the Mongols could not have been all bad. Although known as a ruthless conqueror, Genghis was also looked at by his followers as a generous and fair man who appreciated and often rewarded exceptional bravery and especially loyalty. It is believed the Mongol armies included hundreds of thousands of soldiers from the lands that Genghis conquered; they remained true to him throughout his life and they were rewarded well for this.

Had Genghis been living and in command of the Mongols who first invaded the kingdom of Vietnam and were defeated by the highly outnumbered Vietnamese population, he might have left them alone from thereafter. The Vietnamese did not draw first blood. They merely took up swords and arrows to prevent the total extinction of their people. Genghis would have respected such an adversary.

So, why not the Vietnamese people as God's chosen people? Surely, there has been a divine force present in Southeast Asia over the last several thousand years. How else could the Vietnamese people have survived one massive domination attempt after another, having fewer resources, technology, and numbers of people to defend their borders? Why is this such a far-fetched idea?

As valuable as Israel is as an ally to America in the troubled Middle East, Vietnam could be considered every bit as valuable to America as an ally to balance things in Southeastern Asia. China looms as a major threat to America, and there is no love between China and Vietnam and vice versa.

Throughout the history of civilization, the Vietnamese people have been underestimated. I personally regret how we devastated their land and poisoned their people as well as many of our own we sent over there to stage a war with them. A war that did not have to happen, a war that should not have happened, and yet…a war that is still killing those who fought there and survived.

In North America, Europe, and probably Australia, people consider friendliness as the heart of interpersonal relationships, while in Vietnam, respect is emphasized. Whether it is the relationship among members in a family, colleagues in the workplace, or teachers and students at school, respect is the cornerstone of relationships in Vietnamese society. This universal truth is reflected in the language Vietnamese use in their daily life. They use many terms as personal pronouns when communicating with each other to show different levels of respect, such as "dad," "professor," "uncle," "sister."

Vietnamese Arent' Smart? Some so called economical experts will say that there is a clear positive relationship between a country's economic strength and how well its students perform. However, Vietnam is one of the few low income countries that performs at the same level as many richer countries. In fact, some TIMSS tests show that Vietnamese vastly outperform people in other countries of similar GDP per capital. Their scores are more on par with Canada, Switzerland, Italy etc. and way above other developing countries such as Peru, Columbia, Tunisia, Cambodia etc.

What's their secret? We can probably look at our own less privilege students in our inner city school systems. They aren't any poorer than the Vietnamese. The differences have been surmised in this way - Vietnam invests more in their education systems, Vietnam's parents are more involved with children's academic activities. There are fewer schools in the cities than there are in the villages and small towns. Performances are closely monitored and therefore students take their school work very seriously. Vietnamese students are rarely late for classes, have few unexcused absences and hardly skip classes. There study habits are more dedicated and they do not shy away from doing several extra hours outside of school.

Again, Vietnam is the only low-income country that performs at the same level or higher as more wealthy countries on international academic tests. Looks like it begins at home. Or . . . Vietnamese are just special people. As Confucianism has had a profound impact on societal order in Vietnam, the value of family attachment, one of the most important rules in Confucianism, has gained its influence on social and moral values. Relations between members in family—husband and wife, parents and children, old generation and young generation, distant relatives and close relatives—have been put at the center of relationships in general. Those values are passing from generation to generation.

In Vietnam, age is not a burden but an asset. Accordingly, the elderly enjoy the highest respect in the society, regardless of education, social position, and financial capacity. And Vietnamese society shows great respect for teachers and doctors, whether they are young or old, due to their great contribution to the society. So, another Vietnam War lie debunked.

Those of us who are still hanging around—no one really knows how many of us there are—will most likely never find the answers to why they sent us to die over there or to die back here, prematurely and heartbroken. I may die someday not knowing the answer to one of the many unanswered questions. That single profound question is...**WHY?**

Every Vietnam War veteran who witnessed how our gutsy enemy lived over there, how driven they were to make a life for their families, to protect the rice paddies and jungles they and their ancestors fought so hard to protect at any cost, should take heart in knowing...*they* also respected the heart we had.

My war buddies know WHY we fought as hard as we did against a grubby, fanatical adversary. They know WHY we refused to lose to them. We can be sure that those who spat at us when we came home could not possibly ever understand. Nor do they care to try to understand today. I would never seek out a chat of any sort with the likes of a Laurence Vance, Jane Fonda, or John Kerry. They and others like them represent a breed of people who can quite simply be categorized as the real "deplorables."

What makes people like this tick? Do they even have an ounce of guilt in that it is people like them who divide our country, not the unfortunate patriot who crawled around with scorpions and bamboo vipers, stalking a Viet Cong who was also stalking him at the same time? I could never expect America-haters to understand or appreciate the fabric of this country. That same fabric was put into place by our grandparents and great-grandparents, and this is what America's soldiers and marines were made of who fought together in the Vietnam War. Why do these "deplorable" people remain in this glorious country?

Over there…our brotherhood powered our mission! We grew up together. Maybe not in the same town or in the same state, but we grew up together. We came together from California to Wyoming, from Louisiana, Indiana, Maine, Florida, and all states in between. We came from Twinsburg, from Dallas, Boise, Duluth, Boston, and Coral Gables, and we came together to form a genuine brotherhood, which America's Vietnam vet haters could possibly never appreciate.

Hey, dude, where you from? says the city kid from Detroit to the farm boy from Dubuque. They had almost nothing in common from their childhoods, but in a very short period of time—maybe just a couple of days, but more likely a few weeks—their brotherhood would form and their special bond could last a lifetime, however long that was. Sometimes it took guys a bit longer to get it over there, and many of us began to isolate ourselves because we knew someone we had made the mistake of befriending might not be there the next morning. Eventually though, we did become a family of brothers. It was inevitable, especially those who faced the horrible threat that combat in the bush threw at us.

Our brotherhood wasn't about being Audie Murphy or Private Ryan or John Wayne character. *It* wasn't about each of us as individuals. *It* was about a silent family. We rarely showed our emotions over there, and as many of us haven't opened up even yet, back here. *It* was the squad, the platoon, the M-60 machine gunner, the RTO, the medic, the rifle team, the squad leader, the platoon leader, and the guys back at Cu Chi or Pleiku or Danang who manned the mortar and artillery support. *It* was about the Huey pilot and gunner. Getting *it* was about two boys coming together in an ambush, one from Chicago, the other from Marietta, risking their lives for each other, for the rest of their new family so that more of them could make it just one more day and maybe…maybe make it long enough to see home again.

Our love for each other could be costly. In fact, it inevitably ended that way, over there or back here. We had to move forward or at least try to, even though in many situations we had no one else to cry with than each other.

I constantly envision the faces of each and every one of the 1st Platoon of Bravo Company who came together in March, April, and May of 1968. We were all f—ing new guys thrown into a situation where we were guaranteed to be in a firefight just too soon. *It* was about the bunch of guys before us who we replaced one day, leaving us wondering almost immediately when our time would come to be replaced. We remember the unfortunate times when a guy just could not take it anymore and he went berserk. More often than not, we remember those guys who held their position or maybe advanced during a deadly attack. We remember those guys—they were doing *it* for the rest of us.

Those faces…oh my God, those faces will always be with us—can't help it. I can remember a simple, short, but extremely emotional moment one day in July 1968 that happened—unplanned of course—after a bloody ambush that left us with wounded bodies in every direction. I remember one of our platoon brothers walking up to another who was badly shaken (we all were). In fact, he was still in a state of shock. I remember the faces of both men when one said to the other, "Damn, man, that sure was a great thing you did out there today. I am proud to know you!" The emotion in that exchange, their faces, cannot be described in words. That two-minute exchange of love for each other was like…WOW!

Both of those men made it through their little detour in life called *The Nam*. They came home as changed men, and guess what…they remain close friends to this day and I suspect they always will.

Over there seems like it only happened yesterday, but many times you find yourself wondering if it all really happened…over there.

All of a sudden, it seems, Americans are saying to you "welcome home" from some place in your life that happened forty-plus years ago. Why are they saying this to you now? Didn't they say it when you came home from over there? You can't seem to even remember one way or another; then suddenly, you clearly remember and your heart is broken again.

All we had was each other over there…then in an instant, we had nothing left but memories from over there. Everything after that experience over there seems so insignificant. Why can't the people around you understand you and what happened to you and your brothers…over there?

The Vietnam War was a mess. It was initiated by and fought for reasons understood by no one other than the most cynical Washington politicians. It destroyed an entire generation's faith in our government, leaving permanent scars on all of America that have not healed completely to this day.

Washington dragged that war on and refused to find a way to bring us home because they were more concerned about how to save face without losing their precious global standing than in preventing more of America's sons from rotting away in the jungles of an impending communist-dominated country.

Like every war Americans have ever fought in and sacrificed themselves for their beloved USA, Vietnam War veterans carried on in the battlefield in spite of the burden of fighting and dying in a war...with faith! With faith in our God and in the man in front of us, behind us and alongside us. Even though our nation's heart wasn't in it and did not believe in the fight, and our politicians were never willing to win...we woke up every morning, dreading the task before us, not even believing we would survive one more day, but we went out there and fought a brave, dedicated, elusive enemy who fought us with heart and an iron will that no American military had faced in 240 years.

It worked both ways...indeed, I have spent a lot of time in this book talking about the amazing history of the Vietnamese people, their heart, their resilience, their will, and their mind-boggling tenacity whenever their homeland was invaded or threatened for a possible invasion. Every kudo mentioned in this book about the Vietnamese people is deserved. They brought it to us and we brought it back to them, and just maybe the great leaders of North Vietnam had made their own unthinkable error by underestimating the qualities of the American, Australian, and South Korean soldier boys. Granted, we were not fighting to protect our homeland in this war even though we were brainwashed during our combat training in the States into thinking that we would be doing just that. Our cause was every bit as noble and worthy as that of the Vietnamese military...we were fighting to preserve the lives of our newly formed brotherhood, and believe it, we took that mission very seriously.

America and our allies did not turn tail and run when the communist forces of Ho Chi Minh, backed by China and the Soviet Union, threw everything they had at us in one of history's greatest surprise attacks on another major military force, the Tet Offensive of January and February 1968. This unexpected onslaught had all the makings of a slaughter of American and allied forces, but the counterattack by our forces was awesome and caught the communists completely off guard. The Tet Offensive would end in an overwhelming victory for the Americans and our allies. But...the Ameri-Cong media simply forgot to report it that way. Sour grapes? Hell, no... FACT!

Make no mistake; our brash counterattacks in March and into April did not send the VC and NVA to their knees even though it should have, because a less resilient adversary would have retreated to their safe haven in North Vietnam. No, they did not do that. In fact, the thorough butt whipping we gave them may have awakened Ho Chi Minh to recognize that we would not run either, like all of Vietnam's previous conquerors eventually did, including the French.

In many ways, the January-February 1968 Tet Offensive opened the eyes of America's military leaders, as they came to realize that...**WE NEEDED A BIGGER BOAT!** The reality came abruptly with the Tet Offensive that the Vietnam "conflict" had officially become a war. A war that would leave an everlasting mark on the world's history, especially the United States and Vietnam. Tet would set the stage for escalations on both sides, and both sides would literally "dig in" for what was to come over the next three to five years...a death toll neither side had expected.

The United States, South Vietnam, and North Vietnam suffered their greatest losses of the entire Vietnam War in the months of the VC/NVA Tet Offensive of January and February 1968 and during May's Tet II Offensive, also in 1968. In many ways, 1968 was the most representative year of the war. Yes, indeed, Tet of 1968 was pure hell for those who were over there at that time. However, there would be two months to follow in May and August, which were also two of the bloodiest months of 1968 and the entire war. During this time frame, much of the enemy's concentration had shifted from the north and DMZ area to an area between Cambodia and Saigon called III Corps and War Zone C. This area's list of casualties would come fast and unacceptably hard. An area called War Zone C in III Corps included battle sites which would become regular terms for the men and women who were there from 1967 through 1969, including: the tunnels of Cu Chi, Nui Ba Den, Boi Loi Woods, My Lai, Bien Hoa, Tan Son Nhut, Cholon, Duc Hoa, Hoc Mon, Trang Bang, Tay Ninh, Loc Ninh, Phu Cong, Dau Tieng, Go Dau Ha, The Iron Triangle, and Ho Bo Woods. The list went on and on where one macabre ambush, firefight, or human wave attack after another would take place. Agent Orange spraying was increased in this area, and by the time the Vietnam War had ended, III Corps would be the most often sprayed and most concentrated target of Agent Orange missions of the war. No one would recognize this area in the January-February 1970 timeframe from what it looked like in January-February 1967 or 1968 for that matter.

In Ronald H. Spector's excellent book *After Tet: The Bloodiest Year in Vietnam* (February 1994), he asks emphatically, "How did the United States lose the war in Vietnam?" Mr. Spector notes that most large battles were won in decisive fashion by the American troops, and yet, those battles left nothing decided other than the fact that there would be another one and another and another. We were winning for sure, but the inevitable at best would be a stalemate, as the Korean War ended. While the Americans and the allies fought off every VC ambush and every NVA assault and launched some devastating search-and-destroy operations of their own, the only thoughts of retreat in the minds of the North Vietnamese were...*when will the Americans finally realize that we will never give up and their best move would be to go home?*

As I said, while we were repelling and counterattacking in what we knew were highly successful battles for our side, things were not going well back home, and this would turn the tide against us. This may be old news, as many of us who participated in this unpopular war have made our feelings clear that WE WERE WINNING WHILE WE WERE THERE. If anyone gets tired of hearing this, he or she should be reading about something else, like Mother Goose tales. But as President Johnson said before his last days in office, "The establishment bastards have bailed out on us." In reality, I guess the leaders in Washington, D.C., had decided that there were no longer any safe places left in Vietnam, as Tet had proven to them. If they had asked the "grunts" themselves, we would have most likely told them, "Turn us loose into Cambodia and Laos and we'll let the enemy know they can no longer attack and run to safety." The final decision had already been made, as American troops began to disengage from mid-1970 till the end.

This author wishes to thank those responsible for how we were pulled out of Vietnam, made to look like we cut and ran when we didn't (they did):

- Thanks, McNamara!
- Thanks, Hanoi Jane!
- Thanks, Ameri-Cong Media!
- Thanks, Democratic Congress!

With all due justice to the boneheads in Washington and the media, they did not have a clue how the war was really going or that we were winning, even though our military generals told them so. But they weren't telling Washington about what had happened behind the scenes, that approximately two million Vietnamese civilians (one million KIA) had been casualties during 1968 alone. Sure, most of these unfortunate losses were inflicted by other Vietnamese (VC and NVA), but we had a hand in the killing of civilians. Some of us would justify this by thinking they were all VC anyway, so what would it matter. Besides, I got to put another couple of notches on my belt.

Believe this...the Americans and allies did a ton of wonderful humanitarian acts over there and risked their lives doing them. Did these acts of kindness offset the destruction caused by our Agent Orange spray, our bombs, and our battles in and around their villages with the VC and NV? I would have to say NO WAY!

Personally, I cannot say that I did not witness and was not commanded to be a part of some of the bad, bad shit that happened over there. Hey, it was a war and every day, twenty-four/seven, someone was planning to kill us. Let's just say we were more often than not in a BAD, BAD, MOOD! It worked both ways…

How do I really feel about the Vietnam War today? Well, as I have explained with factual, historical information in this book, the rightful owners to reunite the two Vietnams were the people in the north. Unfortunately, our government heads drove Ho Chi Minh toward communism even though he reached out to the U.S. for help to oust the French from their homeland. Of course, the U.S. refused Ho Chi Minh and his band of Viet Minh, which became the Viet Cong and North Vietnamese Regulars, the eventual winners of two wars over the French and Americans. Had my country minded its own business, the American-Vietnam War would have never happened, and a united, stronger Vietnam would have become a U.S. ally much, much sooner regardless of their communist-style government. Hindsight is twenty-twenty here because a communist takeover of the entire Asian continent would have been a global disaster, so we believed during and after the Korean War. While this is looked at today as being a real threat back then, what was overlooked by the U.S. leaders was that the North Vietnamese did not share the main allegiance with China as the North Koreans did. This is a known fact that the U.S. could have and should have taken advantage, but American arrogance in Washington, D.C. prevailed over common sense.

This mistake reminds me of the two Catholic popes who turned down offers from the Mongols to join together against the Muslims. Imagine what it would be like today had the crusading Christians allowed themselves to overcome their arrogant viewpoint toward the Mongols, as the Muslims were ten times more dangerous to the future of Christianity. The Mongols were never a threat to the Crusaders, and their hate for the Muslims was no secret.

So, some who are unable to appreciate it view history as a "dry" subject. I think not. You can make what you want of it, depending on how deep you are willing to dig. The journey I have taken by going back in time to see what the Vietnamese were really made of and where they came from has been an adventure for me. I feel rewarded for doing it. Today, instead of hating the enemy we fought against in Vietnam, I take my hat off to them; I salute them and they knew what they were here for.

Who are we not to forgive our fellow Americans for their cruelty during the Vietnam War era? Forgiving is easy, but forgetting is very hard—nearly impossible. The journey for the Vietnam War veteran has been one of the longest of any warrior who has ever fought for the USA. Our bond remains strong; this is what we do. **"The two most important days in our lives are the day we are born and the day we finally discover why." —Mark Twain.**

Sudden death, sickening death, Agent Orange, PTSD—we were not to question why. It was our duty to do, and if we must, to die…this is what we do. But now we ask…WHY? We fought with honor, not for recognition. We received neither when it would have counted. We believed in each other. No one else could understand. We expected nothing when we got to Vietnam. When we got home, nothing is what we got. We had only each other then and…still.

I've told you about the great Mongol hordes who conducted three massive invasions by land and sea of the small kingdom that was to be known as Vietnam. In all approximately a million seasoned, battle-hardened, fanatical Mongol soldiers and cavalry men crossed over the borders of Vietnam between the years of 1265 and 1280 with only one goal in mind…to end the lives of all Vietnamese people. Although the Mongols did ravage, rape, and plunder dozens of defenseless villages of civilians and seemingly take complete control for temporary moments in time, the end results were inevitable and totally unfamiliar to the great Mongol Khans and their armies of death. Who could have envisioned what was going to happen, that the armies of death sent to carry out total annihilation of an entire culture would become the annihilated? I personally find it nearly impossible to grasp what happened. Over a million warriors of the world's greatest conquering force sent into retreat for their lives three times, altering the course of history.

Much the same way the Mongols' ruthless attempts to continue their hunger for more conquests had come to a shocking defeat in biblical proportions, the great colonial empire of the French, despite the advantage of western military weaponry, would be humbled shamefully by the inhabitants of the same kingdom that defeated the great dynasties of China and the marauding cutthroats of Mongolia.

Thousands of years of fending off and overpowering great invading armies is the legacy of the Vietnamese people. Courageous and resilient with undying heart. That describes the Vietnamese ancients in 40 AD and 1288 as well as 1954. So, do we add the American empire to that list, who also met humbling defeat in similar fashion? Not so fast.

In fact here is a quote from North Vietnam's victorious General Giap long before the American Democratic Congress threw in the towel and forced the American military to cut and run:

You had us on the ropes. You defeated us at TET, we knew it, and we thought you knew it. Then we were elated to notice your own media helping us by causing more disruption in America than we could on the battlefields. If you had pressed on just a little harder you had us close to surrendering and victory was yours.

—General Nguyen Giap,
North Vietnam Army

More Lies Debunked…Some Continue. During the four-week period leading up to October 26, 2017 when I had slim hopes to close this book, there was a fairly good movie on the Public Broadcast System called ***The Vietnam War***. It lasted ten days and stretched out for eighteen hours. I watched every minute of it twice. Ken Burns and Lynn Novick were the creators, who are not your next-door conservative Americans. They were likely candidates to be reporters against the war during their college days—likely, I say. So naturally my Nam brothers and I carried a bit of skepticism beforehand on how objectively they would be. Many Nam vets did not think they made the grade; however, I ended up grading it with a "B-."

The movie was not completely accurate, and there were some serious events where critically important facts were just not told. In most instances these omissions would have presented more positive evidence in favor of Vietnam veterans. Many Viet vets' reactions went a bit overboard, but it wouldn't take much to do that with guys who have been lied about, dishonored, and betrayed for so long—so they deserve a pardon.

The Vietnam War documentary was very well done and I am glad it was produced. The sound track captivated me. It almost brought me back to the scene at times. The footage was impressive, and so were most of the interviews with Americans and Vietnamese from the North and South. I think too much time was spent on My Lai; after all, the media never forgets to remind America about it every year…give this one a rest.

The documentary protected the student rioters at the May 1970 Kent State riot. Oh BTW, many in that frenzied crowd were not students, nor were they even Ohio residents. Just like today with the Antifa terrorists, the Kent State riots were set up by and instigated by the radical left wing group called SDS.

The Burns-Novick PBS documentary neglected to mention that the protestors/rioters at Kent State were armed with rocks, bricks, bats with protruding nails, golf clubs, broken bottles, and more. NEWS FLASH: This tense atmosphere was injected with another shot of adrenaline—not that it was needed—as it was documented that gunshots went off in the background, which may have set off the "kids" in National Guard uniforms to commence shooting, resulting in a horrible ending.

The Burns-Novick story showed no mercy for the American government's regimes under Kennedy, Johnson, and Nixon. I was shocked and further enraged at the information uncovered here, like telephone conversations between Johnson and Nixon and their staff members. Some of it was sickening to the point I almost puked. The Vietnam War documentary's coverage of how the Vietnamese suffered was difficult to stomach, but it needed to be seen. I'm glad they did this. I was extremely pleased that they showed repeatedly how America's Vietnam vets fought as ferociously as any American military ever fought. We were depicted as fighting like wounded tigers for EACH OTHER!

Drug addiction by Vietnam vets was heavily overblown in the Burns-Novick story. One has to wonder why, as the narrated statement alleged, that "forty thousand" U.S. troops were addicted to heroin. **BULLSHIT!**

Every type of evidence imaginable disproves this unfortunate statement by narrator Peter Coyote, who otherwise did a pretty good job—I thought. Before the story began I had prayed that the episodes would be fair and truthful above all else, and that would help the legacy of my war buddies to regain some of the honor that has been stripped from us. Only time will tell if that will be the result. But promoting myths about Vietnam, myths that have been repeated again and again, won't leave a lot of Vietnam vets with a good taste in their mouths.

At least the Burns-Novick flick proved beyond any reasonable doubt whatsoever that the American bureaucrats who sent us into and left us high and dry after that war were not worthy of our patriotic sacrifices on the field of battle or back here on American soil.

Cheap Shots Continue ... Ignorant intentional?

Who ever said that old soldiers just fade away, could not have known many "real" Vietnam War veterans, still living today, but almost met their maker during the war. There are thousands of them around, still hanging in there with a purpose but many have lost hope. Hope that their war, their purpose and their deeds will be understood properly and honored. Not much to ask for is it?

Why should I be surprised? As I was finally closing this book in December 2018, the Democrats were flexing their muscles with their newly acquired power in Congress, with increased threats of impeaching a President that has clearly done more for America than any other President in many years. And those were protested and fought against the Vietnam War, before they had a clue whether it was a just war or not, continue to take "cheap" shots at those who were sacrificial lambs (the soldiers) as well as the idiots in Washington who sent them there without regret.

Vietnam: An Epic Tragedy, 1945-1975, a monstrous sized book 896 pages launched by author Max Hastings finds ways to continue torturing America's Vietnam War veterans. British born Hastings has impressive credentials as Ken Burns did. A journalist and prolific military historian who has authored nine books and other media deserves some insignificant credit for keeping the Vietnam War's awareness alive in the public eye. To me, no amount of words in just one book can come close to giving a complete and worthy account of America's war that has never ended. Forget some critics complement the work of Hastings and Burns as being comprehensive, balanced, meticulously researched and superbly written. Balanced, NOT! Fair ...Hell No! the rest is open for debate in my opinion and of several other "real"L combat Vietnam War veterans.

We have no beef with Hastings (sir Hastings) deservedly unkind comments toward the Washington bureaucrats who ran the war, Democrat or Republican. He fails to honor America's warriors in that war, living or dead. Neither did Burn's documentary for that matter. If he did, I missed it during my three complete previws of his flick. Hastings constantly belittles the dangerous feats of bravery by the Americans and the war itself as he refers to their time spent there as "just" 12-13 month tours. When in fact it only took a few seconds for a well planned ambush by a determined and experienced hard-core Viet Cong unit to ruin the day for an entire American company of unsuspecting American soldiers or marines.

Unlike most wars before it, in Vietnam the enemy never announced their position or their intentions nor did we all just show up at a designated location and then execute a battle with a prepared adversary in waiting. My war buddies were once ambushed three times in 24 hours and at the end of the day, a larger battle (human wave attack) was dealt with. So what could we possibly experience in "just" 12-13 months? Simply, the horror of the Vietnam War's style of battle presented a never ending threat for a bloody confrontation with an enemy force. Casualties for both sides were guaranteed to be reported for as long as one was in-country anywhere, anytime.

Another critic bestows the honor onto this book as though he has ever written a book so great and probably never ever, will be another. Please spare me, this must have been a relative of Hastings. "He leaves no stone unturned" says another ill informed critic.

Fearing some repetition of earlier information in *Unbreakable Hearts!* Here are a few significant facts that were diminished or completely ignored;

- He constantly points out America's shortcomings in the war, but he was "only" a foreign war correspondent" himself. During my full year in Vietnam I never saw a war correspondent hang with us during an actual firegight.

- There was nothing new in his book that has not already been covered byu those who lived the war.
- Hastings provdes very cruel and unqualified opinions on the health damage by Agent Orange's part in their war.
- He downplays the severity of the war and avloids the facts that … in 1967, 1958 and 1969 over 40,000 Americans died, an average of more than 256 per week or almost forurty lives lost every day during the three peak years.
- Hastings degrades the two thirds of American troops who served in the so-called safe areas, the base camps etc. He pisses on the notion that they were traumatized and even had a right to claim they suffered from PTSD.

Of course there is no doubt that the support troops in large basecamps faced anything even close to the constant dangers that the field troops did on a daily basis. And I have even mentioned this in each of my books. But for sure, the cooks, clerks vehicle drivers etc. sleeping in tents or flimsy hootches that enemy mortar rounds decimate like toothpicks put together by string earned their name placement on The Wall just as every other poor soul did. Bottom line, Hastings and Burns have presented valid reasons why I needed to write this book for my brave brothers and sisters of the world's most senseless and misunderstood war.

Historians seem hell-bent on staying with their incorrect formulations about how the Vietnam War really ended, by ignoring how it almost ended and should have ended. That reason by itself has been enough to motivate me to take on the grueling and somewhat thankless task of writing my stories. I just felt compelled to do it for those young faces that still creep into my life on a daily basis. After all, the only reason I am still breathing and able to write is due to those brave souls who fought so ferociously for no other reason than keeping each other living one more day.

What about that old domino theory? This was supposedly invented to send American and allied armed forces into Southeast Asia to stave off the threat of a massive cancer of communism that would infect every country in that part of the world. Historians and other types of military buffs keep going back and forth on this topic, and either way on the majority's decision, this backyard military history buff (me) is going to throw one more scenario into the mess. A scenario that I think is supportive of the domino theory as being quite real, but for a different reason.

The United States intervened in what was referred to as a Civil War. That Civil War had the so-called good guys (South Vietnamese) fighting the so-called bad guys, the communist-backed North Vietnamese. One problem, the Viet Cong were never part of the communist threat. They didn't know a communist from a Frenchman or an American. Even when the war was over, the Vietnamese population from the reunited Vietnam, south or north, couldn't have told you what communism meant. That being put on the table, what was the real reason for the Vietnam War? What did the North Vietnamese make such huge sacrifices for?

A reminder that those were Soviet-donated tanks and Russian MiGs that stormed over South Vietnam in 1974–1975. If you take that into your old domino theory, then it was as real as the Nixon Watergate Scandal.

Unfortunately, after winning freedom from whoever was the alleged conqueror, America or France or China, the newly christened communist government of the reunited Vietnam tried to force their type of communism on another neighboring country. Oh my, then they fought a war with communist Cambodia, and then communist China attacked Vietnam. What gives here? Is anyone confused?

The domino theory probably was a real threat fifty or sixty years ago, but not for the reasons we were all forced to live with. There was a civil war going on, being fought in the south by the South Vietnamese Viet Cong, supported by their sisters and brothers from North Vietnam, and the only self-serving reasons for the biggest disaster of the century was the reunification back to one free-standing Vietnam.

One could arguably stand behind the belief that the French were the original cause of a civil war between a South and North Vietnam as the French created the two Vietnams and the Americans came over to rescue… **the Wrong Side!**

Vietnam War veterans, great warriors who fought a very worthy adversary face-to-face night and day…betrayed by cold-hearted, gutless politicians, have never needed the support of the American people as we do now as we approach the 2020s. Our battles for due compensation and benefits from the VA are still being withheld from us and in great danger of being completely pushed aside, keeping us from yet another completely deserved victory. We cannot afford to accept another unjustified defeat. We are nearing the end of a long-traveled road of pain and sorrow, and our future is in jeopardy.

I hope that before all Vietnam veterans are gone, America will not look back at the Vietnam War as a meaningless exercise, a walk in the park, where Americans were expendable and fought a small firefight against an insignificant enemy referred to by some as peasants and farmers with knives and pitchforks. Ask the Mongols, Chinese, and French about that.

In my opinion, the Vietnam veteran is America's greatest hero because he fought three enemies—the Viet Cong, the North Vietnamese, and his own countrymen back home…some of whom referred to us as "baby killers." We won most of our battles over there. I am going to say this again. We didn't let America down on the battlefield or off, and then they pulled the plug when...**WE WERE WINNING.**

The world's strongest and best fighting force was just that during the Vietnam War, squaring off with an adversary that had a history of soundly defeating other world powers of their era more than a dozen times. Quite possibly, no other country in history has faced annihilation so many times and come out on top every time. Wow—if the Vietnamese haven't been one of God's favorite people, one would be hard-pressed not to believe it. They have survived the truest sign of time for over twenty centuries.

From Pitchforks to MiGs and SAMs! Chew on this sad and embarrassing scenario, one that none of the Ameri-Cong media would ever tell Americans about back then or even today.

During the time frame of the Democratic Congress-led retreat from Vietnam in 1972 and 1973, North Vietnam's other superpower ally north of China had stepped up its supply chain from Russia to North Vietnam. The timing for this was uncanny and perfect for North Vietnam, disgusting and traitorous for South Vietnam. As North Vietnam was making their move in 1974 to set up their 1975 invasions of the south, it has been reported that the North Vietnam arsenal had been built up with these weapons, compliments of Moscow...

- 2,000 Russian tanks
- 5,500 antiaircraft guns
- 7,000 artillery guns
- 200 surface-to-air missiles (SAMs)
- Tens of thousands of AK-47 rifles

Unfortunately, at approximately the same time all American military support no longer existed, in fact during the 1975 conquest of the South Vietnamese military, they ran out of ammunition, weapon parts for maintenance, and gas/oil to run their war machines to defend themselves.

Does anyone suspect that our Democratic Congress had no idea what was in the process in Vietnam, and they just made it easier for a communist victory? But maybe they saw the handwriting on the wall. Even our air superiority had come to a screeching halt as American B-52s and our F-4 Phantoms were being shot down by the North Vietnamese-operated Russian SAMs and MiGs. I read during the Vietnam War that our side lost more than a thousand aircraft, and North Vietnam lost just 131 planes. This doesn't even take into account how many more "thousands" of American helicopters were destroyed.

In 1965, North Vietnam operated with just thirty MITs while America had seven hundred aircraft to send against the enemy. However in 1966 and from thereafter, the North Vietnamese air force was constantly being bolstered with the most modern MiG-21 interceptors, and American planes were going down in alarming numbers. By the beginning of 1967, Soviet advisors were no longer directly involved in combat along with the North Vietnamese as no more training was needed and the North Vietnamese wanted to shoot down American planes on their own...they were quick studies for mere peasants with pitchforks.

During my time over there, I cannot remember seeing a North Vietnamese Army Regular with anything but an AK-47 for their assault rifle. If our M-16s were so darned good, I would have thought all of the commie forces would have had one and thrown their AK-47s away.

The "River of Aid" was flowing full throttle from Russia to North Vietnam, and by the end of 1969, it is believed that 75 percent of North Vietnam's weapons and technical support came from Russia, even their AK-47s. Believe it, there were some firefights lost to the enemy simply because the AK 47 was a better weapon than the American M-16 was during the early years of the war. As time went on, improvements were made.

Okay, so I have built up the Vietnamese warrior as though they fought like superhumans. They were undoubtedly willing to make tremendous sacrifices, but they were generally smart enough to make those sacrifices count for them. Hanoi's leaders often moved up to a million civilians out of the cities they believed were going to be hit and hid them in the woods of the countryside. Schoolchildren often went to school under cover or camouflaged from the American air attacks. Trucks and tanks were hidden in the jungles by day and brought back out at night.

Le Duan's Rise and Quiet Fall. Things were not always rosy in Hanoiland after the United States began escalating the war in South Vietnam. First Secretary Le Duan, appointed by Ho Chi Minh, was ascending to a more powerful role as Uncle Ho's health was deteriorating. Le Duan was a longtime political rival of Giap and did not show him the respect he had deserved. Le Duan even chose to ignore Giap's vast wisdom and experience by ignoring his strategy to continue with a guerrilla-style war. He chose to operate with a larger scale warfare with human-wave attacks like China had used in the Korean War. This strategy could have destroyed North Vietnam as the Americans won most of the large battles significantly, inflicting heavy casualties on the NVA and almost eliminating the Viet Cong as a fighting force.

Only near the last stages of the war did Giap make a resurgence and lead the North Viets in battles against the South Vietnamese, after the Americans were on their way home. Hindsight tells us now that if we had kept our word to the South Vietnamese and continued to support them, the North Vietnamese could have human waved themselves out and exhausted their manpower. And if North Vietnam had continued with Giap's strategy, the war would have dragged on for several more years—IF the American public would have allowed it, which was very unlikely. Despite all of this, Giap remains an iconic legend in Vietnam, and Le Duan's legacy was known by few after he died of health problems. Critics say that because Le Duan abandoned Giap's guerilla war plan and replaced it with the Chinese/Soviet mass attack warfare, far more blood was spilled than should have been necessary.

Le Duan was remembered as a Vietnamese communist chief who had fallen short of being a great leader such as Ho Chi Minh and General Giap. Although the official reason for his death was mysteriously withheld, rumors came out saying it was kidney failure that ended his life at seventy-eight years old on July 11, 1986.

Many Vietnamese and so-called experts outside of the country supported the belief that Ho Chi Minh was disrespected by Le Duan and shoved him aside on his climb to being a political monarch. Yet others say this was not so, that Uncle Ho was guardedly protected as his failing health prevented him from being a key decision maker in his later years. They say Le Duan remained close to Ho, even read his political will when Ho died. In fact, to honor Ho, Le Duan refused to allow anyone to fill the position that Uncle Ho held, which was the post of chairman.

To his credit, Le Duan was a main contributor to the final defeat of the South Vietnamese and the reunification of Vietnam. However, during the French War he had little influence on the Viet Minh rise and their surprising victory. That credit went entirely to Uncle Ho and Giap. Le Duan was said to be a rigid, secretive man with few intimate friends. He was an accomplished author of more than a hundred books and papers, but a full biography was difficult to find.

In the end the North Vietnamese people (military and civilian) believed that their cause, their mission to reunite Vietnam as it was before the French enslaved them, was a just cause. Amazingly, their morale, patriotism, and yes, nationalism were keys to their eventual victory over every invader in their history. Fifty years ago I was ignorant of these things about the Vietnamese history. Today…I appreciate them.

America's brave soldier boys, the Army, Marines, Navy, Air Force, Coast Guard, and the National Guard did not willingly remove themselves or retreat from the Vietnam War. We were ordered to return home, abandon our battle positions, and leave our allies behind, high and dry. That distinction belongs lock, stock, and barrel to the U.S. Democratic Congress. Either way, we cannot say that the North Vietnamese and Viet Cong were defeated because our leaders did not allow us to finish.

I think before the Vietnam War, most Americans were like me, believed what our presidents said about being an American and serving your country with pride. After the war, most American citizens turned cynical and highly distrustful of our political figureheads in the government. Then of course there was the mainstream media, and oh, how opinions plummeted about them.

As author Karl Marlantes stated…"Vietnam is the war that killed our trust."

Vietnam generated massive lying by the media about war to our leaders in Washington and the American people. No wonder memories of the era continue to torment veterans and civilians exposed to Vietnam. And the torturous memories linger on for many. Naturally, the more current wars in Iraq, Afghanistan, Syria, and our war with terrorism have pushed the Vietnam experience deeper and deeper in Americans' memories. Did we actually fight that war? Did we?

During my growing-up years, I was blessed with frequent social exposure to black Americans. I appreciate those days now as the cultural exchange helped me for the rest of my years in getting along with people socially, in business, sports, and especially in the military. In fact, I did not become so overly familiar with the word "racism" until the Obama years, but I did see it during my military years as so many people were thrown together from coast to coast and they each grew up in different environments.

But in the Vietnam War, underneath all of the horrors of killing, there were special relationships being established on the battlefield as blacks, Hispanics, and whites were forced into serious integration. Whether we liked it or not, we formed bonds and we covered each other's backs. Unfortunately, the trust we formed in Nam would be tested greatly after the war ended as everyone went back to their comfort zones in their old neighborhoods and found that Americans had changed while we bled on the battlefields.

These days many blacks that I meet for the first time appear to be leery of me, finding it to be quite unbelievable when I tell them how I was raised to not harbor any racial prejudices, and we tend to go in different directions. But there was this black marine I met in the neighborhood I lived in during 2013. I told him about my book *Condemned Property?* and he asked to read it, which he did. His reading and believing the stories in that book brought us closer and we enjoyed great bonding conversations, none of which were lacking enough emotional expressions. Unfortunately, Garrett's body and mind were heavily poisoned—worse than mine—from the Agent Orange spraying and severe battle trauma or PTSD. Garrett passed away just two years after our friendship began. Unfortunately, premature dying by Vietnam War vets has plagued our generation, which doesn't make it easier to prepare for.

So, another Vietnam vet bit the dust, still in the prime of his life. So what? Just another bitter memory to fuel my anger and enhance my passion to fight the VA as I've done with each of my books. Garrett's life, his family relationship, and our friendship were cheated by the Vietnam War and the disgraceful way our lying, scumbag politicians stabbed us in our backs over and over again.

"Get over that war, Dusty!" Why do some people continue saying this to us? They don't know shit about the pain and suffering that rotten war laid on us. Little do they know that their words simply motivate me and fuel the fire inside me to prepare for the next battle with VA…and the next one.

An interesting analogy I can offer up to my readers, whether Vietnam vets or not, is this:

Since I married Ginny Brancato (Trimmer) on August 29, 1984, she and I have attended most family members' funerals together. Most of our family members lived to a reasonable age, in their eighties or nineties, and died from natural causes. Her parents, my parents, her aunts and uncles, my aunts and uncles, all lived a pretty good, long life.

But since our marriage, Ginny has experienced with me the premature death of more than a dozen Vietnam War brothers of mine, and not one of them died from natural causes. All of them passed prematurely during their fifties and sixties because of the Vietnam War or inadequate or lack of health care benefits not provided from the Department of Veterans Affairs.

"So, get over that war, Dusty!" Well, I can't and I won't, not as long as there remain Vietnam War veterans who are still battling to make it one more day. How does one fight the fight with or against a large bureaucratic monster like the VA in a calm and mild fashion—without anger, without depression, without passion, tenacity, resilience, and relentless persistence, just like the amazing Vietnamese people have exerted for about three thousand years?

My Vietnam War buddies earned the right to be proud; they deserve the right to remain pissed if they choose. They are still relevant to our society, and many of them (not most) are NOT DEAD YET!

America, Listen Up! America's Vietnam War combat soldier has emotions that are impenetrable, yet his shoulders are soft, flexible, and strong enough to lean on. His hands are firm yet precise in where they are placed. If his arms are wrapped around you, you're either in your final moments of life or the safest place you could possibly be. He's stubborn, has to be, but will let you have your way just to enjoy seeing you smile. He's deadly with the weapons he carries and yet gentle with children. He gambles with the devil, guarding the gates to heaven. He curses, please excuse him, as he can also be a perfect gentleman. He has what is referred to as the "thousand-yard stare," but when you look into his eyes, it's the most comforting thing you've ever felt. The U.S. government trained him to be a human weapon in battle, but his mother raised him to love mankind. He knows every part of his woman. His friends can become his brothers for life. There is no other man like him on the planet. Whether you love him or not, he could be your worst nightmare or best friend, and you should value both. And despite all this some of America's misguided often refer to him as a BABY KILLER?!

In many ways, for many reasons Vietnam veterans were made to believe that the world was against them, and I say that's okay, wouldn't want it any other way. But a word to the wise for the rest of the world (if you are against us). Hell hath no fury like a soldier or marine when his mission is to AVENGE HIS FALLEN BROTHER—BELIEVE IT!

This book has compiled historical data that undoubtedly destroys one of the greatest lies that came out of the Vietnam War. The Vietnamese battle-hardened military was not a third world class, nor were the Vietnamese warriors that America and her allies confronted an inferior fighting force using pitchforks and knives to defend themselves. Vietnam has never been included in discussions about the world's greatest and most powerful conquering forces because all of their wars throughout time have been fought out of necessity to protect their homeland and to win their stolen freedom back time and time again.

Repeating something here. The Americans were caught off guard initially by an adversary that was well prepared to fight off yet another invading force, and the Americans and allies were the invaders in the second Vietnam War. The Americans, to their credit, did not turn tail and retreat like so many world power conquerors of Vietnam did. The American soldiers and marines adjusted and became surprisingly proficient at the style of warfare that had discouraged the Chinese, Mongols, and French—to the point where the Viet Cong's once proud and terrorizing army was almost completely annihilated by the Americans' tenacious counterattacks in spite of the complete lack of motivational support by the American government, the American media, and Americans in general. Know this…no other American fighting force had ever fought a war under such disheartening conditions. Just try to imagine a lost American soldier boy, stalking an enemy at night in the rain in a far-off swamp, trying to convince himself it was worth it, that the folks at home were behind him, so he tries to gut it out and hang on till the day he returns to those folks, his family and friends. But what if there isn't anyone back there supporting you? You have nothing to cling to except your gun. There is nothing but emptiness and darkness.

An Ode to Hanoi Jane: The following paraphrased comments were extracted from a recording of Jane Fonda, which can be located easily online.

> *One thing I have learned beyond a shadow of a doubt since I've been in North Vietnam is that Nixon will never be able to break the spirit of these people; he'll never be able to turn Vietnam, north and south, into a neo-colony of the United States by bombing, by invading, by attacking in any way. One has only to go into the countryside and listen to the peasants describe their lives they led before the revolution to understand why every bomb that is dropped only*

strengthens their determination to resist. I've spoken to many peasants who talked about the days when their parents had to sell themselves to landlords as virtually slaves, when there were very few schools and much illiteracy, inadequate medical care, when they were not the masters of their lives.

But today, despite the bombs, despite the crimes being created—being committed against them by Richard Nixon, these people own their own land, build their own schools with children learning; illiteracy is being wiped out. There is no more prostitution as there was during the French rule. In other words, the people have taken power into their own hands, and they are controlling their own lives.

And after four thousand years of struggling against nature and foreign invaders and the last twenty-five years, prior to the revolution, of struggling against French colonialization—I do think Richard Nixon would do well to read Vietnamese history, particularly their poetry and the poetry written by Ho Chi Minh.

This profound advice from Hanoi Jane was spot-on, but it was about ten years too late. At least four U.S. presidents should have read about the Vietnamese history. If any one of them had, it is quite probable that we would not be reminiscing, suffering, and dying to this day from the war that seems to continue on and on and on. One of the most disgusting scenarios that the U.S. politicians overlooked or ignored was the fact that Ho Chi Minh was a Vietnamese nationalist first and a communist second. He had showed willingness to accept help where he could get it. If the U.S. would have been as willing to provide support to an independent, united Vietnam, it is entirely probable that Ho would have turned his back on communism. As tragic as that error looks now, for certain the most inappropriate and most disgusting terms ever created during this war would have never been uttered from the foul lips and poisoned pens of the cruel media. As a result an entire generation of heroes were robbed of any valor whatsoever, and unfortunately, they were cruelly and disgustingly labeled as...**BABY KILLERS!**

This proud Vietnam vet author has no problem giving accolades to the Kingdom of Dai Viet-Vietnam, for no other nation has accomplished so many military victories against such great odds of biblical proportions—all in defense of their God-given homeland. Throughout time, every invading power made the same critical mistake by...**underestimating their heart!**

Were we as tough as they come? You're damn right. We had to be because our adversary was as tough as they come. But more than likely, a lot of people will remember us as a very confused and misunderstood generation, and unfortunately, I say damn right to that too. One of America's most decorated soldiers of any war once said this after returning home from his service in the Vietnam War:

Serve in an active combat infantry unit in Vietnam for ninety days under constant fire and...live through it. Then you can say that you did something.

—Col. David Hackworth
U.S. Army Veteran of WWII, Korea, Vietnam
(Deceased)

Mind-Boggling Proof that North Vietnam was prepared to extend their suicidal battles with America and South Vietnam is provided in U.S. military records. The military costs accepted by the communist forces were unprecedented historically. Take a close look:

- North Vietnam's battle deaths as a percentage of their prewar population were almost equal to those of Germany / Austria and France combined in WWI.
- They doubled the percentage of the suicidal Japanese in WWII.
- Even more astounding is the North Vietnam percentage was ten times as high as the North Koreans and Chinese in the Korean Conflict.

A scary thought—even if Americans had taken tens of thousands of more lives from the North Vietnam military, a real surrender was still never going to be had. North Vietnam was too committed, too tough, and their hearts were unbreakable. When all was said and done, both sides were willing to claim victory when actually it was at best a stalemate as Korea ended us.

In the end, both sides would fight with Unbreakable Hearts, for different reasons, but nonetheless, it was a fiercely and tenaciously fought battle, day by day and night by night, until there was a victor at any cost.

One of the saddest things about the Vietnam War is that both sides underestimated their opponents' dedication and resolve. The American soldiers would become a family of brothers, fighting with passion to cover each other's backs. On the other hand the North Vietnamese were fighting an unlimited war for these unique reasons:

- Loyalty to the ancestors they worshipped
- Love for their beloved homeland
- Resistance to foreigners

No country in the world, including Germany, England, or Japan with the A-bombs, has been ravaged from airpower as Vietnam was during its war with the USA. They have recovered pretty much on their own and yet the Vietnamese people show little animosity toward the Americans. Think that one over.

The Vietnamese have never been a wealthy society. They have always been poor, but not miserably poor except maybe when they were ruled by the

French, who taxed them heavily and even took possession of their beloved farms. However, they have always refused to become hungry-poor because they were always willing to fish, catch, hunt, and grow food to survive. This makes me think of the ungrateful millionaires around the world who constantly whine about how oppressed they are.

What happened after the defeat of the Trung sisters? Almost a thousand years of intense domination. You can be damn sure that any historical records the Vietnamese had created about the Trung sisters' embarrassing victories over the Chinese during 40–43 AD were trashed. Anyone who even mentioned the Trung sisters would be arrested, interrogated, and possibly executed by the Chinese. As far as Chinese history goes in regards to the Trung sisters: The Trungs were Vietnamese female generals… They raised a small army to fight the Chinese… Their victories were few and short lived… Eventually they lost and died. Everything else about them is and should be treated as folklore, fairy tale, propaganda, or all of them.

In Vietnamese historical documents the Trung sisters' army was so powerful that the Chinese required a hundred men to defeat one sister. There is no chance that such negative stories toward Chinese warriors could possibly remain on record under Chinese rule.

Truly, the Vietnamese have always been peaceful people, but they rose to the occasion and fought like wounded wolverines when backed into a corner. They could be every bit as fierce as a Spartan or Mongol warrior. After all, they were blessed by God, and he gave them…Unbreakable Hearts!

Killing Capabilities Like Never Seen Before! Sure, we had superior firepower and we were given better training than our adversaries had time to wait for as we were racking up the enemy body count at sickening levels from 1967–1969. But the VC and NVA had a boatload of advantages themselves, as I have attempted to bring out in all of my books, especially this one. They had an uncanny desire and the will to win.

What if America's pitiful bureaucrats gave their soldier boys another advantage, one that could make them superior, warriors in battle and able to take more pain than any VC or NVA?

It is common knowledge that American troops were getting high on marijuana and shooting up stronger drugs, mostly in the later years of the war. Maybe 1969, but for sure after that it was almost uncontrollable. And for the most part, this was being done back at the major base camps and fire-support bases, not nearly so much by the grunts doing day and night ambush patrols.

What if there was another advantage being shoved down the throats (literally) of the combat troops out there in the bush, living with and fighting viciously with the enemy? What if?

In his book *Shooting Up*, author/historian Lukasz Kamienski tracks a history of drugs being used in warfare to "juice up the warrior," from the time of the Vikings to the Vietnam War. In April 2016, an article called **"The Drugs That Built a Super Soldier"** explained that intoxicants do not eliminate the causes of stress. Instead, they do what insulin does for us diabetics—treats the symptoms, but the disease continues with its dirty intentions to keep you miserable.

Pep Pills? "A central nervous system stimulant that increases energy and decreases appetite; it is used to treat narcolepsy and depression. Over-doses have been known to cause physical and mental damages like mind altering. These medications should not be taken freely by people, not without professional advice from a medical professional."[47]

David Grossman wrote in his book *On Killing* that Vietnam was "the first war in which the forces of modern pharmacology were fed to combat battlefield soldiers to empower them." So, for the first time in military history, the prescription of potent antipsychotic drugs like chlorpromazine by GlaxoSmithKline, under the brand name Thorazine, became routine. Some alarming facts if you will:

- World War II caused a mental breakdown rate among American soldiers in combat of...10 percent.
- The Korean War had a reported rate of record combat trauma during battle-time of...4 percent.
- In the Vietnam War the recorded rate of complaints about combat trauma was...1 percent.

That is enough to raise questions on why very few combat-exposed American soldiers in the Vietnam War reported or required medical evacuation because combat stress breakdowns had overcome them. However, a reminder that intoxicants do not eliminate the cause of the stress; they only treat the problem.

American armed forces in public society after the war contributed to an unprecedented widespread outbreak of post-traumatic stress disorder (PTSD) among Vietnam War veterans, after their war participation of course. This has been proven to be a result of reckless and overuse of pharmaceuticals and drugs.[48]

The precise number of Vietnam War veterans who claim to be or have suffered from PTSD will probably always remain unknown. I have read estimates ranging from half a million to a million and a half, which baffles

---

47 www.thefreedictionary.com
48 Paraphrased from www.theatlantic.com

me as I'm not so sure there are even a million Vietnam War vets still living as of today (April 1, 2018). Then, to complicate this most unfortunate aftermath of the Vietnam War, Vietnam vets have been unfairly denied compensation claims for PTSD at VAs ever since the end of the war. No one seems qualified to determine who is a "real" Vietnam vet at the VA. That is, no one except probably another "real" Vietnam veteran.

In the book *Flashback*, author Penny Coleman quotes a military psychologist who said, "If drugs are given to a soldier in combat, while the stressor is actually taking place, they will arrest or supersede the development of effectively coping mechanisms, resulting in an increase in the long-term trauma from the resultant stress."

Obviously, not very many psychological examiners at VA's Compensation & Pension departments have read any of these books I've mentioned here. What happened in Vietnam is the moral equivalent of giving a combat-wounded soldier a local anesthetic for shrapnel or bullet wound and then sending him back into combat. (I can relate.)

Supposedly anthropological evidence shows that we are not warlike people, that it can be very difficult to cross the line where we become able to kill fellow humans. But how can one explain how a supposedly docile civilian is turned into a warrior who will kill without having that impacting him psychologically later in life? Major problem here.

Battle Fever goes back to the crazy, nightly, and berserk Viking Northmen who were seized by a fury given to them by their mythical god, Odin. This fury seemed to double their strength, remove any humanity, and seemingly protect them from pain in battle so that they could continue to fight on and on. Historians said the Vikings would even head-butt their shields and howl like a wolf as they charged into battle, and God help whatever was in their way.

Was this Scandinavian genetics? Just take a trip to Minnesota and observe the Norwegian and Swedish population up there. Fairly laid back and gentle people for the most part. The secret for the Vikings superhuman ferocity and killing power was wine and amanita mushroom juice.

I'm part Norwegian genetically and I can't say that I've tried these mushrooms to juice me up or for any reason. But it is said that taking them the right way and in the right quantity can alter one's reality to the point where doing unnatural things—raping and pillaging, what the Vikings became noted for, long before Genghis Khan, Alexander, Napoleon, or Hitler were born—feels natural.

Did the right mixture and quantity of drugs and steroids produce the berserker frenzy of the Vikings?

Well, we who fought in Vietnam became quickly aware of the drugs that the Viet Cong were heavily intoxicated with. How else do you explain a man coming after you after you shot his arm off from the soldier, or when a Viet Cong loses his leg and keeps crawling at you in a "human wave" or kamikaze attack against your heavily fortified and almost impregnable fire base? Normal isn't the word here.

You cannot find it in the history books how the Germans were drugged up to enhance their performance during their invasion of Poland. It was a meth-amphetamine overdose or a form of crystal meth which was nick-named the German "assault pill." It worked so unbelievably well in the Poland invasion that another thirty-five to forty million tablets of Pervitin was ordered for the 1940 offensive on France.

Intersection between Pharmacology and Violence. So, if the Vietnam War was the first pharmacology war, how did it affect us? I can easily pro-vide a few answers to this question, as tens of thousands of Vietnam veterans can...those still living of course.

I recall that after a period of time, we became robotized, working on autopilot so to speak. I don't actually remember taking any "pep pills," but neither do I recollect taking malaria pills. I do remember the salt pills. I hope they were salt pills.

In this irregular and unconventional war, most or all previous battle strategies and principles had become extinct and were useless. The word "normal" did not apply anymore in this war. I now realize and have come to appreciate why the Viet Cong fought the way they did. They never expected our firepower, which dwarfed the French. The VC had to learn how to fight in an unexpected, surprising, and deceptive way to our strengths and to try to exploit our weaknesses...to even the battlefield. Some Americans called the VC cowards—run and hide, take a potshot here, spring ambushes, etc. Trust me, there was nothing cowardly about the VC.

The pharmacological war would bring a level of consumption of psycho-active substances by American combat personnel that was unprecedented in American history, and we are just now finding this out?

Even British Nick Land described the Vietnam War as "a decisive point of intersection between pharmacology and the technology of violence."

No one will ever be able to convince me that America's heroes of uncom-mon valor would not have risen to the occasion to save their brothers from certain death without the adrenaline rush from drugs. I'll keep going with these three things as probable reasons for astounding acts of valor at crunch time in someone's life:

1) Uncommon courage at crisis time
2) Intervention from above...God's will
3) Luck, good or bad, depending on outcome

Oversimplified of course, but that is my view. I could easily add a dozen more reasons why a person displays abnormal emotion during a battle or continues to drive on and on when all hope seems to have evaporated, leaving only one way out, to just give up and allow one's life to end. Possibly just another huge lie about the Vietnam War, kept a secret for half a century.

Many of my Vietnam War brothers gave in to this belief that we were not supposed to come back from that hellhole. Often I have also wondered about this, but that is crazy. Isn't it?

The following heartfelt poem was written by the daughter of a brave Vietnam warrior with whom I had the honor of serving and fighting next to. Shelly Daniels is the daughter of Staff Sergeant Curtis "Tex" Daniels of Bravo Company, 1st Platoon 3rd 22nd-25th Infantry Division, Vietnam in 1968–1969. Curtis succumbed to one of the curses that Agent Orange delivered to hundreds of thousands of Vietnam War veterans.

MY DEAR VIETNAM VETS
My Dear Vietnam vets
To the Vietnam vets of long ago
Of the pain and suffering not often told.
The Sacrifices you made were anything but small
You are not forgotten, someone remembers you all.
The things you saw, you will never forget.
But it wasn't for nothing, My Dear Vietnam vet.
How my heart longs to make your pain disappear
The only One who can is God, who is always near.
Everything you went through, I will surely never know.
For I was not there in that tragic war long ago
How amazing it is that you made it back from that war.
Surely you have a purpose here worth fighting for!
* Love My Viet vet Dad!* ♥ Shelly Daniels

To All the Vietnam veterans:
Don't Give Up! Keep On Fighting!
I am praying for you all!

Shelly Daniels and I have talked many times since the death of her father Curtis, my true brother from the Vietnam War. His premature death, inflicted by the Vietnam War, is still something I have tremendous difficulty in blocking out of my mind. Attending his funeral, seeing the entire family I knew well, was an emotional experience similar to my first visit to the Vietnam

He Was Our Most Special Platoon Buddy!

War Memorial (The Wall). Both experiences will remain with me for the rest of my days, as extremely emotional and unforgettable moments.

Reflections. At the end of the day, or as I close this book, there should be no doubt in most minds that the communist-backed forces of Ho Chi Minh and General Giap from the Viet Minh to the Viet Cong and the North Vietnamese Army sent a wake-up call to the so-called western superpowers, France and the United States of America. Both of their powerful military machines were rudely evacuated from the historic land of Vietnam by an adversary who had a love for their homeland as great as any patriotic society that has ever existed on any continent.

The once mighty military power of France was no match against the heart, spirit, and incomparable resilience of the Vietnamese. The French were chased out of Southeast Asia with their tails between their legs. The American soldier boys never threw up any white flags; they met the enemy and fought them in one "in-your-face" battle after another and were never really defeated in any confrontations of significance. The same can be said for our trusty allies from Australia and South Korea.

While the American soldier was made to walk a fine line in the Vietnam jungles, a line that was between here and nowhere, he discovered something else to hang on to, to help him make it through what seemed like an endless nightmare. The American Vietnam veteran found other Vietnam veterans, and for the most part that was all they ever had.

Most of them came home emotionally dead and filled with anger, and they were quickly misunderstood by most Americans except for the brotherhoods they found during the war. They ended up sharing with other Vietnam veterans because they all knew the unfair price they had to pay.

Taps Doesn't Lie! It's been said often, by many sources, that the death rate of Vietnam War veterans has been greater annually than that of the fathers and uncles who died after WWII had officially ended. I personally found this "rumor" difficult to believe, but not difficult to accept if true. After all, our fathers and uncles are/were twenty-plus years older than we are, so one would not expect them to outlive their sons and nephews from the Vietnam War, right?

I have survived my biological father (ninety-five) and my stepfather (eighty-two) as I continue on this day at age seventy-three to hang in there. I have managed to overcome several post-Vietnam War-related death threats, such as:

- **Suicide Attempt** by wrecking a car at a very high speed (126 mph) in 1972. Multiple surgeries and several weeks of hospital time and God's divine intervention kept me from losing my life at age twenty-eight.
- **Cerebral Vascular Attack** (stroke) following back-to-back transient ischemic attacks (mini strokes) in the same year, October, November, December 2013, and 100 percent carotid artery blockage. I was saved by excellent VA medical care and, of course, God's attention to people's prayers. PTSD and diabetes mellitus Type II were the designated causes.
- **Kidney Cancer** and surgical removal of right kidney and several lymph nodes saved me in the nick of time as the cancer had overtaken the kidney, ending its functionality. The causes were said to be Agent Orange and diabetes II. Another life-threatening Vietnam-related illness was prevented by our great God and the VA's talented surgery team on December 28, 2017.
- **Diabetic Kidney Failure**, the left one, currently at the dangerous level known as stage four in May 2018. Now it's just one day at a time, but I'm hoping and praying for a long run of those days.

All Vietnam War related, although VA's dark side, their Comp & Pen Department, fought each of my disability claims, causing stressful and frustrating delays during all of those years. Still continues. So these unsuccessful brushes with death have allowed me to remain amongst the ranks of the older survivors of the Vietnam War. But tens of thousands or hundreds of thousands Vietnam vets have not enjoyed the opportunity to live into their seventies, sixties, forties, even thirties. This should disturb the rest of America, shouldn't it? Well, it doesn't seem to have, or there seems to be nothing anyone can do about it because the mind-set is...we all have problems.

In the January–June 2018 issues of *Purple Heart Magazine*, the editors listed a special section for deceased members of the Military Order of Purple Heart appropriately titled "Taps."

Obviously, to receive the *Purple Heart Magazine* the primary requirement is to have been wounded in battle and officially awarded the Purple Heart. I have been a loyal subscriber for forty of its eighty-three years of existence. Just a month before finishing this book, I stumbled onto the Taps section of the May/June 2018 issue. Since the editors list the war or conflict of the deceased, I simply counted them up for all of 2018 to date. Here are the fascinating totals, per my counting prowess:

American Veterans Deaths 1/18–6/18[49]

Service		War/Conflict	
Army	1,056 (68.7%)	World War II	599 (38.94%)
Marines	332 (21.6%)	Vietnam	699 (45.44%)
Air Force & Other	150 (9.7%)	Korea & Others	240 (15.62%)
	1,538 (100%)		1,538 (100%)

Surprising facts? To whom, I wonder? But please keep in mind that I am the messenger here, just spreading the information which is available to anyone who cares to search for it. Also keep in mind these numbers probably don't count many or most active duty military who have been wounded as they may not yet be a subscriber of *Purple Heart Magazine*.

Most combat Vietnam War veterans understand and appreciate the courage it took for our WWII fathers to face off with their enemies in direct combat. We had to do that too during countless "human wave" attacks by VC and NVA. Depending on the length of those intense battles and the outcome, both sides usually pulled back to lick their wounds and take a break.

In the Vietnam War, the combat warrior needed to be brave every morning just to get up and square off with another day where they could be blown up at any minute. Every step was a challenge. If you or a buddy took a step in the wrong direction, many lives were endangered.

---

49 Purple Heart Magazine

One thing about the wars of WWII and Vietnam is while neither of them were good wars, most Americans believed WWII was a necessary war, but most Americans saw Vietnam as an unnecessary war. While I understand these things now, imagine trying to convince a combat-wounded Vietnam War veteran who just arrived home, fresh from battles' horror images on his mind, that he fought in and his war buddies were thrown into an unnecessary war!

Total Americans Served (In Theater)[50]

War	Total Served	Still Living	Surviving Spouses / No Benefits
WWII	16,112,566	1,711,000	167,378
Vietnam	2,879,000	1,000,000*	**266,807**
Korea	1,789,000	N/A	75,717
Gulf War	694,550	N/A	28,586
Global Wars on Terror	N/A	N/A	N/A

* Estimated

Estimates on living Vietnam veterans range from 850,000 to 1,200,000. Either way, there are still more WWII veterans living than there are Vietnam War veterans. While I find this disgusting and sadly depressing, what seems even more astonishing is that the number of Vietnam vet widows receiving benefits outnumbers those widows from all of the wars because their husbands died prematurely from various diseases and medical conditions due to Vietnam's killer environment. Note, the last WWI veteran, Frank Buckles, died on February 27, 2011 at age 110.

On December 10, 2013, when I checked into Cleveland's Wade Park VA Hospital, having lost my vision in one eye, with a 100 percent blocked carotid artery due to a sudden life-threatening cerebral vascular attack (stroke), my life was dramatically and permanently changed. Just as it was from the Vietnam War experience fifty years ago during the Tet Offensive of 1968. So, one way or another, Vietnam may inevitably end my life prematurely when it sees fit and how it chooses to. As I conclude this book, I see myself as being extremely blessed so far, in fighting off kidney cancer, compliments of Agent Orange and Super Agent Orange, to add to the stroke I recovered from a few years ago.

And as the VA C&P people continue their evil acts in trying to break us, my brothers and sisters of the Vietnam War continue to fight on just as

---

50 Source U.S. Department of Veterans Affairs

our worthy adversaries did in that unforgettable war, because we are also blessed with...**Unbreakable Hearts!**

It is essential that we document and recount the years of deliberate misinformation about the Vietnam War...to keep on setting the records straight about who fought in Vietnam.

Truth needs to prevail and our comrades' sacrifices must be remembered.

—Col. George "Bud" Day
Vietnam War POW
U.S. Air Force
Medal of Honor Recipient
Deceased 7/27/13

Playing the Waiting Game...With Our Lives! As the VA continues to drag its feet, more Vietnam veterans and their babies continue to suffer from the poisons of Agent Orange. Unfortunately, time is on the VA's side, not the veteran's. The longer the wait, the longer the continued procrastination, as more of us die, the less significant the damage Agent Orange has done, in the public's opinion. And the killing continues.

Still, as I proceed in closing this book, the VA's dreaded Comp & Pen Department is still in a state of denial that our Vietnam combat and Agent Orange exposure were responsible for the severity of our service-connected disabilities, and the war with them and thousands of veterans continues to rage on. But I for one remain hopeful that President Trump, the VA, secretary, and Congress will continue to be caring and responsible to our pleas for an easier path to receiving all of the health care and benefits we have had to fight for which we have earned as warriors for our country. I have searched passionately since the Vietnam War for something that resembles the greatest adventure of my lifetime, the Vietnam War. It was an epic event that I will never be able to get out of my mind, and God knows I have tried.

Amazon basin trips, dozens of treks to the Everglades, and over a hundred rattlesnake hunts in eight states, and still nothing has ever compared to my adventure in...V I E T N A M !

Vietnam nearly killed me countless times in many different ways while I was there, in-country. Vietnam has continued to threaten my life in many more ways after the war. This bewilders me and many around me that I am still here and why. Sometimes I think I should return to that country where I spent the longest year of my life. Should I return to the country that impacted my life unimaginably and spend the rest of my days there with the spirits of those who died there? I wonder, and it's a painful exercise for me.

But other than my own beloved America and the veterans of Vietnam still living and fighting to stay alive, Vietnam and its wonderful people seem like the next best place for me to call home during my last days.

Here we are today and what used to be *then* in our minds has become now. On the following pages are a few images of my brave Vietnam veteran brothers as I remember them. I hope you will enjoy and appreciate them. These are some of the memories I choose to never let go nor am I able to. Please keep in mind that the Vietnam War is an example of hard-core history. But the images on the following pages will show the other side, the soft and gentle side of American warriors. Lots of smiles and lives of thousands of babies being saved. Please spend extra time with these images and... **remember the faces**.

Meet Some of Those Baby Killers!

Guard and Protect

Guarded like they were our own.

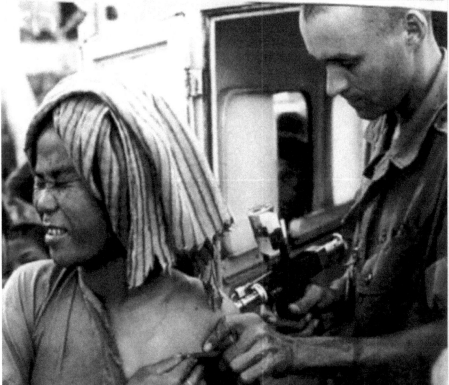

We played with them

EPILOGUE

In love or war if you break their heart, you have broken their will, drained their spirit, and depleted their passion for hope. Historians could have done great justice to their credibility and to the incredible unbreakable hearts shown by both sides in the Vietnam War. Both fought fiercely, honorably, and neither ever quit fighting. The American soldiers and marines did not lose; they were ordered to cease fire and go home. Our adversaries were ordered to fight on and on, which is exactly what they did, until victory was achieved with little opposition at the end.

Nearing the end of the war, it was kept a secret by the Ameri-Cong media that the mission of the American soldiers had changed, or maybe it was gradually changing after the bloody Tet Offensives of 1968. The mission they were trained and paid for, to search and destroy, had become something else which was no less dangerous. They were risking their lives to…**Search and Rescue!**

Some people live an entire lifetime and wonder if they have ever made a difference in the world. A Vietnam War veteran doesn't have that problem.

Many of us left home at nineteen to twenty-four years old. We learned to kill another human before learning to do a tax return. We had friends in college and had friends also in Vietnam. Our friends in college went home for summer…many friends in Vietnam STILL haven't come home.

One Vietnam veteran once said…his biggest challenge after returning home had been coming to terms with his own callousness. He had made a deal with the war and traded his humanity for a ticket home.

What seems to screw us up most after Vietnam is the picture in our heads of how things are and then the opinion of others of how they're supposed to be.

Some people say we Vietnam veterans still live in the past. I don't think we have a permanent residence back there. I just think Nam will always exist in our minds as a place of reference. So, having tried most of my life after Nam to turn back the odometer of time, I don't care anymore if people can't see why I look and think this way, as I've traveled a long way on mostly dirt and muddy roads.

How soon our arrogant politicians seem to forget where we came from. In 1783, the world's most powerful military, Great Britain, was defeated by an upstart, inferior army made up mostly of farmers, and the United States of America was born.

As usual, history would repeat itself when a small three-thousand-year-old nation of farmers in South and North Vietnam rose up to defeat colonial power France in 1954 and fight off the most powerful military in the world's history, earning a bloody stalemate in 1973 against the United States of America.

None of these unexpected victories could have happened without one profound weapon of defense…**Unbreakable Hearts!**

To repeat Mark Twain's profound statement: "The two most important days in our lives are the day we are born and the day we finally discover… WHY." I like to believe that putting out three books, totaling more than 1,700 pages of facts and drama to rectify a wrong, is WHY I was put here and allowed to survive this long after the Vietnam War ended.

Several sources say that there are only 850,000 to 1,000,000 real Vietnam war veterans still living. I am grateful and proud to be one of them. But since the average Vietnam war veteran is seventy-two years old, according to the VA, it appears to be way past due for them to be forgiven and welcomed home…**sincerely!**

They were the very best that America had to offer
from the Baby Boomer Generation...

Vietnam War Veterans.

NOTES ON SOURCES

W hile I had a large selection of images to choose from, shared by men I served with or their families, there is suddenly an over-abundance of Vietnam War photos being presented online and in books. The majority of these photos were taken by the warriors who fought in that war, not by photographers from the media who were rarely outside the perimeter of a firebase or base camp. Therefore, 99 percent of the images in this book are the property of those who fought and died there or were fortunate to come home—where many more of us would die prematurely afterward.

Most of the material and images used in *Condemned Property?* and *Payback Time!* were original from my own experiences and those of my platoon war brothers in Vietnam. After all, we lived those episodes in real life. I used a small sample of that material in *Unbreakable Hearts.* However, as our memories continue to dim, I have been forced to do more research through libraries and the Internet. Many images found online actually appeared in multiple websites, making it impossible to get the original source. I also found images online that originated from our own units with the 25th Infantry Division. I did my best to credit as many sources as possible to the responsible units.

Please note: The Wikimedia Foundation owns almost none of the content on Wikimedia sites. The content is owned, instead, by the individual creators. Also, almost all content hosted on Wikimedia Commons may be used freely (http://freedomdefined.org), subject to few restrictions. In many cases, a statement is not required from the licensor(s).[51]

I am a strong proponent of using as many appropriate images as I possibly can. Why? Because putting together an eye-catching, interesting image does entertain most readers, and it is believed that our brains are able to process images several thousand times faster than words. Remember…a picture is often worth a thousand words. Many of the images used are not identified with a title or caption as I thought they were self-explanatory.

While I have attempted to dedicate myself to arrange the information in this book in a sensible, reader-friendly order, in fact this book has been edited/proofed six times by different people. Still, I am fully aware that there are some organizational hiccups. I do not claim 100 percent accuracy

---

51 Wikimedia Commons

for some of the oral interviews or some of the dated time frames of some happenings. And as I have said in every one of my books, every day began differently, everyone had different views all day, and every ambush began differently and ended differently in each man's mind. Eyes can play tricks on you, and everything happened so fast—and ended so fast—in Vietnam, and we didn't have instant replay then.

BOOK SOURCES FOR INFORMATION

teakdoor.com/arts
mediacenter.smugmug.com
archive.13wmaz.com/images
www.irishtimes.com/polopoly
femmes-guerres.ens-lyon
mphim.net/mg/dien-vien/duc
media-cache-ako.pinmg.com
12.cdn.turner.com
vignette4-wikia.nocookie.net
static.talkvietnam.com
pix.avaxnews.com
162.tinypic.com
media.tumbir.com
tqn.com/y/asianhistory
mattbrown.files.wordpress.com
1.huffpost.com/gen
upload.wikimedia.org
cdn2-be.examiner.com
saloteur265.files.wordpress.com
www.google.com
conservabyte.wpengine
French-new-on-the-fall-dien-bien-phu
taobabe.files.wordpress.com
images.akamai.steamusercontent.com
www.vietnamparadisetravel.com
www.1-kirk.info/scrapbook
http://mediatumblr.com
www.flamsofwar.com
https://libcom.org/files
www.facebook.com/photo.php
http://cherrieswriter.files.wordpress.com/2013
https://s-media-cache
https://upload.wikimedia.org
http://vietnamatwarfrazier
www.transportation.army.mil/museum
http://vovworld.vn/uploaded

http://cdn.theatlantic.com
www.facebook.com/vietnamhell
http://blogspot.com/-uoco
http://baptistcourier.com
http://static01.nyt.com/images
http://www.1-kirk.info.scrapbook
http://peteralanlloyd.com
www.thetoptens.com
www.rantpolitical.com
www.washingtonpost.com
www.insidegov.com
www.nationalinterest.com
www.famouspeopleinfo.com
http://vietnamexploration.com
http://vietnamwithamerica.com
http://indochina54.bree.fr
www.workers.org/articles/wp
www.usmilitiaforum.com
http://huffpost.com/gadgets
http://hochiminh.vn/workspace

IMAGE SOURCES

Bravo 3/22nd scrapbooks
25th Infantry Yearbook, 1968-1969
Bravo & Charlie Co 3/22nd website
Earl Dusty Trimmer Scrapbook
41.media.tumblr.com
cdn.historynet.com
one-six-one.fifthinfantry.com
historyplanet.files.wordpress.com
peteralanlloyd.com
cdn.thedailybeast.com
www.salem-news.com
media-cache-ako

Jane Fonda Images in North Vietnam Found on Following Websites:

Assets 1. Bigthink.com
I.pinning.com
1.bp.blogspot.com
olrag.org/wp-content

cdn3.thr.com
images.search.yahoo.com
2.bp.blogspot.com
1.dailymail.co.uk
myppagesix.files.wordpress.com
frsfreestakes.files.wordpress.com
the gatewaypundit.com
assets.my daily news.com
static.standard.co.uk
commonamericajournal.com
origin.fact check.org

Sources POW/MIA Information Ch. 20

Voices of the Vietnam War 1993, Craig Howes
Vietnam: A History 1983, Stanley Karnow
Five Years to Freedom 1971, James Rowe POW
Advocacy and Intelligence Index for POW-MIA
Powernetwork.org/biios.htm
www.arlington cemetery.net
www.psywarrior.com/rowe

BOOK CREDITS FOR EXCERPTS, PARAPHRASES, IMAGES, ETC.

In Country, B. Mason
Vietnam: Victory Was Never an Option, Col. R. Bayless
A Rumor of War, P. Caputo
Street Without Joy, B. Fall
The Things They Carried, T. O'Brien
A Bright Shining Lie, N. Sheehan
Fields of Fire, J. Webb
Casualties of War, D. Lang
A Piece of My Heart, K. Walker
The Bad War, K. Willenson
Stolen Valor, B.G. Burkett
Dirty Little Secrets of the Vietnam War, J. Dunnigan
The Tunnels of Cu Chi, T. Mangold
The Grunts, C. Anderson
The Tragedy of the Vietnam War, D. Van Nguyen
Aid and Comfort, H. Holzer
Wounded Men—Broken Promises, R. Klein

Vietnam, The Necessary War, M. Lind
Dereliction of Duty, H.R. McMaster
Don't Mean Nothing, S. O'Neill
The Birth of Vietnam, K. Taylor
Everything We Had, A. Santoli
Achilles in Vietnam, J. Shay
Vietnam Order of Battle, S. Stanton
Days of Valor, R. Tonsetic
Vietnam: No Regrets, R. Watkins
Mighty Men of Valor, J.G. Roberts
Condemned Property, E. Trimmer
Payback Time, E. Trimmer
www.Mongol Horde--Yahoo Image Search Results
https:/hinhanhvietnam.corn/wp-content/uploads/2014/09/hue
https://upload.wikimedia.org/Wikipedia/common/c/c8/ThanhPhoNam
Dinh-PhapThuoc3
http://alphahistory.com/vietnamwar/wp-content/uploads/2012/07/vietcong-
trail.jpg
https://file.alotrip.com/photo/Vietnam/society/people-in-hanoi-old-quarter
https://images.search.yahoo.com/yhs/search?p-Vietnam+DeDLY+sNAKES
http:??www.vets-helping-vets.com/images/web_pics/Nam_Pic%27s40.jpg

Sourcing the images for a book takes a lot of time and hard work. Fortunately, I have benefited from being allowed to use dozens of photos from personal collections of other Nam vets whom I came to know through my first four books, including this one:

Vietnam: Our Story—One on One (1991, 1992)
Author: Gary Gullickson, USMC, Vietnam
Several Co-Authors including Earl "Dusty" Trimmer, U.S. Army, Vietnam

Condemned Property? (2013)
Author: Earl "Dusty" Trimmer, U.S. Army, Vietnam

Payback Time! (2015)
Author: Earl "Dusty" Trimmer, U.S. Army, Vietnam

Unbreakable Hearts (2017)
Author: Earl "Dusty" Trimmer, U.S. Army, Vietnam

"NAM TALK" GLOSSARY

ABN	Airborne
Agent Orange	Chemicals used as a defoliant in recent years found to cause medical problems in Vietnam veterans
A-Gunner	Assistant machine gunner
Air Medal	Award for helicopter crewmen and airmobile infantrymen after so many missions
AIT	Advanced Infantry Training
AK-47	A Russian assault rifle
AK-50	Same as AK-47 with folding stock, an NVA favorite
Alpha Bravo	Slang for ambush
Amerasian	Child born of a Vietnamese female and an American male
Ameri-Cong	Term used in *Comrades in Arms* by Roger Canfield, PhD
Ammo Dump	Location where live or expended ammunition is stored
AO	Area of operations
APC	Armored Personnel Carrier used by mechanized infantry units, carries machine guns and an infantry squad
Arc Light	Term to describe a carpet bombing mission by B-52 high-altitude bombers
Article 15	Minor offense under code of military justice
ARVN	Army Republic Vietnam
AWOL	Absent without leave
B-40 Rocket	A shoulder-held rocket-propelled grenade launcher
Baby San	Child of family
Ba mu'o'i ba	Brand name of a Vietnamese beer, also called panther or "tiger piss
BAR	Browning automatic rifle. A .30-caliber magazine-fed automatic rifle used by U.S. troops during World War II and Korea.
Battalion	A military unit composed of a headquarters and two or more companies, batteries, or similar units.
Beehive Round	Artillery round that releases thousands of steel darts
Big Max	Maximum security section of Long Bin Stockade, fashioned out of conex containers. There was one

small hole in each side for light and air; in the sun they grew quite hot. Prisoners were allowed out twice a day to use the bathroom and exercise.

Big Red One   First Infantry Division

Bird   Helicopter

Blood Trail   A trail of blood on the ground left by a fleeing man who has been wounded

Blooper   The M-79 grenade launcher. A 40-millimeter, shotgun-like weapon that shoots spin-armed "balls" or small grenades; also known as a blooker

Boat People   Immigrants from Vietnam, Cambodia, Laos

Body Bags   Plastic zipper bags for corpses

Body Count   The number of enemy killed, wounded, or captured during an operation. The term was used by Washington and Saigon as a means of measuring the progress of the war.

Boom Boom   Sex

Boonies   Out in the field, jungles, swamps, etc.

Bouncing Betty   antipersonnel mine with two charges; the first propels the explosive charge upward, and the other is set to explode at about waist level

Breaking Squelch   Disrupting the natural static of a radio by depressing the transmit bar on another radio set to the same frequency

Brigade   A tactical and administrative military unit composed of a headquarters and one or more battalions of infantry or armor, with other supporting units

Brown Water Navy   Term applied to the U.S. Navy units assigned to the inland boat patrols of the Mekong River delta

Buck Sergeant   First level of NCOs, often squad leaders

Buckle   To fight. "Buckle for your dust" means to fight furiously

Bu-coo   Much or many

Bush, The   Hostile jungle

Bust caps   Marine Corps term for firinig a rifle rapidly

Butter Bar   Freshly arrived second lieutenant

C-127   Transport plane

C-130   Cargo plane used to transport men and supplies

C-141   Large cargo airplane; the Starlifter

C-4   Plastique explosive

Canopy   Layers of jungle foliage

Cao Dai   Religious sect in Tay Ninh area

CAP	Combined Action Platoon
Carbine	Short-barreled, lightweight automatic or semiautomatic rifle
Catche	Hidden supplies
Charlie	Viet Cong
Charlie Oscar	Slang for commanding officer
Cherry	New guy out in the field
Chieu Hoi	Vietnamese government surrender program
Chinook	Army (CH46 Marine) A large, twin-bladed helicopter used for transporting men, materiels, and used in medevacs
Choi oi	Exclamation of surprise
Cholon	Chinese sector of Saigon
Choppers	Helicopters
Chu Hoi	I surrender
CH-47	Helicopter (Chinook)
Claymores	Mine packed with plastique and rigged to spray hundreds of steel pellets
Click	One kilometer
Clusterfuck	Any attempted operation that went bad; disorganized
Cobra	Helicopter gunships heavily armed with rocket launchers and machine guns
Co Cong	Female Viet Cong members
Code of Conduct	Military rules for U.S. soldiers taken prisoner by the enemy
Concertina Wire	Coiled barbed wire, strung around a perimeter
Counterinsurgency	Antiguerrilla warfare
CP	Command Post
C-Rations	Combat food in cans
Crispy Critters	Burn victims
Deuce and a half	Two-and-one-half-ton truck
Di di or Dadi Mau	Vietnamese for "Get out of here"
Dink	Derogatory for Vietnamese
Dinky Dau	To be crazy
Division HQ	Command Headquarters
DAV	Disabled American Veteran
DEROS	Date of estimated returns from overseas
DMZ	Demilitarized Zone
Dong	Vietnamese currency
Dung Lai	Halt or stop
Dust Off	Evacuating wounded by helicopter
Early Out	An early ETS (estimated time of terminating service)

Eggbeater	Helicopter
Electric Strawberry	25th ID patch with red/yellow
EM	Enlisted man
ETS	Estimated time of terminating service
Fire Base	Reinforced bases established to provide artillery fire support for ground units operating in the bush.
Firefight	Gunfire
Fire Mission	Artillery mission exchange with the enemy
FNG	F-ing new guy
FO	Forward Observer
Fragging	Killing an American officer by own troops
Freedom Bird	Jet aircraft taking you from Vietnam to the USA
Free Fire Zone	Area where everyone is deemed hostile
FUBAR	Fucked Up Beyond All Repair
F-4s, F-100s	Jet fighter aircraft
Gooks	Slang for the enemy
Grease Gun	M2-A1 sub-machine gun
Greased	Killed
Grunt	Slang for a combat infantry soldier fighting in Nam
Gung Ho	Military enthusiastic
Gunship	Armed helicopter
G-2	Division intelligence
G-3	Division operations
Hamlet	Cluster of homes; several make a village
Hanoi Hannah	Tokyo Rose of Vietnam
Hanoi Hilton	American POW camp
Heads	Those who were potheads
Hoi Chanh	Returnees under Chieu Hoi program
Hooch/Hootch	Slang for any form of dwelling place (living quarters)
Horn	Radio
Hot LZ	Landing zone under fire
Howitzers	Large cannon
Huey	Helicopter used for transporting troops; medevacs
Humping	Slang for marching with a heavy load through the bush
HQ	Headquarters
Incoming	Receiving enemy mortar or rocket fire
In-Country	In Vietnam
Iron Triangle	Viet Cong dominated area near Cu Chi
Jody	Guy back home who had your girl while you were in Nam

Jolly Green Giant	Heavily armed C-47 aircraft
Juicer	Prefers alcohol over drugs
K-Bar	Combat knife
KBA	Killed by artillery
KCS	Kit Carson scout, usually enemy soldier who surrendered
KIA	Killed in action
Klick, Click	One kilometer (0.62137 mile)
Koonza	Marijuana
Lai Dai	Come here / Come to me
La Vay	Beer
LAW	Light Antitank Weapon
LBJ	Long Binh Jail
Lifer	Career man in the military for life
Lock & Load	Chambering a sound invasion
LP	Listening Post
LRRP	Long Range Reconnaissance Patrol
LZ	Landing Zone
M-1	World War II Vintage American Carbine
MAC-SOG	Military Assistance Command Studies and Observation Group
MACV	Military Assistance Command, Vietnam
Mad Minute	Firing all weapons at once for short time
Mama San	Mother of family
MASH	Mobile Army Surgical Hospital
Mech	Mechanized infantry
Medi/Medevac	Medically evacuating the wounded by chopper or plane
MIA	Missing in action
MIG	Russian fighter jet
Million-Dollar Wound	Just bad enough to get out of the bush, but not serious
Mona	Rain
Monday Pills	Anti-malaria pills
Monsoon	The rainy season in Nam
Montagnard	Mountain people, indigenous people
MOS	Military occupational specialty
MP	Military Police
MPC	Military Payment Certificate
MRE	C-rations
M-14	Rifle used before M-16
M-16	Standard automatic weapon used by American ground forces

M60	A machine gun used by American combat units
M-79	Grenade launcher used by infantry
NAM	Vietnam
Napalm	Jelly-like substance in bombs—burns everything it contacts
NCO	Noncommissioned officers E5 to E9
NDP	Night Defensive Position
NLF	Regulars National Liberation Front—Communists
Numbah one G.I.	Big spending soldier
Numbah ten G.I.	Not a big spender
Numbah ten thou G.I.	The worst spender
NVA	North Vietnamese Army
NVR	North Vietnamese
OCS	Officers Candidate School
Old Man	Commanding officer
OP	Observation Post
Ordinance	Bombs or rockets
Over the Fence	Crossing into Cambodia
Papa San	Father of family
Papa Sierra	Slang for platoon sergeant
PAVN	People's Army of Vietnam
Phantom	A jet fighter (F-4)
Piastres	Vietnamese currency
Point Man	The lead man on a patrol through the bush
PRC25 / PRICK25	Portable radio for ground troops
Puff	A C-47 armed with mini machine guns; 'Puff the Magic Dragon'
Punji Stick	Booby trap with pointed bamboo stakes pointing up
P-38	Can opener worn with dog tag
PX	Post exchange
PZ	Pick-up zone
RA	Regular army
REAL LIFE	Civilian life
Recon	Reconnaissance
Reconnaissance-In Force	Replaced the former term of "search and destroy" in the 1967–1968 timeframe
Red LZ	Landing zone under attack
RIF	Recon in force
Rock N' Roll	Full automatic on an M-16
ROK	Republic of Korea ground troops
RPG	Rocket propelled grenade
R&R	Rest and relaxation

RSVN	Republic of South Vietnam
RTO	Radio-telephone operator
Rucks	Backpacks
Ruff Puff	Regional/popular forces of South Vietnamese militia; usually poorly trained and equipped, not effective in severe combat situations
Saddle Up	Load up, get ready to march
Saigon Cowboys	Officers and noncoms working in base camps or large cities
Sampan	Vietnamese peasant boat
Sappers	Viet Cong infiltrators with explosive charges attached to their bodies
Satchel Charges	Explosive packs carried by VC snipers
Sgt.	Abbreviation for Sergeant
Shake-n-Bake	Slang for instant NCO
Short	Close to the end of your tour in Vietnam
Sin Loi Minoi	Sorry about that, honey
Sitrep	Situation report by radio
SKs	A Russian carbine
Slick	Huey chopper
SOG	Studies and Observations Group
SOP	Standard Operating Procedure
Sortie	One aircraft, one takeoff and landing mission
SOS	Shit on a shingle
Spooky	Plane with electric mini-guns
Starlight	Night vision telescope
Swift Boat	Navy patrol boat used for coastal rivers
Tang-Boat	Armored Personnel Carrier
TDY	Temporary duty
Tee Tee	Vietnamese for "little bit"
TET	Southeast Asia Lunar New Year
The Rock	Guam
The World	Home—USA
Thunder Road	Hwy 13 from Saigon to Loc Ninh
Thumper	M-79 grenade launcher
Tiger Balm	Foul-smelling oil used by Vietnamese to ward off evil
Ti Ti	Small, insignificant
TOC	Tactical Office Command Post
TOP	Company first sergeant
TOT	Time on target
Tracer	A bullet with a phosphorus coating designed to burn and provide a visual indication of the bullet's trajectory

Trip Wire	Thin wire attached to a booby trap
VC	Viet Cong
Viet Cong	The local militias fighting Americans in South Vietnam
VFW	Veterans of Foreign War
Wallabee	Australian Caribou aircraft
Warthog	Slang for A10 aircraft
White Mice	South Vietnamese Police
WIA	Wounded in action
Xin Loi	Too bad, tough shit
XO	Executive Officer
Yards	Montagnard soldiers
Zipperhead	Rarely used slang for Vietnamese
Zulu	Casualty report
105 mm	Howitzer cannon size
81 mm	Mortar shell
50 cal	Heavy-duty machine gun
51 caliber	Comparable to 50 caliber, used by enemy forces

CPSIA information can be obtained
at www.ICGtesting.com
Printed in the USA
BVHW010827170619
550808BV00017B/547/P

9 781457 569975